LEVELS OF ANALYSIS IN PSYCHOPATHOLOGY

Levels of Analysis in Psychopathology draws research from psychiatry, philosophy, and psychology to explore the variety of explanatory approaches for understanding the nature of psychiatric disorders both in practice and research. The fields of psychiatry and clinical psychology incorporate many useful explanatory approaches and this book integrates this range of perspectives and makes suggestions about how to advance etiologic theories, classification, and treatment. The editors have brought together leading thinkers who have been widely published and are well respected in their area of expertise, including several developers of the *Diagnostic and Statistical Manual of Mental Disorders* and authors of the U.S. National Institute of Mental Health's Research Domain Criteria Project (RDoC). Each main chapter has a commentary provided by one of the other authors and an introduction written by one of the editors to create an accessible, interdisciplinary dialog.

Kenneth S. Kendler is a professor and eminent scholar at the Virginia Institute for Psychiatric and Behavioral Genetics and at the Virginia Commonwealth University, USA. He is also a member of the National Academy of Medicine, where he is the recipient of many honors and awards.

Josef Parnas is a clinical professor at the Department of Clinical Medicine and co-founder of the interdisciplinary theoretical institute: The Center for Subjectivity Research at the University of Copenhagen, Denmark.

Peter Zachar is a professor in the Department of Psychology and the associate dean of the College of Sciences at Auburn University Montgomery, USA.

Advance Praise for *Levels of Analysis in Psychopathology*

"The editors continue to deepen the analysis of the conceptual basis of psychopathological science through their astutely framed, thematic book. They have assembled a diverse and expert group of contributors in considering the range of sciences relevant to psychopathology. This volume offers an outstanding pedagogy, including introductory overviews, and insightfully chosen commentaries throughout."

John Z. Sadler, Daniel W. Foster Professor of Medical Ethics and Distinguished Teaching Professor, University of Texas Southwestern Medical Center, USA

"This excellent book combines substantive expertise with philosophical and methodological insights to provide high-level perspectives on essential topics in psychiatry. The editors focus on a topic of central importance: the complicated relation between the biological, psychological, and social levels of analysis that are required for a full understanding of mental disorders."

Denny Borsboom, Professor of Psychology, University of Amsterdam, the Netherlands

"The editors have assembled a wide range of chapters from multiple disciplines, encompassing Anglo-American and European Continental philosophies, to integrate research and clinical perspectives. No matter how well versed a reader may be on the topic, with the breadth of expertise represented in the volume, they will learn something new."

Derek Bolton, Honorary Consultant Clinical Psychologist, South London and Maudsley NHS Foundation Trust's Child and Adolescent Anxiety Service, and Professor of Philosophy and Psychopathology at the Institute of Psychiatry, King's College London, UK

"This is a state-of-the-art conversation between leading psychiatrists and philosophers about the challenges and possibilities of explaining psychiatric disorders across multiple levels."

Carl F. Craver, Professor of Philosophy and Philosophy-Neuroscience-Psychology, University of Washington in St Louis, USA

Levels of Analysis in Psychopathology

CROSS-DISCIPLINARY PERSPECTIVES

Edited by

Kenneth S. Kendler
Virginia Commonwealth University

Josef Parnas
University of Copenhagen

Peter Zachar
Auburn University Montgomery

CAMBRIDGE
UNIVERSITY PRESS

CAMBRIDGE
UNIVERSITY PRESS

University Printing House, Cambridge CB2 8BS, United Kingdom

One Liberty Plaza, 20th Floor, New York, NY 10006, USA

477 Williamstown Road, Port Melbourne, VIC 3207, Australia

314–321, 3rd Floor, Plot 3, Splendor Forum, Jasola District Centre, New Delhi – 110025, India

79 Anson Road, #06–04/06, Singapore 079906

Cambridge University Press is part of the University of Cambridge.

It furthers the University's mission by disseminating knowledge in the pursuit of education, learning, and research at the highest international levels of excellence.

www.cambridge.org
Information on this title: www.cambridge.org/9781108485197
DOI: 10.1017/9781108750349

First published 2020

Printed in the United Kingdom by TJ International Ltd, Padstow Cornwall

A catalogue record for this publication is available from the British Library.

Library of Congress Cataloging-in-Publication Data
NAMES: Kendler, Kenneth S., 1950– editor. | Parnas, Josef, editor. | Zachar, Peter, editor.
TITLE: Levels of analysis in psychopathology : cross-disciplinary perspectives / edited by Kenneth S. Kendler, Josef Parnas, Peter Zachar.
DESCRIPTION: Cambridge ; New York, NY : Cambridge University Press, 2020. | Includes bibliographical references and index.
IDENTIFIERS: LCCN 2019043050 (print) | LCCN 2019043051 (ebook) | ISBN 9781108485197 (hardback) | ISBN 9781108719254 (paperback) | ISBN 9781108750349 (epub)
SUBJECTS: LCSH: Psychology, Pathological.
CLASSIFICATION: LCC RC454 .L466 2020 (print) | LCC RC454 (ebook) | DDC 616.89–dc23
LC record available at https://lccn.loc.gov/2019043050
LC ebook record available at https://lccn.loc.gov/2019043051

ISBN 978-1-108-48519-7 Hardback

Contents

Figures

Tables

Contributors

MORGAN E. BARTHOLOMEW, University of California, Los Angeles

WILLIAM BECHTEL, University of California, San Diego

ROBERT M. BILDER, University of California, Los Angeles

JOHN CAMPBELL, University of California, Berkeley

SHAUN GALLAGHER, University of Memphis, Memphis and University of Wollongong, Australia

STEPHAN HECKERS, Vanderbilt University, Nashville

KENNETH S. KENDLER, Virginia Commonwealth University, Richmond

HANNA M. VAN LOO, University of Groningen, the Netherlands

GREGORY A. MILLER, University of California, Los Angeles

GEORG NORTHOFF, University of Ottawa, Canada

JOSEF PARNAS, University of Copenhagen, Denmark

DANIEL S. PINE, National Institute of Mental Health, Bethesda

JAN-WILLEM ROMEIJN, University of Groningen, the Netherlands

KENNETH F. SCHAFFNER, University of Pittsburgh, Pittsburgh

KATHRYN TABB, Bard College, New York

ERIC TURKHEIMER, University of Virginia, Charlottsville

JAMES WOODWARD, University of Pittsburgh, Pittsburgh

PETER ZACHAR, Auburn University, Montgomery

MAJA ZANDERSEN, University Hospital of Copenhagen, Denmark

Preface

All the chapters of this book began as talks given at a conference held in Copenhagen, Denmark, on May 28–30, 2018. The conference was organized and chaired by the editors of this volume, Kenneth S. Kendler, Peter Zachar, and Josef Parnas.

The conference itself was an exciting three-day experience for the speakers and a packed auditorium of more than 200 people. Each talk was followed by a formal commentary and then an open give-and-take with the audience and other speakers, who were rarely shy in asking challenging questions. So, each speaker who came to the meeting agreed to present a paper of their own, comment formally on another, and to write up both of them for publication.

As with the four prior volumes in this series (Kendler and Parnas, 2008, 2012, 2015, 2017), we have sought to capture the interactive nature of the meeting through the organization of this volume. In addition to a general introduction, written by the editors, each individual chapter has an introduction (written by Kendler, Zachar, or Parnas) and a discussion. We hope that this format will provide readers with a sense of the give-and-take of the actual meeting.

In working on a book like this, we have accumulated a number of debts. Our greatest thanks go to the contributors to the volume. Their willingness to take on their conceptually challenging topics and to work effectively across disciplinary boundaries was vital to the success of this venture. We received many compliments during the meeting about the quality of individual contributions and the stimulating nature of the discussions. While being hardly unbiased observers, all the editors commented on the "buzz" of excitement they felt during our three days together. The conference was funded by Psychiatric Services of the Capital Region of Denmark. The Center for Subjectivity Research is also acknowledged for their financial and institutional support.

As in years past, the editors owe a special thanks to Jill Opalesky for her well-honed organizational skills and perpetual sense of calm and good cheer. She played a central role in all aspects of this project, from the invitation of the speakers, to establishing the schedule, to helping run the meeting, and, especially, in aiding the oft-distracted editors to keep straight all the submitted chapters and comments through their multiple revisions. It was through her gentle but persistent efforts that we were able to deliver this volume to the publishers on time. We also want to express our appreciation to Helene Stephensen, MA, and Merete Lynnerup for their invaluable managerial and administrative assistance. In all of the prior volumes of this series, we have ended the Preface with these words that describe the experience of organizing this conference and editing this volume: "This project was, to use the philosophical term, emergent – in the end, the sum was much more than the individual parts." We are pleased to say that again this accurately describes our experience of organizing and attending the meeting and then editing this volume. We hope you, the readers, will agree with us as you read through this volume.

REFERENCES

Kendler KS, Parnas J. (2008) *Philosophical Issues in Psychiatry: Explanation, Phenomenology and Nosology*. First edn. Baltimore, MD: Johns Hopkins University Press.

Kendler KS, Parnas J. (2012) *Philosophical Issues in Psychiatry II: Nosology*. Oxford: Oxford University Press.

Kendler KS, Parnas J. (2015) *Philosophical Issues in Psychiatry III: The Nature and Sources of Historical Change*. Oxford: Oxford University Press.

Kendler KS, Parnas J. (2017) *Philosophical Issues in Psychiatry IV: Classification of Psychiatric Illness*. First edn. Oxford: Oxford University Press.

General Introduction

PETER ZACHAR AND KENNETH S. KENDLER

We introduce our readers to this volume by sharing the planning of and vision for the conference upon which the chapters are based. Here is what the editorial team (Kendler, Zachar, and Parnas) sent out with our first invitation emails to prospective speakers at the conference. It read:

> Multiple Levels, Explanatory Pluralism, Reduction, and Emergence
>
> The field of psychiatry incorporates more viable explanatory approaches than almost any other discipline in a modern university. Serious scholars have attempted to understand causes of psychiatric illness from the perspective of molecular neurobiology, molecular genetics, cellular neurophysiology, systems neuroscience, neuropsychology, clinical psychology (including a wide diversity of theories incorporating an array of mental constructs such as personality, cognition, and unconscious processes), epidemiology, genetic-epidemiology, sociology, and anthropology. The last decades have seen increasingly sophisticated scientific paradigms that have suggested that many of these levels can indeed yield useful and empirically verifiable risk factors for psychiatric illness. A central conundrum of the field is how to integrate this cacophony of scientific perspectives. Major themes include 1) the importance of reduction – under what circumstances are lower levels of explanation to be preferred? Is wholescale reduction possible or is it more realistic to pursue "small" or "patchy" reductive approaches? 2) How is it best to conceive of the multiple "levels" at which psychiatric illness can be understood? Is levels even a useful term here? 3) What are the advantages and problems of explanatory pluralism versus explanatory monism – when can we truly integrate results across "levels"? 4) given that levels of explanation in psychiatric cross the mind-body divide – the subjective and objective worlds – how can we best span these widely divergent perspectives on reality? 5) A recent survey has shown that truly cross-level research in psychiatry is rare. Why is this

and what scientific, cultural and financial barriers exist to more integrative approaches? 6) Individual researchers and research groups often bring strong commitments to their perspective on psychiatric illness that derive from extra-scientific personal beliefs. Such approaches have often fueled ideological disputes in the field. How can we better understand and reduce such often wasteful debates?

Our email spoke of our efforts to assemble "a mix of philosophers, psychiatrists, and psychologists with an interest in problems of multi-level explanation." We succeeded in assembling a diverse group of scholars. Contributors to the current volume include seven philosophers (Bechtel, Campbell, Gallagher, Romeijn, Schaffner, Tabb, and Woodward), six psychologists (Bilder, Miller and Bartholomew, Turkheimer, van Loo, and Zachar,) and five psychiatrists (Heckers, Kendler, Northoff (also a philosopher), Parnas, and Pine). The philosophers were chosen for diverse reasons but all of them had done philosophical work on psychiatric disorders or their work was directly relevant to the basic themes of the conference and the interests of the other participants. The psychologists and psychiatrists had diverse theoretical orientations, but all had worked on or expressed interest in philosophical issues pertinent to the themes of the conference.

While this is always a somewhat Procrustean solution, we divided the contributions into four topic areas: (1) causes, mechanisms, and levels of analysis; (2) causes, phenomenology, and levels of analysis; (3) classification, explanation, and levels of analysis; and (4) reductionism and levels of analysis. The actual conference had many cross-cutting themes, brought up in the main presentations, the formal commentaries, and the subsequent discussions. These included the strengths and limits of reduction, the central importance of high-level mental functions such as consciousness and the self in the field of psychiatry, the role and potential limits of intralevel and interlevel causal processes, the advantages of a mechanistic approach to the analysis of psychiatric illness, the relative strengths and limitations of the current *DSM* nosology and how that might be complemented by approaches such as the United States' National Institute of Mental Health's (NIMH) Research Domain Criteria (RDoC) initiative, and the appropriate role of phenomenology in psychiatric practice and research.

The structure of the book is as follows. Within each of the topic areas, the fifteen main chapters (2, 5, 8, 11, 14, 17, 20, 23, 26, 29, 32, 35, 38, 41, and 44) are bounded by a prelude/introduction by one of the editors followed by a prologue/commentary from one of the other authors in this volume. Each three-chapter set can stand alone, but to make the shared themes and multiple cross-connections between the chapters more apparent, we provide a brief overview of the whole book here.

Bill Bechtel, in the first main chapter (Chapter 2), goes beyond the standard causal accounts where disorders result either from disease mechanisms that produce them or the failure of mechanisms that are normally health promoting. These models have not worked as well for the heterogeneous disorders classified in the *DSM*. Bechtel, instead, proposes that the heterogeneity of many psychiatric disorders can be explained mechanistically by consideration of control mechanisms. Because control mechanisms are ordered heterarchically and they operate on flexible constraints in a variety of production mechanisms, outcomes can be heterogeneous. He illustrates how this might work using circadian control mechanisms and depression as an example.

In response, Kenneth Kendler applies Bechtel's model to three important explanatory theories in psychiatry: the phenomena of "made actions" in schizophrenia, the suffocation alarm theory of panic disorder, and C4A risk variants for the schizophrenic spectrum. He suggests that this promising model fits some of these explanatory theories in psychiatry, but not all.

In Chapter 5, Bob Bilder takes us on a "levels-informed" tour of the RDoC which was developed in response to a growing concern in the scientific community that the categories of the *DSM* lack validity, one reason for which is that they are too heterogeneous and not well aligned with biology (a view of validity disputed by Turkheimer in his chapter). The RDoC initiative identifies broad neuropsychological domains that can be decomposed into finer-grained constructs that span more than one "unit" of analysis. Bilder's example in this chapter is the construct of working memory from the Cognitive Systems Domain. Ideally, he argues, a more complete RDoC matrix would evolve into what scholars in information sciences call an ontology. An ontology is an attempt to describe with great precision (operationally) what elements exist in a particular domain and the relationships between them. Bilder argues that with an adequate ontology and the use of statistical models that are sensitive to causal patterns, progress can be made in understanding how psychological states emerge from brain activity. However, he acknowledges, it is looking scientifically likely that strong isomorphisms between "levels" will not play a large role in telling that story.

In response, Georg Northoff explores how complicated it may be to work out a satisfactory ontology that offers insights into the link between neuronal changes and psychopathological systems. In a thought-provoking contribution, Northoff argues that the kind of ontologies sought in RDoC represent the mind as composed of various cognitive functions (or faculties; see Kendler's chapter for a closer look). The expectation is that once properly measured by experimental tasks, these faculties will correspond to brain functions. Psychiatric disorders will then be seen as dysfunctions in these faculties. Northoff argues that this cognitive model may be a poor guide for understanding how the brain works. For example, it may not be possible to understand brain function without considering the brain's spontaneous activity and its spatiotemporal structure, which are more global than the local "task activities" measured in cognitive neuroscience. In addition, argues Northoff, it is unlikely that the brain's core features – consciousness and the basic sense of self – can ever be equated with the cognitive faculties alone.

Danny Pine, in Chapter 8, outlines his developmentally informed, clinical neuroscientific research program on anxiety disorders in which he and his colleagues are attempting, within the RDoC framework, to improve treatment options. Pine's work begins with the clinical report of anxiety symptoms from his patients and research participants. His main research tool is fMRI-aided observation of "anxiety circuits" in the brain, aided by psychometrically refined experimental tasks (a practice also emphasized explicitly by Bilder and challenged by Northoff). Drawing on the LeDoux and Pine two-system model, he examines the use of attention behavior modification therapy for people whose excessive anxiety is likely related to *attentional* biases that activate highly conserved, automatic defense-related circuitry. Rodent models have been very informative here. These types of anxiety problems are distinct from anxiety problems related to the *appraisal* of threats. The process of appraisal is affected by developmental changes in self-representations and is less amenable to being studied in rodents. Indeed, for humans, threat appraisal processes differ across development. All the same, says Pine, the research reviewed in this chapter demonstrates that information gleaned from data residing at lower levels of analysis can contribute to making clinically relevant distinctions at higher levels (e.g., distinguishing attentional biases versus appraisal processes within the more coarse-grained notion of anxiety disorders).

In response, Ken Schaffner summarizes Pine's chapter with reference to LeDoux and Pine's paradigm-shifting two-system model of fear and anxiety. The two systems are neural activity (amygdala-based) contributing to automatic defensive behaviors and a more cognitive (cortically engaged) appraisal of threats. Schaffner notes that because the second system's workings depend both on consciousness and self-representations, animal models will be inadequate. He notes, however, that limited, trimmed down aspects of consciousness may still be studied with rodent models. Even primate models, however, may not be adequate for understanding the neuroscience of self-representations – for both ethical and scientific reasons.

In Chapter 11, Shaun Gallagher argues that rather than using a levels of analysis perspective, various forms of body self-awareness (particularly ownership and agency) can be better understood by thinking of them as dynamic gestalts. He defends the notion of a pre-reflective self-awareness (of ownership) from several deflationary critiques, arguing that these critiques are not consistent with the clinical phenomena of depersonalization, dissociation, and affective alienation. He also considers critiques of a pre-reflective self-awareness (of ownership and agency) based on neuroscientific accounts of symptoms associated with schizophrenia spectrum disorders. Instead, he offers a view of basic self-awareness, called the common ground. The common ground refers to the intrinsic, temporal structure of experience. Similar to a claim made by Bechtel in his chapter, Gallagher argues that the concepts that are important in understanding body self-awareness cut across a traditional levels of analysis hierarchy. Some influences may be bottom-up, others top-down, but none can be called more basic because they are constantly interacting in the context of whole persons as agents, embedded in the world.

In response, Jan-Willem Romeijn argues that the distinction between intrinsic self-awareness (argued for by Gallagher) versus derivative self-awareness (the deflationary view) need not be sharply delineated, nor need that distinction exactly parallel the distinction between pre-reflective and reflective self-awareness. With respect to the symptoms of schizophrenia, Romeijn notes that a phenomenological notion of an intrinsic and pre-reflective experience of ownership might suffice for explaining delusions of control, but he does not see how it can ever explain thought insertion. Indeed, he is not convinced that the unity that we gain from the temporal structure of experience is enough to account for the sense of ownership. He concludes by comparing Galileo's work on inertial mass to phenomenological speculation. Galileo presented his findings as if they were arrived at speculatively, but he actually tested them out experimentally with moving bodies. In the same way, Romeijn suggests that the finely tuned conceptual structures of the phenomenologists could indeed improve and supplement the conceptual foundations of even a positivistic psychiatry but are more likely to do so if they were tested in the environment in which they were embodied, such as the clinic.

John Campbell, in Chapter 14, asks whether psychiatry can dispense with mental causation. His example of mental causation is Jaspers' notion of "genetic" understanding, i.e., an understanding of the unfolding of a person's thoughts and feelings over time. For example, someone is insulted and they *get mad* or is complimented and they *feel uncomfortable*. As Campbell notes, this is the kind of understanding typically used to distinguish between primary and secondary symptoms in psychiatry. Jaspers called it empathic understanding (the importance of which is also argued for by Heckers in his chapter). The problem is knowing whether one's reconstruction of another's thought processes is ever accurate, or is just what Campbell calls a cock-and-bull story. Campbell's example here is how LeDoux and Pine's two-system model contradicts common sense notions of emotional causation. Perhaps the real causal work is being done at the level of the brain, which is where we should look instead. Referring to R. G. Collingwood, Campbell argues that we can imaginatively reconstruct the unfolding of another's mental process if we do it in a critical way by figuring out the possible alternatives for action and why the actions selected seem normatively correct to the actor. Campbell argues that looking for the casual connections at the biological level will not illuminate such mental causal pathways. In part, this is because reconstructing local causal processes requires us to consider factors that are not included in general laws, and in part because the key causal connections in mental causation are normatively understandable transitions between psychological states.

In response, Peter Zachar claims that Collingwood's critical approach does not resolve the problem of these imaginative reconstructions potentially being fictional just-so stories, which raises old questions about the proper role of folk psychological constructs in the science of psychopathology. In contrast to the notion of reconstructing another's internal thought processes, he claims that most of the information we use to understand others is based on third-person information, argues that this is how psychotherapists are taught to understand others, and compares that process to Karl Popper's notion of critical rationalism. It is also, he surmises, what Jaspers meant by empathic understanding as well.

In Chapter 17, Josef Parnas and Maja Zandersen argue that the symptom-based categories of the *DSM* do not accurately describe psychopathological phenotypes, but that despite this, they have been reified (a criticism also made by RDoC advocates). Rather than criteria lists, they argue that we should understand the cluster of symptoms we associate with psychiatric disorders as representing Gestalts that emerge from the interaction of multiple causes and contextual factors. To illustrate a broader perspective, they assert that schizophrenic spectrum disorders also involve a disturbance in the core self. The core self is a more fundamental process than other clinical notions of the self, including the psychodynamic-based notions of self-disturbance in the Alternative *DSM-5* Model for Personality Disorders (which are advocated for by Schaffner in his chapter). The core self-disturbances Parnas and Zandersen describe in the chapter may superficially resemble *DSM* symptoms, but are in fact qualitatively different. Rather than segmenting psychopathology into symptoms lists or into neuropsychological faculties, Parnas and Zandersen argue that it is important to understand the structures of subjective life that enable the emergence of symptoms – what they call phenomenal ontology. In their view, this phenomenological perspective can also offer a meta-structure for distinguishing between kinds of disorders and for advancing our understanding of their biology.

In response, Shaun Gallagher lauds their emphasis on core self-disturbances, but notes that it is a mistake to view them as essential to the schizophrenic spectrum. To do so is also a form of reduction, much like reducing complex phenotypes to list of symptoms. As an alternative, he briefly describes the notion of a dynamic self-pattern in which internal and external, and top-down and bottom-up processes are constantly occurring, but none of them is an essential feature of the pattern.

Greg Miller and Morgan Bartholomew, in Chapter 20, provide a broad over-view of the reductionism/anti-reductionism debate that has continued to embroil the field of psychopathology research over recent decades. They take a passionate anti-reductionist position against what they label as naïve reductionism of the Decades of the Brain. With respect to the RDoC initiative, they note that it has some reductive aspirations, but these aspirations do not include the elimination of psychological constructs. They also note that in the past, reductionist terminology has unfortunately been inserted into our public discourse from official NIMH pronouncements such as "science has now shown that schizophrenia is a brain disease." (Such pronouncements are also critiqued by Tabb and Turkheimer in their contributions.) Miller and Bartholomew review other more profitable and defensible ways to view the inter-relationship between psychological and biological processes in psychiatric illness, especially the approach of the new mechanists in the philosophy of sciences such as Craver and Bechtel. According to these thinkers, causal relations are intralevel, not interlevel. (Woodward disputes this in his chapter.) What is interlevel are more often constitutive relations between parts and wholes. In this framework, psychological functions are not caused by the brain, they are implemented in the brain.

In response, Peter Zachar concurs that RDoC had clear non-reductionist aspirations from the beginning, many philosophers continue to criticize it as reductionist. Zachar further notes that RDoC does seem to be eliminativist about *DSM* categories and questions the strategy of blaming the lack of scientific progress on the *DSM* rather than on the inherent complexity of many psychological traits (including psychopathology). He briefly explores some of Paul Meehl's thoughts about why the psychological and behavioral sciences are inherently harder than other sciences. (Turkheimer makes a similar claim in his chapter with a different supporting argument.)

In Chapter 23, Peter Zachar argues that the practice (particularly of many RDoC advocates) of defining descriptive psychopathology as the classification of disorders with respect to manifest signs and symptoms (phenotypes) as opposed to deeper causes is a somewhat superficial construal that does not take into account the various ways that something can be brought under a description. He uses Gilbert Ryle's work to illustrate what philosophers mean by bringing something under a description. That things can be brought under more than one description highlights the importance of re-describing. An important example of re-describing psychopathology is the discovery of panic disorder from which five desiderata for useful descriptions and re-descriptions can be derived. With respect to causes, the elucidation of a causal model for a phenotype can often lead us to notice something descriptively that we had not noticed before in which case the causal model becomes part of a thicker description of the phenotype.

In response, Josef Parnas argues that what Zachar seems to mean by descriptive psychopathology could also be called the science of psychopathology. This science cannot be based only upon quantitative research studies but should incorporate knowledge from a variety of disciplines across the humanities, the social sciences, the behavioral and cognitive sciences, and the natural sciences. In addition, description in psychiatry has to take into account the problem of meaning and how the meanings of psychiatric concepts are embedded in their history; how they have changed, and what has been forgotten. Parnas argues that we need to reinstate a science of psychopathology at the center of our empirical ambitions. Its absence is the real crisis and it cannot be solved by revising classification systems or constructing matrices composed of dimensions and neuropsychological constructs.

Katie Tabb, in Chapter 26, examines the RDoC initiative with respect to its architects' claim that it is a part of the precision medicine movement.

She identifies three commitments of the precision medicine movement – nosological revision, big data, and reductionism. In her view, nosological revision is central to RDoC, big data is optional, and reductionism is harmful. As a paradigm, they are not sufficient for making psychiatric progress, especially without some notion of psychopathology at the level of the phenotype that can bring the clinical relevance of the paradigm into view. She proceeds to raise doubts about the wisdom of the NIMH's funding priorities, especially to the extent that they are based on metaphysical assumptions about mental disorders being brain disorders. In her view, the extensive shift of federal dollars away from research in clinical care and epidemiology toward basic science is ethically questionable. As she notes later in her response to Eric Turkheimer's chapter, even if it is not bad science, it is bad medicine.

In response, Bob Bilder denies that the RDoC initiative is reductionist and believes that Tabb is arguing against a straw man. He lauds her analysis of the foundational elements of both precision medicine and RDoC, but disagrees that the three commitments are bundled together. In his view, the precision medicine initiative and RDoC should be understood in light of the intentions of those who are advocating for them. For example, the leaders of RDoC have tried to avoid using levels of analysis talk in a way that suggests that one "level" is more basic than another – writing instead about units of analysis. In some cases, "lower levels" are studied not because they are more basic but because they are more tractable, i.e., the genome is less complex than the envirome. Ideally, RDoC will attempt to see how all units fit together. He also argues that statistics can be deceptive when they are incomplete or ignore context and disputes that shifts in NIMH priorities have had the inverse impacts that Tabb claims.

In Chapter 29, Jan-Willem Romeijn and Hanna M. van Loo argue that developing psychiatric classifications can be seen as constructing reference classes. Reference classes are groups composed of individuals who are homogeneous on sets of features that license making inferences about other features of interest – such as the likelihood that an intervention will be successful. An important factor in developing these classes is to avoid groups that are too coarse-grained and too fine-grained (examined at more length by Woodward in his chapter). They illustrate how machine learning (and big data) can be used to construct reference classes for predicting the persistence-severity of depression. In their view, in developing and testing mathematical models, the variables used to construct the classes should be selected for their contribution to making successful predictions. The selection should not be constrained by metaphysical concerns about what levels of analysis the variables are taken from. They refer to this as an a-reductionist perspective.

In response, Eric Turkheimer casts doubt on adopting such a strict empirical approach to classification, preferring instead a science that understands reference classes within more substantial theoretical frameworks. He couches this in term of the dissatisfaction in mid-twentieth-century psychology with the strict operational approach to research, famously articulated in MaCorquodale and Meehl's distinction between intervening variables (defined only operationally) and hypothetical (theoretical) constructs. He also notes that in their larger body of work, specifically their work on scientific conventionalism, Romeijn and van Loo also explore the non-empirical aspects of the science of psychopathology.

Ken Schaffner examines LeDoux and Pine's two-system model of fear, suggesting that it can be better developed by adopting two different theories of consciousness (as opposed to LeDoux's preference for a higher order thought theory of consciousness). The two theories are attention theory and global neuronal workspace theory. Another key feature of the two-system model is the importance of self-representations. For this, Schaffner recommends utilizing the descriptions of normal and healthy self-representations in the Alternative *DSM-5* Model for Personality Disorders. He then applies his notion of a temporally extended theory (TET) to the two-system model's relationship with the traditional model of fear and anxiety. With the TET framework, Schaffner can explore how scientific models change over time, and how newer models may replace older ones. A key concept for a TET is the high-level central hypothesis – which for the two-system model is the addition of the consciousness circuit notion to the older fear circuit model. This abstract notion is instantiated in specific mechanisms (which are interlevel) and can be empirically tested.

In response, Bill Bechtel offers an alternative approach to the self (proposed by Ulric Neisser), more along the lines of a traditional empiricism. He also examines Wilfred Sellers' proposal about how linguistic descriptions become the basis for inferences about subjectivity (an important source via Richard Rorty on Zachar's ideas about re-describing in his chapter). Bechtel argues that these empiricist approaches make it easier to incorporate the construct of the self into Schaffner's notion of a temporally extended theory. In Bechtel's view, the temporally extended theory notion is also congruent with the approach of the new mechanists in the philosophy of science because Schaffner's notion of a high-level central hypothesis is similar to the notion of higher-level mechanism sketches, which are filled in with more specific accounts called mechanism schemas. The entities in these schemas reside at different levels of composition. Quite likely, our self-representations conform to this levels structure as well, encompassing both very global hypotheses about what we are like and more specific notions about how we behave in certain situations (which can be decomposed in multiple possible ways).

In one of the more philosophically intricate contributions to the volume, Jim Woodward in Chapter 35 provides a brief review of four leading definitions of "levels": compositional, disciplinary subject matter, abstractness (coarse-versus fine-grained), and interactionist, arguing that talking about levels does some useful work (especially the interactionist conception). After reviewing his interventionist framework for causal analysis, he applies it to the controversial topic of top-down causation. Top-down causation is interlevel causation, something dismissed by new mechanists such as Craver and Bechtel (and Miller and Bartholomew in their chapter). Basically, if you can intervene on a variable at a higher level, and systematically change the value of a variable at a lower level, the higher-level variable is playing a causal role with respect to the lower level variable. This relationship holds, says Woodward, even if the higher-level variable's influence on lower level can be reduced to causal relations at the lower level as long as there is conditional independence. Conditional independence is what occurs when, conditional on the value of the higher-level variable, details about what is occurring at the lower level do not matter for the effect we are trying to explain.

In response, Stephan Heckers agrees with Woodward's defense of a levels approach and illustrates the useful work it does in our understanding of Alzheimer's disease – using several of Woodward's concepts. The important levels for Alzheimer's disease include behavioral and cognitive (dementia), anatomical (medial temporal lobe), neuropathological abnormalities (tangles and plaques), biochemical (amyloid precursor proteins (APP) in plaques), and genetic (the APP gene on chromosome 21). These levels are compositional and they also correspond to the expertise of different disciplinary groups. Dementia is a coarse-grain construct of which Alzheimer's is one type. But the relations between levels have different degrees of invariance. For example, Alzheimer's disease related mutations in chromosome 21 always have misfolded proteins (amyloid plaques), but not all patients with significant plaques manifest the clinical syndrome of dementia. With respect to top-down causation, Heckers suggests that ideally, conditional on making the right kind of interventions at the lower level, the higher-level clinical syndrome might never emerge, but for now the study of the lower levels are not contributing very much to our ability to explain the cognitive and behavioral changes.

In Chapter 28, Kenneth Kendler offers a historical analysis of the role that faculty psychology played in psychiatric nosology. He suggests that the focus of nineteenth-century psychiatry on mood and cognitive/delusional disorders did not arise de novo but in fact was based on earlier developments in philosophy. With this philosophical framework in hand, clinicians could see insanity as disturbances in the faculties. It also let them to try to understand (in Jaspers' sense) disorders with respect to causal effects between faculties – such as when mood alterations drive delusional thinking versus the other way around. It is not the case that the nineteenth-century nosologists proposed the basic syndromes that define psychiatry once they had access to the raw clinical data when it became available in the new asylums and university hospitals, rather what they observed was based on their reliance on the philosophical theory of the faculties. Subsequent work on biopathology could only get to clinical data through the level of the faculties. Indeed, the RDoC initiative in some ways can be seen as a return to a faculty psychology view – but with an updated matrix of which faculties are important.

In response, Greg Miller argues that another legacy of faculty psychology is the categorical approach to classification, which includes the categories of the *DSM* as well as folk psychological dichotomies such as emotion versus cognition. He notes that when they were first defined in *DSM-III*, the categories were expected to be a roadmap for the discovery of biological substrates. It has failed. In contrast, for the RDoC initiative, a construct cannot be included without some prior evidence of implementation in biology. The dimensional constructs used in RDoC are also drawn from the modern psychological sciences rather than folk psychology. Nor is the goal to eliminate psychology in favor of biology – but with a scientifically improved notion of "faculties," psychology can be better understood in light of biology.

Stephan Heckers, in Chapter 41, gives a wide-ranging overview of the kinds of reductionisms that psychiatrists have drawn on to manage clinical problems, focusing on four. The first reduction happens in the psychiatric situation where first-person experiences are reduced to third-person accounts by clinicians. This reduction is practiced differently across settings. The second reduction happens in the heads of the clinician where signs and symptoms are converted into specific disorder constructs. The third reduction happens in the laboratory where psychiatric disorders are reduced to (correlated with) biological markers. Heckers illustrates this with recent work on auditory verbal hallucinations. The fourth reduction happens in the scientific process where disorders are explained causally. This, Heckers notes, has been the least successful of the reductionisms so far. The ultimate constraint on scientific reductionism in psychiatry, he argues, is agency. None of the reductionisms in psychiatry remove the agency of the person, nor can psychiatrists make clinical progress if the discipline does not accept the importance of human agency because without it, the first step in reduction – the psychiatric situation – cannot be established.

In response, John Campbell digs deeper into the relation between what he calls reductionism and patient autonomy. He notes that Heckers is using reductionism more as a synonym for "simplification" or "loss of information" rather than what philosophers usually mean by reductionism. He notes that each one of Heckers' reductionisms could be seen as an attempt to make generalizations about the person. Campbell surmises that however useful these generalizations may be, what Heckers is concerned about is that they leave out the lived, first-person experience of the patient. Campbell, however, is not sure where the autonomy piece fits into this model. To suggest how it might fit, he considers Jaspers' notion of understanding of the unfolding of the thoughts and feelings of the patient. The sometimes one-off causal connections in the mental life of the patient can often be idiosyncratic and unpredictable – running counter to established generalizations. This capacity for one-off mental causation is also something we can generalize about, but it is a generalization which undermines our typical attempt to find generalizations that govern our psychology. That is autonomy.

In Chapter 44, Eric Turkheimer proposes what he hopes is a new approach to thinking about levels of analysis in psychopathology – namely that levels are about entities and their boundaries. This is offered in the context of his long-standing views on complex psychological traits as real patterns in the world. These patterns may be detectable at the genetic level, but what is being detected is not a genetic mechanism for the psychological trait, but one pattern being observed at different level of analysis. In this chapter, he asks us to consider carpets. Carpets are physical entities. Previously he claimed that there is no such thing as *the physics of* carpets, but has subsequently learned that there is for wool engineers. As an entity, a carpet comes into clear focus when we are thinking about home decorating, but it is a blurry entity at the atomic level. Physics can teach us why nylon carpets are easier to clean, but the nylon is not the cause of the carpet. It is part of what the carpet is. (A similar argument about the psychology and biology relationship is offered by Miller and Bartholomew in their chapter.) Despite there being a physics of carpets, we see these interlevel issues of composition clearly. However, we (especially the early biological psychiatrists and some developers of RDoC) still have a tendency to confuse focus questions with compositional questions (in Craver and Bechtel's sense). In contrast to carpets, the existence of a biology and genetics of psychopathology lead people to expect that the entities of psychopathology should come into high focus at the biological level and that brain circuits and genes are the causes of disorders. Not so, says Turkheimer. Many of the various kinds of psychopathology will be detectable but blurry at lower levels of analysis. For clinical categories to be badly aligned with neuroscience therefore, is not necessarily an indictment of the categories.

In response, Katie Tabb agrees that the science of psychiatry has not progressed as the advocates for a biological psychiatry have expected, but that Eric's gloomy prediction about the future is an arm-chair analysis of what should be a set of empirical questions. In her view, psychiatric disorders are unlike carpets and the analogy should not be take too literally. What we consider to be the entities of psychopathology may be revisable so that they do come into clearer focus at lower levels of analysis. However, Tabb argues, the important contrast to Eric's famously "gloomy" view is, just before and after the turn of the last century, the optimistic enthusiasm of some biological psychiatrists regarding how easy it was going to be to discover causal mechanisms for psychiatric disorders. Tabb believes that we should not give up on future success and passively accept the philosophers' pessimistic meta-induction, but ethically she wonders if making very large bets on hypothetical future successes is worth the opportunity costs with respect to more immediate improvements in clinical care.

The actions and interactions at the conference were just the beginning of producing the chapters for this volume. Many of the chapters here are quite different from the main talks presented at the conference because they benefited from the formal commentaries delivered during the conference (represented by the commentary chapters). Both the main chapters and the commentary chapters also benefited from the other talks and interactions at the conference. This iterative process continued to occur during the writing of the book as main chapters and commentaries were exchanged.

We hope that the final products presented in this volume will provide the reader with a rich array of the exciting and challenging conceptual issues current in the field of psychiatry and psychopathology. We tried to demonstrate the extra insights that can occur when dedicated scholars in philosophy, psychology, and psychiatry together try to tackle these problems. We seek, in these meetings and resulting publications, to stimulate cross-disciplinary dialog because we believe that the best of philosophy and of clinical science can emerge in such interactions.

PART I

NEUROSCIENCE, MECHANISMS, AND RDOC

SECTION 1

1

Introduction

PETER ZACHAR

Bill Bechtel is rare breed of philosopher whose writings on mechanistic models are afforded as much respect by scientists in biology and psychology as they are by philosophers. Earlier in his career Bechtel (1988a, 1988b) published two short books written largely for psychologists titled *Philosophy of Mind: An Overview for Cognitive Science* and *Philosophy of Science: An Overview for Cognitive Science*. These books demonstrated that he is adept at writing for a cross-disciplinary audience. His work on mechanisms, however, is of a decidedly technical nature, and nevertheless highly admired outside the philosophy of science.

One important contribution his work on mechanisms made in the philosophy of science was to bring attention to how explanation in the special sciences such as biology and psychology differs from how it has been conventionally construed by philosophers. That is, rather than explanation being governed by laws, as in the deductive-nomological model of Hempel and Oppenheim (1948) or Cronbach and Meehl (1955), explanations in biology and psychology (in theory) describe the mechanisms responsible for producing or maintaining the phenomenon in question (Bechtel, 2008; Bechtel & Abrahamsen, 2005; Bechtel & Richardson, 1993).

Much interesting work has been done applying ideas initially discussed by Bechtel to the topic of psychiatric disorder (Kendler, 2008; Thomas & Sharp, 2019), but in this chapter, a mechanistic approach to psychiatric disorder is pushed forward by Bechtel himself. Rather than looking at the heterogeneity of something like major depressive disorder and claiming that it should be decomposed into homogeneous features that are each subject to a mechanistic account (a Research Domain Criteria [RDoC] strategy), he proposes a mechanistic account that is consistent with the heterogeneity of major depressive disorder.

To begin with, he distinguishes between production mechanisms and control mechanisms. Production mechanisms are what we usually think of as mechanisms. For instance, in medicine a mechanistic account of disease will typically describe a mechanism that produces the disease or describe the failure of a mechanism to function normally. Rather than producing the phenomenon being explained, what control mechanisms do is to regulate the behavior of one or more production mechanisms. In general, production mechanisms are constrained to operate in certain ways. When the constraints are flexible, control mechanisms can alter them in response to information.

One key move Bechtel makes to explain heterogeneity is to assert that the operation of control mechanisms cannot be adequately modeled by thinking of them as organized in a hierarchy. With respect to the topic of this book, in a hierarchical model, the control mechanism resides at a level of analysis above the production mechanism and exerts its influence in a top-down manner. In contrast, in a heterarchical network, there is no fixed ranking of what is higher or lower. For example, in the heterarchy, a control mechanism that might look like it is lower in a hierarchical model can alter a control mechanism that looks like it is higher; it can also alter a control mechanism at the same level or alter a mechanism at a lower level. Any control mechanism that makes direct contact onto a production mechanisms can alter the mechanism somewhat independently, and any production mechanism can be influenced by multiple controllers. There is also indirect control in which a particular control signal can be integrating input from multiple levels. It is useful, therefore, to see control mechanisms as forming a network. In such networks, the contrasts between controller and controlled and between control and production may be more informative than the contrast between higher level and lower level.

Bechtel then proceeds to review evidence, which relate disruption in the circadian clock mechanism to mood disorders and/or anxiety disorders in both human and animal models, with the idea that the circadian clock is a control mechanism operating on flexible constraints in a variety of production mechanisms. The clock itself is also just one mechanism in a wider heterarchical control network. He also uses serotonin to illustrate the potential role of a control mechanism in mood disorders. The problem is how to distinguish between something being correlated with the symptoms of depression and something playing a causal role in the generation of depression. Bechtel argues that for both the circadian mechanism and serotonin, evidence that they are playing the role of control mechanisms would support the causal hypothesis.

In his commentary, Ken Kendler takes three possible different mechanistic models described by Bechtel and speculates on how they might be applied to three causal theories about psychiatric disorder. The three causal theories are a theory about "made action" in schizophrenia, Donald Klein's suffocation alarm theory of panic disorder, and an update to the synaptic pruning theory of schizophrenia based on presence risk variants for the C4A protein on chromosome 6. Although results were mixed, Kendler suggests that looking at alterations in control mechanisms potentially holds great promise for the field of psychiatry.

REFERENCES

Bechtel, W. (1988a) *Philosophy of mind: An overview for cognitive science.* Hillsdale, NJ: Lawrence Erlbaum Associates, Inc.

Bechtel, W. (1988b) *Philosophy of science: An overview for cognitive science.* Hillsdale, NJ: Lawrence Erlbaum Associates, Inc.

Bechtel, W. (2008) *Mental mechanisms: Philosophical perspectives on cognitive neuroscience.* New York: Routledge/Taylor & Francis Group.

Bechtel, W., & Abrahamsen, A. (2005) 'Explanation: A mechanist alternative.' *Studies in History & Philosophy of Biological & Biomedical Sciences, 36*(2), 421–441.

Bechtel, W., & Richardson, R. C. (1993) *Discovering complexity: Decomposition and localization as strategies in scientific research.* Princeton, NJ: Princeton University Press.

Cronbach, L. J., & Meehl, P. E. (1955) 'Construct validity in psychological tests.' *Psychological Bulletin, 52*(4), 281–302.

Hempel, C. G., & Oppenheim, P. (1948) 'Studies in the logic of explanation.' *Philosophy of Science, 15*, 135–175.

Kendler, K. S. (2008) 'Explanatory models for psychiatric illness.' *American Journal of Psychiatry, 165*(6), 695–702.

Thomas, J. G., & Sharp, P. B. (2019) 'Mechanistic science: A new approach to comprehensive psychopathology research that relates psychological and biological phenomena.' *Clinical Psychological Science, 7*(2), 196–215.

2

Rethinking Psychiatric Disorders in Terms of Heterarchical Networks of Control Mechanisms

WILLIAM BECHTEL

2.1 APPROACHING PSYCHIATRIC DISORDERS MECHANISTICALLY

Explanations of biological phenomena, such as oxidative metabolism or muscle contraction, commonly take the form of an account of the mechanism responsible for the phenomenon. Philosophical accounts of mechanistic explanations (Bechtel & Abrahamsen, 2005; Bechtel & Richardson, 1993/2010; Craver & Darden, 2013; Machamer, Darden, & Craver, 2000) present them as identifying the parts of the responsible mechanism, specifying the operations each part performs, and characterizing how, as a result of the organization within the mechanism, the operations are orchestrated so as to generate the phenomenon. Mental phenomena such as visual perception or memory encoding have likewise been viewed to be the result of the operation of specific mechanisms and thought to be explained in the same manner (Bechtel, 2008; Craver, 2007).

Philosophical accounts of mechanisms have typically focused on those operating in healthy organisms. Yet both clinicians and philosophers have also adopted the mechanistic perspective when explaining diseases or disorders. Commonly, one of two strategies has been applied to extend the mechanistic framework to disease: one is to identify a mechanism that brings about the disease and the other is to attribute the disease to an altered mechanism. There are diseases for which both approaches seem applicable. Mechanistic accounts of how viruses infect somatic cells and elicit immune responses provide good accounts of diseases such as

I thank Peter Zachar and Kenneth Kendler for their valuable feedback on earlier drafts of this manuscript. I also thank audience members at the 2018 conference, Philosophical Issues in Psychiatry V, for their many comments and suggestions. Finally, I thank Jason Winning for his highly productive discussions of topics involving constraint and control.

influenza. An account of a mutation in the gene coding for the enzyme phenylalanine hydroxylase, which normally metabolizes the amino acid phenylalanine, explains the disease phenylketonuria (PKU).

Neither approach, however, provides a satisfactory framework for many psychiatric disorders such as major depression, which I will use as my example in this paper. Both approaches tend to focus research on a single mechanism that either is altered or produces the disease state. Although there is research on mechanisms that are involved with moods, there is not a single mechanism that is viewed as responsible for mood and altered in mood disorders such as depression. The quest for a mechanism that brings about depression underlay explanations of depression that appeal to reduced concentrations of monoamines such as serotonin (Lapin & Oxenkrug, 1969). Although the serotonin hypothesis was embraced by many, especially with the claimed success of serotonin reuptake inhibitors such as Prozac in treating the symptoms of depression, more recently it has been subject to multiple criticisms (Cowen & Browning, 2015; Culverhouse et al., 2018; Lacasse & Leo, 2005). One notable shortcoming of the serotonin hypothesis is the lack of an account of how reduced concentrations of serotonin actually generate the symptoms of depression. I will discuss this shortcoming of serotonin hypothesis and what it would take to address it in the final section after I lay out a framework that will make clear the challenges in developing such an explanation.

One feature of psychiatric disorders that makes the prospects of identifying a single mechanism that is responsible or a single mechanism that when altered results in the disease less plausible is the heterogeneity of the symptoms associated with many psychiatric disorders. This heterogeneity is evident in the efforts of the authors of the various editions of the *Diagnostic and Statistical Manual of Mental Disorders (DSM)* to categorize psychiatric disorders. The term "major depressive disorder" was introduced in *DSM-III* in 1980 to group the syndromes manic depression (bipolar) and unipolar depression under one section, while *DSM-5* has split them into separate sections. As with many disorders, the *DSM* identifies multiple symptoms and attributes the pathology to a patient that exhibits a specific number of them. Thus, in *DSM-5*, a diagnosis of major depression requires that five of nine identified symptoms be detected: depressed mood, anhedonia, significant weight loss, insomnia or hypersomnia, psychomotor agitation or retardation, fatigue or loss of energy, feelings of worthlessness or guilt, inability to concentrate and indecisiveness, and thoughts of death or suicide. The result is that a highly diverse set of patients may all be clustered under one diagnosis (Goldberg, 2011; Lux &

Kendler, 2010). The situation is equally heterogeneous if one turns to the various depression scales in current use; they, too, exhibit substantial variability (Fried, 2017). Likewise, one finds considerable heterogeneity if one considers patients actually diagnosed with depression (Chen, Eaton, Gallo, & Nestadt, 2000).

This heterogeneity of symptoms may seem problematic if one expected one mechanism to be responsible for depression. There is, however, a different strategy for developing mechanistic accounts of heterogeneous disorders such as depression. This involves focusing on control mechanisms in biological organisms. Such control mechanisms often constitute heterarchical networks. Different disruptions in heterarchical control networks can generate different patterns of symptoms. Developing this framework requires first distinguishing control mechanisms from production mechanisms, such as those involved in metabolism or muscle contraction. Control mechanisms are, as I will discuss in Section 2, mechanisms that regulate the behavior of production mechanisms. Second, it requires rejecting the assumption that control mechanisms are organized hierarchically, with a top-level controller issuing commands to lower-level control mechanisms until instructions are delivered to production mechanisms. Rather, as I discuss in Section 3, control mechanisms in living organisms are typically organized heterarchically, with multiple different control mechanisms organized into a network through which they jointly regulate production mechanisms. Different disruptions in such control networks can lead to the heterogeneous symptoms associated with diseases. Cancer provides a useful analogy. The various hallmarks of cancer in a cell may each result from disruptions of different control mechanisms. These mechanisms together constitute a heterarchical network that normally maintains the cell in a healthy state. Such a network is subject to numerous alterations that together generate a heterogeneous set of symptoms (Bechtel, 2018).

To apply the control mechanism framework to psychiatric disorders, we must focus on neural mechanisms. Neural mechanisms are examples of heterarchically organized control mechanisms. Although we commonly think of the nervous system as organized hierarchically, with low-level controllers in the spinal cord and the highest-level controller lodged in the cerebral cortex, specifically the frontal lobes, it in fact consists of multiple control mechanisms that each effect some degree of control and together control the operation of physiological and behavioral production mechanisms. The nervous system itself is highly interconnected, realizing what is known as a small-world architecture (Watts & Strogratz, 1998) in which every component is connected to others by relatively short pathways. To illustrate how, within such a network, disruptions of control can result in psychiatric disorders, I examine in Section 4 a neural control mechanism that has been implicated in depression – the circadian clock. While gaps remain in our understanding of how the circadian clock affects different production mechanisms, the general contours of how it does so are becoming clear. In Section 5, I will develop the implications of this perspective for thinking about psychiatric disorders such as depression in mechanistic terms, returning to the serotonin hypothesis to illustrate how it would need to be developed to be a compelling account of depression. The lessons I develop are not specific to the serotonin hypothesis but are applicable to other proposals to explain psychopathologies such as depression.

2.2 RETHINKING MECHANISMS: DISTINGUISHING PRODUCTION AND CONTROL MECHANISMS

As noted above, philosophical accounts of mechanisms have emphasized entities or parts, activities or operations, and organization. Such accounts do not distinguish mechanisms involved in production from those engaged in control. They also leave out an important feature of any mechanism: Mechanisms perform work and to do so they require a supply of materials and free energy (Winning & Bechtel, 2018). We can identify the difference between production mechanisms and control mechanisms by focusing on the work each performs. The primary output of a production mechanism is the synthesis or breakdown of something or its translocation. Protein synthesis results in proteins, glycolysis breaks down glucose and generates ATP, molecular motors move materials through cells, and skeletal muscles generate movement of the whole organism. Control mechanisms also perform work, but the work they perform is on other mechanisms, altering the way in which they operate. They also require energy, but typically much less than production mechanisms require.

A useful concept for clarifying the difference between production and control mechanism is *constraint*. The relevant notion of constraint was introduced in classical mechanics to facilitate explaining the behavior of macroscale objects. (For discussions of the notion of constraint in classical dynamics and its application to biology, see Hooker, 2013; Pattee, 1972/2012.) While Newtonian force laws could be applied to determine the effects on each of six degrees of freedom of each individual particle, it is unnecessary for macroscopic objects in which particles are constrained by bonds that limit the alterations that can be made to individual components. To explain why a glass moves when you push it, you do not need to determine the effects of the push on each particle in the glass; rather, you treat the glass as a macroscale object since the particles constituting the glass are constrained to move together. Constraints not only give rise to macroscale objects, but they allow such objects to perform work by restricting how free energy can dissipate. This is illustrated in human-made machines. A pipe can restrict the flow of steam in a steam engine so that rather than simply diffusing from its source, it is directed to a specific location where it applies a force on the blades of a turbine at the end of the pipe. The moving blades can then transmit energy through the rotor to other mechanical devices to perform the work for which these mechanical devices were designed.

Many constraints, such as the attachment of the blades to the turbine, are unchanging, at least within the timeframe in which the machine operates. But some are changeable, and these open the possibility of control. For instance, if there is a valve in the pipe in the above example, it could be operated upon by another mechanism, thereby altering the work performed by the steam engine. One thing that distinguishes the activity of this second mechanism is that it operates on a constraint in the production mechanism. For this action to count as control rather than just another dynamical effect within the mechanism, however, a further component is needed. The action of the control mechanism must be determined by information, which often results from making a measurement and using that to determine the action. This involves a constraint within the control mechanism being responsive to the variable that is measured and the control mechanism either directly or through a linkage determining the action of the controller (Pattee, 1973/2012).

Feedback control provides a useful example. A thermostat controlling a furnace, for example, measures temperature, which results in a state within the thermostat that constrains it to perform an activity on a constraint in the furnace. Similar feedback control mechanisms are widespread in biology. For example, the glycolytic mechanism in individual cells gates the flow of glucose into the mechanism through an allosteric enzyme. Allosteric enzymes have two binding sites – one that binds to the substrate that it will metabolize and another that binds a molecule that carries information about a measurement. In the key regulatory step in glycolysis, the enzyme binds ATP at both sites, but ATP serves a different function at each site. At the metabolic site, the ATP is transferred to the glucose derivative fructose-6-phosphate. At the control site, ATP binding results in altering the conformation of the protein in a way that blocks access to the first site. The result is that only when ATP is in low concentration will some of it be transferred to the metabolite, enabling it to be oxidized so as to generate more ATP.

With the distinction between control and production mechanisms made, we can focus attention on control mechanisms and how they operate in living systems. While control is important in human-made machines, there are some important differences in how control figures in machines and living systems (Bechtel, in press). First, in machines, there tend to be few constraints on which control operates. Second, control of machines ultimately resides with the human user of the machine. Neither of these is true in biology. Many of the constraints in biological systems are potential targets of control. While initially, allosteric enzymes were thought to be the exception, further examination reveals that many enzymes are allosteric, capable of being controlled by molecules binding at other sites that alter the conformation and reactivity of the enzyme. Moreover, most enzymes are regularly being synthesized and degraded, operations that affect their concentrations and hence their activity. Expression of most genes is regulated in turn by binding of signaling proteins at promoter sites. Second, biological organisms are autonomous; control operations are initiated within individual organisms, not by an external user, and serve to maintain the organism or its lineage (Moreno & Mossio, 2014). One reason control is so important is that biological mechanisms are frequently subjected to processes that would disrupt or destroy them. Accordingly, repair is critical (Rosen, 1991) and many productive mechanisms actually serve to make or repair components of the organism. These repair mechanisms rely on measurements of the activity of the mechanisms they repair so as to perform their operations when needed and not otherwise.

Control is prevalent in all organisms, including those lacking neurons. Production mechanisms in single-celled organisms are often controlled by chemical signals that encode measurements and execute control over them. For example, the chemotactic system in *Escherichia coli* employs a complex measurement mechanism to determine whether the organism is moving up or down chemical gradients (some of the chemicals are nutrients and others are poisons) and integrates that information into a signal that is sent to the motor on the flagellum. That signal operates on a constraint in the motor that determines whether flagella will rotate in a counterclockwise fashion (causing them to form a cohesive whole that can drive the organism forward) or clockwise (causing them to separate and the organism to tumble) (Parkinson, Hazelbauer, & Falke, 2015). Neurons represent a specialized control mechanism that takes in information on its dendrite or cell body and through chemical release from its axon can alter the activity of other cells. One consequence of being a specialized control system is that neurons can operate not just on production mechanisms but can send informational signals to other neurons. This raises the question of organization within control systems.

2.3 HIERARCHICAL VERSUS HETERARCHICAL ORGANIZATION OF CONTROL MECHANISMS

The notion of control gives rise to a specific conception of level;[1] a control mechanism operates on a production mechanism and so is at a higher level than the production mechanism. This framework can easily be extended into a hierarchy as seen in Figure 2.1A. If another control mechanism operates on the given control mechanism, then it is at a still higher level. This is indeed how we conceptualize control in social systems such as the military, government, or corporations. Individuals higher in the hierarchy procure information from those beneath them and, through their decision-making, exercise control over those beneath them. This is, as I suggested above, how we often conceptualize the nervous system as well. In this view, the neocortex is at the top of the hierarchy. Information procured by the

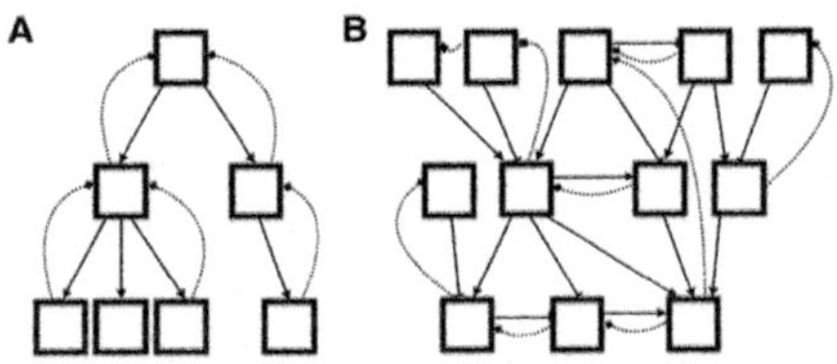

FIGURE 2.1 (A) Hierarchical versus (B) heterarchical control.
Note: Dotted arrows represent informational connections whereas solid arrows represent control operations. While the heterarchical organization is portrayed as layered, one could forego that with little loss and simply show a network of interconnected control nodes.

1 Numerous different notions of level are employed in biology, many of them in the context of mechanisms. One focuses on the fact that mechanisms themselves are high-level structures composed of parts (Craver, 2007). Marr (1982) advanced a different notion, one focused on different types of analysis one might offer of a mechanism. The notion of level of control is distinct from both; it refers in the first instance to the actions of a control mechanism to alter constraints in production mechanisms and in extended contexts to the transmission of information that ultimately changes such constraints.

senses (including proprioception) is funneled up to the neocortex where decisions for action are made and commands sent back down to lower levels of the nervous system until ultimately they are delivered to motor neurons.

Control mechanisms do not have to conform to a hierarchy, and the hierarchical perspective is especially misleading in the case of organisms. Control mechanisms are added to organisms opportunistically in the course of evolution when they serve to facilitate the ability of the organism to maintain and replicate itself as an autonomous system. This does not impose any requirement of hierarchical organization. Multiple control mechanisms, each operating largely independently of each other, can operate on the same production mechanism when each is responsive to different information that allows the organism to better deploy the production mechanism in maintaining itself. Although they could each operate independently, the fact that biological control mechanisms typically deploy the same handful of components creates the possibility of interactions between control mechanisms in which the information procured by one can be transmitted to another. The result may be a heterarchical network of control mechanisms, such as shown in Figure 2.1B.

Earlier, I noted that neurons are cells dedicated to performing control functions in higher organisms. Theorists have puzzled over how neurons could have evolved since we generally view neurons as transmitting signals between sensory and motor systems. Without dedicated sensory systems already in place, neurons would seem to have little function. Keijzer, van Duijn, and Lyon (2013) have advanced a compelling hypothesis that neurons first evolved to facilitate synchronized contraction of multiple muscle cells. In organisms such as the jellyfish, multiple muscles must contract together to move the organism through its environment. Next to the muscles, one finds a nerve network in which individual neurons measure the activity of some muscle cells and control the activity of others. These neurons also receive inputs from each other. Graph theorists have shown that such networks readily synchronize their behavior (Erdös & Rényi, 1960; Ermentrout & Kopell, 1984). As a result, muscle cells contract in synchrony. In jellyfish, the activity of this nerve network is itself controlled by other neurons that convey sensory information, for example, about predators. While these neurons might be viewed to be at a higher level of control, their inputs only serve to modulate the behavior of the nerve network. There is no highest-level executive, but only an integrated network of control mechanisms.

When we think of neural control systems in higher organisms, we tend to focus first on the brain, especially the cerebral cortex. We then construe processing as proceeding from sensory areas of cortex through what are sometimes referred to as association areas until activity reaches motor areas of cortex. This reflects our tendency to view control as hierarchical. But in fact, regions throughout the neocortex receive as many or more projections from and send projections to thalamic and other midbrain regions as they receive or send to other cortical areas. Within the neocortex, there are also at least as many recurrent projections as forward projections. While these are downplayed in the hierarchical perspective, numerous theorists are beginning to view the central nervous system as a network, not a hierarchy (Sporns, 2010, 2012).

One way to move beyond the hierarchical conception in which the neocortex serves as the high-level controller of all behavior is to revisit research from the mid-twentieth century that examined the behaviors that remained in decerebrate (resulting from cuts at the level of the brain stem) and decorticate (resulting from cuts above the thalamus) preparations, typically of cats. A principle that emerged is that centers lower in the nervous system are effective controllers that can be modulated by those situated higher in the nervous typically. For example, cutting just above the pons leads to extended posture of both the upper and lower extremities. Cutting higher, above the thalamus but below the striatum, results in cats becoming hyperactive, but without coordinated behaviors. Input from the thalamus and nearby areas allows the extended posture to be relaxed. If the cut is above the striatum, cats can feed spontaneously, localize auditory stimuli, learn to associate sounds with food, and clean and groom themselves, all without input from the neocortex. Reflecting on this research, Buchwald and Brown (1973) offer the perspective:[2]

> In this view, integration of local reflexes is accomplished at the spinal level by the relatively simple, automatic system of reciprocal and crossed inhibitory reactions seen in the spinal animal. The addition of the brainstem, cerebellum, and diencephalon allows more general

[2] This perspective echoes the one advanced by the nineteenth-century neurologist John Hughlings Jackson (1868–1869/1931), who viewed higher levels of the nervous system as re-representing what is already represented in lower regions of the nervous system. Part of his argument focused on the behavior of patients with cortical damage; they would still exhibit behaviors, often quite coherent.

> motor patterns to emerge, including postural and locomotor reactions which require simultaneous integration of entire groups of spinal reflexes. Thus, a higher level of motor control is superimposed on the lower mechanisms which are used together in groups while still maintaining the selective, sequential inhibition and facilitation of the more primitive response mechanisms. Cortical influences constitute a still more general governing mechanism of motor function, and distance receptors as well as somatic exteroceptors and interoceptors furnish very broad stimulus patterns.

Although highlighting the independence of lower-level controllers, this research still encourages the idea that controllers are organized into a single hierarchy with the neocortex at the top. A further step away from hierarchy to heterarchy comes from considering further the control that is exercised in decorticate preparations. Much of it stems from the hypothalamus, which consists of numerous nuclei that individually control such phenomena as body temperature, intake of food and water, stress responses, ovulation, sleep, and circadian rhythms, many through the release of specific hormones. In some cases, through cortical activity, we can override hypothalamic control for a period; for example, one can consciously drive oneself to remain awake. But hypothalamic regions involved in sleep regulation eventually assert themselves, as is manifest in rebound sleep. Although interconnected in various ways, individual nuclei in the hypothalamus exert relatively independent control over different production mechanisms.

To illustrate this, I focus in the next section on one hypothalamic region that exercises control over many physiological and behavioral regions and that is also implicated in depression. The suprachiasmatic nucleus (SCN), so named because of its location just above the optic chiasm, houses the central circadian clock that exercises regulative effects over activities ranging from body temperature, digestion of food, immune system function, ability to sustain sleep, and reaction times to sensory stimuli. The clock is an endogenous oscillator that maintains a period of approximately 24 hours (hence, these rhythms are referred to as *circadian* – *circa* [about] + *dies* [day]) that can be entrained to the light–dark cycle in the local environment. Once the clock mechanism was discovered, researchers realized that it exists in nearly every cell type. In each cell type, the clock is able to regulate expression of genes specifically relevant to that cell type. However, without the SCN, the clocks in individual cells in these tissues are not synchronized. Because only in the SCN do cells synchronize with each other and because it produces a regular time signal that can entrain the other clocks, the SCN is regarded as the master clock (Welsh, Takahashi, & Kay, 2010).[3]

Although the circadian clock regulates a huge range of physiological and behavioral activities, in none of these cases does it operate alone. Digestive mechanisms are also controlled by the presence of food and sleep by the time from last sleep. The circadian clock interacts with many other control mechanisms in regulating each of these activities. It is just one component in a heterarchical network.

2.4 CIRCADIAN CONTROL MECHANISMS AND DEPRESSION

As is fitting for a control mechanism with widespread effects, disrupted circadian rhythms have been associated with a host of diseases, including psychiatric disorders. Well before any of the details of the circadian clock mechanism were known, researchers identified associations between disrupted circadian rhythms and mood. I will review a variety of evidence for associations between disrupted circadian rhythms and depression. Until recently, there was not compelling evidence that the link was causal, but I will present one study that makes a compelling case that circadian disruption is a causal factor in depression-like behaviors in mice before returning to the question of how to conceptualize these effects in terms of control mechanisms.

One of the first indications of a connection between circadian rhythms and depression focused on the altered sleep patterns manifest in depressed patients. (See Hinton, 1963, for one of the first systematic studies of sleep and depression.) Sleep, however, is only partially under circadian control, and until Boivin et al. (1997) conducted a study that desynchronized sleep from circadian rhythms, it was not possible to show a purely circadian effect on measures related to depression. (Boivin et al. studied perceived happiness.) In the meantime, a variety of other associations were found

[3] The importance of the SCN was demonstrated in a classic study in which Ralph, Foster, Davis, and Menaker (1990) removed the SCN from hamsters and inserted an SCN whose oscillations exhibited a different period into a plastic sac in the ventricle. Remarkably, these hamsters exhibited circadian rhythms of the donor SCN, as reported on a variety of measures, even though the donor SCN was unable to establish any neural connections to other tissues. This indicated that an important component of the signal was hormonal and presumably involved the transmission of one or more transcription factors. Subsequent research, however, has shown that not all circadian rhythms are restored with such transplants, suggesting neuronal signaling mechanisms are also involved. This further supports a heterarchical picture of control.

between disrupted circadian rhythms and mood. Kripke, Mullaney, Atkinson, and Wolf (1978) measured short-period circadian rhythms in manic-depressive patients and proposed that depression resulted from individuals daily experiencing an advance in their circadian phase. They further proposed that the effectiveness of tricyclic and monoamine oxidase antidepressants might be due to their effects in slowing free-running circadian rhythms. While early measurements of altered circadian phase in depressed patients focused primarily on melatonin, Souetre et al. (1989) added measurements of body temperature, plasma cortisol, norepinephrine, and thyrotropin in depressed and recovered patients as well as controls with no diagnosis of depression. They demonstrated that although the phase in the oscillation of these measures remained normal, the amplitude was significantly diminished in depressed participants. Moreover, the amplitude returned to normal after recovery.

A different basis for connecting depression with circadian rhythms came from a report by Lewy, Kern, Rosenthal, and Wehr (1982) that bright light therapy during three hours after awakening considerably reduced the symptoms of a seasonally manic-depressive patient during winter when his depression was greatest. Based on studies with additional patients, Rosenthal et al. (1984) introduced the category *seasonal affective disorder* (SAD) and presented further evidence of temporary reduction in depression with bright light therapy (the effects usually ceased when light treatment was stopped).[4] The researchers went beyond the correlation to propose the *phase shift hypothesis*, which holds that depression results from the delayed phase of circadian rhythms (or, in a few cases, from an advanced phase) and that the therapeutic effect of light on depression resulted from shifting the phase of circadian rhythms earlier (or later in phase-advanced patients). They supported this with correlational evidence of advance (or delay) in the phase of melatonin expression in treated patients (Lewy, Sack, Singer, & White, 1987).

Shortly after these associations between disrupted, circadian rhythms and depression were advanced, circadian researchers began to identify the

[4] Although, starting with *DSM-IIIR*, a "seasonal pattern" modifier has been included for diagnoses of major depression and bipolar disorder, the association between seasonality and depression has been challenged. Traffanstedt, Mehta, and LoBello (2016) conducted a populational study of depression across the United States and found no correlation with latitude, season, or exposure to sunlight. They note that studies claiming such associations typically employed retrospective self-reports and did not employ *DSM* categories for assessing depression. SAD may be an artifact of folk psychologizing, not grounded in reliable data.

components of the mechanism responsible for circadian rhythms. Working on fruit flies, Hardin, Hall, and Rosbash (1990) built on Konopka and Benzer's (1971) discovery of a gene, *period* (*per*) that, when mutated, altered, or totally eliminated circadian rhythms. Hardin et al. showed that concentrations of the protein PER increased several hours after increases in *per* mRNA and proposed a feedback mechanism in which the gene would initially be expressed, but as its product accumulated, expression would be inhibited. As PER degraded, transcription would increase again, generating an oscillation in PER concentration. Subsequent research identified many additional proteins that figure in the clock mechanism and also established that the circadian clock in mammals relies on homologs of the same genes.

A challenge in studying circadian rhythms and their disruptions in humans is that measuring mRNA and protein concentrations requires sacrificing the organism. Li et al. (2013), however, developed a strategy of collecting samples from cadavers and using time of death to create pseudo time-series data. They were thus able to compare changes in protein concentrations in depressed patients and those who died with no indications of depression. Figure 2.2 shows the genes whose expression oscillates (numbers indicate levels of significance; those in Medium grey exhibit the highest level of significance) in six brain regions (dorsolateral prefrontal cortex, amygdala, cerebellum, nucleus accumbens, anterior

A

1 | 0.8 | 0.6 | 0.4 | 0.2 | 0

Symbol	DLPFC	AnCg	HC	AMY	NAcc	CB
ARNTL*	0.0005	0.0005	0.001	0.001	0.0005	0.0005
PER2*	0.001	0.0005	0.0005	0.005	0.008	0.0005
PER3*	0.0005	0.0005	0.0005	0.094	0.0005	0.001
NR1D1*	0.0005	0.0005	0.0005	0.102	0.0005	0.008
DBP*	0.0005	0.0005	0.003	0.066	0.002	0.001
SFPQ	0.0005	0.152	0.013	0.134	0.001	0.029
ITIH5	0.0005	0.021	0.009	0.577	0.007	0.027
LDLR	0.001	0.002	0.004	0.014	0.561	0.204
PER1*	0.0005	0.005	0.008	0.559	0.044	0.071
INSIG1	0.007	0.003	0.001	0.025	0.727	0.183
SLC39A14	0.007	0.0005	0.029	0.067	0.077	0.262
NFIL3*	0.011	0.0005	0.104	0.181	0.03	0.198
SNTB2	0.023	0.038	0.17	0.001	0.013	0.368
PDZRN3	0.002	0.001	0.037	0.333	0.207	0.195
BHLHE40*	0.0005	0.014	0.147	0.42	0.02	0.127
BHLHE41	0.005	0.003	0.997	0.751	0.051	0.003

B **MDD:**

1 | 0.8 | 0.6 | 0.4 | 0.2 | 0

	DLPFC	ACG	HC	AMY	NACC	CB
ARNTL	0.121	0.072	0.732	0.084	0.005	0.141
PER2	0.015	0.083	0.213	0.342	0.075	0.582
PER3	0.42	0.652	0.432	0.999	0.29	0.531
NR1D1	0.04	0.029	0.285	0.097	0.003	0.111
DBP	0.102	0.236	0.025	0.79	0.121	0.118
SFPQ	0.135	0.124	0.165	0.265	0.047	0.089
ITIH5	0.936	0.47	0.117	0.603	0.15	0.832
LDLR	0.012	0.385	0.315	0.307	0.005	0.028
PER1	0.006	0.21	0.137	0.619	0.124	0.061
INSIG1	0.056	0.534	0.668	0.869	0.318	0.88
SLC39A14	0.641	0.21	0.301	0.393	0.157	0.354
NFIL3*	0.565	0.326	0.633	0.478	0.179	0.617
SNTB2	0.928	0.194	0.123	0.765	0.365	0.293
PDZRN3	0.13	0.003	0.503	0.229	0.075	0.139
BHLHE40	0.19	0.897	0.433	0.963	0.14	0.009
BHLHE41	0.497	0.781	0.754	0.433	0.875	0.246

FIGURE 2.2 Top oscillating proteins in six brain tissues in normal controls, and data from patients with major depressive disorder analyzed in the same manner.

Note: (A) Top oscillating proteins in six brain tissues in normal controls in a cadaver study in which time of death was known. Gene names are shown on the left; those shown in bold are known to figure in the circadian clock. The numbers indicate significance levels on a measure of oscillation with darker shading indicating those that oscillate the most. (B) Data from patients with major depressive disorder analyzed in the same manner, making it clear that these genes achieved lower or much lower significance levels in almost all tissues. Reproduced from Li et al. (2013), Figure 2, © 2013 National Academy of Sciences, USA.

cingulate cortex, and hippocampus). Data from patients without indications of depression are shown on the left: many of the oscillating genes are known circadian genes (names shown in bold). In patients with major depressive disorder, shown on the right, oscillation of many of these genes, including especially clock genes, is much reduced.

These studies and numerous others (for a review, see Vadnie & McClung, 2017) demonstrated an association between disrupted circadian rhythms and mood disorders, and many researchers have used these findings to argue for a causal link between disrupted circadian rhythms and depression. Some of these associations are with monoamines, such as serotonin. Both monoamines (Hampp et al., 2008) and their receptors (Logan et al., 2015; McClung, 2007) exhibit circadian oscillations in their concentrations. Specific molecular interactions have been proposed between clock proteins and proteins involved in monoamine synthesis (tyrosine hydroxylase—Th) and degradation (monoamine oxidase—Mao) as well as glucocorticoid receptors that have been implicated in depression (see Albrecht (2017) for a review). These studies, however, fall short of demonstrating that it is disrupted circadian rhythms that explain depression (Bechtel, 2015). Landgraf, McCarthy, and Welsh (2014) point out that many genes are pleiotropic and, even if circadian clock genes have demonstrated effects in processes involved in depression such as monoamine metabolism, the effects may be independent of their role in circadian rhythms. Lazzerini Ospri, Prusky, and Hattar (2017) suggest that alteration of clock proteins and mood disorders could also be effects of a common cause without there being a causal link between them.

A recent study by Landgraf et al. (2016), though, has provided compelling evidence that disrupted circadian rhythms are responsible for depression-like symptoms in mice. They developed a SCN-specific BMAL1 knockdown (KD) in mice that resulted in circadian rhythms with 80% lower amplitude and longer periods. This lengthened period was also manifest in behavior. (The authors note that this corresponds to the lengthened periods exhibited by patients with major depressive disorder.) Landgraf et al. then investigated behavioral changes associated with depression. Prior to any stimulus, the mice spent significantly less time than normal controls in the light compartment of the light-dark box, viewed as an anxiety-like change in behavior. Although they showed change neither in their preference for sweet-sucrose water nor in their latency to approach and eat in novel environments, the knockdown mice gained significantly more weight than controls. They also exhibited increased immobility compared with controls in the tail-suspension test.

When presented with an aversive stimulus from which they could escape, the SCN-BMAL1-KD mice exhibited longer escape latencies and more failures to escape than controls. Most mouse models of learned helplessness require exposure to an inescapable stimulus, leading the researchers to present these mice as "a new genetic animal model of helplessness, despair, and anxiety" (p. 7).

Since the knockdown was limited to the SCN, which is not generally viewed as itself involved in mood regulation, Landgraf et al. propose that the depression-like effects exhibited by their mice are due to altered rhythms generated by the SCN and communicated to other brain regions. Accordingly, they measured cortisol levels in the mice with BMAL1 knocked down in the SCN and showed both that they exhibited a second peak at the end of the activity period, not shown by control mice, and sharply lower corticosterone levels 30 minutes after stress induced by a restrainer. They propose that these reduced corticosterone levels may explain the depression-like behaviors that they observed, although they also acknowledge that the effects could be due to altered rhythms in areas normally orchestrated by the SCN such as the nucleus accumbens and the periaqueductal gray.

There are epistemic challenges in applying results from animal studies to psychiatric disorders in humans (for discussion see papers by Pine and Schaffner, this volume), especially since the mice showed no changes in their preference for sweet sucrose water nor in their latency to approach and eat in novel environments, which are generally regarded as better behavioral indicators of depression. My interest is what they would indicate, if valid, for depression (or perhaps instead for anxiety[5]) about how circadian rhythms manifest these effects. Circadian rhythms affect the expression of 10%–15% of genes in each brain region and bodily tissue (different genes in different tissues), presumably via one or more transcription factors. By releasing transcription factors that regulate gene expression, the circadian clock fits the account offered earlier of a control mechanism – it operates on flexible constraints in production mechanisms, altering the activities they perform. It is important to recognize that it is not the only control mechanism operating on these production mechanisms. Most production mechanisms are also controlled by mechanisms that register information more specific to their activity, e.g.,

5 Depression and anxiety are grouped as internalizing disorders in *DSM-5* and at least some psychiatrists contend they may constitute a spectrum, not well-differentiated disorders.

regulating metabolism according to the need for ATP or regulating muscle contraction in relation to the activity of other muscles or environmental stimuli. Circadian control complements these other control mechanisms so as to enable production mechanisms to generally operate at times when they are most likely to be successful – altering reaction times so as to respond faster to stimuli when they are most likely to arise and limiting metabolic processes to times when nutrients are likely to be available and ATP likely to be needed. Circadian control is often extremely important to the success of organisms in carrying out other activities (we notice the consequences when, as in changing time zones, our activities are not properly coordinated to our local environment), but it spreads its effects diffusely across production mechanisms. It is one component in a heterarchical network that integrates multiple control mechanisms.

The details of how altered circadian rhythms generated in the SCN affect production mechanisms matter for how we understand the role of circadian rhythms on mood. If the effect were directly on the motor mechanisms involved, there would be little basis for linking circadian rhythms to mood. But if the effect is mediated by a more generalized control process such as that associated with cortisol levels, then they might be regarded as one mechanism in a heterarchy control network whose altered operation results in the symptoms of major depression (or anxiety). But when they are, it is important to keep in mind that they are only one among multiple processes that figure in a heterarchical control network.

2.5 IMPLICATIONS OF HETERARCHICAL CONTROL NETWORKS FOR UNDERSTANDING DEPRESSION

I have employed the case of circadian rhythms to illustrate the usefulness and also the challenges of thinking in terms of heterarchical control networks. Because they are embedded in networks, individual control mechanisms have a wide range of effects. Through a network, they are able to regulate expression of many genes and thereby coordinate many aspects of organism physiology and behavior. When they are disrupted, they are also capable of having highly diverse effects. They are thus appropriate systems to which to appeal to explain the diverse effects exhibited in depression. But it also makes it challenging to show that a given causal factor actually has a specific effect. Landgraf et al. were able to overcome this limitation and provide evidence that disrupted circadian rhythms manifest themselves in depression-like symptoms, at least in mice.

Although the serotonin hypothesis that attributed depression to reduced serotonin levels is now rejected by many psychologists as evidence has failed to support it, one could envisage serotonin as operative in a heterarchical control system such that altered levels manifest of serotonin manifest itself in depression.[6] Serotonin certainly plays control roles in the nervous system. Like other neurotransmitters, it is found in a wide range of organisms in which its control activities have been established.[7] Although the fact that serotonin is a versatile control agent makes is a candidate for producing some of the symptoms of depression, it also presents an important challenge. To show that it actually plays such a role, one needs to examine how it operates in control processes to affect symptoms associated with depression in detail. The comments below are intended to make the challenge clear.

In mammalian brains, serotonin is only generated in the neurons in the nine raphe nuclei in the midbrain (Dahlstroem & Fuxe, 1964). Neurons elsewhere in the brain (thalamus, limbic system, retina) possess only the transporters (Gaspar & Lillesaar, 2012). The nine raphe nuclei constitute a diverse collection of nuclei. The six rostral raphe nuclei project to the forebrain, whereas the more caudal nuclei project to the hindbrain (Figure 2.3). Different rostral nuclei are sometimes presented as projecting to different regions of the forebrain, but since the projections form a "dense plexus of axonal processes" (Hensler, 2010, p. 369) with individual neurons having long projections that connect to targets in many different regions (Hale & Lowry, 2011), it is difficult to develop a detailed map. In

6 The serotonin hypothesis continues to have strong adherents, as witnessed by two special recent issues of *Philosophical Transactions* devoted to it (introduced, respectively, by Albert, Benkelfat, & Descarries, 2012, and Albert & Benkelfat, 2013). For its defenders in particular, the issues raised below should be of some urgency.

7 Serotonin appears in organisms lacking neurons, having apparently evolved in photosynthetic cyanobacteria, which produced the molecular oxygen that is required to synthesize serotonin (as well as other molecules such as melatonin and auxin) from tryptophan. Tryptophan is widely distributed amongst prokaryotes and the products synthesized from tryptophan often performed crucial antioxidant activities rendered important by the increase in molecular oxygen. Serotonin occurs widely and in much higher concentrations in plants (where it figures in growth and mitosis) than in animals. In animals, it occurs in cells throughout the organism, not just the brain and has been demonstrated to function in a wide diversity of tissues. In invertebrates, it plays a variety of different roles. In the nematode worm *C. elegans,* it signals the presence of food and Chao, Komatsu, Fukuto, Dionne, and Hart (2004) show how it alters the activity of sensory neurons that respond to the repellant stimulus octanol. In the sea slug Aplysia, Martin et al. (1997) found that it contributed to synaptic plasticity and increasing long-term facilitation. In the leech, Kristan and Nusbaum (1982) identified a pair of serotonin-containing neurons that when stimulated, initiate swimming.

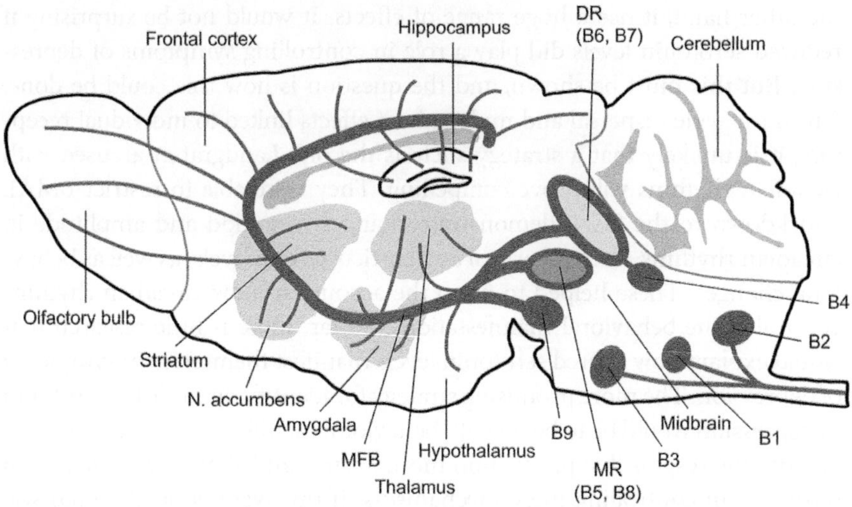

FIGURE 2.3 Serotonin is only synthesized in the nine raphe nuclei, the more rostal of which project diffusely to the forebrain while the more dorsal project to the hindbrain.
Note: Reprinted from Neuron, Vol 76, K.-P. Lesch and J. Walder, Serotonin in the modulation of neural plasticity and networks: Implications for neurodevelopmental disorders, Page 176, Copyright (2012), with permission from Elsevier

addition, within the hippocampus and cerebral cortex, most serotonergic neurons are paracrine or volume transmitters. Rather than forming specific synapses, they diffuse serotonin over a broad region. Accordingly, Figure 2.3 shows one common pathway from several different raphe nuclei projecting to a multitude of brain regions.

The receptors for serotonin are also highly diverse and widely distributed. They have been divided into seven classes, which have different effects of post-synaptic neurons. Receptors in one class (1a), for example, are found in frontal cortex, hippocampus, entorhinal cortex, septum, and amygdala and have been shown to affect addiction, appetite, blood pressure, heart rate, cardiovascular function, memory, pain sensitivity, respiration, penile erection and sexual behavior, sleep, and thermoregulation. They are also found on the cell bodies of serotonin neurons in the dorsal and median raphe bodies where they figure in feedback regulating the activity of these neurons. Among the claims for the 1a receptors is that they are involved in mood and related phenomena such as anxiety.

Two things are immediately notable. On the one hand, serotonin meets the condition of playing a control function in a large heterarchical network. On the other hand, it has a huge range of effects. It would not be surprising if reduced serotonin levels did play a role in controlling symptoms of depression. But this must be shown, and the question is how this could be done. Given the wide dispersal and multitude of effects linked to individual receptors, it is unlikely that a strategy such as the one Landgraf et al. used with circadian rhythms will prove compelling. They were able to restrict BMAL knockdown to the SCN, demonstrate changes in period and amplitude in circadian rhythms, altered cortisol and corticosterone levels, as well as behavioral changes. These helped to fill in the account of how circadian rhythms controlled the behavioral manifestations. So far, there is little research that would explain how altered serotonin levels manifest themselves in symptoms of depression. The more promising strategy for identifying a role for serotonin in depression would be to begin with behavioral manifestations of depression, identify the responsible production mechanisms, and show a specific role of serotonin in controlling these mechanisms. If this were done, it would still leave important challenges in explaining why altered serotonin levels specifically manifested itself in symptoms of depression, but one would at least have the beginnings of an account of its role in control mechanisms affecting symptoms of depression. Lacking such an account, all we have are putative associations between altered serotonin levels and depression.

2.6 CONCLUSION

Independent of the evidence for particular claims, the account I have offered of control mechanisms offers a perspective on how to explain psychiatric disorders such as depression mechanistically. Such disorders, with highly heterogeneous effects, are likely due to disruption of control mechanisms. I have offered an account in which control mechanisms operate on flexible constraints in production mechanisms. I have also argued that neural control, like other instances of control in living organisms, is likely to be organized heterarchically. This allows for both multiple controllers to operate on any given production mechanism and for interactions between controllers that result in diverse consequences when control is disrupted. On the one hand, disruption of control mechanisms offers a promising way to explain the effects of psychiatric disorders with diverse symptoms. But on the other it makes it challenging to support claims linking disorders to control mechanisms. The circadian example, though, suggests that, while difficult, it is possible to fill in the account of control mechanisms sufficiently to provide a compelling explanation.

REFERENCES

Albert, P. R., & Benkelfat, C. (2013) "The neurobiology of depression: Revisiting the serotonin hypothesis. II. Genetic, epigenetic and clinical studies." *Philosophical Transactions of the Royal Society B: Biological Sciences, 368*(1615), 20120535.

Albert, P. R., Benkelfat, C., & Descarries, L. (2012) "The neurobiology of depression – Revisiting the serotonin hypothesis. I. Cellular and molecular mechanisms." *Philosophical Transactions of the Royal Society B: Biological Sciences, 367*(1601), 2378.

Albrecht, U. (2017) "Molecular mechanisms in mood regulation involving the circadian clock." *Frontiers in Neurology, 8*, 30.

Bechtel, W. (2008) *Mental mechanisms. Philosophical perspectives on cognitive neuroscience.* London: Routledge.

(2015) "Circadian rhythms and mood disorders: Are the phenomena and mechanisms causally related?" *Frontiers in Psychiatry, 6*, 118.

(2018) "The importance of constraints and control in biological mechanisms: Insights from cancer research." *Philosophy of Science, 85*(4), 573–593.

(in press) "Living machines: The extent and limits of the machine metaphor." In S. Holm & M. Serban (Eds.), *Philosophical perspectives on the engineering approach in biology: Living machines?* New York: Routledge.

Bechtel, W., & Abrahamsen, A. (2005) "Explanation: A mechanist alternative." *Studies in History and Philosophy of Biological and Biomedical Sciences, 36*(2), 421–441.

Bechtel, W., & Richardson, R. C. (1993/2010) *Discovering complexity: Decomposition and localization as strategies in scientific research.* Cambridge, MA: MIT Press. 1993 edition published by Princeton University Press.

Boivin, D. B., Czeisler, C. A., Dijk, D. J., Duffy, J. F., Folkard, S., Minors, D. S., . . . Waterhouse, J. M. (1997) "Complex interaction of the sleep–wake cycle and circadian phase modulates mood in healthy subjects." *Archives of General Psychiatry, 54*(2), 145–152.

Buchwald, J. S., & Brown, K. A. (1973) "Subcortical mechanisms of behavioral plasticity." In J. D. Maser (Ed.), *Efferent organization and the integration of behavior* (pp. xii, 368 pp.). New York: Academic Press.

Chao, M. Y., Komatsu, H., Fukuto, H. S., Dionne, H. M., & Hart, A. C. (2004) "Feeding status and serotonin rapidly and reversibly modulate a *Caenorhabditis elegans* chemosensory circuit." *Proceedings of the National Academy of Sciences of the United States of America, 101*(43), 15512.

Chen, L., Eaton, W. W., Gallo, J. J., & Nestadt, G. (2000) "Understanding the heterogeneity of depression through the triad of symptoms, course and risk factors: A longitudinal, population-based study." *Journal of Affective Disorders, 59*(1), 1–11.

Cowen, P. J., & Browning, M. (2015) "What has serotonin to do with depression?" *World Psychiatry, 14*(2), 158–160.

Craver, C. F. (2007) *Explaining the brain: Mechanisms and the mosaic unity of neuroscience.* New York: Oxford University Press.

Craver, C. F., & Darden, L. (2013) *In search of mechanisms: Discoveries across the life sciences*. Chicago: University of Chicago Press.

Culverhouse, R. C., Saccone, N. L., Horton, A. C., Ma, Y., Anstey, K. J., Banaschewski, T., . . . Bierut, L. J. (2018) "Collaborative meta-analysis finds no evidence of a strong interaction between stress and 5-HTTLPR genotype contributing to the development of depression." *Molecular Psychiatry, 23*(1), 133–142.

Dahlstroem, A., & Fuxe, K. (1964) "Evidence for the existence of monoamine-containing neurons in the central nervous system. I. Demonstration of monoamines in the cell bodies of brain stem neurons." *Acta Physiologica Scandinavica. Supplementum, 232*, 231–255.

Erdös, P., & Rényi, A. (1960) "On the evolution of random graphs." *Proceedings of the Mathematical Institute of the Hungarian Academy of Sciences, 5*, 17–61.

Ermentrout, G. B., & Kopell, N. (1984) "Frequency plateaus in a chain of weakly coupled oscillators. 1." *Siam Journal on Mathematical Analysis, 15*(2), 215–237.

Fried, E. I. (2017) "The 52 symptoms of major depression: Lack of content overlap among seven common depression scales." *Journal of Affective Disorders, 208*, 191–197.

Gaspar, P., & Lillesaar, C. (2012) "Probing the diversity of serotonin neurons." *Philosophical Transactions: Biological Sciences, 367*(1601), 2382–2394.

Goldberg, D. (2011) "The heterogeneity of 'major depression.'" *World Psychiatry, 10*(3), 226–228.

Hale, M. W., & Lowry, C. A. (2011) "Functional topography of midbrain and pontine serotonergic systems: Implications for synaptic regulation of serotonergic circuits." *Psychopharmacology (Berlin), 213*(2–3), 243–264.

Hampp, G., Ripperger, J. A., Houben, T., Schmutz, I., Blex, C., Perreau-Lenz, S., . . . Albrecht, U. (2008) "Regulation of monoamine oxidase A by circadian-clock components implies clock influence on mood." *Current Biology, 18*(9), 678–683.

Hardin, P. E., Hall, J. C., & Rosbash, M. (1990) "Feedback of the *Drosophila period* gene product on circadian cycling of its messenger RNA levels." *Nature, 343* (6258), 536–540.

Hensler, J. G. (2010) "Serotonin in mood and emotion." In P. M. Christian & L. J. Barry (Eds.), *Handbook of behavioral neuroscience* (Vol. 21, pp. 367–378). London: Elsevier.

Hinton, J. M. (1963) "Patterns of insomnia in depressive states." *Journal of Neurological and Neurosurgical Psychiatry, 26*, 184–189.

Hooker, C. A. (2013) "On the import of constraints in complex dynamical systems." *Foundations of Science, 18*(4), 757–780.

Jackson, J. H. (1868–1869/1931) "Notes on the physiology and pathology of the nervous system." In J. Taylor (Ed.), *Selected writings of John Hughlings Jackson* (Vol. II, pp. 215–237). New York: Basic Books.

Keijzer, F., van Duijn, M., & Lyon, P. (2013) "What nervous systems do: Early evolution, input–output, and the skin brain thesis." *Adaptive Behavior, 21*(2), 67–85.

Konopka, R. J., & Benzer, S. (1971) "Clock mutants of *Drosophila melanogaster*." *Proceedings of the National Academy of Sciences of the United States of America, 89*(9), 2112–2116.

Kripke, D. F., Mullaney, D. J., Atkinson, M., & Wolf, S. (1978) "Circadian rhythm disorders in manic-depressives." *Biological Psychiatry, 13*(3), 335–351.

Kristan, W. B., & Nusbaum, M. P. (1982) "The dual role of serotonin in leech swimming." *Journal of Physiology (Paris), 78*(8), 743–747.

Lacasse, J. R., & Leo, J. (2005) "Serotonin and depression: A disconnect between the advertisements and the scientific literature." *PLoS Medicine, 2*(12), 1211–1216.

Landgraf, D., Long, J. E., Proulx, C. D., Barandas, R., Malinow, R., & Welsh, D. K. (2016) "Genetic disruption of circadian rhythms in the Suprachiasmatic Nucleus causes helplessness, behavioral despair, and anxiety-like behavior in mice." *Biological Psychiatry. 80*(11), 827–835.

Landgraf, D., McCarthy, M. J., & Welsh, D. K. (2014) "The role of the circadian clock in animal models of mood disorders." *Behavioral Neuroscience, 128*(3), 344–359.

Lapin, I. P., & Oxenkrug, G. F. (1969) 'Intensification of the central serotoninergic processes as a possible determinatnt of the thymoleptic effect.' *The Lancet, 293* (7586), 132–136.

Lazzerini Ospri, L., Prusky, G., & Hattar, S. (2017) 'Mood, the circadian system, and melanopsin retinal ganglion cells.' *Annual Review of Neuroscience, 40*, 539–556.

Lesch, K.-P., & Waider, J. (2012) 'Serotonin in the modulation of neural plasticity and networks: Implications for neurodevelopmental disorders.' *Neuron, 76*(1), 175–191.

Lewy, A. J., Kern, H. A., Rosenthal, N. E., & Wehr, T. A. (1982) 'Bright artificial light treatment of a manic-depressive patient with a seasonal mood cycle.' *American Journal of Psychiatry, 139*(11), 1496–1498.

Lewy, A. J., Sack, R. L., Singer, C. M., & White, D. M. (1987) 'The phase shift hypothesis for bright light's therapeutic mechanism of action: Theoretical considerations and experimental evidence.' *Psychopharmacology Bulletin, 23*(3), 349–353.

Li, J. Z., Bunney, B. G., Meng, F., Hagenauer, M. H., Walsh, D. M., Vawter, M. P., . . . Bunney, W. E. (2013) 'Circadian patterns of gene expression in the human brain and disruption in major depressive disorder.' *Proceedings of the National Academy of Sciences of the United States of America, 110*(24), 9950–9955.

Logan, R. W., Edgar, N., Gillman, A. G., Hoffman, D., Zhu, X., & McClung, C. A. (2015) 'Chronic stress induces brain region-specific alterations of molecular rhythms that correlate with depression-like behavior in mice.' *Biological Psychiatry, 78*(4), 249–258.

Lux, V., & Kendler, K. S. (2010) 'Deconstructing major depression: A validation study of the DSM-IV symptomatic criteria.' *Psychological Medicine, 40*(10), 1679–1690.

Machamer, P., Darden, L., & Craver, C. F. (2000) 'Thinking about mechanisms.' *Philosophy of Science, 67*(1), 1–25.

Marr, D. C. (1982) *Vision: A computation investigation into the human representational system and processing of visual information.* San Francisco: Freeman.

Martin, K. C., Casadio, A., Zhu, H., E, Y., Rose, J. C., Chen, M., . . . Kandel, E. R. (1997) 'Synapse-specific, long-term facilitation of Aplysia sensory to motor synapses: A function for local protein synthesis in memory storage.' *Cell*, *91*(7), 927–938.

McClung, C. A. (2007) 'Circadian genes, rhythms and the biology of mood disorders.' *Pharmacology & Therapeutics*, *114*(2), 222–232.

Moreno, A., & Mossio, M. (2014) *Biological autonomy: A philosophical and theoretical inquiry*. Dordrecht: Springer.

Parkinson, J. S., Hazelbauer, G. L., & Falke, J. J. (2015) 'Signaling and sensory adaptation in *Escherichia coli* chemoreceptors: 2015 update.' *Trends in Microbiology*, *23*(5), 257–266.

Pattee, H. H. (1972/2012) 'Laws and constraints, symbols and languages.' In *Laws, language and life* (Vol. 7, pp. 81–89). Netherlands: Springer.

(1973/2012) 'The physical basis and origin of hierarchical control.' In *Laws, language and life* (Vol. 7, pp. 91–110). Netherlands: Springer.

Ralph, M. R., Foster, R. G., Davis, F. C., & Menaker, M. (1990) 'Transplanted suprachiasmatic nucleus determines circadian period.' *Science*, *247*(4945), 975–978.

Rosen, R. (1991) *Life itself: A comprehensive inquiry into the nature, origin, and fabrication of life*. Columbia: New York.

Rosenthal, N. E., Sack, D. A., Gillin, J. C., Lewy, A. J., Goodwin, F. K., Davenport, Y., . . . Wehr, T. A. (1984) 'Seasonal affective disorder. A description of the syndrome and preliminary findings with light therapy.' *Archive of General Psychiatry*, *41*(1), 72–80.

Souetre, E., Salvati, E., Belugou, J. L., Pringuey, D., Candito, M., Krebs, B., . . . Darcourt, G. (1989) 'Circadian rhythms in depression and recovery: Evidence for blunted amplitude as the main chronobiological abnormality.' *Psychiatry Research*, *28*(3), 263–278.

Sporns, O. (2010) *Networks of the brain*. Cambridge, MA: MIT Press.

(2012) *Discovering the human connectome*. Cambridge, MA: MIT Press.

Traffanstedt, M. K., Mehta, S., & LoBello, S. G. (2016) 'Major depression with seasonal variation: Is it a valid construct?' *Clinical Psychological Science*, *4*(5), 825–834.

Vadnie, C. A., & McClung, C. A. (2017) 'Circadian rhythm disturbances in mood disorders: Insights into the role of the suprachiasmatic nucleus.' *Neural Plasticity*, *2017*, 1504507.

Watts, D., & Strogratz, S. (1998) 'Collective dynamics of small worlds.' *Nature*, *393*, 440–442.

Welsh, D. K., Takahashi, J. S., & Kay, S. A. (2010) 'Suprachiasmatic nucleus: Cell autonomy and network properties.' *Annual Review of Physiology*, *72*(1), 551–577.

Winning, J., & Bechtel, W. (2018) 'Rethinking causality in neural mechanisms: Constraints and control.' *Minds and Machines*, *28*(2), 287–310.

3

A Typology of Levels of Mechanisms Involved in the Etiology of Psychiatric Illness

KENNETH S. KENDLER

I have been a fan of Bechtel's writings on the role of mechanisms in the philosophy of science in general and philosophy of biology specifically for many years and often applied them to psychiatric problems. A decade ago, I wrote:

> In suggesting that we adopt a mechanistic approach to explanation in psychiatry, I mean that explanation requires the explication of causal mechanisms and the understanding of how those mechanisms are actually instantiated in the world. Our task is to clarify the mechanisms that underlie and have an impact on central mind/brain processes such as mood, perception, belief formation, and hedonic processes so that we can understand the causal processes whereby they become disordered in psychiatric illness. Mechanistic models occupy a middle ground between the views of hard reduction and hard emergence. As Bechtel succinctly summarizes: "The decomposition required by mechanistic explanation is reductionist, but the recognition that parts and operations must be organized into an appropriate whole provides for a robust sense of a higher level of organization".
>
> (Bechtel, 2007, p. 130; Kendler, 2008,p. 696)

In his essay, working from a mechanistic perspective, Bechtel focuses on the following question: What is the optimal conceptual framework with which to understand the etiology of psychiatric disorders? He begins by articulating two standard mechanistic models used in biomedicine. The first is to postulate a specific mechanism for the disease; think about trying to understand the way in which the many CAG (cytosine–adenine–guanine) triplet repeats in the huntingtin protein produces Huntington's disease or how the HIV virus causes AIDS. Bechtel describes this as "A collection of components whose operation produces the symptoms of a disease as a disease mechanism." The second begins with the identification of a "healthy" or "normal" mechanism – such as the homeostatic control of human blood pressure, blood sugar or bone calcium density – and then looks at the various ways in which that normal mechanism can be disrupted. Bechtel calls this "A broken mechanism that when operating normally performs a function in the healthy organism."

He then writes, "Neither approach, however, provides a satisfactory framework for psychiatric disorders." His reasoning is of particular interest. They are too narrow, he claims, focusing as they do "on a single mechanism that is either broken or that produces the disease state."

So, he proposes a different approach which is succinctly "altered functioning of a network of control mechanisms." Given the focus of this book on the question of "levels," it is noteworthy that in the vernacular, Bechtel is kicking the mechanisms for psychiatric disorders "upstairs" – up a level or two. We shouldn't, he suggests, be looking at lower-level brain mechanisms. Rather, psychiatric disturbances are instantiated neurobiologically at upper-level coordinating systems. He provides what for me is a powerful model for a disease of control mechanisms: cancer. From the perspective of a tumor, it is quite possible to be a "good cancer cell" purring away, reproducing with abandon. From the organism's perspective, of course, it is working with an entirely perverted mechanism that can kill the host. What I take to be the essential point here is that there are many normal mechanisms involved in the control of cell proliferation: oncogenes and tumor suppressor genes code for proteins that serve as signaling molecules in control pathways that affect a range of inhibitory mechanisms and programmed cell death. Multiple different alterations in these the control pathways can all generate what appear as the same type of cancer. He argues that the best way to understand the nature of cancer is at a higher level. In a quote from an earlier draft of his essay, Bechtel well summarizes his main point as follows: "The focus should not be on specific mechanisms but on a network of control mechanisms that is altered and then has widespread consequences including psychopathologies."

This typology of explanatory approaches is quite intriguing, and I decided, in this comment, to take it for a test drive. That is, I try to apply it to three leading etiologic theories of psychiatric disorders – two for schizophrenia and one for panic disorder. I will first briefly present each model and then see how well they fit into Bechtel's typology.

3.1 THEORY 1 – THE PHENOMENON OF "MADE ACTIONS" IN SCHIZOPHRENIA

In a series of papers, Chris Frith and colleagues have proposed a systems neuroscience explanation for what are commonly called passivity symptoms in schizophrenia – the subjective feeling reported by many affected individuals that thoughts, feelings or actions are imposed on them from some outside force (2000). Frith succinctly summarizes his theory as follows:

> The error is due to an inability to distinguish between external events and perceptual changes caused by his own actions. The basis of this failure could be a functional disconnection between frontal brain areas concerned with action and posterior areas concerned with perception.
> (1996, p. 618)

Let me illustrate this in a bit more detail. If I want to touch my nose with my index finger (something most of us can do flawlessly), after I make the "decision" to do this, my motor cortex does two things. First, it sends a series of signals to the spinal cord and hence to the muscles to get the movement started. Second, it sends an "efferent copy" of the planned movement to a "feed-forward center" in premotor cortex of the frontal lobe. Like a guidance system in a missile, the feed-forward center monitors the intended movements, making, if necessary, small mid-course corrections. That is why, when we touch our finger to our nose, the movements look so smooth and well controlled.

Making such a motion, normal individuals have a sense of "mineness" about it. I did it. I made my arm move. How does that sense arise? Frith suggests that at a metaphorical level, you send in an inquiry to the feed-forward center. You ask, "Is it one of ours?" If, in their filing system, they have a record of the plan for that motion from your motor cortex, then the answer is "Yup, one of ours."

What happens if in schizophrenia, the person sends a standard signal to spinal cord which transmits well but the efferent copy to "feed-forward center" degrades. Then, the movement can fail the test of "mineness." Your feed-forward center has no good record that the movement was ever ordered. So, the answer to the query is "No record we ordered it. Somebody else must have moved our arm." The subjective sense – since this is all occurring at unconscious levels – is that the movement gets attributed to an outside agency.

3.2 THEORY 2 – DON KLEIN'S SUFFOCATION ALARM THEORY OF PANIC DISORDER

Klein introduces a key 1993 review paper on his theory as follows:

> A carbon dioxide hypersensitivity theory of panic has been posited. We hypothesize more broadly that a physiologic misinterpretation by a

> suffocation monitor misfires an evolved suffocation alarm system. This produces sudden respiratory distress followed swiftly by a brief hyperventilation, panic, and the urge to flee.
>
> (Klein, 1993, p. 306)

Here is a bit of background. We have in both our brain and periphery sensitive measures of arterial carbon dioxide (CO_2). A slowly rising CO_2 is uncomfortable. I recall when camping on a very cold night, I got into my sleeping bag and closed it all around me to get warm. But after a few minutes, I began to feel uneasy and wanted "fresh air." When I opened the bag and breathed the outside air, the discomfort went away. Although I was not then aware of what was causing my discomfort, it was from the rising levels of CO_2 in my sleeping bag.

But a very rapid rise in CO_2 levels is something quite different. This is what would be experienced if you are pitched overboard from a raft in white water and the current is so strong you could not immediately get to the surface. The feeling is one of panic as suffocation may be imminent. This is an extremely aversive stimulus. Getting to air with its oxygen is vital for survival and you do not have more than a minute or two to make it. Evolution would favor a system where all physical and hormonal resources are put to getting to air as quickly as possible.

Klein suggests that this CO_2 detection system is overly sensitive in a subgroup of individuals with panic disorder. So, the hypothesized mechanism is very simple: Modest "blip" upward in arterial CO_2 for some unknown reason → suffocation alarm system fires inappropriately → panic attack when there is no danger of suffocation.

3.3 MODEL 3 C4A RISK VARIANTS AND SCHIZOPHRENIA

The publication of this etiologic theory for schizophrenia by Sekar et al. (2016) was a major event for the schizophrenia field. The paper is a complex one, so I am over-simplifying their argument somewhat. Here are the key factors. The focus is on genes that express parts of the complement cascade, specifically complement component C4A. This cascade is part of an immune activation system that promotes an immune response to foreign pathogens. Typically, it is something you want to work well if you have a bacterial infection. The gene that codes for the C4A protein lies in a region of the human genome (the HLA region on chromosome 6) long known to be associated with schizophrenia.

So the basic elements of this story are (i) presence of particular C4A risk variants on Chromosome 6 → increased risk for schizophrenia;

(ii) presence of those C4A risk variants on Chromosome 6 → increased C4A expression in brain in mice, (iii) increased C4A expression in post-mortem brain samples in schizophrenics versus controls, (iv) increased C4A expression in brain in mice → increased synaptic pruning and (v) evidence that individuals with schizophrenia, compared to controls, have experienced excess synaptic pruning. So, the putative etiologic scheme here is presence of C4A risk variants on Chromosome 6 → increased C4A expression in brain → increased synaptic pruning → schizophrenia.

3.4 HOW DO OUR THREE EXAMPLES FIT INTO BECHTEL'S TYPOLOGY?

At first glance, Frith's theory about the origins of made actions would seem to fit into Bechtel's second example. That is, the feed-forward system is a mechanism that when operating normally performs an important function in the healthy organism. When it is broken, it can produce symptoms of schizophrenia. However, attempts have been made to generalize Frith's initial work on made actions to a wider array of passivity symptoms commonly experienced in schizophrenia. The effort is to understand how the "mineness" for other aspects of mental functioning arises and could be disrupted. For example, one theory of auditory hallucinations posits that somehow the perception of mineness of our "inner voice" – that silent dialog with ourselves that is a rather constant companion of human consciousness – gets disrupted in a way analogous to the disruption of motor movements. That is, some kind of feed-forward center function is disrupted, and the inner speech no longer has the sense of mineness and becomes attributed to an outside agency – and hence is perceived as "somebody else's" voice. The same could occur for emotions in which case, the patient might experience "made feelings," another common passivity symptom of schizophrenia.

So, if we wanted to expand upon Frith's theory, then Bechtel's third theory ("altered functioning of a network of control mechanisms") would provide a better and more comprehensive explanation for this class of clinical phenomenon in schizophrenia. That is, there might be some common set of mechanisms providing the "mineness" of a host of mental experiences. Understanding what is common across all of them might provide a rather deep insight into the nature of schizophrenia.

Klein's suffocation alarm theory, by contrast, seems to simply fit Bechtel's model 2. As the control of blood sugar becomes perturbed when the insulin producing cells of the pancreas start to die in type I diabetes, so an over-sensitivity of our CO_2 detectors can set off inappropriate panic attacks. This does seem to be an example where a relatively simple mechanism may apply.

The C4A story is harder to fit. It is likely that C4A is part of a finely tuned system that, when working properly, produces an optimal level of synaptic pruning that produces a maximally efficient CNS at low risk for schizophrenia. There are surely a range of control mechanisms that influence this and the genetic variants that upregulates C4A activity is one of many. At our current level of understanding, this simple story again looks more like model 2. Levels of C4A normally produce an optimal synaptic pruning but with these variants, the system goes into overdrive producing disease. But, rather like the story with Frith's theory, we could predict that there are many other ways in which excess pruning could occur which would also predispose to schizophrenia. Then our goal would be to apply Bechtel's model 3 – to understand the entire network of control mechanisms for synaptic pruning – thereby clarifying the multiple lines of disturbances that could predispose to schizophrenia. That more detailed mechanistic understanding would then provide the richest possible sets of points of intervention where therapy might be targeted to prevent or even treat schizophrenia.

3.5 CONCLUSIONS

In his essay, Bechtel has tried to refine a typology of mechanisms and illustrate it with a detailed examination of depression and the associated disturbances in circadian rhythms. His central idea – that a comprehensive understanding of many psychiatric illness can best be captured at a high level of control mechanisms – is intuitively appealing. A small road test with three representative etiologic theories in psychiatry yielded mixed results. One of the theories – suffocation alarm in panic disorder – did not seem to fit well. However, two of our theories, especially when framed in a maximally informative broader way, fit well into his conceptualization. My intuition is that understanding the etiology of the "big" multi-system psychiatric disorders – such as schizophrenia, alcoholism or major depression – that impact many areas of mental functions will likely require a mechanism that will reflect altered functioning of a network of control mechanisms. I am therefore optimistic that Bechtel's further elaboration of a mechanistic theory for psychiatric disorder will prove fruitful for our field.

REFERENCES

Bechtel W. (2007) *Mental Mechanisms: Philosophical Perspectives on Cognitive Neuroscience*. First ed. New York: Lawrence Erlbaum.

Frith C. (1996) 'Neuropsychology of schizophrenia: What are the implications of intellectual and experimental abnormalities for the neurobiology of schizophrenia?' *British Medical Bulletin*, 52:618–626.

Frith C.D., Blakemore S., Wolpert D.M. (2000) 'Explaining the symptoms of schizophrenia: Abnormalities in the awareness of action.' *Brain Research and Brain Research Review*, 31:357–363.

Kendler K.S. (2008) 'Explanatory models for psychiatric illness.' *American Journal of Psychiatry*, 165:695–702.

Klein D.F. (1993) 'False suffocation alarms, spontaneous panics, and related conditions. An integrative hypothesis.' *Archives of General Psychiatry*, 50:306–317.

Sekar A., Bialas A.R., de Rivera H. et al. (2016) 'Schizophrenia risk from complex variation of complement component 4.' *Nature*, 530:177–183.

SECTION 2

4

Introduction

KENNETH S. KENDLER

Robert Bilder takes us on a deep informative dive into the Research Domains Criteria (RDoC) matrix. This National Institute of Mental Health (NIMH) initiative – the brain child of then NIMH director, Tom Insel, and Bruce Cuthbert – has generated a wide range of reactions in the research community. In the context of this book, Bilder provides an insider's view informed from the perspective of the "levels problem." As he articulates it, the progress and controversies in the RDoC initiative

> ... brings us back to directly confront the question of "levels" of analysis and to consider how well we can map "lower" level biological processes to the "higher" levels that encompass psychological functions and psychiatric disorders.

As Bilder makes clear, the birth of RDoC was closely inter-related with growing frustration at the slow pace of etiologic research on the *DSM*-defined psychiatric disorders. Part of the argument underlying the effort was that these syndromally defined diagnostic categories were at the "wrong level" to propel the needed progress. This should come as no surprise as the charge of the *DSM* is to develop clinically useful and reliable categories. Given the probable heterogeneity of psychiatric disorders and the massive many-to-many relationships likely between underlying mind/brain dysfunctions and clinical manifestations of psychiatric symptoms and signs, the expectation of a simple single road from *DSM* categories to etiology is unrealistic. RDoC was based on the assumption that the created matrix, especially the psychological constructs making up the rows, would be a more fruitful focus for etiological research than the *DSM* categories.

Bilder focuses his task by taking us several levels into the "Cognitive Systems" row of RDoC. He starts with one part of that – working memory – which was the focus of the first RDoC consensus conference in 2010. At that meeting, the decision was to divide up working memory into four subconstructs: Active Maintenance, Flexible Updating, Interference Control, and Limited Capacity. He notes an interesting "bump" in the work as it became clear that these constructs were heterogeneous with the first three reflecting processes or functions while the fourth was a property.

It was surprising for me to learn despite the fact that the RDoC columns (genes, molecules, cells, circuits, physiology, behavior, self-reports, paradigms) seemed to cry out "levels-talk," the leaders of the RDoC initiative avoided raising those questions. The potential problem of such an approach is illustrated briefly by Bilder in noting that two of the original initial levels (genes and self-reports) were left out of the more widely accepted levels system adopted by RDoC workers because of conceptual issues: Genes → Cells → Circuits → Physiology → Behaviors.

After raising the tempting question of whether RDoC is or should be defining an ontology of neuropsychological constructs relevant to mental illness, Bilder reviews level issues within RDoC from both the bottom up and the top down. He thereby illustrates a number of the complexities of traversing these levels in this topic area. Going from abstract "levels talk" to the nitty gritty of specific research strategies is not likely to be simple.

He concludes his tour by turning to the ever-important question of causal relationships focusing, much like Woodward in another chapter in this volume, on those that are cross-level. It is one thing to outline putative levels; it is quite another thing to postulate and even harder to prove causal relationships. As Woodward has argued, the a priori assumption that causation should always flow from "lower" to "higher" levels is unlikely to always be valid. In a very interesting short section, Bilder first indicates the many studies showing reliable changes in BOLD fMRI signals or EEGs that arise when subjects are performing some specific psychological test. Then he remarks how challenging it has been for the field to develop rigorous causal interpretation of these now common-place experiments. He acknowledges the rapid rise of causal modeling across a range of fields with the hope that these methods can be applied to relationships between RDoC measures. I will end with what I found to be a poignant and powerful quote, noting that despite the use of very sophisticated instruments for assessing brain function, we are quite far from understanding causal pathways. Bilder writes:

> What is the appropriate definition of this relation between psychological construct and brain activation state? This issue at the core of the RDoC matrix demands a position on the "easy" mind–body problem. Most cognitive neuroscientists accept materialism, and see the psychological states as "emergent properties" of brain activity. But we remain challenged to define precisely what is emerging from what.

5

Wrangling the Matrix: Lessons from the RDoC Working Memory Domain

ROBERT M. BILDER

5.1 INTRODUCTION TO RDOC AND THE MATRIX

The emergence of the National Institute of Mental Health (NIMH) Research Domains Criteria (RDoC) initiative may be appreciated best in a historical perspective. The search for mechanistic bases of mental states in general and mental illness in particular has long involved tensions between biological reductionism and phenomenology in social context, and the controversy over RDoC reflects that tension. Hippocrates (fourth century BCE) is widely credited for attributing intellect and the functioning of the mind to the brain, and Freud's "Project for a Scientific Psychology" (Freud, 1966) represents an explicit effort to develop a systematic mapping of mind function to neural mechanisms. Kraepelin[1] developed taxonomic systems that speculated about etiological background but based classification on syndromal constellations comprising observable symptoms and their courses, generally untethered from their biological roots (Decker, 2007). The Kraepelinian system was temporarily abandoned by American psychiatry in favor of psychoanalysis until the renaissance of biological psychiatry in the 1960s. This fueled the rise of the neo-Kraepelinians at Washington University in St. Louis, which in turn led to the *DSM-III*, which has since remained the prevailing structure for diagnosis of psychiatric disorders. Biological roots have been assumed in *DSM-III*, *-IV*, and *-5*, but biological variables are rarely part of diagnostic

This work was supported by NIH grants R01MH101478, R01MH114152, R03 MH106922, U01MH1055, and R01MH118514.

[1] Kraepelin occupies an interesting position in this history. Despite strong interest in causal biological mechanisms, he was a harsh critic of the "Freudian trend." This critique, however, targeted Freud's later psychoanalytic concepts and those of his "disciples," and was not directed at Freud's "Project for a Scientific Psychology," which was exceptionally mechanistic (and perhaps as a result eminently falsifiable).

criteria.[2] Paradoxically, the continued growth of biological psychiatry, which arguably ushered in the *DSM-III* and its successors, has now provided many examples showing that the taxonomic entities defined by the *DSMs* lack validity with respect to biological, psychological and environmental variables. These failures have driven the creation of RDoC, and stimulated hope that the field can generate alternate categories and dimensions that are better aligned with biology. This pendulum swing brings us back to directly confront the question of "levels" of analysis and to consider how well we can map "lower" level biological processes to the "higher" levels that encompass psychological functions and psychiatric disorders.

While RDoC is explicit in stating that it ". . . is not meant to serve as a diagnostic guide, nor is it intended to replace current diagnostic systems," it does explicitly embrace an alternate view of what are tractable "domains" for scientific study of mental processes relevant to the mission of NIMH, which is to study mental disorders. It makes a series of assumptions, which in turn, have implications for research. First, it aims to "integrate many levels of information (from genomics and circuits to behavior and self-reports)." Second, the goal is to ". . . explore basic dimensions of functioning that span the full range of human behavior from normal to abnormal." An implication of the first aim is that there should be meaningful associations between levels of analysis. RDoC leaders did not specify the ordering of these levels, but many investigators assume that there are "lower" more "basic" molecular and biological entities and "higher" level psychological constructs, as detailed further below. The second aim implies that functions (many or all?) can be represented as dimensional constructs that range from the "normal" to the "abnormal," without there necessarily being clear boundaries between these classes. The second aim further implies that illness is defined by dysfunction in these "psychological/biological" systems. This raises interacting questions about the properties of these dimensions and how variations along biological dimensions may relate to variations on the psychological dimensions.

To identify the domains for further investigation, the RDoC team at NIMH convened a series of expert workgroups to focus on dimensional psychological constructs grouped within broader domains. The workgroup

[2] There are "rule out" criteria, or "attributable to. . ." criteria that refer to medical illnesses, along with rare inclusion of laboratory test results, for example, in the diagnosis of Alzheimer's disease where genetic mutation from family history or genetic testing is considered causative.

participants were selected to represent a diversity of perspectives on each domain and construct, with an aim to consider how the concepts are studied across developmental trajectories and in varied environmental contexts. Expertise was engaged specifically in an effort to understand each construct using methods across levels, including molecular, genetic, neurocircuit, and behavioral. RDoC refers to these levels as "units of analysis" in an effort to avoid the implication that some methods are more "basic" or "fundamental" than others.

The RDoC "matrix" was constructed as a series of rows, each row reflecting a particular concept or construct within each of the five major RDoC domains, which include:

- Negative Valence Systems
- Positive Valence Systems
- Cognitive Systems
- Systems for Social Processes
- Arousal/Regulatory Systems

The columns of the RDoC matrix represent the units of analysis, which include:

- Genes
- Molecules
- Cells
- Circuits
- Physiology
- Behaviors
- Self-Reports
- Paradigms

The last of these columns, representing "paradigms," is designed to enable specification of the experimental approaches that have been useful in validating the specific constructs. It may be noted that "self-reports" is similarly more a measurement approach than it is a discrete unit of analysis, given that self-reports are almost all about "behaviors."

The structure of the RDoC matrix prompts multiple questions, among which we can immediately ask: (1) for rows: How is the validity of these constructs assessed? Are these constructs intended to be independent or interactive? and At what level(s) are these constructs intended to be valid (cognitive? circuit?)? (2) for columns: What entities are included in each unit of analysis? Are these units supposed to be agnostic to interdependencies among units or should these interdependencies be specified? and

(3) for the intersections of rows with columns, How are these specifications related to hypotheses about mental functions and dysfunctions? Should a particular pattern of entries across the rows and columns specify a comprehensive hypothesis about a mental state or mental illness? To explore these questions, the following sections dive into the working memory construct (which is within the RDoC domain of Cognitive Systems) as an example.

5.2 DRILLING INTO THE MATRIX: THE WORKING MEMORY CONSTRUCT

In order to illustrate how the matrix was populated and explore the implications of this framework, it is valuable to drill down to a specific set of constructs. "Working Memory" is one of the RDoC constructs, and indeed it was the first construct to be examined, in part because it was thought to be one of the better operationalized constructs – about which there was both considerable research evidence and reasonable consensus among investigators – forged in part through a prior NIMH initiative (CNTRICS or Cognitive Neuroscience Treatment Research to Improve Cognition in Schizophrenia Project CNTRICS). The construct was subsequently subsumed within the more general domain of "Cognitive Systems," which also include Attention, Perception, Declarative Memory, Language, and Cognitive Control as constructs on the same level as working memory. The experts convened for this initial workshop from July 11 to July 13, 2010. (See www.nimh.nih.gov/research-priorities/rdoc/working-memory-workshop-proceedings.shtml.)

There are many nuances in the conceptualization of Working Memory (WM) as it emerged from this workshop that will not be detailed here. The summary on the abovementioned NIMH website offers the best single source for this information, along with information on areas of agreement and lack of consensus. A key decision was to divide WM into four subconstructs: Active Maintenance, Flexible Updating, Interference Control and Limited Capacity. This division seems to have been an outcome dictated by consensus agreement on the *definition* of WM, which was:

> Definition: Working Memory is the active maintenance and flexible updating of goal/task relevant information (items, goals, strategies, etc.) in a form that has limited capacity and resists interference. These representations: may involve flexible binding of representations; may be characterized by the absence of external support for the internally maintained representations; and are frequently temporary, though this may be due to ongoing interference.

5.3 THE RDOC MATRIX IS A GRAPH WITHOUT EDGES

An unintended consequence of this translation of a definition into a subconstruct specification was the mixture of *processes* with *properties*. This point may at first appear to quibble over semantics, but by mixing the nature of entities that are considered subconstructs, it further emphasizes that the mechanisms involved in these constructs are probably not parallel. The first three subconstructs (active maintenance, flexible updating, and interference control) are all processes, or functions, which conceptually reflect the operation of cognitive systems, and many investigators in turn would say these cognitive systems are mediated by specific brain networks or neural systems. In contrast, *limited capacity* is a property of WM, rather than being a process itself. The workshop did not consider the implications of this distinction, but it is worth considering the factors that lead to the existence of this property because this may constrain theories of the cognitive operations involved in WM and also lead to unique insights about the functional anatomic mediation of this property, which may arise from the operation of mechanisms within each of the other subconstructs, mechanisms that are independent of the other constructs, or a combination of such mechanisms. Considering this property prompts the question: Precisely what structural or functional properties of neuronal assemblies lead to capacity limitations? Are there other (unspecified) processes that lead to this property of WM? Does limited capacity apply to the other processes identified for WM or is this better understood as a description of the "contents" of WM (i.e., the "information" as represented by "items, goals, strategies, etc.")?

This inconsistency in vocabulary further highlights both challenges and opportunities imposed by the structure of RDoC matrix. These features of the RDoC matrix can be appreciated better if we consider explicitly the nature of the entities that exist within the matrix, the ways that these are defined by the rows and columns within which they are nested, and the relations that may exist among these entities.

Like any matrix, the RDoC matrix has a structure defined by its rows, columns, and cell contents (which RDoC calls "elements"). The RDoC matrix does not specify relations among its rows. There is no prioritization or dependency among the five domains, nor within each domain is there a prioritization of constructs (i.e., WM is not considered more important or dependent on other constructs within the domain of Cognitive Systems), nor within the WM construct is there any prioritization or dependency specified among the four subconstructs (active maintenance, flexible updating, etc.). There may, however, be interactions among these subconstructs that remained unspecified in the RDoC matrix, but are implied by theories popular in the field. For example, some theories specify that active maintenance and flexible updating are mediated by shared neural circuit processes that act in opposition, with factors favoring maintenance making flexibility more difficult, and vice versa. Active maintenance is also clearly supported by interference control, although most cognitive and neurophysiological models suggest these depend on mechanisms that are not completely overlapping.

RDoC leaders have generally avoided defining explicit relations among the columns of the matrix, but most investigators believe these exist; indeed, it is these relations among the elements of the matrix that comprise our scientific hypotheses. This is reflected by the frequent replacement of the RDoC term "Units of Analysis" by "levels of analysis" (including occasionally within the RDoC website itself[3]). Many investigators believe there is a mechanistic progression across the "Units" that recapitulates the central dogma of biology: Genes → Cells → Circuits → Physiology → Behaviors. "Molecules" is left out here because in RDoC this term can refer to molecules coded by genes (i.e., proteins; in which case it would logically fit between genes and cells) but can also refer to other non-protein molecules. "Self-reports" is also not included as that is only one kind of behavioral assay, and it is seldom argued that "self-reports" are *caused by* behavior in the same way that protein structure is the product of transcription and translation.

Figure 5.1 illustrates the RDoC matrix as a graph, and represents the elements in the matrix for the working memory construct. The leftmost column indicates the kinds of entities that exist within each unit of analysis (i.e., the descriptive labels, such as "genes" and "molecules"), and the entries in each row are examples nominated by workgroup members as relevant to each unit of analysis. (E.g., "pyramidal cells" were examples of the kinds of cells important to working memory circuits.) What is not specified in the matrix, nor much in the workgroup narrative reports, are the specific relations that are hypothesized to exist among all these entities. For example, the molecule "GABA" was invoked in "distinct types of

[3] "RDoC is a research framework for new approaches to investigating mental disorders. It integrates many *levels of information* [italics added for emphasis] (from genomics and circuits to behavior and self-reports) in order to explore basic dimensions of functioning that span the full range of human behavior from normal to abnormal." From www.nimh.nih.gov/research-priorities/rdoc/index.shtml, accessed 12/17/2018.

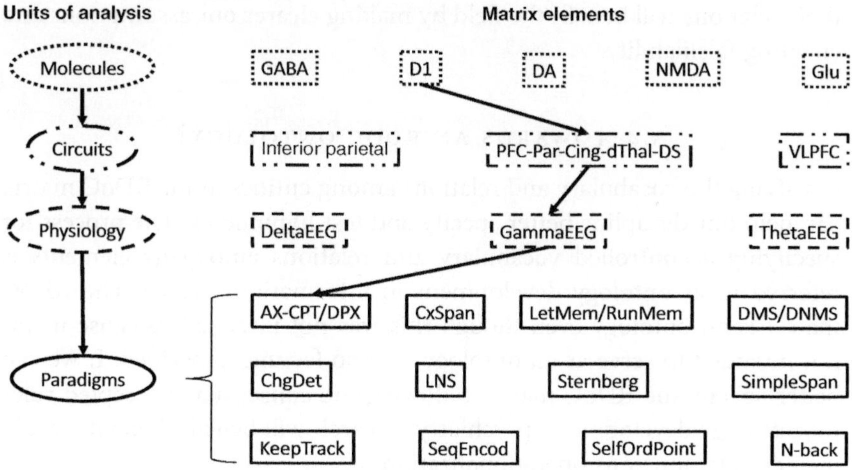

FIGURE 5.1 Schematic representation of RDoC "matrix" for the construct "working memory".

Note: The units of analysis are represented by ovals and the matrix elements, which comprise entities within each unit of analysis, are shown in rectangles. (Note that each unit has a different outline format.) The actual RDoC matrix does not indicate how elements are related to each other, but all hypotheses imply some "edges" (arrows) connecting the different elements. A sample hypothesis is represented suggesting that D1-like dopamine transmission, via its functions with the PFC-parietal-cingulate-dorsal thalamic-dorsal striatal circuit, impacts Gamma oscillations in the electroencephalogram (EEG), and that this activity is important in mediating performance on the "AX-CPT" continuous performance test.

inhibitory neurons" but that dependency is not reflected in the matrix. Every hypothesis, however, can theoretically be considered a special pattern of relations among the entities in the matrix. In this example, it would be valuable to specify exactly what role GABA plays in these inhibitory neurons, and what impact that has on working memory subconstructs. This level of specification is difficult and so far the matrix does not include these details. The figure illustrates how adding "edges" (lines or directional arrows) between nodes in this graph can help specify hypotheses.

Agnosticism about these relations among the entities that represent different units of analysis has the virtue of not being wrong, but it fails to acknowledge considerable knowledge that is widely held to be true (for example, that genetic variation *causes* changes in molecular transcripts that in turn *cause* differences in protein structures that in turn *cause* variations in cellular functions that are the *cause* of variations in circuit functions that are the *cause* of behavioral variations, some of which are considered mental illnesses). I suggest here that more formal specification of these entities and their relations will benefit the field by making clearer our assumptions and enabling falsifiability.

5.4 TOWARDS AN RDOC ONTOLOGY?

Clarifying the vocabulary and relations among entities in the RDoC matrix can help our discipline better specify and test hypotheses. The process for specifying a controlled vocabulary and relations among its elements is referred to as ontology development in information science. The RDoC matrix is an ontology even though this was not intended. Because it was not intended to serve as an ontology, it is so far underspecified. If we can better specify the RDoC matrix following the consensually accepted rules for ontology development, psychiatry research will benefit. Benefits would include unambiguous operationalization of:

- Constructs, so investigators would be able to use or modify the current definitions;
- Relations of constructs to tasks or procedures used to generate indicators of the constructs, so investigators would be able to specify what they measured, and meta-analyses could be conducted on variables assumed to harmonize with each other;
- Relations of constructs to each other, so investigators could test specific hypotheses about the associations between variables, and design experiments to falsify specific hypotheses; and
- The overall scope of the domain, concepts and measurements, so that data can be aggregated into shared knowledge bases, automated inferences can be made based upon these data, and other machine-driven procedures can be applied, for literature mining, data mining, and prioritization of new research.

It may be argued that concretizing the ontology represented by the RDoC initiative is unwieldy, unnecessary, and without benefit. Reducing the unwieldiness is the fact that much of the knowledge included in RDoC is either already formalized, or in a form that poses few theoretical obstacles to its formalization, as will be shown below. Regarding the necessity and potential benefits of formalizing RDoC, it is important to consider the downside of *not* doing so. If we cannot provide adequate and more formal specification of RDoC, it remains a fuzzy target that is difficult to focus upon and difficult to defend. There has been extensive criticism about RDoC prematurely closing key avenues of investigation and attempting to hijack mental health research to focus on unproven theories. Meanwhile, supporters struggle to align their research approaches with the initiative in order to contribute to the shared vision, and reviewers are often confused about the relevance of specific project aims to the overarching goals of the initiative.

It may also be argued that formalizing the ontology implied by the RDoC initiative would stifle innovation. To the contrary, the existence of an RDoC ontology would help clarify exactly what is part of RDoC and what is not, and new projects could be designed to test specific hypotheses implied by the RDoC matrix, and propose alternative hypotheses that could be shown to be superior to those implied by the RDoC matrix. This would also help make clearer for initial review groups and program officers how new proposals relate to the existing RDoC mission, and how they may productively challenge the existing conceptualization.

5.5 TRAVERSING THE MATRIX: BOTTOM-UP AND TOP-DOWN STRATEGIES

It was mentioned above that core elements of an ontology specification exist already for key components of the RDoC matrix. Given the directed graph that is implied by the central dogma of biology, we can start in a "bottom-up" fashion by considering the level (or unit) of "genes." Enormous progress in genetics has been enabled by existence of shared, controlled vocabularies. The National Center for Biotechnology Information (NCBI), in addition to supporting the familiar PubMed database, supports a range of other databases that are particularly well elaborated at the levels of basic biological science. For "Genes & Expression" there are currently 14 databases, including Gene (a searchable database of genes), the Database of Genotypes and Phenotypes (dbGaP), and Online Mendelian Inheritance in Man (OMIM), which is a database of human genes and genetic disorders. Another important project is Gene Ontology (GO), which is one component of a broader bioinformatics initiative known as Open Biomedical Ontologies (OBO). GO includes concepts relating to gene functions (GO terms) and how these functions relate to each other (GO relations), with respect to molecular function, cellular components, and biological processes. Shared vocabularies are further developed by other groups (e.g., the HUGO Gene Nomenclature Committee or HGNC, which approves gene names). These projects all share terminology to enable linking together of concepts ranging from the reagents valuable as probes in genetic studies, through systematic aggregation of gene expression results, to cataloging annotations about experiments linking specific genetic variants to phenotypes in humans and many other species.

Paralleling the robust infrastructure that has been developed for genomics, a similar range of bioinformatics resources already has been assembled to provide controlled vocabularies for proteomics. (For example, NCBI maintains eight databases and eight additional tools for "Proteins".) As noted above, cellular processes are represented to some extent within GO's specification of biological processes and cellular components, and there already exist multiple bioinformatics resources for metabolomics (see http://metabolomicssociety.org/resources/metabolomics-databases), some of which are designed specifically for system biology simulations (e.g., BiGG, at http://bigg.ucsd.edu/). As we ascend further to the level of neural systems, we find diverse tools and resources but the level of integration and interoperability is less obvious. For example, there is a Neuroimaging Tools & Resources Collaboratory (NITRC; www.nitrc.org/), which includes listings for tools like NeuroML (a standardized model description language for computational neuroscience) and Open Source Brain (OSB) but some of these initiatives do not have the scale of community engagement and maintenance of the more basic science offerings.

If we attempt to consider ontology development for mental health concepts from the "top-down" perspective, we find a paucity of formal databases and informatics resources, but a rich array of conceptual models that have been articulated either by fiat or by using statistical methods. The highest levels of mental health concepts in this schema are the "diagnostic entities" or "syndromes" that reflect mental illnesses. These are clearly articulated, indeed algorithmically defined, in the *Diagnostic and Statistical Manual of Mental Disorders*, now in its fifth edition (*DSM-5*). There remains ample controversy about the validity and utility of the *DSM-5*, but the existence of operationalized criteria for assigning people to diagnostic groups is not in question. Indeed, it is the existence of a diagnostic system such as *DSM-5*, and dissatisfaction with its validity with respect to biological concepts, that in part led to the RDoC initiative. Despite its limitations, the *DSM-5* provides a clear target for refinement because it does provide definitions and criteria for its entities. It is falsifiable (and we hope also these criteria will be "modifiable" as we learn more about the causes of mental illnesses, and what features define problems that may benefit from being considered as similar).

Linking mental disorder diagnoses and their criterion symptoms to "lower" behavioral levels is conceptually straightforward, but depends heavily on statistical, principally psychometric assumptions. Psychological and cognitive constructs comprise the heart of the RDoC initiative, insofar as these are the organizing principles around which the domains are orchestrated.[4] Definition of these constructs benefits from a legacy of work in classical and modern psychometric theory. Psychometric methods enable us to assess the validity of a construct based on the covariance of putative measures of that construct; in brief, a construct can reasonably be assumed as valid if multiple measurements of that construct are reasonably well correlated with each other. This fundamental principle (Cronbach, 1951; Cronbach & Meehl, 1955) has been developed further using item response theory, factor analytic strategies, and other methods for covariance structure analysis, to enable robust inferences to be made about how well we can measure specific psychological constructs, determine if we are measuring the same thing in different groups, and determine if individuals' score is likely to be a valid indicator of their true scores (Bilder & Reise, 2019; Embretson & Reise, 2002; Nunnally & Bernstein, 1994). The "magic" of psychometrics is that we can estimate how accurately we can measure true scores, even though we can never actually measure true scores!

The strength of these psychometric approaches is that they provide a clear structure for identifying the patterns of association among constructs at all levels of behavior, whether the measures are self-reported aspects of personality traits or symptoms, or tests of cognitive ability. We can test hypotheses of association among these constructs and apply statistical models to determine the likelihood that some measures are best understood as mediators or moderators of other effects. We can further design experiments to test assumptions about the structure of key constructs by intervening or manipulating conditions under which the data are acquired. Some tests depend on manipulations to measure key constructs. For example, the classic Stroop paradigm manipulates the task demands

[4] The RDoC *domains* are defined as reflecting "human functioning" and the *constructs* within each domain are "behavioral elements, processes, mechanisms, and responses" that are in turn ". . . different aspects of the overall range of functioning" (see www.nimh.nih.gov/research/research-funded-by-nimh/rdoc/definitions-of-the-rdoc-domains-and-constructs.shtml, accessed 6/26/2019). This definition implies that the principle definition of the RDoC domains and constructs is behavioral. The RDoC *matrix*, however, includes the other units of analysis that are putatively relevant to a given domain or construct, and used to *measure* the constructs. This may be confusing because we usually measure things as directly as possible, so including other elements in the RDoC matrix implies that the constructs and domains encompass more than the behavioral constructs. For example, we would not consider a genetic polymorphism in COMT, or a measure of D1 dopamine binding potential to be a measure of working memory. This is a conceptual challenge that would be rectified if the RDoC matrix were formalized using the methods of ontology development.

(in one condition requiring the reading of words, and in another the naming of colors) even though the stimuli are the same (color names printed in different colored ink) in order to identify individual differences in the construct "inhibition of prepotent response tendencies" or "interference control." These methods thus enable quantitative assessment of the relations among constructs from the highest "syndromal" level of analysis down to the constructs measured by the most basic cognitive experiments.

The bottom-up methods provide a methodological infrastructure that can carry us from molecular biology to the functioning of cells and networks of cells. The top-down approaches enable us to model concepts from the level of syndromes down to basic cognitive functions. The remaining challenge involves the traversal from the set of biological processes that are the target of burgeoning bioinformatics representations on one hand, to the set of psychological and behavioral processes that are specified in statistical terms, and putatively are manifestations of the biological processes. Neuroimaging may help us represent this middle ground at the interface of biology and psychology. After all, most functional MRI (fMRI) experiments involve engaging participants in some psychological exercise and viewing the resulting changes in brain function as detected via blood oxygen level dependent contrast effects. Similarly, EEG experiments often involve experimental manipulations that are intrinsically psychological, and examine the resulting patterns of electrical activity monitored on the scalp. A challenge for life scientists and philosophers is to understand the nature of causality that is reflected by these experiments.

It is interesting that despite the prior example of a behavioral intervention resulting in reliable changes in fMRI and EEG signals, there remains a reticence in the field to conclude that psychological processes *caused* brain activity to change. In contrast, if we perform a controlled pharmacological intervention in the same brain, and cause the same change in fMRI or EEG signal, there would be little debate about the agent causing the physiological change. This reflects in part a conceptual adherence to the "bottom-up" conceptualization that dominates biological sciences, but further reflects lack of our current capacity to represent the effects of the behavioral intervention on a neural system level. In theory, we will one day be able to trace the flow of words from the experimenter to impact the auditory cortex of the participant, through the establishment of neural network activation states that generate the fMRI and EEG signals. What is the appropriate definition of this relation between psychological construct and brain activation state? This issue at the core of the RDoC matrix demands a position on the "easy" mind–body problem. Most cognitive neuroscientists accept materialism, and see the psychological states as "emergent properties" of brain activity. But we remain challenged to define precisely what is emerging from what. It is possible that the recent upsurge in methods for assessing causal relations (e.g., Pearl & Mackenzie, 2018) will facilitate formal consideration of emergent properties and identify the constraints or contexts within which psychological states, including subjective states, may be considered to be the specifiable products of brain activity.

How exactly does the "limited storage capacity" of working memory emerge from the stability of neural networks comprising cortical-striatal-pallidal-thalamic loops? We thus continue to see hypotheses stated as if certain low-level molecular entities (e.g., certain genetic polymorphisms) *cause* high-level psychological phenomena. Unfortunately, these hypotheses often fail precisely because they lack attention to missing links in causal chains that involve multiple layers of biological complexity. For example, in 2006, we attempted to use meta-analytic structural equation modeling to test a prevailing hypothesis about the relations of APOE genotype to the memory deficits used to diagnose Alzheimer's disease, as mediated by amyloid deposition (measured using positron emission tomography). The model did not fit! Since then it has become clearer that the adverse effects of APOE genotype may have a range of effects via lipid metabolism and that the functional impacts via amyloid deposition may be only part of the mechanism responsible for cognitive decline. In general, the precision of our hypotheses depends on the precise definitions of entities and their relations, and the greater our ability to specify these hypotheses the more likely we will be able to share and aggregate knowledge. This concern is very similar to that expressed by Denny Borsboom in his classic article "The Attack of the Psychometricians":

> This may be the central problem of psychometrics: psychological theory does not motivate specific psychometric models. It does not say how theoretical attributes are structured, how observables are related to them, or what the functional form of that relation is. It is often silent even on whether that relation is directional and, if so, what its direction is. It only says that certain attributes and certain observables have something to do with each other. But that is simply not enough to build a measurement model.
>
> (Borsboom, 2006, p. 435)

5.6 MOVING FROM "DISEASE" SYNDROME DEFINITIONS TO CAUSAL MODELS

There are further implications of the way we model psychological constructs. Most current models of mental illness rest on an "effect model" in which a particular disease entity is assumed to cause symptoms. This approach may work well in modeling viral infection, where the introduction of the virus causes a range of cellular reactions. It does not work well in the case of most psychiatric syndromes, which in contrast, are defined by constellations of symptoms. For these conditions, it is more accurate to say the symptoms "cause" the syndrome. Borsboom and Cramer (2013) provide an excellent example using the diagnosis of Major Depression (MD). They highlight that it is extremely unlikely that there exists a valid entity "MD" that is the root cause of each of these symptoms, and instead, it is more realistic to assume that certain symptoms (and their associated physiological processes) cause others, and thereby lead to a cluster of symptoms we identify as MD. For example, anxiety may lead to disrupted sleep, which in turn may lead to fatigue, which in turn may cause concentration problems. An adequate physiological model depends on us attempting to specify as realistically as possible what is causing what, and our models need to reflect this understanding as accurately as is possible if we are to advance scientific understanding.

It is interesting that the use of "causal models" has been actively discouraged over multiple decades of statistical teaching, and we are only now beginning to see a renaissance of interest in the topic. The deprecation of causality appears to have arisen as a response to students' frequent misinterpretations of correlations as indications of causation. But Judea Pearl has argued that humans tend to think in causal terms, and that the avoidance of this tendency has led to some unnecessary paralysis in the mathematical and statistical approaches to modeling of causal relations, but now there exists a "calculus of causation" that relies extensively on graph representations and enables causal inferences to be modeled and examined (Pearl & Mackenzie, 2018). New approaches to dynamic causal modeling have also gained traction in neuroimaging (Friston, Li, Daunizeau, & Stephan, 2011).

The rise of these methods for causal modeling enables potentially powerful new approaches to specifying hypotheses that are testable and can lead to more powerful experimental designs. One now classic example of this approach comes from McManus and Bryden (1992) who extracted the assertions specified by Geschwind and Galaburda in their panoramic theory of cerebral lateralization (1985a, 1985b, 1985c, 1987). McManus and Bryden were able to create a structural model with 62 latent concepts and then reduce this to a more manageable set of assertions with only 13 latent variables and 12 putative causal effects, by combining some assertions and concepts and pruning others that were not central to the core hypothesis. In the course of this work, they were able to falsify selected elements of this theory, but more importantly detail specific recommendations for future research on testable hypotheses that were embedded within the original grand theory.

Infrastructure and tools to permit new approaches to causal modeling are under rapid development and may soon enable us to assess the validity of putative causal mechanisms that span multiple levels of analysis, and to create simulations that can further test the validity of the models and suggest interventions based on mechanistic understanding. These models currently span a range of abstractions. At the highest level of abstraction are models that consider observed activation patterns from neuroimaging experiments as a function of the specific manipulations involved in their acquisition. For example, one group used a whole brain model, integrated with a whole-brain density map of the 5-HT_{2A} receptor, along with structural and functional anatomic connectivity data, to predict the functional effects of LSD in healthy people. At an intermediate level are models that directly simulate the functions of neuronal networks to make predictions about the effects of experimental manipulations. Examples of this work are models of prefrontal cortex and basal ganglia circuits that help to explain reinforcement learning, decision making and cognitive control (Collins & Frank, 2018). In another example, a model of cortical and thalamocortical feedforward and feedback connectivity did an excellent job of accounting for a wide range of physiological and functional data that are associated with the "what" and "where" visual pathways (O'Reilly, Wyatte, & Rohrlich, 2017). Finally, detailed biophysical models, constructed to simulate membrane dynamics, and intracellular and extracellular signaling, have been used to model the processes putatively involved in working memory, helping to explain the role of tonic and phasic dopamine transmission, variations in catechol-O-methyl-transferase and monoamine oxidase activity, and possibly explain the limits of working memory capacity (Bilder, Volavka, Lachman, & Grace, 2004; Durstewitz, Seamans, & Sejnowski, 2000a, 2000b; Olesen, Macoveanu, Tegnér, & Klingberg, 2006).

As both knowledge aggregation and computational capacity increase, it is probably a matter of when, not if we will possess simulations capable of replicating the functioning of the human brain, based on realistic biophysical models from the molecular through the systems levels, and which will render behavior in ways that are not easily distinguishable from their human counterparts. These models can ultimately help solve the problems posed by our questions about "levels of analysis" in neuroscience and psychiatry research. Meanwhile, wrangling the RDoC matrix provides useful stimulation of effort to better formalize the links from one level of analysis to the next.

Sticking with our example of working memory, we can immediately identify a series of gaps that deserve attention. First, we recognize that WM is one construct within the domain of Cognitive Systems. Then within the WM construct are four subconstructs (see below). Let us take the first of these subconstructs, "Active Maintenance," and examine its matrix elements within each Unit of Analysis. It should be noted that the level of "Genes" was removed in May 2017, due to increasing concern that some claims of specific associations might be false positives.[5] At the level of Molecules, a series of neurotransmitters is indicated, but their roles are left open. Similarly, a series of "circuits" is listed, but further information about the nature of these circuits can only be gleaned in part from examining the summary of the workshop proceedings (www.nimh.nih.gov/research-priorities/rdoc/working-memory-workshop-proceedings.shtml). The inclusion, for example of the "PFC-parietal-cingulate-dorsal thalamus-dorsal striatum" circuit, is actually a reference to the cortico-striato-pallido-thalamic loops that have been well studied in other contexts (Bilder, Howe, & Sabb, 2013). At the level of "physiology", the matrix refers to Delta, Gamma, and Theta waves, but the workshop discussion was actually about different oscillatory patterns that correlate with WM processes, and it was considered likely that gamma oscillations accompany local ensemble (short range or local) activity, while theta more likely reflected thalamo-cortical activity, and delta cortico-cortical activity. The matrix also does not make clear most of this evidence derives from studies of non-human primates where direct recording of these oscillations is possible. Most of the workshop activity concerned debate about the diverse paradigms that have been

[5] "We [RDoC working group] recognize the clear relevance of investigating genomic aspects of RDoC constructs and domains. However, the current state of the field emphasizes the need for robust evidence of association, generally resulting from adequately powered genome wide association studies, as opposed to candidate gene approaches. As we actively re-evaluate the specifics of information to be included in this column, the RDoC matrix will be updated accordingly." (From www.nimh.nih.gov/research-priorities/rdoc/update-on-genes-in-the-rdoc-matrix.shtml, accessed 12/20/2018).

TABLE 5.1 *RDoC hierarchy of matrix elements for the active maintenance subconstruct of Working Memory*

- Domain: Cognitive Systems
- Construct: Working Memory
- Subconstruct: Active Maintenance
  - Genes: References removed May 2017
  - Molecules: GABA, D1, DA, NMDA, Glu
  - Cells: Distinct types of inhibitory neurons, pyramidal cells
  - Circuits: Inferior parietal, PFC-parietal-cingulate-dorsal thalamus-dorsal striatum, VLPFC
  - Physiology: Delta, Gamma Waves, Theta Waves
  - Paradigms: AX-CPT/DPX, Change detection tasks, Complex Span tasks, delayed match to non-sample, delayed match to sample, keep track task, Letter memory/running memory, letter number sequencing, N-back, Self-Ordered Pointing, sequence encoding and reproduction, Simple Span Tasks, Sternberg Item Recognition
- Subconstruct: Flexible Updating
- Subconstruct: Limited Capacity
- Subconstruct: Interference Control

used to tease apart the various components of WM, and here a more elaborate listing was provided, yet the dissection of which aspects of WM are actually specified within each task is not provided. The contents of the matrix for WM are summarized in Table 5.1 and Figure 5.1.

Thus, while members of the RDoC WM workshop considered individual hypotheses that have been articulated across the Units of Analysis, this is not apparent in the RDoC matrix. It is possible to specify hypotheses that span these units (and many investigators do). For example, we are currently completing a project under the aegis of the RDoC initiative that focuses on the WM construct (R01MH101478). In this project, we are testing the hypothesis that three different kinds of circuit (local cortical, cortico-cortical, and cortico-limbic) mediate the different subconstructs; that local circuits mediate limited storage capacity; while cortico-cortical systems mediate active maintenance, updating interference control processes; and corticolimbic circuits mediate WM when capacity is exceeded. We have specified unique behavioral paradigms to assess the different functional expressions of the subconstructs, along with unique fMRI patterns of activation and EEG oscillatory findings that are hypothesized to serve as indicators of the circuit-level functions. This project critically focuses on how much shared variance exists across the levels (between each set of Units of Analysis). Our preliminary findings suggest that most "cross-level" traversals are associated with shared variance of approximately 10% (Bilder et al., 2018). This is sobering news for those who may have hoped construction of models from the genome to the syndrome would be easy. We are optimistic, however, that this may stimulate research, along the path established by Flint and Munafo (2007) in their review of evidence for the "endophenotype" concept. They found that little variance (often less than 2.5%) was shared between most phenotypes and genotype, regardless of "level," making it clear that there were unlikely to be many complex phenotypes that are "closer" to the level of genes and gene expression. We hope that by assembling evidence in a clearly principled fashion, and exposing our hypotheses about cross-level traversals to falsification, we can continue to pursue the ultimate goal of a deeper understanding of mental illnesses and their causes.

REFERENCES

Bilder, R. M., Howe, A. G., & Sabb, F. W. (2013) 'Multilevel models from biology to psychology: Mission impossible?' *Journal of Abnormal Psychology*, *122*(3), 917–927.

Bilder, R. M., Lenartowicz, A., Rissman, J., Loo, S., Pochon, J. B., Truong, H., ... Sugar, C. (2018) *RDoC working memory constructs spanning levels from disability to structural MRI*. Paper presented at the American College of Neuropsychopharmacology, Hollywood, FL.

Bilder, R. M., & Reise, S. P. (2019) 'Neuropsychological tests of the future: How do we get there from here?' *The Clinical Neuropsychologist*, *33*(2), 220–245.

Bilder, R. M., Volavka, J., Lachman, H., & Grace, A. (2004) 'The catechol-O-methyltransferase polymorphism: Relations to the tonic-phasic dopamine hypothesis and neuropsychiatric phenotypes.' *Neuropsychopharmacology*, *29* (11), 1943–1961.

Borsboom, D. (2006) 'The attack of the psychometricians.' *Psychometrika*, *71*(3), 425.

Borsboom, D., & Cramer, A. O. (2013) 'Network analysis: An integrative approach to the structure of psychopathology.' *Annual Review of Clinical Psychology*, *9*, 91–121.

Collins, A. G., & Frank, M. J. (2018) 'Within-and across-trial dynamics of human EEG reveal cooperative interplay between reinforcement learning and working memory.' *Proceedings of the National Academy of Sciences*, *115*(10), 2502–2507.

Cronbach, L. J. (1951) 'Coefficient alpha and the internal structure of tests.' *Psychometrika*, *16*(3), 297–334.

Cronbach, L. J., & Meehl, P. E. (1955) 'Construct validity in psychological tests.' *Psychological Bulletin*, *52*(4), 281–302.

Decker, H. S. (2007) 'How Kraepelinian was Kraepelin? How Kraepelinian are the neo-Kraepelinians? – From Emil Kraepelin to *DSM-III*.' *History of Psychiatry*, *18*(71 Pt 3), 337–360.

Durstewitz, D., Seamans, J. K., & Sejnowski, T. J. (2000a) 'Dopamine-mediated stabilization of delay-period activity in a network model of prefrontal cortex.' *Journal of Neurophysiology*, *83*(3), 1733–1750.

Durstewitz, D., Seamans, J. K., & Sejnowski, T. J. (2000b) 'Neurocomputational models of working memory.' *Nature Neuroscience*, *3*(Suppl.), 1184–1191.

Embretson, S. E., & Reise, S. P. (2002) *Item response theory for psychologists*. Mahwah, NJ: Erlbaum.

Flint, J., & Munafo, M. R. (2007) 'The endophenotype concept in psychiatric genetics.' *Psychological Medicine*, *37*(2), 163–180.

Freud, S. (1966) *Project for a scientific psychology (1950 [1895])*. London: Hogarth Press.

Friston, K. J., Li, B., Daunizeau, J., & Stephan, K. E. (2011) 'Network discovery with DCM.' *NeuroImage*, *56*(3), 1202–1221.

Geschwind, N., & Galaburda, A. M. (1985a) 'Cerebral lateralization: Biological mechanisms, associations, and pathology: II. A hypothesis and a program for research.' *Archives of Neurology*, *42*, 521–552.

Geschwind, N., & Galaburda, A. M. (1985b) 'Cerebral lateralization: Biological mechanisms, associations, and pathology: III. A hypothesis and program for research.' *Archives of Neurology*, *42*, 634–654.

Geschwind, N., & Galaburda, A. M. (1985c) 'Cerebral lateralization. Biological mechanisms, associations, and pathology: I. A hypothesis and a program for research.' *Archives of Neurology*, *42*, 428–459.

Geschwind, N., & Galaburda, A. M. (1987) *Cerebral lateralization. Biological mechanisms, associations, and pathology*. Cambridge, MA: MIT Press.

McManus, I. C., & Bryden, M. P. (1992) 'Geschwind's theory of cerebral lateralization: Developing a formal causal model.' *Psychological Bulletin*, *110*, 237–253.

Nunnally, J. C., & Bernstein, I. (1994) *Psychometric theory (McGraw-Hill Series in Psychology)* (Vol. 3). New York: McGraw-Hill.

O'Reilly, R. C., Wyatte, D. R., & Rohrlich, J. J. (2017) Deep Predictive Learning: A Comprehensive Model of Three Visual Streams. Available at https://arxiv.org/abs/1709.04654.

Olesen, P. J., Macoveanu, J., Tegnér, J., & Klingberg, T. (2006) 'Brain activity related to working memory and distraction in children and adults.' *Cerebral Cortex*, *17*(5), 1047–1054.

Pearl, J., & Mackenzie, D. (2018) *The book of why: The new science of cause and effect*. New York: Basic Books.

6

Brain and Mind in Psychiatry? Presuppositions of Cognitive Ontology

GEORG NORTHOFF

6.1 INTRODUCTION

Psychiatric disorders have been regarded as disorders of genes, cells, brain regions and networks, experience, emotion, cognition, mind, or/and social environment throughout history. Each of these factors has been investigated extensively in recent years, providing evidence for alterations in basically all levels in disorders like schizophrenia and major depressive disorder (Northoff and Sibille 2014). Moreover, the debate about the nosological classification of psychiatric disorders has flared up intensely in recent years. Clinically, more entity-based classification systems like the *DSM* have been challenged by novel approaches that are more dimension-based. Such dimension-based approaches may apply to the neuronal level of the brain, exemplified by the Research Domain Criteria project (RDoC) (Insel and Cuthbert 2015) and the psychological/cognitive level, exemplified by various cognitive ontology (CO) projects (Bilder et al. 2009, 2013, Poldrack et al. 2011).

Despite the fact that these different classifications operate on different levels – i.e., neuronal, cognitive, personality, etc. – they nevertheless share an allegiance to a dimensionally-based approach. Moreover, they all assume (either implicitly or explicitly) that their respective starting point – i.e., neuronal, cognitive, personality – can be extended to and applied to different levels: this may operate in a bottom-up manner, as in RDoC, from genes and neural circuits to cognitive symptoms and/or personality changes. Or, alternatively, one may proceed, as in CO and the Hierarchical Taxonomy of Psychopathology (HiTOP) in a top-down manner from changes in personality and cognition to the brain and even to the genes.

Crucial to making progress is gaining a better understanding of the link between the brain's neuronal activity changes and the various psychopathological or mental symptoms. Despite extensive research, the exact neural basis and mechanisms underlying psychopathological symptoms (like anhedonia as distinguished from, for instance, major depressive disorder and schizophrenia) remain open. For instance, CO assumes that psychopathological symptoms are cognitive and affective symptoms which can be mapped upon the brain's regions and networks with respective cognitive and affective functions (Bilder et al. 2009, 2013, Poldrack et al. 2011). Apart from such mapping, the underlying mechanisms of how the brain's neuronal activity is transformed into cognitive process remains unclear.

6.2 COGNITIVE ONTOLOGY (CO) – BRAIN, MIND, AND PSYCHIATRIC DISORDERS

CO makes certain presuppositions about brain, mind, and psychiatric disorders which, to a certain degree, remain implicit or tacit. Though we are not able to go into full detail, we here want to shed a brief light on these presuppositions.

CO considers the brain in mainly cognitive terms. The concept of cognitive is here to be understood in a wide sense as referring to all mental processes in a broad sense – including motivation and emotion (Poldrack et al. 2011, footnote 1 on p. 1). The term *cognitive* taken in this wide sense includes various cognitive (as taken in a narrow sense) functions like attention, working memory, central executive functions, etc., as well as affective or emotional functions.

These cognitive and emotional/affective functions are supposed to be mapped onto the brain and even the genes (see, for instance, Figure 4, p. 8 in Poldrack et al. 2011 as well as Poldrack et al. 2011, p. 10). The explicit goal of the cognitive ontology project is to provide a clear conceptual framework for cognitive and emotional/affective functions, a "cognitive atlas," which then can be mapped onto corresponding regions or networks in the brain (Poldrack et al. 2011). For instance, the central executive network in the brain comprises the lateral prefrontal and parietal cortex which are involved in cognitive functions like working memory and goal orientation (Power et al. 2018). Though the focus of CO is not on the level of the brain itself, neural activity in different regions and/or networks is supposed to correspond to the various cognitive constructs included in the cognitive atlas. In other words, for the cognitive ontology project, the brain is a cognitive organ of the mind.

How about the mind? The wide definition of cognitive in terms of all mental processes already makes clear that CO considers the mind in cognitive and affective/emotional terms. The mind is characterized by mental (or cognitive) processes which cannot be directly observed and thus conceived as "latent unobservable constructs" (Poldrack et al. 2011, p. 3) that are defined operationally. This leads us to the distinction between mental processes and mental tasks: mental tasks are experimental tools that can be used to test specific mental processes that operate on or transform mental representations or other, i.e., non-representational forms of mental constructions (Poldrack et al. 2011, p. 3). However, one also needs to consider that one and the same "process" may be operationalized and thus tested in different ways; this makes it necessary to consider both the mental process in question and the experimental measures of said mental process (Poldrack et al. 2011).

The concept of mental representation is thus taken in a loose sense here referring to a "mental entity that stands in some relation to a physical entity or some other mental entity (in that abstract representation)" (Poldrack et al. 2011, p. 3). Note that the concept of mental in both mental processes and representation is ultimately meant in a cognitive or affective/emotional way. Hence, one can speak of cognitive and affective processes and representations.

CO aims to develop a cognitive atlas of the mind's cognitive organization. Different mental processes can be tested experimentally by corresponding mental tasks (i.e., operational definitions/measures). Each mental process supposedly represents a specific mental entity in the atlas. Within the atlas, mental concepts are related to other concepts in a variety of ways. For instance, mental concept A may be identical with another mental concept B, or A could be part of B (mereological relation), or B could result from transformation of A, or A may be the cause of B (Poldrack et al. 2011, p. 5); these are conceptual relations which indicate the logical-conceptual relationships between different mental concepts. How well these conceptual-logical relationships correspond to really existing relations (i.e., empirically confirmable mental or cognitive relationships), remains unclear.

Finally, CO carries major implications for psychiatric disorders. CO aims to provide a "standard ontology for mental function" (Poldrack et al. 2011, p. 10). Such "standard ontology" can, as explicitly stated by the authors, be applied to mental dysfunctions in psychiatric disorders (Bilder et al. 2009, 2013, Hastings et al. 2014, Poldrack et al. 2011). The application of CO to mental dysfunction in psychiatric disorders converges nicely with the development of "cognitive psychopathology" (Halligan and David 2001).

Following traditional psychology and especially cognitive psychology, cognitive psychopathology (CPP) aims to characterize psychopathological symptoms in terms of normal cognitive functions such as working memory and executive function; thereby, CPP will rely on the conceptual framework of cognitive organization developed and provided by CO. Hence, despite their different starting points from either the healthy mind (i.e., CO) or the disordered (i.e., CPP) both CO and CPP consider psychopathological symptoms and psychiatric disorders in general as cognitive (in a wide sense). Finally, CO and CPP also share the ultimate aim of extending beyond the mental or cognitive realm by mapping the mind's cognitive organization (or disorganization) to brain circuits and to lower levels including cellular, molecular, and genetic levels. (See Bilder et al. 2009, 2013, Hastings et al. 2014, Figure 4 in Poldrack et al. 2011.)

6.3 SPATIOTEMPORAL STRUCTURE – BRAIN AND MIND

How about the recent empirical data about brain, mind, and psychiatric disorders? Do they hold up to the presuppositions of CO? Let us start with the brain.

The brain's neural activity can be characterized by task-evoked activity (Morcom and Fletcher 2007) which is related to extrinsic tasks and stimuli as, for instance, mental (i.e., cognitive or affective) tasks as described in CO. The traditional model is that the tasks or stimuli themselves are sufficient for the amplitude as measured in task-evoked activity. This is also called an extrinsic model of brain activity (Northoff 2012, 2014a, 2014b, 2018, Raichle 2009, 2015). However, in addition to task-evoked activity, the brain's neural activity can also be characterized by spontaneous or intrinsic activity which remains independent of specific stimuli or tasks (Logothetis et al. 2009, Northoff 2014a). The role of the brain's spontaneous activity is not yet fully clear.

Recent data show that the spontaneous activity strongly shapes and determines task-evoked activity. For instance, the functional connectivity between different regions during spontaneous activity strongly predicts the pattern during task-evoked activity (Cole et al. 2014, 2016). Task-evoked activity, featured by its amplitude, may primarily increase relative to the ongoing spontaneous activity and its spatiotemporal pattern. The central role of the brain's spontaneous activity is further supported by various studies showing that spontaneous activity – i.e., resting-state activity – predicts task-related mental and behavioral features. (See, for instance, Huang et al. 2016, Ferri et al. 2017.) Since the data suggest a strong molding and shaping of task-evoked activity and related behavioral effects by the spontaneous or intrinsic activity, one can also speak of an "intrinsic model" of the brain activity (Northoff 2012, 2014a, 2014b, 2018, Raichle 2009, 2015).

The assumption of an intrinsic model of brain activity shifts the focus from the brain's task-evoked activity to its spontaneous activity. Recent data show that the spontaneous activity has elaborate spatiotemporal structure as documented in its functional connectivity and network pattern (Cole et al. 2014, 2016, Power et al. 2018) as well as by its various frequencies and the scale-free organization of its power spectrum (He et al. 2010, He 2014, Northoff and Huang 2017). Moreover, the brain's activity as a whole – that is, across its various regions and networks – seems to be centralized. Such holistic (rather than localized) neural activity can be measured in fMRI by what is called the "global signal" which may not just reflect noise or artifacts in the fMRI signal (Power et al. 2015, 2017), but meaningful neuronal activity (specifically, the infraslow frequency domain (0.01–0.1Hz)) (Liu et al. 2018, Schölvinck et al. 2010).

How about the mind and its mental processes? Consciousness is considered one, if not the hallmark, feature of the mind. Consciousness, put briefly, refers to the subjective experience of oneself, one's own body, and of the environment or world (Northoff 2014b, Northoff and Huang 2017). (See below for more details about the concept of experience.) If CO is right to assume that mental processes are cognitive processes (see above), one would expect consciousness and self, as prototypical features of mind, to be sufficiently accounted for by cognitive functions like attention or working memory.

However, empirical data strongly suggests that this is not the case. Empirical studies demonstrated that consciousness (in the sense of a basic experience) cannot be equated with cognitive functions such as working memory or attention (Northoff 2014a, 2014b, 2018). Moreover, focusing only on cognitive functions might even confound those neural mechanisms and correlates specifically associated with consciousness (as experience). Some authors even suggest research should use "no-report paradigms" rather than "report paradigms" (Tsuchiya et al. 2015). By no-report paradigms they mean using various non-verbal indicators of conscious experience rather than introspective reports of experience.

The characterization of consciousness and self as distinct from cognitive function and processes is further supported by neuronal data. Studies on altered states of consciousness such as loss of consciousness in sleep, anesthesia, or coma have demonstrated changes in spontaneous activity's spatiotemporal structure (i.e., its functional connectivity), its power spectrum, and scale-free activity (Huang et al. 2018, Tagliazucchi et al. 2013, 2016, Zhang et al. 2018), and its global signal (Huang et al. 2016). Moreover, studies using the construct of the self show strong overlap between self-related activity and resting-state activity (D'Argembeau et al. 2005, Davey et al. 2016, Qin and Northoff 2011, Whitfield-Gabrilie et al. 2011). More importantly, the spontaneous activity's spatiotemporal structure predicts the degree of subjectively experienced self-relatedness, i.e., self-consciousness or sense of self (Bai et al. 2016, Huang et al. 2016, Wolff et al. 2019).

6.4 CONCLUSION

Taken together, these neuronal findings strongly suggest that mental features like consciousness and self are rooted in the brain's spontaneous activity and its overall spatiotemporal structure rather than the brain's cognitive functions. Most importantly, they support the assumption that the mind, as featured by consciousness and self, cannot be sufficiently and exhaustingly characterized by cognitive functions or processes even if taken in the broad sense as advocated for in the cognitive ontology project.

REFERENCES

Bai Y, Nakao T, Xu J, Qin P, Chaves P, Heinzel A, Duncan N, Lane T, Yen NS, Tsai SY, Northoff G. (2016) 'Resting state glutamate predicts elevated pre-stimulus alpha during self-relatedness: A combined EEG-MRS study on "rest-self overlap".' *Society for Neuroscience*. 11(3):249–63.

Bilder RM, Sabb FW, Parker DS, Kalar D, Chu WW, Fox J, Freimer NB, Poldrack RA. (2009) 'Cognitive ontologies for neuropsychiatric phenomics research.' *Cognitive Neuropsychiatry*. 14(4–5):419–50.

Bilder RM, Howe AG, Sabb FW. (2013) 'Multilevel models from biology to psychology: Mission impossible?' *Journal of Abnormal Psychology*. 122(3):917–27.

Cole MW, Bassett DS, Power JD, Braver TS, Petersen SE. (2014) 'Intrinsic and task-evoked network architectures of the human brain.' *Neuron*. 83(1):238–51.

Cole MW, Ito T, Bassett DS, Schultz DH. (2016) 'Activity flow over resting-state networks shapes cognitive task activations.' *Nature Neuroscience*. 19(12):1718–26.

D'Argembeau A, Collette F, Van der Linden M, Laureys S, Del Fiore G, Degueldre C, Luxen A, Salmon E. (2005) 'Self-referential reflective activity and its relationship with rest: A PET study.' *NeuroImage*. 25(2):616–24.

Davey CG, Pujol J, Harrison BJ. (2016) 'Mapping the self in the brain's default mode network.' *NeuroImage*. 132:390–97.

Ferri F, Nikolova YS, Perrucci MG, Costantini M, Ferretti A, Gatta V, Huang Z, Edden RAE, Yue Q, D'Aurora M, Sibille E, Stuppia L, Romani GL, Northoff G. (2017) 'A neural "tuning curve" for multisensory experience and cognitive-perceptual schizotypy.' *Schizophrenia Bulletin*. 43(4):801–13.

Halligan PW, David AS. (2001) 'Cognitive neuropsychiatry: Towards a scientific psychopathology.' *Nature Reviews Neuroscience*. 2(3):209–15.

Hastings J, Frishkoff GA, Smith B, Jensen M, Poldrack RA, Lomax J, Bandrowski A, Imam F, Turner JA, Martone ME.(2014) 'Interdisciplinary perspectives on the development, integration, and application of cognitive ontologies.' *Frontiers in Neuroinformatics*. 8:62.

He, BJ. (2014) 'Scale-free brain activity: Past, present, and future.' *Trends in Cognitive Sciences*. 18(9):480–87.

He BJ, Zempel JM, Snyder AZ, Raichle ME. (2010) 'The temporal structures and functional significance of scale-free brain activity.' *Neuron*. 66(3):353–69.

Huang Z, Zhang J, Wu J, Qin P, Wu X, Wang Z, Dai R, Li Y, Liang W, Mao Y, Yang Z, Zhang J, Wolff A, Northoff G. (2016) 'Decoupled temporal variability and signal synchronization of spontaneous brain activity in loss of consciousness: An fMRI study in anesthesia.' *NeuroImage*. 124(Pt A):693–703.

Huang Z, Zhang J, Wu J, Liu X, Xu J, Zhang J, Qin P, Dai R, Yang Z, Mao Y, Hudetz AG, Northoff G. (2018) 'Disrupted neural variability during propofol-induced sedation and unconsciousness.' *Human Brain Mapping*. 39(11):4533–44.

Insel TR, Cuthbert BN. (2015) 'Medicine. Brain disorders? Precisely.' *Science*. 348(6234):499–500.

Liu X, de Zwart JA, Schölvinck ML, Chang C, Ye FQ, Leopold DA, Duyn JH. (2018) 'Subcortical evidence for a contribution of arousal to fMRI studies of brain activity.' *Nature Communications*. 9(1):395.

Logothetis NK, Murayama Y, Augath M, Steffen T, Werner J, Oeltermann A. (2009) 'How not to study spontaneous activity.' *NeuroImage*. 45(4):1080–89.

Morcom AM, Fletcher PC. (2007) 'Does the brain have a baseline? Why we should be resisting a rest.'*NeuroImage*. 37(4):1073–82.

Northoff G. (2012) 'Immanuel Kant's mind and the brain's resting state.' *Trends in Cognitive Sciences*. 16(7):356–9.

Northoff, G. (2014a) *Unlocking the Brain. Volume I: Coding*. New York: Oxford University Press.

Northoff, G. (2014b) *Unlocking the Brain. Volume II: Consciousness*. Oxford: Oxford University.

Northoff, G. (2018) 'The brain's spontaneous activity and its psychopathological symptoms; "Spatiotemporal binding and integration".' *Progress in Neuro-Psychopharmacology & Biological Psychiatry*. 80(Pt B):81–90.

Northoff G, Huang Z. (2017) 'How do the brain's time and space mediate consciousness and its different dimensions? Temporo-spatial theory of consciousness (TTC).'*Neuroscience and Biobehavioral Reviews*. 80:630–45.

Northoff G, Sibille E. (2014) 'Why are cortical GABA neurons relevant to internal focus in depression? A cross-level model linking cellular, biochemical and neural network findings.' *Molecular Psychiatry*. 19(9):966–77.

Poldrack RA, Kittur A, Kalar D, Miller E, Seppa C, Gil Y, Parker DS, Sabb FW, Bilder RM. (2011) 'The cognitive atlas: Toward a knowledge foundation for cognitive neuroscience.' *Frontiers in Neuroinformatics*. 5:17.

Power JD, Schlaggar BL, Petersen SE. (2015) 'Recent progress and outstanding issues in motion correction in resting state fMRI.' *NeuroImage*. 105:536–51.

Power JD, Plitt M, Laumann TO, Martin A. (2017) 'Sources and implications of whole-brain fMRI signals in humans.' *NeuroImage*. 146:609–25.

Power JD, Plitt M, Gotts SJ, Kundu P, Voon V, Bandettini PA, Martin A. (2018) 'Ridding fMRI data of motion-related influences: Removal of signals with distinct spatial and physical bases in multiecho data.' *Proceedings of the National Academy of Sciences of the United States of America*. 115(9):E2105–14.

Qin P, Northoff G. (2011) 'How is our self related to midline regions and the default-mode network?' *NeuroImage*. 57(3):1221–33.

Raichle ME. (2009) 'A brief history of human brain mapping.' *Trends in Neuroscience*. 32(2):118–26.

Raichle ME. (2015) 'The brain's default mode network.' *Annual Review of Neuroscience*. 38:433–47.

Schölvinck ML, Maier A, Ye FQ, Duyn JH, Leopold DA. (2010) 'Neural basis of global resting-state fMRI activity.' *Proceedings of the National Academy of Sciences of the United States of America*. 107(22):10238–43.

Tagliazucchi E, von Wegner F, Morzelewski A, Brodbeck V, Jahnke K, Laufs H. (2013) 'Breakdown of long-range temporal dependence in default mode and attention networks during deep sleep.' *Proceedings of the National Academy of Sciences of the United States of America*. 110(38):15419–24.

Tagliazucchi E, Chialvo DR, Siniatchkin M, Amico E, Brichant JF, Bonhomme V, Noirhomme Q, Laufs H, Laureys S. (2016) 'Large-scale signatures of unconsciousness are consistent with a departure from critical dynamics.' *Journal of the Royal Society Interface*. 13(114):20151027.

Tsuchiya N, Wilke M, Frässle S, Lamme VAF. (2015) 'No-report paradigms: Extracting the true neural correlates of consciousness.' *Trends in Cognitive Science*. 19(12):757–70.

Whitfield-Gabrieli S, Moran JM, Nieto-Castanon A, Triantafyllou C, Saxe R, Gabrieli JD. (2011) 'Associations and dissociations between default and self-reference networks in the human brain.' *NeuroImage*. 55(1):225–32.

Wolff A, Di Giovanni DA, Gómez-Pilar J, Nakao T, Huang Z, Longtin A, Northoff G. (2019) 'The temporal signature of self: Temporal measures of resting-state EEG predict self-consciousness.' *Human Brain Mapping*. 40(3):789–803.

Zhang J, Magioncalda P, Huang Z, Tan Z, Hu X, Hu Z, Conio B, Amore M, Inglese M, Martino M, Northoff G.(2018) 'Altered global signal topography and its different regional localization in motor cortex and hippocampus in mania and depression.' *Schizophrenia Bulletin*. 45(4):902–10.

SECTION 3

7

Introduction

KENNETH S. KENDLER

Daniel Pine is a child psychiatrist and clinical neuroscientist who has spent the bulk of his research career studying childhood anxiety disorders. His chapter represents such a useful contribution to this volume because it documents the conceptual and empirical work of a working scientist who "lives" the levels problem. Pine's science is conducted on three major "levels," the highest of which assesses subjective first-person reports of the clinical symptoms of anxiety disorder in subjects. The lowest level assesses brain function by various imaging methods, especially fMRI. In between these two levels sits neuropsychological assessments – objective measures of specific kinds of mental functioning. Pine is interested in two specific functions: attention and appraisal. The neuropsychological measures function as a bridge between the mental and the systems neuroscience. So, his work sits squarely on the boundary of mind and brain. As Pine summarizes it: "The goal for such work is to explain mental phenomena experienced in the first person at the level of 'mind' based on functioning within high-level neural circuitry, at the level of 'brain.'"

Unlike the clinical symptoms which can largely just be recorded, those mental functions instantiated in various neuropsychological paradigms can be pushed, probed and, especially importantly, delivered while individuals are in the scanner. This permits the joint assessment, at the same time, of specific forms of mental processes and those levels of brain functioning revealed by level of cerebral blood flow. His neuropsychology ". . .provide(s) a middle level that can be targeted to generate insights on higher, clinical-level constructs and lower, neural-level constructs, which flank this middle level."

To add to the complexity of this picture, Pine and his collaborator Le Doux have postulated two different neural instantiations of anxiety, one of which is conscious (threat-related attention) and other unconscious (defensive survival circuitry). Obviously, the research approach to these two "pathways" needs to be different. Neuropsychological constructs can be used for both, but only the conscious pathway can be examined through reporting of first-person experiences.

A final exciting feature of Pine and others on the neuropsychology and neurobiology of anxiety disorders is an effort to translate insights obtained from this mechanistic research into the therapy, one key example being attention bias modification therapy.

One of the fun parts of editing a volume like this is sometimes gently suggesting changes to the authors in the first drafts of their manuscripts. With several of the philosophers, part of the task was to urge them to put in more psychiatric details or examples. With Dr. Pine, the approach was the opposite – to encourage him to put more philosophical "levels talk" into his chapter. He was a quick learner. His chapter represents a thoughtful attempt to frame an active clinical-neuropsychological-systems neuroscience psychiatric research program as a project to integrate multiple levels of research to both aid etiologic understanding and support the development of effective therapies.

8

Tackling Hard Problems: Neuroscience, Treatment, and Anxiety

DANIEL S. PINE

8.1 INTRODUCTION

This chapter reviews findings from research attempting to use neuroscience to inform clinical practice on the diagnosis and treatment of mental disorders. In general, progress in research on mental illnesses has been steady over the past 30 years. Nevertheless, calls to quicken the pace of discovery have led some leaders to prioritize research on neuroscience, as exemplified by the Research Domains of Criteria (RDoC) (Cuthbert & Insel, 2013; Insel, 2014). The current chapter reviews research related to such prioritization. While the chapter adopts a relatively broad perspective on mental illness, research on clinical application of neuroscience involves many complexities that are difficult to overcome with a broad perspective. Attempts to move the field forward, in the face of these complexities, benefit from a narrow focus on specific varieties of mental illness. As a result, the current chapter focuses narrowly on anxiety disorders, leveraging this focus in ways that allow research on anxiety disorders to serve an exemplary foundation that might be followed in research on other forms of mental illness.

The chapter unfolds in four stages. The first portion provides an overview of problems and progress in attempts to create a clinical neuroscience field pertinent to mental illnesses. This section broadly describes research goals and challenges for such clinical neuroscience applications. Next, the chapter describes one narrow area of neuroscience, related to the orienting of attention, where progress in clinically relevant domains has been steady. The third section summarizes work on appraisal, a process closely connected to consciousness. As compared to research on attention

Supported by NIMH Intramural Research Program Project ZIAMH-00278.

orienting, research on appraisal less profoundly impacts clinical thinking. Finally, the chapter concludes by summarizing problems confronting future attempts to establish a clinical neuroscience approach to mental disorders, problems which are difficult to solve due to unique aspects of human thought.

8.2 OVERVIEW: RESEARCH GOALS

Progress in research over the past 30 years followed when leading agencies established objective criteria for mental illnesses that could be assessed with relatively high degrees of reliability (Pine, 2013). By enhancing the quality of scientific communication, this focus on objective criteria defined the impact on health from mental illnesses while also demonstrating these illnesses' relatively high levels of stability and familial aggregation. Finally, this focus established clinical standards for specific treatments, which could be broadly applied to families of mental illnesses, such as the psychoses, mood disorders, and syndromes characterized by excessive anxiety.

Despite these notable successes, progress on novel therapeutics has stalled in the past 20 years. Most new treatments arose through modification of established treatments discovered by serendipity and careful clinical observation (Insel, 2014).While current research shows mental disorders as a group of relatively stable entities, group-level data do not readily translate to the individual; clinicians are not able to predict outcome with much confidence for individual patients. Recent emphasis on neuroscience as reflected in the Research Domain Criteria (RDoC) and similar projects arises from a desire to catalyze the discovery of novel treatments and biomarkers capable of predicting long-term outcome or response to a treatment in a way that is relevant for individual patients (Cuthbert & Insel, 2013).

For tools from neuroscience to be clinically useful, they must provide information that surpasses the insights that arise from state-of-the-art clinical assessments. Research in other branches of medicine suggests that this information can be discovered through an iterative process involving dialogue between basic and clinical scientists (Pine & Leibenluft, 2015). From the clinical perspective, research with patients initially can identify targets that correlate with clinical features of a syndrome, and these targets then can be studied in other species using invasive techniques and experimental methods inappropriate for use with people. However, identifying such targets is difficult in psychiatry, due to the greater complexity of the brain and the greater difficulty in directly assessing functions of this complex bone-encased organ, as compared with other organ systems. Despite this difficulty, progress can be made. From the basic science perspective, this can proceed from the initial identification of targets in patients to research in rodents, non-human primates, and other organisms. This basic research has the advantage of being able to use experimental approaches to define candidate mechanisms. Such mechanisms can then be shown to possibly generate the observed relationships in patients between a measure of brain function and behavior, through alterations in computations performed by the brain. These insights in turn may refine the measure of brain function to be quantified in patients. Success in this process arises when this quantifiable measure is used to either inform treatment or predict outcome.

Initial forays into clinical neuroscience largely have been disappointing. Thus, more than a decade of research in neuroscience has minimally, if at all, impacted treatment or outcome prediction for most impairing mental disorders. This chapter describes one set of such attempts, which involve research on behaviors, emotions, and cognitions evoked by threats – stimuli capable of harming the organism (J. E. LeDoux & Pine, 2016). Clinically, such behaviors often are classified as a feature of an anxiety disorder, typically expressed in the form of either clinically significant avoidance or extreme reports of distress. Thus, anxiety disorders represent conditions where threats evoke an excessive response. Moreover, many conditions besides anxiety disorders, such as the psychoses, involve clinical features that resemble those that occur in the anxiety disorders. For these conditions, recent conventions recommend restricting use of the term "anxiety" to these phenomena as they occur in people, where it defines the state of subject distress that people report when they confront danger (J. E. LeDoux & Pine, 2016). For non-human primates and rodents, more narrow terms, such as "defensive behavior", are used when describing behaviors or physiological responses evoked by specific dangers.

The current chapter describes work that operates at three fundamental levels. At the highest level, the work targets clinical symptoms, which are expressed in patients' reports, observations from others, and assessments by clinicians. At the lowest level, work targets brain function, as assessed through imaging techniques, with the goal of articulating large-scale neural networks in human subjects, what some might call systems neuroscience. Work aimed at the neuropsychological level operates at a middle level, to bridge assessments of clinical presentation and brain function. Such mid-level work quantifies mental constructs that can only be assessed indirectly, based on individual's behaviors, typically evoked by psychological experiments.

Research on behavior evoked by threats provides a particularly rich avenue for bridging these three levels. This work is based in a range of conditions that manifest atypical responding to threats. The goal of creating a clinical neuroscience approach to the patient seems relatively tractable for this group of conditions due to the strong cross-species conservation in brain–behavior relations evoked by threat exposure. In other words, the linked changes in brain function and behavior that are evoked by threats in rodents resembles the changes that occur in non-human primates and people (Davis, Walker, Miles, & Grillon, 2010; J. E. LeDoux & Pine, 2016). This facilitates a multi-level approach, by providing a knowledge base from other areas of science to link the three levels of inquiry examined in the current chapter. These other areas of science typically utilize non-human species where more invasive techniques can be employed to generate understandings, some at a lower level – that of molecular neuroscience or much finer-scale systems neuroscience than is possible in humans. In other branches of medicine besides psychiatry, such cross-species conservation facilitates the iterative dialogue between basic and clinical scientists that has proved successful in cardiology, infectious disease management, and oncology (Pine & Leibenluft, 2015). Nevertheless, despite cross-species conservations, complexities in both clinical phenomena and neuroscience significantly hinder these efforts for the anxiety disorders.

8.2.1 Development and Psychopathology

The developmental nature of mental disorders represents one major clinical complexity impacting these efforts. Most mental disorders represent developmental conditions, where the initial clinical signs of the disorder manifest before adulthood (Pine & Fox, 2015). As illustrated in Figure 8.1, disorders can be divided into three groups, based on heterogeneity in clinical features and levels of genetic contribution. The anxiety disorders lie within a broader group of emotional disorders. These conditions involve marked degrees of heterogeneity. Thus, Figure 8.1 depicts a wide curve for the emotional disorders, reflecting variable clinical expressions over time; children who display high levels of separation anxiety often mature to become adolescents with social phobia who in turn face high risk for major depressive disorder (Beesdo, Knappe, & Pine, 2009). Similarly, individuals who continue to manifest symptoms as they mature often

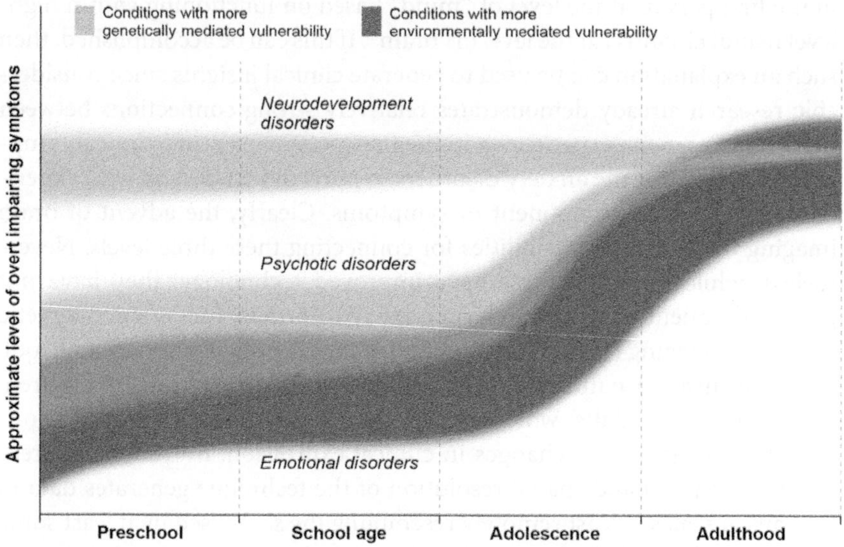

FIGURE 8.1 Changes in psychopathology with development.
Note: On the y-axis, the figure depicts approximate levels of impairment from psychiatric symptoms. The x-axis depicts changes in these levels across development. High variability in the emotional disorders is depicted as a persistently thick line across development and an increasing trajectory in levels of impairment. Adapted from a published paper (Pine & Fox, 2015)

display a steady worsening in their condition. Such complexity complicates attempts to define a corresponding disturbance in brain function. A changing clinical expression must involve an as-of-yet defined changing substrate that must be assessed in longitudinal research. Finally, as reviewed below, this variability in the expression of emotional disorders may reflect the influence of multiple component processes. Some of these may manifest similarly in disorders across ages, accounting for stable components of illnesses. Others may manifest differently at different ages, accounting for heterogeneity.

8.2.2 Connecting Brain, Mind, and Clinical Presentations

Steady advances in brain imaging provide fertile ground for scientists attempting to create a clinical neuroscience field that adopts a multi-level approach. The current chapter focuses on bridging three levels, encompassing brain, mind, and clinical presentation, or more precisely high-level systems neuroscience, neuropsychology, and subjective first-person reports. The goal for such work is to explain mental phenomena experienced in the first person at the level of "mind" based on functioning within high-level neural circuitry, at the level of "brain". If this can be accomplished, then such an explanation can be used to generate clinical insights since considerable research already demonstrates relatively strong connections between mental phenomena experienced in the first-person level and clinical symptoms. After all, for the anxiety disorders, reports of first-person level experiences form a vital component of symptoms. Clearly, the advent of brain imaging opens many possibilities for connecting these three levels. Nevertheless, while these advances have improved technology, they have not impacted patients. For research on anxiety disorders, functional magnetic resonance imaging (fMRI) provides a particularly powerful, promising tool. The non-invasive nature of the technique facilitates studies in children, adolescents, and adults, which can adopt a developmental approach consistent with age-related changes in clinical expression. Moreover, the reasonable temporal and spatial resolution of the technique generates data in humans at scales at least remotely resembling the scale used in at least some research on brain–behavior relations in other species.

Most fMRI research in psychiatry involves case–control comparisons, and results from these studies illustrate some problems arising in imaging research. With this approach, groups of patients are compared with one another and with non-affected, healthy subjects. In general, this research does find differences among healthy and various groups of affected patients. Nonetheless, the magnitude of these differences is not large, far below the level that would be needed for the differences to be diagnostically useful (Goodkind et al., 2015; McTeague et al., 2017). Moreover, findings are highly heterogeneous. For some findings, similar differences from healthy individuals manifest in patients with various diagnoses, even when they are classified as nosologically distinct. Conversely, for other findings, even among subjects in the same diagnostic group, differences with healthy individuals manifest in only a subset of the affected group.

Figure 8.2 provides a diagram for attempting to address this problem, focusing the field on defining "core psychological processes", which are entities that lie between measures of brain function and clinical states. This intermediate set of entities can be considered features of the "mind", referring for the anxiety disorders to information-processing functions that are deployed upon exposure to threats. Moreover, unlike clinical features, which are defined based on patients' problematic behaviors and feelings, these core psychological processes are defined based on neuroscience research. Thus, Figure 8.2 displays a process for using the mind to bridge research on brain function and clinical presentations.

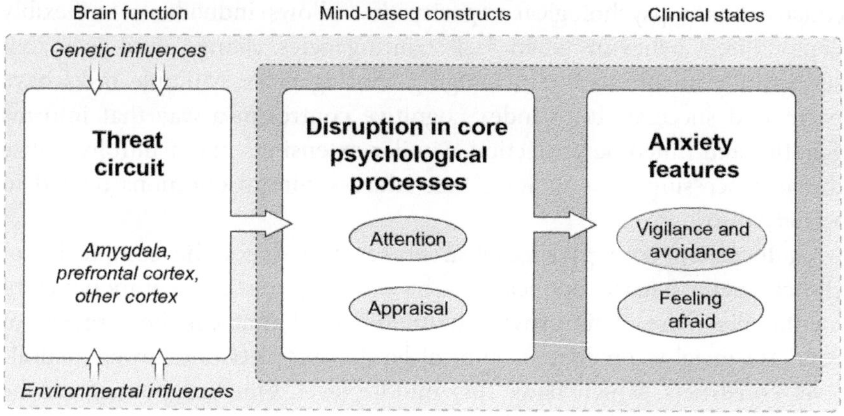

FIGURE 8.2 Depicts relationships among brain function, mind-based constructs, and clinical states.

Note: The figure shows how core psychological processes, constructs represented conceptually at the level of the mind, bridge measures of brain function and clinical states. The figure illustrates this bridging for two processes, attention, which manifests similarly across mammalian species, and appraisal, which manifests uniquely in humans.

8.2.3 Assessing Core Psychological Processes

Many difficulties hinder attempts to use assessments of core psychological processes to bridge measures of brain function and clinical status. Here, the concept of "core psychological process" refers to phenomena that operate at the middle "mental" or "neuropsychological" level, connecting brain to clinical entities on opposite poles adjacent to this middle level. One of the most important difficulties concerned assessments of core psychological processes related to issues of psychometrics. Because core psychological processes represent constructs that influence behavior, assessments of behavior can be used to index these constructs. This involves the creation of psychological tasks, where stimuli are presented to subjects or animals in ways that evoke relevant behaviors. For the assessment of anxiety-related constructs, these tasks often present subjects or animals with threats. When such tasks are used, acceptable reliability represents a prerequisite for establishing the validity of a construct, but scant psychometric research using tasks to assess anxiety-related constructs in people finds better than moderate reliability. Research on core psychological processes in areas beyond anxiety provide clues for addressing this problem. Multiple tasks can be deployed to index the underlying latent construct that influences performance on these tasks. Successful application of this approach examined the construct of cognitive control (Miyake & Friedman, 2012). This construct is a psychological capacity that allows individuals to flexibly deploy their behavior when task contingencies change in a way that successfully adapts to these changing contingencies. Multiple tasks have been used successfully to index cognitive control in a way that informs genetics and outcome prediction. Similar extensions may fruitfully utilize threat-processing tasks in ways that address clinical questions related to anxiety disorders.

A focus on core psychological processes reduces the complexity of clinical neuroscience applications by isolating distinct components of mental disorders. This provide a middle level that can be targeted to generate insights on higher, clinical-level constructs and lower, neural-level constructs, which flank this middle level. One component can be targeted for in-depth research, when extensive information exists on the underlying neural correlates. LeDoux and Pine put forth one such framework for research on anxiety disorders (J. E. LeDoux & Pine, 2016). This framework isolates two components of anxiety disorders, one of which exhibits particularly strong cross-species conservation and another of which manifests uniquely in humans. Both components operate at the same middle, neuropsychological level. As such, both components effectively bridge brain to clinical presentations. However, one of these areas exhibits tighter connections to the brain than clinical presentations, whereas the other exhibits tighter connections to clinical presentations than the brain. The next section of the chapter review findings arising from these two areas of research. The chapter focuses first on defensive survival circuitry, where existing research forges strong links between brain-based and psychological levels. The chapter then ends by focusing on cognitive appraisal circuitry, where existing research forges strong links between psychological and clinical levels.

8.3 DEFENSIVE SURVIVAL CIRCUITRY

8.3.1 Conceptualization

LeDoux and Pine conceptualize anxiety disorders as related to two sets of components, both operating at the middle, psychological level. One set involves core psychological processes related to defensive survival circuitry. This set of components manifests similarly in rodents, non-human primates, and humans, reflecting the output of brain circuitry that is highly conserved across species. The behaviors that are regulated by this circuitry are deployed on a relatively rapid time scale, and they are expressed in a relatively stereotyped or non-flexible manner. Some of the most extensive research in this area examines forms of stimulus–response learning quantified through an experimental task termed "threat conditioning" (J. LeDoux, 2007; J. E. LeDoux, 2014). In a threat conditioning task, a neutral stimulus, such as a tone or light, is paired with an aversive stimulus, such as an electrical shock. This pairing leads the animal to learn the association between the neutral conditioned stimulus and the aversive unconditioned stimulus. After this occurs, exposure to the previously neutral conditioned stimulus unleashes a set of rapidly deployed stereotyped responses typically indexed by freezing in rodents and by changes in autonomic activity in non-human primates and people. The importance of threat conditioning arises from research on the underlying circuitry that supports this form of learning. This research traces the neural connections supporting the process in multiple mammalian species, and this work reveals similar patterns of brain–behavior relationships (Duits et al., 2015; J. E. LeDoux & Pine, 2016).

Research on threat conditioning highlights the utility of reflexive behaviors, such as autonomic responses, as outputs of defensive survival circuitry. Many such behaviors are engaged immediately following threat exposure, and research examining such circuitry effects on attention provide one avenue where knowledge has begun to approach clinical utility. Attention refers to a collection of processes that allow organisms to adapt to the capacity-limited nature of the brain, which precludes a full evaluation of every detail in a complex stimulus array (Corbetta, Patel, & Shulman, 2008; Moore & Zirnsak, 2017). Attention processes regulate allocation of these capacity-limited neural resources in ways that facilitate adaptation to the environment. Attention orienting represents one component of attention, which can be rapidly deployed in situations where mammals confront danger. Threats have the capacity to consume attention resources in mammals, presumably because mammalian ancestors benefited from a selective advantage when they exhibited such reflexive responding to threats (Barberini, Morrison, Saez, Lau, & Salzman, 2012). The prototypical instance of such attention capture occurs when a human, when otherwise engaged in an enjoyable stroll through a forest, suddenly notices a snake.

8.3.2 Attention Orienting

Various tasks can be used to assess threat-related attention orienting in primates (Bar-Haim, Lamy, Pergamin, Bakermans-Kranenburg, & van Ijzendoorn, 2007; Barberini et al., 2012; Lazarov, Pine, & Bar-Haim, 2017).

These tasks share a few fundamental features. Typically, the organism is engaged in a neutral motor act during these tasks, analogous to a stroll through the woods for a person enjoying the afternoon. In this context, a threat appears, such as a picture of a threatening individual or a predator in the context of a cognitive task or a live snake in the context of an afternoon stroll through a forest. The capture of attention in these scenarios can be indexed based on differences between features of the neutral motor act performed in the presence of a threat, as compared to features of the neutral motor act performed in the presence of a control stimulus. This effect is designed to mirror the effect on behavior following appearance of a snake in the woods, whereby an individual's gait changes and their eyes closely attend to the snake.

The dot-probe task, depicted in Figure 8.3, represents one of the most commonly deployed attention tasks (Briggs-Gowan et al., 2016; White, Degnan, et al., 2017; White, Sequeira, et al., 2017). Here, measures of reaction time slowing or slowing of saccadic eye movements index biasing in attention orienting. While relatively extreme threats evoke orienting among most individuals, mild threats, which do not capture attention in healthy individuals, evoke orienting among individuals with anxiety disorders and other clinical conditions associated with excessive fear. This task has been used to assess clinical correlates of the anxiety disorders, their relationship to brain function, and their malleability through experiments designed to alter attention (Bar-Haim et al., 2007; White, Sequeira, et al., 2017).

8.3.3 Conceptualizing Pathological Orienting

Considerable research relates attention orienting to many clinical entities. The best replicated findings demonstrate a concurrent association between the degree of orienting towards threat and the clinical severity of anxiety (Bar-Haim et al., 2007). Other findings provide additional insights on the nature of this pathological responding. For example, in dangerous scenarios, research finds that healthy individuals, who typically ignore threats in safe contexts, manifest high levels of orienting towards threats (Wald et al., 2011, 2013). In fact, when exposed to combat, the pattern of attention orienting typically associated with an anxiety disorder in a safe environment may be protective, manifesting in healthy and resilient individuals but not in individuals who develop post-traumatic problems with anxiety (Badura-Brack et al., 2015).

Defensive survival circuitry is expected to develop relatively early in the life of the organism. As a result, one would expect to observe broadly

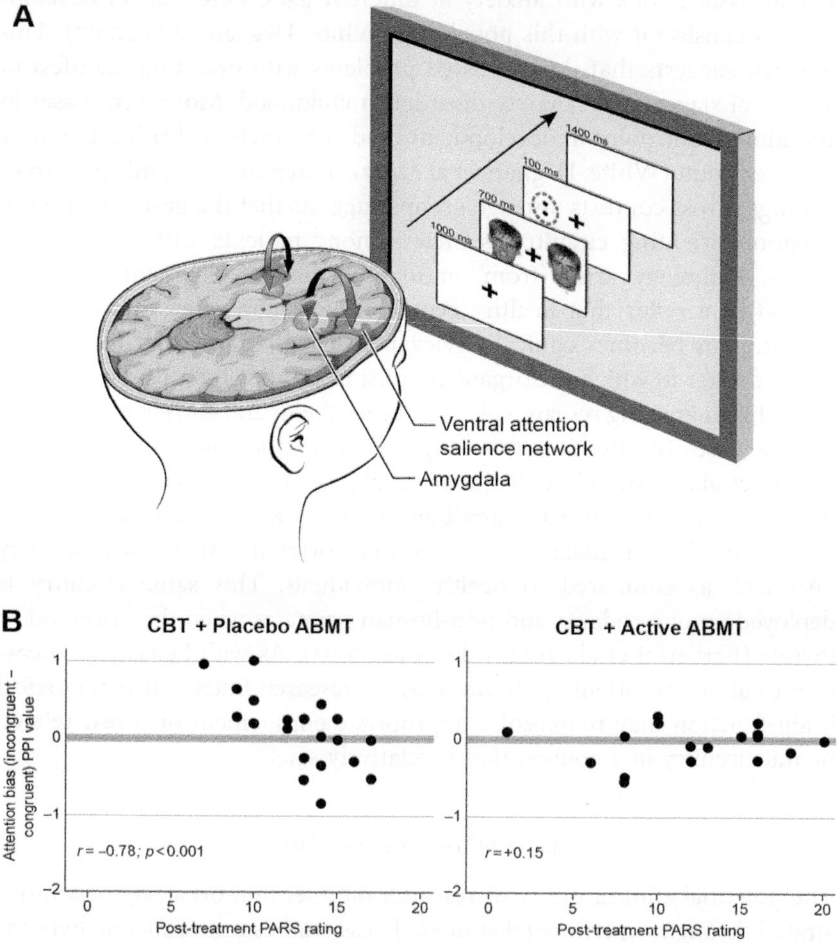

FIGURE 8.3 Changes in symptoms and brain function relationships.

Note: The top half of the figure (A) displays events for the dot-probe task on a computer screen. In a trial shown on the screen, a plus-sign signals the beginning of the trial, which is followed by a display of two faces, one threatening and another neutral, which in turn, if followed by a target to be identified, is expressed as a colon. The schematic of a person viewing this trial illustrates circuitry connecting the amygdala to the ventral prefrontal cortex, which relates to the brain's ventral attention network. The bottom half of the figure (B) shows data in two groups of pediatric patients with anxiety disorders from the published paper. The figure shows that functioning of amygdala-based circuitry prior to treatment predicts outcome only in the group of patients who are not randomized to an active form of attention bias modification treatment (ABMT). Adapted from a published paper (White, Sequeira, et al., 2017) similar associations with anxiety at different ages. Research on development is consistent with this possibility (White, Degnan, et al., 2017). This research suggests that threat-related problems with orienting manifest in the initial stages of an anxiety disorder in childhood. Moreover, biases in attention at one point in development predict an increased risk for anxiety at a later point (White, Degnan, et al., 2017). Taken together, this pattern of findings across contexts and age groups suggests that the basic function of attention orienting circuitry is intact among patients with anxiety disorders. Pathology arises from an inappropriate deployment in a safe context of a reflex that healthy people only deploy when they confront danger. This becomes clinically relevant when it is deployed in contexts where danger to which the organism must respond is not present. Considerable brain imaging research also examines the neural correlates of threat-related biases in attention orienting, where comparable findings emerge (Monk et al., 2008; White, Sequeira, et al., 2017). This research finds that the dot-probe and similar paradigms more powerfully engage circuitry connecting the amygdala to the prefrontal cortex in patients with anxiety disorders, as compared to healthy individuals. This same circuitry is deployed among rodents and non-human primates when they respond to threats (Barberini et al., 2012; J. LeDoux, 2007). As with behavioral measures of attention orienting, brain imaging research finds that pathological brain function may represent inappropriate engagement of threat-related neural circuitry in a context that is relatively safe.

8.3.4 Brain–Mind Symptoms

The potential clinical utility of research on attention orienting is demonstrated through experimental studies. These studies test falsifiable hypotheses on the nature of associations among brain functions, mental phenomena, and clinical entities, thereby effectively linking the three levels of brain–mind clinic. Such experimental studies manipulate attention with the goal of changing clinical end points, thereby attempting to causally demonstrate the clinical relevance of mental phenomena. As such, these studies manipulate the middle, mind-level construct to alter the flanking brain-level and clinic-level (or subjective self-report) constructs. The best developed approach to research in this area uses a procedure called attention bias modification therapy (ABMT) (Price et al., 2016; White, Sequeira, et al., 2017). Considerable ABMT research utilizes the dot-probe task as a therapeutic tool. Neuroscience research suggests that threat-related attention orienting reflects functions of a rapidly deployed defensive survival circuit. Therefore, changing attention orienting is thought to require techniques suited for altering such reflexive behaviors. Rather than explicit techniques utilized in treatments such as cognitive behavioral therapy (CBT), ABMT exposes the patient to many hundreds of trials in the dot-probe task, where a probe consistently appears in the opposite hemifield from where a threat had appeared. This leads to changes in attention orienting through implicit forms of learning. More than 20 randomized controlled trials utilize ABMT as a treatment for anxiety (Cristea, Kok, & Cuijpers, 2015; Price et al., 2016). While the effect size for this treatment is not large, it is significantly greater than seen with appropriate experimental control conditions. Two other aspects of ABMT research use neuroscience to extend the reach of these studies.

One set of studies considers the complimentary nature of ABMT and CBT (Lazarov, Marom, et al., 2017; White, Sequeira, et al., 2017). These two therapies may target distinct components of anxiety. Of note, both therapies still might target the same, middle neuropsychological-level construct that connects brain to the clinic. However, for ABMT, circuitry would be targeted that links closely to the neural-psychological connection established from research on neuroscience. For CBT, in contrast, circuitry would be targeted that links more closely to the clinical-psychological connection, established from research on psychological processes.

As noted above, ABMT targets implicitly learned, rapidly deployed threat reactions maintained by defensive survival circuitry. CBT uses declarative techniques where subjects are explicitly taught to regulate their levels of anxiety when exposed to a threat. This form of therapy may target distinct circuitry, as reviewed in the next section of the current chapter. Randomized controlled trials are beginning to test the complimentary nature of these techniques. Emerging data suggest that an active form of ABMT provides a more substantial clinical benefit than a placebo form of ABMT when added to CBT (Lazarov, Marom, et al., 2017; White, Sequeira, et al., 2017). Therefore, targeting distinct mental components brings additive clinical benefit.

Another set of studies examines relationships between brain function and ABMT. White and colleagues used fMRI to show that patterns of function in defensive survival circuitry predicted outcome to ABMT augmentation of CBT in pediatric anxiety disorders (White, Sequeira, et al., 2017). This suggests that individual differences in brain function identify subgroups of patients most responsive to treatments that target these brain functions. Britton and colleagues also used fMRI in another study of ABMT, here delivered as a stand-alone therapy (Britton et al., 2015). This work demonstrated a distinct effect on function in defensive survival circuitry from active relative to placebo ABMT. Taken together, combing brain imaging data with an experimental targeting of attention orienting effectively bridges research connecting the brain, the mind, and clinical presentation. These studies provide a sound example to illustrate how clinical neuroscience research on psychiatric disorders can, and perhaps needs to operate at multiple levels. Thus, these studies operate at a clinical level (i.e. first person subjective reports), by examining changes in symptoms associated with the experimental and control interventions. Moreover, these studies also operate at the level of the mind and brain – by manipulating attention – as measured using neuropsychological methods, and examining effects on brain function as assessed by fMRI.

8.3.5 Summary

Research on attention orienting represents one of the more successful attempts to use neuroscience to generate clinical insights, thereby operating at multiple levels of analysis. As noted above, these levels encompass clinical, psychological, and neural constructs, all examined in the same research studies. This research highlights the role of evolutionary conserved circuitry in regulating functions that are rapidly deployed when mammals confront danger. The research also leverages techniques from neuroscience to effectively alter these functions as part of experimental studies. Finally, initial attempts to combine such experimental studies with brain imaging are beginning to leverage research on the mind to bridge neural and clinical entities. This further bases the work in a multi-level approach. With this approach, interventions can target a mid-level construct that is a component of the mind, such as attention. Effects of this targeting can then be examined at a relatively high level, in terms of clinical endpoints, and at a relatively low level, in terms of brain function.

8.4 COGNITIVE APPRAISAL CIRCUITRY

8.4.1 Conceptualization

Clearly, research on attention orienting and function of defensive survival circuitry provides one reasonable path towards developing a clinical neuroscience field. Nevertheless, research in this area fails to address many fundamental components of anxiety disorders. LeDoux and Pine call attention to such failures by distinguishing functions of defensive survival circuitry from functions of a second anxiety disorder component infrequently studied in past neuroscience-focused research (J. E. LeDoux & Pine, 2016). This component relates to reports of distress associated with experienced or imagined exposures to danger, which are a primary factor leading patients to see treatment. LeDoux and Pine attribute this second component to functions of a cognitive circuit and argue that neuroscience research has failed to isolate this component from components related to functioning of defensive survival circuitry.

This work operates at the same three levels described in the research on attention orienting. Moreover, the work manipulates processes operating at a middle level to gauge the effects that occur at both higher and lower levels. Thus, symptoms are assessed at a clinical level; subjectively reported responses to threatening events delivered in the context of an experimental paradigm, operates at the middle level, and brain function operates at the lowest brain-based level. However, in other ways, work on cognitive appraisal is quite different from work on attention. In particular, as compared to the work on attention, in the realm of distress following threat exposure, relatively few studies in neuroscience map connections between the neural and middle level, whereas a much greater wealth of research examines connections between the middle and clinical level. As such, work on reported feeling states compliments work on attention orienting. The two areas of research differ largely based on the complexity of the associated mental–psychological constructs and connections with associated neural and clinical entities. As one aspect of cognitive circuitry function, the current chapter focuses on attempts to understand mechanisms supporting the patient's reported experience of distress that occurs during threat exposure; the psychological process that enables these experiences is termed "threat appraisal".

Far less progress accrues in research on threat appraisal as compared with research on attention orienting. Many factors contribute to this difference. Threat appraisal involves the reporting of a conscious experience evaluated by the self. This is considered an immediate self-report of an evolving mental state, operating at a psychological level. Much like clinical assessments, threat appraisal involves self-report of subjective states. However, unlike a clinical assessment, threat appraisal only involves the immediate response to a threatening event, as it occurs in real time. Neuroscience research on such phenomena related to consciousness or the self is far less advanced than research on processes such as threat conditioning or attention orienting. This relates at least partly to the difficulty of conducting cross-species research on consciousness. Moreover, to the extent that such research has been conducted, it finds far less conservation in brain–behavior relations as compared to research on defensive survival circuitry. Finally, attention orienting shows broadly similar associations with anxiety disorders across development (Bar-Haim et al., 2007; White, Degnan, et al., 2017). In contrast, as reviewed below, various aspects of appraisal are expressed differently in children, adolescents, and adults, which further complicates research in this area. Whereas longitudinal research on clinical aspects of anxiety reveals strong relations between pediatric and adult symptomatology, research on threat appraisal finds discontinuity. This suggests that anxiety disorders evolve during development through influences of dissociable components. Some of these components, such as attention orienting, operate similarly over this period, whereas others, such as those related to threat appraisal, operate differently at different ages.

8.4.2 Self-Report and Development

Clinical research on reported feeling states provides one piece of evidence on developmental change in threat appraisal. Three notable findings demonstrate the presence of such age-related differences. First, the stability of an individual's reported feeling states increases from childhood through adulthood (Shaffer et al., 1996; Shaffer, Fisher, Lucas, Dulcan, & Schwab-Stone, 2000). That is, test–retest reliability is generally stronger in parents reporting on their child's anxiety than in children reporting on their own anxiety (Rappaport, Pagliaccio, Pine, Klein, & Jarcho, 2017). This difference may relate to a second difference related to the reporting of feeling states. Specifically, this reporting of a current feeling state typically involves a reference to one's typical feeling state, which involves a concept of "the self", as an entity that exists in some stable form over time. As noted above, this concept is conceptualized at the psychological or mental level, bridging work on the brain and clinical entities. Marked changes occur for an individual's descriptions of concepts related to the self, which provides a foundation when evaluating feeling states that occur at a point in time (Harter, 1992; Harter, Bresnick, Bouchey, & Whitesell, 1997). Given that such descriptions provide a reference for feeling states manifesting at a specific point in time, changes in descriptions of the self will affect changes in reported feeling states. Finally, independent of these changes, the accuracy of self-report also increases through the adolescent years. In research on such changes, accuracy is typically assessed based either on an independent observer's rating of the reporter's behavior or based on some other objective measure. For example, Davis-Kean and colleagues examined the accuracy with which children rated their cognitive and emotional capacities as these children matured throughout adolescence (Davis-Kean et al., 2008). Accuracy was evaluated based on third-person reports or scores on standardized tests of cognitive capacity. This data showed that accuracy steadily improved over the adolescent years.

Neuroscience research has only begun to map the brain circuits that support conscious reporting of events. Due to the complexity of research in this area, much of this work focuses on perceptual events, which can be readily manipulated using an experimental approach. This leaves few studies that explore the neural correlates of feeling states, which are less easily manipulated and verified in research participants. Such work is vital when attempting to examine multiple levels of processing in patients. In particular, work is needed to bridge assessments of brain function, engagement of psychological processes, and clinical endpoints. In work on perception, one framework suggests that subjective experience arises through interactions between prefrontal cortex and posterior association cortex that functions in object representation (J. E. LeDoux & Brown, 2017; van Vugt et al., 2018). Lau and colleagues extended this approach to research on fear, as a reported feeling state, as it relates to development (Lau et al., 2011). This study reports results from one relevant study, comparing neural correlates of fear appraisal in healthy youth and adults. This study used threat-conditioning procedures, whereupon research participants were exposed to conditioned and unconditioned stimuli while lying in an MRI scanner. Typically, studies of threat conditioning quantify functions in the defensive survival circuitry, by relying on reflexive behaviors or autonomic outputs. However, Lau and colleagues used a different approach: to engage circuitry related to appraisal, subjects were required to rate their level of fear when viewing stimuli. Two main findings emerged from this study. First, adults were better able to discern stimulus contingencies, manifesting a greater difference than youth for the level of rated fear evoked by the threat and safety cues appearing in the experiment. That is, over time, ratings of fear among adults showed steady divergence, with greater ratings of fear to the conditioned than non-conditioned stimulus. In youth, the levels of divergence were less pronounced. Second, this ability in adults to discern stimulus-related threat features more accurately was reflected in functioning of the dorso-lateral prefrontal cortex (DLPFC), a brain region relatively unique to primates. This region also is implicated in perception, whereby engagement of the dlPFC is linked to the reporting of one or another object. These findings are broadly consistent with other research demonstrating developmental change in brain functions associated with self-appraisal.

8.4.3 Cognitive Appraisal Circuitry and Developmental Psychopathology

Linking brain function to reported feeling states in any population is a difficult task, and it is even more difficult to differentiate the way in which such functions uniquely relate to feeling states across age groups. A final layer of complexity arises when attempting to define differences in circuitry function and fear appraisal as they relate to both development and psychopathology. Accordingly, very few studies provide insights on the nature of these differences. Nevertheless, studies of psychological processes reviewed above establish robust age-related differences in key features of reported feeling states as they relate to anxiety disorders. Therefore, one would expect to find equally robust age-related differences in the neural correlates of fear appraisal in pediatric relative to adult anxiety disorders.

A few notable findings inform understandings of developmental differences in fear appraisal among anxious and healthy individuals. Studies have begun to use paradigms like the one used by Lau and colleagues, exposing healthy and anxious youth and adults to fear-related stimuli while they rate their experienced fear. In general, findings suggest that the neural correlates of feeling states in pathological anxiety differ in youth and adults (Gold et al., 2016). Moreover, healthy as compared to anxious adults generally manifest large differences in brain function during fear appraisal (Gold et al., 2016). Findings in youth reveal relative few differences. This suggests that deficits in circuitry supporting cognitive appraisal may be easier to detect in adult relative to pediatric anxiety disorder patients.

The early state of research on neural correlates of appraisal creates significant problems for advancing research. In research on defensive survival circuitry, clear ideas regarding the nature of dysfunction led to relatively clear tests of hypotheses that involved experimental manipulations targeting the mind. In the absence of such clear ideas regarding fear appraisal, comparable ideas for experimental approaches remain similarly unclear. This problem is compounded by the presence of developmental differences. For research on attention orienting, studies in adult anxiety disorder generated clear ideas for studies based in youth. For threat appraisal, such a clear path does not exist, in light of fundamental age differences in brain–behavior relations.

8.4.4 Summary

Research on appraisal provides a useful contrast with research on attention orienting. In attention orienting, the underlying circuitry has been at least partially mapped. Functioning of this circuitry has been linked to both the presence of clinical anxiety and response to treatment. For appraisal, the underlying circuitry is only incompletely understood. Moreover, one major set of findings suggests that functioning of this circuitry changes in fundamental ways during development. As such, unlike for attention orienting, studies in adults provided only limited guidance for designing studies in youth.

8.5 CONCLUSIONS ON PROGRESS AND PROBLEMS IN CLINICAL NEUROSCIENCE

The current chapter summarizes problems encountered when seeking clinical neuroscience applications in mental illnesses, and the chapter describes one approach to addressing these problems. Thus, the need for advances in treatment and outcome prediction led some experts to emphasize a role for neuroscience in attempts to improve aspects of psychiatry. This emphasis created problems when understandings in neuroscience did not map cleanly onto understandings of nosology. From the perspective of research on the anxiety disorders, for example, identical patterns of perturbations in attention occur in anxiety disorders that are categorized as nosologically extinct. Specifically, the nature of attention bias that occurs in specific phobia appears similar to the nature of bias that occurs in social anxiety disorder, panic disorder, separation anxiety disorder, and generalized anxiety disorder. As a result, neuroscience findings only partially conform to clinical findings. Whereas these anxiety disorders are categorized as distinct in the *Diagnostic and Statistical Manual*, they express comparable attention-related perturbations at a psychological level, specifically the middle level where neuropsychological tests are employed.

One solution to this problem has been to decompose mental disorders into components based on understandings of mental phenomena emerging from neuroscience. In anxiety disorders, perturbations in attention – which operate on implicit level – are distinguished from perturbations in appraisal, which operate on a level involving conscious experiences. These perturbations in attention can be targeted with a treatment, designed based on successes in other research areas, changing rapidly deployed motor actions. Of note, this approach of component dissection has been used in research on other mental illnesses, also with some success. In schizophrenia, perturbations in working memory are distinguished from perturbations in perception, and treatments have been developed based on their capacity to influence one or another component. This process of decomposition has been linked to experimental manipulations, as is done in randomized controlled trials. For example, ABMT emerged as a potentially useful, novel treatment based on its capacity to alter perturbations in attention orienting and its underlying neural correlates. While this initial set of studies has been useful, this initial set has created other problems.

Problems with this component-based approach to mental illness reflect the complex nature of mental disorders. Insights from philosophy may clarify how to confront such complexity. Due to such complexity, the influence of any one component on clinical aspects of a disorder tends to be small. Thus, the association between biased attention orienting and clinical levels of anxiety is not large, nor is the effect of ABMT on clinical anxiety. Moreover, in neuroscience, cross-species data typically apply to relatively simple phenomena, such as attention orienting, which can be modeled in many organisms. Mental illnesses involve perturbations in higher cognitive functions that are not so easily translatable to studies in rodents or non-human primates. A major challenge for future research on mental disorders relates to a plan for charting future research. Insights from philosophy may help inform the charting of this path. Clearly, more progress is possible by focusing relatively narrowly on processes like attention orienting. These processes, which operate similarly in many species, support iterative approaches to research involving deep dialogue between clinicians and basic scientists. However, processes that are unique to humans also are likely to impact aspects of mental illness, and research approaches to mental illness remain incomplete without a focus on these other aspects. Such processes include threat appraisal and other functions related to consciousness. Basic research has only begun to examine these processes in levels of depth comparable to those applied in research on attention orienting. As a result, a focus on this set of processes brings both risks and opportunities, and philosophical insights may help guide in finding an approach that balances these tensions.

REFERENCES

Badura-Brack, A. S., Naim, R., Ryan, T. J., Levy, O., Abend, R., Khanna, M. M., . . . Bar-Haim, Y. (2015) 'Effect of attention training on attention bias variability and PTSD symptoms: Randomized controlled trials in Israeli and U.S. combat veterans.' *American Journal of Psychiatry*, *172*(12), 1233–1241.

Bar-Haim, Y., Lamy, D., Pergamin, L., Bakermans-Kranenburg, M. J., & van Ijzendoorn, M. H. (2007) 'Threat-related attentional bias in anxious and nonanxious individuals: A meta-analytic study.' *Psychological Bulletin, 133*(1), 1–24.

Barberini, C. L., Morrison, S. E., Saez, A., Lau, B., & Salzman, C. D. (2012) 'Complexity and competition in appetitive and aversive neural circuits.' *Frontiers in Neuroscience, 6*, 170.

Beesdo, K., Knappe, S., & Pine, D. S. (2009) 'Anxiety and anxiety disorders in children and adolescents: Developmental issues and implications for *DSM-V*.' *Psychiatric Clinics of North America, 32*(3), 483–524.

Briggs-Gowan, M. J., Grasso, D., Bar-Haim, Y., Voss, J., McCarthy, K. J., Pine, D. S., & Wakschlag, L. S. (2016) 'Attention bias in the developmental unfolding of post-traumatic stress symptoms in young children at risk.' *Journal of Child Psychology and Psychiatry, 57*(9), 1083–1091.

Britton, J. C., Suway, J. G., Clementi, M. A., Fox, N. A., Pine, D. S., & Bar-Haim, Y. (2015) 'Neural changes with attention bias modification for anxiety: A randomized trial.' *Social Cognitive and Affective Neuroscience, 10*(7), 913–920.

Corbetta, M., Patel, G., & Shulman, G. L. (2008) 'The reorienting system of the human brain: From environment to theory of mind.' *Neuron, 58*(3), 306–324.

Cristea, I. A., Kok, R. N., & Cuijpers, P. (2015) 'Efficacy of cognitive bias modification interventions in anxiety and depression: Meta-analysis.' *British Journal of Psychiatry, 206*(1), 7–16.

Cuthbert, B. N., & Insel, T. R. (2013) 'Toward the future of psychiatric diagnosis: The seven pillars of RDoC.' *BMC Medicine, 11*, 126.

Davis-Kean, P. E., Huesmann, L. R., Jager, J., Collins, W. A., Bates, J. E., & Lansford, J. E. (2008) 'Changes in the relation of self-efficacy beliefs and behaviors across development.' *Child Development, 79*(5), 1257–1269.

Davis, M., Walker, D. L., Miles, L., & Grillon, C. (2010) 'Phasic vs sustained fear in rats and humans: Role of the extended amygdala in fear vs anxiety.' *Neuropsychopharmacology, 35*(1), 105–135.

Duits, P., Cath, D. C., Lissek, S., Hox, J. J., Hamm, A. O., Engelhard, I. M., . . . Baas, J. M. (2015) 'Updated meta-analysis of classical fear conditioning in the anxiety disorders.' *Depression and Anxiety, 32*(4), 239–253.

Gold, A. L., Shechner, T., Farber, M. J., Spiro, C. N., Leibenluft, E., Pine, D. S., & Britton, J. C. (2016) 'Amygdala–cortical connectivity: Associations with anxiety, development, and threat.' *Depression and Anxiety, 33*(10), 917–926.

Goodkind, M., Eickhoff, S. B., Oathes, D. J., Jiang, Y., Chang, A., Jones-Hagata, L. B., . . . Etkin, A. (2015) 'Identification of a common neurobiological substrate for mental illness.' *JAMA Psychiatry, 72*(4), 305–315.

Harter, S. (1992) 'Visions of self: Beyond the me in the mirror.' *Nebraska Symposium on Motivation, 40*, 99–144.

Harter, S., Bresnick, S., Bouchey, H. A., & Whitesell, N. R. (1997) 'The development of multiple role-related selves during adolescence.' *Development and Psychopathology, 9*(4), 835–853.

Insel, T. R. (2014) 'The NIMH Research Domain Criteria (RDoC) project: Precision medicine for psychiatry.' *American Journal of Psychiatry, 171*(4), 395–397.

Lau, J. Y., Britton, J. C., Nelson, E. E., Angold, A., Ernst, M., Goldwin, M., . . . Pine, D. S. (2011) 'Distinct neural signatures of threat learning in adolescents and adults.' *Proceedings of the National Academy of the Sciences U S A, 108*(11), 4500–4505.

Lazarov, A., Marom, S., Yahalom, N., Pine, D. S., Hermesh, H., & Bar-Haim, Y. (2018) 'Attention bias modification augments cognitive-behavioral group therapy for social anxiety disorder: A randomized controlled trial.' *Psychological Medicine, 48*(13), 2177–2185.

Lazarov, A., Pine, D. S., & Bar-Haim, Y. (2017) 'Gaze-contingent music reward therapy for social anxiety disorder: A randomized controlled trial.' *American Journal of Psychiatry, 174*(7), 649–656.

LeDoux, J. (2007) 'The amygdala.' *Current Biology, 17*(20), R868–R874.

LeDoux, J. E. (2014) 'Coming to terms with fear.' *Proceedings of the National Academy of the Sciences U S A, 111*(8), 2871–2878.

LeDoux, J. E., & Brown, R. (2017) 'A higher-order theory of emotional consciousness.' *Proceedings of the National Academy of the Sciences U S A, 114*(10), E2016–E2025.

LeDoux, J. E., & Pine, D. S. (2016) 'Using neuroscience to help understand fear and anxiety: A two-system framework.' *American Journal of Psychiatry, 173*(11), 1083–1093.

McTeague, L. M., Huemer, J., Carreon, D. M., Jiang, Y., Eickhoff, S. B., & Etkin, A. (2017) 'Identification of common neural circuit disruptions in cognitive control across psychiatric disorders.' *American Journal of Psychiatry, 174*(7), 676–685.

Miyake, A., & Friedman, N. P. (2012) 'The nature and organization of individual differences in executive functions: Four general conclusions.' *Current Directions in Psychological Science, 21*(1), 8–14.

Monk, C. S., Telzer, E. H., Mogg, K., Bradley, B. P., Mai, X., Louro, H. M., . . . Pine, D. S. (2008) 'Amygdala and ventrolateral prefrontal cortex activation to masked angry faces in children and adolescents with generalized anxiety disorder.' *Archives of General Psychiatry, 65*(5), 568–576.

Moore, T., & Zirnsak, M. (2017) 'Neural mechanisms of selective visual attention.' *Annual Review of Psychology, 68*, 47–72.

Pine, D. S. (2013) 'A 60-year climb on the mountain of nosology.' *Journal of the American Academy of Child and Adolescent Psychiatry, 52*(12), 1251–1254.

Pine, D. S., & Fox, N. A. (2015) 'Childhood antecedents and risk for adult mental disorders.' *Annual Review of Psychology, 66*, 459–485.

Pine, D. S., & Leibenluft, E. (2015) 'Biomarkers with a mechanistic focus.' *JAMA Psychiatry, 72*(7), 633–634.

Price, R. B., Wallace, M., Kuckertz, J. M., Amir, N., Graur, S., Cummings, L., . . . Bar-Haim, Y. (2016) 'Pooled patient-level meta-analysis of children and adults completing a computer-based anxiety intervention targeting attentional bias.' *Clinical Psychology Review, 50*, 37–49.

Rappaport, B. I., Pagliaccio, D., Pine, D. S., Klein, D. N., & Jarcho, J. M. (2017) 'Discriminant validity, diagnostic utility, and parent-child agreement on the Screen for Child Anxiety Related Emotional Disorders (SCARED) in treatment- and non-treatment-seeking youth.' *Journal of Anxiety Disorders, 51*, 22–31.

Shaffer, D., Fisher, P., Dulcan, M. K., Davies, M., Piacentini, J., Schwab-Stone, M. E., . . . Regier, D. A. (1996) 'The NIMH Diagnostic Interview Schedule for Children Version 2.3 (DISC-2.3): Description, acceptability, prevalence rates, and performance in the MECA study. Methods for the epidemiology of child and adolescent mental disorders study.' *Journal of the American Academy of Child and Adolescent Psychiatry*, *35*(7), 865–877.

Shaffer, D., Fisher, P., Lucas, C. P., Dulcan, M. K., & Schwab-Stone, M. E. (2000) 'NIMH Diagnostic Interview Schedule for Children Version IV (NIMH DISC-IV): Description, differences from previous versions, and reliability of some common diagnoses.' *Journal of the American Academy of Child and Adolescent Psychiatry*, *39*(1), 28–38.

van Vugt, B., Dagnino, B., Vartak, D., Safaai, H., Panzeri, S., Dehaene, S., & Roelfsema, P. R. (2018) 'The threshold for conscious report: Signal loss and response bias in visual and frontal cortex.' *Science*, *360*(6388), 537–542.

Wald, I., Degnan, K. A., Gorodetsky, E., Charney, D. S., Fox, N. A., Fruchter, E., . . . Bar-Haim, Y. (2013) 'Attention to threats and combat-related posttraumatic stress symptoms: Prospective associations and moderation by the serotonin transporter gene.' *JAMA Psychiatry*, *70*(4), 401–408.

Wald, I., Lubin, G., Holoshitz, Y., Muller, D., Fruchter, E., Pine, D. S., . . . Bar-Haim, Y. (2011) 'Battlefield-like stress following simulated combat and suppression of attention bias to threat.' *Psychological Medicine*, *41*(4), 699–707.

White, L. K., Degnan, K. A., Henderson, H. A., Perez-Edgar, K., Walker, O. L., Shechner, T., . . . Fox, N. A. (2017) 'Developmental relations among behavioral inhibition, anxiety, and attention biases to threat and positive information.' *Child Development*, *88*(1), 141–155.

White, L. K., Sequeira, S., Britton, J. C., Brotman, M. A., Gold, A. L., Berman, E., . . . Pine, D. S. (2017) 'Complementary features of attention bias modification therapy and cognitive-behavioral therapy in pediatric anxiety disorders.' *American Journal of Psychiatry*, *174*(8), 775–784.

9

Commentary on Daniel S. Pine

KENNETH F. SCHAFFNER

9.1 INTRODUCTION

Dr. Daniel Pine's chapter (Pine 2020) has four sections that constitute a well-integrated set of perspectives on a neuroscience-based clinical approach to a pervasive psychiatric disorder – anxiety (and more generally fear disorders). The chapter starts with a brief summary of a shift from (1) a traditional *DSM*-oriented approach to psychiatry to (2) exploring whether a more genetic and especially neuroscience-oriented perspective might assist progress on anxiety- and fear-related disorders. In psychiatry, a neuroscience-based psychiatric approach is noted to be much more difficult than in somatic medicine; this due to the complexity of the human brain and severe ethical difficulties with invasive manipulation of brain circuits.

Pine suggests that appropriate use of related animal model studies might ameliorate this problem in using neuroscience, writing:

> When possible, however, from the basic-science perspective, following initial identification of targets in patients, research in rodents, non-human primates, and other organisms might use experimental approaches to define candidate mechanisms that generate observed relationships between a measure of brain function and behavior in patients, through alterations in computations performed by the brain.

Further, below I will briefly address this important issue of animal model studies in psychiatry.

The second part of Pine's chapter mainly focuses on a fairly narrow psychological construct – the orientation of attention for which there have been reliable patient-based tests developed to assess the aspect of "attention." The third section of Pine's contribution summarizes psychological and neuroscience-oriented work on *appraisal*, a process closely connected to the contentious topic of consciousness. The final part of the chapter is more general and speculative, summarizing and reviewing the problems raised in the first three sections, and calling for "a plan for charting future research" in which "insights from philosophy may help inform the charting of this path."

The backdrop theme of Pine's chapter, explicitly cited from time to time in the text below, is the paradigm-shifting (and contentious) "two-system model" (TSM) of fear and anxiety in humans (LeDoux and Pine 2016, Fanselow and Pennington 2017, LeDoux and Brown 2017, Pine and LeDoux 2017, Fanselow and Pennington 2018).

The TSM is compared to and differentiated from the traditional fear model. (For a very helpful diagrammatic form of the contrasting models taken from LeDoux and Pine (2016), see my chapter in this volume (Schaffner 2020)). Both models are initiated by a vague "threat" (call this stage 1) – perhaps by an *organism* such as a snake or a wasp, or perhaps by an avalanche, or virtually by anything. This threat then is perceived by an organism's "sensory system" (stage 2) *as* a *threat,* and that directly influences a "fear circuit" (stage 3), creating in turn a set of innate fear *responses* (stage 4). The latter stage 4 responses are *both* physiological and behavioral. In the contrasting TSM, it is only at the fear circuit stage 3 that the TSM model becomes more complex, where it divides into two circuits. In the TSM, the sensory signal affects a "defensive survival circuit," but simultaneously also stimulates a separate *cognitive circuit* involving working memory. Thus, although in the traditional fear model responses can be the sole consequence of the survival circuit, in the TSM that survival circuit may also affect the cognitive circuit. And critically, it is the *cognitive circuit* that produces *fear* – an extremely important point for LeDoux and Pine, since "fear" is *only* to be *defined* in a *subjective* phenomenological sense. (For further details on this point, see my chapter.)

9.2 CORE PROCESSES, ATTENTION, APPRAISAL, AND A CLINICAL TRIAL

Though research from a neuroscience perspective on emotion in general and on fear and anxiety in particular is difficult, there are several approaches that Pine suggests that might help make some progress. One of his suggestions is to focus on "core psychological processes," which are "entities that lie between measures of brain function and psychological states" (p. 96). Pine adds:

> This intermediate set of entities can be considered features of the "mind", referring for the anxiety disorders to information-processing functions that are deployed upon exposure to threats. Moreover, unlike clinical features, which are defined based on patients' problematic behaviors and feelings, these core psychological processes are defined based on neuroscience research.
>
> (p. 96)

It can be problematic to develop reliable and valid measurements for these processes, but the TSM that LeDoux and Pine has proposed for anxiety disorders offers evidence that such processes can be assessed by following a two-part strategy: appealing to something old and something new – albeit in terms of circuits and behaviors.

The first or "old" strategy appeals to core psychological processes (CPP) arising in response to threats that relate to *evolutionarily older* and strongly conserved *defensive survival behaviors* and their circuitry. (The old circuits and behaviors are common both to the traditional model and the TSM.) Similar old behaviors and circuits can be found in rodent and primate models, as well as in humans. I first discuss the older processes, and then the newer ones.

9.2.1 Attention Processes

In humans, these types of older defensive survival behaviors can potentially be modified by "attention" processes. Pine defines attention as follows:

> Attention refers to a collection of processes that allow organisms to adapt to the capacity-limited nature of the brain, which precludes a full evaluation of every detail in a complex stimulus array. Attention processes regulate allocation of capacity-limited neural resources in ways that facilitate adaptation to the environment. Attention orienting represents one component of attention, which can be rapidly deployed in situations where mammals confront danger.
>
> (p. 99)

It is "attention orienting" (or AO) that is one psychologically-based, and also putatively clinically-based, intervention that has been taken up by Pine and his colleagues in testing treatments for anxiety. I prefer to think of the AO kind of attention approach that Pine proposes as falling under the rubric of a "thin" attention theory, by which I mean an attention theory that does not claim that it explains *all of* consciousness, as does philosopher Jesse Prinz's influential attention account (Prinz, 2012). (Philosophers frequently use "thin" in this sense as opposed to "thick," where a "thick" account means a full, robust, and nearly complete analysis is available.[1]) Such a thin attention theory can still be very useful in itself within its bounds and also apparently embraces the empirical work on fear and anxiety by Pine (White et al. 2017, Pine 2019).

Here I will only briefly mention several ways that Pine and his colleagues have made use of attention in two of its forms – bottom-up as well as top-down forms of attention. (More specifically, bottom-up implicates "attention orienting," and appraisal appears to involve top-down attention. (An account of appraisal is to come below.)[2]

Attention orienting (AO) is accordingly one component of attention that in connection with danger signals has been well conserved in evolution. In humans, the prototype is its activation upon coming across a dangerous snake during a leisure forest stroll. AO also seems to differ between normal and anxiety-prone individuals, and if that difference can be reliably assessed with an appropriate test, corrective training using this process might be able to ameliorate unwanted pathological anxiety. This is a major theme of the Pine and colleagues 2017 study (White et al. 2017) described below. The test that Pine and colleagues employed to assess AO is termed the dot-probe task, and is shown in Figure 8.3 of Pine's chapter. This AO type of attention can also be affected by Attention Bias Modification Therapy (ABMT), which was employed therapeutically in the White et al. (2017) study, and also has been used in some twenty other anxiety treatment trials (Pine, p. 103).

9.2.2 Appraisal Processes

This first, or "older," AO strategy of examining evolutionarily older and strongly conserved defensive survival behaviors and their circuitry is *complemented* by a second strategy addressing a different "newer" component

[1] For a comprehensive review of a variety of attention theories of consciousness see Wu (2014).

[2] On these two general notions, Katsuki and Constantinidis (2014) define them succinctly, writing as follows:

> This process of information selection is referred to as attention. Attention is commonly categorized into two distinct functions: bottom-up (or exogenous) attention, an externally induced process in which information to be processed is selected automatically because of highly noticeable features of stimuli; and top-down (or endogenous) attention, an internally induced process in which information is actively sought out in the environment based on voluntarily chosen factors (refs are in original) (p. 509).

Bottom-up attention is also typically related to the older circuits that signify danger, or possibly related to a novel stimulus.

of anxiety involving a presumptively different circuit. Humans, and primates at least, also seem to have another danger alerting process that involves *conscious* thought as well as memories, a proposal that points to the second system of "two-system" model (TSM). This second process Pine terms "appraisal," and in the framework of the TSM, it will utilize largely different brain circuits and potentially be addressable by different forms of therapy, including cognitive behavioral therapy (CBT) (White et al. 2017). Appraisal, however, is not that well understood, it probably involves a form of top-down attention in addition to other related processes, and is the subject of active investigations regarding both clinical and neuroscience research projects. Still more will be said about appraisal below, after I provide some additional details of the study by White et al. (2017).

9.2.3 Two Clinical Interventions to Test the Two System Model

Though the ABMT mentioned may target rapid, implicit threat reactions, CBT may target more slowly developing threat responses, and thus could be used in a test of the two systems of the TSM. The authors of the White et al. (2017) study also used fMRI to measure amygdala-based connectivity during a threat-attention task and a randomized controlled trial design to evaluate potential complementary features of these treatments. The focus in the trial was on *pediatric* anxiety disorders. For this trial, the investigators recruited some 85 young people (8–17 years old) with anxiety disorders as well as healthy comparison participants. Participants were all assigned to CBT, but also randomly assigned either to active or placebo ABMT. In addition, patients' "pretreatment amygdala-based connectivity profiles were compared among patients with varying levels of clinical response."

There were three findings reported in this study, namely

1. Compared with the CBT plus placebo ABMT group, the CBT plus active ABMT group exhibited less severe anxiety after treatment.
2. The patient and healthy comparison groups differed in amygdala-insula connectivity during the threat-attention task.
3. Patients whose connectivity profiles were most different from those of the healthy comparison group exhibited the poorest response to treatment, particularly those who received CBT plus placebo ABMT. (White et al. 2017, p. 775).

Pine and his colleagues added that "The study provided evidence of enhanced clinical effects for patients receiving active ABMT. Moreover,

ABMT appears to be most effective for patients with abnormal amygdala-insula connectivity. ABMT may target specific threat processes associated with dysfunctional amygdala-insula connectivity that are not targeted by CBT alone. This may explain the observation of enhanced clinical response to CBT plus active ABMT." (White et al. 2017, p. 775)

This study was thus guided by, and confirmed, the TSM model by using two complementary therapies that targeted the two components of the TSM.

9.2.4 Appraisal Redux and the "Self"

The most intriguing innovations of the "two-system model" (TSM) in its contrast with the traditional fear model are (1) the addition of the consciousness dimension to fear and anxiety studies and (2) its cognitive circuit pathway(s) that are involved in appraisal. One of the more salient difficulties with the cognitive pathway, however, is that it involves the "self" and its evaluation of experience. This "self" problem also ties in to a second problem, one raised by the use of animal models and hinted at above.

First, regarding the "self" issue, Pine writes:

> Far less progress accrues in research on threat appraisal as compared with research on attention orienting. Many factors contribute to this difference. Threat appraisal involves the reporting of a conscious experience evaluated by the self, and neuroscience research on phenomena related to consciousness or the self is far less advanced than research on processes such as threat conditioning or attention orienting. This relates at least partly to the difficulty of conducting cross-species research on consciousness.
>
> (p. 105)

As I note in my chapter in this volume, the range of the literature on the "self" comprises philosophical, psychological, psychiatric, and neuroscientific analyses and it is vast, diverse, and diffuse in all of these four fields. The Alternative Model of Personality Disorders (AMPD) approach that I propose for analysis of the self is sketched in my chapter and need not be discussed here, except to agree with Pine that further research on the "self" is an area that sorely needs further philosophical and empirical research. The need for an analysis of the "self" also reappears in Pine's comments on the contrast between AO and appraisal, where he notes that in appraisal, a stable self is needed to ascertain when one's feeling has changed, whether that be in the short run or developmentally across different ways the self matures as the individual ages.

Turning to the issue of cross species research on consciousness, Pine also notes that using such species, "neuroscience research has only begun to map the brain circuits that support conscious reporting of events, and that "due to the complexity of research in this area, much of this work focuses on perceptual events, which can be readily manipulated using an experimental approach," in contrast to "feeling states" which are central to fear and anxiety. Pine is correct in these assessments concerning the focus on largely perceptual (usually visual) research. Pine also has commented (see the quote on page 1 of this commentary) that a variety of species might be used to identify mechanisms relating brain and behavior. But Pine may be underestimating the difficulties of research in using *appropriate* animal models, such as primates in contrast to rodents.

On this point, Joshua Gordon, the current director of the NIMH, has also stressed the need for more evolved animal models, and questioned the rodent model. Gordon asked:

> How do we determine the precise neuroanatomical location of functional microdomains on an individual basis in a heterogeneous genetic and environmental context? How do we achieve comprehensive infection or illumination of a brain region that in mice might measure a few hundred microns in diameter, but in humans several millimeters or more? And what about the prefrontal cortex, a complex amalgam of regions in humans that clearly plays a crucial role in psychiatric dysfunction, yet is ridiculously simplified and comparatively miniscule in mice?
>
> (Gordon 2016)

Gordon continued:

> All of these issues point to a crucial conclusion: intermediate models are necessary if we are to advance circuit technologies from mice to men [sic]. . . . [F]or . . . questions. . . such as how to direct gene expression to specific prefrontal cortical regions, only primate models will suffice. Given the current societal pressures against nonhuman primate research, strong ethical as well as scientific foundations will be required in order to facilitate this important work.

Even primate models might not suffice for TSM investigations if primates do not possess an approximation to human consciousness nor exhibit something akin to a "self." This is a concern that LeDoux has expressed (personal communication, 2018)

Such a primate research program will also encounter ethical and social difficulties, suggested by Gordon, not only in the United States but also in the European Union. Such a program might only be pursuable in a different society, such as in China where reports indicate that extensive primate research is already in operation (Cyranoski 2016). A very recent in-depth analysis of the social, political, and scientific issues on animal models can be found in Grimm (2018), and for strategies and ethical analyses of animal model use also see van der Staay et al. (2009).

Again, turning back to the topic of consciousness, another difficulty with appraisal research is that there are a number of differing approaches that have been taken to characterize the nature of consciousness and its related neural circuits (for more on this see my chapter (Schaffner 2020) in this volume). There is also no consensus in this area, and many speculative non-empirical assumptions are made by a large variety of theories concerning this topic of consciousness, thus compounding experimental assessments. Also in my chapter, and along with Pine, I also accept an "attention" oriented approach to consciousness, though in my account I label it a "thin" theory of attention. That said, I also have suggested in my chapter that *more* than an "attention" theory will be needed for the analysis of consciousness, and have proposed that one of the best more general theories may come from the extensive but still ongoing work of Dehaene and colleagues on the Global Neuronal Workspace (GNW) theory (Dehaene and Changeux 2011, Dehaene et al. 2014).

Regarding Dehane's theory, it may be worth noting that in a recent article (Dehaene et al. 2017), Dehaene and his colleagues usefully distinguish two types of consciousness within the GNW into "Global Availability" (i. e., information available to the conscious workspace) abbreviated as C1, and "Self-Monitoring," or C2. They also suggest that this C2 is "orthogonal" to C1 but still related to C1. And about C2 they write:

> It (C2) refers to a self-referential relationship in which the cognitive system is able to monitor its own processing and obtain information about itself. . . . This sense of consciousness corresponds to what is commonly called introspection, or what psychologists call "meta-cognition"— the ability to conceive and make use of internal representations of one's own knowledge and abilities [and thus the "self"].
>
> (pp. 486–487)

I think this approach and proposal is plausible, if still incomplete, and also relevant to the "self" concept that I hold. I also think Dehaene's approach here is consistent with Pine's concerns about a self being able to monitor itself over time.

That said, a follow-up of these possibilities must wait for additional research.

9.3 CONCLUDING COMMENTS

In general, the two-system model (TSM) is an exciting substantive "paradigm shift," involving extensive appeals to analyses of phenomenal consciousness in the area of fear and anxiety, and also positioned in the context of brain science. The radical nature of this modification of the traditional fear circuit model in this scientific area cannot be overemphasized. The promise of this shift is that adding in the second system allows a reorientation not only of diagnosis of fear-related mental disorders, including panic disorder, generalized anxiety disorder, and additional fear disorders, but it could point the way to better treatments both of a pharmacological type and behavioral type. (For specific suggestions regarding treatment see Pine and LeDoux 2017.) The TSM may also be a paradigm shift for analytical philosophy of consciousness, bringing another dimension of that discipline's extensive consciousness studies into contact with empirical psychiatry. As such, analytical philosophy joins a long-standing, but more phenomenological, tradition that has had significant earlier influences in psychosis and schizophrenia studies (Parnas et al. 2005, Parnas 2011, Zahavi 2014, 2018).

One final comment regarding "philosophy." Pine suggests that "A major challenge for future research on mental disorders relates to a plan for charting future research. Insights from philosophy may help inform the charting of this path."

This inquiring mind would like to know more – namely what philosophical topics, and which authors, might provide some assistance in charting such a "research path."

REFERENCES

Cyranoski, D. (2016) 'Monkey kingdom.' *Nature* 532(7599): 300–302.

Dehaene, S. and J. P. Changeux (2011) 'Experimental and theoretical approaches to conscious processing.' *Neuron* 70(2): 200–227.

Dehaene, S., L. Charles, J. R. King and S. Marti (2014) 'Toward a computational theory of conscious processing.' *Current Opinion in Neurobiology* 25: 76–84.

Dehaene, S., H. Lau and S. Kouider (2017) 'What is consciousness, and could machines have it?' *Science* 358(6362): 486–492.

Fanselow, M. S. and Z. T. Pennington (2018) 'A return to the psychiatric dark ages with a two-system framework for fear.' *Behaviour Research and Therapy* 100: 24–29.

(2017) 'The danger of LeDoux and Pine's two-system framework for fear.' *American Journal of Psychiatry* 174(11): 1120–1121.

Gordon, J. A. (2016) 'On being a circuit psychiatrist.' *Nature Neuroscience* 19(11): 1385–1386.

Grimm, D. (2018) 'Opening the lab door.' *Science* 360(6396): 1392–1395.

Katsuki, F. and C. Constantinidis (2014) 'Bottom-up and top-down attention: Different processes and overlapping neural systems.' *Neuroscientist* 20(5): 509–521.

LeDoux, J. E. and R. Brown (2017) 'A higher-order theory of emotional consciousness.' *Proceedings of the National Academy of Sciences of the United States of America* 114(10): E2016–E2025.

LeDoux, J. E. and D. S. Pine (2016) 'Using neuroscience to help understand fear and anxiety: A two-system framework.' *American Journal of Psychiatry* 173(11): 1083–1093.

Parnas, J. (2011) 'A disappearing heritage: The clinical core of schizophrenia.' *Schizophrenia Bulletin* 37(6): 1121–1130.

Parnas, J., P. Moller, T. Kircher, J. Thalbitzer, L. Jansson, P. Handest and D. Zahavi (2005) 'EASE: Examination of anomalous self-experience.' *Psychopathology* 38(5): 236–258.

Pine, D. S. (2020) 'Tackling hard problems: Neuroscience, treatment, and anxiety.' In *Levels of Analysis in Psychopathology: Cross-Disciplinary Perspectives*, K. S. Kendler, J. Parnas and P. Zachar (eds.). New York: Cambridge University Press.

Pine, D. S. and J. E. LeDoux (2017) 'Elevating the role of subjective experience in the clinic: Response to Fanselow and Pennington.' *American Journal of Psychiatry* 174(11): 1121–1122.

Prinz, J. (2012). *The conscious brain: How attention engenders experience*. New York: Oxford University Press.

Schaffner, K. F. (2020) 'Approaches to multi-level models of fear: The what, where, why, how, and how much?' In *Levels of Analysis in Psychopathology: Cross-Disciplinary Perspectives*, K. S. Kendler, J. Parnas and P. Zachar (eds.). New York: Cambridge University Press.

van der Staay, F. J., S. S. Arndt and R. E. Nordquist (2009) 'Evaluation of animal models of neurobehavioral disorders.' *Behavioral and Brain Functions* 5: 11.

White, L. K., S. Sequeira, J. C. Britton, M. A. Brotman, A. L. Gold, E. Berman, K. Towbin, R. Abend, N. A. Fox, Y. Bar-Haim, E. Leibenluft and D. S. Pine (2017) 'Complementary features of attention bias modification therapy and cognitive-behavioral therapy in pediatric anxiety disorders.' *American Journal of Psychiatry* 174(8): 775–784.

Wu, W. (2014) *Attention*. London; New York: Routledge.

Zahavi, D. (2014) *Self and Other: Exploring Subjectivity, Empathy, and Shame*. New York: Oxford University Press.

(2018) *The Oxford Handbook of the History of Phenomenology*. New York: Oxford University Press.

PART II

PHENOMENOLOGY, BIOLOGICAL PSYCHOLOGY, AND THE MIND–BODY PROBLEM

SECTION 4

10

Introduction

JOSEF PARNAS

If you ask the question "where is the mind located?" or "where do consciousness and cognition take place?" a typical answer from the layperson and most of the neuroscientists will be "in the brain" or "in the skull." This is a usual view of our mentation: It is produced by the brain and is therefore confined to the skull. This theoretical perspective is frequently called "internalism." Sometimes it is also called "Cartesian materialism": The brain and its world are in a constant energetic exchange. The information that impinges on the brain comes through the sensory channels as physical or chemical stimuli. This is all that we know directly about the world. It is the task of the brain to make a model of the world on the basis of computation of those elementary sensory data. Needless to say, such a view of cognition is fraught with several difficulties such as solipsism and skepticism. Over the recent decades, this view has been increasingly questioned and this questioning can be traced to many phenomenological philosophers such as Maurice Merleau-Ponty or Martin Heidegger. This opposite perspective, often called "externalism" claims that mental contents and processes are not only constituted by the brain but implicate, in a strong sense, the body and the environment. One radical version of externalism considers cognition as being embodied, extended, embedded, and enactive (EEEE) (Rowlands, 2010). This view sees the cognitive processes as constitutively and dynamically involving the entire body, the environing world, intersubjective and cultural frameworks, and our own activity in this world. Shaun Gallagher is a phenomenologist, very much inspired by Merleau-Ponty, and he has worked for many decades in cognitive science promoting the notion of the "embodied mind" (Gallagher, 2005, 2017). In this chapter, he provides an account of our sense of agency and ownership as a dynamical self-organizing system/Gestalt that is not reducible to the modular or hierarchical views of cognition. If our cognitive activities are widely distributed, involving disparate elements of the brain, body, and world, then it has profound consequences for our pathogenetic research in psychopathology. In the following commentary, there is an attempt to question and clarify some of Gallagher's claims as well as more general assessments of the role of phenomenology in contemporary psychiatry.

REFERENCES

Gallagher, S. (2005) *How the Body Shapes the Mind.* Oxford, UK: Clarendon Press.
(2017) *Enactivist Interventions: Rethinking the Mind.* Oxford, UK: Oxford University Press.
Rowlands, M. (2010) *The New Science of the Mind: From Extended Mind to Embodied Phenomenology.* Cambridge, MA: MIT Press.

11

Body Self-Awareness: Multiple Levels or Dynamical Gestalt?

SHAUN GALLAGHER

The issues surrounding questions of body self-awareness are complex ones. One contentious issue concerns whether there is a minimal, pre-reflective body self-awareness involved in action or more generally in all experience. This question has been addressed in terms of contrasting a sense of mineness or ownership with a sense of agency, and a pre-reflective awareness with a reflective consciousness. Further distinctions have complicated this conceptual landscape. For example, Elisabeth Pacherie has suggested that the sense of agency may include "awareness of a goal, awareness of an intention to act, awareness of initiation of action, awareness of movements, sense of activity, sense of mental effort, sense of physical effort, sense of control, experience of authorship, experience of intentionality, experience of purposiveness, experience of freedom, and experience of mental causation" (Pacherie 2007, 6). Not all of these factors, however, will show up in the actual first-order phenomenology, and in some respects, they may be the product of reflection or of purely theoretical considerations. Further complications are introduced when one attempts to sort causal from constitutive processes, and to locate these processes on different explanatory levels or in the framework of different time scales, from elementary neural processes to integrative pre-reflective processes, to reflective introspective or narrative processes, to longer-term processes of social and cultural structures. These are issues that concern not only phenomenology and philosophy of mind, but also neuroscience, psychopathology, psychiatric understanding, physio- and psychotherapy, performance studies, as well as feminism and race theory.

In this chapter, I review some of these issues and show that various aspects of body self-awareness can be organized in a relatively coherent manner by thinking of them in terms of dynamical gestalts. I'll argue that taking this approach moves us away from thinking of these issues as involving multiple or different levels, or conceiving of them under hierarchical descriptions that refer to 'top-down' versus 'bottom-up' processes. By thinking of body self-awareness on the model of a dynamical gestalt, we can start to see how different forms of pre-reflective and reflective self-awareness are related in a more holistic fashion. The analysis here will need to work through a lot of material that is typically framed in the current literature in terms of hierarchical levels. For this reason my analysis will remain suggestive rather than definitive, and it should be understood in that way.

The first step is to say something about various notions of body self-awareness, including senses of ownership (mineness) and agency. I'll review some terminological and conceptual issues, and then discuss various objections that have been raised against these notions in general. I'll then move on to consider specifically the role they play in understanding psychiatric disorders.

11.1 TERMINOLOGICAL AND CONCEPTUAL ISSUES

Before moving on to the substantial issues, it may be helpful to consider some terminological and conceptual distinctions and confusions. Most of these considerations circulate around the concept of the sense of ownership or mineness (see Table 11.1).

11.1.1 Phenomenology's Two-Fold Distinction: Reflective versus Pre-reflective

One distinction made by phenomenologists, from Husserl to Sartre to Merleau-Ponty to Zahavi, is between reflective and pre- (or non-) reflective experience. The phenomenological view is that experience (consciousness) involves or is characterized as, first of all, pre-reflective self-awareness as an

TABLE 11.1 *The sense of ownership versus the sense of agency.*

	Ownership	Agency	
Pre-reflective	SO – Mineness	SA	Perspectival
Reflective	AO – Attribution/ judgment-Subjectivity	AA – Attribution/ judgment-Authorship	Personal

Note: SO = sense of ownership; SA = sense of agency; AO = attribution of ownership; AA = attribution of agency intrinsic structure. To say it is intrinsic means that it is a form of self-awareness that is built into the perspectival structure of experience in such a way that it does not require an extra or transitive (reflective) act of self-awareness which takes one's experience, (or movement, or body) as an object. The sense of ownership or mineness, on this account, is an aspect of this intrinsic pre-reflective self-awareness and nothing over and above it (Gallagher and Zahavi 2012, 2014). Accordingly, this first-order, pre-reflective sense of mineness is distinguished from a reflective (e.g., retrospective) judgment about one's body or one's experience (Vosgerau and Newen 2007).

11.1.2 Phenomenology of Ownership versus Agency

In the 1990s, psychologists, neuropsychologists, and philosophers were using phrases like 'sense of ownership' and 'sense of agency' (e.g., Campbell 1999; Frith 1992; Gallagher and Marcel 1999; Martin 1995) without making a systematic distinction between them. Although pre-reflective experiences of ownership and agency are tightly integrated in everyday experience, they are phenomenologically distinguishable, for example, in the case of involuntary movement.

> **Sense of agency**: The sense that I am the one who is causing or generating an action.
>
> **Sense of ownership**: The sense that I am the one who is undergoing an experience. For example, the sense that my body is moving regardless of whether the movement is voluntary or involuntary.
>
> (Gallagher 2000, 15)

Some authors made similar or correlated distinctions at the reflective or narrative level, distinguishing between attributions (or judgments) of ownership (or subjectivity) and attributions (or judgments) of agency (Stephens and Graham 2000). Alternatively, John Campbell (1999) suggested that these are really two forms of ownership. On the one hand, a person may regard a bodily experience *as her own* just because she finds it to be part of her stream of experience or happening within the boundaries of her body. On the other hand, a person can claim a bodily experience – for example the experience of a movement – *as her own* because she originated or caused the movement, i.e., she recognizes herself to be the agent of this movement. The use of the phrase 'as my own' signifies for some authors that the distinction on the reflective level involves a conceptual (identifying) judgment (Hutto and Ilundáin-Agurruza 2018). This distinction seems equivalent to Stephens and Graham's attributions of ownership and agency respectively, the latter sometimes referred to as authorship (see e.g., Bortolotti and Broome 2009). We'll see that these distinctions play into several debates about schizophrenic symptoms. Importantly, the sense of ownership or mineness applies not only to one's body or one's body parts; it also applies to one's movement, one's action, and even to one's experience itself. I may have a sense that this is *my* action, or *my* thinking, or, most basically, *my* experience (Gallagher 2000; Guillot 2017).

11.1.3 A Further Two-Fold Distinction

Another distinction originally introduced by Miri Albahari (2016) has also figured into discussions of the sense of ownership. This is the distinction between *personal* ownership and *perspectival* ownership. Personal ownership involves an explicit act of self-identification with an experience or action, and seems akin to a reflective attribution of ownership, although it may involve a kind of emotional investment as well. Perspectival ownership for the experience or action simply means that the experience or action presents itself in a distinctive manner to the subject (Albahari 2016, 53–54). It lines up with the idea that, for example, an action is mine if it is given to me in first-person perspective (see Zahavi 2018). In phenomenology there is an implicit link between the first-person perspectival character of experience and the pre-reflective sense of agency.

These terminological and conceptual distinctions may vary from one study to another, or even within a single study. Despite that difficulty Braun et al. (2018) have done an excellent and extensive review of these concepts in the recent scientific literature, including discussions of different experiments and ways of characterizing and implicitly or explicitly measuring these complex and non-unitary phenomena, their neuroscientific underpinnings, and their relevance to clinical and therapeutic contexts. Their review clearly shows that the scientific discussion of these concepts is framed by defining different neurological and phenomenological levels of explanation. James Moore (2016) provides a general overview of the research on the experience of agency and shows why this concept is important in health, psychiatric and ethical contexts. Although both reviews acknowledge the relevance of these concepts for both philosophy and psychiatry, neither of them look precisely at some of the contentious debates that have formed around these concepts as they relate to basic questions about self-awareness, nor do they question the idea that these issues are best framed in terms of different levels. I'll focus on these questions in the following sections.

11.2 THE BODY AND THE GORILLA

Let me start at the supposed top, i.e., with the issue of a higher-order *reflective* self-awareness that on some accounts reifies or takes the body as an object. This is frequently the way it is described in the phenomenological literature. If I reflectively attend to my body, or specifically to a body part, I regard it as one object among others, although still in some sense the most proximate object and one that is in some way connected with my subjectivity. If, for example, I have a pain in my foot, I can examine it as a physician might examine it, consider what reasons there may be for the pain, and decide to treat the pain with some medicine or exercise. Throughout this attending I can acknowledge that this is *my* foot – and for that reason it is a case of body self-awareness. Indeed, the pain itself keeps me attuned to this. At the same time I can distance myself from the *mineness*, and treat it as if it were other than me – as if it were a foot in general to be examined and treated. If I do this, perhaps we would say that I am dialing back on the mineness aspect, dialing back from what might be considered 100% explicit body self-awareness with mineness intact.

Drew Leder (1990) has contrasted this reflectively objectified body (*Körper*) with what he calls the absent body. Here he continues in a phenomenological line of thought expressed in Husserl and Merleau-Ponty, employing the distinction between *Leib* and *Körper*. With respect to how we live or experience the body, as *Leib*, when we are fully engaged in action we are not reflectively attending to the body as an object. In that case, what precisely is the status of body self-awareness? For Merleau-Ponty (on one reading), for Sartre (on a reading by Howell and Thompson [2017]), for Leder, for Hubert Dreyfus, and others, the body disappears – i.e., the agent is not aware of his body (or more generally, not self-aware). The body is much like the gorilla in the famous inattentional blindness/selective attention experiment – the one where, as our focus is entirely on a task of counting the passing of a ball among a group of people, a person dressed in a gorilla costume walks into the middle of the action, and yet, typically, we do not see the gorilla (Simons and Chabris 1999). Here one might think that since the gorilla is doing its dance right in front of our eyes, we must actually see it and it simply fails to register. But the phenomenology is precisely that we do not see the gorilla. Similarly, the phenomenology of engaged action is said to be such that we are simply not self-aware of our bodies. Body self-awareness = 0.

It turns out that there is a significant ongoing debate about the phenomenology of body self-awareness between the extremes of 0 and 100%. Is it really the case that the body is like the gorilla? Are we not always in some minimal sense (above 0) aware of our bodies, even if we are immersed in the flow of an action? Is there not at least what Gibson (1979) calls an ecological self-awareness of our general posture (sitting, standing, etc.) or movement (walking, running, etc.)?

One such debate revolves around the notion of expertise, indeed, the expertise involved in everyday motoric performance. Dreyfus (2007), for example, argues for a mindless performance. When an expert athlete, for example, engages in action, he or she lacks all body self-awareness. On this view, in most cases, or at least in our expert everyday performance, and setting aside instances where we might be suffering some pain, there is no explicit awareness of our feet, or how we are moving, when we are walking across the room in order to answer the door, in the same way that we are typically unaware of our posture. Our attention is elsewhere.

Perhaps it is a caricature of Dreyfus's position to say that our *full* awareness is elsewhere. It's not clear that he (or Merleau-Ponty) would deny that we have a pre-reflective awareness of what we are doing, even if we are not aware of the fine details of our movements. If I am reaching to grasp my cup to take a drink, outside of my field of awareness my hand shapes itself in a specific configuration that relates to the shape of the cup or cup handle. Phenomenologists, ecological psychologists and some neuroscientists tend to agree that I can be aware of *what* I am doing (I can easily respond "I'm grasping the cup," or more likely, "I'm getting a drink"), but that I am not aware of *how* I am doing it (that I am shaping my fingers thus and so) (see Gallagher 2005; Jeannerod 2003; Jeannerod and Gallagher 2002). Clearly, some parts of my action are non-conscious, but some are a matter of self-awareness.

If we leave Dreyfus to defend the 0 (or the close-to-0) position, most other phenomenologists want to dial things up to a default setting of 10–20%. Let's take this as an arbitrary setting for pre-reflective self-awareness, and specifically pre-reflective body self-awareness. The body, in this case, is not the explicit object of our awareness – not an *object* of awareness at all. As I express it, "I'm getting a drink" rather than "I am moving my hand" or "shaping my grasp." My attention is on the task or the world. My report describes something about the action or my intention, rather than something about bodily movement. On the supposition that this type of report, although in some sense reflective, is a report on pre-reflective experience, the claim is, I am implicitly or marginally aware of my bodily action, and this self-awareness is an intrinsic aspect of my experience and action. Moreover, this minimal self-awareness can be specified as involving a first-person perspective, a sense of ownership and, in cases when I am acting, a sense of agency (e.g., Gallagher and Zahavi 2012). Much of the debate begins here, with the claim that, as embodied agents, we are not just mindless gorillas.

11.3 THE SENSE OF OWNERSHIP: CLOSING THE DOOR ON THE FRIDGE LIGHT PROBLEM

As we've noted, some phenomenologists claim that when the experiencing agent moves, she has a sense of ownership (SO) for the movement, without having to turn her reflective attention to it. The phenomenological view is that this sense of ownership or mineness is experienced as a pre-reflective self-awareness that is intrinsic to everyday (non-pathological, non-exceptional) experience. It does not require an extra or transitive act of reflection which takes one's experience, or movement, or body as an object. This pre-reflective experience of ownership for my bodily movement is accomplished, in part, by way of sensory feedback, including somatic proprioception (position sense) and kinaesthesis (movement sense). Philosophers and psychologists distinguish between non-conscious proprioceptive/kinaesthetic *information* (i.e., physiological signals in the body), and proprioceptive/kinaesthetic *awareness* (Bermúdez, Eilan, and Marcel 1995; Gallagher 1996). To the extent that there is proprioceptive/kinaesthetic awareness, it seems reasonable to claim that the agent has some feeling or sense of her bodily movement. The 'proprio' in 'proprioception' signifies a very basic form of *self*-awareness. Unless I am *subject A* in an odd thought experiment where *subject A's* proprioceptive system is hooked up to *subject B's* body, if I proprioceptively experience a body, the body that I experience is mine (Evans 1982). Indeed, on this basis Evans and others argue that this self-experience is immune to error through misidentification – that is, *via* proprioception, I cannot mistakenly take it to be someone else's body.

It's clear, from the odd thought experiment, that this has to be a contingent claim – contingent on the proper working of the proprioceptive system. In addition, cases of deafferentation point to the possibility that without somatic proprioception and, in an ideal case, without the proprioceptive (or ecological) characteristics of the other senses, a subject may not have pre-reflective body awareness (Gallagher and Cole 1995). Deafferented subjects require more reflective means – cognitive effort and visual perception – to keep track of and control their body. This is the case for IW, who lacks proprioception and touch below the neck. He nonetheless does have temperature sense, and experiences of fatigue and deep pain, and this gives him some sense of ownership for his own body.

Not everyone accepts the idea that we have a minimal, pre-reflective body awareness in the form of a sense of ownership (mineness). José Bermúdez, for example, regards the phenomenological claim that there is a sense of mineness implicit in our experience of self-movement and action as inflationary. Bermúdez (2011, 2017) rejects the idea that there is a positive first-order (non-observational) phenomenology of ownership or feeling of 'mineness', and he offers a deflationary account. 'On a deflationary conception of ownership the sense of ownership consists, first, in certain facts about the phenomenology of bodily sensations and, second, in certain fairly obvious judgments about the body (which we can term judgments of ownership)' (2011, 162). Bermúdez contends that an experience of ownership only comes up when we explicitly turn our reflective attention to our bodily experience and attribute that experience to ourselves. It is only this reflective, second-order experience that can count as an experience of ownership, and only on this basis does he say "[w]hen we [reflectively] experience our bodies we experience them as our own . . . there is a phenomenology of ownership" (Bermúdez 2015, 38). The phenomenology of ownership is thus derived, top-down, from the judgment of ownership (AO). This is the light in the fridge scenario. An experience of ownership results (the light comes on) as a product of this judgment (opening the door), but it is not something that is there to begin with. "There are facts about the phenomenology of bodily awareness (about position sense, movement sense, and interoception) and there are judgments of ownership, but there is no additional feeling of ownership" (2011, 166; see Schear 2009).

According to Bermúdez (2011), then, SO, as "a specific feeling of ownership – a qualitative 'feel' that one has in all and only those body parts that one experiences as one's own" (2017) is a philosophical fiction. Although one does experience a sense of body boundedness and connectedness, as well as proprioception and other bodily sensations, one does not experience, in addition, ownership as a separate and independent feeling. Barry Dainton (2008) makes a similar point. When I experience some sensation, e.g., a pain, I experience it 'against the backdrop of various other forms of consciousness: a range of bodily experience, tactile sensations, visual and auditory experience, intentional or willed bodily movements, conscious thinking . . . [etc.]' (2008, 239–240). This experienced 'phenomenal background' includes an elusive set of bodily experiences, thoughts, memories, and so on, and it contributes to (and perhaps constitutes) 'the feeling of what it is typically like to be *me* (or *you*)' (240). Like Bermúdez, however, Dainton does not think that this feeling consists of a separable experience, and specifically, he argues, it does not consist of a pre-reflective self-awareness or sense of mineness or ownership, "something over and above the changing stream of thought, perception, volition, emotion, memory, bodily sensation, and so on" (240).

Neither Dainton nor Bermúdez want to deny that we can have a proprioceptive and kinaesthetic awareness of bodily (and limb) posture and movement, or a complex set of background sensory experiences of the body. Dainton argues, however, that if we subtract all of these various experiences, there would be nothing of experience left; therefore, there is nothing *over and above* just these experiences – no extra or additional experience that we would identify as the experience of mineness. Like Bermúdez he claims that "we can account for the phenomenology of *mineness* without positing any primitive 'ownership' quality" (2008, 243).

As we've seen, however, for the phenomenologists, to say that SO is an intrinsic aspect of proprioceptive and kinaesthetic experiences is to agree that it is not an additional or independent feeling, but rather, a sense 'already inherent within' the phenomenology of bodily sensations (Martin 1995, 278). On the phenomenological view, and in contrast to Bermúdez and Dainton, this intrinsic aspect is pre-reflective in the sense that one has this intrinsic experience of ownership without having to make a reflective judgment about ownership. This can be read in a deflationary way, so that the phenomenologists can agree that there is no additional feeling of ownership independent of proprioceptive and kinaesthetic sensations. The claim is rather that such proprioceptive experience is an integrated pattern of body awareness that includes an intrinsic experience that it is *my* bodily experience. That's the *proprio* in proprioception. Phenomenologists describe SO as an *intrinsic* aspect of experience, not as something extra that is added, or an additional quality that one experiences in addition to experiencing pain, or bodily sensations, etc. (see Gallagher and Zahavi 2014).

11.4 DEPERSONALIZATION AND THREE CHALLENGES TO DEFLATIONARY THEORIES OF SO

"Bodily experience gives us a *sense of ownership*," Jerome Dokic suggests. "The very idea of *feeling* a pain in a limb which does not seem to be ours is difficult to frame, perhaps unintelligible" (2003, 325). According to Alexandre Billon (2017), however, some cases of depersonalization present us with precisely such unintelligible instances. Billon outlines three challenges for various conceptions of SO. The first challenge, which he calls the 'centrality challenge,' applies to accounts that focus only on the question of body ownership (e.g., Bermudez 2011, 2017; de Vignemont 2007, 2017; Martin 1995). These accounts "ground the sense of bodily ownership on something that cannot readily explain other forms of self-awareness [violated in depersonalization] as well (the sense of mental ownership, agency and oneself)" (Billon 2017, 197). That is, these accounts identify spatial features or body schematic aspects as the ground for SO; but these features do not apply to "mental ownership," which refers to the experience of one's own mental states (including sense-experiences) as one's own. The phenomenological account, however, can meet this challenge since it takes the SO most basically to be part of the implicit pre-reflective structure of the givenness (the how it feels) of any experience. Of course, what needs to be explained is precisely what this structure is, which Billon calls the 'common ground C' of any 'central theory' that would account for SO in all cases – the sense that this is my body, my action, my pain, my thought, etc. I address the question of what this pre-reflective structure (C) is in Section 6, below.

The second challenge identified by Billon is the "dissociation challenge." Billon argues that in the case of depersonalization, the spatiality of sensation, as well as interoceptive, motor and cognitive processes/experiences are all relatively normal despite the fact that patients experience a lack of ownership for their bodies. Accordingly the example of depersonalization seems to defeat any theory of SO based on such factors – again trouble for Martin, Bermúdez, and de Vignemont. This might also suggest trouble for the phenomenological account since the claim is that SO is part of the intrinsic structure of any experience, whether sensory, motor or cognitive. If sensory, motor and cognitive experiences are intact, SO should be also. One important question, however, is whether depersonalization actually involves a lack of SO. Billon claims that it does and he cites clinical evidence to this effect, namely the reports of patients. But let's take a close look at those reports.

First, note that these are all reports provided by the patients. As such, the patient is reflecting on his or her experience and trying to find the right words to express it. Billon cites several reports. Consider the following examples.

(1) I do not feel I have a body. When I look down I see *my legs and body* but it feels as if it was not there. When I move I see the movements

as I move, but I am not there with the movements. I am walking up the stairs, I see *my legs* and hear footsteps and feel the muscles but it feels as if I have no body. I am not there (Dugas and Moutier 1911; cited and translated in Billon 2017, 194, emphasis added).

(2) I feel like a robot, like I am listening to someone else talking, like I am looking at myself from the outside, but it is not another voice or body, *it is mine*, it is me, it just doesn't feel like it (Baker et al. 2003, 431; cited in Billon 2017, 194–195, emphasis added).

(3) When I wash myself . . . *my hand* is insensitive.. . . Yesterday when I kissed my daughter . . . *my lips* did not feel anything. . .. *My eyelids* are insensitive.. . . I do not feel *my back* (Leroy 1901, cited and translated in Billon 2017, 195, emphasis added).

(4) I feel pains in *my chest*, but they seem to belong to someone else, not to me (Mayer-Gross 1935, 114; cited in Billon 2017, 195–196, emphasis added).

(5) I watch me acting as I would watch someone else. *My voice, my gestures and my computations* seem to me like things combined in advance, that I would have decided but that I would not be accomplishing (Hesnard 1909, cited and translated in Billon 2017, 203, emphasis added).

It is clear that something is amiss. But is it the pre-reflective sense of ownership (SO)? In these cases the patients seem to have no problem referring to "my legs and body," "my voice or body," "my hand," "my lips," "my eyelids," "my chest," "my voice," and "my gestures." That is, the patients are not having trouble tracking which of the various bodies or body parts in the room are their own. They don't mistake your leg for their own leg. The complaint is something like "*my* leg doesn't feel right, it feels insensitive, it feels alien." What exactly that means may be unclear. Case (5) seems to be a problem with the sense of agency. That is, my bodily movement or speech seems consistent with what I might decide to do or say, but it doesn't seem that I am accomplishing, i.e., generating the movement or speech. Case (3) however, seems to be about an insensitivity in my body. More generally, if it is something to do with ownership, it may be a problem with my reflective judgment of ownership, i.e., the reflective attribution of ownership (AO). These are, after all, reflective reports about experience. The patient's experiences all seem anchored in what the patient tracks as her own body, but for some reason in her reflective awareness or judgment she feels alienated from her body.

I note that the difference between pre-reflective SO, which allows the patient to track her own body, and the reflective AO may not register in

Billon's theory. Billon (2013) equates the experience of ownership with a more complex definition of ownership proposed by John Campbell (1999, 2002). Speaking of inserted thoughts, he states:

> A thought will seem fully mine both (i) if it is . . . 'accessible through introspection' and (ii) if it seems to be caused by me, that is, if I have a sense of agency or authorship for the thought.
>
> (Billon 2013, 299)

The first clause identifies the experience of ownership with reflective (introspective) AO. The second clause follows a realignment of the distinction between the experiences of agency and ownership. As in Campbell, the experience of agency is simply one necessary feature of, or one particular form of the experience of ownership. For that reason case (5) looks like a problem with ownership to Billon. To be clear, however, it's not the second clause that Billon wants to make the demanding part of the definition; rather, Billon takes the first clause to be the important one. The phenomenology of ownership is purely a second-order (reflective) phenomenology. In other words, there is no perspectival, pre-reflective sense of ownership (SO). In this regard he agrees with Bermúdez. There is no pre-reflective, first-order phenomenology of ownership pertaining to one's body or one's experience. The experience of ownership is entirely a matter of reflective attribution.

If Billon is right, however, the mineness of "*my* body, *my* arm, etc." experienced by the patient derives from the patient's reflective attribution. In that case the patient has all the ownership that she needs, or that anyone else has, and depersonalization, *contra* Billon, is not a problem with ownership. If the phenomenological view is right, however, then the patient's ability to say "my body, my arm, etc." is based on a pre-reflective SO which is still intact, along with intact sensory, motor and cognitive factors, and the problem is a problem of reflective attribution, AO, which is consistent with the first-clause of Billon's definition of ownership. Accordingly, if Billon want's to argue that depersonalization really does involve a problem with ownership as AO, he has to accept that there is something like pre-reflective SO, or admit that there is no explanation for the patient's ability to track her own body.

The third challenge identified by Billon is what he calls the 'grounding challenge'. This challenge is similar to the centrality challenge but is applied to arguments that base the experience of ownership on affectivity. Since in some cases of depersonalization the patient experiences an alienation from their own affective states, which nonetheless remain relatively normal, there must be some other factor than affect that explains this failure. As in the centrality challenge we end up looking for some independent factor, C, that would explain how we can be alienated from our own affective states in depersonalization. Indeed, this is where Billon ends up. Although he does not name C, he conceives of it as something that has to be over and above affectivity, and likewise over and above the spatiality of sensation, as well as interoceptive, motor and cognitive processes/experiences. This third challenge, like the first two, is a challenge to deflationary theories that would reduce the experience of ownership to a particular affect, the spatiality of sensation, etc. According to Billon, this "naturally suggests a theory to the effect that all my mental states have a mark of mineness that tags them as mine, and that grounds all forms of self-awareness, including the sense of bodily ownership" (210). In this sense the experience of ownership is a "primitive" (ibid.).

If this conclusion causes trouble for deflationary views, it also causes trouble for Billon's earlier conception of the experience of ownership (2013). In any case it is difficult to reconcile the deflationary view that there is no pre-reflective SO but only a reflective (introspective) AO (which would be in agreement with Bermúdez, for example), and the view that the experience of ownership is a primitive experience not dependent on "sensory, interoceptive, sensorimotor, or affective dispositions" (210), since this would be what Bermúdez would call an inflationary theory.

11.5 EXPERIENCES OF OWNERSHIP AND AGENCY IN SCHIZOPHRENIA

The kinds of objections raised against the notion of a sense of ownership also arise against the notion of a sense of agency, and specifically in the context of explaining schizophrenic symptoms of thought insertion and delusions of control. Here I'll consider objections made by Bortolotti and Broome (2009) to what they call the now standard idea that thought insertion and delusions of control involve problems with the experience of agency (e.g., Campbell 1999; Frith 1992; Frith and Gallagher 2002; Gallagher 2000). This standard view sometimes runs as follows: In typical cases of involuntary movement, efferent signals are missing and, in most situations, so is the sense of agency; but a pre-reflective sense of ownership for the movement is maintained because of the presence of afferent sensory feedback. In such cases, my experience is that I (or *my* body) am (is) moving, but I did not initiate the movement. The same logic may explain some aspects of schizophrenic delusions of control. If, for example, there are neurological problems with efference copy, it may result in a loss of the sense of agency for the action (Frith 1992).[1]

I have argued elsewhere (Gallagher 2004) that the explanation developed by Frith in terms of the failure of a comparator mechanism to generate the sense of agency, may work, theoretically, for delusions of control, but for phenomenological and other reasons will not work to explain thought insertion. Accordingly, I'll try to reframe the objections raised by Bortolotti and Broome, which usually involve thought insertion, in terms of delusions of control (where the subject feels as if his body or movement is being controlled by some external agency) since that also brings us closer to the question of body self-awareness.

Bortolotti and Broome (2009) deny that delusions of control and thought insertion involve problems with a pre-reflective sense of agency. Rather, they propose that such delusions involve problems with the experience of ownership. Like Billon (2013), Bortolotti and Broome (2009) embrace the 'more demanding' concept of ownership suggested by John Campbell. They emphasize the reflective nature of this experience, where a subject acknowledges the thought as her own. "[That is] the subject can ascribe the thought [or action] to herself on the basis of introspection, psychological information about herself or consideration of the reasons" that favor attribution of that thought or action (217).

This leads Bortolotti and Broome to a characterization of ownership in terms close to what Stephens and Graham (2000) define as the attribution of subjectivity or ownership (AO), which Bortolotti and Broome then contrast with the reflective attribution of authorship (AA). They equate the latter with a retrospective attribution or judgment of agency. In other words, they define the concepts of agency and ownership in a way that is consistent with the definitions offered by Stephens and Graham, but they then disagree with the latter's explanation that the schizophrenic symptoms involve problems with the attribution of agency. Rather, they claim that the problem concerns the attribution of ownership.

[1] Note that the explanation of delusions of control in terms of the sense of agency cannot be the complete story, since more is involved – namely the attribution of agency for a particular movement or action to something or someone other than the subject who experiences the delusion (Gallagher 2004). Billon and Kriegel (2014) suggest that rather than there being 'something missing' (a sense of agency), delusions of control and thought insertion really involve 'something added' – namely a phenomenology of alienation, which is reflected in the subject's claim that someone or something else is making or causing his actions.

Applied to delusions of control this means that the subject does not experience ownership for the movement or action, which they claim is caused by someone else. The movement is accessed directly and reported first-personally, but it is not reported as the subject's action. "It is 'mineness' as [reflective] entitlement to the [action] which is the crucial and distinguishing feature of this account of ownership; and it is this 'mineness' which is conspicuously missing from the [schizophrenic] subject's phenomenology" (Bortolotti and Broome 2009, 217).

Bortolotti and Broome may be correct that the person's retrospective report reflects an absence of ownership, as they define it. If we ask why the subject reflectively disowns the action, however, or why he says that the action is not his despite the fact that he has experienced it directly or proprioceptively, two answers still seem possible, and indeed, consistent with one another.

(1) The action doesn't seem to fit with his self-narrative (as suggested by Stephens and Graham), or is not "endorsed" by the subject since he is not able to provide reasons for acting in that way (as suggested by Bortolotti and Broome). We might call this a *semantic coherency problem.*

(2) The action actually feels or is experienced as alien – a first-order experience that may have initially motivated the second-order reflection that led to (1).[2] This first-order feeling of alienation in relation to the action performed by his own body, may modulate or disrupt the pre-reflective sense of agency for generating that action. We can call this a *process problem* involving neurological and first-order experiential disruptions.

Even if Bortolotti and Broome are right that the person's second-order, retrospective report indicates a problem with ownership as they define it, and as outlined in (1), this retrospective problem may be due to a first-order, experiential problem with the sense of agency, as outlined in (2). Bortolotti and Broome, however, try to rule out the second option. They provide three reasons to reject the loss-of-agency account (2009, 219–221).

2 With respect to inserted thoughts, the inserted thought may not be inconsistent with the person's own thoughts. The inserted thought may be as innocuous as a comment such as "That's a good idea." It still feels inserted and alien, however. In such cases the lack of the sense of agency or ownership cannot be explained simply by semantic incoherency at the reflective level.

Again, although they frame this in terms of thought insertion, I'll reframe it in terms of delusions of control.

a) Loss-of-agency accounts cannot distinguish between 'alien' movements and, for example, involuntary movements.

Bortolotti and Broome are correct that an account solely in terms of a sense of agency, as 'something missing' cannot be the full explanation, since in both these cases a sense of agency may be missing. Once we start to think about 'something added' – namely, a sense of alienation – we may start to get an account for this difference. If the sense of alienation is something added, however, it may also be something missing. On the one hand, as we saw in the case of depersonalization, one's sense of alienation from one's sensory, motor, cognitive or affective experiences may be due to a missing sense of ownership. On the other hand, the sense of alienation may simply be the flip side of the loss of the sense of agency, since an experience of movement may feel alien precisely because I do not have a sense of agency for it.

b) Loss-of-agency accounts cannot explain differences between delusions of control and other phenomena where there is a loss of agency. Consider the difference between delusions of control and Anarchic Hand Syndrome (AHS). In both cases there is a purported loss of a sense of agency; but in the case of AHS, the subject does not attribute the action of the anarchic hand to someone else. So it is definitely correct to say that the sense of agency cannot explain the difference between delusions of control and AHS.

But again, the claim is not that loss of the sense of agency provides a complete explanation. Indeed, in both schizophrenic delusions of control and AHS, a pre-reflective sense of ownership still seems to be intact (*my* body is being controlled; *my* arm is doing this), and has to enter into the explanation. In neither of these cases does the subject disown the body/body part (something we do find in somatoparaphrenia), even if they reflectively or retrospectively disown the action. Again, one cannot rule out that this may be motivated by either the absence of a sense of agency plus the feeling of alienation, or by discordance with the agent's self-narrative (or by both).

c) Finally, loss-of-agency accounts seemingly ignore significant differences between motor control issues and thought processes – so delusions of control and thought insertion are not similar enough that an explanation in terms of the sense of agency will explain both.

This is a point that should be made more precise. Rather than a problem with an explanation in terms of the loss of the sense of agency, it's more likely a problem with the comparator model explanation of the sense of agency that does not easily transfer to the issue of thought insertion (Gallagher 2004; see footnote 1 above).

Accordingly, none of these objections shows that we should rule out problems with the sense of agency as at least part of the explanation of these schizophrenic symptoms. In such symptoms what's missing is the sense that I am the one who is generating the action – the action is just there, and I come upon it as already formed. Which is to say that I experience the action as alien (which may signal a problem with either the pre-reflective senses of ownership and/or agency). Accordingly I do not attribute the action to myself, precisely because I did not experience myself generating it. Once again, however, the claim is not that a full explanation can be given exclusively in terms of the sense of agency or its absence.

11.6 C

On the basis of the logic of the centrality challenge and the grounding challenge Billon concludes that there needs to be a 'common ground', which he terms 'C', that would account for the sense of ownership across all instances of ownership, that is, the sense of body ownership, mental ownership, action-ownership, affect-ownership, etc., or in other words, the sense that this is *my* body, *my* thought, *my* action, *my* pain or emotion, etc. If we were to follow Bermúdez or Billon or Bortolotti and Broome we might start looking for C in our reflective or introspective attributions. Adopting the standard framework of thinking about these issues in terms of levels, this would be what some theorists would call a high-level or top-down account. If we were to pursue the phenomenological path, we would want to investigate the basis of the low-level pre-reflective or first-order sense of ownership and provide a bottom-up account. Of course an even lower-level neurological account framed in terms of comparators (or predictive processing) might be sought. Since there is not yet a clear consensus on what the phenomena of ownership and agency are, however, and despite all of the work that has already been done on the neuroscience of the sense of agency and sense of ownership (Braun et al. 2018), it may be prudent to set aside the search for a neurological explanation and to focus on the phenomenology. The phenomenology would need to include both the reflective (higher-level) and pre-reflective (lower-level) experience of ownership and agency.

The question then is about C, the common ground. The phenomenological solution to this proposes that the intrinsic temporal structure of experience is relevant to both the senses of agency and ownership, and to pre-reflective and reflective levels. This is the basic phenomenological answer to C, because this intrinsic temporal structure is the common structure of all typical experience, whether it is the experience of body, action, perception, affect or reflective thought. By 'intrinsic temporal structure' I am referring to what Husserl called inner-time consciousness or the retentional-impressional-protentional structure of consciousness which also applies to action (Gallagher 2011; Husserl 1991).

The analysis of the intrinsic temporal structure of experience (for example, the experience of listening to a melody, to use Husserl's favorite example) not only posits

(1) a retentional awareness of just-past experience(the perception of the notes that have just elapsed), together with
(2) the primal impression of the present event (i.e., the perception of the current note), and
(3) the protentional awareness of what is just about to occur (i.e., the anticipations of the notes that are just about to sound)

– all of this over an integrative timescale of seconds – but also a double intentionality:

(a) a "transverse" awareness of the temporal object (i.e., the melody), and
(b) a "longitudinal" awareness of *my experience of* the temporal object (i.e., a self-awareness).

That is, the retentional awareness of the just past note is effected via a retentional awareness of what I have just experienced. Husserl thus explains the way that one's consciousness is unified (via retentional structure) over time (see Figure 11.1). My awareness of the past is effected through my retentional self-awareness (awareness of my own experience) of what I have just heard. My consciousness of the just past, in retention, and of the just-about-to-be, in protention, is integrated into the flow or process structure of perception. The retentional structure constitutes a continuum across the just past set of my experiences; the protentional structure constitutes an anticipation of what I will experience. The double intentionality that Husserl describes (of the melody and of *my experience* of the melody) is similar to Gibson's notion of ecological perception – the idea that when I perceive the world I also gain information about myself –

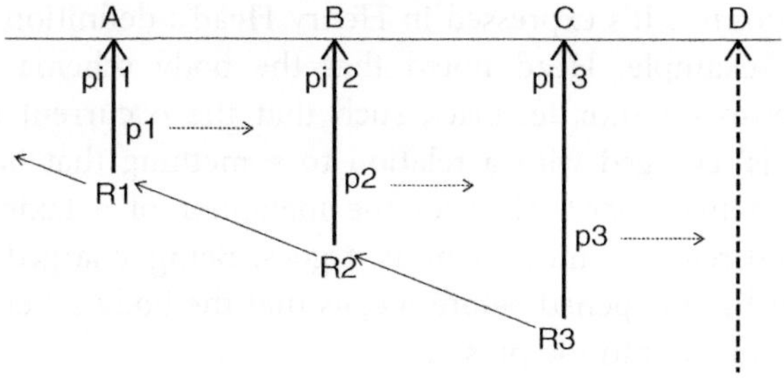

FIGURE 11.1 Husserl's model of intrinsic temporality.

Note: The horizontal line ABCD represents a temporal object such as a melody of several notes. The vertical lines represent abstract momentary phases of an enduring act of consciousness. Each phase is structured by three functions: *Primal impression* (pi), allowing for the consciousness of an object (a musical note, for example) that is simultaneous with the current phase of consciousness; *Retention* (R), which retains previous phases of consciousness and their intentional content; *Protention* (p), which anticipates experience that is just about to happen. In the current phase, simultaneous with C, there is a retentioning (R3) of the previous phase of experience, and this just-past phase includes its own retentioning of the prior phase. Thus a retentional continuum – R3(R2 [R1]), and so forth – stretches back over recent prior experience, on the order of seconds. There is also a double intentionality to this retentional aspect. Retention retains the prior phases of consciousness (longitudinal intentionality), but since those phases include primal impressions of the then current notes (B and A, respectively), retention also retains the prior notes of the melody (transverse intentionality), in the sequential order in which we heard them, which generally reflects the order in which they were sounded. Protention, in turn, provides consciousness with an intentional sense that something more will happen.

the fact that I am standing still, or moving, or sitting, or swimming. This is part of the ecological structure of perception, and if we think of perception as dynamic and embodied, then this is a temporal-ecological structure.

This intrinsic, temporal, double-intentional structure provides a basic longitudinal sense that I am the one who is undergoing this experience (a sense of mineness for the experience of hearing the melody, for example, or of moving through the world, or of feeling this pain, or of thinking this thought). In the phenomenological analysis, this retentional–protentional structure constitutes the sense of ownership for experience, whether this is bodily experience, motor experience, affective experience, cognitive experience, or some mix of experiences. Importantly, retentional (or protentional) awareness is not a specific act of cognition (something over and above the flow of consciousness, e.g., an act of memory/recollection or expectation), but part of the structure of cognition, whether it's an act of perception, memory, imagination, etc. Even reflection has this basic structure, so that when I engage in reflection, I have a sense that I am the one reflecting.

As Alain Berthoz has suggested, the Husserlian analysis of the intrinsic retentional–protentional structure of experience applies to action as well

(Berthoz 2000, 16). It's expressed in Henry Head's definition of the body schema, for example. Head noted that the body schema dynamically organizes sensory-motor feedback such that the occurrent sensation of my posture is 'charged with a relation to something that has happened before' (Head 1920, 606). He uses the metaphor of a taximeter, which computes and registers movement as it goes. Being 'charged with a relation' to what has happened before means that the body schema incorporates past moments into the present:

> At each moment in a movement, the preceding instant is not forgotten, but rather is somehow fit into the present, and, in short, the present perception consists in taking up the series of previous positions that envelop each other by relying upon the current position.
>
> (Merleau-Ponty 2012, 141)

Such retentional aspects of movement are integrated into a process that includes ubiquitous anticipatory or prospective aspects. Empirical research shows that anticipatory processes are pervasive in low-level sensorimotor actions. The infant's mouth opens in anticipation of its hand (Butterworth and Hopkins 1988; Lew and Butterworth 1995). Visual tracking involves moment-to-moment anticipations concerning the trajectory of the target. Our gaze anticipates the rotation of our body when we turn a corner (Berthoz 2000, 126). Similar to the mouth's anticipation of the hand, when I reach down to the floor to grab something, my body angles backward in order to adjust its center of gravity so it doesn't go off balance and fall over when I bend forward (Babinski 1899). Reaching for an object involves feed-forward components that allow last minute adjustments if the object is moved. On various models of motor control, for example, a copy of the efferent motor command (efference copy) is said to create 'anticipation for the consequences of the action' (Georgieff and Jeannerod 1998) prior to sensory feedback, allowing for fast corrections of movement. Forward control models involve an anticipatory character so that, for example, the grasp of my reaching hand tacitly anticipates the shape of the object to be grasped, and does so according to the specific intentional action involved (see Jeannerod 2001; MacKay 1966; Wolpert, Ghahramani and Jordan 1995). My grasp moves in a teleological fashion. In this sense, anticipation is 'an essential characteristic' of motor functioning, and it serves our capacity to reorganize our actions in line with events that are yet to happen (Berthoz 2000, 25). Since these prospective processes intrinsic to action are pervasive, even in infants, the 'conclusion that [anticipatory processes] are immanent in virtually everything we think or do seems inescapable' (Haith 1993, 237).

What is inescapable and pervasive with respect to action is not just the anticipatory aspect, but the full intrinsic temporality of the processes involved. On the phenomenological analysis, the intrinsic temporality of action includes the double intentionality of (a) the action-intention-to-goal (a transverse sense of what I am doing) and (b) a sense that I am the one doing it – the pre-reflective sense of agency, the awareness that I am generating and guiding my action, which is intrinsic to action itself.

Accordingly the intrinsic temporal structure of experience and action is the common structure, the C, of both the pre-reflective sense of ownership for my body, my action, my affective and cognitive experiences, and the sense of agency for my actions. Furthermore, on the phenomenological analysis, reflection depends on this pre-reflective structure. I can reflect and report on my ongoing experience (without a full-fledged act of recollection being involved) because the retentional structure of experience makes my just-past experience immediately available and marks it as mine, not by some kind of special marker of ownership, but by its intrinsic longitudinal–intentional structure.

Consider what experience would be like if this were not the case. If every experience I had was momentary and completely dissipated when finished, it would be one flash of experience after another, but I would not even be able to experience a succession or flow of experience. And if I were unable to anticipate what was about to happen, I wouldn't even be constantly surprised, since surprise requires something like an unfulfilled expectation. Without retention or protention, experience would lack integration and seem chaotic. If the retentional–protentional structure remained intact but was significantly disturbed in its dynamics, motivated by some disturbed affect, for example (Gallagher and Varela 2003), my experience might be disjointed or disrupted in any number of ways, approaching the schizophrenic symptoms of disordered thought, the inability to anticipate or the feeling of constant surprise (see, e.g., Frith and Done 1988), or a failure in the sense of agency, or in my reflective attribution of ownership, etc. A different dynamical pattern could lead to the feelings of alienation found in some delusional experiences or in depersonalization.

11.7 CONCLUSION: LEVELS OR DYNAMICAL GESTALT?

Should we think of the intrinsic temporal structure of experience as the ultimate common ground (C) that explains the pre-reflective senses of ownership and agency? Surely one can argue that there is some explanatory level below the intrinsic temporal structure of retentions and protentions – a level of neural mechanisms that will provide a more ultimate explanation of this structure. We would need to wrestle with questions about whether comparator models instanciated in neural circuits, or perhaps predictive processing (PP) models (Braun et al. 2018; Friston 2011; Synofzik, Vosgerau, and Newen 2008) offer the best accounts. Hohwy, Paton, and Palmer (2016), for example, have offered a prediction error minimization model of the intrinsic temporal structure (looking specifically at Husserl's account), its role in movement initiation, and its disruption in autism. This PP model itself posits different levels of cortical hierarchy: the higher levels instanciate a generative model formed in the course of retained prior experience, which then anticipates patterns in the dynamics of the incoming sensory input that occur over longer time scales. The flow of experience slows or speeds up depending on the amount of mismatch (prediction error) occurring between the predicted input and the current input. In autism, the authors hypothesize, there are problems with the precision of the protended predictions leading to "weak central coherence" (Happé and Frith 2006). The authors mention agency only in passing, but they do cite evidence that these problems lead to modulations in motor control processes of the sort that can disrupt movement preparation and initiation (Enticott et al. 2013; Rinehart et al. 2006), processes that are thought to generate a pre-reflective sense of agency (Gallagher 2000; Gallagher and Marcel 1999; Haggard and Eimer 1999; see Hohwy 2007 for a fuller account of the sense of agency in PP terms). Even allowing for the authors' provisos concerning differences across the autism spectrum, they indicate that this remains a speculative account, but it provides an example of how a neuroscientific account of the intrinsic temporal structure might work.

The full story about the sense of agency is not told merely in terms of motor control processes, whether we frame such accounts in terms of comparator models or predictive processing (Gallagher 2012). Since we are embodied agents in the world, whether we accomplish what we set out to do matters. Indeed, there are much larger, social and cultural factors that can disrupt the intrinsic temporal structure and that impinge on our senses of ownership and agency. In any fuller account, these factors must be taken into account. Accordingly, there is more to body awareness than just the motoric and affective state of one's individual body; intersubjective relations and social arrangements play a large role.

For example, one can become self-conscious of one's bodily appearance in a variety of ways in the presence of others. Others can make us feel ashamed of or proud of our bodies. The expression on a caregiver's face can convince a child that he feels less or more pain or affective discomfort from a scraped knee. Importantly, there are more systemic social and cultural effects on how we think of and feel about our bodies, and how we posture and move. Measuring one's body against male or female ideal body types can lead to body self-awareness that is characterized as a dissatisfaction that motivates cosmetic surgery, eating disorders, and so forth (e.g., Olivardia et al. 2004). Such effects impinge upon body-schematic, motor-control processes that shape our most basic pre-reflective self-awareness. This is made clear in a set of criticisms leveled against phenomenological accounts, especially in regard to the work of Merleau-Ponty (2012). Specifically, his analysis of body schematic processes has been criticized for ignoring factors that have to do with race, gender, and cultural differences. Merleau-Ponty tended to universalize a white-male model of the body schema that fails to take into account the effects of race and gender norms (e.g., Alcoff 1999; Butler 1988, 1989; Fanon 2008; Weiss 2015; Wieseler 2016; Young 2006).

Frantz Fanon, for example, suggested that for Merleau-Ponty body schematic processes are said to operate for the 'normal' subject recessively in the background.

> [This] is impossible for those whose bodies are deemed inherently inferior, that is, for those who are ruled out, from the outset, from achieving the status of 'normal' subjects. Being viewed and treated as a 'normal' subject [is] an inherited privilege that white bodies enjoy and that non-white bodies do not.
>
> (Weiss 2015, 86; see Yancy 2014)

Reflective processes of deliberation, intention formation and motivation to act are not simply mental states in one's head, or reducible to causal brain states. Rather, they are often processes or states co-constituted with others in processes of communication, subject to peer pressure, implicit or explicit social referencing, or one's habitual behavior in the presence of others. Such phenomena may detract from or increase one's feeling of agency and ability to act. It is also the case that specific types of long-standing social arrangements, such as apartheid, can have prolonged effects on a person's (or a people's) long-term sense of agency,[3] essentially robbing them of possibilities for action (Gallagher 2013).

[3] Elisabeth Pacherie (2007, 6) defines the long-term sense of agency as "a sense of oneself as an agent apart from any particular action, i.e., a sense of one's capacity for action over time, and a form of self-narrative where one's past actions and projected future actions are given a general coherence and unified through a set of overarching goals, motivations, projects and general lines of conduct."

The complexity involved in neural dynamics, as they are embedded in bodily dynamics, which in turn are situated in physical, social, and cultural environmental dynamics, all of which are characterized by dynamical looping effects that make the entire system plastic (or meta-plastic – see Malafouris 2013), does not allow for easy explanations of how a system can go wrong. Any attempt to map out different explanatory levels and to identify some as more basic than others is an exercise that is sometimes useful, but many times an oversimplification.

On some hierarchical characterizations, concrete coping behaviors involve the bottom-up and fast pre-reflective integration of many factors, while retro-introspective reflection is top-down, top-heavy and abstract. Alternatively, one might think of the arrangement of these different factors in terms of a dynamical gestalt, ruled by a gestalt principle that is nicely summarized by Goldstein and Scheerer.

> Although the normal person's behaviour is prevailingly concrete, this concreteness can be considered normal only as long as it is embedded in and co-determined by the abstract attitude. For instance, in the normal person both attitudes are always present in a definite figure-ground relation.
>
> (Goldstein and Scheerer 1964, 8)

Thinking of a system in terms of a dynamical gestalt of figure-ground rather than in terms of a hierarchy of levels suggests that pre-reflective versus reflective aspects of experience, the sense of agency versus the sense of ownership, something added versus something missing, are, rather than binary distinctions, better treated as matters of degree that above a certain threshold shift between figure and ground. In some cases pre-reflective senses of agency or ownership may be modulated or go missing either because of some neurological disruption, or because they are dominated by reflective or hyperreflective attitudes, or because they are constrained by cultural attitudes that involve oppression or racism. In a dynamical gestalt, a change in any one of these factors above a certain threshold can result in readjustments in the organization of all other factors.

REFERENCES

Albahari, M. (2016) *Analytical Buddhism: The Two-Tiered Illusion of Self*. Heidelberg: Springer.

Alcoff, L. (1999) 'Toward a phenomenology of racial embodiment. *Radical Philosophy* 95: 15–26.

Babinski, J. (1899) 'De l'asynergie cérébelleuse.' *Revue de Neurologie* 7: 806–816.

Baker, D., Hunter, E., Lawrence, E., Medford, N., Patel, M., Senior, C., Sierra, M., Lambert, M. V., Phillips, M. L., and David, A. S. (2003) 'Depersonalisation disorder: Clinical features of 204 cases.' *The British Journal of Psychiatry* 182 (5): 428–433.

Bermúdez, J. L. (2011) 'Bodily awareness and self-consciousness.' In S. Gallagher (Ed.), *Oxford Handbook of the Self* (pp. 157–179). Oxford: Oxford University Press.

(2015) 'Bodily ownership, bodily awareness and knowledge without observation.' *Analysis* 75(1): 37–45.

(2017) 'Ownership and the space of the body.' In F. de Vignemont and A. Alsmith (Eds.), *The Subject's Matter* (pp. 117–144). Cambridge, MA: MIT Press.

Bermúdez, J. L., Marcel, A. J., and Eilan, N. (Eds.) (1995) 'Introduction.' In *The Body and the Self*. Cambridge, MA: MIT Press

Berthoz, A. (2000) *The Brain's Sense of Movement*. Cambridge, MA: Harvard University Press.

Billon, A. (2013) 'Does consciousness entail subjectivity? The puzzle of thought insertion.' *Philosophical Psychology* 26(2): 291–314.

(2017) 'Mineness first: Three challenges to the recent theories of the sense of bodily ownership.' In F. de Vignemont and A. Alsmith (Eds.), *The Subject's Matter* (pp. 189–216). Cambridge, MA: MIT Press.

Billon, A. and Kriegel, U. (2014) 'Jaspers' dilemma: The psychopathological challenge to subjectivity theories of consciousness.' In R. Gennaro (Ed.), *Disturbed Consciousness* (pp. 29–54). Cambridge, MA: MIT Press.

Bortolotti, L. and Broome, M. (2009) 'A role for ownership and authorship in the analysis of thought insertion.' *Phenomenology and the Cognitive Sciences* 8(2): 205–224.

Braun, N., Debener, S., Spychala, N., Bongartz, E., Sorös, P., Müller, H. H. O., and Philipsen, A. (2018) 'The senses of agency and ownership: A review.' *Frontiers in Psychology* 9: 535.

Butler, J. (1988) 'Performative acts and gender constitution: An essay in phenomenology and feminist theory.' *Theatre Journal* 40(4): 519–531.

(1989) 'Sexual ideology and phenomenological description: A feminist critique of Merleau-Ponty's. *Phenomenology of Perception*.' In J. Allen and I. M. Young (Eds.), *The Thinking Muse: Feminism and Modern French Philosophy* (pp. 85–100). Bloomington: Indiana University Press.

Butterworth, G. and Hopkins, B. (1988) 'Hand-mouth coordination in the newborn baby.' *British Journal of Developmental Psychology* 6: 303–314.

Campbell, J. (1999) 'Schizophrenia, the space of reasons and thinking as a motor process.' *The Monist* 82(4): 609–625.

(2002) 'The ownership of thoughts.' *Philosophy Psychology and Psychiatry* 9(1): 35–39.

Dainton, B. (2008) *The Phenomenal Self*. Oxford: Oxford University Press.

de Vignemont, F. (2007) 'Habeas corpus: The sense of ownership of one's own body.' *Mind & Language* 22(4): 427–449.

(2017) 'An agentive conception of the sense of bodily ownership: The bodyguard hypothesis.' In F. de Vignemont and A. Alsmith (Eds.), *The Subject's Matter* (pp. 217–236). Cambridge, MA: MIT Press.

Dokic, J. (2003) 'The sense of ownership: An analogy between sensation and action.' In J. Roessler (Ed.), *Agency and Self-Awareness: Issues in Philosophy and Psychology* (pp. 321–344). Oxford: Clarendon Press.
Dreyfus, H. L. (2007) 'The return of the myth of the mental.' *Inquiry* 50(4): 352–365.
Dugas, L. and Moutier, F. (1911) *La depersonalization*. Paris: Felix Alcon.
Enticott, P. G, Kennedy, H. A., Rinehart, N. J., Bradshaw, J. L., Tonge, B. J., Daskalakis, Z. J., and Fitzgerald, P. B. (2013) 'Interpersonal motor resonance in autism spectrum disorder: Evidence against a global ëmirror systemí deficit.' *Frontiers in Human Neuroscience* 7: 248.
Evans, G. (1982) *Varieties of Reference*. Oxford: Oxford University Press.
Fanon, F. (2008) *Black Skin, White Masks*. Trans. R. Philcox. New York: Grove Press.
Friston, K. (2011) 'What is optimal about motor control?' *Neuron* 72(3): 488–498.
Frith, C. D. (1992) *The Cognitive Neuropsychology of Schizophrenia*. Hillsdale, NJ: Lawrence Erlbaum Associates.
Frith, C. D. and Done, D. J. (1988) 'Towards a neuropsychology of schizophrenia.' *British Journal of Psychiatry* 153: 437–443.
Frith, C. D. and Gallagher, S. (2002) 'Models of the pathological mind: An interview with Christopher Frith.' *Journal of Consciousness Studies* 9(4): 57–80.
Gallagher, S. (1996) 'The moral significance of primitive self-consciousness.' *Ethics* 107(1): 129–140.
(2000) 'Philosophical conceptions of the self: Implications for cognitive science.' *Trends in Cognitive Sciences* 4(1): 14–21.
(2004) 'Neurocognitive models of schizophrenia: A neurophenomenological critique.' *Psychopathology* 37: 8–19.
(2005) *How the Body Shapes the Mind*. Oxford: Oxford University Press.
(2011) 'Time in action.' In C. Callender (Ed.), *Oxford Handbook on Time* (pp. 419–437). Oxford: Oxford University Press.
(2012) 'Multiple aspects in the sense of agency.' *New Ideas in Psychology*, 30(1): 15–31.
(2013) 'Ambiguity in the sense of agency.' In A. Clark, J. Kiverstein, and T. Vierkant (Eds.), *Decomposing the Will* (pp. 118–135). Oxford: Oxford University Press.
Gallagher, S. and Cole, J. (1995) 'Body schema and body image in a deafferented subject.' *Journal of Mind and Behavior* 16: 369–390.
Gallagher, S. and Marcel, A. (1999) 'The self in contextualized action.' *Journal of Consciousness Studies* 6(4): 4–30.
Gallagher, S. and Varela, F. (2003) 'Redrawing the map and resetting the time: Phenomenology and the cognitive sciences.' *Canadian Journal of Philosophy*. Supplementary Volume 29: 93–132.
Gallagher, S. and Zahavi, D. (2012) *The Phenomenological Mind*. London: Routledge.
Gallagher, S. and Zahavi, D. (2014) 'Phenomenological approaches to self-consciousness.' In E. N. Zalta (Ed.), *The Stanford Encyclopedia of Philosophy*. https://plato.stanford.edu/archives/win2016/entries/self-consciousness-phenomenological/.

Georgieff, N. and Jeannerod, M. (1998) 'Beyond consciousness of external events: A 'who' system for consciousness of action and self-consciousness.' *Consciousness and Cognition* 7: 465–477.

Gibson, J. J. (1979) *The Ecological Approach to Visual Perception*. Boston, MA: Houghton-Mifflin.

Goldstein, K. and Scheerer, M. (1964) *Abstract and Concrete Behavior: An Experimental Study with Special Tests*. Evanston, IL: Northwestern University. Reprint of *Psychological Monographs* 53(2), 1941.

Guillot, M. (2017) 'I me mine: On a confusion concerning the subjective character of experience.' *Review of Philosophy and Psychology* 8(1): 23–53.

Haggard, P. and Eimer, M. (1999) 'On the relation between brain potentials and the awareness of voluntary movements.' *Experimental Brain Research* 126: 128–133.

Haith, M. M. (1993) 'Future-oriented processes in infancy: The case of visual expectations.' In C. Granrud (Ed.), *Carnegie-Mellon Symposium on Visual Perception and Cognition in Infancy* (pp. 235–264). Hillsdale, NJ: Lawrence Erlbaum Associates.

Happé, F. and Frith, U. (2006) 'The weak coherence account: Detail-focused cognitive style in autism spectrum disorders.' *Journal of Autism and Developmental Disorders* 36(1): 5–25.

Head, H. (1920) *Studies in Neurology*. Volume 2. Oxford: Clarendon Press.

Hesnard, A. (1909) *Les troubles de la personnalité dans les états d'asthénie psychique*. Paris: Felix Alcan.

Hohwy, J. (2007) 'The sense of self in the phenomenology of agency and perception.' *Psyche* 13: 1–20.

Hohwy, J., Paton, B., and Palmer, C. (2016) 'Distrusting the present.' *Phenomenology and the Cognitive Sciences* 15(3): 315–335.

Howell, R. J. and Thompson, B. (2017) 'Phenomenally mine: In search of the subjective character of consciousness.' *Review of Philosophy and Psychology* 8(1): 103–127.

Husserl, E. (1991) *On the Phenomenology of the Consciousness of Internal Time (1893–1917)*. Collected Works IV. Trans. J. Brough. Dordrecht: Kluwer Academic. Translation of (1966) *Zur Phänomenologie des inneren Zeitbewußtseins (1893–1917)*. Husserliana 10. Den Haag: Martinus Nijhoff.

Hutto, D. D. and Ilundáin-Agurruza, J. (2018) 'Selfless activity and experience: Radicalizing minimal self-awareness.' *Topoi* 1–12.

Jeannerod, M. (2001) 'Neural simulation of action: A unifying mechanism for motor cognition.' *Neuroimage* 14: S103–S109.

(2003) 'Self-generated actions.' In S. Maasen, W. Prinz, and G. Roth (Eds.), *Voluntary Action: Brains, Minds, and Sociality* (pp. 153–164). Oxford: Oxford University Press.

Jeannerod, M. and Gallagher, S. (2002) 'From action to interaction.' *Journal of Consciousness Studies* 9(1): 3–26.

Leder, D. (1990) *The Absent Body*. Chicago, IL: Chicago University Press.

Leroy, E.-B. (1901) 'Sur l'illusion dite dépersonalization.' *L'Année Psychologique* 8(1): 519–522.

Lew, A. and Butterworth, G. E. (1995) 'Hand-mouth contact in newborn babies before and after feeding.' *Developmental Psychology* 31: 456–463.

MacKay, D. (1966) 'Cerebral organization and the conscious control of action.' In J. C. Eccles (Ed.), *Brain and Conscious Experience* (pp. 422–445). New York: Springer.

Malafouris, L. (2013) *How Things Shape the Mind.* Cambridge, MA: MIT Press.

Martin, M. G. F. (1995) 'Bodily awareness: A sense of ownership.' In J. L. Bermúdez, T. Marcel, and N. Eilan (Eds.), *The Body and the Self.* Cambridge, MA: MIT Press.

Mayer-Gross, W. (1935) 'On depersonalization.' *British Journal of Medical Psychology* 15(2): 103–126.

Merleau-Ponty, M. (2012) *Phenomenology of Perception.* Trans. D. A. Landes. London: Routledge.

Moore, J. W. (2016) 'What is the sense of agency and why does it matter?' *Frontiers in Psychology* 7: 1272.

Olivardia, R., Pope Jr, H. G., Borowiecki III, J. J., and Cohane, G. H. (2004) 'Biceps and body image: The relationship between muscularity and self-esteem, depression, and eating disorder symptoms.' *Psychology of Men & Masculinity* 5(2): 112.

Pacherie, E. (2007) 'The sense of control and the sense of agency.' *Psyche* 13(1), http://psyche.cs.monash.edu.au/.

Rinehart, N. J., Tonge, B. J., Bradshaw, J. L., Iansek, R., Enticott, P. G., and Johnson, K. A. (2006) 'Movement-related potentials in high-functioning autism and Asperger's disorder.' *Developmental Medicine & Child Neurology* 48(4): 272–277.

Schear, J. C. (2009) 'Experience and self-consciousness.' *Philosophical Studies* 144: 95–105.

Simons, D. J. and Chabris, C. F. (1999) 'Gorillas in our midst: Sustained inattentional blindness for dynamic events.' *Perception* 28(9): 1059–1074.

Stephens, G. L. and Graham, G. (2000) *When Self-Consciousness Breaks: Alien Voices and Inserted Thoughts.* Cambridge, MA: MIT Press.

Synofzik, M., Vosgerau, G., and Newen, A. (2008) 'Beyond the comparator model: A multifactorial two-step account of agency.' *Consciousness and Cognition* 17 (1): 219–239.

Vosgerau, G. and A. Newen. (2007) 'Thoughts, motor actions, and the self.' *Mind & Language* 22(1): 22–43.

Weiss, G. (2015) 'The normal, the natural, and the normative: A Merleau-Pontian legacy to feminist theory, critical race theory, and disability studies.' *Continental Philosophy Review* 48: 77–93.

Wieseler, C. M. (2016). 'A Feminist Contestation of Ableist Assumptions: Implications for Biomedical Ethics, Disability Theory, and Phenomenology.' Graduate Theses and Dissertations, University of South Florida. http://scholarcommons.usf.edu/etd/6433

Wolpert, D. M., Ghahramani, Z., and Jordan, M. I. (1995) 'An internal model for sensorimotor integration.' *Science* 269: 1880–1882.

Yancy, G. (2014) 'White gazes: What it feels like to be en Essence.' In E. S. Lee (Ed.), *Living Alterities: Phenomenology, Embodiment, and Race* (pp. 43–64). Albany, NY: State University of New York.

Young, I. M. (2006) 'Lived body vs. gender: Reflections on social structure and subjectivity.' In *"Throwing Like a Girl" and Other Essays* (pp. 12–26). Oxford: Oxford University Press.

Zahavi, D. (2018) 'Consciousness, self-consciousness, selfhood: A reply to some critics.' *Review of Philosophy and Psychology* 9(3): 703–718.

12

Commentary on Gallagher "Body Self-Awareness: Multiple Levels or Dynamical Gestalt?"

JAN-WILLEM ROMEIJN

12.1 INTRODUCTION

Shaun Gallagher's chapter exemplifies a phenomenological approach to conceptual issues in psychiatry. The chapter is concerned with body self-awareness, namely the experience or realization that one's body belongs to oneself. This is relevant to psychiatry because some psychiatric patients, specifically schizophrenics, experience their own body or mind as being controlled by something or someone else, or as somehow not belonging to themselves. Patients report experiences of depersonalization or alienation: "When I look down I see my legs and body but it feels as if it was not there" and "I feel pains in my chest, but they seem to belong to someone else, not to me." These reports reveal that, on the one hand, patients consider their body parts as belonging to themselves, experiencing a "sense of ownership," while on the other hand they consider the body parts as separate or even alien. How are we to make sense of such experiences? And can we make sense of alienation with regard to cognitive and affective states in a similar way?

Gallagher's contribution is to claim that such experiences and realizations can be integrated in a theory of "dynamical Gestalts," a view of the self that derives from Husserl's phenomenological theory of consciousness. Gallagher arrives at this claim after carefully considering and evaluating different views on the origin and nature of our body self-awareness, and on our wider sense of ownership over cognitive and affective states. The chapter discusses proposals by Dreyfus, Bermudez, Dainton, Campbell, and Bartolotti and Broome. A recurring concern in the discussions is whether we can think of body self-awareness as being derivative of introspective insights or more basic experiential facts, like proprioception and sensorimotor responses, through an act of reflection. Gallagher's conclusion is that such "deflationary" accounts of body self-awareness cannot properly make sense of the double nature of the afore-mentioned experiences of alienation. Our sense of ownership cannot be based on a reflective insight into the cognitive, affective, or physical aspects of oneself, because that would leave unexplained why we consider the items from which we feel alienated as, after all, belonging to ourselves, despite the overriding feeling of alienation.

Gallagher's claim is that the theory of dynamical Gestalt does offer an adequate account of such alienation experiences while ensuring the basic unity of the self. According to this theory, a basic sense of ownership is weaved into the very fabric of our pre-reflective experiences. Body parts are automatically experienced as belonging to their owner. Against this backdrop of mineness, generated pre-reflectively and as part of experience, those body parts may subsequently seem alien, or controlled by forces outside of oneself, as a result of disturbances in the sense of agency or in the reflective relations that obtain between a patient and their body parts. In much the same way, the pre-reflective experiences of mental and affective states have a sense of ownership weaved into them. Disturbances in one's experiences of these states may then bring about a feeling of alienation without impinging on the mineness of the states.

12.2 THIS COMMENTARY

In what follows I will discuss Gallagher's arguments and conclusions in three parts. First I consider the intricate dialectic on reflective and pre-reflective senses of ownership between Bermudez, Dainton, and Gallagher, questioning its conceptual exactness and empirical content. Then I consider the rejection of the intrinsic sense of ownership by Bartolotti and Broome, investigating if it matters that their arguments pertain primarily to thought insertions rather than bodily alienation. Finally, I focus on the implications that the dynamical Gestalt theory has for the issue of explanatory levels, arguing that the theory is in need of further development. Towards the very end of my commentary, I consider the phenomenological approach to psychiatry more broadly, commending particular aspects of it. This ends with concrete suggestions on how the approach might offer improvements to current psychiatric science, relying on insights that derive from the history of the natural sciences and the reception of this history in the work of Husserl.

12.3 CONCEPTUAL DISTINCTIONS

Gallagher's chapter starts by drawing up a number of distinctions. Sense of ownership is set apart from sense of agency and a distinction is made between personal and perspectival ownership. Personal ownership involves an explicit act of self-identification while perspectival ownership derives from the fact that the subject occupies a special position with regards to what is experienced as belonging to itself, which therefore leaves open the possibility that the subject experiences a sense of ownership pre-reflectively. These distinctions help Gallagher to focus the discussion, namely on sense of ownership, and to locate the phenomenological view, namely as involving pre-reflective experience. The accounts of self-awareness by Bermudez, Dainton, Bartolotti and Broome are criticized from this phenomenological standpoint. Dreyfus' idea that awareness of the body is entirely absent in many automated tasks is discussed in a separate section but then more or less left aside, because most authors agree that some body awareness is involved in all activity.

Bermudez and Dainton acknowledge that a sense of ownership is mostly present in our bodily activity. But, by the lights of Gallagher's discussion, they present it as following from the complex of experiences of the subject and her specific perspective on her own actions. According to Bermudez and Dainton, the sense of ownership is nothing over and above these bodily experiences, and it manifests when attention is actively directed at them. The metaphor is that of the "fridge light"; it only switches on when the door of the fridge is opened. Gallagher rejects these conceptions of sense of ownership by pointing to its pre-reflective nature. In the phenomenological view the sense of ownership does not derive from the experiences as an add-on; it is inherent to it. Note that the distinctions drawn here are multiple: the issue is whether the sense of ownership is derived from the experiences of oneself, and accessed in an act of reflection, as opposed to intrinsic to these experiences, and already available pre-reflectively. The opposition is therefore between reflective and pre-reflective, but also between derivative and intrinsic.

In response to this first part of the paper, I would like to raise two concerns. First, as a relatively uninformed reader, I do not find it apparent that the categories of experience used in the discussion are sharply delineated, nor that they exhaust the space of experiential possibilities. I can imagine reflective awareness to come in degrees rather than in binary format, and I can only draw the exact dividing line between derivative and intrinsic when further assumptions on ontological dependence are put in place. Furthermore, admittedly after some mental yoga, it seems possible to entertain reflective experiences in which the sense of ownership is intrinsic, thereby escaping the double opposition that Gallagher identifies.

A second concern ties in with this first one. We might try to settle the above concerns over unsharp concepts and distinctions by tying them to experience in a systematic way. Naturally this need not, and perhaps cannot, be the experimental operationalization known from psychological science. A proceduralization along the structuralist lines of Titchener may be more feasible. However, at present it is unclear how we are to relate the concepts and distinctions to our private experiences. How can we connect the concepts to experiences, or to phenomena, let alone to empirical fact? I will return to this concern at the end of my comments.

12.4 CRITICISMS OF AN INTRINSIC SENSE OF OWNERSHIP

After discussing Billon's challenges to accounts of sense of ownership, and endorsing the requirement that they must clarify experiences of alienation in the bodily, mental and affective realm in equal measure, Gallagher moves on to discuss Bartolotti and Broome. Their view pertains primarily to delusions of control and thought insertions, and therefore in first instance to the loss of a sense of agency. Bartolotti and Broome hold these experiences ultimately hinge on a lacking sense of ownership. However, they explicitly reject that this sense of ownership is pre-reflective and intrinsic, advancing three problems for an account based on such an intrinsic notion. All three problems, in one way or another, indicate that making the sense of ownership inherent to the experience itself does not give us enough of a conceptual grip on the alienation experiences, and that we need to involve a reflective self-narrative to explain them.

In all three cases, Gallagher's response is that the intrinsic sense of ownership is indeed not the full story about these experiences, but that such an intrinsic sense of ownership provides the basis for that story. And insofar as the alienation experiences are concerned with body self-awareness, Gallagher's response might well be right: it seems that the phenomenological theory can be developed to resolve the problems that Bartolotti and Broome put forward. In fact the solutions that Bartolotti and Broome themselves offer, which turn on the subject's reasons for acting, can be given a phenomenological underpinning, by tracing the disturbance in the reflective self-narrative back to pre-reflective experiential disruptions. Gallagher can subsume the ideas of Bartolotti and Broome under his own account.

It is less clear to me, however, that the response is adequate if the problems signalled pertain not to delusions of control but to thought insertions, which is what Bartolotti and Broome seem to focus on. If the states from which a subject feels alienated are themselves mental, i.e., cognitive or affective, then it is entirely natural to look for the source of the feelings of alienation in the reflective response to an initially aberrant thought. After all, the thought item that generates the alienation is itself already located in the mental realm. It seem somewhat contrived to me to insist that ultimately the feelings of alienation originate in a disruption of the pre-reflective experience of having the thought, without involving the inevitable reflective response to the thought. Now Gallagher indicates in his chapter that a phenomenological account of thought insertion cannot be developed in parallel to an account of delusions of control, and perhaps this is why the response seems less natural or adequate to begin with. On the other hand, one of Billon's challenges is precisely that an account of the feelings of alienation has to cover the bodily, mental and affective realm in equal measure. A complete phenomenological account will also have to answer to the problems for thought insertions that Bartolotti and Broome outline. At present it is, as far as I can see, missing from the discussion.

12.5 THE PHENOMENOLOGICAL APPROACH

In the final two sections of the chapter, Gallagher presents the phenomenological theory of dynamical Gestalt in more detail. The theory is offered as a response to Billon's challenges to provide a "common ground C" among all instances of a sense of ownership. The accounts of Bermudez, Bartolotti, or Broome all look for this common ground in reflective or introspective attributions. Such attributions are most easily associated with what is normally deemed a higher explanatory level. Against this, Gallagher proposes to follow a phenomenological approach, and start from a pre-reflective sense of ownership, which is more naturally associated with so-called lower explanatory levels. The direct experiential sense of ownership then serves as a basis for further reflective and pre-reflective experiences.

What eventually provides this basis is Husserl's retentional–protentional structure of experience: the way in which our experiences are embedded in time, in how we live from moment to moment. Experiences just passed are folded into the present moment to provide context, and future experiences are brought into the present moment through anticipation. Gallagher claims that it is inherent to our way of relating to the passage of time that the experiences that have just passed, and the actions we are preparing, are felt as belonging to us. This is presumably what makes the sense of ownership intrinsic to pre-reflective experience.

Now it seems right that our ability to tie together our experiences and entertain them as sequential is key to our experiential integrity. And, following a Humean conception of personhood, it might indeed be all there is to our experience of self. We therefore get the sense of ownership as an immediate consequence of the nature of experience itself. More cautiously, I would say that the unity of experience, as described by Husserl, is a pre-requisite for any account that ties the experiences to a notion or conception of self. It is not evident to me that the sense of ownership follows from the unity of experience alone. That it is me experiencing these things cannot be derived just from the temporal unity of the experiences.

Quite apart from this, it is not clear where the phenomenological approach to the sense of ownership leaves us in the debate over the salience of, or relations between, explanatory levels. The emphasis on pre-reflective awareness and experience might suggest that lower-level processes take precedence in our accounts of alienation. But Gallagher rightly points to the complex interplay between levels in experiences of alienation, ranging all the way from motor control processes to social, cultural and political factors. Examples of alienation through racial discrimination from Fanon show, convincingly in my view, that the roots of experiences of alienation may lie on any of these levels. It speaks very much in favor of the theory of dynamical Gestalt that it is versatile in this respect, and that it allows us to bring any of these factors into focus. However, both on the point of the intrinsicality of our sense of ownership and on the point of explanatory levels, the phenomenological account of body self-awareness is in need of further development.

12.6 CONCEPTUAL CHANGES

The comments of the foregoing are directed at certain arguments and conclusions in Gallagher's chapter, and mostly selected for their critical content. If we zoom out and look at the chapter as part of a bigger project on the conceptual foundations of psychiatry, the text has a lot to recommend itself. Witnessing Husserl's own description of phenomenology in "The Crisis of the European Sciences" (Husserl 1954/1970), one of its central goals was to provide the sciences of the mind with a conceptual framework of their own, in which our specific introspective access to the mental realm could be accommodated. It is in my view very fitting that modern phenomenology is put to work in clearing up conceptual issues in psychiatry, and in developing theoretical notions for it. As illustrated in Gallagher's chapter, phenomenology may help psychiatry to obtain a better conceptual grip on the empirical phenomena under study. And depending on one's philosophical tastes, it thereby also benefits philosophy, because the application will direct phenomenology away from more speculative or, more critically, self-involved endeavors.

While philosophical phenomenology will have a lot to offer to more positivistic psychiatric science, which has been focused mostly on what can be inter-subjectively ascertained, I would like to end my commentary with a positivist suggestion. Consider Husserl's own example of conceptual construction, as a parallel to what phenomenology might achieve for the sciences of the mind, namely Galileo's attempts to frame and thereby illuminate the movements of massive bodies. Following the arguments from the *Discorsi*, it may be thought that Galileo came upon the notions of inertial mass and impetus, and onwards to the success of the new mechanics, by purely speculative means. But historians of science have long since concluded that Galileo did conduct physical experiments, dipping lead balls in ink and flipping them up to study their trajectories along an inclined plane, rather than merely speculating mathematically on their paths. The suggestion is that he was able to develop his mechanics by cleverly matching theoretical terms to experimental practice (cf. van Dyck 2006). The development of new concepts is best undertaken, it seems, when one is immersed in the practical application of a science, and in direct contact with the topic under scrutiny. Scientific knowledge thereby gets embodied in an experimental setup or in an environment that manifests, by how it is constructed, a partly theoretical reality.

Hence my suggestion would be to take phenomenology's finely tuned conceptual instruments from their bookish surroundings, and start using them, first and foremost in the clinic, to see how they can aid the psychiatrist and the patient in their therapeutic contact, and then also in the lab, where they might inform the decisions of psychiatric scientists. By analogy to Galileo's conceptual achievements, our best hope of coordinating the concepts from phenomenology onto the raw phenomena of mental disorder lies in the focus on a practice. That is where distinctions between reflective and pre-reflective experience, and between intrinsic and derived sense of ownership, can ultimately be grounded and prove their value.

REFERENCES

Husserl, E.G.A. (1954/1970) *The Crisis of European Sciences and Transcendental Phenomenology*. Translated by D. Carr. Evanston, IL: Northwestern University Press.

van Dyck, M. (2006) An Archaeology of Galileo's Science of Motion. PhD thesis. University of Gent.

SECTION 5

13

Introduction

JOSEF PARNAS

In Chapter 14, John Campbell, a renowned analytic philosopher, is discussing the issue of mental causation and its possible replacement by neuroscientific explanatory models. What is a mental causation? In this moment, you the readers are engaged in a perceptual-motor activity by reading these lines. You probably have a desire to read this particular book and believe that you can obtain a copy from the Amazon service. You have bought the book and are now reading it either in a paperback or in a Kindle version. Your desire to read this book is most likely embedded in a wider interest in theoretical issues of psychiatry. This example illustrates how mental processes can cause a particular behavior. It is our common sense self-understanding and understanding of others that is based on the phenomena of mental causation. If you by any chance got an impulse to buy this book because you felt some forces of external influence emanating from your government, then our common sense understanding of mental causes would apparently break down and we would perhaps look for neuroscientific explanations of the influence phenomena. The issue of mental causation is linked to, but not identical with, the so-called mind–body problem. The distinction between explanation and understanding was introduced at the beginning of the twentieth century to characterize the methods of natural sciences and human sciences, respectively. In psychiatry, it was Karl Jaspers who most clearly introduced this distinction in his famous *General Psychopathology* (Jaspers 1913–1963). A very good example of the relationship between explanation and understanding can be found in Bleuler's treatise on schizophrenia (Bleuler 1911/1950). In the section on theory of the symptoms, Bleuler distinguished between the so-called primary and secondary symptoms (not to be confused with the fundamental and accessory division). Primary symptoms comprised, e.g., a tendency to stereotypes and loosening of associations which were, according to Bleuler, psychologically irreducible and, therefore, called for a neuroscientific explanation. Secondary symptoms such as delusions or certain catatonic phenomena were psychologically understandable and were consequences of primary symptoms caused by biological deficit.

We have not advanced dramatically since the time of Bleuler, and Campbell shows very clearly how neuroscientific models of psychopathology typically are concerned with only the first step of the causative change with the remaining steps morphing into processes of mental causation.

REFERENCES

Bleuler, E. (1950) *Dementia Praecox or the Group of Schizophrenias* (J. Zinkin, trans.). New York: International Universities Press.

Jaspers, K. (1963) *General Psychopathology* (7th ed., J. Hoenig & M. W. Hamilton, trans.). Chicago, IL: University of Chicago Press.

14

Can Psychiatry Dispense with the Appeal to Mental Causation?

JOHN CAMPBELL

14.1 HOW DO WE KNOW ABOUT MENTAL CAUSATION?

Suppose we consider a clinician interviewing a psychiatric patient. On the face of it, we can make a broad distinction between two approaches the clinician might take. (They are different approaches, but of course not mutually exclusive; a good clinician might constantly move back and forth between the two approaches in the course of the interview). One approach is to get inside the patient's mind, to understand how the world seems from their vantage-point, to see things from their perspective. We might call this a 'subjective' approach. The other is to regard the patient in terms of checklists of symptoms: ideally, the patient will be found to meet a checklist that suggests an established diagnosis, for which in turn there are familiar treatments. Karl Jaspers, in the classic discussion of this distinction, put it in terms of a contrast between (1) 'subjective psychopathology (phenomenology)' and (2) 'objective psychopathology':

1. We sink ourselves into the psychic situation and *understand genetically by empathy* how one psychic event emerges from another.
2. We find by repeated experience that a number of phenomena are regularly linked together, and on this basis we *explain causally* (Jaspers 1913/1959, p. 301)

Now both approaches can make free use of psychological terms: understanding 'genetically by empathy' how one psychic event emerges from another presumably involves thinking in psychological terms, but the 'regularly linked phenomena' that we appeal to on the second approach could themselves be psychological just as well as physical; we can find regular linkages between social humiliation and major depression just as well as we can find regular linkages between serotonin imbalances and major depression. Moreover, though the 'understanding' described under 'subjective psychopathology' is contrasted with 'causal explanation', it seems to require establishing causal relations between mental events ('how one psychic event emerges from another') and, as Christoph Hoerl (2013) points out, Jaspers' examples of 'subjective' psychopathology seem to concern insight into causal relations between psychological states:

> In the natural sciences we find causal connections *only* but in psychology our bent for knowledge is satisfied with the comprehension of a quite different sort of connection. Psychic events 'emerge' out of each other in a way which we understand. Attacked people become angry and spring to the defence, cheated persons grow suspicious. The way in which such an emergence takes place is understood by us, *our understanding is genetic*. Thus we understand psychic reactions to experience, we understand the development of passion, the growth of an error, the content of delusion and dream; we understand the effects of suggestion, an abnormal personality in its own context or the inner necessities of someone's life. Finally, we understand how the patient sees himself and how this mode of self-understanding becomes a factor in his psychic development.
>
> (pp. 302–303)

These examples all concern knowledge of what makes what happen in the mind. Jaspers says they concern 'internal' causation, rather than the 'external' causation that is grounded in laws; and looking at the examples, this seems to be a contrast between two types of causation, rather than a contrast between something that isn't causation and something that is. But it's natural to wonder how seriously we should take the deliverances of the imagination as to what makes what happen. Perhaps this Jaspers-style empathy is important in a clinical context, in making for easier communication between patient and therapist, while being of no value at all in determining the analysis of a disorder. What does it matter if in imagination you can spin together a way of putting the patient's symptoms into a 'comprehensible' whole? Adolf Grunbaum gave a blunt expression of this concern:

> [N]arratives replete with mere hermeneutic elucidations of thematic affinities are explanatorily sterile or bankrupt; at best, they have literary and reportorial value; at worst they are mere cock-and-bull stories.
>
> (Grünbaum, 1990, 575f)

But the situation here is somewhat puzzling, for the appeal to mental causation – the imaginatively discovered causal connection between one psychological state and another – is pervasive in psychiatry. One obvious place is in the distinction between 'primary' and 'secondary' delusions, where the idea is that the subject has an initial delusion which then plays a role in bringing it about that the patient then has further delusions, affecting their content and volume. Cognitive neuroscience models of psychiatric problems generally have the form: cognitive mechanism X is described by the researcher, the disorder is hypothesized to begin with a breakdown in cognitive mechanism X, generating a psychological state Y, and the rest of the disorder is thought to follow by psychological causation from Y. For instance, in Andy Young's model of the Capgras delusion (Ellis et. al. 1997), the supposition is that there is a breakdown in the system processing one's affective response to faces; this results in a perception of a familiar face that does not involve the familiar affect associated with that face; and mental causation is presumed to be responsible for the further symptoms the patient has, such as ideas about what exactly has happened to their loved one and the particular identity of the imposter. Similarly, Christopher Frith's (1992) cognitive neuroscience model of schizophrenia aims to explain how an organic breakdown results in the patient having the feeling that thoughts in their mind have been 'inserted'; further symptoms, such as exotic beliefs about who is doing the insertion, and so on, are generated by mental causation. Once the key organic breakdown has been identified, the knock-on impacts on the subject's psychology are lightly sketched. There is generally no attempt here to find laws governing the development of those knock-on effects. In practice, the knock-on effects seem to be so idiosyncratic and diverse as to defy the discovery of general laws. Suppose that, as Frith suggests, there is some single organic malfunction that is responsible for the core symptoms of schizophrenia. The knock-on effects can be so various: one patient thinks that a group of French revolutionaries is assailing their mind, another thinks that their next-door neighbor is trying to cause him social embarrassment by speaking in their head at parties, and so on. There may be no stateable general laws governing the elaboration of delusion here, even though the whole process is imaginable 'from the inside'. Jaspers famously said that delusions are 'un-understandable', of course, but what he had in mind here was the generation of a primary delusion; its elaboration may be quite understandable.

If we think, with many theorists, that the only way to establish causation is by establishing general laws, then Grunbaum's attack seems quite convincing; the idea that 'imaginative understanding' can give us any knowledge at all of knock-on causation is a fantasy. So the current situation, in which cognitive neuroscience models of disorders ultimately lean on our imaginative understanding of the generation of secondary delusions, is not really tenable. In the end, we will have to investigate the generation of secondary delusions by finding regularities governing their production. Our assurance that we are doing this correctly may ultimately have to come, in this line of thought, from knowledge of the brain mechanisms underpinning the elaboration of secondary delusions. There is absolutely no advance guarantee that this will vindicate the assessments we make on the basis of our imaginative understanding of patients.

On the other hand, it seems to me that the common-sense reaction to this idea is that grinding through the perhaps literally endless complexity involved in making explicit laws governing the unfolding of secondary delusions would be a complete waste of time; we already understand reasonably well what the knock-on effects might be of a primary delusion; that knowledge is provided by our imaginative understanding of the patient, and is not likely to be significantly revised by any subsequent discovery of general laws.

I think that there is a lot to this common-sense response, and that we should regard our ordinary imaginative understanding of one another as providing knowledge of causal relations among mental states. But it is puzzling to know how this can be; why imaginative understanding isn't merely providing a 'cock-and-bull' story about what's going on. Where does the authority of imaginative understanding come from, and if we regard it as providing knowledge of 'causal relations' among mental phenomena, what concept of causation are we using? If causal relations have to be grounded in laws, how can imaginative understanding be providing insight into them?

14.2 SIMULATION VS. IMAGINATION

In the cognitive science literature, the capacity for imaginative or empathetic understanding of another person is usually thought of in terms of the ability to 'simulate' another person. This is a matter of 'taking on board' the other person's beliefs and objectives, where they differ from one's own, and seeing what one would do next oneself. This whole exercise has to be decoupled from action, of course, since otherwise one would actually be executing actions and behaviors that are in the service of the other person's motivations, rather than one's own. So what you have to do, in an 'off-line' way, is make adjustments for the differences between your own and the other person's wants and beliefs. You take on board their wants and beliefs, holding the rest of your psychology constant, and then 'run the simulation', to see what you would do next. To use a famous example from Gordon's (1986) article, suppose you are trying to predict what your friend would do on hearing footsteps in the basement:

> I imagine, for instance, a lone modification of the actual world: the sound of footsteps from the basement. Then I ask, in effect, "What shall I do now?" And I answer with a declaration of immediate intention, "I shall now . . ." This too is only feigned . . ..
>
> (Gordon 1986, p. 161)

The trouble is that 'simulation', as conceived in the cognitive science tradition, is fundamentally a predictive device. So this 'off-line' approach cannot distinguish between causal pathways and mere correlations. That is, in the simulation, you take on, for example, the belief that you can hear footsteps in your basement. And perhaps you find next, within the simulation, that you are nervous. It may be that the footsteps cause you to be nervous. But it may also be, though this would be a slightly unusual case, that it is only when you are nervous that you ever pay enough attention to what is going on in the basement to hear footsteps there; perhaps the footsteps add nothing to your original nervousness. In either case, when you simulate the hearing of footsteps in the basement, you will, off-line, be nervous. But the simulation will not of itself tell you which causal route is operating to generate the nervousness; whether the footsteps cause the nervousness or the nervousness is a precondition of hearing the footsteps.

This kind of point is graphically illustrated by LeDoux and Pine's 'two-systems' model of fear (Figure 14.1). Suppose you encounter something dangerous. You feel afraid, and then you run, let's suppose. That natural model is that perception of the thing caused you to feel fear, and that feeling of fear was what propelled you out of the area. As LeDoux and Pine (2016) put it, this is the natural model:

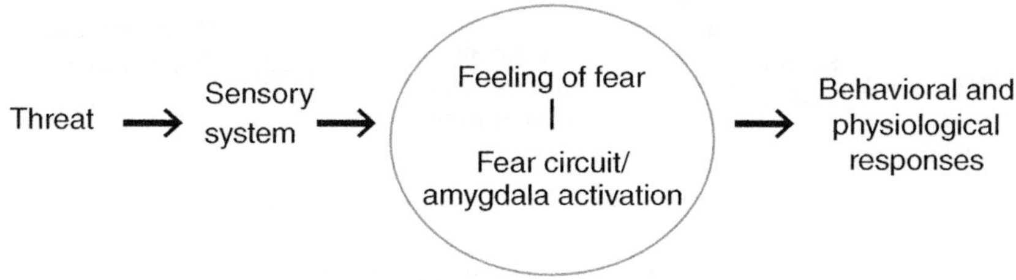

FIGURE 14.1 The fear center model.

According to LeDoux and Pine, though, this model does not really fit the data: feelings of fear are not well correlated with defensive behaviors or physiological responses; subliminal perception of threatening stimuli generates defensive physiological and behavioral responses in the absence of any feeling of fear; blindsight patients respond defensively to threatening stimuli without reporting any feeling of fear; and although damage to the amygdala interferes with the production of physiological and behavioral responses to threatening stimuli, the feeling of fear is still produced. Taken together, these points suggest that there are actually two systems in play here (Figure 14.2): one, non-conscious, running through the amygdala, generates the physiological and behavioral responses; the other runs from the sensory system through to the cortex and generates the feeling of fear.

Even if there are two different systems here, there must be many connections between them; for example, the defensive survival circuits may 'modulate' the experience of fear.

The distinction between a 'one-system' and a 'two-systems' view of the fear–anxiety circuit matters when we consider the use of animal models to test potential treatments for related disorders. It has proven difficult to get effective treatments by this route, and the 'two-systems' analysis suggests a reason why. The animal models are tested by looking for changes in the

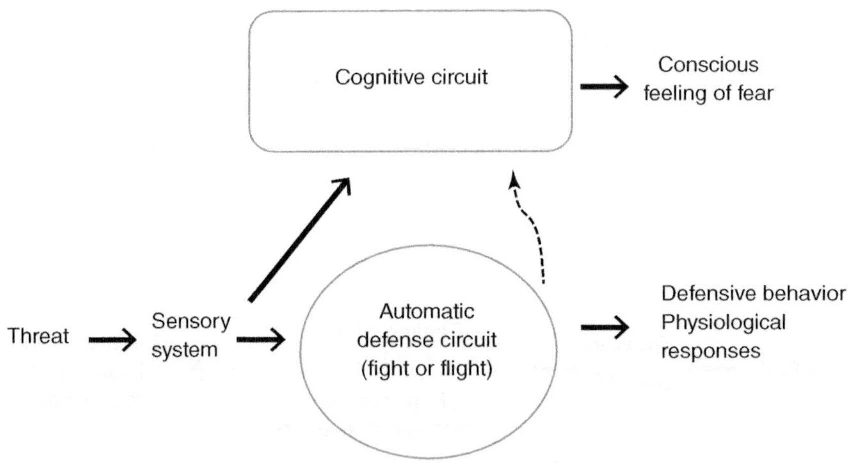

FIGURE 14.2 The two-system model.

animal's defensive responses to stimuli. But in humans, the efficacy of treatment is tested by looking for amelioration of the feelings of fear and anxiety. If there is just one fear–anxiety circuit, then this approach makes perfect sense. Suppose a treatment for fear, such as threat extinction (repeated presentation of the threatening stimulus without anything bad happening), is administered. In animals, the reduction of fear is exhibited principally by looking at the defensive responses of the animal. In humans, we look for amelioration of the feeling of fear as exhibited in verbal report. The two-systems analysis suggests, however, that a treatment that works well in the animal models may be addressing a system that does not implicate the feeling of fear at all: the circuit, remote from consciousness that generates defensive behaviors. The system that is being monitored in humans, however, is the system that generates feelings of fear or anxiety and exhibits those feelings in verbal behavior. So it is perhaps not all that surprising that treatments that work well on one system are not having much impact on the other system. That's not to say that previous work will be of no help with human disorders. Humans may have disorders of either or both of those circuits. And animal work may well help when humans have problems with the defensive behavior circuit. To address the feelings of fear or anxiety, however, a different approach is required. And here, it seems possible that clinical work, perhaps using cognitive-behavioral therapy, will be more valuable.

Suppose for the moment that the two-systems view is correct. Suppose that, not knowing any of this data, you try to simulate the condition of someone feeling fear. Well, you would likely only be feeling the fear if you had perceived a threatening stimulus. And if you had perceived a threatening stimulus, likely enough, your non-conscious fear circuit would have been activated, so you might be engaging in defensive behaviors. So when you simulate, off-line, the feeling of fear, and run the simulation, you will get the upshot that in that case, you will be engaging in defensive behavior. But the fact that that the simulation, when executed correctly, delivers that upshot, does nothing to suggest that the feeling of fear caused the defensive behavior. That was not the point or promise of the exercise of simulation. The upshot was not a causal hypothesis, but merely a prediction that when feeling the fear, you will also engage in defensive behavior. The correctness of that prediction could be underpinned by any of a wide variety of causal structures, and the simulation exercise of itself is not an attempt to specify which causal structure is in question here.

14.3 THE 'PROCESS' PICTURE OF CAUSATION

This suggests a sharp contrast between Jasper's conception of imaginative understanding and the cognitive science model of simulation. As I read him, Jaspers conceives of imaginative understanding of another's train of thought and feeling as the tracing of a causal pathway. When you observe and empathize with your friend, who has been cheated many times, growing suspicious, you are tracing the pathway by which your friend's suspicion was generated. You are not merely predicting their suspicion. You are following the process which produced the suspicion.

Now the two-systems model of the fear raises a question for this way of thinking of imaginative understanding, too. I said that the simulation model cannot distinguish between the case in which the feeling of fear causes defensive reactions and the case in which the presence of the defensive reactions is caused by an external stimulus which also, independently, causes the feeling of fear. That is not a problem for the simulation model, properly understood, because the simulation model, properly understood, is merely a predictive device whose point is to use encountered correlations to predict, rather than to attempt to provide insight into causation. But in Jaspers' picture, imaginative understanding is trying to provide insight into causal relations between psychological events. So suppose, you are watching as someone encounters, say, a rattlesnake, and freezes. It may seem to you that you are following the trajectory of the patient's mind perfectly. You see them come across the rattlesnake, and you follow in imagination what happens next: the feelings of fear that perception arouses, all the way to the 'consequent' freezing. But if the two-systems account is correct, that's an error. The problem this raises for a Jaspers-style account is to explain how, if this is possible, we can have the right to take it that this isn't the general case. That is, maybe our ordinary appeals to mental causation are typically wrong, and, when right, right only by accident. Don't we always need some scientific enquiry to establish when a claim of mental causation is right? Or was Jaspers – and ordinary common sense – right in thinking that the appeal to imaginative knowledge of causation does have some kind of epistemic authority?

Even to get this question correctly framed requires some effort. In this section, I suggest that the question should be framed in terms of a 'process' conception of causation. In the next section, I suggest that the key role for imaginative understanding is in our knowledge of singular causal relations between particular psychological states of affairs. Let's begin with framing the role of imagination in understanding mental causal processes.

(1) Recall that when we are discussing causation at all, it is difficult to go for long without appealing to the idea of a 'causal process'. We do have to recognize that when we have a system governed by dynamical laws – I mean, laws governing the development of the system over time – it's natural to suppose that if we consider the total state S1 of the system at one time, and the total state S2 of the system at a later time, and the laws demand that S1 be followed by S2, then S1 caused S2. And here there isn't any appeal to the notion of a 'process'. But, as Russell pointed out, this kind of idea can only apply to *global* states of a system. And, we usually think of causation as a *local* phenomenon. We think, for example, that a cue shot can be what caused the red ball to go into the pocket. But there aren't going to be any local laws to say that cue shots always get the ball to go into the pocket. Although we sometimes talk of the pool table as though it's a relatively closed system, in fact, it isn't: there can always be outside interference, if for example the ceiling collapses onto the table immediately after the ball has been hit. Even if we are in a deterministic universe, we would have to consider an initial state encompassing the whole world in order to find a law that implies that the initial state must be followed by the ball going into the pocket. We have to rule out the passing meteors or light showers that might interfere with the ball going into the pocket. But we don't usually think of causation in these global terms. The reason is that we think of causation in terms of local processes, such as the movement of a ball and its collisions with other balls, connecting causes and effects, and we don't think of the causation in terms of exceptionless laws at all. The trouble is to explain what concept of 'process' we are using.

(2) Russell made some helpful remarks about this. He says, 'When two events belong to one causal line [that is, there is a causal process connecting the two events] the earlier may be said to "cause" the later. In this way laws of the form "A causes B" may preserve a certain validity' (1948, p. 334).

He says: 'I call a series of events a "causal line" if, given some of them, we can infer something about the others without having to know anything about the environment' (1948, p. 333).

'A causal line may always be regarded as a persistence of some thing, a person, a table, a photon, or what not. Throughout a given causal line, there may be constancy of quality, constancy of structure, or gradual changes in either, but not sudden change of any considerable magnitude' (1948, pp. 475–477).

(3) Now the notion of a 'causal line' or 'causal process' is sketched out by Russell only for the physical case. It seems, indeed, to be only the physical conception of causal process that is needed by cognitive-science approaches to the brain. The ascription of representational content, in beliefs or desires, hopes or fears, is not, in this view, the level at which we find causal processes.

Just to fill this out a little: in a cognitive-science approach to the brain, typically what happens is that the researcher tries to find the significance of a particular group of cell-firings. The question the researcher asks is: to what external stimulus are these cell-firings a response? The researcher finds that they are, let's say, responsive to the presence of particular light wavelengths at particular locations. We then hypothesize that the cell-firings are representing the presence of that stimulus. We confirm the hypothesis by looking at how these cell-firings are connected to other cell-firings (for example, cells that sample our first round of cell-firings to look at the ratios of light of various wavelengths being reflected from particular positions), and finding some plausible adaptive reason why there might be cells that represent just the external magnitudes we are considering (e.g., to differentiate objects from their backgrounds). In this picture, the causal processes by which one state generates another are biological. The mechanisms of causal connection are found at the biological level. (This was Fodor's (1987) argument for the existence of a 'language of thought' – that the mechanisms by which we move from one representational state to another must be biological, and that the systematic nature of the representational demands that there be a systematicity in the underlying mechanisms that generate one representational state on the basis of another.)

This, of course, is not how we think of causal processes in commonsense psychology. When we want to understand just how someone got to a particular feeling about a person, for example, finding them annoying or intriguing, we think in terms of thoughts and emotions generating the outcome. In the mental just as in the physical case, we do have a distinction between mere counterfactual dependence of one state on another, and the causal generation, or causal production, of one state by another. In the physical case, we might illustrate the point by considering causation by omission. You didn't turn the switch off; consequently, the machine overheated. But 'not turning the switch off' is not itself an element in the process by which the overheating was generated. For the actual process, you would have to consider the flow of electricity through the resistors and so on. Similarly, if you ask me why I'm in my office, the answer might be that I'd forgotten that we had a department meeting now. But 'forgetting' is not itself an element in the process that propelled me to my office. In this case, we'd think of the 'process' as involving the factors that positively justify me or rationalize my going to my office.

As a first approximation, we might say that the notion of a 'mental process' connecting X and Y that we use every day in common-sense psychology is the idea of a sequence beginning with X, and perhaps recruiting other factors along the way, that *justifies* or *rationalizes* Y. ('Forgetting' in itself does not rationalize or justify; it rather explains why your rationalization or justification took the form that it did.)

It seems that we have two conceptions of 'causal process', mental and physical. What I've said is that cognitive neuroscience models of disorders typically appeal to both, physical or biological processes, when describing the organic damage that results in cognitive malfunctioning; and then, when considering the consequences of the cognitive malfunction, to the psychological, or rationalizing processes that generate the knock-on impact of the initial psychological state that one gets into because of this cognitive malfunctioning. The question I want to raise is whether it's realistic to suppose that in principle, the talk about mental causation could ultimately be replaced by talk in terms of physical processes. There seem to be (at least) three possibilities:

(a) Talk about mental causation and mental processes is legitimate in its own right and can't be replaced by talk about physical causation.
(b) Talk about mental causation is legitimate, but can be reduced to talk about physical causation. Consistent with this broad general picture, you might acknowledge that there are points at which our understanding of mental causation can be corrected by what we find at the biological level, as with the 'two-systems' model of fear.
(c) Typically, there is nothing to be found at the biological level that corresponds to our ordinary talk of mental causation and mental processes and – unlike the picture in (a) – for that reason, talk about mental causation should ultimately be abandoned in favor of more rigorous biological explanations of what's going on.

All of these views seem to be consistent with physicalism, or at least, consistent with a physicalism that says only that the mentalistic facts globally supervene on the physical.

Already, I think, we can see that options (a) and (c) here seem to be quite far-reaching in their consequences. If option (a) is correct, then mental causation can't be understood in terms of an underlying level of physical causation. Even though this position is consistent with the supervenience of the mental on the physical, it would seem to be a bit of a blow to the idea of physicalism if we can't understand the dynamics of the mind at a physical level. Option (c) is in effect a kind of epiphenomenalism, devastating to ordinary social life and to civilization generally: we ordinarily hang a great deal on our interpretations of mental causality in everyday life. You and I are in a crowded elevator: did you stand on my toe because you saw your opportunity, or because you were pushed? These kinds of things drive our ordinary social relations. If we accepted that these kinds of questions are simply not legitimate, because the only causation here is to be found at a strictly neural level that can't be interpreted in terms of psychological causation, our ordinary social relations with one another would simply seize up. Similarly, more formally, in the law, we should simply not know how to proceed if we could not ask about mental causation: about the motives that caused the accused to act as they did. So on a first look, most of us would, I think, hope that something like option (b) is correct. My aim in this chapter is to fill out a little more what sustaining option (b) would come to, and to indicate some of the significant difficulties we face in pursuing it.

14.4 CAUSAL PROCESSES IN THE MENTAL

I suggest that the starting point for a characterization of the idea of 'causal pathway' that we need in the mentalistic case is provided by Jasper's notion of a 'meaningful' or 'intelligible' sequence of thoughts and feelings. It can happen that a subject has one thought and then another thought that is not intelligibly related to it. And in that case, we would usually assume that there is no causation here. Of course, philosophers have often highlighted the idea of 'rationality' as mattering, and there certainly is a notion of 'instrumental rationality' at work when we soberly consider the best way to achieve a predetermined objective. But often, the mental life engages with the world without the benefit of a predetermined overriding objective – as, for example, when we are trying to figure out what our objectives should be – and then the concept of instrumental rationality seems less helpful.

Jaspers also pointed out that the way we ordinarily know about the causal pathways taken by someone's thoughts and feelings is through the use of imagination, or empathy. This is the fundamental role for empathy, to allow us to follow the twists and turns of someone's thinking and feeling.

There is, indeed, a question as to whether we can explain the concept of a 'causal pathway' in the mentalistic case otherwise than as the mere correlate of 'empathy'. That is, we could say: for subject A there was a causal pathway from X to Y means simply that an observer could empathetically or imaginatively understand the progression from X to Y. And there might be no deeper account to be given of the idea of a mentalistic causal pathway. That would be disappointing, but we have to keep the possibility in mind.

I think it's instructive here to compare Jasper's conception of imaginative understanding with Collingwood's conception of historical understanding. Collingwood (1959) is plainly operating with the idea of trying to follow someone's thought processes through various twists and turns, but he is more explicit about why 'imagination' is the right notion here. His point is that a mental process can only be understood by locating it in a space of alternatives, and recognizing why one path through that space, rather than another, seemed normatively correct to the subject.

> The historian of philosophy, reading Plato, is trying to know what Plato thought when he expressed himself in certain words. The only way in which he can do this is by thinking it for himself. This, in fact, is what we mean when we speak of 'understanding' the words. So the historian of politics of warfare, presented with an account of certain actions done by Julius Caesar, tries to understand these actions, that is, to discover what thoughts in Caesar's mind determined him to do them. This implies envisaging for himself the situation in which Caesar stood, and thinking for himself what Caesar thought about the situation and the possible ways of dealing with it. The history of thought, and therefore all history, is the re-enactment of past thought in the historian's own mind.
>
> This re-enactment is only accomplished, in the case of Plato and Caesar respectively, so far as the historian brings to bear on the problem all the powers of his own mind and all his knowledge of philosophy and politics. It is not a passive surrender to the spell of another's mind: it is a labor of active and therefore critical thinking. The historian not only re-enacts past thought, he re-enacts it in the context of his own knowledge and therefore, in re-enacting it, criticizes it, forms his own judgement of its value, corrects whatever errors he can discern in it. This criticism of the thought whose history he traces is not something secondary to tracing the history of it. It is an indispensable condition of the historical knowledge itself. Nothing could be a completer error concerning the

history of thought than to suppose that the historian as such merely ascertains 'what so-and-so thought', leaving it to someone else to decide 'whether it was true'. All thinking is critical thinking; the thought which re-enacts past thoughts, therefore, criticizes them in re-enacting them . . ..

. . . Suppose, for example, he is reading the Theodosian code, and has before him a certain edict of an emperor. Merely reading the words and being able to translate them does not amount to knowing their historical significance. In order to do that, he must envisage the situation with which the emperor was trying to deal, and he must envisage it as that emperor envisaged it. Then he must see for himself, just as if the emperor's situation were his own, how such a situation might be dealt with; he must see the possible alternatives, and the reasons for choosing one rather than another; and thus he must go through the process which the emperor went through in deciding on this particular course. Thus he is re-enacting in his own mind the experience of the emperor; and only insofar as he does this has he any historical knowledge, as distinct from a merely philological knowledge, of the meaning of the edict.

(In Gardiner (ed.), pp. 253–255)

The point here is that understanding someone's train of thought is not merely a matter of going over things they have said or thoughts and feeling they have had; it *requires* critical understanding, sensitivity to the possibility of alternative trains of thought, seeing why the path not taken was not taken. Now it is not straightforward to find a physical correlate of this kind of mental process. We would have to find a sequence of physical states that are physically causally connected – one set of cell-firings causing another set of cell firings, and so on – and it would have to be essential to our understanding of this sequence as a causal sequence that we have some sensitivity to the counterfactuals governing other possible firings that did not but could have occurred, and some sense that the firings that did happen were happening because of their normative correctness. It is not easy to see how this would go. Of course, one can make the claim that a particular set of cell-firings realizes a particular representation in the brain, and that another set of cell-firings, perhaps caused by the first, realizes another representation in the brain. But if we consider the cell-firings merely as cell-firings, it is difficult to see how we will find a notion of 'normative correctness', recognizable at a merely biological level of description, that allows one to do an analog of the Collingwood exercise at the level of brain biology. If we work with Collingwood's picture of what we are doing when we follow someone else's thought processes, locating it in a space of possible alternatives, there is no apparent way in which we will be able to locate the biological sequence in an isomorphic space of alternatives, with one path through the space being followed because of its normative correctness. I do not say that the thing is impossible, only that I do not see how it is to be done. Notice that there is way of talking about the brain that is very often used by those who know a little bit about it, where you simply translate back and forth freely from psychological terms to neural terms, as when someone says, 'That cake shop really stimulates my endorphins, so I'll go there'. Here the talk about endorphins is simply a dummy, a stand-in for ordinary psychological talk. Suppose, for example, that the Emperor is making the decision that the law courts should close during Holy Week. We can re-enact the train of thought leading up to the decision, just as Collingwood describes: weighing the problems the closure will raise against the benefits, and so on. And we could describe a sequence of biological states and claim that each one of these constitutes a realization of one of the Emperor's judgments along the way. We could say that the biological sequence takes the form it does because of what thoughts are being realized, and apply Collingwood-style understanding to the sequence of thoughts. But what is hard to understand is how the biological sequence, understood at the biological level, could be thought to be a causal process in the same way that the mental process realized is a causal process. Of course there are biological processes, but they do not seem to be answerable to anything like the constraints to which thought processes are answerable. The disordered thoughts of a schizophrenic patient exhibiting formal thought disorder, for example, may be biologically comprehensible in just the same way as any other, even though we do not have a psychologically comprehensible causal process here in Jaspers' or Collingwood's senses. There is a sense in which the Emperor Theodosian's thought processes constitute a causal process, and the thoughts of the disordered patient do not stack together to constitute a causal process, and it is hard to see how the distinction can be biologically grounded.

This is not the same as the mind-body problem, as usually conceived. The usual picture is that conscious experience has a distinctive 'qualitative character', and the mind-body problem is to explain how that qualitative character can be grounded in the brain. But the puzzle I am raising here does not, in any immediate way at any rate, depend on the idea of qualitative character. It has to do with whether the way we think of causal processes in the mental can be grounded in the way we think of causal processes in biology.

Jaspers, of course, famously pointed out that primary delusions are not 'understandable' in anything like Collingwood's sense. He said:

> If we try to get some closer understanding of these primary experiences of delusions, we soon find we cannot really appreciate these quite alien modes of experience. They remain largely incomprehensible, unreal and beyond our understanding.
>
> (Jaspers 1913/1959, p. 98)

Now on one reading of it, the problem here has to do with the 'qualitative character' of the patient's experiences. The patient in 'suspicious mood', where everything seems full of hidden significance, or the patient who feels that her body has been taken over by an alien force, these may seem quite unimaginable because the static experience at a single moment, of feeling like that, seems so different to our own. But there is another dimension to 'un-understandability'. Consider the patient who believes that thoughts from her mother are being transmitted to her mind, and that she can feel them entering her head. With this patient we cannot do what Collingwood's historian did with the Emperor Theodosian, and critically evaluate her line of thought. Suppose the patient says that the thoughts are being transmitted by way of the air conditioner. Can we argue that by the patient's own lights, it should be the fireplace, rather than the air conditioner, that is the likeliest candidate for being the vehicle by which the thoughts are transmitted? Should we ask whether electrical outlets affect the movement of thoughts? We really have not the first idea how to engage in Collingwood's critical thinking here. For that reason, we cannot conceptualize the patient's thinking in terms of 'mental processes'. But they may nonetheless have the same kind of biological grounding as the thought processes of Theodosian.

There may be a broader, more schematic level at which the patient's thinking can be recognized as subject to normative constraints. Roberts (1992) wrote:

> Delusion formation can be seen as an adaptive process of attributing meaning to experience through which order and security are gained, the novel experience is incorporated within the patient's conceptual framework, and the occult potential of its unknownness is defused ... Lansky ... speaks for many in asserting that 'Delusion is restitutive, ameliorating anxieties by altering the construction of reality'.
>
> (Roberts 1992, p. 305)

In a similar vein, Bortolotti more recently argued that there are epistemic benefits in the elaboration of delusion. For a patient in the early stages of schizophrenia, learning is difficult because attention is constantly drawn toward irrelevant stimuli and prediction errors are registered inappropriately (Mishara and Corlett 2009, p. 531). But the full onset of the delusions means that learning becomes possible again:

> the delusion is stamped into the agent's memory and reinforced every time a new prediction error is registered. The shift back to the habitual and automated learning processes enhances the capacity to respond to cues in the environment and the delusion plays a dominant role in providing explanations for the phenomena previously found to be puzzling and anomalous
>
> (Bortolotti 2016, p. 887)

This does not mean that the patient's thoughts become comprehensible in anything like the way that Jaspers or Collingwood had in mind. It does mean that we might understand something about why the patient's delusional thinking takes the general form that it does; but it cannot show that the patient's thoughts can be subjected to the kind of 'critical re-enactment' that Collingwood described.

In this section, I've tried to sketch the reason why option (b), set out in Section 14.3, is difficult to sustain: namely, that we seem to have a conception of causal processes in the mental that is difficult to find mirrored at the biological level. If the difficulty is as big as it looks right now, that would mean that we must either regard mental causation as not answerable to findings about biology, or that we should dispense with talk about mental causation and replace it with talk about biological processes. Neither of those options seems immediately attractive.

14.5 REVIEW AND CONCLUSIONS: LAWS VS. PROCESSES

Suppose we consider different models of how we know about causation. One possibility is that we have a system governed by deterministic laws, so that given enough information about the current state of the system and knowledge of the laws governing it, we can predict what will happen next. Then we can say that an earlier state of the system, A, caused an outcome, B, if, given the laws governing the system, and given A, B was bound to happen. And knowing that A caused B will be a matter of knowing the condition A, knowing the relevant laws, and being able to predict on that basis that B would occur.

There seem to be plenty of cases in which we know about causation but not in a way that this model explains. Consider, for example, billiard ball causation. This is usually taken to be a good case for illustrating the kind of nomological model of causation I just set out, but it is nothing of the sort. A billiard table with a number of balls rolling around on it is a textbook example of a chaotic system. Variations in the initial condition of the system that are too small to be measurable in practice may make big difference to the outcome. That is, very small differences in the force or direction of a cue shot, or in the positioning of just one ball – differences too small to be measurable in practice – may make a big difference to the outcome; may make a difference to whether the red goes in a pocket, for example. Even for someone who knows the relevant laws, and who knows, as far as is practicable, the relevant facts about the initial positions and movements of the balls on the table, for example, and the force and direction of the cue shot, may be quite unable to predict whether or not the red ball will go into a pocket. Nonetheless, once the cue shot is taken and the balls roll, with the red going into a pocket, the causal pathway from the cue shot to the ball going into the pocket is almost childishly easy to trace. You simply have to follow the cue shot from the initial ball struck, through its collisions with other balls, and their collisions with further balls, to find a causal pathway from the cue shot to finally the red ball going into the pocket. What makes this tracing of the causal pathway possible is that our knowledge of causation is not instructed merely by our knowledge of laws. We have further the conception of a 'causal pathway' from one event to another. In this case, it is easy to say what the components of the pathway are. We have (a) the trajectory of an individual ball over time, transmitting causal influence from one location to another. That is, within a single ball over time we have the transmission of causation: it is because of the initial cue shot that there is now, a second later, that same ball going past a particular place at a particular speed. Causation has been transmitted from the initial cue shot to that later place. But we also have (b) the transmission of causation from one ball to another when they collide. So causation can be transmitted from the cue shot to a later placing of the ball struck, to another ball, through the collision. It is because we have that conception of a 'causal pathway' from the initial shot to the dropping of the red into the pocket that we know what caused the red to drop into the pocket, even though we could not have predicted, even probabilistically, that the red would go into the pocket. We have a postdictive knowledge of causation that does not seem to depend on our knowledge of laws, but rather on our grasp of the conception of a causal pathway, put together from (a) the trajectories of individual balls and (b) collisions between balls. Of course, there is a subterranean level at which the system is law-governed – and indeed, for all I have said, these underlying laws may be deterministic – but the relation between (1) the existence of causal pathways and our knowledge of causal pathways and (2) this underlying level at which we have law-governedness, is at best indirect. On the face of it, it may be that the existence of causal pathways and our knowledge of them does not at all depend on the existence of the underlying level at which we have governance by law. At any rate, if there is a dependence here, it would take quite a deep investigation to establish it. There doesn't, for example, seem to be an obvious contradiction in the idea of a system in which there are causal pathways and there is knowledge of them, even though there is no underlying level at which the system can be described as strictly law-governed.

The billiard-table here seems to me to provide quite a good model for our knowledge of mental causation. Of course, there may be an underlying level at which the whole system is governed by laws, perhaps even deterministic laws. The brain, is, on the face of it, at best a probabilistic system; it's hard to find regularities in brain functioning that are even probabilistic, let alone deterministic; but perhaps, there will turn out to be a level, perhaps the level of fundamental particles, at which the brain can be described as governed by deterministic laws. It seems quite evident, however, that knowledge of the laws at work here and how they apply to particular events is not what we use to establish mental causation. Suppose you are talking through with a close friend some big decision they're about to make – should they take the post they've just been offered in Canada? You can follow their train of thought through all the different options and factors weighed, you may indeed have more insight than your friend into what factors are counting and why. You might not be able, at the start of the discussion, to predict the outcome, but postdictively, you can trace the causal pathways through your discussion, and know definitively just what the causal path was to their decision. That's not to say that you are infallible: it can happen that the discussion is a charade and there is some hidden factor you don't know about that all along was determining your friend to decide one way rather than another. Similarly, in the billiard ball case, it can happen that there's an unseen magnet, or a bias in the table, unsuspected by that observer, that is really what's making the ball travel in one direction rather than another. But in both cases, it can also happen that the observer does get all the relevant causal factors and has the right to say decisively that they know what caused the outcome. Now in the case of the billiard balls, it's fairly straightforward, as we saw, to start to characterize the notion of 'causal pathway' that we need, even if it will clearly take substantial work to find a characterization that will generalize to other cases of physical causation. In the case of mental causation, however, it's harder to know exactly where to start to describe the notion of 'causal pathway' that we need. It does not seem to be to the point to begin with a description of underlying brain pathways because someone who knows about the causal trajectory of a person's thought and feeling may not even be aware that the subject has a brain. We need to be considering the subject's psychological states as such, whether ephemeral or sustained, and the dynamics of the relations among them as they unfold over time. In effect, what I have suggested is that we should take the notion of a 'mental process' to be the complement of the kind of discovery processes described by Jaspers and Collingwood, where we regard mental processes as 'imaginatively understandable' in Jaspers' sense, and subject to the kind of 'critical re-enactment' described by Collingwood.

I began this essay by pointing out that cognitive neuroscience models of disorders typically take the form of (a) description of an organic malfunction that's thought to generate the 'primary delusion', with it being assumed that (b) the generation of 'secondary delusions' from the first, primary delusion, will be understood in terms of mental causation. I asked whether this is merely a temporary situation, or if we will ultimately be able to analyze all the causation here in biological terms. My claim has been that the notion of 'causal process' that we have for the mental cannot be regarded as grounded in, or validated by, any conception of 'causal process' for the biological. It, therefore, looks as though the appeal to mental causation, discovered by imagination, cannot be dispensed with.

REFERENCES

Bortolotti, L. (2016) 'Epistemic Benefits of Elaborated and Systematized Delusions in Schizophrenia.' *British Journal for the Philosophy of Science*, 67, 879–900.

Collingwood, R. G. (1959) 'History as Re-enactment of the Past Experience.' In Patrick Gardiner, ed., *Theories of History: Readings from Classical and Contemporary Sources*. Glencoe, IL: Free Press, pp. 251–262.

Ellis, H. D., Young, A. W., Quayle, A. H., and De Pauw, K. W. (1997) 'Reduced Autonomic Responses to Faces in Capgras Delusion.' *Proceedings of the Royal Society of London B – Biological Sciences*, 264, 1085–1092.

Fodor, J. (1987) *Psychosemantics*. Cambridge, MA: MIT Press.

Frith, C. (1992) *The Cognitive Neuropsychology of Schizophrenia*. London: Psychology Press.

Gordon, R. (1986) 'Folk Psychology as Simulation.' *Mind and Language*, 1, 158–171.

Grünbaum, A. (1990) '"Meaning" Connections and Causal Connections in the Human Sciences: The Poverty of Hermeneutic Philosophy.' *Journal of the American Psychoanalytic Association*, 38, 559–577.

Hoerl, C. (2013) 'Jaspers on Explaining and Understanding in Psychiatry.' In Giovanni Stanghellini and Thomas Fuchs (eds.), *One Century of Karl Jaspers' General Psychopathology*. Oxford: Oxford University Press, pp. 107–120.

Jaspers, K. (1913/1959) *General Psychopathology*. Manchester: Manchester University Press.

LeDoux, J. E. and Pine, D. S. (2016) 'Using Neuroscience to Help Understand Fear and Anxiety: A Two-System Framework.' *American Journal of Psychiatry*, 173, 1083–1093.

Mishara, A. L. and Corlett, P. (2009) 'Are Delusions Biologically Adaptive? Salvaging the Doxastic Shear Pin.' *Behavioral and Brain Sciences*, 32, 530–531.

Roberts, G. (1992) 'The Origins of Delusion.' *British Journal of Psychiatry*, 161, 298–308.

Russell, B. (1948) *Human Knowledge*. New York: Simon and Schuster.

15

Folk Psychology and Jaspers' Empathic Understanding: A Conceptual Exercise?

PETER ZACHAR

John Campbell's thoughts about the impracticality and unfeasibility of reducing talk about mental causation to talk about physical causation has many interesting implications. His notion of mental causation refers to how, in understanding another person, we attempt to grasp the unfolding of their thoughts and feelings over time. One of his examples is understanding the meaningful connections between a friend being offered a new job in another country and the various personal and professional factors causing her to feel ambivalent and indecisive about whether to accept the offer. Jaspers (1923/1963) called this genetic understanding – with genetic likely meaning something like "developmental." According to Jaspers, we understand someone genetically by empathy.

The problem, Campbell notes, is how are we to know that our empathic understanding is accurate, and not a fictional construction of our imagination? Can this even be said to be causality at all – especially causality as it is understood by scientists?

This problem touches on a fundamental issue regarding the proper role of folk psychology in the sciences of psychiatry, psychology, and psychopathology. What is folk psychology? It is a theoretical framework that we use to understand (and explain) behavior using concepts such as belief, desire, emotion, motivation, sensation, perception, and so on.

Certainly, how we understand and explain ourselves using the tools of this theoretical framework can be false. Campbell gives an example of one potentially mistaken folk psychological explanation. In the traditional Jamesian scenario, according to the folk psychological notion of emotional causation: I see a bear and then feel afraid, which causes me to run away. In biological psychology's fear center model, the initiation of the fear reaction is coordinated by the amygdala. According to LeDoux and Pine (2016), however, the amygdala coordinates the physiological and behavioral responses only, whereas the experience of "fear" is implemented in a distinct pathway involving the cortex. The "cortical" feeling of fear does not cause the flight or fight response. Indeed, that response occurs whether or not fear is felt. If LeDoux and Pine are correct, the feeling of fear does not cause me to run away. That explanation is a fictional construction of the imagination.

Campbell mentions R. G. Collingwood approvingly, but shouldn't we also be worried about Collingwood's notion of trying to reconstruct the thoughts and motivations of a figure such as Plato or of a Roman Emperor living in the fourth century CE? Even if the historian critically used all the information he has at his disposal, how would we discriminate between an accurate reconstruction and a well-narrated just-so story? It is particularly worrisome that we cannot avoid being at least a little whiggish about people from a different culture and a different time – like Plato.

Campbell notes that Jaspers himself believed that empathic understanding does not always work. For example, the delusions of people who are psychotic are not readily understandable. We cannot empathically understand and recreate the experience that leads a person with schizophrenia to believe that the air conditioner is transmitting another's thoughts into his head. The experience does not correspond to our norms of understanding.

Empathy failures, however, do not apply to states of psychosis only. It is also difficult to get into the head of someone with borderline personality or psychopathic personality. This may also be true of adults trying to understand children or anyone trying to understand someone from a different culture. Most people are not natural method actors who can adopt the mindset of another person – and even if someone has the talent to attempt it, the risk of empathy failure is tremendous.

So how do we develop our understandings of others? My main point in this commentary is that both simulation and imaginative understanding play a necessary, but relatively small role in understanding others. We develop our understanding of others from many sources of information, but mostly based on what we can see and hear. Information obtained from the third-person perspective drives the bus.

One of the most important things we can do is to follow behavioral patterns – noting what the person has done in the past and how she or he typically reacts to situations. It is also important to ask other people what they have observed. Observation here includes observing how others react to her and how you react to her as well.

Also very useful is to have some idea of how other people like her, behave, think, and feel. These generalizations are like mini theories. For example, having a conceptual model of people with borderline personality disorder or people with psychopathy can aid understanding. The same for trying to understand things like extroversion and cultural differences. We can learn a lot by grouping people into kinds and seeing what they have in common.

The *most important* way to combat empathy failure is to ask the person themselves about what they are thinking and feeling. That is not to say the people always have accurate self-knowledge or that they are willing to disclose, but the value of self-report is underrated.

Understanding another does not require putting oneself into the head of the other person and reconstructing the unfolding of their thoughts bit by bit. Indeed, some accurate understanding can be aided by doing just the opposite – temporality suspending your notions of what the person is like and how they see things, turning them into something of a mystery and not having expectations. The value of this occasional exercise is that instead of attending to things that fit your expectations, you may notice things that you would have otherwise ignored.

My proposal for what we do when trying to understand another has more in common with Popper's (1963) notion of critical rationalism than with Collinwood's critical understanding and sensitivity to potential alternative trains of thought. By critical rationalism, Popper meant an active process of making conjectures about what we are trying to understand, but then putting those conjectures to the test and modifying them accordingly. His contrast with critical rationalism was dogmatic thinking, by which he meant a kind of confirmatory hypothesis testing in which people seek evidence to support what they already believe.

As I noted, the best way to test out a conjecture is to ask the person themselves, but that is only one of many different strategies. This conjecture-driven, trial- and- error process is one of the basic skills taught to people learning general psychotherapy (e.g., Egan, 1986; Martin, 1983). It is a kind of empathy, but of a more conceptual or cognitive sort. From this perspective, our genetic understanding of another person can have some epistemic authority, but the authority resides in our commitment to the process – to the hard work of understanding in which our conjectures are subject to correction by further information.

Let us return to our friend pondering whether to take the job in another country. As she is giving expression to her reluctance, she declares that it is a long way to move, selling a house is a pain, and she has a lot of friends in her current town. Having had many conversations with her over the years, you also bring up her only brother who has autism and the fact that her parents are just past 70 years old. Perhaps she is worried about not being there to assume care of her brother 10 or 12 years from now? Is that a good reason to not take the job? Are there options for making this work? This may not be accurate, but it is a fair conjecture and worth asking about.

But what about our patient who has delusions of thought insertion? Perhaps you have spent enough time listening to him over the years as well and you have noticed that when he claims that the air conditioner is inserting another's thoughts into his head, it often is indicative of an imminent period of dysphoria. Fireplace thought insertions, in contrast, suggests an increase in irritability and oppositionality. If so, you might even say "Are sure you mean the air conditioner? You have been fidgety lately, which is more consistent with your believing that the fireplace is being used to insert thoughts into your head." Again, maybe not – but is a reasonable conjecture and worth asking about.

I am not claiming that understanding never involves having a sense of what it is like for the other person, far from it. What I am describing is like detective work, but it is not an impersonal inquisition. Understanding another is an affect- laden and deeply interpersonal process. For instance, as much as any other piece of information you utilize, nothing can be more useful than to follow the emotion and affect – and that does include having a sense of the other's subjectivity. But that is never separated from what else you also have learned about the person.

Perspective-taking also plays an important role in common courtesy. You are probably more likely to talk during a movie or not wait your turn in line if you fail to take the perspective of other people. But we can teach courtesy to young children; it is important but psychologically, a little cursory. Nor need perspective- taking involve reconstructing other people's thought processes. Often, it involves an awareness of the basic situations (plot elements) of life and knowing how people react to things. (Morally, however, such perspective-taking is not cursory and people don't do it as much as they should.)

Indeed, this cognitive (or conceptual) empathy is not so different from what Jaspers wrote about. Jaspers identified two different types of understanding. The first he called static understanding, the second genetic understanding. By static understanding, Jaspers seemed to mean an awareness of what we might call the basic experiences of human psychology, for example, that people enjoy it when their team wins a big game or are upset when they get rejected. We understand this directly in our own case. For others, given the proper body language and/or verbal accounts, Jaspers thought that we understand it immediately without making inferences because the experience for all of us is basically the same. According to Mike Gorski (2015), this is the kind of understanding that we cannot apply to people with delusions. Delusions are not (static) psychological universals.

Campbell, however, is writing about genetic understanding. For Jaspers, this was the understanding of the meaningful connections between people's mental states as they unfold. But according to Gorski, the "empathy" here is guided by concepts or ideal types (in Weber's sense). So, for example, people with pathological narcissism deal with intense anger and rage by regulating their emotions by adopting a (highly positive emotional) grandiose sense of self. If, however, the grandiosity is ever deflated by being challenged, what you will see is the rage until the grandiose defense is re-established. That is an understanding of meaningful connections, but it is conceptually guided; typically, you learn it initially from a book or in a lecture.

The important point for Campbell's notion of mental causation is the understandable unfolding of the connections according to normative considerations. As he notes, even when we are thinking of causality in terms of general causal laws, when we apply the laws to the particular events, we go local. When following the local psychological connections, the various potential confounds may need to be considered and ceteris paribus assumptions cannot always be made – and these complications may not be systematically represented at the neural levels of analysis. Furthermore, in genetic understanding, those connections are transitions between psychological contents such as the experience of thought insertion and subsequent beliefs about how those thoughts are being transmitted. Even if the thought insertion experience can be explained mechanistically, and the unfolding that follows supervenes on physical processes, the meaningful connections are still going to be the psychological transitions.

If, however, my suggestions about the conceptual bases of genetic understanding are valid, there is plenty of room for cognitive neuroscience and RDoC to make a difference in how we understand the unfolding, not only in terms of general causal patterns (explanation), but with respect to the psychological causal line itself. The way in which the two-system framework described earlier can alter how we understand and respond to a person's fear response is one example. In an earlier paper, Kendler and Campbell (2014) referred to this as *explanation-aided understanding*, which they saw as expansion of the boundaries for the limits of our understanding. Here, the neuroscience does not reduce the psychology; it enriches it.

REFERENCES

Egan, G. (1986) *The skilled helper: A systematic approach to effective helping.* Monterey, CA: Brooks/Cole.

Gorski, M. (2015) Karl Jaspers (1883–1969). In R. L. Cautin & S. O. Lilienfeld (Eds.), *The encyclopedia of clinical psychology* (Vol. III, pp. 1583–1589). Chichester, UK: John Wiley & Sons.

Jaspers, K. (1923/1963). *General psychopathology* (J. Hoenig & M. W. Hamilton, trans.). Chicago, IL: University of Chicago Press.

Kendler, K. S., & Campbell, J. (2014) 'Expanding the domain of the understandable in psychiatric illness: An updating of the Jasperian framework of explanation and understanding.' *Psychological Medicine*, *44*, 1–7.

LeDoux, J. E., & Pine, D. S. (2016) 'Using neuroscience to help understand fear and anxiety: A two-system framework.' *American Journal of Psychiatry*, *173*(11), 1083–1093.

Martin, D. G. (1983) *Counseling and therapy skills.* Belmont, CA: Brooks/Cole.

Popper, K. (1963) *Conjectures and refutations: The growth of scientific knowledge.* London: Routledge.

SECTION 6

16

Introduction

PETER ZACHAR

Ranging from disdain to contempt, the dissatisfaction with *DSM* and ICD categories takes many forms. Some reject the value of official, shared classifications (Caplan, 1995; Markon, 2013). Others believe that the descriptive categories of the *DSM* have prevented the discovery of successful treatments and should be replaced with constructs based on etiology and pathogenesis (Hyman, 2011; Insel, 2013). Still others question the use of diagnostic categories derived from clinical tradition and prefer a more quantitative, dimensional approach to classification (Krueger et al., 2018; Livesley, 2012). In contrast, Parnas and Zandersen deride neither the classification of psychopathology, descriptive psychopathology per se, nor the use of categories/kinds, but instead critique the use of the *DSM* symptom based, operational approach to classification in the absence of an integrative theoretical framework.

The symptom-based syndromes of the *DSM* and the ICD can be considered phenotypes, but, argue Parnas and Zandersen, these symptoms alone cannot accurately characterize phenotypes. Instead they look back to the rich tradition of description in psychiatry that was jettisoned when the operational approach was adopted with *DSM-III* in 1980.

One possible point of confusion here is that the term phenomenology can be used with two somewhat different senses in psychiatry and in philosophy. In nineteenth-century psychiatry, the observable features of a disorder were called its *clinical phenomenology*. (See Kendler's Chapter 38 for a closer look at nineteenth-century clinical phenomenology.) The alternative approach to describing the primary features of disorders that Parnas and Zandersen advocate is drawn from an early twentieth-century innovation in philosophy, called the "phenomenological" study of the structure of consciousness. Many different dimensions to the structure of consciousness have been studied by philosophical phenomenologists. In this chapter, Parnas and Zandersen look at the dimension of selfhood.

They begin with a brief review of the concepts of self and identity in the *DSM* and in psychoanalysis. These are not completely distinct due the important role played by psychoanalysis in twentieth-century American psychiatry. Generally, the various *DSM*s use concepts such as self and identity without defining them. This changed with the *DSM-5* in which the concept of the self in the Alternative *DSM-5* Model for Personality Disorders is closely based on psychodynamic conceptualizations. (See Schaffner's Chapter 32 for a summary of the Alternative *DSM-5* Model.)

In their review of psychoanalytic approaches, they emphasize Otto Kernberg's (1975) integration of the work of the ego psychologists and the object relations theorists into a multifaceted theory about disturbances in self-structure for conditions that lie in a borderline region between the neuroses and the psychoses (i.e., certain personality disorders such as borderline, schizotypal, and narcissistic). In their view, the psychoanalytic views of the self are focused mostly on the self as a relational structure. This contrasts with a phenomenological view of the self as an ongoing awareness that one exists.

Turning to philosophical phenomenology, they note that over our lifetime we can be characterized by many shifting traits, values, and relationships that are all parts of a single identity (or one self-narrative). This oneness is grounded in *how* all individual experience manifests for the person as *my experience*. They call this ground the core self as opposed to the narrative self. The core self is so fundamentally ingrained in our experience that we do not notice it, nor spontaneously describe it. However, schizophrenia involves a disturbance of the core self – and because it manifests in consciousness, the self-reports of people with schizophrenia do express that disturbance. It can, however, be tricky to differentiate between disturbances of the narrative self and disturbances of the core self, but doing so is important especially when what looks like a typical disturbance of the narrative self (such as identity uncertainty) is a manifestation of a core self-disturbance. For instance, they argue that in many cases what looks like on the surface to represent an identity disturbance for someone with a borderline personality organization may be better classified as the manifestation of core self-disturbance in someone on the schizophrenic spectrum.

Despite the long history of alterations in modes of consciousness and existence being recognized in psychiatric phenomenology, neither the *DSM*/ICD approach to psychopathology nor the more modern object relations and relational approaches to psychoanalysis have concepts referring to them, i.e., to the "how" of the experience rather than to the "what" of experience. The "how" of experience refers to the structures of subjective life that enable the emergence of symptoms. The "what" of experience is the symptomatic content such as hallucinations and delusions, feeling empty, or having poorly defined boundaries between self and others.

This failure to take disturbed structures of subjectivity into account is somewhat frustrating for Parnas because such disturbances have been "operationalized" in *The Examination of Anomalous Self-Experience Scale* (EASE) for use in empirical research. Parnas and Zandersen also raise the possibility that these types of disturbances might be conceptualized as residing on a separate "mesoscopic" level of analysis that bridges microscopic biology and macroscopic phenomenology and behavior. This sounds very much like a new kind of endophenotype. Endophenotypes were originally akin to biomarkers (Gottesman & Gould, 2003), but as the endophenotype concept has been redefined to also include latent psychological variables such as neuroticism, it can certainly incorporate core self-disturbances as well.

Shaun Gallagher is a phenomenological philosopher whose work is closely informed by empirical research in the cognitive sciences. For example, in his commentary, he alerts readers to the fact that insights about the role of the self in psychopathology can also be found in the cognitive neurosciences. He also pushes back on Parnas and Zandersen's presentation of core self-disturbances as akin to the essence of schizophrenic spectrum disturbances. As a contrast, Gallagher describes his own notion of the dynamic self-pattern. The dynamic self-pattern is constituted by a cluster of features at many levels of analysis and that are known in a variety of ways. A unique and recognizable self-pattern emerges from these features, but no feature (or combination of features) is ever an essential feature of that self-pattern (Gallagher, 2013). In Gallagher's view, any attempt to make any one feature essential is itself a kind of reductionism. With respect to clinical psychiatry, he argues that unlike in a conventional disease model, in a dynamical systems approach there is no such thing as the single correct intervention that will fix "the problem"; rather, there may be multiple ways of intervening that can then disrupt the current dynamic self-pattern in a way that leads to positive changes.

REFERENCES

Caplan, P. J. (1995) *They say you're crazy: How the world's most powerful psychiatrists decide who's normal.* Reading, MA: Addison-Wesley.

Gallagher, S. (2013) 'A pattern theory of self.' *Frontiers in Human Neuroscience, 7*, 443–443.

Gottesman, I. I., & Gould, T. D. (2003) 'The endophenotype concept in psychiatry: Etymology and strategic intentions.' *American Journal of Psychiatry, 160*, 636–645.

Hyman, S. E. (2011) 'Diagnosis of mental disorders in light of modern genetics.' In D. A. Regier, W. E. Narrow, E. A. Kuhl, & D. J. Kupfer (Eds.), *The conceptual evolution of* DSM-5 (pp. 3–17). Arlington, VA: American Psychiatric Publishing, Inc.

Insel, T. (2013) 'Director's blog: Transforming diagnosis.' Retrieved from www.nimh.nih.gov/about/director/2013/transforming-diagnosis.shtml

Kernberg, O. F. (1975) *Borderline conditions and pathological narcissism.* New York: Jason Aronson.

Krueger, R. F., Kotov, R., Watson, D., Forbes, M. K., Eaton, N. R., Ruggero, C. J., . . ., Zimmermann, J. (2018) 'Progress in achieving quantitative classification of psychopathology.' *World Psychiatry, 17*(3), 282–293.

Livesley, W. J. (2012) 'Tradition versus empiricism in the current *DSM-5* proposal for revising the classification of personality disorders.' *Criminal Behavior and Mental Health, 22*, 81–91.

Markon, K. E. (2013) 'Epistemological pluralism and scientific development: An argument against authoritative nosologies.' *Journal of Personality Disorders, 27*(5), 554–579.

17

Phenomenology of a Disordered Self in Schizophrenia: Example of an Integrative Level for Psychiatric Research

JOSEF PARNAS AND MAJA ZANDERSEN

17.1 INTRODUCTION

The contemporary discussion about levels of explanation and description in psychiatry as well as the debate between proponents of categorical and dimensional classifications are all indirectly associated with the failure of neo-Kraepelinian biological reductionism that flourished in the wake of the introduction of *DSM-III* and which was believed to result in an etiology-based *DSM-IV*. The etiological hopes associated with molecular genetic research to discover few major genes responsible for main mental disorders evaporated with the realization that psychiatric disorders are massively polygenic with limited likelihood of reductionist magic bullet. Moreover, the accumulated empirical research points to a bewildering multiplicity of risk factors for mental disorders and so far, the biological findings have not been translated into palpable progress in clinical psychiatry.

The contemporary interest in the level approach became popular because the basic neurosciences advanced very rapidly in their diverse specific domains. It is becoming obvious that in order to arrive at practically relevant models of the disorders of the mind–brain system, we need some serious integration. The venerated bio-psycho-social model has not resulted in more than an additive accumulation of biological, psychological, and social risk factors without a true comprehension of their mutual interplay (Ghaemi, 2009). The "level talk" is in a certain sense a reaction to the failure of that model. Any chance of integration between the levels presupposes some sort of integrative framework, which is itself not a purely empirical issue.

The categorical systems such as *DSM-IV* and *DSM-5* are increasingly criticized for reification of entities, high and incomprehensible levels of comorbidity, and a continual proliferation of diagnostic categories whose number now approaches 400. One of the basic problems of current classifications is that they lack a conceptual meta-structure, which could allow for rational modifications of the system with empirical progress. If a system consists of 400 *descriptively defined* categories, it must entail significant overlap with consequences for differential diagnosis. Adding any new category will have a systemic domino effect. This problem is one of the sources of extremely high comorbidity. In other words, the student of the *DSM/ICD* is not informed about the difference in *kind* between suffering from a schizotypal condition and prolonged grief disorder. Both are considered just "mental disorders".

The literature portrays the revolutionary aspects of the introduction of *DSM-III* as being a novelty in its operational definitions and abandonment of etiopathogenic theorizing behind the diagnostic classes. However, it is seldom mentioned that *DSM-III* in fact reproduced the major categories of *DSM-II* and *ICD-9* but without the clinical, theoretical, and conceptual considerations that aggregated single disorders into larger groups. As already pointed out by Andreasen (2007), the *DSM-III* revolution converted psychiatric description into simple common-sensical statements deprived of theoretical and clinical considerations (from which they originally derived), which has led to an oblivion of the rich psychopathological knowledge accumulated before *DSM-III* (Parnas & Bovet, 2015). Dimensional approaches to psychopathology are currently being proposed as a remedy (Krueger et al., 2018). Such approaches have their main origin in personality research, and it is unclear as to what extent they are applicable to psychiatric syndromes (Jablensky, 2018; Kendler, 2018).

Here we come to the basic problem of classification and integration of levels, namely the issue of the psychiatric phenotype. No matter how much neurosciences advance, the principle object of psychiatry is the state of mind of the psychiatric patient that may cause subjective suffering, interpersonal, social, or occupational dysfunction. Addressing the *phenotypic level* is therefore an indispensable prerequisite for any further investigation (Parnas, Sass, & Zahavi, 2013).

Contemporary psychiatric research considers symptoms and signs as well-demarcated ontological entities that have mutually independent object-like properties and can be unproblematically and acontextually described and quantified from the third-person perspective (Nordgaard, Sass, & Parnas, 2013; Parnas & Urfer-Parnas, 2017). In the diagnostic manuals, there is an overwhelming dominance of descriptions favoring the so-called objective, behavioral data. We have repeatedly argued that such an approach is epistemologically misguided and that psychiatric symptoms and signs are wholes or Gestalts emerging from the interaction of multiple and contextual factors (Zandersen, Henriksen, & Parnas, 2019). Moreover, psychiatry traditionally favors mental contents – e.g., the fact that the patients suffer from persecutory delusions – rather than the *modes* of experiences – i.e., the nature of delusional consciousness. The consideration of the nature of psychiatric symptoms reinforces our point made above about the importance of the meta-structure of psychiatric classification that could inform differential diagnostic distinctions between a temporary fleeting disorder, perhaps a reaction to environmental stress, and a more enduring disorder linked to more basic psychological changes (e.g., prolonged grief vs schizotypal disorder).

This brings us to our major claim, namely that the phenotypic level, over and above purely symptomatic description, requires addressing the level of the structures of subjective life that enables the emergence of symptoms and signs. Such a structural approach (phenomenal ontology) may serve as a basis for principles of meta-classification and function as an integrative axis for empirical research. How can we envisage such an ontology? Contemporary furniture of the mental is to a large degree based on surviving elements of faculty psychology, comprising in a minimal version the domains of cognitive, affective, and volitional life. Such mental faculties have a certain intuitive appeal but are based on common sense considerations dating back to antiquity. Adopting a phenomenological approach could avoid some of the pitfalls of the inherited common sense segmentation of mental life[1]. Phenomenal ontology is concerned with the modes of being of consciousness and existence (Parnas & Sass, 2008; Zahavi, 2018b), modes that constrain the mundane manifestations of psychological life, e.g., a relationship between disorder of temporality and specific symptoms of melancholia (Fuchs, 2001, 2013). At the most basic level of phenomenal ontology, we find the dimensions of intentionality, selfhood, temporality, intersubjectivity, and embodiment.

Of course, such basic ontology cannot be exhaustive or sufficient for an understanding of the psychological life. There are other structural relations which are of relevance. The psychodynamic structures such as defense mechanisms described in psychoanalytic literature probably reflect

[1] A phenomenological method should not be confused with introspectionism, which considers mental phenomena as thing-like objects. Moreover, a phenomenological study is only rarely dependent on introspective experience but more often on a potentially public experience of the world. For example, a phenomenological study of perception does not consist of some inner gaze directed to perceptual processing but to the ways in which the perceived object appears (Parnas & Sass, 2008).

a more developmentally and psychologically sophisticated level of mental functioning. Finally, psychological life is co-determined by neurocognitive functions, which in most cases, however, are constructs and not, as it is widely believed, well-demarcated *natural kinds* and the origin of those constructs goes back to faculty psychology.

In this chapter, we will illustrate how the ontological dimension of selfhood and the derived concept of identity may be useful for phenotypic distinctions and illustrate its potential for an integrative approach in psychiatric research in schizophrenia. We begin with reviewing the notion of selfhood and the closely related notion of identity as they appear in the *DSM* system. We then describe the contributions of psychoanalysis and propose a phenomenological model to which we subscribe. We will discuss two cases of schizophrenia spectrum disorders. In the concluding section, we will summarize how the study of pathologies of selfhood may contribute to scientific and clinical progress.

17.2 SELF AND IDENTITY IN THE *DSM*

In the *DSM-III*, we find a definition of identity as "the sense of self, providing a unity of personality over time" (APA, 1980, p. 361). This definition links disturbance of identity to schizophrenia, borderline personality disorder, and identity disorder but offers no definition of the term "sense of self". *DSM-IV* and *DSM-IV-TR* have no definitions of identity. Identity *disturbance* is described only as a criterion of borderline personality disorder in terms of uncertainty concerning self-image, sexual identity, career choices, values, goals, and friendship patterns. In the *DSM-5*, the alternative model for personality disorders included in section III provides a more elaborate description of identity disturbance (psychoanalytically inspired) along a severity dimension and a definition of identity as the "experience of oneself as unique, with clear boundaries between self and others; stability of self-esteem and accuracy of self-appraisal; capacity for, and ability to regulate, a range of emotional experience" (APA, 2013, p. 762). Noteworthy, none of the *DSM* editions offer a definition of the term "self".

17.3 PSYCHODYNAMIC APPROACHES TO SELFHOOD

The contemporary understanding of the notion of self in psychiatry is very much influenced by psychoanalysis despite its disappearance from psychiatric academia. In psychoanalysis, we find a range of concepts regarding self and identity, most of which come from ego psychology and object relations theory, e.g., *self representation* (Hartmann, 1950), *identity* (Erikson, 1956), *self-feeling* (Jacobson, 1964), and *cohesive self* (Kohut, 1977). Kernberg (2016) synthesizes several of these constructs and also adds a *self concept*. Likewise, concepts such as *a false self* (Winnicott, 1965), *as if personality* (Deutsch, 1942), and *identity diffusion* (Erikson, 1956; Kernberg, 1967) have been used to express a disturbance of identity or sense of self.

Identity in psychoanalytic literature refers to a theoretical construct describing a developmental process beginning in infancy, reaching a crucial period of identity *formation* in adolescence and continuing its development throughout life (Erikson, 1956; Marcia, 2006). It was Erikson who introduced and strongly influenced the term *identity* in psychoanalytic thought. In his writings, the term *identity* expresses "a mutual relation in that it connotes both a persistent sameness within oneself (self-sameness) and a persistent sharing of some kind of essential character with others" (Erikson, 1956, p. 57). A sense of identity gives a "feeling of being at home in one's body, a sense of 'knowing where one is going', and an inner assuredness of anticipated recognition from those who count" (p. 74). Although this sense of identity is not established once and for all, but something that is "constantly lost and regained" (ibid.), there is in late adolescence a configuration of identity reflecting a synthesis of earlier identifications yet transcending these particular identifications.

Identity *diffusion*, on the other hand, manifest in various features such as a disintegration of the sense of inner continuity and sameness, difficulties in committing to occupational choices, and difficulties with intimacy because of "narcissistic mirroring". Kernberg (1985) refers to identity diffusion as "the lack of an integrated self concept and an integrated and stable concept of total objects in relationship with the self" (p. 39). This formulation (apparently kept on a *sub-personal* [unconscious] level) draws on Klein's (1946) description of the mechanism of "splitting" and the association between excessive splitting and a disturbance in "the feeling of the ego", which she believed to be the roots of some forms of schizophrenia. The concept of splitting, when referring to a fundamental disintegration of self, became a core concept in the psychoanalytic descriptions of schizophrenia.

According to Kernberg, the development of *basic trust* facilitates the linking between positive and negative representations of self and others (see also Mahler, 1971). This leads to an integrated view of self and others that constitutes *normal identity*. Identity *diffusion* is a result of a failure of this developmental process. In identity diffusion, contradictory self and object images are permanently split rather than being synthesized into a more coherent image. A range of disturbances in ego functions, including defensive structures, the integrative function, and affect modulation accompany this fixation of splitting processes. With respect to the more *experiential* level, i.e., the level of phenomenal symptoms, Kernberg finds identity diffusion to be reflected in the patients' incapacity to give an integrated description of self and significant others. They are uncertain about their major interests, their behavior patterns are chaotic, and their commitments to work and other people are unstable.

Psychoanalytic writings contain rich clinical descriptions and discussions and many of those ideas can be identified in contemporary phenomenological psychopathology. It is quite clear, however, that identity in psychoanalysis is formulated mostly as a psychological structure concerning the sense of *who* one is (in relation to others). The *self* as an ongoing awareness *that* one exists has not been clearly delineated by ego psychologists as a constituent factor in the formation of identity as a psychoanalytic concept. Moreover, in psychoanalysis, the boundary between descriptions at a phenomenological (phenomenal) level of symptoms and behavior and descriptions of sub-personal, unconscious hypothetical constructs is blurred, and this constitutes a crucial problem in psychopathology and classification.

17.4 A PHENOMENOLOGICAL APPROACH TO SELFHOOD AND IDENTITY AS A STRUCTURAL LEVEL OF PSYCHOPATHOLOGY

Personal identity and selfhood are a perennial topic of philosophy. Here, we present a phenomenological approach that has been consistently used in recent psychopathological research (Zandersen & Parnas, 2019b). In a common sense psychological understanding, *personal* identity refers to a set of persisting features that identify and individuate a person. If asked on the street "who are you?" a by-passer may answer "I am John Smith" and he may proceed with a list of biographical, characterological, and cognitive characteristics. In this type of understanding, we pay no attention to the *structure* or *form* (the "how") of the underlying experience.

The French philosopher Paul Ricoeur (1992) characterized personal identity as emerging in the triangle of idem-identity (sameness), ipse-identity (selfhood), and interpersonal relations. Idem-identity, or sameness, refers to persisting yet malleable personal features such as personality traits, character, temperamental dispositions, and values, which change over the span of life in our social interactions. All these features may be expressed in linguistic (propositional) terms and may be contemplated upon in self-reflection.

The sameness of the changing idem-identity is assured by the selfhood or ipse-identity (ipse=self or itself). The *who* or the elusive subjectivity of experience remains persistent over the lifespan and is exemplified by Ricoeur with the notion of keeping a promise: If I keep a promise made when I was 20 years old until I am 80, the keeper of the promise is the *who* of personal identity. The *who* or the first-person perspective is normally never a theme or object of explicit awareness and attention but simply a tacit structure of experience. Contemporary phenomenology and cognitive science make an analogous distinction between the 'narrative' self and the 'minimal' or 'core/basic' self[2]. The notion of core self refers to the first-personal manifestation of all experience, i.e., an experience is never anonymous but manifests always itself as *my* experience. In other words, our *experiencing* articulates itself in the first-person perspective, entailing an elusive pole of self-presence as an abiding and sourcing feeling of "I-me-myself" (perhaps also addressed by Erikson in his description of self-sameness). This sense of I-me-myself is a sense of a unique but propertyless self-familiarity and identity around which the more sophisticated and personal features of identity coalesce (Hart, 2009). The concept of core self may be extended to imply a sense of self-coincidence, temporal persistence, privacy of our inner world and the "me/not me" demarcation, psychosomatic unity (embodiment), and an experience of one's being as "having begun in or around birth and liable to extinction with death" (Laing, 1960, p. 42).

It is upon this core self that the narrative self is developed in social and linguistic interactions. The core self is a prerequisite of the narrative self. It implies the *who* (in Ricoeur's term) for a person to be introverted, ambitious, and friendly. In normal experience, the structure and the content of experience are interwoven and the structure of experience usually does not become the object of our reflection (i.e., the object of experience). The by-passer John Smith mentioned above would probably not include in his answer to us that he is experiencing the world in the first-person

[2] In the philosophy of mind, there is an ongoing debate on how minimal the concept of minimal self must be (Zahavi, 2018a). Of course, certain features of core self, such as a sense of subjectivity are more fundamental than other features, e.g., embodiment. However, for our discussion and for the purpose of our presentation, we will not enter into this debate.

perspective. Patients with schizophrenia, however, can describe such structural disturbances of self-experience, e.g., various distortions of first-person perspective, incomplete sense of substantiality-embodiment, and an ephemeral sense of self-presence. In psychopathology, there may be disturbances at either one or both levels of selfhood, though also in a clinical setting these levels may not be easy to differentiate. Usually, disturbance of the structural level of selfhood, entailing an instability of the basic subject–world relation, will also manifest as disturbance of narrative features, including interpersonal functioning, emotional regulation, and direction in life. However, disturbance of the narrative level of selfhood will not in itself cause structural disorders of the core self. Being confused about career choice or being impulsive typically does not entail problems with demarcation or self-presence (see also the clinical vignette below).

As mentioned above, the features of narrative selfhood can be thematically/reflectively represented but also the features of the core self are phenomenally accessible when we reflect upon the way in which we experience something. Thus, neither the concept of narrative or core self appeals to unconscious or sub-personal structures or mechanisms, and this possibility of phenomenological descriptions makes these concepts useful in psychopathology. Below, we will demonstrate their utility with the help of two clinical vignettes.

17.5 CLINICAL ILLUSTRATION

17.5.1 Vignette 1

A 23-year-old woman, single, has a high school degree with good marks. Since then, she has been ambivalent about her future education and dropped out of two university programs. She lives in a dormitory and is on a sick leave. She was admitted to a psychiatric facility one year ago after her second suicide attempt. At this admission, she reported a tendency to act impulsively and mentioned occasional episodes of cutting herself. She described herself as sometimes agitated and restless and with difficulties sustaining relations. She felt "depressed", without energy, cried a lot without knowing any reason, and did not attend school.

During the research interview, she reported feeling different from her peers during childhood as if she was somehow "not on the same side" as them. In adolescence, this feeling has intensified and changed into a vague sense of uniqueness or superiority, perhaps being "brighter" than other people. However, she does not think that she is more intelligent than others are but that she perhaps has a better insight into the conditions of human existence. This sense of difference may change into a feeling as if in a bubble and not truly part of the world.

She has no idea who she is. When trying to describe herself, the only adjectives that come to her mind are "lazy" and "energetic". She cannot point to any specific personal values, preferences, or interests. Her "personality" solely depends on the role she chooses to take. When looking in a mirror, she sometimes has a feeling as if looking at an unfamiliar person. At times, her thoughts and feelings become somehow anonymous and "free flowing" as if not truly related to her. She also describes how her memories feel detached from her, as if her childhood was not her own but someone else's.

Her lack of identity feels as a sort of emptiness, "there is *nothing* inside of me, nothing like a *soul* or anything". She describes this emptiness as "a black hole" and as "a gap" in the middle of her chest. She senses this gap in a concrete way, specifying its size. Previously, she felt that the hole became smaller when having a boyfriend, but it was always there. Then she tried having two boyfriends at the same time, but that did not help. Now she wonders if she needs to have several simultaneous boyfriends in order to make it disappear.

The feeling of emptiness is linked to a feeling of not being at one with her body. She experiences her body only as "a tool", which is there in order for her "to walk from A to B". Her thoughts and feelings are in her head; her body is empty. At the peak of such experiences, she feels a sort of painful restlessness and anxiety without autonomic symptoms. She feels as a "fluent existence", as a "fluent blob" in the air instead of a whole person. She reports her 'I' as being so blurry that she sometimes thinks she cannot even die because there is no "core" that can be "taken out of the game". When walking on the street, she may experience that strangers stare at her and she wonders whether it is because that they can see that she is empty.

(Modified from Zandersen & Parnas, 2019b)

The patient fulfills criteria for both schizotypal and borderline personality disorder according to *DSM-5*. It is quite clear that the identity problem is the central feature of this clinical picture, affecting the patient's interpersonal life and educational career. This is evident on the level of what we have called narrative selfhood, e.g., she reports that she has no personal values, preferences, or interests. However, her identity problems seem not only to be located at the level of narrative selfhood but also to entail disturbances of a very basic and structural level of experience. For example, she experiences a pervasive sense of diminished or insecure self-presence: she has no abiding and substantial feelings of an "I/me/myself".

She expresses a fundamental difference from others. This feeling of difference is of an ontological kind which means that the patients' own being-in-the-world feels different from that of other people. This feeling becomes only secondarily thematized by some adjectives ("I am more ugly than others" etc.). In other words, the sense of difference precedes finding out *what* is different. This phenomenon has been known in German psychiatry under the term "Anderssein" (Motobayashi et al., 2016) and as quite specific to the schizophrenia spectrum disorders but practically unknown in contemporary psychiatry. It is a sense of another ontological position, which obviously the patient cannot easily conceptualize and verbalize and very often uses the vague but comprehensive term "I felt wrong". The above patient's first-person perspective becomes distorted with the ensuing anonymization of thought processes and memories, which sometimes lose the character of 'mineness'. Her ambivalence and lack of direction in life, which are manifest on the narrative level of selfhood, are in our view linked to her pervasively diminished sense of self-presence or even existence. In fact, she describes a fundamental loss of centrality of being (e.g., she feels as a fluent blob in the air). From this perspective, it is the disturbance of the core self that infuses her narrative identity with instability and a feeling of always playing a role. She describes further disturbances of the core self, comprising spatialization of experience (e.g., she senses her emptiness in a very concrete spatialized manner) and a loss of the ordinarily unproblematic sense of psychophysical unity or embodiment. Her thought processes reveal a tolerance for contradictions ("lazy" and "energetic") and psychosis-near reasoning (e.g., increasing number of boyfriends would diminish her sense of emptiness). In sum, the patient presents a range of disorders of the core self characteristic of the schizophrenia spectrum disorders (see below) with clear consequences on the level of narrative identity. In general terms, we witness a profound and persisting psychological disintegration bringing the patient close to the psychotic end of psychopathology.

17.5.2 Vignette 2

A 31-year-old, unmarried woman (always single) biochemist, works in a hospital lab. She has always been isolated and felt uncomfortable in the company of others. She always enjoyed being alone and engaged herself in "analyses", i.e., trying to think through important existential questions. Often, she could become so self-absorbed that she felt as disembodied or even non-existent. She reported two former episodes of what she calls "depression" where she stayed at home with inverted day-night rhythm, spending her time on the internet. She was admitted to a psychiatric ward because she was disturbed by thoughts about being switched at birth with another infant. Asked about her name and age, she replied that she could not answer, because she did not know who she was born as and therefore did not know her "true identity." The substitution became clear to her when, during a period of restlessness and global feelings of insecurity, she was reading some old family letters. The style of the letters and some variation in handwriting made it clear to her that the letters signaled the hidden message about her substitution as an infant. She then searched online to find her biological roots and found out that she was a secret descendant of a Jewish, mystical family known from 200 BC. She had the impression that strangers in the street knew that she was the secret descendant and that other people somehow could read her thoughts.

She was relieved to discover the explanation because she had always felt that there was something "wrong" and that something "didn't add up." She always had the feeling that she was "weird" or "just wrong," and she always had the tendency to observe herself when talking to other people as if there was an "extra consciousness" about how she should say things, how her face and hands looked. She always felt that when people were talking to her, they never addressed her true self but somehow talked "past" her: "*When people talk to me, they talk to the other child, and not the real me. That is because I'm substituted with the other child ... Communication [with other people] goes awry from the beginning because I don't have my real identity and I'm being judged as a wrong person ... There is no connection between who I am and who the other child is, they do not know who I am and I do not know it either. I couldn't explain that before. All my life, it was just a question mark: Why do I not belong?*"

As with the first patient, the problem of the sense of self and identity dominates this case, which moreover is clearly delusional and the patient fulfills criteria for schizophrenia in both *DSM-5* and *ICD-10*. Both patients describe feeling different from their peers and other people since early childhood (*Anderssein*). Our second patient also manifests a phenomenon of "involuntary self-witnessing" where the sense of subjectivity seems doubled during interaction with other people (Stephensen & Parnas, 2018). This is not an instance of self-reflection because neither of the "two consciousnesses" assumes a truly subject role in a unified reflective moment. Our patient develops what Jaspers, Schneider, and others called a primary delusion or a delusional perception. What is characteristic of this type of delusion is that it lacks a clear intentional subject–object structure;

rather it arises as a process designated by Henry Ey (1973) as alterization: It is a part of self that so to say becomes the thematic object of delusion. Typically, such delusional formation is associated with increased affective, pathic tension with atmospheric quality (Conrad, 1959). The delusion in our particular case seems to have some sort of effect of psychological resolution. Clearly, her delusion is not an epistemic statement about the world (a "false belief") but rather reflects an altered structure of the self (an "autistic-solipsistic delusion"), which is characteristic of schizophrenia (Parnas, 2004).

Thus, both patients reveal disturbances of the core self but with rather different symptomatic constellations. Although we are ignorant of pathogenetic processes that differ between those cases, it seems clear to us that in both cases the disorder of core self plays a generative role in psychopathology. Phrased differently, there is a similarity of structure or form of experience whereas there are significant differences in the manifest content of psychopathology. In our view, the disorder of self provides a phenotypic commonality between these two cases.

17.6 SELF IN SCHIZOPHRENIA: PAST AND PRESENT

17.6.1 History

Descriptions of a disturbance of identity or sense of self in schizophrenia spectrum conditions are as old as the concept of schizophrenia itself. Among the prominent German psychiatrists who considered self-disintegration as a fundamental feature of schizophrenia are Kraepelin (1899), Pick (1903), Gruhle (1929), Bleuler (1950), and Schneider (1950). In the beginning of the twentieth century, there was a line of research in the so-called Ich-Störungen, i.e., self-disorders. Bleuler (1950) reports a patient who "is not really herself, she is merely a reflection of herself" (p. 145) and other patients who report that they "can't catch up with themselves" or that they "have lost their individual self" (p. 143). Bleuler considered these disorders as part of the fundamental symptoms of schizophrenia. When Bleuler claimed that the essential feature of schizophrenia was a peculiar "alteration of thinking, feeling and relation to the external world which appears nowhere else in this particular fashion" (p. 9), or when Jaspers (1997) talked about "process phenomena" inaccessible to psychological understanding, they seem to indicate a confrontation with the illness features that are located at a *structural* level of experience. As we indicated in the previous sections, this level concerns the "how" of the experience rather than the "what" (the content) of experience. The French psychiatrist Eugene Minkowski, a pupil of Bleuler, who introduced the concept of schizophrenia in France, considered disorders of the core self as the essential feature of schizophrenia.

In the pre-*DSM-III* era, the experiential self-disorders were emphasized in articles on "pseudoneurotic schizophrenia" (Hoch & Polatin, 1949; Hoch & Cattell, 1959), referring to patients with temporally unstable clinical pictures and fluctuation of seemingly neurotic symptoms in the presence of fundamental schizophrenia symptomatology. In his existential-phenomenological study of schizoid and schizophrenic persons, Laing (1960) described their experiences of a lack of autonomous identity, personal consistency, and temporal continuity. Such disturbances were in fact part of the schizophrenia definition in the *ICD-8* and *ICD-9*, stating that schizophrenia entails "a fundamental disturbance of personality [...that] involves its most basic functions, those that give the normal person his feeling of individuality, uniqueness, and self-direction" (WHO, 1974, p. 27).

As already mentioned, in psychoanalytic literature, the notion of severe self-disturbance was seen as a part of schizophrenia psychopathology. Klein maintained that severe splitting was associated with schizophrenia. Kernberg's concept of borderline personality organization applies to several psychosis-near categories such as paranoid, schizoid (and presumably schizotypal) personality disorders.

17.6.2 Contemporary Research

During the last 20 years, disorders of selfhood have been conceptualized as *structural changes of the patient's self*, operating at a non-thematic level of consciousness (the 'ipseity disturbance model' [Sass & Parnas, 2003]). The scientific interest in self-disorders was motivated by clinical experience with first-admission schizophrenia spectrum patients (Parnas et al., 1998; Møller & Husby, 2000). In 2005, a psychometric instrument to identify and register clinical phenomena such as disorder of core self was published (The Examination of Anomalous Self-Experience Scale [EASE]; Parnas et al., 2005). It was a product of a cooperation among Danish, German, and Norwegian psychiatrists with input from the philosophy of mind and philosophical phenomenology. The EASE contains five domains of experience (stream of consciousness, self-presence, embodiment, transitivism, and existential reorientations). The first two domains of the EASE reflect most closely a disordered sense of subjectivity and individuality, whereas the subsequent three domains contain items covering consequential experiences in the domain of demarcation, embodiment, and world relation.

The EASE scale has been used in series of empirical studies. These studies have shown that self-disorders selectively hyper-aggregate in schizophrenia and schizotypal disorder but not in bipolar psychosis and other non-psychotic disorders (e.g., Parnas, Handest, Sæbye, & Jansson, 2003; Parnas, Handest, Jansson, & Sæbye, 2005; Raballo, Sæbye, & Parnas, 2009; Raballo & Parnas, 2010; Haug et al., 2012; Raballo & Parnas, 2012; Nordgaard & Parnas, 2014; Raballo et al., 2016). An Australian study (Nelson, Thompson, & Yung, 2012) demonstrated that self-disorders predict psychotic breakdown in ultra-high-risk individuals. A recent prospective study of non-psychotic adolescents predicted schizophrenia spectrum disorder seven years later (Koren et al., in press). Three independent studies demonstrated a highly significant moderate stability and similarity of pattern of self-disorders across the span of five to seven years (Parnas et al., 2011; Nordgaard et al., 2017, 2018). Two recent studies have demonstrated the value of self-disorders in differential diagnosis. In the first study (Zandersen & Parnas, 2019a), a thorough psychopathological examination of a group of patients treated for borderline personality disorder (BPD) in an outpatient clinic revealed that more than two-third of the sample in fact fulfilled the criteria for schizophrenia spectrum disorders (schizophrenia and schizotypal [personality] disorder). These patients had significantly elevated EASE scores comparable to those reported from previous studies of schizophrenia spectrum patients. In the second study (Rasmussen, Nordgaard, & Parnas, 2019), a similar examination of a clinical sample of patients with obsessive-compulsive disorder (OCD) showed that two-third of the sample also fulfilled the criteria of schizophrenia, other non-organic psychosis, or schizotypal personality disorder. Also in this study, the schizophrenia spectrum subgroup scored significantly higher on the EASE-scale and with severity levels comparable to those typically identified in the schizophrenia spectrum. Both BPD and OCD represent disorders, whose definitions have been gradually expanded in the *DSM* to include patients with psychotic or near-psychotic symptoms. The results from these studies point to a potential usefulness of self-disorders as a differential diagnostic tool.

In sum, the empirical research is consistent with the hypothesis that self-disorders constitute the core phenotype of schizophrenia. One could perhaps consider this statement as a banality or a tautology since the very concept of schizophrenia was constitutively associated with the clinical evidence of self-disintegration (Bleuler, 1950). Accordingly, hebephrenia or disorganized schizophrenia was phenotypically considered the most characteristic form of schizophrenia. Unfortunately, this diagnosis is today extremely rarely used and such patients are frequently misdiagnosed as suffering from BPD (Parnas, 2012; Zandersen, Henriksen, & Parnas, 2019). Likewise, the concept of schizotypal disorder, originally evolved from Bleuler's idea of fundamental symptoms, is rarely clinically used (Nordgaard, Jessen, Sæbye, & Parnas, 2016) and is increasingly blurred and blending with other personality disorders and neurotic conditions (Zandersen, Henriksen, & Parnas, 2019; Zandersen & Parnas, 2019b).

17.7 DISCUSSION AND CONCLUSIONS

The history of clinical research in schizophrenia has been characterized by many attempts to articulate a specific clinical core of this condition. (For a more detailed account, see Parnas, 2011.) Bleuler's concept of fundamental symptoms and especially autism was one of these attempts. Rümke (1958) talked about the praecox feeling, phenomenologists talked about fundamentally altered existential structures (*Daseinsweise*) (Wyrsch, 1946; Krauss, 1999), and Schneider (1950) listed the so-called first-rank symptoms considered as qualitatively changed modes of experience. Another aspect of the concept of schizophrenia was a nearly universal recognition of the fact that schizophrenia was a disorder of a different ontological kind than other mental disorders such as depression, anxiety, or phobias. However, both the specificity of the phenotype and the question of the ontological order were difficult to articulate because of insufficient conceptual resources (Parnas, 2011).

If our assumption of the structural disorders of core self as the most essential feature of the schizophrenia spectrum is correct, then it provides a conceptual and pragmatic tool to address the issue of specificity and ontological order. The contemporary concept of schizophrenia is basically dependent on delusions and hallucinations with the regrettable oblivion of basic expressive and experiential phenomena, and previous and sophisticated distinctions of the psychotic symptomatology. There is a general pressure to replace the concept of schizophrenia with the generic concept of psychosis which is probably detrimental to research and treatment because it homogenizes qualitatively different phenomena. The concept of structural disorders of self provides a phenotypic indicator of specificity and thus determines the boundaries of the schizophrenia spectrum. As the research in borderline conditions (Zandersen & Parnas, 2019a), obsessive-compulsive disorder (Rasmussen, Nordgaard, & Parnas, 2019), and most recently autistic spectrum disorders (Nilsson et al., 2019) indicates, the phenotype of self-disorder may provide a useful marker of differentiation between the cases truly belonging to the schizophrenia spectrum and those which are most likely outside. It seems, therefore, that a structural approach (in our case the disorders of the self) may provide a rational tool for an erection of a meta-structure of classification with important consequences also for the empirical research into the determinance of mental disorders. For example, one could envisage a differentiation between the disorders in which there is an apparent alteration of basic ontological structures (Fuchs, 2013, 2018) and disorders which reflect involvement of more sophisticated mental structures including cognitive dysfunctions. Thus, in addition to the level of surface symptoms, neurobiological processes, and neurocognitive functions, there is a subtle phenotypic level of ontological structures which may constitute an intermediate level ("mesoscopic level"; Roy, Petitot, Pachoud, & Varela, 1999) of description and explanation, serving as a binding element between biology ("microscopic level") and phenomenality and behavior ("macroscopic level").

Research in pathogenesis of schizophrenia has advanced the so-called neurodevelopmental hypothesis, supported by a multitude of behavioral data from the prospective high-risk studies (Parnas, Bovet, & Innocenti, 1996). Typically, the neurodevelopmental hypothesis has been studied solely on a biological level with different theories concerning neuronal migration, pruning, maturation, and even degeneration, etc. The notion of self-disorders as a fundamental feature of schizophrenia opens up a possibility of a more interdisciplinary study of not only neural but the concomitant psychological development in schizophrenia. The disordered self must have its specific ontogenesis, also involving environmental interactions with caregivers early in life. The formation of the human self is very much dependent on the adequacy of early preverbal contact to caregivers involving reciprocity, rhythmicity, and predictability (Stern, 1985).

The notion of structure is also of value in pathogenetic theorizing about mental causation involved in evolution of symptoms. On the basis of social network analyses, it has been proposed that it is unnecessary to postulate separate dysfunctional neurobiological modules or networks for the evolution of symptoms. Rather, the evolution of symptoms is understandable from the relations between the symptoms. The most frequent example cited is that fatigue may lead to lowered mood. In this case, we do not need to postulate separate mechanisms for each of the symptoms but only concentrate on those, which apparently play a generative role. What is interesting about this model is that it narrows the gap between Jaspers' notion of understanding and explanation. Understanding implies empathic grasps of meaningful psychological connections, whereas explanation is concerned with neurobiological causal mechanisms. The introduction of structure and structural disorders narrows this gap even more and probably in a more sophisticated and fruitful way. This illustrates that the analysis of the mesoscopic level has a relevance both to explanation and understanding. For instance, difficulties with self-demarcation may be conductive to passivity phenomena of external influence. In fact, a recent study (Nelson et al., 2019) showed a high correlation between disorders of core self and experimentally measured source monitoring deficits. A similar line of thinking may be applied to other Schneiderian first-rank symptoms such as primary delusion (see above) (Parnas & Henriksen, 2016) and hallucinations (Parnas & Urfer-Parnas, 2017).

In conclusion, we think that psychopathology is enriched by a phenomenological approach, which enables us with access to subjective experience and the conceptual means to articulate the empirical findings. We have tried to demonstrate how the notion of selfhood may be thought of as playing a crucial role in solving classification issues and aiding neuroscientific research in relation to the schizophrenia spectrum conditions. In more general terms, we have proposed that psychopathology needs to concern itself with the phenotypic level of psychological structures, which may turn out indispensable in a construction of rational classification of mental disorders and provide integrative levels for etiological research.

REFERENCES

American Psychiatric Association. (1980) *Diagnostic and statistical manual of mental disorders*, 3rd ed. Washington: American Psychiatric Association.

(2013) *Diagnostic and statistical manual of mental disorders*, 5th ed. Arlington: American Psychiatric Association.

Andreasen, N. C. (2007) "*DSM* and the death of phenomenology in America: An example of unintended consequences." *Schizophrenia Bulletin*, *33*(1), 108–112.

Bleuler, E. (1950) *Dementia praecox or the group of schizophrenias* (trans. J. Zinkin). New York: International Universities Press.

Conrad, K. (1959) *Die Beginnende Schizophrenie*. Stuttgart: Thieme.

Deutsch, H. (1942) "Some forms of emotional disturbance and their relationship to schizophrenia." *The Psychoanalytic Quarterly*, *11*(3), 301–321.

Erikson, E. H. (1956) "The problem of ego identity." *Journal of the American Psychoanalytic Association*, *4*(1), 56–121.

Ey, H. (1973) *Traité des Hallucinations*. Paris: Masson.

Fuchs, T. (2018) *The ecology of the brain: The phenomenology and biology of the embodied mind.* Oxford: Oxford University Press.
(2001) "Melancholia as a desynchronization: Towards a psychopathology of interpersonal time." *Psychopathology, 34*(4), 179–186.
(2013) "Temporality and psychopathology." *Phenomenology and the Cognitive Sciences, 12*(1), 75–104.
Ghaemi, N. S. (2009) *The rise and fall of the biopsychosocial model: Reconciling art and science in psychiatry.* Baltimore: Johns Hopkins University Press.
Gruhle, H. W. (1929) *Psychologie der Schizophrenie.* Berlin: Springer.
Hart, J. (2009) *Who one is. Meontology of the "I": A transcendental phenomenology.* Berlin: Springer.
Hartmann, H. (1950) "Comments on the psychoanalytic theory of the ego." *The Psychoanalytic Study of the Child, 5*(1), 74–96.
Haug, E., Lien, L., Raballo, A., Bratlien, U., Øie, M., Andreassen, O. A., . . . Møller, P. (2012) "Selective aggregation of self-disorders in first-treatment *DSM-IV* schizophrenia spectrum disorders." *The Journal of Nervous and Mental Disease, 200*(7), 632–636.
Hoch, P. H., & Cattell, J. P. (1959) "The diagnosis of pseudoneurotic schizophrenia." *Psychiatric Quarterly, 33*(1), 17–43.
Hoch, P., & Polatin, P. (1949) "Pseudoneurotic forms of schizophrenia." *Psychiatric Quarterly, 23*(2), 248–276.
Jablensky, A. (2018) "The dialectic of quantity and quality in psychopathology." *World Psychiatry, 17*(3), 300–301.
Jacobson, E. (1964) *The self and the object world.* New York: International Universities Press.
Jaspers, K. (1997) *General psychopathology* (trans. J. Hoenig & M. W. Hamilton). London: John Hopkins.
Kendler, K. S. (2018) "Classification of psychopathology: Conceptual and historical background." *World Psychiatry, 17*(3), 241–242.
Kernberg, O. F. (1985) *Borderline conditions and pathological narcissism.* Northvale: Jason Aronson.
Kernberg, O. (1967) "Borderline personality organization." *Journal of the American Psychoanalytic Association, 15*(3), 641–685.
(2016) "What is personality?" *Journal of Personality Disorders, 30*(2), 145–156.
Klein, M. (1946) "Notes on some schizoid mechanisms." *International Journal of Psycho-Analysis, 27*, 99–110.
Kohut, H. (1977) *The restoration of the self.* Chicago: The University of Chicago Press.
Koren, D. (in press) "Basic self-disturbance in adolescence predicts schizophrenia-spectrum disorders in young adulthood: A 7-year follow-up study among non-psychotic treatment-seeking adolescents." *Schizophrenia.* https://doi.org/10.1016/j.schres.2019.12.022
Kraepelin, E. (1899) Psychiatrie: Ein Lehrbuch für Studirende und Aerzte, 6. Auflage. Leipzig: Johann Ambrosius Barth.
Krauss, A. (1999) "The significance of intuition for the diagnosis of schizophrenia." In M. Maj & N. Sartorius (Eds.), *Schizophrenia* (pp. 47–49). Chichester: John Wiley & Sons.

Krueger, R. F., Kotov, R., Watson, D., Forbes, M. K., Eaton, N. R., Ruggero, C. J., . . . Bagby, R. M. (2018) "Progress in achieving quantitative classification of psychopathology." *World Psychiatry, 17*(3), 282–293.

Laing, R. D. (1960) *The divided self: An existential study in sanity and madness.* London: Penguin Books.

Mahler, M. S. (1971) "A study of the separation-individuation process: And its possible application to borderline phenomena in the psychoanalytic situation." *The Psychoanalytic Study of the Child, 26*(1), 403–424.

Marcia, J. E. (2006) "Ego identity and personality disorders." *Journal of Personality Disorders, 20*(6), 577–596.

Motobayashi, Y., Parnas, J., Motobayashi, Y., Kimura, B., & Toda, D. L. (2016) "The 'schizophrenic' in the self-consciousness of schizophrenic patients", by Mari Nagai (1990). *History of Psychiatry, 27*(4), 493–503.

Møller, P., & Husby, R. (2000) "The initial prodrome in schizophrenia: Searching for naturalistic core dimensions of experience and behavior." *Schizophrenia Bulletin, 26*(1), 217–232.

Nelson, B., Lavoie, S., Gaweda, L., Li, E., Sass, L. A., Koren, D., . . . Allott, K. (2019) "Testing a neurophenomenological model of basic self disturbance in early psychosis." *World Psychiatry, 18*(1), 104–105.

Nelson, B., Thompson, A., & Yung, A. R. (2012) "Basic self-disturbance predicts psychosis onset in the ultra high risk for psychosis 'prodromal' population." *Schizophrenia Bulletin, 38*(6), 1277–1287.

Nilsson, M., Arnfred, S., Carlsson, J., Nylander, L., Pedersen, L., Mortensen, E. L., Handest, P. (2019) "Self-disorders in Asperger syndrome compared to schizotypal disorder: A clinical study." *Schizophrenia Bulletin.* https://doi.org/10.1093/schbul/sbz036

Nordgaard, J., Handest, P., Vollmer-Larsen, A., Sæbye, D., Pedersen, J. T., & Parnas, J. (2017) "Temporal persistence of anomalous self-experience: A 5 years follow-up." *Schizophrenia Research, 179*, 36–40.

Nordgaard, J., Jessen, K., Sæbye, D., & Parnas, J. (2016) "Variability in clinical diagnoses during the ICD-8 and ICD-10 era." *Social Psychiatry and Psychiatric Epidemiology, 51*(9), 1293–1299.

Nordgaard, J., Nilsson, L. S., Sæbye, D., & Parnas, J. (2018) "Self-disorders in schizophrenia-spectrum disorders: A 5-year follow-up study." *European Archives of Psychiatry and Clinical Neuroscience, 268*(7), 713–718.

Nordgaard, J., & Parnas, J. (2014) "Self-disorders and the schizophrenia spectrum: A study of 100 first hospital admissions." *Schizophrenia Bulletin, 40*(6), 1300–1307.

Nordgaard, J., Sass, L. A., & Parnas, J. (2013) "The psychiatric interview: Validity, structure, and subjectivity." *European Archives of Psychiatry and Clinical Neuroscience, 263*, 353–364.

Parnas, J. (2004) "Belief and pathology of self-awareness a phenomenological contribution to the classification of delusions." *Journal of Consciousness Studies, 11*(10–11), 148–161.

(2011) "A disappearing heritage: The clinical core of schizophrenia." *Schizophrenia Bulletin, 37*(6), 1121–1130.

(2012) "*DSM-IV* and the founding prototype of schizophrenia: Are we regressing to a pre-Kraepelinian nosology?" In K. S. Kendler & J. Parnas (Eds.), *Philosophical issues in psychiatry II: Nosology* (pp. 237–259). Oxford: Oxford University Press.

Parnas, J., & Bovet, P. (2015) "Psychiatry made easy: Operation(al)ism and some of its consequences." In K. S. Kendler & J. Parnas (Eds.), *Philosophical issues in psychiatry III: The nature and sources of historical change* (pp. 190–212). Oxford: Oxford University Press.

Parnas, J., Bovet, P., & Innocenti, G. M. (1996) "Schizophrenic trait features, binding, and cortico-cortical connectivity: A neurodevelopmental pathogenetic hypothesis." *Neurology, Psychiatry and Brain Research, 4*(4), 185–196.

Parnas, J., Handest, P., Jansson, L., & Sæbye, D. (2005) "Anomalous subjective experience among first-admitted schizophrenia spectrum patients: Empirical investigation." *Psychopathology, 38*(5), 259–267.

Parnas, J., Handest, P., Sæbye, D., & Jansson, L. (2003) "Anomalies of subjective experience in schizophrenia and psychotic bipolar illness." *Acta Psychiatrica Scandinavica, 108*(2), 126–133.

Parnas, J., & Henriksen, M. G. (2016) "Mysticism and schizophrenia: A phenomenological exploration of the structure of consciousness in the schizophrenia spectrum disorders." *Consciousness and Cognition, 43*, 75–88.

Parnas, J., Jansson, L., Sass, L. A., & Handest, P. (1998) "Self-experience in the prodromal phases of schizophrenia: A pilot study of first-admissions." *Neurology Psychiatry and Brain Research, 6*(2), 97–106.

Parnas, J., Møller, P., Kircher, T., Thalbitzer, J., Jansson, L., Handest, P., & Zahavi, D. (2005) "EASE: Examination of anomalous self-experience." *Psychopathology, 38*(5), 236–258.

Parnas, J., Raballo, A., Handest, P., Jansson, L., Vollmer-Larsen, A., & Sæbye, D. (2011) "Self-experience in the early phases of schizophrenia: Five-year follow-up of the Copenhagen Prodromal Study." *World Psychiatry, 10*(3), 200–204.

Parnas, J., & Sass, L. A. (2008) "Varieties of 'phenomenology': On description, understanding, and explanation in psychiatry." In K. S. Kendler & J. Parnas (Eds.), *Philosophical issues in psychiatry: Explanation, phenomenology, and nosology* (pp. 239–278). Baltimore: John Hopkins University Press.

Parnas, J., Sass, L. A., & Zahavi, D. (2013) "Rediscovering psychopathology: The epistemology and phenomenology of the psychiatric object." *Schizophrenia Bulletin, 39*(2), 270–277.

Parnas, J., & Urfer-Parnas, A. (2017) "The ontology and epistemology of symptoms: The case of auditory verbal hallucinations in schizophrenia." In K. S. Kendler & J. Parnas (Eds.), *Philosophical issues in psychiatry IV: Classification of psychiatric illness* (pp. 201–216). Oxford: Oxford University Press.

Pick, A. (1903) "Zur Pathologie des Ich-Bewusstseins." *European Archives of Psychiatry and Clinical Neuroscience, 38*(1), 22–33.

Raballo, A., Pappagallo, E., Dell'Erba, A., Lo Cascio, N., Patane', M., Gebhardt, E., . . . & Girardi, P. (2016) "Self-disorders and clinical high risk for psychosis: An empirical study in help-seeking youth attending community mental health facilities." *Schizophrenia Bulletin, 42*(4), 926–932.

Raballo, A., & Parnas, J. (2012) "Examination of anomalous self-experience: Initial study of the structure of self-disorders in schizophrenia spectrum." *The Journal of Nervous and Mental Disease*, *200*(7), 577–583.

(2010) "The silent side of the spectrum: Schizotypy and the schizotaxic self." *Schizophrenia Bulletin*, *37*(5), 1017–1026.

Raballo, A., Sæbye, D., & Parnas, J. (2009) "Looking at the schizophrenia spectrum through the prism of self-disorders: An empirical study." *Schizophrenia Bulletin*, *37*(2), 344–351.

Rasmussen, A. R., Nordgaard, J., & Parnas, J. (2019) "Schizophrenia-spectrum psychopathology in obsessive-compulsive disorder: An empirical study." *European Archives of Psychiatry and Clinical Neuroscience*. https://doi.org/10.1007/s00406-019-01022-z

Roy, J-M., Petitot, J., Pachoud, B., & Varela, F. J. (1999) "Beyond the gap: An introduction to naturalizing phenomenology." In J-M. Roy, J. Petitot, B. Pachoud, & F. J. Varela (Eds.), *Naturalizing phenomenology: Issues in contemporary phenomenology and cognitive science* (pp. 1–80). Stanford: Stanford University Press.

Ricoeur, P. (1992) *Oneself as another*. Chicago: The University of Chicago Press.

Rümke, H. C. (1958) "Die klinische Differenzierung innerhalb der Gruppe der Schizophrenien." *Der Nervenarzt*, *29*, 40–53.

Sass, L. A., & Parnas, J. (2003) "Schizophrenia, consciousness, and the self." *Schizophrenia Bulletin*, *29*(3), 427–444.

Schneider, K. (1950) *Klinische Psychopathologie* (3. Vermehrte Auflage der Beiträge zur Psychiatrie ed.). Stuttgart: Thieme.

Stephensen, H., & Parnas, J. (2018) "What can self-disorders in schizophrenia tell us about the nature of subjectivity? A psychopathological investigation." *Phenomenology and the Cognitive Sciences*, *17*(4), 629–642.

Stern, D. N. (1985) *The interpersonal world of the infant: A view from psychoanalysis and developmental psychology*. New York: Basic Books.

World Health Organization (WHO). (1974) *Glossary of mental disorders and guide to their classification: For use in conjunction with the International Classification of Diseases, 8th Revision*. Geneva: WHO.

Winnicott, D. W. (1965) *The maturational processes and the facilitating environment*. London: Hogarth Press.

Wyrsch, J. (1946) "Über die Intuition bei der Erkennung der Schizophrenen." *Schweizerische Med Wochenschrift*, *46*, 1173–1176.

Zahavi, D. (2018a) "Consciousness, self-consciousness, selfhood: A reply to some critics." *Review of Philosophy and Psychology*, *9*(3), 703–718.

(2018b) *Phenomenology: The basics*. London: Routledge.

Zandersen, M., Henriksen M. G., & Parnas, J. (2019) "A recurrent question: What is borderline?" *Journal of Personality Disorders*, *33*(3), 341–369.

Zandersen, M., & Parnas, J. (2019a) "Borderline personality disorder or a disorder within the schizophrenia spectrum? A psychopathological study." *World Psychiatry*, *18*(1), 109–110.

(2019b) "Identity disturbance, feelings of emptiness, and the boundaries of the schizophrenia spectrum." *Schizophrenia Bulletin*, *45*(1), 106–113.

18

Who Is the Psychiatric Subject?

SHAUN GALLAGHER

One motivation for framing our understanding of psychopathology in terms of symptoms rather than broad categories of disorders concerns the specificity required for doing science. Schizophrenia is perhaps the clearest example. As Chris Frith explains, each case of schizophrenia "is so different from the next that it is difficult to say what they have in common. Schizophrenia is so varied in its manifestations and course that some [psychiatrists] have questioned whether it is a single entity at all" (1992, p. 3). Not only are disorders ill defined, requiring us to think of them in terms of spectrums rather than neatly delineated categories, but also patients often present with co-morbidities. Hence, it seems much more precise to specify the symptom or set of symptoms that manifest in any particular patient, and to take the symptom as the *explanandum*. Indeed, once we have a precisely defined symptom, it is easier to think about its underlying etiology, which leads to even more productive precisions at the levels of neurons and genes. This opens the door to scientific explanation. The direction of explanatory and diagnostic analysis is clear: start with a symptom and then descend to the subpersonal material processes that underpin it. This approach also offers some *rough* directions for treatment, primarily in terms of medications that can address the neurological aspects of the disorders. 'Rough' so far because much of the precision is still a promise rather than a reality. And whether science will deliver on the promise will ultimately depend on understanding how the brain works – which may be very different from our current understanding.

Parnas and Zandersen push back on this type of scientific reductionism. Although it may be useful in some regards to gain neuronal specificity or genetic specificity, these gains must not be won by losing the experiential specificity of the existential subjects who are manifesting the symptoms. As they put it, their major claim is that working at "the phenotypic level, over and above purely symptomatic description, requires addressing the level of the structures of subjective life that enable the emergence of symptoms and signs." Importantly, this is not to give up the scientific quest for diagnosis and explanation, but is a necessary part of this quest of which we should not lose track. Symptoms and behavioral signs come along with "a phenomenal ontology," a set of experiential structures that involve personal-level phenomena such as embodiment, temporality, intentionality, selfhood, and intersubjectivity. What's at stake is not the life of the gene or the neuron; it's the life of the patient. Parnas and Zandersen focus specifically on the notion of selfhood as an attempt to define who the psychiatric subject is.

As they note, the various editions of the *DSM* fail to offer a systematic definition of self; indeed, mentions of self-related phenomena are scarce and scattered among discussions of identity and things like self-esteem and self-appraisal. In psychiatric theory and practice, Parnas and Zandersen suggest that psychoanalytic concepts have been important. It is also the case that more recently cognitivist models have been informing psychiatry – models of self that are framed in terms of brain function, comparators, predictive processing, and so on (e.g., Northoff, 2007, 2014; Picard & Friston, 2014). In any case, as Parnas and Zandersen note, the existential concept of "the *self* as an ongoing awareness *that* one exists" is ignored.

To approach this idea, they turn to a phenomenological analysis of personal identity and the structure of experience, the most basic aspect of which is ipseity or the first-person minimal (core, basic) experiential aspect of self. Some accounts of the minimal self include a sense of ownership and/or a sense of agency (Cermolacce, Naudin, & Parnas, 2007; Frith & Gallagher, 2002; Gallagher, 2000). As Parnas and Zandersen point out, we can learn some things about these minimal aspects of self when they break down, as in cases of schizophrenia. Problems and disruptions in the narrative aspect of self also reflect these anomalous experiences at the level of ipseity. Importantly, both minimal and narrative aspects of self manifest themselves consciously and this provides an opportunity for phenomenological analysis.

In the analysis of their vignettes, Parnas and Zandersen focus on the "very basic and structural level of experience." At the same time, they acknowledge the complexity of the subject's situation and in fact throughout the vignettes and their analysis, one finds a number of different dimensions or variables related to the self. In the first vignette, for example, we find a description of the person's situation, including her educational background and her current treatment. We also find descriptions of her behavior (cutting, impulsive actions), her affective experience (feeling agitated, restless, depressed, alienated), her social relations (including her relations with boyfriends), her sense of embodiment, and her self-concept and self-narrative. Some issues might be characterized as cognitive, the "anonymization of thought processes and memories," but, as Parnas and Zandersen point out, these are also clearly about the very basic sense of 'mineness' and lack of self-presence. The vignette is short and incomplete, of course, and there are likely other important aspects of this person's existence that are relevant for clinical understanding. But we already can discern disruptions or anomalies across a pattern of aspects, and not just with respect to the minimal level of experience. To get a full picture, one needs to recognize a pattern of the many variables that make up her life. This pattern is a set of relations between her basic self-experience, her behavior, her intersubjective interactions, her life-situation, her self-concept, her cognitive processes, her narrative, etc. All of these variables and their dynamical relations are what I call a self-pattern that would be relatively unique to that person (Gallagher, 2013; Gallagher & Daly, 2018). The different "symptomatic constellations" in the subject of the second vignette is to be expected as part of a different self-pattern even if there is some structural similarity with the first in the form of experience.

One can attempt to grasp the self-pattern through the lens of any one of these variables – through a phenomenology of basic embodied and affective experiences, for example. In addition, the narrative aspect may reflect all of the other aspects; it thus offers an excellent analytic (and perhaps even a therapeutic) tool. Any attempt to reduce the complexity of the dynamic self-pattern to just one variable, however, is a form of reductionism, not so different from an attempt to explain everything in terms of neuronal processes or genetics. Reductionism lends itself to a particular conception of etiology, that is, a standard one-way, bottom-up, or top-down account where processes at one level will account for processes at another level. In contrast, thinking of the self in terms of a pattern of variables offers a different way of thinking about causality and about levels. Causality may in fact be dynamically reciprocal and loopy. For example, problems in early social relations may lead to distorted ipseity experience, or disruptions in the sense of agency, which may lead to further problems with intersubjective interactions and to problems with self-concept that show up in both the content and the formal structure of narrative. These different factors or variables form a kind of dynamical gestalt such that an intervention on any one variable can upset the dynamical organization of the pattern and have multiple recursive effects on the other variables. Thinking of the pattern in terms of a gestalt is clearly quite different from thinking of it in terms of hierarchical levels. In a gestalt, there is no top or bottom.

None of this downplays the importance of the existential-phenomenological approach since this provides the important inside story of how precisely these changes to the self-pattern are experienced by the patient. More than that, phenomenological analysis offers rich insights about certain twists and turns in this experience, examples of which Parnas and Zandersen indicate under the headings of *Anderssein*, alterization, self-witnessing, spatialization of experience, and so on. The notion of a self-pattern lends itself to taking into account multiple perspectives, that is, first-, second-, and third-person perspectives in psychiatric explanation, diagnosis, and therapy. With respect to the latter, one can think of therapeutic practices as interventions made on different variables of the self-pattern: bodily interventions (as in movement therapy); narrative interventions; cognitive-behavioral interventions; social and situational interventions (which may involve changing the patient's environment or field of affordances) (Gallagher, 2018). Given the variability of symptoms across individual self-patterns, the type of phenomenological analysis that Parnas and Zandersen outline may give us a good idea of precisely which type of therapeutic intervention would be appropriate in each case.

REFERENCES

Cermolacce, M., Naudin, J., & Parnas, J. (2007) "The 'minimal self' in psychopathology: Re-examining the self-disorders in the schizophrenia spectrum." *Consciousness and Cognition, 16*(3), 703–714.

Frith, C. (1992) *The neuropsychology of schizophrenia*. London: Psychology Press.

Frith, C., & Gallagher, S. (2002) "Models of the pathological mind." *Journal of Consciousness Studies* 9(4), 57–80.

Gallagher, S. (2000) "Philosophical conceptions of the self: Implications for cognitive science." *Trends in Cognitive Sciences* 4(1), 14–21.

(2013) "A pattern theory of self." *Frontiers in Human Neuroscience* 7(443), 1–7.

(2018) "The therapeutic reconstruction of affordances." *Res Philosophica* 95(4), 719–736.

Gallagher, S., & Daly, A. (2018) "Dynamical relations in the self-pattern." *Frontiers in Psychology* 9, 664.

Northoff, G. (2007) "Psychopathology and pathophysiology of the self in depression – Neuropsychiatric hypothesis." *Journal of Affective Disorders* 104(1–3), 1–14.

(2014) "How is our self altered in psychiatric disorders? A neurophenomenal approach to psychopathological symptoms." *Psychopathology* 47(6), 365–376.

Picard, F., & Friston, K. (2014) "Predictions, perception, and a sense of self." *Neurology* 83(12), 1112–1118.

SECTION 7

19

Introduction

KENNETH S. KENDLER

This chapter provides a broad overview of the reductionism – anti-reductionism debate that has continued to boil in the field of psychopathology research over the last few decades. Miller and Bartholomew (M&B) touch on many themes with clarity and some passion.

As Miller has done in past papers (see especially this wonderful review [Miller, 2010]), M&B point out the excesses in "brain-talk" that have characterized many recent pronouncements from the NIMH and NIDA. I have often pondered what is meant and what might be learned from these statements which usually take the form of "Schizophrenia (or panic disorder or drug abuse) is a **brain** disease." At one level, unless you are a dualist, this is a self-evident claim. Where else in the body might these disorders be biologically instantiated? For alcoholism, the liver probably plays a non-trivial role, but schizophrenia?

But that doesn't capture it entirely. Often, in coded words, this claim seems to mean "Schizophrenia is **only** a brain disease." As M&B point out, this is an incoherent claim. Many of the criteria for this disorder (symptoms such as auditory hallucinations and delusions) derive from first-person reports of patients about their mental experiences. Perhaps eliminative materialist would disagree, but common sense surely suggests that such symptoms exist in mental space, as manifestations of mind.

Another covert meaning of this claim can be understood from the perspective of the "disciplinary" definition of levels (see essay by Woodward, Chapter 35). That is, what this claim ("Schizophrenia is a brain disease") really means is that "Schizophrenia *belongs* to neuroscience and soft-headed clinical psychologists and psychiatrists should stay away from studying it and, certainly, not expect to get any grant funding to do so." A final meaning for this claim, made more often by patient advocates than NIMH officials – and the one with which I have the most sympathy – is as a cry for respect. When the National Alliance of Mental Illness claims that "Schizophrenia is a Brain Disease," I think this is a code that means: i) This is a real disorder and those suffering from it deserve respect and not stigma and ii) Insurance companies should treat it as a real disorder and reimburse at full rates just like strokes, cancer, and diabetes.

As is likely clear by now, M&B vigorously stake out the anti-reductionist perspective. They give a brief history of this recent debate in the psychopathology circle, and conclude, correctly in my opinion, that the reductionist wave has crested and is somewhat receding. Congruent with my own view on these matters, they do not take the opposite extreme (that brain research on mental illness is useless) but seem to settle on what I would consider the "sweet-spot" of explanatory pluralism, that there are a number of valid scientific approaches to psychopathology including reductionists' molecular neuroscience and molecular genetics. The real problem with the hard-biological reductionists in our field is not their advocacy for the value of molecular and systems neuroscience research, but their claim that that is the only valid approach and the only one in which NIH or other large-scale funders should invest.

They put the current debate in a broader historical context, noting that Griesinger in mid-nineteenth-century Germany initiated a first version of hard reductionism for psychiatric disorders. They could also have cited the increasing use by Karl Japers and others of the lovely phrase "brain mythology" which he applied to the neurological theories of psychiatric illness developed by Meynert and Wernicke in the late nineteenth century (Hafner, 2015). This term still has some currency today.

M&B also examine the helpful perspective on the tangle of the mind-brain problem of *instantiation* and *implementation* – that the mind is instantiated in brain and that the brain implements the functions of the mind. How could we possibly study the brain without knowing what its functions are? How could there be a neuroscience without a psychology to conceptualize and measure the relevant outputs of the brain? Evolutionary pressures that have shaped the development of our brain will not occur directly on the brain tissue but on the functional productions of brain. Many of these are traits we now measure in psychology. These fields are inextricably linked although they don't always optimally get along.

M&B conclude by examining the contributions of the "new mechanists" well represented in this book by one of the founders of that school of thought – William Bechtel. They note the utility of this synthetic approach and the degree to which it can avoid the, by now, stale reductionist–anti-reductionist debate.

This chapter provides a wonderful overview of the several issues central to the conference themes. M&B are to be congratulated for how hard they work to integrate their views with those expressed by the other participants. While writing with fervor for their point of view, they avoid the sharp-edged polemics which can sometimes characterize these discussions.

REFERENCES

Hafner, H. (2015) "Descriptive psychopathology, phenomenology, and the legacy of Karl Jaspers." *Dialogues in Clinical Neuroscience*, *17*, 19–29.

Miller, G. A. (2010) "Mistreating psychology in the decades of the brain." *Perspectives on Psychological Science*, *5*, 716–743.

20

Challenges in the Relationships between Psychological and Biological Phenomena in Psychopathology

GREGORY A. MILLER AND MORGAN E. BARTHOLOMEW

The Decade of the Brain, which began in 1990, carries on into its fourth decade, with no sunset in sight. A widespread premise in this era has been that psychological phenomena can and should be reduced to biological phenomena. Commonly, that goal is understood as eliminative reductionism, such that constructs and phenomena that can be framed as psychological need not be – that biological constructs and phenomena will eventually suffice to characterize and account for what we have traditionally conceived of as psychological entities. (See Lilienfeld, 2007, for discussion of types of reduction and applications in the psychopathology literature.) Thus (Bechtel & Abrahamsen, 2008, p. 559):

> The goal of reduction is seen as completely explaining the phenomenon of interest at the lowest possible level (e.g., in terms of genes and biochemistry), thereby supplanting and rendering superfluous the kinds of accounts typically offered by cognitive scientists or even those of systems neuroscientists. . . . That is, if one can account for and predict

Based on an invited lecture presented at the "Philosophical Issues in Psychiatry V: The Problems of Multiple Levels, Explanatory Pluralism, Reduction and Emergence" conference, Copenhagen, May 29, 2018. This chapter benefited from the formal commentary on the lecture that Peter Zachar presented at the conference and from informal discussions with him and other conference participants, especially William Bechtel, John Campbell, Stephan Heckers, Eric Turkheimer, Kathryn Tabb, and James Woodward, as well as review by Paul Sharp of any earlier draft. The authors acknowledge current support from grant R01 MH110544S1 from the U.S. National Institute of Mental Health to Gregory A. Miller, Keith H. Nuechterlein, and Cindy M. Yee-Bradbury. The author is a member of the US National Institute of Health (NIH) National Advisory Mental Health Council (NAMHC) and is one of two co-chairs of its Workgroup for Revisions to the RDoC Matrix. The views expressed herein are those of the author and do not necessarily reflect the official policy or position of NIH or its NAMHC.

> all that happens in terms of the lowest-level parts and operations.... The psychological narrative is at best epiphenomenal (that is, psychological processes result from the lower-level processes and have no causal efficacy of their own).

Piccinini and Craver (2011, p. 285) characterized this viewpoint: "Many of these authors conclude that psychological explanations either reduce to or ought to be replaced by neuroscientific explanations...." Crucially for the psychopathology literature, in her lecture at the Copenhagen conference Tabb (2018) noted that "Reduction is leading the way in psychiatry." Pursuit of eliminative reductionism regarding mental illness is of much more than academic interest because of its now well-cemented grip on research on, research dollar allocation for, and public perceptions of mental health and illness, all of which have enormous implications for understanding, preventing, assessing, and treating mental illness.

Fortunately, the primacy of the premise of biological reductionism has crested. It remains widely accepted, but its infeasibility is becoming better recognized (e.g., Borsboom & Cramer, 2013; Borsboom, Cramer, & Kalis, 2019; Franklin, Jamieson, Glenn, & Nock, 2015; Kendler, 2005; Kendler, Zachar, & Craver, 2011; Miller, 1996, 2010; Miller & Keller, 2000; Schwartz, Lilienfeld, Meca, & Sauvigné, 2016; Sharp & Miller, 2019), and more nuanced and feasible alternatives are beginning to take root (e.g., Sharp & Miller, 2019; Thomas & Sharp, 2019). In parallel, a number of authors have noted that the benefit to clinical science of the long evolution of the editions of the *Diagnostic and Statistical Manual of Mental Disorders* seems to have asymptoted (e.g., Beauchaine & Klein, 2017; Berenbaum, 2013; Carpenter & Davis, 2012; Frances, 2014; Hyman, 2010, 2012; Yee, Javitt, & Miller, 2015), having achieved a great deal for standardization in clinical practice but virtually none of the hoped-for translation of fundamentally psychological disorders into biological disorders. (The criticism is not merely that the *DSM*s have not achieved this *yet*; we argue here and in previous papers that that translation is not even feasible, though it has motivated much of the psychopathology literature.) Indeed, the past 40 years of development and evaluation of the *DSM*s have improved reliability far more than validity. For example, former US National Institute of Mental Health (NIMH) Director Hyman (2010, p. 155, 169) argued that "the modern *DSM* system, intended to create a shared language, also creates epistemic blinders that impede progress toward valid diagnoses. Insights that are beginning to emerge from psychology, neuroscience, and genetics suggest possible strategies for moving forward." and concluded that, "Far from providing the predicted validation of schizophrenia or any other mental disorder as categories delineated from all others, family and genetic studies have dramatically undercut the Robins and Guze (1970) approach to classifying psychopathology" which provided the foundation upon which the 1980 and subsequent editions of the *DSM* were rebuilt and refined.

One manifestation of that epistemic blindness is inattention to comorbidity or cross-diagnostic phenomena, fostering a siloed clinical research literature out of touch with clinical practice, where, for example, medication practices often do not follow diagnostic boundaries. Until recently, remarkably few studies were looking across traditional diagnostic boundaries. Almost 90% of the articles reporting studies about the nature of pathophysiology or psychopathology in the 2012 volumes of the *American Journal of Psychiatry* and *Biological Psychiatry*, early in the third Decade of the Brain, compared a single *DSM* diagnosis to healthy controls. Only 12% compared multiple *DSM* disorders, and none examined subtypes or dimensions that cut across disorders (former NIMH Acting Director B. N. Cuthbert, personal communication, January 21, 2019). By 2010, the US National Institute of Mental Health had concluded that the *DSMs'* emphasis on established, categorical disease entities was not sufficiently facilitating research on phenomena that cross category boundaries or that differentiate subtypes within categories (Cuthbert, 2015). Fortunately, several developments in the past decade are converging on a way forward.

In terms of clinical research frameworks, over the past decade, NIMH has launched the Research Domain Criteria (RDoC) initiative (Cuthbert, 2015; Cuthbert & Insel, 2010, 2013; Insel & Cuthbert, 2009; Insel et al., 2010; Kozak & Cuthbert, 2016; Morris & Cuthbert, 2012; Sanislow et al., 2010), designed to improve diagnostic validity by applying criteria for inclusion of psychological domains and constructs in what has become known as the RDoC matrix that emphasize grounding in neural circuits or systems. RDoC was conceived as protean, designed to evolve more rapidly than the *DSM*, in step with accumulating research evidence. The concepts defining the rows of the initial draft of the RDoC matrix reflected the relatively well understood neural circuitry supporting the emotion of fear, reward processes, cognitive control, etc. The initial matrix was not designed to be an exhaustive map subsuming all forms of psychopathology because, in many cases, neural circuits or systems have not been well characterized. Rather, RDoC was designed to provide a framework for advancing on all fronts, with elements to be filled in and boundaries expanded as data and understanding accrue. To that end, NIMH is now ramping up its efforts to validate RDoC in its initial form (e.g., https://grants.nih.gov/grants/guide/rfa-files/rfa-mh-19-240.html and https://grants.nih.gov/grants/guide/rfa-files/rfa-mh-19-242.html) and to revise it in light of advancing research (e.g., www.nimh.nih.gov/news/science-news/2018/nimh-releases-updates-to-its-rdoc-framework.shtml and www.nimh.nih.gov/news/science-news/2019/sensorimotor-domain-added-to-the-rdoc-framework.shtml?utm_source=APS+Emails&utm_campaign=5d18f18796-PSU_011819_FULLMEMB&utm_medium=email&utm_term=0_d2c7283f04-5d18f18796-62625779).

In terms of clinical research strategies, the growing interest in what is sometimes called computational psychiatry (though what it refers to would be better captured by computational psychobiology, computational cognitive neuroscience [broadly conceived], or computational psychopathology (e.g., Friston, Stephan, Montague, & Dolan, 2014; Montague, Dolan, Friston, & Dayan, 2012; Stephan & Mathys, 2014) fits quite well with this RDoC approach. A report on an NIMH-sponsored workshop on computational psychiatry in 2017 foregrounded this synergy (Ferrante, Redish, Oquendo, Averbeck, Kinnane, & Gordon, 2018, p. 2, 4):

> It has become clear that computational approaches are a key to understanding how properties inter-relate across levels of analysis (e.g., molecular, neuronal, circuit, system, behavioral, societal), particularly as these levels can interact in complex ways (e.g., societal changes affect behavior, which affects learning, which is stored as molecular changes in neurons and circuits). There was a general consensus that all levels of analysis are important, as is the integration between them.

and

> The use of RDoC and other conceptual frameworks as the means of framing experimental questions in human subjects may allow for better comparison between animal and human data because the data from both subjects would be taken at the level of translatable constructs (working memory, attention, etc.) rather than trying to find animal models of DSM diagnoses. An understanding of the behaviors mediated by circuitry relevant to psychiatric disorders may further improve dimensional approaches.

In terms of metatheoretical support for the clinical research enterprise, the recent "new mechanist" movement in the philosophy of science is developing a sophisticated approach to relationships among psychological and biological concepts and phenomena, providing scaffolding necessary for credibly escaping the strictures of the failed premise that eliminative biological reductionism in psychopathology is feasible. This movement and its relevance to the psychopathology literature are discussed below. (See also Thomas & Sharp, 2019, for a compelling presentation.)

Another promising reconceptualization that similarly offers a more viable framing of relationships between biological and psychological entities than the widely accepted reductionist view is the so-called network approach to psychopathology (a narrower notion than the term implies). Borsboom and Cramer (2013, p. 116–117) provided a review, faulting simplistic use of the usual "levels of analysis" metaphor and arguing:

> Traditionally, researchers tend to think of these levels as being intrinsically ordered, in the sense that genes cause brains and brains cause behaviors. However, in our view it is extremely likely that once researchers start taking the dynamics of symptomatology seriously, they will find feedback loops that cross the borders of traditional thinking. Naturally, genetic differences may predispose to the development of disorders, but persistent symptomatology (e.g., insomnia or loss of appetite) may cause differential gene expression just as well; in turn, such changes may affect a person's brain state and ultimately feed back into the environment, as in the extended feedback loops discussed previously in this review (see also Borsboom, Cramer, Schmittmann, Epskamp, & Waldorp, 2011, and Thomas & Sharp, 2019). In our view, it is highly unlikely that one particular level of analysis will, in the end, be able to claim causal priority
>
> (see also Kendler, 2012a).

20.1 A BRIEF CRITIQUE OF NAÏVE REDUCTIONISM IN THE PSYCHOPATHOLOGY LITERATURE

Even prior to the first Decade of the Brain, it was becoming common to characterize mental illness as, instead, physical illness. Miller (1996, 2010; Miller & Keller, 2000) cited numerous examples of this misconstrual. During that first Decade, National Institute on Drug Abuse Director Leshner (1997, p. 46) stated: "That addiction is tied to changes in brain structure and function is what makes it, fundamentally, a brain disease." NIMH Director Hyman (1998, p. 36) similarly took the position that "Mental illnesses are real, diagnosable, treatable brain disorders." This reductionist premise is remarkably longstanding, dating at least to psychiatric pioneer Wilhem Griesinger (1854), quoted by Maj (2013): "all mental illnesses are cerebral illnesses."

The abstract of a *Nature* paper in the third Decade of the Brain (Brennand et al., 2011, p. 211) began with the announcement that

"Schizophrenia…is a debilitating neurological disorder…" and ended with reference to it being "…a complex genetic psychiatric disorder." But schizophrenia is not a neurological disorder, nor a genetic disorder, at least not in a common or meaningful sense of those terms. There is no question that genes (or more precisely gene expression, driven by environment and other genes) make a significant and potentially clinically important contribution to psychopathology. But, as present and former NIMH Directors Gordon (2018) and Hyman (2010) have noted and Kendler (2005, p. 1250) has explained, "The impact of individual genes on risk for psychiatric illness is small, often nonspecific, and embedded in causal pathways of stunning complexity… Although we may wish it to be true, we do not have and are not likely to ever discover 'genes for' psychiatric illness."

Yet 20 years ago, mental illness looked, to many, ready to have its genetic code cracked. NIMH Director Hyman (1998, p. 38) said that "psychiatric illnesses are fully and unquestionably viewed as part of the next challenge in mainstream genetics." As the official completion of the human genome sequencing project neared in 2003, statements of the form "Now that we have the genome…" became common, often finishing with grand claims about imminent achievements, including about mental illness. Now going on two decades later, it is notable that one never hears such statements any more. We do still have the genome. Now that we have had the genome for a while, it has become all the more evident that having the genome, by itself, is of no value in understanding mental illness. Seeking the "genetic basis" of mental illness, a goal so commonly trumpeted in scientific and popular media in the Decades of the Brain (Miller, 2010), is a misunderstanding of the crucial role genes play. What we need to do about genes is identify what role they play.

We have not done so. We may.

Increasingly, calls for research on genetic contributions to psychopathology assert the need for what would have been, until recently, unthinkably large sample sizes – in the thousands or even hundreds of thousands. From the standpoint of mainstream inferential statistics (Cohen, 1988), the need for such enormous samples in order to detect effects with confidence means that the effects in the population are extremely small. That does not mean that the effects are unimportant, scientifically or clinically. An effect that is quite causally strong when a particular set of genes and/or environments converge can be quite statistically weak when that convergence is rare. Framing this issue in terms of classical reliability or dependability theory (Clayson & Miller, 2017), one could profit from a set of measures with very low internal reliability, in that each item would be a poor predictor of the other items – because they are rare and largely uncorrelated in the population. As Golden and Meehl (1979) explained some years ago, a measure able to detect a rare convergence may be a superb means of detecting a syndrome that is heavily driven by that convergence, even though the measure has very poor reliability in the usual psychometric sense; in fact, low internal reliability is a virtue in such cases. The present argument is not against the importance of genetic or other biological contributions to psychopathology, even if the effects are often quite small at the population level. The argument is that the widespread assumption that mental illness *is* genetic (or neurological, etc.) is untenable logically and dangerous as a foundation for public policy. One may also argue whether the best use of large sums of precious research funds is on mega-sample genetic studies vs. other types of studies. In any case, at present, it seems a safe bet that progress on genetic contributions will require such large-scale investments.

The problem of biological reductionism is not confined to the overvaluing of genetics research. A leading mental illness research foundation recently offered a Webinar titled: "What's new with TMS for depression and other brain diseases" (BBRF, 2018). But depression is not a brain disease. A more common version of this error is the claim that depression "is" a chemical imbalance. It is not, cannot be, a chemical imbalance, on logical grounds. Per *DSM-5* (American Psychiatric Association, 2013), "the common feature of all [depressive] disorders is the presence of sad, empty, or irritable mood, accompanied by somatic and cognitive changes that significantly affect the individual's capacity to function." Nearly all of the elements of that statement are psychological. Depression is a mood disorder, and mood is a psychological construct, not a neural construct nor a chemical construct. Transcranial magnetic stimulation (TMS) is clearly a biological intervention in that modulation of magnetic fields modifies neural current flows. That there is growing evidence that such treatment is associated with reduction in depressed mood (e.g., George et al., 2010; Perera et al., 2016) is an important research direction, but it is not evidence that depression is a brain disease, rather than a psychological disease. What the term "depression" as currently defined refers to is psychological, even if TMS or another biological method advances to the point that it is a sufficient treatment for (brain circuit dysfunction in) depression, and even if the term "depression" is someday redeployed to refer to something entirely biological. Similarly, pharmacological interventions sometimes reduce depression symptoms, but that does not mean that chemistry can provide an adequate account of depression. Given that depression is a fundamentally a psychological construct, one needs psychological mechanisms to account for it (see also Marr, 1982, and Sharp & Miller, 2019). For decades, interest has ebbed and flowed in what was called the dopamine theory of schizophrenia (e.g., Davis, 1976; Laruelle, 2013; Yang & Tsai, 2017), but it was never a theory of schizophrenia. It was a theory of dopamine's role in schizophrenia. The literature was never able to identify causal mechanisms relating dopamine to thought disorder or other key symptoms, let alone to explain how dopamine phenomena can account for the whole of schizophrenia. The general point: "Seeking to understand causal mechanical processes in psychiatric illness at a basic biological level is a highly valuable research approach that has yielded important insights. This method cannot, however, be extrapolated to many important classes of causal variables in psychiatry and so is too restrictive to be used as a general approach to causation in our field." (Kendler & Campbell, 2009, p. 884)

Naïve biological reductionism is not confined to studies focused on biological mechanisms. Intelligence is, clearly, a psychological construct. Bates, Lewis, and Weiss (2013) added to a growing literature showing that conventionally defined intelligence is not inherited, in the general sense, it is widely assumed to be – that one's genes essentially determine one's intelligence. Heritability is quantified not in general but in a specific population in a specific environment. Bates et al. reported that heritability of adult intelligence approached zero in participants who experienced low SES in childhood, whereas they reported high heritability of adult intelligence in participants who experienced high SES in childhood. Indeed, "...the magnitude of genetic influences on intelligence was proportional to SES. By contrast, [the contributions of other] environmental influences were constant." (p. 2111) Thus, the respective roles of genes and environment in intelligence depend on environment. Remarkably, however, the press release about this article, from a leading psychology research society, claimed that this study "supports a biological model of intelligence in which supportive environments lead to maximal genetic effects." The paper provided no grounds for construing what is a clearly gene x environment model as (solely) biological rather than (equally) environmental. Even psychologists are not immune to the current allure of portraying psychological phenomena as biological.

That allure, it happens, is not new. The following characterization reads like a rueful retrospective on the Decades of the Brain written long after they passed:

> ...an entire generation of researchers...tended to reduce psychiatry to neuropathology. However, this wave of brain research never lived up to

> its promises, and, increasingly, as the expected breakthroughs from neuropathological research failed to materialize, critics began searching for alternative approaches.
>
> (Engstrom & Kendler, 2015, p. 1190)

But the "entire generation" the authors were writing about were the students, circa 1885, of Griesinger. Engstrom and Kendler identified Kraepelin as one such critic and noted (p. 1192) that Kraepelin "insisted vehemently that the notion of psychiatry as nothing more than a special branch of neuropathology or neurophysiology...would never be able to deliver on its promise of a comprehensive understanding of mental disorders. No understanding of 'brain mechanisms' could entirely incorporate mental processes." Kraepelin, another psychiatric pioneer, died almost a century ago. It would not be fair to fault Griesenger, who died 150 years ago, for the modern resurgence of naïve biological reductionism regarding mental illness. That is on us.

The research policy of the NIMH exemplified this resurgence, as reference to the "biological basis" of one or another mental illness became commonplace in scientific and popular literature in the second Decade of the Brain. In 2003, the Clinical Neuroscience Research Branch of the NIMH was divided into three funding programs (www.nimh.nih.gov/diva/index.htm#cnrb, accessed 4/26/03, emphasis added):

- The Molecular and Cellular Basis of Schizophrenia, Mood, and *other Brain Disorders* Program
- The Integrative Neuroscience of Schizophrenia, Mood and *other Brain Disorders* Program
- The Developmental Neuroscience of Schizophrenia, Mood and *other Brain Disorders* Program

Each of those three program titles construed these types of mental illnesses as "brain disorders." Allegedly, the "basis" of these disorders had come to be seen as molecular and cellular. In 2005, and even in 2009 at the dawn of the RDoC initiative, the same Research Branch advertised that it "supports programs of research, research training, and resource development aimed at understanding *the neural basis of mental disorders*" (www.nimh.nih.gov/datr/a3-ns.cfm, accessed 1/31/05 & 1/18/09, emphasis added). Was the message that some – or all – of the basis (though it is not clear what "basis" means here) of mental illness is such low-level biology? Was this no longer the National Institute of *Mental* Health?

The premise was not just that there is or at least may be a crucially important story to be discovered in molecular and cellular phenomena but that those phenomena were *the* place to invest research dollars in order to understand and ameliorate mental illness.

20.2 THE PENDULUM BEGINS TO SWING BACK

Despite how widespread biological reductionism had apparently become at the NIMH, the impact of the RDoC initiative was rapid. By 2011, the NIMH Neuroscience and Basic Behavioral Science Branch described its agenda as "ensuring that relevant basic science knowledge is generated and then harvested to create improved diagnosis, treatment, and prevention of mental and behavioral disorders" – not "brain disorders" (www.nimh.nih.gov/about/organization/dnbbs/index.shtml, accessed 05/25/11). Similarly, the NIMH Molecular, Cellular, and Genomic Neuroscience Research Branch "supports research aimed at developing an integrative understanding of basic brain–behavior processes that provide the foundation for understanding mental disorders" – not "brain disorders" – in order to "elucidate how cognitive, affect, stress, and motivational processes interact and their role(s) in mental disorders through functional studies spanning levels of analysis (genomic, molecular, cellular, circuits, behavior" (www.nimh.nih.gov/about/organization/dnbbs/molecular-cellular-and-genomic-neuroscience-research-branch/index.shtml, accessed 05/25/11). By 2015, all six "Areas of High Priority" at the NIMH Neuroscience and Basic Behavioral Science Branch centrally involved psychology, such as the first two (www.nimh.nih.gov/about/organization/dnbbs/index.shtml, accessed April 19, 2015, unchanged February 2, 2019, emphasis added):

- Develop new and use existing physiological and computational models to understand the biological functions of genes, gene products, cells, and brain circuits *in normal and abnormal mental function.*
- Elucidate how cognitive, affect, stress, and motivational processes interact and their role(s) *in mental disorders* through functional studies spanning levels of analysis (genomic, molecular, cellular, circuits, behavior) during development and throughout the lifespan.

Notably, the target was once again "mental disorders", not "brain disorders".

Commonly in our literature, claims that mental illness is genetic – or neurological, or chemical, or cellular, or a brain disease – are offered to mean that it is *only* such things, is not psychological, and also that it is not to any important extent a function of poverty or nutrition or exercise or health care or immunological compromise or alimentary fauna. Such claims seriously misdirect the attention of clinicians, researchers, policymakers, journalists, and the public away from substantial clinical research literatures that have already established the contributions of every one of those other domains to mental illness. This miscontrual has serious implications for the quality of our science, the focus of our clinical practice, the funding of our science and our practice, the priorities of our policymakers, and the choices of and resources available to our citizens (Miller, 2010).

There can be no argument that biological interventions can be associated with psychological changes. There also can be no argument that psychological interventions can be associated with biological changes. The clinical research literature provides numerous examples of the latter (Miller, 2010, cited several), though these are routinely ignored due to the premise that biological reduction of psychological phenomena is the goal. When we assume that the hunt should be solely for biological ways to alter psychopathology (whether biological or psychological aspects of it), we systematically overlook psychological ways to alter psychopathology (whether biological or psychological aspects of it) as well as strategies that marshal both, even when combinations have already been shown to be generally superior to either modality alone.

By the third Decade of the Brain, more and more clinical scientists were lamenting how far this naïve biological reductionism had gone. Phillips (2014, p. 41) suggested that "The siren call of biological fixes for biopsychosocial problems has dominated medical research for decades. . .." Frances (2014, p. 48), a leader in the development of the *DSM-IV*, faulted clinical science policymakers:

> NIMH was at the center of the neuroscience enthusiasm. . .betting the house on a narrow biological agenda to replace what had been a more balanced portfolio. . . NIMH turned itself into a 'brain institute' rather than an 'institute of mental health'. Its efforts have succeeded in producing wonderful science, but have failed in helping patients. . .it is a dangerous myth to assume that patients who meet criteria for 'schizophrenia' suffer only from a brain disease.

Even some NIH policymakers who were widely perceived as having pushed the pendulum far toward biological reductionism expressed doubts. After stepping down as NIMH Director, psychiatrist Hyman (2005, p. 1414) came to see addiction as "a disease of learning and memory", which are clearly psychological constructs. After stepping down as NIDA Director, psychologist Leshner (2007, p. 953) noted that "there is no evidence that we will be able to understand all aspects of the mind simply in molecular neurobiological terms." After stepping down as NIMH Director, psychiatrist Insel (quoted by www.wired.com/2017/05/star-neuroscientist-tom-insel-leaves-google-spawned-verily-startup/?mbid=social_twitter_onsite share, accessed 01/21/19) reflected:

> I spent 13 years at NIMH really pushing on the neuroscience and genetics of mental disorders, and when I look back on that I realize that. . .I think $20 billion – I don't think we moved the needle in reducing suicide, reducing hospitalizations, improving recovery for the tens of millions of people who have mental illness. I hold myself accountable for that.

NIMH's swing toward the hyper-reductionistic "mental illnesses are brain disorders" premise had proved to be profoundly disappointing. Thirty (now 40) years of research based on modern *DSMs* (1980+) had failed to connect mental illness to biology. A decade ago, *DSM-5* was taking shape and was no more biologically grounded than its predecessors, despite NIH (and pharmaceutical companies) spending billions on *DSM*-driven research. Inside mental illness and beyond, not one instance had emerged in the literature in which researchers had worked out the full reductionist causal chain from biology to a nontrivial psychological construct. Growing evidence that having the genome, or having a brain connectivity map, cannot provide a full account of psychological phenomena spawned the realization that Kraepelin was right: eliminative reduction is not an option.

Based on extensive literature reviews, NIMH developed a new approach to conceiving a research agenda for mental illness. Borrowing somewhat from the perspective of the new mechanists discussed below, NIMH launched the RDoC initiative, as described by Kozak and Cuthbert (2016, p. 292):

> . . .the RDoC guidelines accord no a priori theoretical precedence to any particular unit of analysis [biological or psychological]. . .. All measurement classes are potentially relevant in examining the role and functioning of the constructs. The RDoC internal workgroup's aphorism for this idea was, "Behavioral science studies what the brain does, and neuroscience studies how the brain does it"; both are essential to an understanding of adaptive functioning. This consideration constitutes a major postulate of the overall RDoC framework, consistent with the goal of promoting an integrative, rather than a reductionist, approach
> (Bechtel, 2007; Wright & Bechtel, 2007).

Not realizing how radical a change RDoC represented, and in light of sometimes confusing messaging from NIMH leadership (discussed below), some audiences initially have found RDoC too psychological (with psychological constructs now in the forefront), while others found it too biological (due to limiting the emphasis to psychological constructs for which neural circuits and systems are relatively well known), even accusing RDoC of the same infeasible reductionism (e.g., Goldfried, 2016; Lilienfeld, 2014; Lilienfeld & Treadway, 2016). But RDoC is explicitly agnostic about the relationships between psychology and biology, and is intended to foster integration of the two domains (Berenbaum, 2013; Cuthbert & Kozak, 2013; Kozak & Cuthbert, 2016; Miller, Rockstroh, Hamilton, & Yee, 2016; Sanislow et al., 2010). The constructs that label the rows of the RDoC matrix are clearly psychological, and in fact psychological constructs have returned to the center of the NIMH research agenda: "The RDoC matrix is a tool for use by researchers to help them structure their study designs around behavioral or cognitive concepts." (www.nimh.nih.gov/news/science-news/2018/nimh-releases-updates-to-its-rdoc-framework.shtml, accessed 01/21/19) Yee et al. (2015, 1159–1160) argued that:

> The RDoC initiative. . .is at once more biological and less biologically reductionistic than the DSMs. . .. The RDoC matrix is not under consideration as a replacement of the DSM in clinical practice. Instead, the RDoC premise is that clinical research should build on the best available genetic, neuroscience, and psychological science concepts, findings, and relationships.

RDoC's restoration of psychology to the center of the NIMH research agenda, without loss of the emphasis on neural circuits and systems fostered by the Decades of the Brain, is manifest in many public-facing areas of NIMH. In a town hall teleconference hosted by the Coalition for the Advancement and Application of Psychological Science (November 1, 2017), NIMH Director Gordon offered that "When we say biological, we include psychological" and "Psychological and biological measures as far as we're concerned are biology." Even NIMH's genomic agenda has embraced the RDoC approach. "Heritability is shared across psychiatric disorders, as well as across related dimensional traits. Understanding the relevant biological pathways requires analysis not only of traditional disease categories, but also of functional domains (e.g., valence, cognition) affected by mental illnesses." (National Advisory Mental Health Council Workgroup on Genomics, 2018)

RDoC has also been widely misunderstood as intended to replace the *DSM/ICD* approach to diagnosing and treating mental illness. (See Lake, Yee, & Miller, 2017, Lilienfeld & Treadway, 2016, Miller et al., 2016, Miller &

Yee, 2015, and Yee et al., 2015, for discussions of a number of common misunderstandings of RDoC.) But RDoC was explicitly developed to foster research, not to replace the *DSM* categorical approach in clinical practice. Borsboom et al. (2016, p. 1567) argued against a false choice, which mirrors the agnosticism RDoC emphasizes about how to construe psychopathology: "the structure of constructs may be continuous for some individuals but categorical for others. . .the kinds–continua distinction is considerably more subtle than is often presupposed in research; in particular, the hypotheses of kinds and continua are not mutually exclusive or exhaustive." A recent announcement from NIMH (https://grants.nih.gov/grants/guide/notice-files/NOT-MH-18-053.html, dated Oct 2, 2018) communicates clearly how RDoC dimensions relate to *DSM* categories:

> The essence of RDoC is to identify organizing dimensions that cut across multiple psychiatric disorders as traditionally defined, and to promote research according to these dimensions, complementing traditional diagnostic categories that addresses both psychological and biological theory and phenomena. The RDoC matrix depicts functional domains of behavior that are relevant to mental disorders and provides a framework for future research on psychopathology.

20.3 The Pendulum's Return Has Not Been Smooth

Much of the confusion around reductionism in RDoC comes from problems in the early communication about the initiative. In particular, early RDoC framing from NIMH leadership sometimes included the familiar language of naive reductionism, e.g. ". . .schizophrenia is now viewed and treated as a developmental brain disorder" (Insel, 2010, p. 44). ". . .depression is fundamentally a brain disorder" (Insel, 2010, p. 46). ". . .mental disorders can be addressed as disorders of brain circuits" (Insel et al., 2010, p. 749). ". . .mental illnesses are presumed to be disorders of brain circuits" (Morris & Cuthbert 2012, p. 33). These words renewed the legacy of previous NIMH leadership, which had embraced the original Decade of the Brain, not only fostering untenable assumptions but undermining what the RDoC initiative can achieve. Very recently, the current NIMH Director foregrounded the biological story in psychopathology, not citing the psychological story (Gordon, 2019, p. 425):

> Patients, families, and communities bearing the burden of mental illnesses in the here and now deserve continued progress even while we wait for this long-promised future. Standing in the way of such

> progress is the complexity of the biological problem that faces us. The brain, the organ from which the symptoms of mental illness emanate, is the most complex biological system. . ..

Indeed, the biological problem we face in psychopathology research is remarkably complex, but it is by no means obvious that the psychological problem we face in psychopathology research is any less complex. The RDoC initiative engages that complexity by thoroughly developing the psychological constructs for which it demands well-researched psychological and biological data.

But problems in the messaging from NIMH leadership can be overstated. Granted, the widely cited overview of the RDoC provided by Insel et al. (2010) proposed to regard mental disorders as brain disorders, which we have argued here and elsewhere is untenable, because of the infeasibly reductionistic implications widely drawn from such a view. However, Bolton (2013, p. 24) argued that the position taken in the 2010 paper is:

> plainly not reductionistic. By this, I mean that they do not suppose that neural dysfunctions are the only causes of mental disorders, but rather recognize developments in mental health sciences showing that causes or risks of mental disorders may operate at many levels, including the genetics and the neural, the individual, the family environment, and the social context. Crucially, this view of multifactorial or multilevel view [sic] of causation (or risk) acknowledges and is intended to accommodate the fact that interventions at these various levels may affect onset and course, playing parts in primary prevention and management and treatment after.

The space that Bolton created is essentially that one can take the position that some portions of the mental illness story are biological without requiring that all other portions of it be reducible to biological constructs and phenomenon. Bolton (2013, p. 24) noted that the RDoC initiative does not assume that biology (genetic, neuroscience, etc.) is sufficient or even merely more fundamental or more important in general:

> reductionism might be right in some cases and in some cases it is already known to be right; in other cases, the psychosocial might be more important, account for more of the variance in incidence or outcomes, than, for instance, genetic factors. In short, the new sciences for which RDoC provides a framework make discriminations between conditions in these respects. [These new sciences] emphasize the interplay between the internal biology, the environment, and individual differences.

Finally, Bolton (2013) emphasized that because RDoC also urges researchers to study normal function, it allows for a more comprehensive understanding of the interplay between biology, environment, and individual differences. It is not the case that RDoC rejects categorical constructs, phenomena, or methods, but its bet on continuity underlies its (compensatory) emphasis on dimensional phenomena and specifically on grounding research on mental illness as much as possible in available biological science, especially neural circuits and related phenomena at various scales. A guiding principle in the original and the ongoing development of the RDoC matrix is that there should be good science available for the biology (especially neural circuits) involved in candidate constructs (the rows, generally psychological) for those constructs to be admitted to the matrix. Cuthbert and Insel (2013, p. 131) corrected earlier framings of RDoC as biologically reductionist, noting that RDoC "is intended to provide a structure that places equal weight on behavioral functions and upon neural circuits and their constituent elements – that is, to be an integrative model rather than one based primarily on either behavior or neuroscience." In an articulation of the relationship of developmental processes to RDoC, Casey, Oliveri, and Insel (2014, p. 351) stated:

> Inherent within the neurodevelopmental framework is the utility of parallel nonhuman animal work for delineating mechanisms... The mechanistic advantages inherent in research on nonhuman animals can advance the RDoC agenda, and science more generally, by improving specification and validation of constructs.

Cuthbert (2015, p. 77) described the research-based principles that various domain-expert workgroups applied to select and define domains and the constructs underneath them:

> Each construct had to meet three empirical criteria to be included in the system. First, there had to be evidence for the validity of the construct as a functional unit of behavior or cognitive processes; second, there had to be evidence for a neural circuit or system that played a primary role in implementing the construct's function; and third, the construct had to evince relevance for understanding some aspects of psychopathology.

These principles, including the importance of available biological research, remain central in ongoing efforts of the National Institute of Health National Advisory Mental Health Council Workgroup for Revisions to the RDoC Matrix. New or substantially reconceptualized domains and constructs are evaluated in part for how well they are informed by available research on relevant circuits and systems.

20.4 UNDERLYING PHENOMENA UNDERLYING MECHANISMS

Having documented that NIMH has made substantial progress in recovering from the naïve reductionism of the Decades of the Brain, we note that the psychopathology literature (and the scientific literature more generally) has yet to reach consensus on a workable framework regarding the relationship between psychological and biological constructs and phenomena (besides the new mechanists discussed below, see Marr, 1982, and Thomas & Sharp, 2019, for promising approaches). As noted above, to date there is not yet a single example of a thoroughly worked out causal story about mechanisms by which biological events account for nontrivial psychological events (Miller, 2010, argued that there cannot be such a story). Yet, in the Decades of the Brain, the widespread assumption has been that biological phenomena "underlie" psychological phenomena and that, as an instance of eliminative reductionism, an adequate account of the former will either provide an account of the latter or remove the need for it. One illustration, from a Nobel Prize winner and a past President of the Society for Neuroscience, early in the first Decade (Kandel & Squire, 1992, 143): "Cognitive neuroscience...begins with localization within the brain of various cognitive abilities.... It has now become possible to localize mental functions to particular sets of regions..." But psychological functions do not have locations in space. Neuroimaging localizes neural activity, not psychological function. More fundamentally, it is not at all clear whether biology "underlies" psychology, or psychology "underlies" biology, or whether "underlies" is even an appropriate way to characterize their relationship (Berenbaum, 2013; Miller, 1996, 2010; Miller & Keller, 2000).

In RDoC, it is the psychological constructs that underlie expressions of mental illness (Casey et al, 2014, p. 350):

> ...different levels of analysis (molecular, circuit, behavior, symptom) in RDoC instantiate dimensional constructs that are presumed to underlie core symptoms of mental disorders. These constructs (e.g., fear, attention, memory, arousal) will rarely bear one-to-one relationships with traditional disorder categories; rather, they are expected to cluster and combine in various degrees to apply to multiple disorders as traditionally defined.

The choice of the word "instantiate" here is fortunate and telling. The array of types of measurements one can bring to bear (the columns in the RDoC matrix) are diverse means of assessing the psychological constructs that form the rows in the RDoC matrix. RDoC constructs are what MacCorquodale and Meehl (1948) called "hypothetical constructs", distinct from observables and not reducible to observables (see Kozak & Miller, 1982, for extended discussion applying this distinction to psychopathology and measurement of it). Berenbaum (2013, p. 895) similarly argued that "mental disorders (regardless of whether they are thought to be categorical or dimensional) can be thought of as hypothetical constructs." Accordingly, the RDoC framework strongly endorses the value of measuring biological (and psychological) phenomenon without endorsing naïve reductionism of psychological constructs and phenomenon to biological constructs and phenomenon. In the meantime, banishing "underlying" from our vocabulary, with its implications about what is more important, fundamental, or explanatory, would be prudent.

20.5 THE NEW MECHANISTS: A STRATEGY FOR UNDERSTANDING BIOLOGY AND PSYCHOLOGY IN MENTAL ILLNESS

In stark contrast to the faith in hyper-biological reductionism that the Decades of the Brain have both assumed and fostered, accounts of psychopathology will surely require "...causal processes that act both at micro levels and macro levels, that act within and outside of the individual, and that involve processes best understood from biological, psychological, and sociocultural perspectives" (Kendler, 2008, p. 695). "...we will need to move away from the traditional hard medical model that requires that we ground our diagnoses in single biological essences, and focus instead on fuzzy, cross-level mechanisms, which may more realistically capture the true nature of psychiatric disorders." (Kendler, 2012b, p. 11) Elements of the recent "new mechanists" literature in the philosophy of science offer an appealing framework for such accounts, although it is an evolving rather than a settled approach.

Bechtel (2017, p. 256), a pioneer in this literature, defined mechanisms as "highly interactive modules within a larger network that are capable of exhibiting complex dynamics." He explained modules using graph theory, which is seeing increasing use in neuroscience (e.g., Bartholomew, Yee, Heller, Miller, & Spielberg, 2019). With this methodology, the complexity and dynamic nature of a psychological construct are better captured via modules representing various manifestations of the construct (e.g., chemical, neural, cognitive, interpersonal, etc.) that can exert influence on or relate to each other in a non-linear and non-hierarchical manner (see also

Woodward, Chapter 35). Importantly, Bechtel discussed how readily causal relations within and among modules in such a mechanism can produce feedback effects that a traditional reductionist approach would not allow for. Such feedback effects immediately complicate simplistic notions of causal relationships between biological and psychological phenomena.

Sharp and Miller (2019) described the manner in which the new mechanists rely on an uncommon notion of "levels" as being different scales of organization within mechanisms and how they provide new perspectives on how to think about the autonomy of each level vs. its potential reduction to another level (see also Miller & Kozak, 1993):

> At the core of the mechanistic proposal is a characterization of what mechanisms are and how they serve to explain phenomena in the life sciences. A mechanism is defined as a dynamic system realizing a phenomenon in virtue of the orchestrated functioning of its component parts and activities (Bechtel & Abrahamsen, 2008). Thus, to explain a phenomenon (e.g., cellular respiration), one must decompose relevant parts and activities of physical structures and their spatiotemporal organization. For psychological phenomena, a mechanism must also be described functionally, which describes the various information processing activities carried out within the physical system.

The reduction that such an approach envisions is quite different from what has been widely assumed in the psychopathology literature during the Decades of the Brain:

> Systems neuroscientists have suggested, for instance, that explaining how dynamical properties such as oscillations across different brain modules arise will not require an appeal to the causal structure of the brain at the level of single neurons (Sporns, 2013). Thus, reductionism within mechanisms does not privilege a priori the lowest level one could appeal to in one's explanation. One need not always end up at physics; reductionism does not entail eliminative reductionism. In fact, for some purposes, physics is no help at all, even though it is clear that there IS a physics unfolding.

The latter point exemplifies Fodor's (1968) distinction between necessary and contingent identity. There is no question that a given person with major depression is a corporeal being in whom biochemistry is constantly unfolding and crucial to the overt manifestation of the depression. But, as noted above, the biochemistry is not the depression, contrary to the popular mantra that "depression is a chemical imbalance." There is always a contingent identity between a person being depressed and that person having some (no doubt relevant) chemistry, but the specific chemistry may vary greatly. As a consequence, there is no necessary identity between a particular depressed state and a particular chemical state. There is no chemistry that provides the specific etiology of depression (see also discussion of Kendler & Campbell, 2009, below).

The notion of levels as different scales of organization within mechanisms sets up a perspective for understanding the meaning of causation in psychopathology. Early on in the new mechanist movement, Craver and Bechtel (2007, p. 562, 547, 550) proposed that:

> . . .causal relations are exclusively intralevel. . .. Mechanistically mediated effects are hybrids of constitutive and causal relations in a mechanism, where the constitutive relations are interlevel, and the causal relations are exclusively intralevel.. . .we find no metaphysical puzzle imagining that items in the proper domain of one science, however that domain is defined, interact with items in the proper domain of another science.

In this approach, lower-level biological phenomena do not cause higher-level psychological phenomena, and there is no hint of eliminative reductionism. One can take a further step and not assume that biology is the lower level and psychology the higher level. In fact, lower and higher are not viewed as helpful specifiers for "levels." These new mechanists are explicit that they reject cross-level reduction entirely (Piccinini & Craver, 2011, 284):

> Our argument. . .is not an argument for reductionism, either as it has been classically conceived (as the derivation of one theory from another) or as it is now commonly conceived (as the idea that lower-level mechanisms are explanatorily privileged).

Chapter 35 by Woodward offers an alternative new mechanist perspective that does allow inter-level causation but similarly rejects reductionism and the privileging of lower-level accounts. He provides a typology of different meanings of the level-of-analysis metaphor. For example, levels may be compositional, such that objects at a higher level are composed or made up of objects at lower levels (atoms, molecules, cells. . .). As an example, he notes that we typically view psychosocial stressors as at a higher level than genes, while implicitly employing a compositional notion of levels, which then requires an account of how this could be possible – the mechanisms by which causal arrows can cross levels. The psychopathology literature provides many (and more and more) examples of gene × environment interactions, yet such an interaction seems incoherent if psychosocial environmental factors are reducible to biological phenomena in the compositional sense, as is widely assumed in the Decades of the Brain: it does not make sense to say that parts can cause wholes of which they are a part (Craver & Bechtel, 2007). Nor does it make sense to say that something psychological is composed of something biological, though the assumption that that is viable is widespread in the Decades of the Brain. The psychopathology literature is utterly lacking in such accounts, raising fundamental doubts about such conceptualizations.

On a different meaning of the "levels of analysis" metaphor, levels may involve realization or implementation, such as how Marr's (1982) famous book on vision distinguishes computation, algorithm, and hardware. In such a notion of levels, an algorithm is not a spatiotemporal part of the computation that implements it logically, nor is the algorithm composed of the hardware that implements it physically. Similarly, the hardware does not cause the algorithm, even as it instantiates it. Sharp and Miller (2019) argued accordingly that:

> If psychology comprises the algorithms of the mind, and biology their physical instantiation, then it makes no sense to talk about them being causally related, given that they are not physically or temporally separate events. Rather, the former is implemented in the latter, and two noncompeting causal stories may be told regarding the temporal cascade of information processing (psychology) and the spatiotemporal sequence of biological events (biology) that occurs simultaneously.

Another view of levels that Woodward (Chapter 35) describes involves abstractness or granularity. One may construe the behavior of a group of people as the net effect of its individual members' behavior, without claiming that there is no property of the group that is more than the sum of all the individual behavior. Woodward goes on to describe a fourth, interactionist concept of levels, wherein systems that interact are at the same level. In this view, gene expression and psychosocial stressors are at the same level to the extent that they interact. The problem of how to reduce the latter to the former would not arise because no reductionistic relationship between them is assumed. Woodward argues that, if one adopts the "levels" metaphor, finding the right level for modeling or theorizing is often crucial, in fact among the most important methodological and philosophical issues raised by level talk. He notes that whether causation can happen across levels is a matter of active discussion. (E.g., Chapter 35 in this volume disputes some of the contentions of

Craver & Bechtel, 2007) and suggests that applying the levels metaphor to distinguish scientific disciplines such as biology and psychology is not useful:

> . . .researchers operate with many different understandings of levels and how to distinguish them. . .which level or levels are most appropriate turns out to be an empirical matter. . .it is a mistake to suppose that we always improve the quality of an explanation or causal analysis by invoking lower-level variables. . .we can do nuclear physics without doing chemistry and vice versa. . .there is no problem in principle with the notion of inter-level causation, including the notion of downward causation from "upper" [e.g., psychology] to "lower" levels. The temptation to think otherwise results, at least in part, from thinking of levels too exclusively in compositional terms. . .. We can establish the truth of upper-level causal claims. . .without making use of "underlying" lower-level information.

Kendler and Campbell (2009) offered a very compatible exposition of what they called an interventionist model of causation, wherein whether one should emphasize psychological or biological causal factors varies empirically. (See also the case studies that concluded Sharp & Miller, 2019.) In some cases, a single, biological, final, common pathway may play a key role in mental illness, as a downstream consequence of various psychological inputs; or diverse biological inputs may foster a single psychological phenomenon, with the latter the better place to focus assessment and/or intervention. For example (p. 885), "there may. . .be no unified 'biology of humiliation' that is sufficiently consistent across individuals to give much explanatory power." The authors emphasized that this interventionist perspective is "non-reductive and agnostic to issues of mind–body problem" (p. 881). Woodward (Chapter 35) describes and endorses the interventionist type of account as well.

Chapter 44 by Turkheimer notes that we do not ask what physical properties cause something to be a carpet, nor do we look for the physics equivalent of biomarkers of carpets. There is not some single, crucial physical property of carpets that make them carpets, even though every actual carpet has a physical composition. He suggests metaphorically that a bad choice of level can take an entity out of focus, such as a carpet, were one to focus on its physics. (Woodward, Chapter 35, argues similarly about the consequences of focusing on irrelevant details.) Turkheimer argues that Huntington's disease gene does not cause the disease. Rather, the gene *is* Huntington's disease. The gene is the crucial entity that is disordered (and the symptoms are not the disorder; they are symptoms of it). Thus,

Huntington's disease is in focus at a genetic level and not at the level of behavioral symptoms. But he points out that mental illness being most in focus at a genetic level is very unusual. We would go further: no traditional category of psychopathology has been shown to *be* the genes or genes that contribute to it. Again quoting Kendler (2005, p. 1250), "...we do not have and are not likely to ever discover 'genes for' psychiatric illness."

The new mechanist approach shows great promise for advancing our understanding of the relationship between the biological and the psychological. Thomas and Sharp (2019, p. 2) recently provided a very accessible entrée to the new mechanist framework and an extension of it to the psychopathology literature that fits perfectly with the RDoC approach: "In contrast to typical practices in psychological science, mechanistic science requires that psychological scientists constrain their conceptions of psychological functions to those that might plausibly be implemented in living systems." The authors provided a particularly useful notion of units of organization as an alternative to the fraught "levels" metaphor. (See Craver, 2007, Hardcastle, 1996, Miller, 2010, Woodward Chapter 35, and Wright & Bechtel, 2007, for further analyses and criticisms of the "levels" metaphor, in part for encouraging indefensible reification). Thomas and Sharp's concept is distinct from though highly compatible with the "units of analysis" dimension of the RDoC matrix.

20.6 CONCLUSIONS AND DIRECTIONS

This chapter engaged three of the major conference themes identified by the organizers in advance, and it has argued for these conclusions:

Theme 1: "The importance of reduction – under what circumstances are lower levels of explanation to be preferred? Is wholescale reduction possible or is it more realistic to pursue 'small' or 'patchy' reductive approaches?"

Conclusion: Eliminative reduction is not a viable option for relating psychological and biological concepts and phenomena. As we enter the fourth Decade of the Brain, eliminative reduction is nevertheless widely embraced in basic and clinical neuroscience. This greatly limits what the psychopathology literature can contribute to science, practice, and public policy.

Theme 2: "How is it best to conceive of the multiple 'levels' at which psychiatric illness can be understood? Is 'levels' even a useful term here?"

Conclusion: The "levels" metaphor is underspecified and encourages naïve reductionism. In the psychopathology literature, the "levels" metaphor is unnecessary, and, worse, it is often invoked casually and confidently, as if its meaning is obvious, but it is rarely explicated and commonly misleading. The new mechanist approach in recent philosophy of science provides promising if unfinished alternatives for understanding how the parts of complex phenomena relate, including causal relations, without the premise of hierarchical relationships between systems.

Theme 4: "Given that levels of explanation in psychiatry cross the mind-body divide – the subjective and objective worlds – how can we best span these widely divergent perspectives on reality?"

Conclusion: First, the psychopathology research literature, the policymakers and funding sources who shape its agenda, and the popular media that shape public perceptions should stop assuming that eliminative reduction is the goal of clinical science. Second, we should have the humility to acknowledge how little clinically applicable progress we have made over many decades of ardent clinical research. Third, we should explore and challenge the new mechanist school as a potential antidote to longstanding naïve reductionism by articulating fresh notions of causation and of relationships within and between psychology and biology in general and crucially in psychopathology. With help from that new approach, the categories and traditions of the *DSMs* and the dimensional constructs and diverse units of analysis now being actively developed under the RDoC framework may bring our science closer to comprehension, prevention, assessment, and treatment of mental illness.

REFERENCES

American Psychiatric Association. (2013) *Diagnostic and statistical manual of mental disorders (DSM-5).* Washington, DC: American Psychiatric Publishing.

Bartholomew, M. E., Yee, C. M., Heller, W., Miller, G. A., & Spielberg, J. M. (2019) "Reconfiguration of brain networks supporting inhibition of emotional challenge." *NeuroImage, 186,* 350–357.

Bates, T. C., Lewis, G. J., & Weiss, A. (2013) "Childhood socioeconomic status amplifies genetic effects of adult intelligence." *Psychological Science, 24,* 2111–2116.

Beauchaine, T. P., & Klein, D. N. (2017) "Developmental psychopathology and the diagnostic and statistical manual of mental disorders." In T. P. Beauchaine &

S. P. Hinshaw (Eds.), *Child and adolescent psychopathology* (3rd ed., pp. 33–67). Hoboken, NJ: Wiley.

Bechtel, W. (2007) "Reducing psychology while maintaining its autonomy via mechanistic explanations." In M. Schouton & H. L. de Jong (Eds.), *The matter of mind: Philosophical essays of psychology, neuroscience, and reduction* (pp. 172–198). Malden, MA: Blackwell.

(2017). "Explicating top-down causation using networks and dynamics." *Philosophy of Science, 84*(2), 253–274.

Bechtel, W., & Abrahamsen, A. (2008) "From reduction back to higher levels." *Proceedings of the 30th Annual Meeting of the Cognitive Science Society* (pp. 559–564). Austin, TX: Cognitive Science Society.

Berenbaum, H. (2013) "Classification and psychopathology research." *Journal of Abnormal Psychology, 122*, 894–901.

Bolton, D. (2013). "Should mental disorders be regarded as brain disorders? 21st century mental health sciences and implications for research and training." *World Psychiatry, 12*(1), 24.

Borsboom, D., & Cramer, A. O. (2013) "Network analysis: An integrative approach to the structure of psychopathology." *Annual Review of Clinical Psychology, 9*, 91–121.

Borsboom, D., Cramer, A. O. J., & Kalis, A. (2019) "Brain disorders? Not really: Why network structures block reductionism in psychopathology research." *Behavioral and Brain Sciences, 42*(e2), 1–63.

Borsboom, D., Cramer, A. O. J., Schmittmann, V. D., Epskamp, S., & Waldorp, L. J. (2011) "The small world of psychopathology." *PLoS ONE 6*, e27407.

Borsboom, D., Rhemtulla, M., Cramer, A. O. J., Van der Maas, H. L. J., Scheffer, M., & Dolan, C. V. (2016) "Kinds versus continua: A review of psychometric approaches to uncover the structure of psychiatric constructs." *Psychological Medicine, 46*, 1567–1579.

Brennand, K. J., Simone, A., Jou, J., Gelboin-Burkhart, C., Tran, N., Sangar, S., . . . McCarthy, S. (2011) "Modelling schizophrenia using human induced pluripotent stem cells." *Nature, 473*(7346), 221–225.

BBRF/Brain & Behavior Research Foundation. (2018, April) "What's new with TMS for depression and other brain diseases." https://us3.campaign-archive.com/?u=c6e89b4de3dfd70e795490632&id=7b7ae091ba&e=1a018af71d, accessed 04/05/18.

Carpenter Jr, W. T., & Davis, J. M. (2012) "Another view of the history of antipsychotic drug discovery and development." *Molecular Psychiatry, 17*, 1168.

Casey, B. J., Oliveri, M. E., & Insel, T. (2014) "A neurodevelopmental perspective on the Research Domain Criteria (RDoC) framework." *Biological Psychiatry, 76*, 350–353.

Clayson, P. E., & Miller, G. A. (2017) "Psychometric considerations in the measurement of event-related brain potentials: Guidelines for measurement and reporting." *International Journal of Psychophysiology, 111*, 57–67.

Cohen, J. (1988) *Statistical power analysis for the behavioural sciences* (2nd ed.). Hillsdale, NJ: Lawrence Erlbaum Associates.

Craver, C. F. (2007) *Explaining the brain: Mechanisms and the mosaic unity of neuroscience.* Oxford: Oxford University Press.

Craver, C. F., & Bechtel, W. (2007) "Top-down causation without top-down causes." *Biology and Philosophy*, *22*, 547–563.

Cuthbert, B. N. (2015). "Research Domain Criteria: Toward future psychiatric nosologies." *Dialogues in Clinical Neuroscience*, *17*(1), 89.

Cuthbert, B. N., & Insel, T. R. (2010) "Toward new approaches to psychotic disorders: The NIMH Research Domain Criteria project." *Schizophrenia Bulletin*, *36*, 1061–1062.

(2013) "Toward the future of psychiatric diagnosis: The seven pillars of RDoC." *BMC Medicine*, *11*, 126.

Cuthbert, B. N., & Kozak, M. J. (2013) "Constructing constructs for psychopathology: The NIMH research domain criteria." *Journal of Abnormal Psychology*, 122, 928–937.

Davis, J. M. (1976) "Recent developments in the drug treatment of schizophrenia." *American Journal of Psychiatry*, *133*, 208–214.

Engstrom, E. J., & Kendler, K. S. (2015) "Emil Kraepelin: Icon and reality." *American Journal of Psychiatry*, *172*, 1190–1196.

Ferrante, M., Redish, A. D., Oquendo, M. A., Averbeck, B. B., Kinnane, M. E., & Gordon, J. A. (2018) "Computational psychiatry: A report from the 2017 NIMH workshop on opportunities and challenges." *Molecular Psychiatry*, *24*(4):479–483.

Fodor, J. A. (1968) *Psychological explanation*. New York, NY: Random House.

Frances, A. (2014) "RDoC is necessary, but very oversold." *World Psychiatry*, *13*, 47–49.

Franklin, J. C., Jamieson, J. P., Glenn, C. R., & Nock, M. K. (2015) "How developmental psychopathology theory and research can inform the research domain criteria (RDoC) project." *Journal of Clinical Child & Adolescent Psychology*, *44*, 280–290.

Friston, K. J., Stephan, K. E., Montague, R., & Dolan, R. J. (2014) "Computational psychiatry: The brain as a phantastic organ." *The Lancet Psychiatry*, *1*, 148–158.

George, M. S., Lisanby, S. H., Avery, D., McDonald, W. M., Durkalski, V., Pavlicova, M., . . . Holtzheimer, P. E. (2010) "Daily left prefrontal transcranial magnetic stimulation therapy for major depressive disorder: A sham-controlled randomized trial." *Archives of General Psychiatry*, *67*, 507–516.

Golden, R. R., & Meehl, P. E. (1979) "Detection of the schizoid taxon with MMPI indicators." *Journal of Abnormal Psychology*, *88*, 217–233.

Goldfried, M. R. (2016). "On possible consequences of National Institute of Mental Health funding for psychotherapy research and training." *Professional Psychology: Research and Practice*, *47*(1), 77.

Gordon, J. A. (2018) "Towards a genomic psychiatry: Recommendations of the Genomics Workgroup of the NAMHC." *Director's Messages* published online March 29, 2018. www.nimh.nih.gov/about/director/messages/2018/towards-a-genomic-psychiatry-recommendations-of-the-genomics-workgroup-of-the-namhc.shtml, accessed 01/06/18.

(2019) "From neurobiology to novel medications: A principled approach to translation." *American Journal of Psychiatry*, *176*, 425–227.

Griesinger, W. (1854) *Die Pathologie und Therapie der psychischen Krankheiten*. Stuttgart: Krabbe.

Hardcastle, V. G. (1996) *How to build a theory in cognitive science.* Albany, NY: SUNY Press.

Hyman, S. E. (1998). "NIMH during the tenure of Director Steven E. Hyman, MD: The now and future of NIMH." *American Journal of Psychiatry, 155*(Suppl.), 36–40.

(2005). "Addiction: A disease of learning and memory." *American Journal of Psychiatry, 162*, 1414–1422.

(2010) "The diagnosis of mental disorders: The problem of reification." *Annual Review of Clinical Psychology, 6*, 155–179.

(2012) "Revolution stalled." *Science Translational Medicine, 4*, 155cm11.

Insel, T. R. (2010, April) "Faulty circuits." *Scientific American, 302*(4), 44–51.

Insel, T. R., & Cuthbert, B. N. (2009) "Endophenotypes: Bridging genomic complexity and disorder heterogeneity." *Biological Psychiatry, 66*, 988–989.

Insel, T. R., Cuthbert, B. N., Garvey, M. A., Heinssen, R. K., Pine, D. S., Quinn, K. J., . . . Wang, P. S. (2010) "Research domain criteria: Toward a new classification framework for research on mental disorders." *American Journal of Psychiatry, 167*, 748–751.

Kandel, E., & Squire, L. (1992) "Cognitive neuroscience: Editorial overview." *Current Opinion in Neurobiology, 2*, 143–145.

Kendler, K. S. (2005) "'A gene for. . .': The nature of gene action in psychiatric disorders." *American Journal of Psychiatry, 162*, 1243–1252.

(2008) "Explanatory models for psychiatric illness." *American Journal of Psychiatry, 165*, 695–702.

(2012a) "The dappled nature of causes of psychiatric illness: Replacing the organic functional/hardware-software dichotomy with empirically based pluralism." *Molecular Psychiatry*, 17, 377–388.

(2012b) "Levels of explanation in psychiatric and substance use disorders: Implications for the development of an etiologically based nosology." *Molecular Psychiatry, 17*, 11–21.

Kendler, K. S., & Campbell, J. (2009) "Interventionist causal models in psychiatry: Repositioning the mind–body problem." *Psychological Medicine, 39*, 881–887.

Kendler, K. S., Zachar, P., & Craver, C. (2011) "What kinds of things are psychiatric disorders?" *Psychological Medicine, 41*, 1143–1150.

Kozak, M. J., & Cuthbert, B. N. (2016) "The NIMH research domain criteria initiative: Background, issues, and pragmatics." *Psychophysiology, 53*, 286–297.

Kozak, M. J., & Miller, G. A. (1982). "Hypothetical constructs versus intervening variables: A re-appraisal of the three-systems model of anxiety assessment." *Behavioral Assessment, 14*, 347–358.

Lake, J. I., Yee, C. M., & Miller, G. A. (2017) "Misunderstanding RDoC. Mechanisms of mental disorders special issue," *Zeitschrift für Psychologie, 225*, 170–174.

Laruelle, M. (2013) "The second revision of the dopamine theory of schizophrenia: Implications for treatment and drug development." *Biological Psychiatry, 74*, 80–81.

Leshner, A. I. (1997). "Addiction is a brain disease, and it matters." *Science, 278*, 45–47.

(2007) "Behavioral science comes of age." *Science, 316*, 953.

Lilienfeld, S. O. (2007) “Cognitive neuroscience and depression: Legitimate versus illegitimate reductionism and five challenges.” *Cognitive Therapy and Research*, *31*, 263–272.

(2014) “The research domain criteria (RDoC): An analysis of methodological and conceptual challenges.” *Behaviour Research and Therapy*, *62*, 129–139.

Lilienfeld, S. O., & Treadway, M. T. (2016) “Clashing diagnostic approaches: DSM-ICD versus RDoC.” *Annual Review of Clinical Psychology*, 12, 435–463.

MacCorquodale, K., & Meehl, P. E. (1948). “On a distinction between hypothetical constructs and intervening variables.” *Psychological Review*, *55*, 95–107.

Marr, D. (1982) *Vision: A computational investigation into the human representation and processing of visual information.* New York: Freeman.

Maj, M. (2013) “Mental disorders as ‘brain disorders’ and Jaspers’ legacy.” *World Psychiatry*, *12*, 1–3.

Miller, G. A. (1996). “Presidential address: How we think about cognition, emotion, and biology in psychopathology.” *Psychophysiology*, *33*, 615–628.

(2010) “Mistreating psychology in the decades of the brain.” *Perspectives on Psychological Science*, *5*, 716–743.

Miller, G. A., Clayson, P. E., & Yee, C. M. (2014) “Hunting genes, hunting endophenotypes.” *Psychophysiology*, *51*, 1329–1330.

Miller, G. A., & Keller, J. (2000) “Psychology and neuroscience: Making peace.” *Current Directions in Psychological Science*, *9*, 212–215.

Miller, G. A., & Kozak, M. J. (1993) “A philosophy for the study of emotion: Three-systems theory.” In N. Birbaumer & A. Öhman (Eds.), The structure of emotion: Physiological, cognitive and clinical aspects (pp. 31–47). Seattle, WA: Hogrefe & Huber.

Miller, G. A., Rockstroh, B. S., Hamilton, H. K., & Yee, C. M. (2016) “Psychophysiology as a core strategy in RDoC.” *Psychophysiology*, *53*, 410–414.

Miller, G. A., & Yee, C. M. (2015) “Moving psychopathology forward.” *Psychological Inquiry*, *26*, 263–267.

Montague, P. R., Dolan, R. J., Friston, K. J., & Dayan, P. (2012) “Computational psychiatry.” *Trends in Cognitive Sciences*, *16*, 72–80.

Morris, S. E., & Cuthbert, B. N. (2012) “Research domain criteria: Cognitive systems, neural circuits, and dimensions of behavior.” *Dialogues Clinical Neuroscience*, *14*, 29–37.

National Advisory Mental Health Council Workgroup on Genomics. (2018) “Report of the National Advisory Mental Health Council Workgroup on Genomics: Opportunities and Challenges of Psychiatric Genetics Research Recommendations Summary.” [Internet]. National Institute of Mental Health. Available from: www.nimh.nih.gov/about/advisory-boards-and-groups/namhc/reports/namhc-genomics-workgroup-research-recommendations-summary.shtml, accessed 29/06/19.

Perera, T., George, M. S., Grammer, G., Janicak, P. G., Pascual-Leone, A., & Wirecki, T S. (2016) “The Clinical TMS Society consensus review and treatment recommendations for TMS therapy for major depressive disorder.” *Brain Stimulation*, *9*, 336–346.

Phillips, M. R. (2014) “Will RDoC hasten the decline of America’s global leadership role in mental health?” *World Psychiatry*, *13*, 40–41.

Piccinini, G., & Craver, C. (2011) "Integrating psychology and neuroscience: Functional analyses as mechanism sketches." *Synthese, 183*, 283–311.

Robins, E., & Guze, S. B. (1970) "Establishment of diagnostic validity in psychiatric illness: Its application to schizophrenia." *American Journal of Psychiatry, 126*, 983–987.

Sanislow, C. A., Pine, D. S., Quinn, K. J., Kozak, M. J., Garvey, M. A., Heinssen, R. K., . . . Cuthbert, B. N. (2010) "Developing constructs for psychopathology research: Research domain criteria." *Journal of Abnormal Psychology, 119*, 631–639.

Schwartz, S. J., Lilienfeld, S. O., Meca, A., & Sauvigné, K. C. (2016) "The role of neuroscience within psychology: A call for inclusiveness over exclusiveness." *American Psychologist, 71*, 52–70.

Sharp, P. B., & Miller, G. A. (2019) "Reduction and autonomy in psychology and neuroscience: A call for pragmatism." *Journal of Theoretical and Philosophical Psychology, 39*(1), 18–31.

Sporns, O. (2013) "The human connectome: Origins and challenges." *NeuroImage, 80*, 53–61.

Stephan, K. E., & Mathys, C. (2014) "Computational approaches to psychiatry." *Current Opinion in Neurobiology, 25*, 85–92.

Tabb, K. (2018, May) "Can psychiatry be precise?" Invited lecture at the "Philosophical Issues in Psychiatry V: The Problems of Multiple Levels, Explanatory Pluralism, Reduction and Emergence" conference, Copenhagen.

Thomas, J. G., & Sharp, P. B. (2019) "Mechanistic science: A new approach to comprehensive psychopathology research that relates psychological and biological phenomena." *Clinical Psychological Science, 7*(2), 196–215.

Wright, C., & Bechtel, W. (2007) "Mechanisms and psychological explanation." In P. Thagard (Ed.), *Handbook of the philosophy of science: Volume 4. Philosophy of psychology and cognitive science* (pp. 31–79). New York, NY: Elsevier.

Yang, A. C., & Tsai, S. J. (2017) "New targets for schizophrenia treatment beyond the dopamine hypothesis." *International Journal of Molecular Science, 18*, e1689.

Yee, C. M., Javitt, D. C., & Miller, G. A. (2015) "Replacing DSM categorical analyses with dimensional analyses in psychiatry research: The research domain criteria initiative." *JAMA Psychiatry, 72*, 1159–1160.

21

Non-reductionism, Eliminativism, and Modularity in RDoC: Thoughts about a Progressive Mechanistic Science

PETER ZACHAR

Greg Miller and Morgan Bartholomew advance an argument for the non-reductionist aspirations of the Research Domain Criteria (RDoC). They are particularly insightful about the shortcomings of the levels of analysis metaphor. In this commentary, I will focus on their philosophical claims about the Research Domain Criteria (RDoC) initiative because RDoC became the most contentious topic at the 2018 Copenhagen conference.

I argue that in their defense of the non-reductionist and psychological focus of RDoC, Miller and Bartholomew give short shrift to one of RDoC's great promises, but which is, by its very nature, potentially eliminativist. With respect to a mechanistic science, I suggest that that the mapping out of mechanisms for psychological processes cannot completely escape some intrinsic limitations (or complexities) of research programs in scientific psychology. I also express some worries about the neural circuit metaphor, which may be unnecessarily constraining mechanistic approaches by adopting too modular a theory of mind.

In the initial articulations of the RDoC project, the different architects were not in agreement about its conceptual basis (Bilder, Howe, & Sabb, 2013; Cuthbert & Kozak, 2013; Hyman, 2010; Insel, 2013; Miller, 2010). Several of them were biological psychiatrists who entered the field in the late 1970s when it seemed that the Nobel Prizes for discovering the biological bases of psychiatric disorders were just a little further up the road. They never made it that far, but RDoC was going to be the difference-maker they had been waiting for. In justifying RDoC, these psychiatrists voiced a contempt for the descriptive diagnostic systems of the *DSM* and ICD, blaming *DSM* categories for the lack of progress in the validation of psychiatric disorders – with "validity" meaning discovering the etiology and pathogenesis of disorders. Claims about mental disorders being brain disorders and some aspects of the emphasis on neural circuits likely reflect these commitments.

In addition to biological psychiatrists, however, the genesis of the RDoC initiative included scientific psychologists. Tanya Luhrmann (2000) has written about how physicians learn to see the world through a biological lens.

> What doctors are taught, what they assimilate more deeply than any other professional, is that we are creatures of the body, and that bodily processes, which they know in excruciating detail, are our life.
>
> (p. 87)

To earn a doctoral degree in psychology, however, even in biological psychology, you need to learn about developmental, social, and cognitive psychology; these provide a conceptual framework that medical school is less likely offer. The incorporation of scientific psychology into psychiatry is also paired with a disdain for *DSM* and *ICD* categories, but for different reasons. Statistically, latent trait models usually fit the data better than do latent class models (Haslam, Holland, & Kuppens, 2012). Nevertheless, the incorporation of psychology adds a non-reductionist flavor to RDoC. Greg Miller is one of the most dedicated anti-reductionists within the RDoC initiative (Miller, 2010; Miller & Keller, 2000).

Miller and Bartholomew – with a hint of triumphalism – suggest that the introduction of RDoC initiated a change at the NIMH away from eliminative reductionism, but I have to wonder if RDoC did that or the language in certain policy statements changed after the psychologist Bruce Cuthbert became the acting director of the NIMH in 2015. In an early draft of this commentary I wrote that their articulation of the non-reductionist aspirations of RDoC is welcome clarification, but I deleted that because I never thought it needed to be clarified. From its inception, RDoC represented an incursion of cognitive neuroscience constructs and factor analytic dimensional models from psychology into biological psychiatry – and its antipathy to eliminative reductionism was clear (Cuthbert, 2014; Cuthbert & Kozak, 2013). Many of my colleagues in philosophy did not see it that way. They key issue for them has not even been a matter of following what the NIMH does (shift money to basic science and animal models) rather than what some RDoC proponents say ("We do not advocate for biological reductionism!") because requiring that there be evidence that a psychological variable is implemented in a neural circuit is always included in what they say. And thus the philosophers continue to critique.

What is the argument for RDoC being a psychological rather than a diseased-based model? The argument is that we can potentially learn how psychological functions are implemented in the brain (and body), but *what* is implemented will remain psychological – and the goal is to better understand and modify those psychological functions (and in psychiatry and clinical psychology understand and modify psychological dysfunctions). Part of the RDoC project, claim Miller and Bartholomew, involves reduction, but it is not reduction aimed at eliminating the psychological in favor of the biological. This argument certainly rings true.

I remain a little puzzled, however, by what Miller and Bartholomew mean by claiming that depression cannot be either a brain disease or a chemical balance *on logical grounds*. Would that be analogous to someone in the nineteenth century saying that mood changes in general paresis of the insane cannot be symptoms of an infectious disease on logical grounds alone? Is this like saying Reginald Dwight cannot be Elton John on logical grounds alone or that the morning star cannot be the evening star on logical grounds alone? This raises complicated philosophical ideas about language and reference that need not be delved into here, but psychological concepts and biological concepts do not HAVE to be segregated into parallel tracks. The referents of *some* psychological concepts might be more plastic (or inscrutable). Psychological descriptions could integrate biological referents into the semantics of their concepts without losing their psychological focus.

I also worry that the functionalism and token identity theory Miller and Bartholomew use in promoting RDoC's non-reductionist credentials potentially draws attention away from one of RDoC's great promises. For example, in the classic functionalist picture, how pain is implemented physically might differ drastically between species, including for life forms from other worlds (like Vulcans or Gallifreyans) and even for advanced artificial life forms – and thus pain cannot be reduced to any one way it happens to be implemented. Pain in this picture is a like a universal concept. The important clinical question asks: how is pain implemented in mammalian bodies, and more specifically in human bodies. One of the great promises of the RDoC initiative is that in learning how psychological processes such as pain or depression are implemented in bodies, we can possibly discover a better way of carving up and conceptualizing those processes. In theory, future generations could possess psychological concepts and explanatory models that are practically unimaginable from within the constraints of our current knowledge.

My first major foray into the philosophy of psychiatry was an analysis of eliminativism in psychiatry and philosophy from the perspective someone trained in psychotherapy (Zachar, 2000). To my mind, even the non-reductionist approach to RDoC maintains some eliminativist goals. For instance, Miller and Bartholomew's description of the criteria for being a good RDoC construct is informative. A good RDoC construct must represent some cognitive or behavioral function, it must be relevant to psychopathology, and there must be some evidence that it is implemented in a neural circuit. They leave out that it is better if it is dimensional. There also seems to be a secret criterion; it is even better if it is applicable to animal models.

Will the "good" RDoC constructs become the new basic concepts for understanding the domain of psychopathology? If so, it is not just *DSM* and *ICD* categories that are targets for elimination. A whole cluster of folk and scientific psychological concepts that do not meet criteria may be targeted as well – consciously or not.

Let me return to something I mentioned earlier, a tendency on the part of some to suggest that the categorical model used in the *DSM* and the *ICD* bears some blame for lack of scientific progress. One can of course say we have not made the hoped-for progress using categorical approaches so let's try other approaches, but many of the comments one sees about categorical models are not so measured in tone. As I have noted elsewhere (Zachar, 2018), I am not in agreement with the contempt for the *DSM*. It is not because I prefer categories to dimensions, although I do favor kind concepts as a practical tool (Zachar, 2015). My disagreement is more along the lines of thinking that if we spent more time learning to be psychopathologists, some of the things that the *DSM* is so often indicted for would be seen a) as inherent limitations of any attempt to classify human psychological processes and behaviors and b) as providing important information about the complexity of the domain of psychopathology.

An alternative diagnosis of the problem would be to say that progress has been difficult because psychopathology is so complex and hard to figure out. Instead of saying psychiatry, psychology, and psychopathology are a lesser sciences due to a stubborn attachment to categorical models, one could just they are harder than a lot of other sciences Why harder? One of the best thought-out answers to that question was offered by Paul Meehl (1978) who suggested 20+ reasons why it has been and will continue to be difficult to make scientific progress. Interestingly, descriptive clinical psychiatry was listed in the five "noble traditions" (p. 817) that Meehl believed had permanent merit; this just prior to the publication of the *DSM-III*.

Let me say more about one item on Meehl's list which I select primarily because Ken Schaffner, Eric Turkheimer, and I recently revisited it

(Zachar, Turkheimer, & Schaffner, forthcoming). Even for those psychological concepts that may be more subject to reductive definitions, there are important limitations. In short, psychological concepts are abstractions and too "open" to nail down with metaphysical specificity. Let me explain further.

Open concepts are concepts whose meanings are subject to future correction in the light of new facts and therefore their definitions cannot be fixed. Meehl believed that open concepts are more intrinsic to psychology than they are to the natural sciences.

Consider this overlapping list of psychological processes: pride, self-satisfaction, self-centeredness, positive emotionality, gratification, honor, dignity, arrogance, grandiosity, and conceit. Pride and arrogance are different concepts, but in understanding behavior, they cannot always be neatly separated. Having vague boundaries, these processes can merge together in numerous ways. Also consider the variety of ways that that these processes can be exercised in what people think, say, and do – across the life span, across time, and across cultures. For instance, pride may manifest differently in a culture that rewards self-promotion versus in a culture that discourages it. With such diversity, how we understand any of these concepts can always be rethought in the light of new evidence.

In psychological science, such concepts are regimented with operational definitions, but because of their shifting degrees of overlap and the variety of ways they can be exercised, they cannot be reduced to any one operational definition. Because the concepts remain open, operational definitions are always partial definitions (Carnap, 1936, 1937; Poldrack & Yarkoni, 2016; Sullivan, 2017). Quite likely what we taken as the boundaries of mechanisms and the components of mechanisms for psychological processes will be influenced by such partial definitions. Understanding such intrinsic limitations of the science is an important part of training in psychology, and this understanding is potentially always in the background, but rarely explicitly asserted.

In their chapter, Miller and Bartholomew note that the "allowed" RDoC constructs such as attention, arousal, and positive emotionality are unlikely to have one-to-one relationships with *DSM* categories. Indeed, *DSM* categories such as depression seem like unlikely candidates for being implemented in neural circuits because as processes, they tend to draw on a whole cluster of psychological functions including perception, attention, arousal, expectation, memory, and so on – and those processes are distributed throughout the brain, not crammed not into a depression circuit. But the same can be said about arousal and positive emotionality – processes that also draw on perception, attention, memory and so on in the ways that they function. I would not go so far as to call for a return to the mass action perspective on mind and brain, but the pendulum may have swung a bit too far to the localization side.

The notion of a "neural circuit" is also a metaphor. With respect to complex psychological traits, talk about "circuits for" is not much better than talk about "genes for" or "genetic mechanisms for" (Kendler, 2005; Turkheimer, Horn, & Pettersson, 2014). Thinking about psychological processes as organized into distinct modules likely motivates the notion of dedicated mechanisms/circuits, but a mechanistic perspective does not require modules (Donald, 2001). Some complex psychological traits (both normal and abnormal), at least, may be akin to perfect storms, produced by complicated combinations of events, except that rather than being rare, we are built in such a way that such synergies continuously emerge. That is not an argument against pursuing a more mechanistic science of psychopathology, but a warning that the science of psychopathology will still be harder than a lot of other sciences and those mechanisms are probably not just a little further up the road.

REFERENCES

Bilder, R. M., Howe, A. G., & Sabb, F. W. (2013) "Multilevel models from biology to psychology: Mission impossible?" *Journal of Abnormal Psychology*, *122*, 917–927.

Carnap, R. (1936) "Testability and meaning." *Philosophy of Science*, *3*, 419–471.

(1937) "Testability and meaning—continued." *Philosophy of Science*, *4*, 104.

Cuthbert, B. N. (2014) "Response to Lilienfield." *Behaviour Research and Therapy*, *62*, 140–142.

Cuthbert, B. N., & Kozak, M. J. (2013) "Constructing constructs for psychopathology: The NIMH research domain criteria." *Journal of Abnormal Psychology*, *122*(3), 928–937.

Donald, M. (2001) *A mind so rare*. New York: W. W. Norton & Company.

Haslam, N., Holland, E., & Kuppens, P. (2012) "Categories versus dimensions in personality and psychopathology: A quantitative review of taxometric research." *Psychological Medicine*, *42*(5), 903–920.

Hyman, S. E. (2010) "The diagnosis of mental disorders: The problem of reification." *Annual Review of Clinical Psychology*, *6*, 155–179.

Insel, T. (2013) "Director's blog: Transforming diagnosis." Retrieved from www.nimh.nih.gov/about/director/2013/transforming-diagnosis.shtml

Kendler, K. S. (2005) "'A gene for': The nature of gene action in psychiatric disorders." *American Journal of Psychiatry*, *162*(7), 1243–1252.

Luhrmann, T. M. (2000) *Of two minds: An anthropologist looks at American psychiatry*. New York: Vintage Books.

Meehl, P. E. (1978) "Theoretical risks and tabular asterisks: Sir Karl, Sir Ronald, and the slow progress of soft psychology." *Journal of Consulting and Clinical Psychology, 46*(4), 806–834.

Miller, G. A. (2010) "Mistreating psychology in the decades of the brain." *Perspectives on Psychological Science, 5*(6), 716–743.

Miller, G. A., & Keller, J. (2000) "Psychology and neuroscience: Making peace." *Current Directions in Psychological Science, 9*(6), 212–215.

Poldrack, R. A., & Yarkoni, T. (2016) "From brain maps to cognitive ontologies: Informatics and the search for mental structure." *Annual Review of Psychology, 67*, 587–612.

Sullivan, J. A. (2017) "Coordinated pluralism as a means to facilitate integrative taxonomies of cognition." *Philosophical Explorations, 20*(2), 129–145.

Turkheimer, E., Horn, E. E., & Pettersson, E. (2014) "A phenotypic null hypothesis for the genetics of personality." *Annual Review of Psychology, 65*, 515–540.

Zachar, P. (2000) *Psychological concepts and biological psychiatry: A philosophical analysis.* Amsterdam, Netherlands: John Benjamins.

(2015) "Psychiatric disorders: Natural kinds made by the world or practical kinds made by us?" *World Psychiatry, 14*, 288–290.

(2018) "Quantitative classification as (re-)descriptive psychopathology." *World Psychiatry, 17*(3), 294–295.

Zachar, P., Turkheimer, E., & Schaffner, K. F. (forthcoming) "Defining and redefining phenotypes: Operational definitions as open concepts". In A. G. C. Wright & M. N. Hallquist (Eds.), *The Cambridge handbook of research methods in clinical psychology.* Cambridge: Cambridge University Press.

PART III

TAXONOMY, INTEGRATION, AND MULTIPLE LEVELS OF EXPLANATION

SECTION 8

22

Introduction

JOSEF PARNAS

Peter Zachar's chapter is devoted to the issue of description and descriptive psychiatry. Description is one of the discursive modes, the other being argumentation, narration and exposition. In practical use, all four components frequently co-exist. The purpose of description is a linguistic attempt to make an object, a person or a state of affairs more clear, articulated and vivid. The issue of description, taken on a theoretical or philosophical level, is an immense topic with connections to linguistics, semiotics, philosophy of language, pragmatics of language use, concept formation, philosophy of mind and metaphysics. Neither the chapter nor the following commentary have an aspiration to branch into all those domains. Peter Zachar is primarily concerned with the notion of the so-called descriptive psychiatry which is usually considered as a sort of inferior kind of psychiatry, only useful in our attempt to create explanatory models. Zachar tries to demonstrate that this is in fact not the case and he touches upon several important issues in psychiatric description. The commentary is a supplement to, rather than a critique of, Zachar's chapter that focuses upon the specific conditions of contemporary description in psychiatry that came into being in the wake of the so-called operational revolution (Parnas and Bovet, 2015). The commentary points to the fact that the aspiration of operationalism to achieve a simple, immutable and reliable description has failed with dramatic and negative consequences for psychiatry.

REFERENCE

Parnas, J., & Bovet, P. (2015) 'Psychiatry made easy: Operation(al)ism and some of its consequences.' In K. S. Kendler & J. Parnas (Eds.), *Philosophical Issues in Psychiatry III: The Nature and Sources of Historical Change* (pp. 190–212). Oxford: Oxford University Press.

23

Descriptive Psychopathology: A Manifest Level of Analysis, or Not?

PETER ZACHAR

23.1 INTRODUCTION

Descriptive psychopathology is often defined as classifying disorders with respect to manifest symptoms, course, and outcome, not underlying causes. This descriptive approach is exemplified by the operationalized diagnostic criteria of the *Diagnostic and Statistical Manual of Mental Disorders* (*DSM*) and the *Mental and Behavioral Disorders* section of the *International Classification of Diseases* (ICD).

Such a definition of descriptive psychology is problematic. A broader descriptive psychopathology encompasses most of the words, concepts, theories, and narratives used to depict psychopathology, all of which have undergone significant transformations over time (Berrios, 1996). The main purpose of the *DSM* and the *ICD* is to detect and identify disorders efficiently, not to describe them comprehensively. Thus neither should be thought of as a textbook of psychopathology (Zachar, 2018).

Descriptive psychopathology has also been characterized as an activity that defines scientifically immature stages of classification, with more mature scientific classifications being grounded in causal models (Hempel, 1961). To the extent that descriptive psychopathology is analogous to a table of contents that specifies what is included in the psychiatric domain rather than serving an explanatory role, this characterization has some merit. Unfortunately, this characterization misleadingly depicts a great chasm between description and explanation, leading to the disparagement of descriptive psychopathology as shallow, based only on surface features and mere appearances.

Interestingly, descriptive classification was central to the natural history approach to medicine that was articulated by leading thinkers of the scientific revolution in opposition to the speculative hypotheses of the

Galenic model (Anstey, 2011; Zachar & Kendler, 2017). Its advocates included Robert Boyle, John Locke, and Thomas Sydenham. Sydenham's contribution in particular initiated extensive work on classification in both medicine and biology.

Throughout the eighteenth century and the early part of the nineteenth century, however, medical classification readily included speculation about unseen essences and life forces. Important work on pathological anatomy in the mid-eighteenth century initiated the shift toward a more scientifically-based medicine, but in psychiatry, this shift led to what has been called the anatomoclinical model, which often as not, replaced speculation about essences with speculation about nerves and brain states. Dissatisfaction with anatomoclinical speculation by thinkers such as Kraepelin led to a resurgence of a more descriptive, empiricist approach in the late nineteenth century (Engstrom & Kendler, 2015).

In this chapter, I intend to move beyond a somewhat superficial construal of descriptive psychopathology as a listing of signs and symptoms by exploring philosophical perspectives about psychological descriptions. I will explicate what philosophers mean by bringing something under a description, give examples of re-descriptions in psychopathology, and articulate some norms for useful descriptions. I will also critically examine the claim that descriptions are shallow and explanations are deep by arguing that, many times, what we want from explanations that make them good explanations is that they make a difference in the psychological descriptions we are able to articulate. Following up on this analysis, I suggest that to talk about a descriptive level of analysis often involves running together several distinctions in a misleading way.

23.2 UNDER A DESCRIPTION

The philosopher Gilbert Ryle is often identified as a behaviorist, but if one examines his larger body of work, it is clear that he was not a behaviorist (Tanney, 2015). To call Ryle a behaviorist is to project onto him metaphysical commitments that he did not hold. Ryle rejected the Cartesian theory that beliefs, sensations, and intentions are entities in some ghostly realm called the mind, but he did not reject mentalist or psychological descriptions. One can describe behavior in Skinnerian terms, but also describe behavior using psychological idioms. In contrast to thin behavioral descriptions, Ryle considered psychological descriptions to be *thick descriptions*.

To illustrate, it is often said that we know other people's purposes and intentions by what they say and do, but as we can keep purposes to ourselves and not express them, they are not reducible to behaviors. Nevertheless, we largely tend to know our own purposes much like we know the purposes of others, through descriptions. We learn about our purposes by describing them to ourselves and others. Ryle's former student, Daniel Dennett (1996), renamed giving such descriptions as adopting the intentional stance. Indeed, any approach to psychopathology that refers to psychological concepts will, in part, be a descriptive psychopathology.

One important feature of descriptions is that the same 'event' can be subject to different descriptions. For instance, consider these distinctions offered by Ryle (1949) in his book *The Concept of Mind*:

Flying south versus migrating
Moving pieces on a board versus playing chess
Slipping versus pratfall

Both sides of these contrasts refer to the same behaviors, but they are different descriptions. Take the third contrast, slipping versus pratfall. Under the descriptions 'falling,' 'slipping,' and 'tumbling,' these are uncoordinated behaviors, but under the descriptions 'slapstick' and 'physical comedy,' they are intentional and skillful actions. We slip by accident, but comedic pratfalls are purposeful.

Ryle claims that in giving psychological descriptions, we look beyond the behavior, but not to shadowy mental operations. We look to other things the person says and does that are tied together by threads of implication. The description 'accidental falling' and the description 'skillful pratfall' have different implication threads. A pratfall is the result of hours of practice. A pratfall is repeated on demand. A pratfall occurs mainly during performances. A pratfall is often performed for pay. These additional descriptions have their own implication threads. Performed for pay implies that the person is a professional rather than an amateur comedian.

Together, this cluster of descriptions supports articulating higher order psychological descriptions such as 'being done on purpose' or 'being done intentionally.' According to Ryle, in this example there is not a mental event called the intention and a behavioral event, there is just one thing – the pratfall – which is intentional.

The phrase 'under a description' is nebulous and it is not always clear what work it does, but psychologists and psychiatrists use descriptions all the time. For instance, 'I am an anxious person' is a description. Anxiety is also an abstract concept that needs to be explicated. One way to explicate it is to offer further descriptions such as 'I worry so much that I cannot think clearly,' 'I always expect the worst to happen,' and 'I have nightmares every few nights.' The diagnostic criteria of the *DSM* and much of what psychologists call operational definitions are descriptions. In addition, descriptions can be metaphorical such as 'I often feel as if I am going to fall to pieces.' We know our own and others' psychology primarily through descriptions. Those who can give more elaborate descriptions are called psychologically minded.

Nor are descriptions relevant only to the concepts institutionalized in our official nosologies. For instance, Henriksen and Parnas (2017) describe disorders of the self in schizophrenia. According to them, disorders of the self 'are not psychotic phenomena,' 'are trait-like,' and 'date back to childhood.'

Parnas and colleagues' semi-structured interview titled the *Examination of Anomalous Self-Experience* (*EASE*) was developed on the basis of patient self-descriptions (Parnas et al., 2005). Patient descriptions of *a diminished sense of basic self* include "A feeling of total emptiness frequently overwhelms me, as if I ceased to exist" (p. 245) and "It as if I am not part of this world; I have a strange ghostly feeling as if I was from another planet. I am almost nonexistent" (p. 245).

To link descriptions in continental phenomenology with Ryle's framework is not a stretch. Although I will emphasize the empiricist credentials of the descriptive approach throughout this chapter, Dennett (2000) reports that Ryle had a deep knowledge of Husserl and phenomenology. According to Dennett, most of Husserl's topics can be found in *The Concept of Mind*.

The notion of implication threads also bears some similarity to the nomological network in clinical psychology (Cronbach & Meehl, 1955). The nomological network for a psychological concept such as generalized anxiety disorder (GAD) includes the ways in which it is observed/measured and how its meaning is partly specified by reference to other constructs such as "GAD is a psychiatric disorder" and "GAD and depression share vulnerability genes." The references to other constructs are implication threads. One problem with the nomological network is that it is a term of art inspired by logical positivism, a somewhat outmoded philosophy of science with which people are increasingly unfamiliar. To elaborate the nomological network, however, is also to build more elaborate descriptions.

23.3 RE-DESCRIPTION

The phrase 'under a description' is most often associated with Elizabeth Anscombe's (1957) work on intentional action. According to Anscombe, behaviors can be intentional under one description and not another. For example, the behavior of raising one's hand up and down is not intentional under the description 'flexing the muscles,' but under the description 'pumping water' it is intentional.

What is interesting about alternative descriptions is the possibility of re-describing – and how descriptions can change over time. One philosopher who has been very interested in the introduction of new descriptions is Ian Hacking (1995, 2002). In his view, certain behaviors are not acts of a particular kind until the descriptions under which those acts fall are historically available.

For example, 'having sexual relations with an eleven-year-old' and 'committing child abuse' are different descriptions. The various descriptions associated with child abuse such as: *the child is too immature for sex, this child is powerless, inappropriate sexual activity predisposes children to psychiatric distress later in life, abused children grow up to be abusers themselves,* and *sex with minors is illegal* are part of the conceptual network of child abuse. Hacking even suggests that the description 'this is child abuse' only became available in the 1960s; child abuse was not observed beforehand.

Articulating descriptions allows us to see things anew. Let's look at how this works for psychopathology. A historically important example of re-descriptive psychopathology is Donald Klein and Max Fink's (1962) elucidation of panic disorder. In the late 1950s, Klein and Fink were working at Hillside Hospital on Long Island, a voluntary treatment center specializing in psychodynamic psychotherapy. Within this setting, they had the opportunity to study the mode of action of newly discovered drugs such as imipramine. Klein wrote all the prescriptions in the hospital and in collaboration with the hospital staff followed the patients weekly to document what changes, if any, could be observed after beginning the medication.

Based partly on an interview of Klein for an article on the discovery of panic disorder, Felicity Callard (2016) reports that the first clue to panic disorder came from the treatment of a specific patient. He was referred to Klein by his therapist with a suggested diagnosis of schizophrenia, but had gotten worse on an anti-psychotic. Klein disagreed with the schizophrenia diagnosis, describing the patient instead as anxious, dependent, and demanding. Rather than altering the antipsychotic dosage to treat schizophrenia, he prescribed imipramine. Over the next few weeks, neither the patient, his resident therapist, nor the therapist's supervisor observed any difference while on the imipramine.

The nursing staff, however, did not agree. Their reasoning was articulated by one of the nurses who Klein described as a "good observer." The difference was that the patient no longer ran to the nurses' station every few hours in fear that he was dying.

It might seem obvious to us that the patient stopped running to the nurses' station because the imipramine had reduced the severity and frequency of his panic attacks, but when Klein asked him why he no longer ran to the nurses' station, the patient himself said he realized that they could not do anything for him. It was only after careful questioning that the role of panic and the reduction in panic became apparent.

Soon thereafter, Klein and Fink distinguished between the episodic anxiety associated with panic attacks and the expectant anxiety associated with phobic avoidance. Later, they proposed new descriptions such as 'this is a syndrome,' 'these are uncued panic attacks,' and 'you have panic disorder.' Once described, panic disorder was easy to notice.

23.4 FIVE DESIDERATA FOR USEFUL DESCRIPTIONS AND RE-DESCRIPTIONS

In this section, I will articulate some norms for useful descriptions and re-descriptions. Not every description needs to meet all five norms to be useful.

First, re-descriptions in particular should enhance noticing and observing. To illustrate, Klein and Fink did not discover panic attacks. Panic had been part of the psychiatric landscape at least since Freud (1895/1962) published 'On the grounds for detaching a particular syndrome from neurasthenia under the description "anxiety neurosis".' Neurasthenia, in current terms would be a mixed anxiety-depression presentation with clinically significant fatigue and somatic complaints. Freud described anxiety neurosis as a syndrome characterized by irritability, fearful catastrophizing, and panic attacks.

Yet Klein and Fink did not see panic *disorder* until their patient's running to the nurses' station was brought under the description of a panic attack rather than nested under the descriptions of 'schizophrenia' or 'anxiety neurosis.' Once described, however, they could say that panic disorder was there all along.

Second, although descriptions guide observation, those descriptions that cannot withstand further scrutiny are best abandoned. For instance, according to Freud, anxiety neurosis is a manifestation of sexual excitation without completion. In Freud's description of a panic attack, the rapid heartbeat and shallow breathing that normally occur during sexual intercourse occur instead in exaggerated form in a non-sexual context. In addition to judging that this was a mistaken causal hypothesis, we can also say it does not cohere with other descriptions of panic. Nor does it cohere in an interlocking way with descriptions of the sexual lives of people with irritability, chronic worry, and panic attacks.

To be historically fair, I should also note that when Freud introduced anxiety neurosis, it was an advance. For instance, Berrios (1996) reports that both Carl Westphal and Moritz Benedikt believed that panic attacks were the manifestation of an inner ear disorder, initiated by vertigo. Freud re-described the development of agoraphobia as a disorder of anxiety. According to Freud, the conventional notion that agoraphobia begins as a reaction to vertigo is incorrect because if people have an attack of vertigo without anxiety, their behavior does not become restricted. It is only after vertigo is combined with the other symptoms of anxiety that the restrictions develop. Agoraphobia, said Freud, is a disorder of anxiety.

Descriptions have multiple implication threads. Although a proposed description (such as 'this is anxiety neurosis') may later be rejected as inadequate, certain of its implication threads ('this is a disorder of anxiety') may be incorporated into another description ('this is panic disorder') and live on.

Third, descriptions may be, but need not be, antithetical to explanations. I readily acknowledge that distinguishing between describing and explaining is useful for some purposes. However, explanations offered on the basis of suitable information would themselves be elaborate descriptions that answer various 'why' and 'how' questions. This includes explanations of panic disorder with respect to avoidance learning or with respect to maladaptive cognitive assumptions. The kind of explanations sought by clinical scientists are those for which there is a higher bar to meet for adequacy – usually some epistemic norm or convention such as "an explanation should describe how psychological process are implemented in the brain" or "an explanation should describe targets for successful therapeutic intervention."

Fourth, descriptions and re-descriptions should provide more than summaries of behaviors. 'You are having a panic attack' is a description, but it is more than a concatenation of concrete descriptions such as rapid heartbeat and shallow breathing. "This is a panic attack" is the description of a kind or of a whole, and rapid heartbeat and shallow breathing are properties of the kind or parts of the whole.

A fifth desideratum for descriptions and re-descriptions is that they should facilitate the acquisition of new information not contained in the description itself. For instance, the description articulated to make sense of the restricting and avoiding behaviors associated with agoraphobia was 'the fear of open spaces.' Once Klein and Fink brought panic attacks into the foreground, they learned that in addition to avoiding open spaces, such patients will also avoid crowded theaters. This would have seemed like a very puzzling feature of the fear of open spaces, but once agoraphobia is brought under the description of panic disorder, one can see that patients who have panic attacks will avoid any situation where escape is difficult or they cannot easily get to a safe place – which includes large open spaces and crowded theaters.

23.5 DESCRIPTIONS: SHALLOW AND DEEP

In this next section, I want to challenge what has become a common characterization of descriptive psychopathology, that its focus on symptoms is shallow and analogous to diagnosing a fever rather diagnosing the different causes of fevers.

Historically at least, this is a faulty understanding of descriptive psychopathology. Kendler and Engstrom (2017) show that descriptive psychopathology was introduced as a dual critique of two nineteenth century nosological practices. The first was proposing diagnostic categories based on the presence of only single symptoms such as cough, fever, or dropsy (edema). The second was speculating about brain pathology. For instance, Theodor Meynert proposed that mania resulted from increased supply of blood in the cortex and depression resulted from a decreased supply of blood (Dalzell, 2018).

In contrast to single symptom diagnoses and neurological speculation, Kahlbaum, Hecker, and Kraepelin believed that it is important to carefully describe something akin to disease forms. Their example was general paresis of the insane which at that time was clearly a syndrome, but without an established etiology or pathophysiology. Descriptive psychopathology is often reduced to the descriptions it gives, such as symptoms lists, with little consideration afforded to what it is attempting to describe (psychological forms, patterns, and kinds). (Interestingly, representing how the nosological pendulum swings back and forth over the ages,

Stephan Heckers (2008) has proposed that emphasizing the search for natural disease units rather than studying individual clinical features such as reality distortion or mood abnormalities has held psychiatric research back).

Soon after the science of genetics was founded at the beginning of the twentieth century, the botanist Wilhelm Johannsen distinguished between the underlying elements or "genotype" and the observable "phenotype." An important contribution of the Mendelian model is that the same phenotype can be produced by different underlying biological genotypes. In psychology and psychiatry, this has become associated with a cluster of distinction such as:

Biological versus psychological
Cause versus effect
Deep versus shallow
Reality versus appearance

When these are all conflated or run together, psychology becomes an effect, shallow, and about how psychopathology appears. Biology becomes deep and the domain of real causes.

Something akin to this metaphysical view is suggested by Steven Hyman's (2010) claim that descriptive psychopathology is less valid in comparison to deeper etiologically-based and patho-physiologically-based approaches. In Hyman's view, the *DSM* classification of disorders according to observable signs and reported symptoms (phenomenology) is akin to the classification of species by phenotype – both of which emphasize surface features. In an interview for another article, Hyman labeled surface classifications as descriptive phenotypes and classifications that reveal what has gone awry in the brain mechanistic phenotypes (Delude, 2015).

One of Hyman's examples of classifying by phenotype is grouping together all organisms with wings as being of the same kind. Interestingly, this would be a taxonomic sibling of single symptom diagnoses. According to Hyman, if we consider deeper evolutionary relationships, it is evident that bat wings, bird wings, and insect wings evolved separately and are not homologous structures, i.e., they are different kinds of things. The wings of bats are more like the forelimbs of land dwelling mammals and the pectoral fins of whales than they are like bird or insect wings.

Many people are impressed by this argument, but it is a little deceptive. It was descriptively clear long before the introduction of evolutionary science and genetics that bat, bird, and insect wings are different kinds of things. Bat wings have hair, bird wings have feathers, and insect wings have neither. Readily observable morphology also showed how different they are – with bat wings being structured like hands, bird wings not so much, and insect wings not at all. It is not the case that these distinctions were shallow when made on the basis of appearances and became deep when they were made using data from paleontology and genetics. What evolutionary science and genetics did was to elaborate on these descriptions differences in scientifically meaningful ways.

23.6 MORE ON THE ARTICULATION OF NEW PSYCHOLOGICAL DESCRIPTIONS

In the first Copenhagen volume, I compared psychiatric nosology to biological taxonomies (Zachar, 2008). One of those taxonomic approaches is cladism. An attractive feature of cladism is that it groups things together in ways that would be counterintuitive if you just examined the readily observable phenotype. The realization that dinosaurs are closer to birds than they are to reptiles is one contribution of the cladistic approach. It has also altered scientific ideas about the dinosaur phenotype. There may be an analogous process in psychiatric taxonomy – namely the articulation of new psychological descriptions that were not previously obvious.

One possible example of calling attention to something not previously noticed is what we learn by looking at panic attacks with respect to the autonomic nervous system. The autonomic nervous system is conventionally divided into the sympathetic and parasympathetic nervous systems. One way of describing the escalation phase of a panic attack is to note that it is a sympathetic nervous system response and the de-escalation phase is a parasympathetic response. The sympathetic nervous system is tightly integrated anatomically because many of the cell bodies of the pre- and post-ganglionic neurons are located in close proximity to each other and can be activated at about the same time. A description of sympathetic activity would be that in the escalation of a panic attack, the rapid heartbeat, dizziness, sweating, and nausea all begin in close approximation to each other.

The de-escalation is a parasympathetic response. In the parasympathetic nervous system, the post-ganglionic cell bodies are located near the organs that their axons innervate. A description of parasympathetic activity would be that in the de-escalation of a panic attack, the dizziness dissipates before the heart rate and breathing return to normal.

If the panic attack can be brought under the description 'autonomic response,' and it calls our attention to something about panic that we did not notice before, that new description might be called deeper. This would include not only noticing the time course of the panic response, but seeing that these differences between the escalation and de-escalation are adaptive. When a threat situation suddenly appears, it is adaptive to quickly enter a fight or flight mode. Once it appears that the threat situation has passed, it is adaptive to keep the blood oxygenated with an accelerated breathing and heart rate for a while longer just in case the threat returns.

One implication of this example is that, if the description of a causal model contributes to the articulation of new, thicker psychological descriptions, then causal models are not antithetical to descriptive psychopathology. If biological activity such as sympathetic activation makes a difference at the phenotypic level, it may become *part of the description* of a panic attack. But rather than a mechanistic phenotype, it is better thought of as a re-described phenotype. Deeper is a metaphysically loaded term. From an empiricist standpoint, if the description of nervous systems activity becomes a part of our description of a panic attack, these descriptions are part of one thing, a thick description of a panic attack.

Is the same thing going on when we describe strong feelings of being close to someone as an oxytocin rush, describe someone who is impulsive as hypofrontal, or describe someone with PTSD as having an overactive HPA axis? It all depends.

Richard Rorty (1979) used a science fiction thought experiment to write about a humanoid species from another planet with advanced neuroscience who learned to report, upon being injured, that a particular bundle of c-fibers was firing. In the course of visiting this planet and learning the inhabitant's languages, philosophers from Earth were frustrated that they could not get the new species to also report that they also had "mental sensations of pain." The aliens readily agreed that c-fiber firings were unpleasant but they did not understand the notion of mental events that occur in addition to c-fiber activity.

If such a role for c-fibers were scientifically supported, Rorty says it would be possible to teach children that when they bump their head, this particular bundle of c-fibers is firing, when they get burned this bundle of c-fibers is firing, and c-fiber firings hurt. In contrast, our children are taught that when you bump your head and cry out, it hurts; when you burn your hand and pull it back, it hurts and when you are stuck with a pin and grimace, it hurts; and what unites them is they all involve the experience of pain which is in the mind, not the body.

The point Rorty is making does not depend the empirical plausibility of his thought experiment in which c-fiber firings are type identical with the experience of pain. Like with c-fibers, when learning language, if people learned that 'what parents feel toward newborn babies' and 'the strong intimacy of young love' have in common is called an oxytocin rush, then oxytocin rush would play a descriptive role. The same would be true of behaviors under the description hypofrontal and overactive HPA axis.

The descriptive roles in these cases would be a somewhat shallow though. Names are arbitrary, so we can call something 'feelings of closeness,' 'sensación de proximidad,' or 'oxytocin rush.' For something like an oxytocin rush to come to play an informative descriptive role rather than just being another option in a list of arbitrary labels, it should make a descriptive difference. The chemical and physiological explication should lead us to notice something psychologically and behaviorally that we might have not otherwise noticed.

In fact, making a descriptive difference is one way of thinking about the project of *deep phenotyping* in precision medicine. As described by Peter Robinson (2012), the current goal of deep phenotyping is to describe the full spectrum of abnormal variation associated with any diagnostic construct. In other words, deep phenotyping is an attempt to be *descriptively comprehensive*, in theory, doing the work of thousands of good describers.

In information science, this project includes specifying how the phenotypes are measured. From a levels-of-analysis perspective, a deep phenotype would be one that can be paired with a mechanistic explanation of some kind. Here the focus is on the search for the mechanisms. A related but different end goal might be not the search for mechanisms, but to use information about mechanisms to re-describe phenotypes, i.e., to offer new psychological descriptions.

23.7 DESCRIPTIONS AND LEVELS OF ANALYSIS

With respect to psychopathology, Gregory Miller has argued that "levels of analysis" is a metaphor (Miller, 2010; Miller & Keller, 2000). As a metaphor, we can examine the various ways it breaks down if taken too literally. Muhhamed Khalidi (2013) also argues that the levels metaphor is misleading because it assumes that kinds are ordered in a hierarchy in which lower levels underlie higher levels, but in some cases the lower level is irrelevant to what is a valid kind at a higher level.

The levels of analysis metaphor also incorporates a cluster of largely metaphysical implication threads that are often run together. These threads include:

Biological versus psychological
Cause versus effect
Deep versus shallow
Reality versus appearance

Two additional threads are

Theoretical versus descriptive
Latent versus manifest

These distinctions are meaningful, but thoughtlessly running them together can be misleading. As I argued earlier, when we mindlessly run these together, observable psychology becomes an effect, shallow, an appearance, descriptive, and manifest. Likewise, descriptive psychopathology becomes shallow, manifest appearances, and so on.

To say that there are things in the world called psychological events, which are appearances, and which are best explained with respect to biological causes that reside at lower levels of analysis is not a fact, but cluster of metaphysical conventions. To call such lower level explanations deeper is to offer a metaphysical compliment.

For example, are panic attacks mere appearances that represent a shallow and manifest level of analysis? As we saw with Klein and Fink's ur-patient, the role of panic with respect to his running to the nurse's station was not at all manifest or apparent, until so described. Nor was panic's causal contribution to avoiding crowded theaters and avoiding open spaces manifest until they were brought under the description of panic disorder.

When I was in my late 20s, I spontaneously began having physiological reactions to scenes in films with copious amounts of blood. I remember the first time it happened. The movie was *Interview with a Vampire.* In this scene, the vampire Lestat presents the reluctant vampire Louis with a wine glass full of human blood. As the scene progressed, I started sweating and felt a little dizzy, so stepped outside into the lobby. I assumed it had gotten hot in the theater because I had no conscious aversion to blood. After this first incident, I would occasionally get dizzy when I donated blood to the Red Cross. The first time that happened, I thought it was a reaction to loosing blood. With respect to movies, the dizziness and sweating became an occasional but bothersome reaction, and I learned to close my eyes or look away if there was likely to be a scene with copious amounts of blood.

Several years later, I was in front of a class describing the symptoms of a panic attack as I had done many times before. I went through the list of symptoms and got to sweating, dizziness, nausea and in the middle of the lecture I had a sudden insight, went silent for a moment, and blurted out "Oh my God, I have had limited symptom panic attacks!" Soon thereafter, I realized that my dizziness when giving blood was also panic-related. It seems obvious in retrospect and I am not sure how I missed it, but my missing it makes it equally obvious that panic attacks are not "manifest" until brought under the description "this is a panic attack." Indeed, one of the first interventions in the treatment of panic disorder is to tell people that they should not be afraid that they are dying; rather they are having a panic attack.

Psychological descriptions of behavior are not just manifest; they have to be articulated. This is especially true in psychopathology. Consider the following members of the descriptive psychopathology zoo: delusions, feelings of worthlessness, inflations of self-esteem, obsessions, intrusive thoughts, magical thought processes, identity disturbances, and feeling entitled. These are abstract descriptions that have to be explicated with more behavioral examples and none of them are manifest before being so described. Nor do they represent a single descriptive level of analysis because we need varying degrees of causal models and theories in order to articulate descriptions. If the theory is elaborate, we will have thicker descriptions.

23.8 CONCLUSIONS: THE SCOPE OF DESCRIPTIVE PSYCHOPATHOLOGY

Things like working memory and extroversion are abstractions – they do not have a shape, size, color, or state of motion. They are psychological descriptions that we apply to patterns of behavior – both our own and others' behavior. As stated, we know our own and others' psychology through descriptions.

One obvious worry about a descriptive psychopathology is that it includes too much under its scope. If we only know about psychopathology through descriptions, then descriptive psychopathology becomes all there is.

This raises an important question: to what do we contrast descriptive psychopathology? For abstractions, we need contrasts. We understand empiricism by contrasting it with rationalism and liberalism by contrasting it with conservatism. If there is no contrast, then it isn't a meaningful conceptual distinction. One thing that is certain is that descriptive psychopathology is not a contrast to psychoanalytic, biomedical, and cognitive behavioral theories. These all involve descriptions.

Several years ago, Ken Kendler and I listed the contrast 'causal versus descriptive' as part of our conceptual taxonomy for psychiatric nosology (Zachar & Kendler, 2007). This is often a meaningful contrast. For instance, when I teach personality testing to psychology graduate students, one of the problems I encounter is that they want to use an elevation on one scale to explain an elevation on another scale. Let's say Mr. X obtained high scores on scales measuring passivity, submissiveness, and social anxiety. In a psychological report, students will write "because Mr. X is passive and submissive, he avoids relationships and as a result, is highly anxious around other people." One of my constant refrains is "Stop trying to explain the elevations and just describe this person. He is passive, submissive, and anxious around other people is what you can legitimately say." But as we have seen, this contrast can be misleading as well because causal models are not always antithetical to descriptions.

I began the chapter by briefly mentioning the roots of descriptive psychopathology in Baconian natural history. Overtime, the natural history approach evolved into the philosophical empiricism of John Locke, David Hume, and John Stuart Mill. When seen as a part of the empiricist tradition, descriptive psychopathology becomes a metatheoretical perspective on the classification of psychopathology.

It emphasizes regularities and patterns and is cautious about making metaphysical inferences about causes. It rejects talk about hidden essences. It is nominalist and pragmatist, viewing things as alike in some ways and different in some ways. We can use similarities to describe things as belonging to the same kind for certain purposes, but for other purposes we may emphasize different groupings. These features of descriptive psychopathology emphasize the possibilities of re-describing. Given its historical association with empiricism, an alternative contrast to descriptive psychopathology is speculative psychopathology.

To construe descriptive psychopathology as a general theory of psychopathology, therefore, would be to mis-classify it. There are too many things that fall under descriptive psychopathology to say they are part of a single general theory. Yet descriptions are always there.

REFERENCES

Anscombe, G. E. M. (1957) *Intention*. Cambridge, MA: Harvard University Press.
Anstey, P. R. (2011) *John Locke and natural philosophy*. Oxford, UK: Oxford University Press.

Berrios, G. E. (1996) *The history of mental symptoms.* Cambridge, UK: Cambridge University Press.

Callard, F. (2016) 'The intimate geographies of panic disorder: Parsing anxiety through pharmacological dissection.' *Osiris, 31,* 203–226.

Cronbach, L. J., & Meehl, P. E. (1955) 'Construct validity in psychological tests.' *Psychological Bulletin,* 52(4), 281–302.

Dalzell, T. G. (2018) *Freud's Schreber between psychiatry and psychoanalysis.* Abingdon, UK: Routledge.

Delude, C. M. (2015) 'Deep phenotyping: The details of the disease.' *Nature,* 527 (7576), S14–S15. Retrieved from www.nature.com/articles/527S14a

Dennett, D. C. (1996) *The intentional stance.* Cambridge, MA: The MIT Press.

(2000) 'Re-introducing the Concept of Mind.' In G. Ryle (Ed.), *The concept of mind* (pp. vii–xvii). Chicago, IL: University of Chicago Press.

Engstrom, E. J., & Kendler, K. S. (2015) 'Emil Kraepelin: Icon and reality.' *American Journal of Psychiatry, 172,* 1190–1196.

Freud, S. (1895/1962) 'On the grounds for detaching a particular syndrome from neurasthenia under the description of "anxiety neurosis."' In J. Strachey (Ed.), *The standard edition of the complete psychological works of Sigmund Freud* (Vol. 3), (1893–1899) Early psychoanalytic publications (pp. 87–116). London: Hogarth Press.

Hacking, I. (1995) *Rewriting the soul: Multiple personality and the sciences of memory.* Princeton, NJ: Princeton University Press.

(2002) *Historical ontology.* Cambridge, MA: Harvard University Press.

Heckers, S. (2008) 'Making progress in schizophrenia research.' *Schizophrenia Bulletin, 34,* 591–594.

Hempel, C. G. (1961) 'Introduction to problems of taxonomy.' In J. Zubin (Ed.), *Field studies in the mental disorders* (pp. 3–22). New York: Grune & Stratton.

Henriksen, M. G., & Parnas, J. (2017) 'Clinical manifestations of self-disorders in schizophrenia spectrum conditions.' *Current Problems of Psychiatry, 18*(3), 177–183. doi:10.1515/cpp-2017-0014

Hyman, S. E. (2010)' The diagnosis of mental disorders: The problem of reification.' *Annual Review of Clinical Psychology, 6,* 155–179. doi:10.1146/annurev.clinpsy.3.022806.091532

Kendler, K. S., & Engstrom, E. J. (2017) 'Kahlbaum, Hecker, and Kraepelin and the transition from psychiatric symptom complexes to empirical disease forms.' *The American Journal of Psychiatry, 174*(2), 102–109. doi:10.1176/appi.ajp.2016.16030375

Khalidi, M. (2013) *Natural categories and human kinds.* Cambridge, UK: Cambridge University Press.

Klein, D. F., & Fink, M. (1962) 'Psychiatric reaction patterns to imipramine.' *The American Journal of Psychiatry, 119,* 432–438.

Miller, G. A. (2010) 'Mistreating psychology in the decades of the brain.' *Perspectives on Psychological Science, 5*(6), 716–743. doi:10.1177/1745691610388774

Miller, G. A., & Keller, J. (2000) 'Psychology and neuroscience: Making peace.' *Current Directions in Psychological Science, 9*(6), 212–215. doi:10.1111/1467-8721.00097

Parnas, J., Møller, P., Kircher, T., Thalbitzer, J., Jansson, L., Handest, P., & Zahavi, D. (2005) 'EASE: Examination of Anomalous Self-Experience.' *Psychopathology*, *38*(5), 236–258. doi:10.1159/000088441

Robinson, P. N. (2012) 'Deep phenotyping for precision medicine.' *Human Mutation*, *33*(5), 777–780. doi:10.1002/humu.22080

Rorty, R. (1979) *Philosophy and the mirror of nature*. Princeton, NJ: Princeton University Press.

Ryle, G. (1949) *The concept of mind*. Chicago, IL: The University of Chicago Press.

Tanney, J. (2015) 'Gilbert Ryle.' In E. N. Zalta (Ed.), *The Standford encyclopedia of philosophy*. Retrieved from https://plato.stanford.edu/archives/spr2015/entries/ryle

Zachar, P. (2008) 'Real kinds but no true taxonomy: An essay in psychiatric systematics.' In K. S. Kendler & J. Parnas (Eds.), *Philosophical issues in psychiatry: Explanation, phenomenology, and nosology* (pp. 327–367). Baltimore, MD: Johns Hopkins University Press.

(2019) 'Diagnostic nomenclatures in the mental health professions as public policy.' *Journal of Humanistic Psychology*, *59*(3), 438–445.

Zachar, P., & Kendler, K. S. (2007) 'Psychiatric disorders: A conceptual taxonomy.' *The American Journal of Psychiatry*, *164*(4), 557–565. doi:10.1176/appi.ajp.164.4.557

(2017) 'The philosophy of nosology.' *Annual Review of Clinical Psychology*, *13*, 49–71.

24

Psychiatry without Description

JOSEF PARNAS

In the beginning was the Word
The Gospel of John

Peter Zachar in his text touches upon multiple aspects of description. It is difficult to disagree with his presentation of these issues. However, their articulation invites some comments. Furthermore, I will address certain crucial topics that Zachar significantly omits, namely the particular nature and role of description in psychiatry and its evolution and contemporary problems. One point mentioned by Zachar which is worth reemphasizing is that descriptive psychopathology is more than a list of disorders and descriptions of symptoms and signs, but contains a large body of concepts, theories, accumulated clinical experience (recorded in many "classic" texts) and attempts of its generalizations – systematically acquired empirical knowledge from different fields – and explanatory models. Rather than calling it "descriptive psychopathology," we should perhaps call it the science of psychopathology. Zachar ascribes the origin of descriptive psychopathology to the era of Kraepelin and the birth of the anatomo-clinical model. However, we can find in-depth psychiatric descriptions already in the first half of the nineteenth century French and German psychiatry (e.g. Leuret, 1834). Moreover, the anatomo-clinical model preceded Kraepelin and is still very much alive today.

A proper science of psychopathology can never be a purely empiricist enterprise. In the contemporary scientific approach, the notion of "empirical" – say in "empirically derived classification" – can be depicted as a reception of objectively existing "raw" sensory data, undistorted by any figurative or conceptual effort of the mind. This approach is reflected in numerous studies using large patient samples examined with self-questionnaires and with conclusions derived from mathematical operations not guided by any hypothesis or clinical and conceptual considerations. This is an empirical model which antedated logical empiricism and which has forgotten everything about Karl Popper. This "empiricist" approach dominates today's academic psychiatry and is reflected in an immense body of exceedingly boring research literature. The science of psychopathology is in its essence interdisciplinary and contains or should contain concepts and ideas from anthropology, philosophy, sociology, biology and many other sciences. The most ambitious attempt to provide a comprehensive treaty of psychopathology was made by German psychiatrist and philosopher Karl Jaspers who first published his *General Psychopathology* in 1913 followed by several revised editions, the latest being in 1954 (Parnas, Sass, & Zahavi, 2013). Jaspers' psychopathology had a strong influence on continental psychiatry, but was translated into English only in 1963 and unfortunately exerted practically no impact on the Anglophone psychiatry.

Zachar rightly emphasizes that the current diagnostic manuals describing single disorders should not be mistaken for the textbooks of psychiatry but treated as merely useful guidelines to what he calls "efficient diagnosis." Zachar does not tell us what is efficient in this diagnosis nor where the truly informative textbooks of psychiatry for residents or consultants are to be found. Psychopathology in contemporary textbooks consists of reprints of *DSM*/*ICD* criteria and although all these criteria derive from psychopathological pre-*DSM* literature, the knowledge of these original texts has gone into oblivion. There are perhaps only few persons among contemporary psychiatrists who would be able to reconstruct this old accumulated knowledge in the form of a textbook.

We are now approaching the crucial issue, namely the status of language and the *DSM-III* epistemological revolution. Psychiatry is today eager to be considered as a real medical science (Cuthbert, 2014; Insel & Cuthbert, 2015). However, there is a profound dis-analogy between, let us say, oncology and psychiatry. An oncologist specialized in the treatment of small-cell pulmonary carcinoma will not read historical texts describing first surgical interventions in lung cancer. The texts which he would be reading will contain concepts (often abbreviated into acronyms) with a specific reference to genetic profiles and thematic processes and other laboratory findings. This is an entirely different matter from trying to describe a specificity of the delusions or hallucinations in schizophrenia which are standard psychiatric questions related to psychopathology. Psychiatric description is concerned with the phenomena of meaning either on the subjective or intersubjective and existential level. Psychiatric terms do not refer to real kind-like entities (Parnas & Urfer-Parnas, 2017). In other words, psychiatric description is very much influenced by the problems of meaning, signification and the issues involved in describing phenomenal experience. Such a description is often confronted with the problem of matching technical terms and the patient's personal experience. Unfortunately, it is common today to consider language as a tool only, which is useful for communication. This is reflected in the *DSM* system in the formulation of the so-called operational criteria. These criteria are not operational in any scientific or philosophical sense (Parnas & Bovet, 2015). Rather, they are simple lay language superficial descriptions of symptoms and signs. It is unlikely that the process leading to the creation of *DSM-III* was strongly influenced by theoretical and conceptual considerations and most importantly by the psychopathological and phenomenological corpus of knowledge (Parnas & Bovet, 2015; Parnas, Sass, & Zahavi, 2013). The criteria were believed to be uniformly understood by the entire profession, by patients and by the international psychiatric community. It was also believed that they would not undergo any semantic drift with time.

The *DSM-III* categories of disorders were basically replicated from pre-*DSM* diagnostic systems. However, the literature attached to those previous systems stopped being of interest and is largely unread. The *DSM-III* replicated categories, which were defined contextually and prototypically, with a list of sufficient criteria without any concern if a translation from prototype to component criteria would remain stable over time. Unfortunately, criteria acquired their own life disconnected from the founding prototype. The original categories and their component criteria have undergone dramatic semantic changes. We can here mention a few examples. The concept of depression has been expanded to cover any kind of human malaise (Parnas, 2012) and clinicians today are very often unable to detect a true melancholia. The concept of borderline personality disorder – which was intended to express extraverted, dramatic, and manipulating patients – has been transformed into an over-inclusive category also containing psychotic disorders (Zandersen et al., 2019; Zandersen & Parnas, 2019a, 2019b). Something similar has happened to the concept of obsessive compulsive disorder and in this process, the notion of what an obsession essentially is has been forgotten (Rasmussen et al., 2019). These examples point to the fact that description and language are complex phenomena that cannot be understood and properly employed from a perspective of a narrow medical model. French philosopher Merleau-Ponty distinguished *La langue* and *La parole* (language and speech) (Merleau-Ponty, 1962). Language, in his view, is a system of significations which has its own autonomous life independent of the individual speaker. There are occasions when it is language that speaks through me, rather than me that speaks the language. The signifying function of a term or a concept is heavily contextually determined and is very much dependant on relations of dissimilarity to other words (concepts). When we introduce a new word, say "cool", then all other similar adjectives somehow change in their linguistic value (Saussure, 1959). Language is often metaphorical; in fact, the metaphor is one of the most basic functional units in any language (Lakoff, 1987). It has a special importance in the psychiatric context. Often, the patient is trying to describe an experience which is pre-conceptual and pre-linguistic, and the only way to achieve a description is to make a recourse to metaphor. Thus, psychiatric description cannot be hoped to function as a stable, unchanging set of terms with fixed reference, but will have a much more fluid, contextual and historically bound status. All these banalities have profound consequence for conceptualizing psychiatric terms, validating those terms in the specific nature of the patient's experience and in professional communication (Nordgaard et al., 2013). This has also profound consequences for the conducting of a psychiatric interview. We have previously argued on epistemological (Nordgaard et al., 2013) and empirical (Nordgaard et al., 2012) grounds that contemporary *DSM*-style description is inadequate and that structured interviews are not a solution to overcome the problems of interpersonal communication.

What has been said about psychiatric categories may also be said about single psychopathological phenomena, i.e. symptoms and signs. In the current *DSM* vocabulary, there is a homogenization of the phenomena of anxiety, depression, delusion, hallucination, etc. The contemporary definitions and descriptions fail to capture profound differences in the manifestations of the phenomena, differences that may indicate dissimilarities of kind. It is helpful to mention certain examples: In the *DSM-III*, delusion is defined as a false personal belief based on incorrect inference about external reality and firmly sustained in spite of what almost everyone else believe and in spite of what constitutes incontrovertible and obvious proof of evidence to the contrary. This definition has been heavily criticized in nearly all its components (Bovet & Parnas, 1993; Cermolacce et al., 2010; Parnas, 2004) and it has morphed in the *DSM-5* to "fixed ideas" not amenable to correction. These defining permutations illustrate an intrinsic difficulty in trying to define psychopathological phenomena by simple criteria, which are not supported by a richer description of prototypical cases and conceptual considerations. Because language is not only a tool but a medium, it is also formative for our culture, self-understanding, and our understanding of mental life. Zachar quotes an example from Rorty about the extra-terrestrials who instead of using the word "pain," describes "firing in the C-fibres." This example is supposedly showing that with increasing biological explanatory power, we could replace mental terms with the terms referring to brain events. However, Rorty's example is flawed from the start: In his example, the extra-terrestrials mention unpleasant sensation, which they call firing of C-fibres. In other words, they do make a reference to a subjective experience or phenomenology. But perhaps we do not need to go through Rorty to look for examples. It is not uncommon that instead of saying that they feel unhappy, patients state that their brain is lacking serotonin or that psychiatrists, instead of saying to the patient that he suffers from psychosis, tell him that he has too much dopamine in his synaptic clefts. Apart from the doubtful truth of such statements, it is in itself alarming because it is pointing to a possible future simplification and homogenization of our language. This mixture of phenomenal and sub-personal terminology is unfortunately also characteristic of today's cognitive science and psychiatry. In other words, we find texts that purport to description of phenomenology, but which nonetheless use an admixture of sub-personal terms. A good example is the RDoC definition of perception as "computation of sensory data."

In sum, we are witnessing today a crisis of psychiatry and a crisis of psychiatric description. As we have repeatedly argued elsewhere (Zandersen et al., 2019; Zandersen & Parnas, 2019b), psychiatry needs to reinstate the science of psychopathology at the centre of its empirical ambitions. Only then can we expect a translation of neuroscientific progress into a progress in the everyday clinical work.

REFERENCES

Bovet, P., & Parnas, J. (1993) 'Schizophrenic delusions: A phenomenological approach.' *Schizophrenia Bulletin, 19*(3), 579–597.

Cermolacce, M., Sass, L., & Parnas, J. (2010) 'What is bizarre in bizarre delusions? A critical review.' *Schizophrenia Bulletin, 36*(4), 667–679.

Cuthbert, B. N. (2014) 'The RDoC framework: Facilitating transition from *ICD/DSM* to dimensional approaches that integrate neuroscience and psychopathology.' *World Psychiatry, 13*(1), 28–35.

Insel, T. R., & Cuthbert, B. N. (2015) 'Brain disorders? Precisely.' *Science, 348*(6234), 499–500.

Lakoff, G. (1987) *Women, Fire, and Dangerous Things: What Categories Reveal about the Mind.* Chicago: University of Chicago Press.

Leuret, F. (1834) *Fragments Psychologiques sur la Folie.* Paris: Crochard.

Merleau-Ponty, M. (1962) *Phenomenology of Perception.* London: Routledge & Kegan Poul.

Nordgaard, J., Revsbech, R., Sæbyt, D., & Parnas, J. (2012) 'Assessing the diagnostic validity of a structured psychiatric interview in a first-admission hospital sample.' *World Psychiatry, 11*(3), 181–185.

Nordgaard, J., Sass, L. A., & Parnas, J. (2013) 'The psychiatric interview: Validity, structure, and subjectivity.' *European Archives of Psychiatry and Clinical Neuroscience, 263*, 353–364.

Parnas, J. (2004) 'Belief and pathology of self-awareness a phenomenological contribution to the classification of delusions.' *Journal of Consciousness Studies, 11*(10–11), 148–161.

(2012) 'A sea of distress.' In K. S. Kendler & J. Parnas (Eds.), *Philosophical Issues in Psychiatry II: Nosology* (pp. 229–233). Oxford: Oxford University Press.

Parnas, J., & Bovet, P. (2015) 'Psychiatry made easy: Operation(al)ism and some of its consequences.' In K. S. Kendler & J. Parnas (Eds.), *Philosophical Issues in Psychiatry III: The Nature and Sources of Historical Change* (pp. 190–212). Oxford: Oxford University Press.

Parnas, J., Sass, L. A., & Zahavi, D. (2013) 'Rediscovering psychopathology: The epistemology and phenomenology of the psychiatric object.' *Schizophrenia Bulletin, 39*(2), 270–277.

Parnas, J., & Urfer-Parnas, A. (2017) 'The ontology and epistemology of symptoms: The case of auditory verbal hallucinations in schizophrenia.' In K. S. Kendler & J. Parnas (Eds.), *Philosophical Issues in Psychiatry IV: Classification of Psychiatric Illness* (pp. 201–216). Oxford: Oxford University Press.

Rasmussen, A. R., Nordgaard, J., & Parnas, J. (2019) 'Schizophrenia-spectrum psychopathology in obsessive-compulsive disorder: An empirical study.' *European Archives of Psychiatry and Clinical Neuroscience*. doi: 10.1007/s00406-019-01022-z. [Epub ahead of print]

Saussure, F. D. (1959) *Course in General Linguistics*. New York: The Philosophical Library.

Zandersen, M., Henriksen M. G., & Parnas, J. (2019) 'A recurrent question: "What is borderline?"' *Journal of Personality Disorders, 33*(3), 341–369. doi:10.1521/pedi_2018_32_348

Zandersen, M., & Parnas, J. (2019a) 'Borderline personality disorder or a disorder within the schizophrenia spectrum? A psychopathological study.' *World Psychiatry, 18*(1), 109–110.

(2019b) 'Identity disturbance, feelings of emptiness, and the boundaries of the schizophrenia spectrum.' *Schizophrenia Bulletin, 45*(1), 106–113.

SECTION 9

25

Introduction

PETER ZACHAR

In her chapter, Katie Tabb focuses on one of the major selling points used in the rollout of the Research Domain Criteria initiative (RDoC), specifically the claim that RDoC aspires to be a part of the precision medicine revolution in medicine (Insel, 2014). From this perspective, a *DSM* diagnostic category such as major depressive disorder is too coarse-grained to guide treatment selection. The hope of RDoC is that genetic and physiological biomarkers for neuropsychological dimensions that cut across conventional diagnostic boundaries may identify more homogeneous patient groups who respond to treatment in similar ways.

Tabb argues that the precision medicine movement has been presented as a kind of Kuhnian paradigm shift for disrupting conventional practices that are not working. Like the way that new paradigms disrupt what Kuhn calls normal science, the hope is that in the precision medicine movement, new unforeseen solutions will emerge leading to the development of more successful practices. According to Tabb, this precision medicine paradigm is composed of three core commitments nosological revision, big data, and reductionism.

Nosological revision includes under its scope the core justifications for RDoC. One, *DSM* and *ICD* categories are too heterogeneous to support the identification of causal mechanisms. Two, treatments in psychiatry are also nonspecific, only loosely bound to one's diagnosis and not based on validated theories of etiology or pathogenesis.

Big data was not a part of the original vision for RDoC, but has become more important since Joshua Gordon became the director of the National Institute of Mental Health (NIMH) (Gordon, 2017a, 2017b). In this chapter, big data refers to the creation of publically available data sets with hundreds of variables and tremendous sample sizes, and thus a high degree of statistical power for finding effects. Tabb suggests that large data sets will not alter the inherent complexity of psychiatric disorders. She also questions the RDoC approach to big data which places a high priority on the data of the neuroscience (see Romeijn and van Loo Chapter 29 for an alternative view of big data).

This bring us to the third commitment of the precision medicine paradigm: reductionism. Tabb succinctly summarizes the reductive assumptions of precision medicine: *lower-level mechanisms are causal in a way that facilitates intervention on higher levels outcomes of interest.* Tabb then proceeds to lay bare the strongly reductionist, disease-oriented commitments of Thomas Insel who was the director of the NIMH when RDoC was developed. She supports her claims with statistics showing a substantial shift in NIMH funding priorities away from clinical research to basic research during Insel's time as NIMH director.

In the second part of the chapter, Tabb asks two questions. Is precision necessary for progress and is precision sufficient for progress? The first thing she does is to question whether progress requires commitment to nosological revision, big data, and reductionism. She suggests that nosological revision is necessary, big data can be helpful but is not necessary, reduction is potentially harmful, and precision, writ large, is not sufficient.

Tabb is sympathetic to the critiques of *DSM* categories from a variety of perspectives in psychology and psychiatry – none of which advocate for biological reductionism, but she also mentions Ken Kendler's explicitly pro-*DSM* notion of iteration and incremental changes. In the sharpest part of her chapter, she offers some socially penetrating criticisms of how the NIMH is using public funds that have been allocated to reduce the nation's mental health burden. Rather than fund projects that could have important, more immediate impacts on people's lives, she says, the NIMH preferentially funds projects based on some philosophically suspect metaphysical assumptions about the causes of mental disorder. Nearer the end of the chapter, she puts on her philosopher of science hat and offers a clear summary of what a challenge it is to validate the attribution that some condition is a disorder, and why having a biological substrate or representing an extreme value on some dimension of functioning cannot sufficiently validate disorder status.

During the conference, Katie's talk was the most contentious, especially for several of the leaders of the RDoC initiative who were in attendance and there was a spirited but professionally conducted discussion. Katie certainly held her own and stuck to her guns. Chapter 20 by Greg Miller and Morgan Bartholomew is in some respects a response to Katie's talk as is Bob Bilder's commentary on Katie's chapter. For instance, with respect to NIMH funding priorities, Bilder suggests that her use of statistics is selective and provided a distorted picture of NIMH funding policies.

Like in Miller and Bartholomew's chapter, Bilder disputes the charge that the RDoC initiative represents a philosophically and scientifically naïve advocacy of biological reductionism or that it is specifically tied to big data, suggesting that Katie Tabb is arguing against a straw man – with one exception. On the topic of nosological revision Bilder asserts that Tabb remains far too sympathetic to the *DSM* nosology.

His main message is that the RDoC leaders are psychologists and psychologically oriented psychiatrists who do not have metaphysical commitments to biological reductionism, far from it. In their view, a lot of what is going to be discovered in neuroscientific research program won't lead to adequate theories of human psychopathology until they are also conceptualized ecologically, meaning as having broader functions best understood in various psychosocial, developmental, environmental, and cultural contexts.

REFERENCES

Gordon, J. (2017a) 'The future of RDoC.' *Director's Messages*. Retrieved from www.nimh.nih.gov/about/director/messages/2017/the-future-of-rdoc.shtml

Gordon, J. (2017b) 'RDoC: Outcomes to causes and back.' *Director's Messages*. Retrieved from www.nimh.nih.gov/about/director/messages/2017/rdoc-outcomes-to-causes-and-back.shtml

Insel, T. R. (2014) 'The NIMH Research Domain Criteria (RDoC) project: Precision medicine for psychiatry.' *American Journal of Psychiatry*, 171(4), 395–397.

26

Should Psychiatry Be Precise? Reduction, Big Data, and Nosological Revision in Mental Health Research

KATHRYN TABB

26.1 INTRODUCTION

The National Institutes of Health's Precision Medicine Initiative, introduced under the Obama administration in 2015, has been portrayed as a paradigm shift in American medicine (Lesko 2007, De Grandis and Halgunset 2016, Juengst et al. 2016, Fernandes et al. 2017). Renamed "All of Us" in October 2016, the initiative aims to recruit a nationally representative research cohort of one million people in order to "accelerate our understanding of individual variability and its effect on disease onset, progression, prevention, and treatment."[1] Along with a burst of public funding for cancer genomics, the Initiative was part of a national embrace of *precision medicine*, which the National Research Council defines as "the tailoring of medical treatment to the individual characteristics of each patient" (2011); the National Cancer Institute describes it as "an approach to patient care that allows doctors to select treatments that are most likely to help patients based on a genetic understanding of their disease."[2] One immediate effect of the growing interest in precision medicine has been a reallocation of resources toward genetics and other basic sciences that promise to generate the sort of discoveries that will transform clinical diagnostics in these ways.

The author thanks Maël Lemoine, Scott Lilienfeld, Jan-Willem Romeijn, Jim Tabery, and Hanna M. Van Loo for discussions about these themes and feedback on this chapter.

1 National Institutes of Health Precision Medicine Initiative (PMI) Working Group, https://acd.od.nih.gov/working-groups/pmi.html. Accessed December 20, 2018. In the first decades of the twenty-first century, "precision medicine" came to eclipse other popular terms, such as "personalized medicine" or "individualized medicine," in the American context – so I use it here. For a discussion of the rhetoric of the movement, see De Grandis and Halgunset (2016), Juengst et al. (2016), and Lemoine (2017).

2 National Cancer Institute, www.cancer.gov/about-cancer/treatment/types/precision-medicine. Accessed December 20, 2018.

American psychiatry, as represented by the National Institute of Mental Health (NIMH), enthusiastically joined in the precision medicine movement in the first years of the twenty-first century. The NIMH introduced the Research Domain Criteria (RDoC) project, an alternative classification protocol by which psychiatric researchers can present their proposals to the funding body without relying on psychiatry's traditional diagnostic categories. In this sense, RDoC aspires to mirror precision medical developments in other fields, for example, oncology, where genetic signatures have been discovered that cross-cut traditional taxonomic groupings of tumors based on organ of origin. The NIMH has also refocused its research priorities on the neural circuitry thought to cause mental illness, including the search for neurophysiological markers of disease. By 2014 its director, Thomas Insel, could herald RDoC as "precision medicine for psychiatry" (Insel 2014). While the number of proposals ultimately funded under RDoC has been modest, the scheme has come to carry great symbolic weight as a challenge to business as usual in psychiatry, where the accepted targets for research have long been the types of psychopathology codified in the *Diagnostic and Statistical Manual of Mental Disorders* (*DSM*).[3]

The aim of this chapter is to evaluate what precision psychiatry has amounted to in the early years of the twenty-first century, specifically with respect to its role in the fortunes of reductionism in psychiatric research. Medical reductionism can be understood as those approaches – often characterized as "biomedical" or "naturalist" – that prioritize the discovery of underlying mechanisms (at, e.g., the level of the gene or the neural circuit) that can explain higher-level phenomena such as phenomenology, behavior, or measures of well-being.[4] I will argue in Section 2 that precision medicine is best understood as the pursuit of this reductionist commitment together with two other medical commitments. The first is *nosological revision,* the improvement or transformation of traditional diagnostic categories. The second is *big data*, the compilation of research that makes use of innovative large-scale data collection and analysis techniques of the sort employed by the All of Us Initiative.

3 See, e.g., the February 2014 issue of *World Psychiatry* (13:1) for an overview of different stances on RDoC from a number of prominent psychiatrists; for attention from philosophers, see contributions in Kincaid and Sullivan (2014) and Poland and Tekin (2017).

4 For an overview of medical reductionism, see Andersen (2016). For a broader orientation to debates over reduction in the life sciences, see Kaiser (2015, chapter 2).

To argue that precision is a new *paradigm* for medicine is to imply that the commitments grouped together under the precision label must be jointly fulfilled in order to achieve medical progress. The appeal to Thomas Kuhn's theory of scientific change is a way to imply that, in more contemporary language, the combination of nosological revision, big data and reduction will "innovatively disrupt" medical business as usual, solving the crises of stalled psychopharmacological research and ineffective treatments (Lilienfeld and Treadway 2016, 443); as Carpenter has put it, RDoC is "motivated by the limited success of traditional paradigms" (2016, 563). The adoption of the language of precision psychiatry has, in some cases, been quite self-conscious, an attempt to "assist in creating a stronger identity" for a new vision of psychiatric progress (Fernandes et al. 2017). But while critical taxonomic projects, the trawling of enormous datasets, and the search for lower-level mechanisms have each proved revolutionary in some fields of medicine, these successes do not prove that the paradigm of precision is a recipe for transformative medicine across the board.

One way to characterize the way in which the precision paradigm aims to disrupt traditional practices is in its reversal of the usual relationship between its three commitments. Whereas taxonomic revision has broadly been theorized as a driver for the collection and analysis of data concerning the mechanisms underlying disease, precision medicine encourages a bottom-up approach, in which nosology is the outcome, rather than the starting place, for research. The primary place of pathology in shaping medical inquiry is handed over to the basic and translational sciences. In psychiatry, robust arguments have been made for the urgent need for nosological revision, not only by the NIMH but by a variety of stakeholders. Prioritizing the search for reductive breakthroughs using innovative methodological tools is often taken to be an obvious corollary. However, there is little consensus that the other two precision commitments, to big data and to reduction, are either necessary or sufficient to bring about the kind of taxonomic transformation that psychiatry seems to need. If reduction and big data are not necessary for taxonomic revision, precision as a paradigm may not be appropriate for psychiatry; or so I argue in Section 3. In Section 4, I make the case that fulfillment of the three precision commitments are also not sufficient for psychiatric progress, because the project of nosological revision is incoherent without psychopathology, which neither reductionism nor big data alone can provide. I conclude that the value of each precision's commitments for psychiatry is better assessed independently and circumstantially.

26.2 THE THREE COMMITMENTS OF PRECISION MEDICINE

As noted above, precision medicine is usually defined in terms of the matching of patients with appropriate therapies on the basis of the presence or absence of certain diagnostic features, or biomarkers. The website for the White House Initiative describes precision medicine as "an innovative approach that takes into account individual differences in people's genes, environments, and lifestyles. It gives medical professionals the resources they need to target the specific treatments of the illnesses we encounter, further develops our scientific and medical research, and keeps our families healthier."[5] The successful application of this approach to an outstanding medical problem requires two achievements. A therapeutic intervention must be demonstrated to be effective for some population of patients and a biomarker must be discovered – most commonly a gene variant, but possibly also a blood product, neural signature, behavior, etc. – that identifies individuals who can be successfully matched with the therapy. Some scientists have worried that variation in drug response might not typically be predictable at any particular lower level, like the genetic level (Senn 2001, 2018). In psychiatry, an even broader skepticism about the value of biomarkers for clinical practice has been voiced on the grounds that the pathways to mental illness are too complex to allow for stratification by, e.g., genetic profiling for therapeutic purposes (Lemoine 2016; Turkheimer, this volume).

Perhaps in response to this sort of skepticism, biomarkers are often taken to not simply indicate correlative relationships between classes of patients and specific drug responses, but to explain these correlations. In other words, precision medicine is taken to ideally deliver a new understanding of disease etiology and the mechanisms through which therapeutic agents do their work. For example, Hey and Kesselheim describe the aim of precision medicine as

> [T]o discover and harness a true biological explanation for why a drug will work for an individual patient. Hypotheses take the form: "Treatment T is effective for condition C, as defined by testing positive for biomarker B, where B is determined by diagnostic assay A." Additional assumptions – why A is a reliable test for B; why B should predict

[5] The Precision Medicine Initiative, https://obamawhitehouse.archives.gov/precision-medicine. Accessed December 20, 2018. Since the change of administration following the 2016 presidential election, this page has been archived.

> activity of T against C – are now "built into" the hypothesis, so decisive tests of PM cannot be agnostic about underlying theory.
>
> (2016, 448)

Precision medicine is thus more than an approach to treatment that considers individual variation; it is an approach to research that privileges the discovery of biomarkers that play a key role in the etiology of disease, allowing them to act as both therapeutic targets and diagnostic tests. Driving this is the search for reticent causal mechanisms that can only be revealed through the analysis of powerful datasets, and that can be used to ground new medical taxonomies. I consider the rationale for this sort of nosological revision in psychiatry in the next section, before turning to big data and finally reduction in Sections 2.2 and 2.3, respectively.

26.2.1 The First Commitment: Nosological Revision

The precision medicine ideal is that treatment decisions will be based on a demonstrable relationship between a diagnostic marker and an intervention, rather than on a statistical norm. While precision treatments will not be "personal" – patients will still be treated as members of a group having or lacking certain biomarkers – precision medicine aims to bring about a much more complex and nuanced re-stratification of the patient population than is afforded by traditional diagnostics. Some of the most dramatic examples have been new taxonomic groupings resulting from the identification of so-called Mendelian conditions, rare disorders caused by single-gene mutations (Haendel et al. 2018). Existing taxonomies have also been reformed, for example, for certain cancers (Curtis et al. 2012), cystic fibrosis (Paranjape et al. 2018), diabetes (Meigs et al. 2008), and epilepsy, where new classifications based on etiological discoveries are already being used clinically (Zuberi and Brunklaus 2018).

Within psychiatry, the need for a nosological revolution was brought into view by critics of the *DSM* at the beginning of the twenty-first century. The worry was growing that the *DSM*'s categories had become "reified," treated as entities even though they did not represent natural kinds. Steven Hyman, then the acting director of the NIMH, wrote in 2010 that that the *DSM*'s categories do not refer to real types in nature, but only to diagnostic constructs that gather together heterogenous cases of psychopathology (Hyman 2010). I have argued elsewhere that the problem Hyman identified had less to do with the metaphysics of mental disorders – the *DSM*, after all, explicitly recognizes that its categories are constructed – than with the fact that the *DSM*'s categories group patients together in ways that do not allow for relevant facts about mental disorder to be discovered (Tabb 2015, 1049). For example, in a grant application under the RDoC scheme, the psychologists Benjamin Lahey and David H. Zald give the following rationale for their proposal: "Categorical mental disorders do not 'line up' one-to-one with variations in the functioning of neural circuits. Rather, neural circuits align with narrower neurobehavioral constructs that are themselves related to psychopathology in cross-cutting fashion."[6]

The aim of the Research Domain Criteria scheme, then, was to produce an alternative classification protocol for psychiatric research that did not rely on the *DSM*'s categories, but rather on the sort of "neurobehavioral constructs" that Zald and Lahey describe. It consists of a matrix on which scientists identify the objects of their study; the columns of the matrix are units of analysis from genes up to behaviors, while the rows are constructs borrowed not from psychopathology but from cognitive science, such as "auditory perception" and "cognitive control." Finding a conflict between scientific innovation and clinical precedent, the NIMH chose scientific innovation. In effect, they rejected what has been called the "vindication project," the attempt to validate psychiatry's categories through the discovery of underlying mechanisms (Murphy 2014, Tabb 2015). Despite its powerfully negative stance toward traditional nosology, however, RDoC's advocates have emphasized that it is not, itself, a project of nosological revision, but rather a piece of a larger scheme which will ultimately bring about the appropriate changes:

> [RDoC] begins with the humble realization that we do not know enough to develop a precision medicine approach to mental disorders. We need a decade of intense scientific work – from molecular factors to social determinants – to understand normal and abnormal behavior, based on a deep understanding of mechanisms.
>
> (Insel 2014, 396)

The thought is that once our scientific understanding of physiology has improved, our understanding of pathophysiology will follow, and will be the foundation on which new treatments can be developed. While the distal aims of the RDoC scheme may be to "validate tasks for use in clinical

[6] Project # R01MH098098-01, "RDoC Constructs: Neural Substrates, Heritability, and Relation to Psychopathology." https://ndar.nih.gov/edit_collection.html;jsessionid=7F67694A8D01CBF01AE45243F43A5C9C.node3?id=2099&source=RDoCdb&funding=NIH+-+Extramural. Accessed January 24, 2019.

trials, identify new targets for treatment development, define meaningful clinical subgroups for the purpose of treatment selection, and provide a pathway by which research findings can be translated into changes in clinical decision making" (Morris and Cuthbert 2012, 29), these activities will emerge out of "a decade of intense scientific work."

26.2.2 The Second Commitment: Big Data

The precision medicine paradigm can be seen in part as a response to transformations in how medical data are collected and used. As Monteith et al. note, "Healthcare is one of the fastest growing segments of the digital world, with healthcare data [including provider- and patient-reported data and biomedical research data] increasing at a rate of 50% per year" (2015). The widespread adoption of electronic health records, along with the dropping costs of data accumulation and storage, has resulted in vast new public (e.g., the Cancer Genome Atlas and the All of Us initiative) and private (datasets belonging to hospital systems and research institutions) reservoirs of information that can be integrated with demographic and clinical data. When precision medicine is described as a revolution in the way data are collected and utilized, one of two things is usually meant: either that the patient's clinical experience will be transformed by the availability and integration of their past clinical records, lifestyle information, and -omics profiles or that vast new stores of biomedical information will, in aggregate, transform medical discovery (Prainsack 2015). Accordingly, individuals are encouraged to participate in the All of Us Initiative both by an appeal to self-interest (the hope of better personal care) and to altruism (the promise of future scientific breakthroughs).

These two projects come together in the precision ideal of making data collection more systematic such that it is useful not only for clinical purposes but for research ones; this requires that patients are "deeply classifiable" in order to make their data available for inferential methods like machine learning and statistical analysis (Haendel et al. 2018). "Big Data" is used to refer to data sets so large and complex that they cannot be analyzed using traditional statistical methods and instruments. One way to conceive of precision medicine is as the set of theories that are struggling to reduce unruly masses of data using new bioinformatics platforms – and not always succeeding (Prainsack 2015, Lemoine 2017). Indeed, the fortunes of precision medicine are tied to the viability of these advances in data organization and analysis, which give rise not only to empirical challenges but to ethical ones surrounding the collection and distribution of personal information.[7] Concerns about information overload – not only for individuals who offer up their own medical information, but also for the variety of researchers and clinicians who make use of it – are growing. There are calls for transparency about what data are useful in the clinical setting versus the research setting, and for a greater scrutiny of the potential for analysis and integration of data that are often not collected in standardized ways (Prainsack 2015).

A big challenge for medical big data is the integration of information from methods collectively referred to as the "omics" of precision medicine: those studying everything from the genome, to the proteome, to the microbiome, and recently, the "exposome" – the totality of an organism's environmental exposure (Topol 2014). The complete picture of the individual that might come into view through a mosaic of all these different "omics" – what has been called the "panoromic" (Topol 2014) – holds obvious clinical appeal. A group of Stanford scientists gathered exhaustive data on one of their number in order to demonstrate the value of an integrative personal omics profile, and the resulting "Snyderome" did indeed impact the lifestyle of the scientist in question, Michael Snyder (Chen et al. 2012, Snyder 2012). But the gathering of information at the level of the individual and the use of big data to make discoveries about biological correlates for phenotypes of interest are very different tasks, both of which have been subsumed within the project of precision. This has been facilitated by the ambiguity of the word "biomarker" which, as noted above, is used to refer to both a diagnostic property (of a patient) and a causal factor (of a disease process). The term "biomarker" thus can refer to a relation between different sorts of relata: signs/symptoms and underlying mechanisms, phenotypes and treatment responses, and lower-level and higher-level mechanisms (see Lemoine and Tabb, in progress).

Genome-wide association studies (GWAS) have become a significant new tool for discovering genetic markers for disease. By looking at the entire genomes of people sharing a symptom profile and comparing them to genomes of healthy people, it has become possible to discover not only chromosomal regions but the actual gene variants that are associated with certain phenotypes. For some conditions, the discovery of a genetic biomarker can be transformative for our understanding of a disease and, sometimes, for its treatment in the clinic. For example, using methods

[7] These ethical aspects of the precision medicine paradigm fall outside of the scope of this paper, but for an orientation towards these issues, see Prainsack (2015), Juengst et al. (2016), and Eyal et al. (2018).

such as GWAS and other genomic study designs like exome sequencing, rare Mendelian conditions have been identified and treatments have been found on the basis of this precise classification. For example, in one notable case a young patient displaying mysterious neurological symptoms was discovered to carry a mutation of the *SLC52A2* gene, and the known association between *SLC52A2* and Brown-Vialetto-Van Laere syndrome 2 pointed the way to a completely different course of care that proved life-changing (Petrovski et al. 2015).

There is reason to think this sort of success story using GWAS cannot be expected as readily in psychiatry. Diseases whose clinical treatment are likely to be transformed through genetic research, Lemoine has argued, share four key attributes: they can be reliably diagnosed on the phenotypic level, they are heritable, they reach a certain level of frequency in the population, and they are caused by a specific mechanism that is relatively simple (Lemoine 2016). But heterogeneity is a structural feature of psychiatric nosology (Olbert et al. 2014) and high rates of comorbidity are a fact of clinical life, indicating that traditional disease classifications do not represent diseases with discrete causal pathways (van Loo et al. 2013). While the heritability of neuropsychiatric disorders has been, for a long while, recognized to be collectively robust, individual diagnostic categories have not been shown to be distinctly heritable (Gandal et al. 2016) – relatives of an individual with schizophrenia have a higher chance of having that disease themselves, and also of having multiple other affective and cognitive disorders (Sullivan et al. 2017). While many psychiatric disorders have disturbingly high prevalence rates, no single causal pathway has been discovered that can explain even one of the common categories of psychopathology. The Psychiatric Genomics Consortium, after a decade of concentrated study, has declared that there are no common genetic variants with large effect sizes to be discovered in the field. The need to instead locate rare genetic variants of large effect and/or common ones of small effect makes the utility of GWAS more dependent than ever on enormous sample sizes, difficult to obtain even for relatively common psychiatric disorders (Sullivan et al. 2017). Even once they are obtained, a host of statistical errors and artifacts must be understood and avoided, requiring innovation and refinement of traditional analytic techniques.

Psychiatric neuroscience faces even greater challenges of this sort; given the expense of magnetic resonance imaging (MRI), neuroscientific data are much more time-consuming and expensive to collect than genetic data, and datasets are accordingly much more limited in size. And when precision psychiatry advocates call for new efforts at data collection and organization, they are often not referring to genetic but to neuroscientific research. This is at the heart of the NIMH's vision for progress in psychiatry, captured in the first strategic objective of the Institute, "Define the Mechanisms of Complex Behaviors," which is framed in terms of focusing "on the basic science required for understanding mental illnesses." The RDoC framework has been described as having its foundation in three postulates:

> First, mental illnesses are presumed to be disorders of brain circuits. Secondly, it is assumed that the tools of clinical neuroscience, including functional neuroimaging, electrophysiology, and new methods for measuring neural connections can be used to identify dysfunction in neural circuits. Third, the RDoC approach presumes that data from genetics research and clinical neuroscience will yield biosignatures that will augment clinical signs and symptoms for the purposes of clinical intervention and management.
>
> (Morris and Cuthbert 2012, 33)

Insel himself is the author of publications with titles like "Psychiatry as a Clinical Neuroscience Discipline" (2005) and "Brain Disorders? Precisely" (2015).

The RDoC matrix is not just a framework but also a cache of the sort of information that the NIMH views as valuable for cutting-edge psychiatric research. The information included in each cell is not meant to indicate that the research on that construct at that unit of analysis is complete, but rather to provide "a convenient repository of tasks and measures for when [researchers] are writing grants, or a useful resource when they are approaching a new topic of research. One way that the RDoC matrix may help to facilitate the scientific review culture is to provide a place for common terms and approaches."[8] One particular aim of RDoC is the establishment of a large database – "RDoCdb," housed within the NIH/NIMH's data repository – that will give researchers a significant shared resource to draw on, already conforming to the matrix structure.

26.2.3 The Third Commitment: Reduction

Andersen has recognized three forms that reductionism can take in the medical context. It can refer to the aim of reducing a system to its

8 RDoC's FAQ, from www.nimh.nih.gov/research-priorities/rdoc/rdoc-frequently-asked-questions-faq.shtml. Accessed January 23, 2019.

component parts; of reducing a set of models to a single, unifying model; or of reducing of a complex system to a simpler causal model (Andersen 2016, 81). These methods are mutually informative, and can contribute to the aim of isolating the part of a causal pathway leading to a disease state where clinicians can best intervene. In the context of precision, reductionism is best understood as the valuing of any and all of these methods, leading to the preference for research that aims to identify the lower-level signal in the noise of higher-level malfunction. Precision medicine, as a paradigm, rests on the assumption that lower-level mechanisms are causal in a way that facilitates intervention on higher-level outcomes of interest, that is, disease states. In this assumption, the two aspects of precision medicine I identified above – the matching of patients to therapies and the furthering of biomedical knowledge – come together.

To take one success story commonly rehearsed by advocates of precision medicine, the discovery of the overexpression of the HER2/neu receptor by certain tumors allowed for the development of trastuzumab (branded as Herceptin), a chemotherapy that targets only tumors caused by *HER2* gene amplification. Diagnostic tests can now identify either the amplification of the gene or the overexpression of the protein, allowing tumors that are responsive to trastuzumab to be diagnosed as such, regardless of their clinical presentation. This transformative medical advance was due to the reduction of diverse causal pathways leading to the signs and symptoms of certain cancers to a disfunction at the genomic and proteomic levels. However, as Lemoine has argued, the success of monoclonal antibodies like trastuzumab may be attributable to specific molecular features of this class of drug, leaving open the question of how representative the invention of Herceptin and ensuing nosological revision in oncology will turn out to be (2017, 20).

Nonetheless, this sort of combination of reductive and integrative methods is starting to bear certain fruit in psychiatry, as with, for example, the finding in 2016 of gene variants that increase the expression of a gene called complement component 4A that plays a role in synaptic pruning, a process that scientists have identified as causally relevant to schizophrenia using animal models (Sekar et al. 2016). Scientists working in neuropsychiatry and genetics are confident this is just the beginning (Gandal et al. 2016), but while the C4A discovery is unusual in so far as it has shed light on the causes of a major psychiatric disorder, it is far from clear how it could lead to clinical innovation. As noted above, some scientists have expressed doubt that GWAS hits that are similarly illuminating will be forthcoming for psychiatric disorders, despite successes in related fields, like neurodegenerative disease (Need and Goldstein 2016, 245). In any event, such discoveries would differ from success stories like the discovery of various monoclonal antibodies, and fall short of what precision medicine has promised; not only a transformation in diagnosis and etiology, but also in treatment (Lemoine 2017, 19).

Perhaps in part because of the disappointments psychiatric genetics met with early in the twenty-first century, the NIMH has turned its attention to the connectome. In discussing the rationale for RDoC, two of its architects describe the following pitfalls of the *DSM*'s use in the research setting:

> [T]he current system imposes three constraints upon the independent variable (i.e., group classification) in psychiatric studies: first, symptoms are the unit of analysis that must be utilized; second, particular constellations of symptoms must be employed (i.e., the DSM polythetic criteria or their ICD [International Classification of Diseases] equivalents); and third, the symptoms must be employed (with rare exceptions) simply to render a binary, diagnosis present/absent decision rather than being quantified in any way. RDoC is intended to free investigators from these constraints
>
> (Morris and Cuthbert 2012, 32)

The RDoC initiative funds proposals that present research in terms of cognitive neuroscientific constructs, investigating relationships between different levels of analysis. One way to see this shift is that rather than determining the appropriate targets for psychiatric research, the NIMH encourages researchers to simply use the matrix to identify their objects of study to the funding body. As will be discussed further below, researchers need not specify a pathological lesion or process – the RDoC initiative supports investigations of normal function, as well as recognized factors in pathology. Another key motivation of the RDoC initiative is to limit the role that the phenomenological level – that is, psychopathology itself – plays in guiding what research should be identified as (and funded as) "psychiatric."

Under Insel's guidance, the operating budget for the NIMH's Division of Neuroscience and Basic Behavioral Science increased by 28% between 2005 and 2014, while the budget for research into epidemiology, treatment, and health services decreased by 16.7%.[9] Insel wrote in his

[9] Intel, Thomas, "Anatomy of NIMH Funding," from www.nimh.nih.gov/funding/funding-strategy-for-research-grants/the-anatomy-of-nimh-funding.shtml. Accessed January 24, 2019.

Director's Blog, "Applicants who are not funded frequently assume that NIMH has stopped funding their area of science: clinical researchers complain that NIMH only cares about basic science and basic scientists rue the assumed emphasis on clinical research. The reality is that NIMH has maintained a diverse portfolio of basic, clinical, and services research, but many worthy projects are not funded in each of these areas" (ibid.). However, as he acknowledges, there was a $35 million-dollar reduction in spending on clinical trials between 2011 and 2014 – a cut by almost a third. Over all, the budget of the Division of Translational Research was reduced by 12.8% between 2005 and 2014, in order, Insel writes, that contracts might be shifted from clinical trials "to next generation 'experimental medicine' trials that will be more informative of disease mechanisms" (ibid.).

Insel argues that neuroscientific findings "are forcing psychiatrists to rethink the causes of mental illness," and to see psychopathology as biological, rather than mental. He cites evidence that, after centuries of ignorance about the workings of the brain, neuroscience can now show how "the malfunction of entire circuits may underlie many mental disorders" (Insel 2010, 44). While a ubiquitous one in the literature, the term "underlie" is ambiguous (Miller 2010, 720); but it would seem from the previous quote that Insel believes neurobiological malfunction to cause mental disorder, rather than just correlating with it. For example, he explains how OCD can be reduced by cutting the axons that link the orbitofrontal cortex to the caudate, and argues, "such a clear effect produced by physically altering the connections within a brain circuit offers strong evidence for the principle that symptoms of mental disorders can arise from the dysfunction of a specific circuit" (Insel 2010, 47). In response to this kind of claim, Schwartz and his co-authors, all psychologists, write, "Although we certainly applaud the increasing incorporation of the biological level of analysis and of biological indicators in conceptualizations of psychopathology, conceptualizing mental disorders as brain diseases is both logically confused and confusing" (Schwartz et al. 2016, 60). Describing psychological phenomena – such as, for example, the mechanisms by which psychotherapy works – in neurological terms can amount to "neuroredundancy," insofar as nothing explanatory is gained by characterizing the phenomenon at the neural level that was not already known at higher levels of description. For purposes of nosological revision, as Wakefield has put it, many contributory causal factors of small effect are "about as diagnostically informative as listing "gravity" when trying to explain a plane crash" (2014, 39).

26.3 IS PRECISION NECESSARY FOR PSYCHIATRIC PROGRESS?

What is to be gained by championing precision medicine as a paradigm? By subsuming the three commitments just described under the label of "precision," advocates suggest that they come as a package: those who are committed to one of precision's projects should be committed to the others. But this packaging begs the question of whether nosological revision, big data, and reduction are all in fact necessary for medical progress across the board. When the conceptual underpinnings of the precision medicine movement are scrutinized, it is not obvious why the commitments *should* be concomitantly required, or how, when taken together, they give a comprehensive answer to the question of what twenty-first century medicine needs. In the case of psychiatry, I argue in this section, there is little consensus that precision's three commitments are all necessary or even always helpful for psychiatric progress. In particular, while there is a broad consensus around nosological revisionism, there is extensive debate about the appropriateness of reductionism as a project for psychiatry.

In Section 2.1, I described the case made by precision psychiatrists for nosological revision, based on worries about the appropriateness of *DSM* categories as research targets for biomedicine. But it is worth noting that other constituencies besides biomedical psychiatrists have long been frustrated with the *DSM*. The majority of the manual's detailed structure and content is ignored by clinicians, who tend to use the same narrow set of diagnostic categories as a means to secure insurance reimbursements for patients and to communicate with other clinicians (First and Westen 2007). Diagnoses are often given not because they fit the clinical phenomena, but because they facilitate care decisions that clinicians make on the basis of their expertise (Bowker and Star 1999, Whooley 2010). Indeed, it has been recently argued that what is needed is not just a new taxonomic system but a new approach to the place of diagnosis within psychiatric practice more generally, due to the oversized and ineffectual role the *DSM* has taken in patient care (Maj 2018).

There is, then, a broad consensus that nosological revision is past due. Other means of reform besides the NIMH's have been advocated for, however, they do not qualify as precision medicine because they are not reductive and/or do not privilege big data. Kendler has offered a proposal for nosological revision through what Chang (2004) has called "epistemic iteration," a process of scientific change that is fundamentally theory-driven rather than big data-driven. Kendler agrees that psychiatrists for decades "have hunted for big, simple neurochemical explanations for psychiatric disorders and have not found them." But he is less sanguine than Insel that nosological revision can simply follow along after bottom-up scientific discovery, writing, "We need to regard our nosological systems as structures of substantial value to our young field. We should seek to pass them on to our successors in yet better shape than we found them" (2012, 320). In Kendler's view, nosological revision should motivate research, not just fall out of it, and he sketches out an iterative process by which the application of different validators to psychiatric categories can shift them over time from historical clinical syndromes to etiologically based diagnoses.

Other critics have offered proposals that use data-forward techniques to bring about nosological revision without embracing reductionism, focusing on symptoms instead of either disease categories or underlying mechanisms (e.g., Wanders et al. 2016, Borsboom et al. 2018). Attempts to implement non-reductionist, data-driven projects of nosological revision at scale include the Roadmap for Mental Health Research in Europe (ROAMER), an initiative of the European Union that ran from 2011 to 2015 and that aimed to bring about a transformation in mental healthcare by financing research into not only biomedicine but five other relevant domains: infrastructures and capacity building, psychological research and treatments, social and economic issues, public health, and well-being (Haro et al. 2014). More recently the Hierarchical Taxonomy of Psychopathology (HiTOP) project has aimed to introduce an alternative nosology to the *DSM* by using quantitative methods like factor analysis to group together symptoms, producing a dimensional psychopathology that can be used in the place of traditional categories in the clinic and research settings (Kotov 2017). These efforts are of a piece with broader revisionary projects that keep medicine focused on higher-level targets, such as psychological or phenomenological data or social and environmental factors, while still advocating for nosological change and embracing quantitative methods. These have included explicit calls for data-driven "precision" medicine that eschews reductionism (Khoury 2016) as well as attempts at nosological revision which do not subscribe to either reductionism or big dataism, such as the *Psychodynamic Diagnostic Manual*, a joint effort put out in 2006 by psychoanalytically oriented psychiatrists, psychologists, and social workers.

Some clinicians and researchers view reductionism as not only unnecessary for progress in psychiatry but even counterproductive; according to these critical voices, uncertain prospects for clinical application makes basic science research a worrisome place to invest public funds that have been earmarked for improving the nation's mental health burden. The NIMH's prioritization of reductionistic approaches has made some researchers feel that "the not-so-implicit message" of RDoC, as one psychiatrist and global health expert has opined, "is that economic realities, social factors and cultural preferences should wait until the neuroscientists have discovered the 'truth' and then fall into line accordingly" (Phillips 2014, 40). The NIMH's funding priorities were referred to in 2012 by the editorial board of *Nature* as leaving research into psychosocial interventions "scandalously underfunded" (Nature Editorial Board 2012). An interdisciplinary group of scholars, all of whom have served on the NIMH National Mental Health Advisory Council, recently wrote of their concern that an overenthusiasm for neuroscience was stripping funding from research into the sources of mental health disparities and means of overcoming them (Lewis-Fernandez et al. 2016, 508). There has been a recent call for more funding for clinical psychological research on the grounds that this research can, more quickly and more reliably, transform clinical diagnostics and care in alignment with the NIMH's goals, even if it does not provide the kind of reductionistic research that the NIMH is prioritizing (Teachman et al. 2019).

Whereas traditionally, clinical studies have collected data in order to solve specific challenges to diagnosis and care, there have been increasing calls for collections of data that, like other -omics banks, could be mined to answer a broad variety of hypotheses about psychopathology. In psychiatry especially, big data has shown promise in augmenting randomized controlled trials (RCTs), which use atypical patient populations, with information about actual service users including populations excluded from or underrepresented in RCTs (Monteith et al. 2015). Data mining also has the potential to discover biomarkers that correlate with treatment response and allow for risk prediction, even without elucidating the mechanisms that explain therapy efficacy (Paulus 2015). It has also been argued that results from machine learning analyses of data would be a boon for clinical research even if they provided only modest probabilistic guidance about which treatments to pursue (Gillan and Whelan 2017). But not all useful data need be "big" data. Clinical studies of psychopathology that require the qualitative evaluation of individual subjects cannot approach the sample sizes of GWAS, but can be invaluable. Data about clinical service utilization, for example, have been used for epidemiological research, to assess healthcare disparities, to track immunity and vaccination, and to evaluate outcomes of inpatient treatments. There have already been discoveries about drug response that, while not amounting to novel causal explanations of mental disorder, are clinically fruitful (Harper and Topol 2012).

On the theoretical side, a robust variety of anti-reductionist theoretical frameworks have been proposed to counter the NIMH's official position that mental disorders are brain disorders. Gillett and Harré have argued that mental disorder is a sort of psychological dysfunction in the relationship between "a human organism, the psyche, and the world of speech in which the psyche is formed" and have therefore concluded that "psychiatry impoverishes itself by focusing on biology to the exclusion of human discourse and the (partly symbolic) structure of our life-world" (2014, 307). To right this wrong in the research setting, the phenomenology of the mentally ill would need to take center stage. Accordingly, methodological arguments have also been made against reductionism: Mishara and Schwartz have emphasized that phenomenology is "precisely the step required to translate the patient's subjective experience of symptoms, etc., into workable operationalizable hypotheses which can be quantifiably measured using the experimental methods of clinical neuroscience" (2013, 128). The case has been made that phenomenology can actually constrain and direct neuroscientific research, delineating the proper targets for psychiatric investigation. An instrument assessing ipseity disturbance, for example, has been used to differentiate schizophrenia-spectrum disorders from other forms of psychosis (Parnas and Henriksen 2014) and is an example of a subjective experience useful for psychiatric researchers that "has no analogue in somatic medicine and therefore requires a suitable method, a phenomenology" (Parnas and Sass 2008, 251). Beyond arguing against the necessity of reductionism for psychiatric progress, these sorts of approaches suggest a case against its sufficiency.

26.4 IS PRECISION SUFFICIENT FOR PSYCHIATRIC PROGRESS?

"[I]t is clear," Cuthbert and Kozak have written in a discussion of RDoC, "that a diagnostic system based upon empirical data from genetics, neurobiology, and behavioral science is desirable to move toward an era of precision medicine where patients are diagnosed and treated according to accurate and appropriately fine-tuned assessments" (2013, 929). But as critics have pointed out, precision alone cannot guide nosological revision. Even an abundance of explanatory clarity about the causes of variation in mental functioning cannot amount to normative clarity about what counts as a disorder. For example, Broom and Bertolotti have written that "concretely speaking, a brain scan, genetic abnormality, blood test, and so on, can never *a priori* serve as the sole criterion for the diagnosis of mental illness . . . how would one decide whether dopamine quantal size, functional MRI activation, or repeats of genetic polymorphisms were abnormal in the absence of a disordered person?" (Broome and Bortolotti 2009, 38). Kendler has argued that insofar as the central goal of psychiatry as a medical discipline is the alleviation of human suffering, it must continue to rely on descriptions of first-person experiences. He is committed to the idea that "the human first-person world of subjective experience emerges from and is entirely dependent upon brain functioning" (Kendler 2005, 434). However, even from this monist perspective, Kendler argues, we can still say meaningfully that "thoughts, feelings and impulses matter not only because they are responsible for huge amounts of human suffering but because they do things" (ibid.).

Traditionally, the question of what count as appropriate objects of study for the psychiatric researcher has been determined by what signs and symptoms count as pathological, which in turn has been decided by nosological precedent. The *DSM* grew out of a body of clinical wisdom which had roots in the influential taxonomies of nineteenth-century psychiatric greats like Emil Kraepelin, but also in the Freudian theoretical apparatus that was so influential in the United States in the first decades of the twentieth century. It has adapted to accommodate new trends, and incorporated, to a modest degree, the results of scientific investigations of psychopathology and the "drug cartographies" implicitly applied to the landscape of clinical nosology by discoveries in psychopharmacology (Radden 2003). Without the normative parameters provided by the *DSM*, it is unclear what will guide the collection of new empirical data, much less the construction of a new taxonomy based on them. As Wakefield has put it, "*DSM*/ICD provides the only thoughtful guidance to what conditions the RDoC must explain in terms of malfunctioning circuits." In ignoring the manuals' central role in guiding research, RDoC "gets the relationship wrong between itself and *DSM*/ICD" (Wakefield 2014, 38).

The *DSM* has long been criticized for the manner in which it delineates the pathological from the normal. These criticisms have grown out of the worry that cultural, racial, sexual, or political minorities are at risk when the label of "pathological" is applied at will by an authoritative source like the American Psychiatric Association. Psychiatry certainly has a nefarious history, ranging from the experiments of Nazi physicians to the forced sterilizations of tens of thousands deemed mentally degenerate in the United States to the pathologization of homosexuality through the early

1970s by the APA. It is also important to note, however, that there is no widely agreed upon conceptual analysis of biological dysfunction to be appealed to (Lemoine 2013, Murphy 2015). In its absence, biological difference must fail to provide a satisfactory alternative to subjective judgments about pathology. Without an acceptable theory of disease as a biological dysfunction, it is fallacious to conclude that if a mental condition has a physiological basis, its status as a psychiatric object is established and those who meet its criteria are diseased. It is imperative, then, that the NIMH's ambitious transformation of psychiatric research methodology include an explication of "alternative models for dysfunction in psychobiological systems (e.g., lesion, hyperactivity, or hypoactivity in the functioning of these systems; a network model in which there are bidirectional causal relations among diagnostic signs and symptoms)" (Lilienfeld and Treadway, 2016, 456).

Instead, Insel and others at the NIMH have simply described psychopathology as a problem in neural circuitry, which has often been interpreted to mean that high circuit activation indicates disorder (Wakefield 2014, 39). According to its architects, RDoC's goal is to explain basic dimensions of functioning using the cutting-edge science of the day, and "[t]hen, in this light, mental disorders [will be] considered as extremes at one or both tails of these normal distributions" (Insel and Cuthbert 2010, 312). The fallacy of conflating the abnormal with the pathological, however, is easily brought into view; high IQ, for example, shows that not all extremes of mental functioning are pathological, while tooth plaque shows that not all types of medical pathology are atypical. In many cases, to be sure, one or both extremes on a dimension are used to diagnose pathology (consider, for example, hypertension and hypotension, or scales of neuroticism) and dimensional thinking is generally on the rise in psychiatry (Sonuga-Barke 2014, Hengartner and Lehmann 2017, Maj 2018). Nonetheless, statistical abnormality has been dismissed as a viable universal criterion for demarcating the pathological (Boorse 2011), and more complex biostatistical approaches available in the literature have also been shown to be deeply problematic (Amundson 2000). Few scientists or philosophers defend what might be called a "simple" naturalism, in which disorder is understood only as an atypicality in functioning, without an appeal to normative considerations.[10] Researchers have raised concerns that because it decontextualizes biological variance from subjective measures of

[10] See Murphy (2015) for overview and discussion.

suffering, RDoC will be unable to distinguish physiological risk factors from manifest psychopathological states, which may only be discernable at the level of behavior (Lilienfeld and Treadway 2016).

The fact that RDoC's "behavioural domain principles do not put a strict demarcation line between normality and pathology" has been praised as a benefit of the scheme, since it "justifies the search for neurobiological correlates of pathology on a basis of conceptual findings in normal/healthy subjects" (Anderzhanova et al. 2017, 50). Basic scientists are able to appeal to the NIMH as a funding resource, along with the National Science Foundation; The NIMH states that "basic scientists are welcome to propose research involving further study of the RDoC constructs at a preclinical level"[11] as long as some conceptual connection can be drawn to the signs or symptoms of mental suffering. Accordingly, psychopathology has no presence on the RDoC matrix itself – the extent to which researchers should engage with a clinical population is left open. It is at the discretion of researchers applying to the NIMH for support, and to the review committees that make funding decisions, to determine how promising the clinical applicability of each proposal is. Implicit assumptions about the relevance of biological pathways to the identification and prevention of mental disorders, then, take the place of explicit enforcement of traditional nosological categories in the research setting. This is by design, since, as discussed above, psychopathology is viewed as the endpoint, rather than a prerequisite, for psychiatric research. Quite intentionally, precision itself gives no normative guidance.

26.5 CONCLUSION

The most vocal advocates of precision in psychiatry have been committed to nosological revision, big data, and reduction. But they have not been equally committed to all three: while nosological revision is most often voiced as a central aim of precision psychiatry, in practice it has been treated as a distal one, and the resources of the NIMH have been focused instead on supporting research into lower-level mechanisms and ambitious schemes of data collection and analysis (Teachman et al. 2019). This is a reversal of the traditional relationship between psychiatric nosology and research, where the dominant taxonomy of the discipline, the *DSM*, was long used to determine what researchers should investigate. The rejection

[11] RDoC FAQ, from www.nimh.nih.gov/research-priorities/rdoc/rdoc-frequently-asked-questions-faq.shtml. Accessed December 29, 2018.

of traditional classifications comes at the cost of a principled means for distinguishing the normal from the pathological, and therefore for distinguishing scientific research projects from medical ones.

Ironically, as I argued in Section 3, it is nosological revision that has had the widest support among the diverse constituencies that have a stake in psychiatric funding, while both reductionism and big dataism have been more contentious. Nonetheless the language of a precision "paradigm" has made it easy to think of precision's commitments as forming a unity, one that is necessary if psychiatry is to stay in step with other areas of medicine that seem to be progressing by leaps and bounds. The powerful notion of a paradigm may encourage those who are dubious about the value of reduction or big data to accept them as necessary steps toward a better taxonomy for psychiatry. But as discussed above, improvements to classification and diagnostics might fruitfully proceed non-reductively, and without innovation in data collection and analysis. Therefore, the prioritization of reduction and big data are not justifiable solely based on widespread nosological revisionist sentiment among psychiatrists.

This does not, of course, mean that they are unjustifiable *tout court*. New methods like brain imaging and genetic association studies may well allow for the discovery of causal mechanisms that translate into clinical advances, and which can propel psychiatry out of its rut. In an article written in 2005 with Remi Quirion, Insel envisioned the decade between 2005 and 2015 to be one of transformative discovery, to be followed, starting in 2016, by a decade of translation (see Chapter 45, Figure 45.1). The authors were certainly right that there is a huge amount of work to be done applying new information about pathogenesis to diagnostics. At my time of writing, however, it is clear that they were overly optimistic about the expediency with which basic science research would advance sufficiently to generate discoveries with clear clinical application. The frustration of some critics of precision comes from their feeling that clinicians – and patients – cannot afford to wait for these ambitious expectations to be realized. Teachman et al. have written that "a steady drift toward prioritizing biomedically oriented research at the expense of more psychosocially oriented research over the past 20 years[. . .] has [. . .] hampered our ability to link biological processes to the human environments, social factors, and behaviors that shape and define mental illnesses and psychological disorders" (2019, 12). Since the NIMH is the only major public funding body for psychiatric research in the United States, it can feel like a zero-sum game for those with competing research priorities.

I have argued that reductionist projects, and those that center on the collection and analysis of big data sets, are not psychiatry's only hope for progress. As a result, the precision paradigm's discouragement of higher-level, smaller-data research should be suspect. I have also argued that successes from basic science will be insufficient for reforming psychiatric nosology if not accompanied by a robust psychopathology that can bring their clinical relevance into view. Precision medicine's common conflation of disease and statistical abnormality will not do; its reductionist orientation excludes other, more convincing approaches to defining pathology, including those from public health, which may focus on what is outside the individual, not within (Bayer and Galea 2015) and from psychology and psychometrics, which may focus instead on phenomenology and clinical data (Parnas and Henriksen 2014, Kotov et al. 2017, Borsboom et al. 2018). Precision medicine is an expensive gambit in which American taxpayers have invested heavily. A less tangible, but still substantial, cost of adopting this new paradigm is the muting of critical debate over the identification and treatment of mental illness.

REFERENCES

Amundson R. (2000). 'Against Normal Function.' *Studies in History and Philosophy of Science Part C: Biology and Biomedical Science* 31(1):33–53.

Andersen H. (2016) 'Reduction in the Biomedical Sciences.' In M Solomon, J Simon, and H Kincaid (eds), *Routledge Companion to Philosophy of Medicine*. Abingdon, UK: Routledge.

Anderzhanova E, Kirmeier T, and Wotjak CT. (2017) 'Animal Models in Psychiatric Research: The RDoC System as a New Framework for Endophenotype-Oriented Translational Neuroscience.' *Neurobiology of Stress* 7 (December): 47–56.

Bayer R, and Galea S. (2015) 'Public Health in the Precision-Medicine Era.' *New England Journal of Medicine* 373 (6): 499–501.

Boorse C. (2011). 'Concepts of Health and Disease.' In F Gifford (ed), *Handbook of the Philosophy of Science*, Vol. 16: Philosophy of Medicine. Amsterdam, the Netherlands: Elsevier BV.

Borsboom, D, Cramer A, and Kalis A. (2018) 'Brain Disorders? Not Really... Why Network Structures Block Reductionism in Psychopathology Research.' *Behavior and Brain Sciences* (Jan 14): 1–54.

Bowker GC, and Star, SL. (1999) *Sorting Things Out: Classification and Its Consequences*. Cambridge, MA: MIT Press.

Broome, MR, and Bortolotti L. (2009) 'Mental Illness as Mental: In Defence of Psychological Realism.' *Humana Mente* 11:25–43.

Carpenter WT. (2016) 'The RDoC Controversy: Alternate Paradigm or Dominant Paradigm?' *American Journal of Psychiatry* 173 (6): 562–63.

Chang H. (2004) *Inventing Temperature: Measurement and Scientific Progress.* Oxford: Oxford University Press.

Chen R, Mias GI, Li-Pook-Than J, Jiang L, Lam HY, Chen R, Miriami E, Karczewski KJ, Hariharan M, et al. (2012) 'Personal Omics Profiling Reveals Dynamic Molecular and Medical Phenotypes.' *Cell* 148: 1293–307.

Curtis C, Shah SP, Chin SF, Turashvili G, Rueda OM, Dunning MJ, Speed D, et al. (2012) 'The Genomic and Transcriptomic Architecture of 2,000 Breast Tumours Reveals Novel Subgroups.' *Nature* 486 (7403): 346–52.

Cuthbert BN, and Kozak MJ. (2013) 'Constructing Constructs for Psychopathology: The NIMH Research Domain Criteria.' *Journal of Abnormal Psychology* 122 (3): 928–37.

De Grandis G, and Halgunset V. (2016) 'Conceptual and Terminological Confusion around Personalised Medicine: A Coping Strategy.' *BMC Medical Ethics* 17 (1): 1–12.

Eyal G, Sabatello S, Tabb K, Adams R, Jones M, Lichtenberg FL, Nelson A, et al. (2019) 'The Physician–Patient Relationship in the Age of Precision Medicine.' *Genetics in Medicine* 21 (4): 813–15.

Fernandes BS, Williams LM, Steiner J, Leboyer M, Carvalho AF, and Berk, M. (2017) 'The New Field of "Precision Psychiatry."' *BMC Medicine* 15 (1): 1–7.

First MB, and Westen D. (2007) 'Classification for Clinical Practice: How to Make ICD and DSM Better Able to Serve Clinicians.' *International Review of Psychiatry* 19 (5): 473–81.

Gandal MJ, Leppa V, Won H, Parikshak NN, and Geschwind, DH. (2016) 'The Road to Precision Psychiatry: Translating Genetics into Disease Mechanisms.' *Nature Neuroscience* 19 (11): 1397–407.

Gillan CM, and Whelan R. (2017) 'What Big Data Can Do for Treatment in Psychiatry.' *Current Opinion in Behavioral Sciences* 18 (December): 34–42.

Gillett G, and Harré R. (2014) 'Discourse and Diseases of the Psyche.' In KWM Fulford, M Davies, RGT Gipps, G Graham, JZ Sadler, G Stanghellini, and T Thornton (eds)*The Oxford Handbook of Philosophy and Psychiatry.* Oxford University Press, 307–20. doi:10.1093/oxfordhb/9780199579563.013.0022

Harper AR, and Topol EJ. (2012) 'Pharmacogenomics in Clinical Practice and Drug Development.' *Nature Biotechnology* 30 (11): 1117–24.

Haendel MA, Chute CG, and Robinson PN. (2018) 'Classification, Ontology, and Precision Medicine.' *New England Journal of Medicine* 379 (15): 1452–62.

Haro JM, Ayuso-Mateos JL, Bitter I, Demotes-Mainard J, Leboyer M, Lewis SW, Linszen D, et al. (2014) 'ROAMER: Roadmap for Mental Health Research in Europe.' *International Journal of Methods in Psychiatric Research* 23 (S1): 1–14.

Hengartner MP, and Lehmann SN. (2017) 'Why Psychiatric Research Must Abandon Traditional Diagnostic Classification and Adopt a Fully Dimensional Scope: Two Solutions to a Persistent Problem.' *Frontiers in Psychiatry* 8 (June): 101.

Hey SP, and Kesselheim AS. (2016) 'Countering Imprecision in Precision Medicine.' *Science* 353 (6298): 448–49.

Hyman S. (2010) 'The Diagnosis of Mental Disorders: The Problem of Reification.' *Annual Review of Clinical Psychology* 6: 155–79.

Insel TR. (2010) 'Faulty Circuits.' *Scientific American* 302 (4): 44–51.

—(2014) 'The NIMH Research Domain Criteria (RDoC) Project: Precision Medicine for Psychiatry.' *American Journal of Psychiatry* 171 (4): 395–97.

Insel TR, and Quirion R. (2005) 'Psychiatry as a Clinical Neuroscience Discipline.' *JAMA* 294 (17): 2221–24.

Insel TR and Cuthbert B. (2010). 'The Data of Diagnosis: New Approaches to Psychiatric Classification.' *Psychiatry: Interpersonal and Biological Processes* 73 (4): 311–14.

Insel TR, and Cuthburt B. (2015) 'Brain Disorders? Precisely.' *Science* 348 (6234): 498–99.

Juengst E, McGowan ML, Fishman JR, and Settersten RA Jr. (2016) 'From "Personalized" to "Precision" Medicine: The Ethical and Social Implications of Rhetorical Reform in Genomic Medicine.' *Hastings Center Report* 46 (5): 21–33.

Kaiser M. (2015) *Reductive Explanation in the Biological Sciences*. Cham: Springer.

Kendler KS. (2005) 'Toward a Philosophical Structure for Psychiatry.' *American Journal of Psychiatry* 162 (3): 433–40.

—(2012) 'Epistemic Iteration as a Historical Model for Psychiatric Nosology: Promises and Limitations.' In KS Kendler and J Parnas (eds), *Philosophical Issues in Psychiatry II: Nosology*. Oxford: Oxford University Press.

Khoury MJ, Iademarco MF, and Riley WT. (2016) 'Precision Public Health for the Era of Precision Medicine.' *American Journal of Preventive Medicine* 50 (3): 398–401. doi:10.1016/j.amepre.2015.08.031.

Kincaid H, and Sullivan JA (eds). (2014) *Classifying Psychopathology*. Cambridge, MA: MIT Press.

Kotov R, Krueger RF, Watson D, Achenbach TM, Althoff RR, Bagby RM, Brown TA, et al. (2017) 'The Hierarchical Taxonomy of Psychopathology (HiTOP): A Dimensional Alternative to Traditional Nosologies.' *Journal of Abnormal Psychology* 126 (4): 454–77.

Lemoine M. (2016) 'Molecular complexity: Why has psychiatry not been revolutionized by genomics (yet)?' In G Boniolo and M Nathan (eds), *Foundational Issues in Molecular Medicine*. London: Routledge, 81–99.

Lemoine M. (2013) 'Defining Disease beyond Conceptual Analysis: An Analysis of Conceptual Analysis in Philosophy of Medicine.' *Theoretical Medicine and Bioethics* 34: 309–25.

—(2017) 'Neither From Words, nor From Visions: Understanding P-Medicine From Innovative Treatments. *Lato Sensu: Revue de la Société de Philosophie des Sciences* 4 (2): 12–23. doi:10.20416/lsrsps.v4i2.793

Lesko LJ. (2007) 'Personalized Medicine: Elusive Dream or Imminent Reality?' *Clinical Pharmacology & Therapeutics* 81: 807–16.

Lewis-Fernandez R, Rotheram-Borus MJ, Betts V, Greenman L, Essock SM, Escobar JI, Barch D, et al. (2016) 'Rethinking Funding Priorities in Mental Health Research.' *The British Journal of Psychiatry* 208 (6): 507–9.

Lilienfeld SO, and Treadway MT. (2016) 'Clashing Diagnostic Approaches: DSM-ICD versus RDoC.' *Annual Review of Clinical Psychology* 12 (1): 435–63.

Maj M. (2018) 'Why the Clinical Utility of Diagnostic Categories in Psychiatry Is Intrinsically Limited and How We Can Use New Approaches to Complement Them.' *World Psychiatry* 17 (2): 121–22.

Meigs JB, Shrader P, Sullivan LM, McAteer JB, Fox CS, Dupuis J, Manning AK, Florez JC Wilson PW, D'agostino RB Sr, and Cupples LA. (2008) 'Genotype Score in Addition to Common Risk Factors for Prediction of Type 2 Diabetes.' *New England Journal of Medicine* 359: 2208–19.

Miller, GA. (2010) 'Mistreating Psychology in the Decades of the Brain.' *Perspectives on Psychological Science* 5 (6): 716–43. doi:10.1177/1745691610388774.

Mishara AL, and Schwartz MA. (2013) 'What Does Phenomology Contribute to the Debate about DSM-5?' In J Paris and J Philips (eds), *Making the DSM-5: Concepts and Controversies*. New York: Springer, 125–42.

Monteith S, Glenn T, Geddes J, and Bauer M. (2015) 'Big Data Are Coming to Psychiatry: A General Introduction.' *International Journal of Bipolar Disorders* 3 (1): 21.

Morris S, and Cuthbert B. (2012) 'Research Domain Criteria: Cognitive Systems, Neural Circuits, and Dimensions of Behavior.' *Dialogues in Clinical Neuroscience* 14 (1): 29.

Murphy D. (2014) 'Natural Kinds in Folk Psychology and in Psychiatry.' In H Kincaid and JA Sullivan (eds), *Classifying Psychopathology: Mental Kinds and Natural Kinds*. Cambridge, MA: MIT Press, 105–22.

Murphy D. (2015) 'Concepts of Disease and Health.' In EN Zalta (ed), *The Stanford Encyclopedia of Philosophy* (Spring 2015 Edition). https://plato.stanford.edu/archives/spr2015/entries/health-disease/.

Nature Editorial Board. (2012) 'Therapy Deficit.' *Nature* 489: 473–74.

National Research Council (US) Committee on a Framework for Developing a New Taxonomy of Disease. (2011) 'Toward Precision Medicine: Building a Knowledge Network for Biomedical Research and a New Taxonomy of Disease.' Washington, DC: National Academies Press (US).

Need AC, and Goldstein DB. (2016) 'Neuropsychiatric Genomics in Precision Medicine: Diagnostics, Gene Discovery, and Translation.' *Dialogues in Clinical Neuroscience* 18 (3): 237–52.

Olbert CM, Gala GJ, and Tupler LA. (2014) 'Quantifying Heterogeneity Attributable to Polythetic Diagnostic Criteria: Theoretical Framework and Empirical Application.' *Journal of Abnormal Psychology* 123(2): 452–62.

Paranjape SM, and Mogayzel PJ. (2018) 'Cystic Fibrosis in the Era of Precision Medicine.' *Paediatric Respiratory Reviews* 25 (January): 64–72.

Parnas J, and Sass LA. (2008) 'Varieties of 'Phenomenology.' In KS Kendler and J Parnas (eds), *Philosophical Issues in Psychiatry: Explanation, Phenomenology, and Nosology*. Cambridge, UK: Cambridge University Press, 239–77.

Parnas J, and Henriksen MG. (2014) 'Disordered Self in the Schizophrenia Spectrum: A Clinical and Research Perspective.' *Harvard Review of Psychiatry* 22 (5): 251–65.

Paulus MP. (2015) 'Pragmatism Instead of Mechanism.' *JAMA Psychiatry* 72 (7): 631–32.

Petrovski S, Shashi V, Petrou S, Schoch K, McSweeney KM, Dhindsa RS, Krueger B, Crimian R, Case LE, Khalid R, El-Dairi MA, Jiang YH, Mikati MA, Goldstein DB. (2015) 'Exome Sequencing Results in Successful Riboflavin

Treatment of a Rapidly Progressive Neurological Condition.' *Cold Spring Harbor Molecular Case Studies* 1 (1):a000257. doi:10.1101/mcs.a000257
Phillips MR. (2014) 'Will RDoC Hasten the Decline of America's Global Leadership Role in Mental Health?' *World Psychiatry* 13 (1): 40–41.
Poland J, and Tekin S (eds). (2017) *Extraordinary Science and Psychiatry: Responses to the Crisis in Mental Health Research*. Cambridge, MA: MIT Press.
Prainsack B. (2015) 'Through Thick and Big: Data-Rich Medicine in the Era of Personalisation.' In J Vollman, V Sandow, S Wäscher, and J Schildmann (eds), *The Ethics of Personalised Medicine*. Farnham: Ashgate, 161–72.
Radden J. (2003) 'Is This Dame Melancholy?: Equating Today's Depression and Past Melancholia.' *Philosophy Psychiatry and Psychology* 10 (1): 37–52.
Schwartz SJ, Lilienfeld SO, Meca A, and Sauvigné KC. (2016) 'The Role of Neuroscience within Psychology: A Call for Inclusiveness over Exclusiveness.' *The American Psychologist* 71 (1): 52–70.
Sekar A, Bialas AR, de Rivera H, Davis A, Hammond TR, Kamitaki N, Tooley K, et al. (2016) 'Schizophrenia Risk from Complex Variation of Complement Component 4.' *Nature* 530 (7589): 177–83.
Senn S. (2001) 'Individual Therapy: New Dawn or False Dawn?' *Drug Information Journal* 35: 1479–94.
(2018) 'Statistical Pitfalls of Personalized Medicine.' *Nature* 563 (7733): 619–21.
Snyder M. (2012) 'Q & A: The Snyderome.' *Genome Biology* 13(3): 147.
Sonuga-Barke EJS. (2014) 'Editorial: 'What's Up, (R)DoC?' – Can Identifying Core Dimensions of Early Functioning Help Us Understand, and Then Reduce, Developmental Risk for Mental Disorders?' *Journal of Child Psychology and Psychiatry* 55 (8): 849–51. doi:10.1111/jcpp.12293.
Sullivan PF, Agrawal A, Bulik CM, Andreassen OA, Børglum AD, Breen G, Cichon S, Edenberg H, et al. (2017) 'Psychiatric Genomics: An Update and an Agenda.' *American Journal of Psychiatry* 175 (1): 15–27.
Tabb K. (2015) 'Psychiatric Progress and the Assumption of Diagnostic Discrimination.' *Philosophy of Science* 82 (5): 1047–58.
Teachman BA, McKay D, Barch DM, Prinstein MJ, Hollon SD, and Chambless DL. (2019) 'How Psychosocial Research Can Help the National Institute of Mental Health Achieve Its Grand Challenge to Reduce the Burden of Mental Illnesses and Psychological Disorders.' *The American Psychologist* 74 (4): 415–31.
Topol EJ. (2014) 'Individualized Medicine from Prewomb to Tomb.' *Cell* 157 (1): 241–53.
Wakefield JC. (2014) 'Wittgenstein's Nightmare: Why the RDoC Grid Needs a Conceptual Dimension.' *World Psychiatry* 13 (1): 38–40.
Wanders RBK, van Loo HM, Vermunt JK, Meijer RR, Hartman CA, Schoevers RA, Wardenaar KJ, and de Jonge P. (2016) 'Casting Wider Nets for Anxiety and Depression: Disability-Driven Cross-Diagnostic Subtypes in a Large Cohort.' *Psychological Medicine* 46 (16): 3371–82.
Whooley O. (2010) 'Diagnostic Ambivalence: Psychiatric Workarounds and the *Diagnostic and Statistical Manual of Mental Disorders*.' *Sociology of Health & Fitness* 32 (3): 452–69.

van Loo H, Romeijn JW, de Jonge P, and Schoevers R. (2013) 'Psychiatric Comorbidity and Causal Disease Models.' *Preventive Medicine* 57 (6): 748–52.

Zuberi, SM, and Brunklaus A. (2018) 'Epilepsy in 2017: Precision Medicine Drives Epilepsy Classification and Therapy.' *Nature Reviews Neurology* 14 (2): 67–68. doi:10.1038/nrneurol.2017.190.

27

Commentary on "Should Psychiatry Be Precise? Reduction, Big Data, and Nosological Revision in Mental Health Research"

ROBERT M. BILDER

An old adage states that when the title of a scholarly paper ends in a question mark, the answer is invariably "no." Would we believe that psychiatry should not be precise? In her chapter, Kathryn Tabb captures our attention and leads us to question the fundamental premises underlying major efforts by NIH in general and NIMH in particular to focus on "precision" medicine, and in particular the National Institute of Health (NIH) Precision Medicine Initiative (PMI). Tabb carefully constructs an argument that the paradigm of precision medicine may be inappropriate for psychiatry research. In the process, she makes multiple compelling points that should be considered seriously by leaders of the relevant initiatives, and by all investigators in psychiatry research: both those who are "believers" in precision medicine and those who are "skeptics" about its relevance to their work. Accompanying these valuable points, however, there are elements of this argument that I believe misrepresent the initiatives. In the spirit of open collegial exchange, I aim to challenge these, in hopes that this may help advance our shared understanding of the complex issues at hand.

The chapter focuses on three elements linked to precision medicine initiatives, including reduction, nosological revision, and big data. Among the valuable points, Tabb's discussion of reductionism is trenchant, and citing Andersen (2016), she usefully identifies how simplification and identification of causal mechanisms can contribute to understanding of both disease and intervention targets. The chapter also makes excellent points about the desirability of clearer logic in describing "levels" of

The author thanks Daniel S. Pine and Josef Parnas for providing valuable comments. This work was supported by NIH grants R01MH101478, R01MH114152, R03MH106922, U01 MH1055, and R01MH118514.

analysis in psychiatry research. Schwartz et al. (2016) and Wakefield (2014) are quoted to highlight the problems of mixing levels of analysis in attempts to specify causal relations. Here, Tabb identifies a major problem and potential source of confusion that is faced in any attempts to identify causal relations when the phenomena span different levels of analysis. Precision medicine initiatives also share a focus on nosological revision, and Tabb indicates that there is relatively good consensus that nosological revision is a reasonable aim, with several caveats that are explored below. The chapter further identifies multiple challenges to our ability to effectively leverage big data, including analytic challenges involved in assuring data quality, appropriate statistical inference, appropriate drawing of conclusions from statistical tests, and serious ethical concerns that highlight how difficult it may be to appropriately apprise individuals of the risks and benefits of participating in large-scale data aggregation efforts.

While making these points that I believe reflect shared conceptualizations of precision medicine, Tabb offers pointed criticisms, which I agree are vital to help shape the future direction and provide "course correction" for such large endeavors. But this criticism may be most helpful when it acknowledges fully the complexity of the challenges and provides a balanced perspective. I believe the chapter could be more constructive if the PMI perspective were reflected more accurately. Instead, Tabb concludes that the PMI is an "expensive gambit" that has caused a "...muting of critical debate over the identification and treatment of mental illness." To arrive at these conclusions, Tabb first defines and then analyzes the PMI in terms of "commitments" to reductionism, big data, and nosological revision. She paints the National Institute of Mental Health (NIMH) Research Domains Criteria (RDoC) initiative with the same brush. Given the nature and severity of these criticisms, which suggest that taxpayer funds are being misappropriated and that the NIH is stifling critical feedback, it is particularly important to evaluate these arguments in further detail.

The chapter presents logical arguments about the foundational elements that Tabb considers essential to PMI and RDoC, identifies limitations in the elements either independently or conjointly, and then claims that the composite is necessarily and fundamentally flawed. I believe these arguments would be more compelling if they attended more carefully to the intentions and contextual factors that guided NIH and academic leaders to develop these initiatives. As stated, I believe these arguments may primarily alienate those who may be most likely to effect change. Why?

In my opinion, the argument presented in this chapter amounts to a straw man that fails to represent either the intentions or implementation of PMI or RDoC. First, the term "paradigm" (a term which, incidentally, was not used in the Obama Administration's announcement of the PMI, Francis Collins' NEJM elaboration of his vision for the PMI, or on the NIMH website to describe the RDoC initiative) is defined to ". . .imply that the commitments (reductionism, big data, and nosological revision) grouped together under the precision label must be jointly fulfilled in order to achieve medical progress." In other words, the chapter first constructs PMI as a three-legged stool that requires all legs, working together, to remain useful. While this may accurately reflect Thomas Kuhn's use of the term "paradigm," it is doubtful that either the founders or most current scientists would see PMI/RDoC as a "paradigm" in this sense of the word, or that the success of these initiatives is necessarily tied to these three elements bundled together.

But Tabb suggests further that PMI/RDoC initiatives see reduction as directional in a way that may deviate from the intents of the framers of these initiatives. Specifically, she indicates that PMI "rests on the assumption that lower-level mechanisms are causal in a way that facilitates intervention on higher-level outcomes of interest" (p. 318). While many presentations of PMI and RDoC concepts state what are "lower" and "higher" levels of analysis, generally following the central dogma of biology that suggests directionality in the flow of information from DNA structure to protein, cellular, and other functions, most current investigators are well aware of complexities in virtually all biological processes that challenge such directional hypotheses. The RDoC initiative has specifically committed to agnosticism with respect to its different "units of analysis," and has assiduously avoided labeling some units (e.g., symptoms) as being "higher" than others (e.g., genes). The allure of genetic research has been at least partially based on its tractability. The "genome" is finite, one-dimensional, and based (in humans) on only about three billion variables. In contrast, the "envirome" is infinite and its dimensionality is unknown. Subjective experience is similarly infinite. Thus, the prioritization of some basic biology projects may be more due to their feasibility than consensus that these units of analysis contain all the answers.

Turning to the critiques of big data, most of the scientists involved in either PMI or RDoC see big data now as a relatively generic (and likely overused) buzzword that refers to any large-scale aggregation of observations (e.g., genetic repositories, collections of electronic health records, or intensively sampled data acquired from mobile platforms). Big data may be useful, but problems with naïve analyses of big data are already legendary and not a prerequisite for the PMI or RDoC. A large body of scholarly work already describes overfitting, the GIGO (garbage in, garbage out) principle, and the manifold pitfalls of applying various machine learning, "AI," and other "deep learning" classifiers to large datasets, often generating uninterpretable sets of features that are hard to replicate. The opportunity to use big data can be great when useful, but like any data, only as good as careful analysis and interpretation can support. One can thus agree completely with Tabb's arguments that big data are not "privileged," and that big data should not drive all theories, without faulting either PMI or RDoC for leveraging big data when useful.

Nosological revision is indeed an aim of both PMI and RDoC. PMI sees current taxonomies as limited, given that we do not understand the biological bases of most diseases, and thus we face myriad problems treating or researching a "diagnosis" rather than better-defined and circumscribed syndromes or symptoms. RDoC further emphasizes the challenges posed by the current diagnostic taxonomy of mental disorders, because these taxonomic definitions have traditionally defined almost all research projects, which are then bound to reify the diagnostic entities if any differences are found between groups, or to claim "null" findings (or worse, to conclude that there is "comorbidity") if they fail to find differences between taxonomic entities. Tabb's concern with nosological revision is principally that she sees it as "bundled" with the other "commitments" in the three-legged stool of PMI. Tabb actually agrees that nosological revision is desirable, albeit only if it is "unbundled" from other "commitments," that is – big data and reductionism. Given that those involved in PMI and RDoC do not bundle these concepts together as Tabb has done, this argument does not undermine the validity of PMI or RDoC.

The chapter states further, however, that "rejection of traditional classifications comes at the cost of a principled means for distinguishing the normal from the pathological, and therefore for distinguishing scientific research projects from medical ones" (pp. 327–328). There are at least three problems with this statement. First, it is not clear that the current taxonomy is highly principled, and there is good evidence that the principles upon which it is founded are invalid. We can hope that new approaches to distinguishing "normal" from "pathological" are based on stronger principles than the current taxonomy, but in the meantime, neither PMI nor

RDoC are asserting that assessment of human suffering, which most often marks the threshold between health and disease, should be replaced.

Second, the statement assumes that distinguishing normal from pathological is always desirable or even possible. The distinctions between normal and abnormal may be useful in some circumstances, but this dichotomization also comes with costs, for example, of associating mental "illnesses" with stigma and treating those with the "diagnosis" as "different," when in fact, two people may be virtually identical but happen to fall on different sides of "cutoffs" based on different intra-individual and environmental contexts. Even more dramatically, the *same* person may be considered to have a mental illness by one diagnostician but not another, simply due to unreliability of a diagnostic process based principally on patient self-report.

Third, it is unclear what benefit we derive from splitting "scientific" from "medical" research projects. In this era marked by major threats to the entire scientific enterprise from replication failures and lack of rigor, it is hoped that all of our medical projects will also be scientific. It is not clear that nosological revision as envisioned in PMI and RDoC undermines Kendler et al.'s (2005) call for continued attention to "the human first-person world of subjective experience." It could be of enormous value for researchers dedicated to subjective experience to demonstrate the explanatory power of these methods in the context of PMI and RDoC research so that we can define more clearly how these factors emerge from brain functioning (Kendler 2005).

In another critique of nosological revision, the chapter states that the PMI is based on "... a bottom-up approach, in which taxonomy is the outcome..." (p. 310). This is not exactly true and may be misleading. Instead, the models used in precision medicine are usually bidirectional, with disease entities being reframed by biological observations, and new ideas about what comprises illness syndromes or relevant symptoms leading to further refinements in what biological measures to make. In contrast, assuming that the current taxonomy of mental disorders is valid for biological research runs into immediate problems as a "top-down" formalization that constrains hypotheses, and leads to biases well identified in statistical inference due to the sampling of extreme groups (see Preacher et al., 2005). The PMI/RDoC initiatives are further completely congruent with efforts such as Borsboom's (e.g., Borsboom et al., 2018) to identify causal relations within units of analysis, for example, among different symptoms. The PMI/RDoC initiatives embrace modeling of constructs within units of analysis, and modeling of relations across units of analysis, in ways that do not violate either philosophical or scientific conventions.

Tabb suggests that NIMH is encouraging investigators "... to simply use the matrix to identify their objects of study..." (p. 319). As an investigator who has had multiple projects submitted for NIMH support under the aegis of the RDoC initiative, I am not aware that NIMH has ever encouraged such a strategy, nor would that approach likely hold up very well under the lens of peer review. If this were a winning strategy, there would be no need for grant applications at all, and the NIMH could simply fund a project to naively study associations among the various elements in the RDoC matrix. I believe most of us who served on RDoC workgroups and witnessed the population of the matrix with elements by committee would be the first to indicate that these elements were at best examples and starting points that helped summarize some of the work ongoing in biological psychiatry research labs. It may be useful for investigators to cite the matrix in support of their ideas, but I believe the ideas continue to be evaluated by peers in a way that does not naively endorse the matrix as commandments handed down to us by higher powers.

Tabb states that a "key motivation of the RDoC initiative is to limit the role that the phenomenological level – that is psychopathology itself – plays in guiding what research should be identified as (and funded as) 'psychiatric'" (p. 319). Setting aside the concern that this statement comprises an accusation about the "motivation" of RDoC to limit a specific approach to research, it is problematic that it misstates the goals of the initiative, which remains agnostic about subjective experience. Parnas and Henriksen (2014) framed this well, acknowledging that RDoC is highly limited in considering patient "self reports" and fails to consider "... the complications of what philosophers call the "explanatory gap," "the hard problem of consciousness or the defiant distinctiveness of the ontology (nature of being) and epistemology of human consciousness." There is hope that one day we may make progress in understanding subjective experience and even consciousness so that these can be better integrated into frameworks like PMI and RDoC (see LeDoux et al., 2018). Meanwhile, it seems more productive to aspire to include these features, and propose specific methods to add them to modern research programs, than to declare that PMI/RDoC are without value because these features are not yet specified. Environmental and social effects are also not explicated in the RDoC matrix, but no one would argue that we should not consider environmental or social contexts in psychopathology research.

A salient thread in the chapter is tied to money. It is suggested that funding has been diverted away from more clinical and phenomenological investigation toward basic scientific work. Tabb acknowledges that funding for RDoC has been modest, in part, undermining the argument that the PMI and RDoC have drained resources from other clinical research areas. The changes in definitions of what constitutes a "clinical trial" (increasing the administrative burden on many investigators), along with demands that clinical trials demonstrate "target engagement" (precipitating fundamental questions about what are the molecular-, cellular-, or system-level targets of drugs or other therapies), have generated substantial angst in the psychiatry clinical research community. But it remains unclear that the shifts in NIMH priorities have had the adverse impacts on investigation of psychopathology that are alleged in this chapter.

It is also suggested that "American psychiatry" is represented by the NIMH, but the publication of *DSM-5* is just one of many examples showing how the American Psychiatric Association (which more accurately reflects American psychiatry as a discipline) came into stark conflict with NIMH. Indeed, two prior NIMH directors (Hyman and Insel) have been extremely critical of the *DSM-5* and long called for a fresh scientific perspective to rectify major flaws in the taxonomy. If we are seeking to discern how money may distort progress in psychopathology research, perhaps it would be valuable to assess the impact of the American Psychiatric Press (publisher of the *DSM-5* and related materials) to determine if promotion of this work raises any concerns.

To return to the original question: Should psychiatry be precise? While this chapter highlights reasons that the answer should be "no," I believe the overall argument targets a straw man that does not represent the current direction of psychiatry research as this is expressed in NIH programs and priorities. With respectful disagreement, I would assert that psychiatry should aim to be more precise. It is not clear that our current efforts to revise nosology, leverage big data, or find mechanistic explanations of psychological phenomena will succeed. But by exploring these avenues and freeing investigation from the shackles of a flawed taxonomy I believe we will be in a stronger position. I further believe that many points made in this chapter are valuable for the advancement of psychiatry research. We need to be clearer about how we understand and test causal models, appreciating distinctions among levels of analysis. We need to be more precise in our use of terms and definitions of constructs. And we need to do better at specifying exactly how the "highest" levels of human subjective experience fit into a research agenda that embraces findings at every level, and guides our work for the benefit of humanity.

REFERENCES

Andersen H. (2016) 'Reduction in the Biomedical Sciences.' In M. Solomon, J. Simon, & H. Kincaid (eds.), *Routledge Companion to Philosophy of Medicine.* London: Routledge.

Borsboom, D, Cramer A, and Kalis A. (2018) 'Brain Disorders? Not Really. . .: Why Network Structures Block Reductionism in Psychopathology Research.' *Behavior and Brain Sciences* 42: 1–54.

Kendler KS. (2005) 'Toward a Philosophical Structure for Psychiatry.' *American Journal of Psychiatry* 162 (3): 433–40.

LeDoux J, Brown R, Pine D, and Hofmann S. (2018, January) 'Know Thyself: Well-Being and Subjective Experience.' In *Cerebrum: The Dana Forum on Brain Science.* New York: Dana Foundation.

Parnas J and Henriksen MG. (2014) 'Disordered Self in the Schizophrenia Spectrum.' *Harvard Review of Psychiatry* 22 (5): 251–265.

Preacher KJ, Rucker DD, MacCallum RC, Nicewander WA. (2005) 'Use of the Extreme Groups Approach: A Critical Reexamination and New Recommendations.' *Psychological Methods*;10 (2):178

Schwartz SJ, Lilienfeld SO, Meca A, and Sauvigné KC. (2016) 'The Role of Neuroscience within Psychology: A Call for Inclusiveness over Exclusiveness.' *The American Psychologist* 71 (1): 52–70.

Wakefield, JC. (2014) 'Wittgenstein's Nightmare: Why the RDoC Grid Needs a Conceptual Dimension.' *World Psychiatry* 13 (1): 38–40.

SECTION 10

28

Introduction

PETER ZACHAR

Several chapters in this volume address the heterogeneity problem in psychiatric classification, i.e., that constructs such as major depressive disorder and generalized anxiety disorder have turned out to be too coarse-grained to support the discovery of underlying mechanisms or to guide clinicians in selecting disorder-specific treatments (Bilder Chapter 5, Miller Chapter 20, although see Bechtel Chapter 2 for a different view on mechanisms and heterogeneity). Bringing a more statistical perspective to the heterogeneity issue, Jan-Willem Romeijn and Hanna M. van Loo refer to this as the reference class problem.

A reference class is a group of individuals that share some set of characteristics that license making inferences. The example they give is the rolling of dice. Let's say what we want to predict is the chances of rolling a 1. To simplify, assume some dice have six sides labeled 1 through 6 and others have six sides with three sides labeled 1 and three sides labeled 4. If so, these dice could be grouped into two practically useful reference classes. In the first class, the chances of rolling a 1 are 1/6. In the second class, the chances are 1/2. All the dice in the same class are alike in important ways, and the predictions that we make based on class membership are pretty different. Very importantly, these groups were constructed empirically – based only on how well they facilitate the prediction of the variable of interest. The color, size, and composition of the dice were not used to construct the reference class because they were irrelevant to the predictions sought.

To say that the construct of major depressive disorder has not supported the discovery of either causal mechanisms or the selection of efficacious treatments is to say that the diagnostic criteria of major depressive disorder do not identify a practically useful reference class. Using these criteria to construct a reference class seemed like a good idea to Spitzer,

Endicott, and Robins (1978), but the classes they proposed have not been validated for making the inferences they expected. In philosopher's terms, the strong disregard for *DSM* categories among those psychiatrists and psychologists working on the RDoC initiative is based on the view that *DSM* categories are entrenched, but not projectable (see Chapters 5, 20, 27, and 39 by Bilder and Miller for more on RDoC).

The resolutely empirical commitments adopted by Romeijn and van Loo lead to what they call an *areductionist* perspective. Certain versions of reductionism claim that lower levels of analysis have ontological priority and therefore explanatory authority. Various non-reductionist views deny this, and argue that explanatory authority might be found at higher levels of analysis or that using information from a plurality of levels can be informative. The areductionist view does not see a need to adopt any metaphysical commitments about the ontological priority or the explanatory authority of "levels." Rather than segregating potential criteria into distinct levels of analysis, any criterion that can be used to define a reference class that supports the practical goals of accurate prediction and successful intervention is a potentially valid criterion.

They illustrate how this might work using an example of statistical model selection guided by machine learning. In a preliminary study using a very large data, set Kessler et al. (2017) develop multivariate mathematical models to predict the persistence and severity of depression. The best fitting model identified three reference classes, those with a low risk, those with an intermediate risk, and those with a high risk for a severe course of depression (see Tabb Chapter 26 for a critical look at big data approaches in psychiatric research).

Of course, there are also differences between people within a reference class, but grouping people together in classes and seeing what they have in common is the basis of making diagnostic inferences. The trick is to find a balance between groups that are too large or too small. Groups that are too large ignore systematic variations within the group that might have predictive value; those that are too small have been constructed using random variation. In statistical modeling, these mistakes are called underfitting and overfitting, respectively. It is not a matter of discovering the correct groups but of constructing groups that have an acceptable ratio of benefits and costs with respect to one's predictive goals.

We might also find that groups that work for one goal such as predicting course are less useful for another goal such as predicting response to a particular form of treatment. Perhaps the classifications of the future can be calibrated to one's goals rather than being used for all purposes come what may. (See my chapter from an earlier Copenhagen conference for a complimentary view about the role of goals in validation using the concept of a practical kind (Zachar, 2012).)

Romeijn and van Loo suggest that reference group thinking may be used in many ways to develop more informative classification schemes. In their chapter, they illustrate a different way of looking at confounding variables and causal networks. Let me illustrate reference class thinking with another example. When scientific psychologists are learning statistics, they sometimes take an interaction effect in a 2 × 2 factorial analysis of variance and make sense of it for themselves by converting it to a one-way analysis of variance. For example, they make take the finding that there is an interaction effect between alcohol and barbiturate use on job performance, and try to make sense of it by creating four groups: (a) no alcohol use, no barbiturate use; (b) alcohol use, no barbiturate use; (c) no alcohol use, barbiturate use; and (d) alcohol use and barbiturate use. In the analysis of variance, with performance as the dependent variable, the interaction would manifest as the alcohol and barbiturate use group being significantly different compared to all other groups. Likely because so many of the people in that group end up missing work and/or being compromised when at work. Group (d) is a reference group about which important inferences can be made.

In his commentary, Eric Turkheimer suggests that Romeijn and van Loo are adopting too strict an empiricism in which references classes are constructed only because they have some predictive value with respect to a narrow outcome variable, but little value or import beyond that. He compares this to the history of a very strict operationalism in scientific psychology, which was at the same time a very strict empiricism. What psychologists did not like about strict operationalism is that it had a reductionist flair to it in which, for example, an MMPI depression scale was nothing more than a tool for making inferences about people. As Paul Meehl (1945) argued in his classical rationale for interpreting MMPI scale elevations, all that mattered were the empirical correlates of the scales.

Meehl soon modified his thinking, a bit.[1] In 1948, Kenneth MacCorquodale (a student of B.F. Skinner) and Paul Meehl (a student of Starke Hathaway who co-developed the MMPI), borrowing some ideas from the logical positivists, introduced the notion of hypothetical constructs into psychology (MacCorquodale & Meehl, 1948). Applying these ideas to the

[1] Meehl (1954) continued to advocate for the superiority of statistical algorithms when making predictions.

clinical realm a few years later, Cronbach and Meehl (1955) argued that whatever meaning the term depression has via the MMPI items, it also has surplus meaning that cannot be captured by the content and the empirical correlates of those items alone. The surplus meaning is embedded in a theoretical framework in which we understand depression. Turkheimer is fine with the predictive tools, but wants the theoretical frameworks as well.

This calls to mind John Stuart Mill's (1843/1973) notion of a real kind. As opposed to a narrower reference class constructed for a particular task, classes that form real kinds have an uncountable number of properties in common, and many possible inferences can be made about them.

All three interlocutors in this discussion have pragmatist sympathies and like other pragmatists can end up on either side of the line separating scientific antirealism and scientific realism, depending on the issue. In response to Eric's shifting his weight onto his realist foot, Jan-Willem and Hanna might argue that the problem with major depressive disorder is not that it cannot be a real kind in Mill's sense, but that it is not the kind of real kind that we need to make predictions about how best to intervene – and if a different reference class does a better job, whether it is a real kind or not is irrelevant.

REFERENCES

Cronbach, L. J., & Meehl, P. E. (1955) 'Construct validity in psychological tests.' *Psychological Bulletin*, 52(4), 281–302.

Kessler, R. C., van Loo, H. M., Wardenaar, K. J., Bossarte, R. M., Brenner, L. A., Ebert, D. D., . . . Zaslavsky, A. M. (2017) 'Using patient self-reports to study heterogeneity of treatment effects in major depressive disorder.' *Epidemiology and Psychiatric Sciences*, *26*(1), 22–36.

MacCorquodale, K., & Meehl, P. E. (1948)' On a distinction between hypothetical constructs and intervening variables.' *Psychological Review*, 55(2), 95–107.

Meehl, P. E. (1945) 'The dynamics of "structured" personality tests.' *Journal of Clinical Psychology*, *1*(4), 296–303.

(1954) *Clinical versus statistical prediction*. Minneapolis, MN: University of Minnesota Press.

Mill, J. S. (1843/1973) *A system of logic*. Toronto: University of Toronto Press.

Spitzer, R. L., Endicott, J., & Robins, E. (1978). Research diagnostic criteria. *Archives of General Psychiatry*, 35(6), 773–782.

Zachar, P. (2012) 'Progress and the calibration of scientific constructs: The role of comparative validity.' In K. S. Kendler & J. Parnas (Eds.), *Philosophical issues in psychiatry II: Nosology-definition of illness, history, validity, and prospects* (pp. 21–34). New York: Oxford University Press.

29

Psychiatric Classification: An A-reductionist Perspective

JAN-WILLEM ROMEIJN AND HANNA M. VAN LOO

29.1 INTRODUCTION

Many psychiatric disorders capture heterogeneous classes of patients, in terms of their etiology, course of illness, and response to treatment (Nandi et al. 2009, Baumeister and Parker 2012,). For instance, of all patients with a first episode of major depression, about one-third will have only one lifetime episode, whereas two-thirds will suffer from recurrent or chronic episodes (Eaton et al. 2008). This variation in patients with the same diagnosis hampers prediction and treatment assignments in clinical practice. It has evoked continuing efforts to improve psychiatric disease classification such as the *Diagnostic and Statistical Manual of Mental Disorders* and *International Classification of Disease* (cf. Kupfer et al. 2008).

Recently, the American Psychiatric Association has invited researchers worldwide to contribute to improving the *DSM*, and propose alternative disease or subtype definitions based on empirical evidence according to the so-called empirically-driven continuous improvement model (Kendler 2013, First et al. 2017). Several validators – e.g., familial aggregation, biological markers, course of illness, response to treatment – have been proposed as criteria to judge whether new proposals will improve on current disease definitions (Kendler 2013). If there is clear evidence that alternative definitions outperform the current ones in terms of validity, reliability, or clinical utility, this might lead to a change in specific diagnostic categories (First et al. 2017).

Note that performance is put in terms of validity, reliability, and clinical utility. All of these, we note, relate to the more general goals of accurate

We would like to thank Ken Kendler, Kathryn Tabb, Eric Turkheimer, and Peter Zachar for helpful discussions.

prediction and effective intervention. Consider the aforementioned validators. Biomarkers and familial aggregation signal robust predictive properties, and both expected course of illness and response to treatment relate to therapeutic interventions. And much like the measure of validity, the measures of reliability and clinical utility relate to prediction and intervention: the reason to aim for them is that it is desirable that different clinicians have similar expectations, similar views on what is wrong with the patient, and similar ideas on what can best be done. Therefore, without suggesting in any way that these goals exhaust the purposes of psychiatric classification, we maintain that classifications are generally better when they lead to improved opportunities for prediction and intervention (cf. Cartwright and Hardie 2012). This will be true for clinicians, researchers, and patients, although all these stakeholders will have differing predictive concerns.[1]

But how to identify classes of patients that improve prediction and intervention, and outperform the existing classifications? The focus of this chapter will be on how statistical methods can be utilized to contribute to this goal.[2] Our outlook on the improvement of psychiatric classification, moreover, will offer insight into the fact that classification schemes can include characteristics that pertain to entirely different theoretical domains, or explanatory levels. Is it problematic when a classification scheme sorts individuals by means of specific pathophysiological characteristics, as well as by psychological and social ones? Toward the end of this chapter, we will answer this question in the negative, and motivate our position.

This chapter is structured as follows. First we will show that the problem of finding the right categories is equivalent to the so-called

[1] One possible criticism of viewing psychiatric classification this way is that it ignores one of its most important purposes. A classification may also support an understanding of disorders, an explanation of a course of events, and thereby be an instrument for therapists and a consolation for those who suffer from mental disorder. For researchers, understanding is similarly important, even if they will have a different use for it. For now, we want to suggest that the value of understanding and explanation is often in the empirical consequences that they have. Insight into a disorder helps us to apply our ideas more adequately and reliably, to gain a sense of control, to support our decisions in dealing with the disorder. Therefore, to some degree we view the explanatory value of a classification as derivative.

[2] While there are certainly other possible approaches to psychiatry, e.g., medical casuistics or single-case research, current medical research is dominated by the practice of statistics, i.e., the collection of data and the use of statistical methods to investigate mental illness. In this chapter, we approach psychiatric research from this statistical angle.

reference class problem, an essentially statistical problem well-known from the philosophy of science literature (Section 29.2). Then we discuss how model construction and selection and causal modeling methods can be used to identify adequate classes of individuals (Sections 29.3 and 29.4). Next we argue that these methods promote a so-called a-reductionist perspective toward the variety of explanatory levels in psychiatry (Section 29.5). We conclude by giving a brief summary of what we have claimed (Section 29.6).

29.2 PSYCHIATRIC CLASSIFICATION AS A REFERENCE CLASS PROBLEM

We introduce a statistical perspective on the problem of psychiatric classification and then show how it coincides with the problem of the reference class.[3] Toward the end, we look ahead and indicate how our perspective links up with a particular view on explanatory levels.

29.2.1 Classification as Statistical Model Building

A classification scheme generates a grouping of the population based on certain characteristics assigned to the individuals. Depending on the granularity of the classification, the groups will be larger or smaller. For a system that only contains two binary variables, for instance "depression yes/no" and "psychosis yes/no", there will be 2×2, hence four groups. For a very rich classification scheme, on the other hand, every individual might be contained in their own group. Of course, the usual disease classifications will have a granularity that sits in between such extremes, and that is endowed with further structure. The *DSM-5*, for instance, specifies a grouping into a large number of disorders, into the hundreds, by means of a collection of even more symptoms. These characterizations in terms of symptoms allow us to define very many subgroups within these disorders, of which some will be clinically meaningful while others are not (cf. Olbert et al. 2014).

In general, the problem of classification is that of finding the relevant set of characteristics in individuals. Viewed in this way, classification sits close to the core tasks of psychiatric scientists. Finding out about the factors that matter to the prediction of, and intervention on psychiatric disorders

[3] To avoid terminological confusion: the notion of reference class here is different from the reference class in analyses of categorical variables.

encompasses much of their research. It involves measuring, constructing, and then selecting the right variables, and determining relations among them by means of experimental and observational studies. In the philosophy of science, this is often referred to as the construction and evaluation of "models" (cf. Morgan and Morrison 1999). Several of the other chapters in this volume are directly or indirectly concerned with models. The construction of a model is at stake in, for instance, "designing control panels" by which we judge a clinical course of action (Campbell [Chapter 14]), pitching the patient descriptions at the right level (Pine [Chapter 8]), and even in crafting new concepts in the psychosocial realm, by means of which we can capture the experiences or raw empirical facts of a clinical practice (Parnas and Gallagher [Chapters 17 and 11]).

A key problem in psychiatric classification is that of identifying homogeneous and maximally distinct groups. We look for inter-class heterogeneity, i.e., classes that are dissimilar on variables of interest, and intra-class homogeneity, i.e., classes of similar individuals with respect to these variables. As said, in this chapter, we consider the role of statistical methods in the task of classification, and we take classification to have the purpose of supporting predictions and interventions. Accordingly, what it means for patients in the classes to be similar, and between classes to be dissimilar, is that they are alike and different in terms of the characteristics salient for what we want to predict and control. There is intra-class homogeneity when within the classes we find little variation among characteristics that matter for those goals, and there is inter-class heterogeneity when between the classes we find large variation among those characteristics.

It is extremely rare that membership of some class, i.e., having a certain combination of characteristics, fully determines a particular course of illness, or a particular result of an intervention. The normal situation is that a class is associated with chances, not certainties. In this statistical context, intra-class homogeneity, and hence the similarity of members of the class, means that all the members have roughly the same chance for some event or result. Inter-class heterogeneity, in the same vein, means that those chances vary widely when moving from one class to the next. For a homogeneous class, then, the proportions within the class will be good estimations of the chances for the members of the class. A classification that satisfies intra-class homogeneity thus identifies groups for which we can build up statistical knowledge, by observing proportions within the group and taking them as estimates for chances that then apply to the individuals in that group. This is arguably the core idea of statistics.

29.2.2 The Problem of the Reference Class

In the philosophy of science, groups on which we can base chance ascriptions are termed "reference classes" (Reichenbach 1949, Hájek 2007). A useful reference class for an individual is a group to which that individual belongs such that we can infer stable chances for the individual from the observed proportions of the group. Say that we offer a certain treatment to all individuals labeled with a disorder from our classification scheme, record the proportion of recoveries within that group, and then take the proportion as indicative of the chance of recovery for any person suffering from the disorder. If the classification scheme groups the individuals together in the right way, the chance ascriptions to individuals will be predictively accurate and useful in making the intervention decisions. The problem that we are facing when classifying mental disorders is precisely the problem of the reference class: what individuals shall we group together for the purpose of determining these chances?

By analogy, say that we are asked to sort a large collection of dice, with a varying number of sides, of which an unknown number of sides shows a 1. Note that this need not only be six-sided dice, and that the numbering on the dice might have duplications, e.g., when several sides all show a 1; see Figure 29.1.

Now imagine that our aim is to predict whether we will roll a 1 with a randomly selected die. We then do best to disregard the color and weight of the dice, and focus only on the number of sides showing 1 and on the total number of sides when we make a grouping. Further, if we are asked to make groups, we might decide to isolate a set of dice for which rolling a 1 has a low chance, one for which the chance is high. Depending on the collection of dice given to us, we might find that there really are two

FIGURE 29.1 A collection of dice with different numbers of sides. (With permission from skullsplitterdice.com)

distinct sets of dice, one with dice that have between ⅔ and ¾ of the sides marked 1, and another that do not have any 1s, or else a single 1 among at least ten sides. Such sets show high intra-class homogeneity, with little variation in the chances for each individual die within the set, and high inter-class heterogeneity because the difference between the chances of rolling a 1 between the two sets is large. But we might be less lucky with our dice collection, with the chances on a 1 spread over the whole spectrum between 0 and 1 without any sort of grouping. However this may be, we will group the dice according to the predictive goals we set ourselves, and we will focus on characteristics that are relevant for determining the salient chances.

Next to this example with dice, consider a concrete psychiatric example that is structurally the same. Say we want to determine the intensity of monitoring for an individual patient who just recovered from a first episode of major depression. Then it would be useful to know the probability of this patient on long-term remission versus chronic or recurrent episodes of depression. Suppose that, in general, for patients who recovered from a first episode of depression, this chance is roughly 50%. Could we imagine a better reference class for this individual patient? A good reference class would be a sub-class of patients recovered from a first episode of major depression who are similar in such a way that we can infer the probability for this individual patient from the group average; we want this chance ascription to be stable. Ideally, chances in this reference class would be extreme, i.e., very low or very high. The percentage for all patients recovered from a first episode of major depression, to wit, 50%, is not very informative.[4]

From the example, it will be apparent what it means for a grouping, and hence for a model or a classification scheme, to generate useful reference classes. The classification of the individuals must facilitate accurate predictions of, and effective interventions on the phenomena that we care about. Optimizing a psychiatric classification scheme is, at least in part, that kind of exercise: it concerns the selection of criteria for the formation of groups that can serve as reference classes for stable and distinct chance ascriptions to variables of interest, either for the purpose of accurate predictions or for

[4] Readers with philosophical inclinations may wonder if chances for the individual can make sense at all, but ideas from the philosophy of science can help us ground the requisite notion of chance conceptually. By employing ideas from emergentism and multiple realizability, we can overcome reductionist challenges to the coherence of single-case chances, including chances assigned to variables and events that are characterized at a high level of description.

effective intervention. Importantly, this is an empirical issue: we determine the groupings not on the basis of some preconceived notion of natural kind, or on the basis of a preconceived explanatory level, but primarily by the empirical facts of which characteristics facilitate prediction and intervention.[5]

29.2.3 Looking Ahead

The remainder of this chapter is devoted to working out some of the consequences of viewing nosological reform in this way, namely, as ultimately a statistical affair of forming groupings based on the characteristics of the individuals (cf. Grove and Meehl 1996). The next two sections point to specific statistical methods that may help us to identify groupings with relevantly similar individuals for which distinct and stable chances can be determined. In the section following that, we consider the more theoretical implications of our perspective on nosological reform, in particular the non-committal position in the reductionism debate that is entailed by it. We can already note that nothing in the foregoing suggests that we have to limit our search for salient characteristics to a specific explanatory level, for instance, by looking only to neurological variables, or cognitive and social ones. Any characteristic of an individual is in principle suitable for inclusion into the classification scheme, and they can all be treated on a par. In what follows, we will keep returning to this a-reductionist implication of our view on classification.

29.3 MODELS: CONSTRUCTION AND SELECTION

In this section, we devote our attention to the two research phases of model construction and model selection because they hold particular promise for the design of classifications. Moreover, as we argue at the end, the statistical tools that help us construct and select models are neutral toward explanatory levels, and therefore support the afore-mentioned position of a-reductionism.

5 This empirically driven way of classifying individuals is reminiscent of Hathaway and McKinley (1940) and the development of the Minnesota Multiphasic Personality Inventory (MMPI), a standardized psychometric test of adult personality and psychopathology. It also reminds of Meehl (1956), who discusses the MMPI extensively. We thank Peter Zachar and Marcus Eronen for pointing us to these respective parallels.

29.3.1 Statistical Methods for Classification Design

What statistical methods can be used to contribute to the design of such classification schemes? For one, ordinary statistical analysis, carried out against the backdrop of a model, can be highly instrumental: hypothesis tests, parameter estimations, and statistical inferences may all contribute to the design of classifications, e.g., by determining the relative importance of characteristics that are taken into consideration. However, we also find methods that are suited to the task in the research phase that precedes statistical analysis namely in the construction of a statistical model, and in the phase that follows it namely in the evaluation of those models. We concentrate now on these methods.

On the side of model construction, certain statistical learning methods can be used to discern similarity patterns in characteristics of patients that were not known beforehand (Lubke and Muthén 2005, James 2013), and thereby suggest specific classifications. The advantage of using statistical learning methods is that these can evaluate vast numbers of patient characteristics in large samples of subjects. Based on similarity patterns in these patient characteristics, these methods can divide subjects into subgroups with high intra-class homogeneity, and pronounced inter-class differences. The resulting statistical models might underpin alternative classifications.

A good example comes from the research into more homogenous subtypes for depression (cf. Baumeister and Parler 2012). How can we use statistical methods to improve on current subtypes, such as the traditional division into melancholic and atypical depression (American Psychiatric Association 2013)? In a recent study, we used data of the World Mental Health Survey (Kessler and Ustun 2008) of more than 8,000 subjects with a lifetime depressive episode (van Loo et al. 2014, Wardenaar 2014). These subjects were interviewed about a range of clinical characteristics, such as their symptoms during the depressive episode, their age when they became first depressed, psychiatric comorbid disorders, and whether their parents also suffered from depression. The subjects also reported on the course of their depressive illness, i.e., on the number of depressive episodes they had, the chronicity of these episodes, whether they were ever hospitalized for depression, and whether they were disabled to work.

Statistical learning methods were then deployed to discover classes of patients with similar course of illness patterns, based on these clinical characteristics. Using penalized regression methods, we constructed a variety of models, ranging from more to less complex in terms of the numbers of included clinical characteristics. After a phase of model

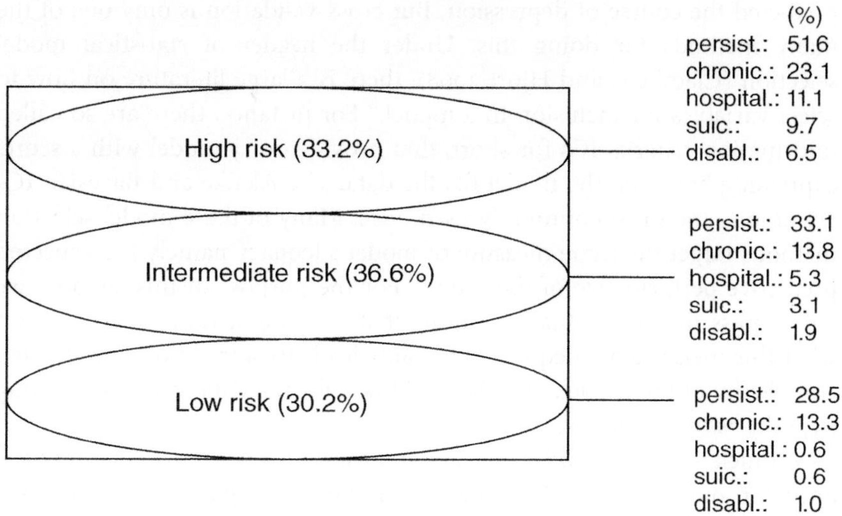

FIGURE 29.2 Association of identified risk clusters with course of illness after 10–12 years in 1,056 subjects with lifetime depression in the US National Comorbidity Survey (Kessler et al. 2016).

Note: This figure presents prospective associations between initial cluster scores (1990–1992) and subsequent persistence and severity of course of depression (2001–2003). The outcomes measured at follow-up concern percentages of years with depressive episodes (persist.; persistence), the episodes lasting most of the year (chronic.; chronicity), hospitalization (hospital.; hospitalization), and suicide attempts since baseline (suic.; suicide attempts), and current disability (disab.; disability), in the NCS data. Area under the curves (AUCs) for the three cluster classification varied between 0.60–0.69 for the outcomes indicating years with (chronic) episodes, and 0.70–0.73 for outcomes indicating severity (hospitalization, suicide attempts, and disability).

construction and statistical analysis, we assessed the performance of the models by means of cross-validation. We selected the model that best predicted the course of illness and defined three subtypes of depression with a low, intermediate and high risk for a severe course of illness. When we tested the accuracy of this model in new data, the proposed subtypes indeed differentiated between subjects with a more severe, intermediate, or mild course of illness (Figure 29.2, Kessler et al. 2016).

29.3.2 Assessing Models: Finding the Sweet Spot

Notice that these previous studies (van Loo et al. 2014, Wardenaar et al. 2014) used cross-validation to select the statistical model that best predicted the course of depression. But cross-validation is only one of the many methods for doing this. Under the header of statistical model selection (Claeskens and Hjort 2008), there is a large literature on how to select variables for inclusion in a model.[6] For instance, there are so-called information criteria, ICs for short, that provide every model with a score, expressing how well the model fits the data. The Akaike and Bayesian ICs are among the most commonly used ones. Many of these model selection methods target the same measure of model adequacy namely the expected predictive performance of the model. For the purpose of this chapter, we will bypass the conceptual questions that this might raise, and focus on what this measure of adequacy invariably leads to: a trade-off between the complexity of the model, and the likelihood for the data of the best-fitting hypothesis in the model.

A quick illustration will make apparent why this is of particular importance for our purposes. Consider a sample of people suffering from a mental disorder, and two classification schemes or models that may be used to fit the data of the patients. The first of these has very few classes, lumping together large patient groups, while the second has so many of them that every individual occupies their own group. The problem with the first classification is that it will not be sufficiently differentiating, for example, between patients with a severe course of illness versus a mild course of illness. It will lead to highly heterogeneous groups, and therefore to inaccurate predictions. The second classification will also be problematic though, albeit for a different reason. If the classification is so fine-grained that everyone will be the sole datum for their own grouping, there is hardly any basis for extrapolating from the observed individuals to other individuals in the population: a single data point might give some information about the class to which that individual belongs, but it is far too little for reliable predictions. The upshot is that the predictions stemming from the classification will be unreliable. For either model, the predictive performance will thus be found wanting.

The point of all the model selection methods is to find the sweet spot between these two extremes. On the one hand we want to avoid overfitting, i.e., picking up on noisy or unimportant individual differences in the data

[6] The suggestion of model "selection" is somewhat misleading because the model selection methods merely evaluate and compare models. The researcher's act of selecting one model is more akin to making a decision than forming a judgment, and therefore something best understood by means of decision theory. It involves more than assessing evidential relations between data and model; it also concerns the utility of the outcome.

and viewing them as signals, thereby identifying too many subgroups. This corresponds to optimizing on inter-class heterogeneity: we want to avoid distinguishing groups that are not all that different. On the other hand we want to avoid underfitting, i.e., failing to pick up on signals in the data because we lack the means to detect genuine differences among the individuals. This corresponds to optimizing on intra-class homogeneity: we do not want to miss out on salient distinctions among patients. Model selection methods help us to make this trade-off in a broadly data-driven way, and thus optimize the expected predictive performance.

29.3.3 Discussion: Subject-Specific Knowledge and Explanatory Levels

A few comments on these statistical methods are in order. First, there are numerous model discovery and selection methods and they all strike the balance between fit and complexity in a slightly different way. We certainly do not want to suggest that the issue of how to strike the balance can be delegated to a statistics department. Application of these methods is only helpful if it is combined with detailed knowledge about clinical psychiatry, and with a good understanding of the assumptions that underpin the methods. Second, the results of model selection methods will depend strongly on the predictive targets that we set. There is no guarantee that the set of variables that appears to be the sweet spot for predicting the course of one particular illness, will also be the sweet spot for predicting treatment response. It may well be that we have to maintain several task-specific models. Although we cannot develop this idea in any detail, it is in principle possible to select a set of variables for optimal performance on a range of predictive tasks, simply by finding a compromise between the demands placed by the different predictive goals. How accurate these predictions are, will depend on the nature of the compromise but also on how regular and noisy the phenomena themselves are.

Finally, notice that in the foregoing, we did not discuss the level of description of variables that are considered for inclusion in the classification scheme, or the scientific discipline from which they originate. That is simply irrelevant to the application of the model selection methods: all variables, from biological and behavioral to cognitive and social, are treated on a par by the statistical methods under consideration. The methods thus offer a particular grip on the classification of disorders for which multiple explanatory levels are implicated. In practice it may not always be easy to combine data from different levels, e.g., genetic data with data from the cognitive and social realm, for example, because there are few large data sets in which all these characteristics are combined. The point we want to make is that the statistical approach to psychiatric classification that is under discussion here does not constrain us to a single level. All that matters is the role of a variable in improving the predictive performance of the classification scheme.

29.4 CAUSAL MODELING

This section considers the role of causal network models, a statistical tool for determining causal relations, in the design of psychiatric classifications. After introducing them in a worked example, we argue for their usefulness and touch on their fit with our a-reductionist viewpoint.

29.4.1 The Importance of Interventions

Besides predicting events, an important goal of science is to intervene. This is true in particular for medical science with its focus on treatment. A core desideratum for psychiatric classification is that it allows us to intervene on, and change the course of mental disorders for the better: the classification needs to guide treatment decisions. The desideratum for a classification is therefore that individuals from different classes of patients respond to treatment options in the same way, and that for each group of patients there is at least one treatment option that offers a high probability of success. For each individual patient, an optimal treatment can then be determined by referring back to the classification. Accordingly, the classification can then support the organization of treatment programs.

To facilitate maximally effective clinical interventions, it is helpful when our classification meshes with the causal structure of the disorder. Insight into the causal structure will reveal what factors initiate, promote, moderate, mediate, or otherwise modify the disorder, and how we can influence these factors to positive effect. Unfortunately, silver bullets are a rarity in a therapeutic context, but we might hope that the causal structure among the factors gives us a statistical grip, in the sense that we gain some control over the chances of recovery. For steering nosological reform, a crucial question is therefore whether the classification scheme facilitates interventions with good statistical properties: we want to include variables or characteristics if they are useful in the specification of treatments that are effective, in the sense that they increase the recovery chances. Importantly, it is not thereby required that we fully expose the mechanisms that are driving the disorders because we can also gain causal knowledge, and hence control, through derivative variables.

The statistical toolbox of the psychiatric researcher already includes designs and methods that help evaluate treatment: randomized controlled trials, hypothesis testing and parameter estimation, e.g., regression analysis, and various ways of controlling for confounders. However, if the aim is to lay our hands on causal structure, statistics has its well-known shortcomings, as laid down in the slogan "correlation is not causation". It is received wisdom that statistical relations between variables cannot help us establish the causal ties between the underlying events.

Fortunately, the past three decades have seen the development of new statistical methods, developed in statistical science but also in computer science and philosophy, aimed at determining causal structure (Glymour, Spirtes, and Scheines 2001). The methods go by the name of causal networks, or sometimes causal Bayesian networks even though many of the statistical methods involved in using these methods are not Bayesian but frequentist. In our view, causal networks are underused in the sciences, considering their potential value. As we will argue below, psychiatric classification seems especially suitable for their application.

29.4.2 Causal Network Models

The key idea of causal networks is that correlations and dependency relations between variables can be captured in a network. The variables are the nodes in such networks and the arrows in between represent statistical dependencies. These arrows are then interpreted causally, so that the graph helps us to determine what we can expect after we have changed the value of one of the variables. This is what makes causal networks different from other statistical methods that help us to determine the effects of treatments: they offer an explicit grip on the interventions. For our purposes, it suffices to discuss a few of the basic ideas by means of an example. Our goal with this is to illustrate how causal networks can be instrumental to making decisions over the salience of variables, and hence over their inclusion into a classification scheme.[7] For further detail on causal network models, we refer to Glymour et al. (2001) and, more accessible, Pearl (2018).

[7] The narrative of this section also illustrates Simpson's paradox (Pearl 2000, Chapter 6), which can be illuminated very well by means of causal networks. But the emphasis will not be on the paradox itself.

FIGURE 29.3 A simple causal network for treatment with SSRI and self-reported recovery. The observation study suggests a negative connection, but the RCT shows a positive impact.

Say that we have done an observational study recording whether or not individuals with panic disorder received treatment with a selective serotonin reuptake inhibitor, here denoted simply as *SSRI*, and also whether or not they reported a recovery after 8 weeks, denoted *RepRec*. Imagine that we found a *negative* correlation between the two, $P(RepRec|SSRI) < P(RepRec)$, i.e., somewhat surprisingly the treatment seems to have a negative effect on recovery. We can now construct a simple network that expresses this correlation, interlinking the variables and tentatively marking the link as negative. Moreover, considering that the treatment event preceded the recovery and interpreting the link as casual, we can orient the relation, as depicted on the left in Figure 29.3.

Imagine that we have also carried out a randomized controlled trial (RCT) on the efficacy of the SSRI compared to placebo treatment in panic disorder. And that, despite the negative correlation in the field study, actively administering the treatment, denoted as *Do*[*SSRI*], to a randomly selected set of individuals has a positive impact on their recovery, as depicted on the right of Figure 29.3. What might explain this seeming inconsistency? The answer to this question is that in the observational study, the explaining variable *SSRI* is "confounded": it is correlated with other variables, not present in our narrative thus far, that have an impact on the outcome variable *RepRec*. Doing an RCT allows us to determine the separate impact of SSRI on recovery, by removing the correlations with all other relevant variables, or at least attempting to remove them.

A development of the narrative brings the confounder into view. Say that, in the field study, further characteristics of the population before the treatment were recorded, namely their age, gender, and whether they had comorbid depression, denoted by *DiaDep*. Including age and gender as nodes in the causal network shows no moderation of the negative association between SSRI and *RepRec*, but the variable *DiaDep* does (Figure 29.4). In the field study, subjects with panic disorder and depression were more often treated with an SSRI, and *DiaDep* was therefore highly correlated with SSRI use. Furthermore, and crucially, the prospects of recovery from panic disorder are much worse if there is comorbid depression (Roy-Byrne

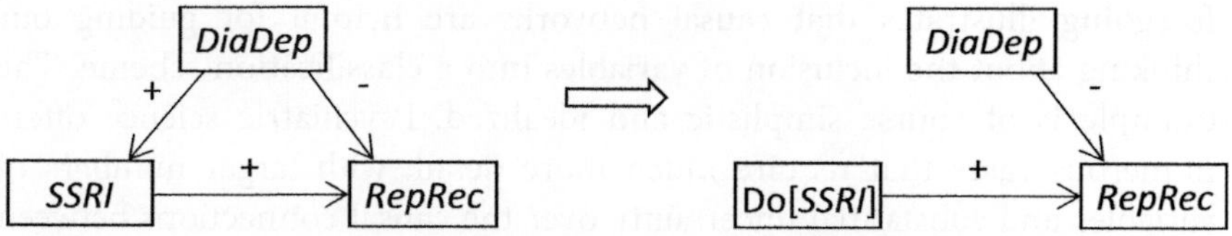

FIGURE 29.4 A more complete causal network for treatment and recovery, and the corresponding RCT network. Notice that there is an impact of DiaDep on SSRI, but that the intervention variable Do[SSRI] is not correlated to DiaDep.

et al. 2000). In the observation study, the recovery rate for individuals who received SSRI will therefore be lower. This is not because the SSRI treatment itself is detrimental to recovery. It is because the individuals who were given SSRI were by and large those individuals who had comorbid depression symptoms, and who will therefore recover less easily.

Figure 29.4 provides a more complete network among the salient variables on the left, as well as a network corresponding to the RCT on the right. Note the marked difference between merely recording whether or not the SSRI treatment was given, as expressed in the variable *SSRI* on the left, and actively administering the SSRI treatment, which we will denote by the variable Do[*SSRI*] on the right. In the observation study, the positive impact of SSRI on recovery is masked by the negative correlation that is established through the comorbid depression. Administering SSRI irrespective of comorbid depression removes this correlation, so that the positive impact of SSRI on recovery can come to the fore.

29.4.3 The Merits of Causal Networks

The foregoing merely illustrates the idea of causal networks. It shows the benefits of classifying patients with panic disorder into two subgroups, those with and those without comorbid depression. If we do not distinguish the subgroups and work with the coarse-grained classification, we misread field data on the efficacy of SSRI treatment, and this may lead us astray when we are considering whether or not to administer an SSRI. Getting to a more complete causal structure, and adapting the classification accordingly, helps us to determine effective clinical interventions.

The more standard statistical treatment, based on RCTs and the methods for identifying confounders, would seem perfectly fine for using comorbid depression as a means to create subgroups of patients with panic disorder. So what is the use of the causal network models? We think the foregoing illustrates that causal networks are helpful for guiding our thinking about the inclusion of variables into a classification scheme. The example is of course simplistic and idealized. Psychiatric science offers numerous cases that require much more detail, with larger numbers of variables and substantial uncertainty over the causal connections between them. We can easily expand the networks above, up to the point where our intuitions fail and standard statistical tools become clunky and unclear. The theory of causal networks is a well-developed and complete toolkit for investigating the causal structure of systems of variables, and for determining what difference certain interventions make to the chance of recovery in distinct subgroups of patients. Decisions about the inclusion or not of a variable in a classification can thus be supported by causal modeling.

Another important advantage of causal networks is that, also in much more involved narratives and models, they offer a formally precise grip on interventions. The administering of SSRI, for example, can be represented precisely in terms of an operation on the original network structure, as illustrated in Figure 29.4. This is helpful in at least two ways: we can systematically determine what our current model and its model estimates entail about the results of interventions; and we have a systematic means to adapt our model if our predictions about the results of interventions are not borne out. Specifically, in the example, the first network that linked SSRI to recovery negatively turned out to be at variance with the results of the intervention study. And this led us to search for, and eventually identification of confounding variables. The networks, in short, are convenient tools in the construction of models, and in the derivation of predictions following interventions.

As a further motivation for using this methodology, the theory of causal networks is undergoing rapid development. There is active research on causal methods in statistics, machine learning, and philosophy, and there are many interesting areas of research that deserve mention here. We want to end this section by mentioning a development that we find particularly important for psychiatric classification. One pressing problem in psychiatry is that it is causally complex. Disorders may be triggered by a multitude of factors, manifesting on different explanatory levels. We are typically presented with a cacophony of inter-dependent variables that are all salient, and among which there is no clear order of relative prominence. It becomes virtually impossible to say in general what caused a disorder: everything did to some extent. Recent work on causal feature learning (Chalupka et al.2017) may provide the start of a solution to this. Machine learning techniques can construct macroscopic variables from large collections of factors in such a way that these macroscopic variables play the requisite causal role. The method enables us to identify global characteristics of systems, in this case of individual patients, that are causally relevant for the course of illness. We are not yet in the position to apply this machinery to the case at hand, but the idea of causal feature learning is promising.

A final remark pertains to the issue of explanatory levels. As before, we did not discuss the level of description of variables that show up in causal networks. This is irrelevant to the methods on offer: all variables, from biological and behavioral to cognitive and social, are treated on par by the causal modeling methods. Much like model selection methods, causal networks therefore offer a grip on multi-level disease classification.

29.5 A-REDUCTIONISM IN PSYCHIATRY

We are now in a position to relate the current chapter to the central theme of this book on explanatory levels. Psychiatry is inherently multilevel; risk factors for psychiatric disorders are widely dispersed across biological, psychological, and environmental levels (Kendler 2013, 2014). Over two-thirds of studies have a within-level focus (Kendler 2014), and some researchers give a higher priority to factors from one level, such as genetic factors or other biological factors (cf. Eronen 2019). But the levels all have their own concepts and their own relevance to the core issue of psychiatry. The benefit of our data-driven approach to classification is that we can involve multiple levels in nosological reform. We do not judge any level as *a priori* more important for classification.

The idea that science needs to be done in terms of concepts stemming from one particular domain or level is very influential. Most commonly this is the domain of the physical, e.g., of the cells and their composition. An important motivation sometimes given for this is metaphysical: science should only be concerned with what exists, and one particular level, typically the material one, has a unique claim to existence. By contrast, epistemic reductionism is the claim that there is a single domain, again typically the material, in terms of which we can ultimately predict, control, and explain all the facts about the target system, in our case psychiatric disorders. Weaker versions of the same idea might admit that concepts from other domains will come in handy when explaining the facts, but minimally they will maintain that these concepts are explanatory in virtue of a translation that can be made toward the concepts belonging to the fundamental domain.

So-called epistemic anti-reductionism denies that one single domain takes explanatory priority. The positive claim of the anti-reductionist is that for a full understanding of psychiatric disorders, we need concepts from different domains. An important argument for this view is that facts expressed in terms of different domain vocabularies require explanations in terms of those different domains, because the domain vocabularies contain terms that resist translation. This radical untranslatability even motivates some theorists to endorse metaphysical anti-reductionism. If some facts can only be explained by reference to, e.g., concepts from the social domain, then it might seem reasonable to bestow some kind of existence upon the referents of those concepts as well.

The pragmatic and empiricist position that we have developed in the foregoing is deliberately non-committal when it comes to the debate over epistemic reductionism: it is an a-reductionist point of view. The positive claim we want to make is that this reductionist issue can be resolved empirically and pragmatically. In search of a better classification of mental disorders, we can take all manner of variables into consideration. The methods that we have advertised in order to decide over inclusion into the classification scheme do not favor one domain over another, and they do not restrict us to a specific domain at the outset. Relative to the predictive and interventionist goals that we determine ourselves, we will find that some set of variables will perform best. For certain disorders, this may turn out to be a set of variables stemming from one single explanatory domain, whereas for other disorders it will be a set that includes variables from multiple domains. That will all depend on which variables will benefit the goals of the classification scheme, viz. prediction and intervention, most.

Perhaps this attitude seems to preselect a classification scheme that includes variables from multiple domains. Do we not have any principled reasons to prefer a classification scheme that involves only one such domain? Clearly, if we think that certain concepts help science progress faster, take precedence metaphysically, or fit better with our overall world view, then the choice of variables should be constrained. But our point is precisely that adopting such constraints at the outset, by choosing a set of natural kinds for instance, is unnecessary, and that it might hamper our ability to predict and intervene.[8] If we find use for intervention variables on

[8] Tabb (2015, 2017) argues that the centrality of the *DSM* presents obstacles to the identification of salient patient groups, and Tabb [this volume] presents arguments against a particular take on precision-medicine. Our views are similar to hers in that she

the explanatory level of behavior, or if it turns out that certain biological, social, or cultural factors help us to predict the course of illness, then we should avail ourselves of these conceptual means, without regard for the explanatory level from which they originate.

The drive toward a physicalist vocabulary in psychiatry will in some cases be motivated by a sentiment of "smallism" and "physics envy". This refers to the idea that descriptions in terms of component parts are always more fundamental, better for scientific progress, or that the components have more of a claim to reality than the composites.[9] It is a view often associated with the natural sciences, in particular with fundamental physics. However, as the history of the natural sciences abundantly shows, the search for adequate concepts is ultimately an empirical matter (e.g., Kuhn 1962), and the design and selection of these concepts is arguably what made these sciences so successful. It would be an error to rob psychiatry of one of science's most effective means to support prediction and intervention namely the freedom to come up with new conceptions of classification criteria. The characteristics eligible for inclusion in psychiatric classification range from biomarkers to environmental factors, and a drive toward the micro-level will only stand in the way of making optimal classification choices.

29.6 CONCLUSION

The foregoing was informed by a discussion from the philosophy of science which, we argue, sits at the very center of all classification efforts. It is the discussion on the so-called reference class problem, the problem that the ascription of chances to an individual requires us to see the individual as a member of a group of similar individuals. In the case of psychiatry, as explained in Section 2, the reference class problem is that we can only determine the chance of recovery of an individual patient once we have located the patient in a group of relevantly similar patients. Classification schemes aim to provide us with such homogeneous patient groupings.

argues against taking one specific conceptual schema as the be-all and end-all of psychiatric science. Our attitude here should be a pragmatic one.

9 Turkheimer [this volume] also critically discusses a tendency to take the smaller scale as more fundamental, arguing that we should instead search for the level of description that brings our entities sharply into focus. We agree with this but replace entities by statistical relations.

The identification of the problem of psychiatric nosology with the reference class problem suggests a specific approach to nosological reform. Broadly speaking, if the problem of classification is one of finding statistically homogeneous patient groups, specific statistical methods may help us to identify such groups. Sections 3 and 4 discussed two such statistical methods, to wit, the construction and selection of statistical models and the statistical analysis of causal relations respectively. While these discussions will not build a complete case for the application of these methods and remain rather programmatic, we hope that they will invite researchers to frame their research efforts in the way that we outline, and reconsider the statistical methods that serve their goals. We do not claim warranted optimism about finding intra-homogeneous and inter-heterogeneous patient groups in this way, but we think our approach to be a plausible way forward.

Another benefit of these methods is that they can deal with the inherent multilevel nature of risk factors that are implicated in psychiatry, such as biological, psychological, and environmental risk factors. We support an empiricist and pragmatic approach to psychiatric nosology in which inclusion of a characteristic into a classification scheme depends on whether or not this improves our predictions or interventions. Whether or not something is an improvement may vary from one classification effort to another, but the goal of prediction and intervention is generic. Most relevant to the theme of this book, there is no presupposition on the so-called explanatory level that the characteristic is associated with. The classification scheme may include characteristics from a multitude of levels if this is what serves the purpose of predicting and intervening best.

REFERENCES

American Psychiatric Association (2013) *Diagnostic and Statistical Manual of Mental Disorders: DSM-5* (5th ed). American Psychiatric Publishing, Washington, DC.

Baumeister H, Parker G (2012) 'Meta-review of depressive subtyping models.' *Journal of Affective Disorders* 139, 126–140.

Cartwright N, Hardie J (2012) *Evidence-Based Policy*. Oxford University Press, New York.

Chalupka K, Eberhardt F, Perona P (2017) 'Causal feature learning: An overview.' *Behaviormetrika* 44, 137–164.

Claeskens G, Hjort N (2008) *Model Selection and Model Averaging*. Cambridge University Press, Cambridge, UK.

Eaton WW, Shao H, Nestadt G, Lee BH, Bienvenu OJ, Zandi P (2008) 'Population-based study of first onset and chronicity in major depressive disorder.' *Archives of General Psychiatry* 65, 513–520.

Eronen MI (2019) 'The levels problem in psychopathology.' *Psychological Medicine*, 1–7. https://doi.org/10.1017/S0033291719002514
First MB, Kendler KS, Leibenluft E (2017) 'The future of the DSM Implementing a continuous improvement model.' *JAMA Psychiatry* 74, 115.
Glymour C, Spirtes P, Scheines R (2001) *Causation, Prediction, and Search* (2nd ed). MIT Press, Cambridge, MA.
Grove WM, Meehl PE (1996) 'Comparative efficiency of informal (subjective, impressionistic) and formal (mechanical, algorithmic) prediction procedures: The clinical–statistical controversy.' *Psychology, Public Policy, and Law* 2, 293–323.
Hájek A (2007) 'The reference class problem is your problem too.' *Synthese* 156, 185–215.
Hathaway SR, McKinley JC (1940) 'A multiphasic personality schedule (Minnesota): Construction of the schedule.' *Journal of Psychology* 10, 249–254.
James G, Witten D, Hastie T, Tibshirani R (2013) *An Introduction to Statistical Learning with Applications in R.* Springer, New York.
Kendler KS (2013) 'A history of the DSM-5 scientific review committee.' *Psychological Medicine* 43, 1793–1800.
(2014) 'The structure of psychiatric science.' *The American Journal of Psychiatry* 171, 931–938.
Kessler RC, van Loo HM, Wardenaar KJ, Bossarte RM, Brenner LA, Cai T, Ebert DD, Hwang I, Li J, de Jonge P, Nierenberg AA, Petukhova M V, Rosellini AJ, Sampson NA, Schoevers RA, Wilcox MA, Zaslavsky AM (2016) 'Testing a machine-learning algorithm to predict the persistence and severity of major depressive disorder from baseline self-reports.' *Molecular Psychiatry* 21, 1366–1371.
Kessler RC, Ustun TB (eds) (2008) *The WHO World Mental Health Surveys: Global Perspectives on the Epidemiology of Mental Disorders.* Cambridge University Press, New York.
Kuhn, T. (1962) *The Structure of Scientific Revolutions.* Chicago University Press, Chicago, IL.
Kupfer DJ, Regier DA, Kuhl EA (2008) 'On the road to DSM-V and ICD-11.' *European Archives of Psychiatry and Clinical Neuroscience* 258, 2–6.
van Loo HM, Cai T, Gruber MJ, Li J, de Jonge P, Petukhova M, Rose S, Sampson NA, Schoevers RA, Wardenaar KJ, Wilcox MA, Al-Hamzawi AO, Andrade LH, Bromet EJ, Bunting B, Fayyad J, Florescu SE, Gureje O, Hu C, Huang Y, Levinson D, Medina-Mora ME, Nakane Y, Posada-Villa J, Scott KM, Xavier M, Zarkov Z, Kessler RC (2014) 'Major depressive disorder subtypes to predict long-term course.' *Depression and Anxiety* 31, 765–777.
Lubke GH, Muthén B (2005) 'Investigating population heterogeneity with factor mixture models.' *Psychological Methods* 10(1), 21–39.
Meehl PE (1956). 'Wanted—a good cook-book.' *American Psychologist,* 11(6), 263–272. http://dx.doi.org/10.1037/h0044164
Morgan M, Morrison M (1999) *Models as Mediators.* Cambridge University Press, Cambridge, UK.
Nandi A, Beard JR, Galea S (2009) 'Epidemiologic heterogeneity of common mood and anxiety disorders over the lifecourse in the general population: A systematic review.' *BMC Psychiatry* 9, 31.

Olbert CM, Gala GJ, Tupler LA (2014) 'Quantifying heterogeneity attributable to polythetic diagnostic criteria: Theoretical framework and empirical application.' *Journal of Abnormal Psychology* 123(2), 452–462.

Pearl J (2000) *Causality*. MIT Press, Cambridge, MA.,

(2018) *The Book of Why*. Basic Books, New York.

Reichenbach, H (1949) *The Theory of Probability*. University of Chicago Press, Chicago, IL.

Roy-Byrne PP, Stang P, Wittchen H-U, Ustun B, Walters EE, Kessler RC (2000) 'Lifetime panic–depression comorbidity in the National Comorbidity Survey.' *British Journal of Psychiatry* 176, 229–235.

Tabb, K. (2015) 'Psychiatric progress and the assumption of diagnostic discrimination.' *Philosophy of Science* 82, 1047–1058.

(2017) 'Philosophy of psychiatry after diagnostic kinds.' *Synthese* 196(6), 2177–2195. doi:10.1007/s11229-017-1659-6.

Wardenaar KJ, van Loo HM, Cai T, Fava M, Gruber MJ, Li J, de Jonge P, Nierenberg AA, Pethukova M V, Rose S, Sampson NA, Schoevers RA, Wilcox MA, Alonso J, Bromet EJ, Bunting B, Florescu SE, Fukao A, Gureje O, Hu C, Huang YQ, Karam AN, Levinson D, Medina-Mora ME, Posada-Villa J, Scott KM, Taib NI, Viana MC, Xavier M, Zarkov Z, Kessler RC (2014) 'The effects of co-morbidity in defining major depression subtypes associated with long-term course and severity.' *Psychological Medicine* 44, 3289–3302.

30

Double Black Diamond

ERIC TURKHEIMER

Romeijn and van Loo's outlook on psychiatric classification is practical, quantitatively based, and as they say, a-reductionist. In a domain that is sometimes inclined to overcommitment to favored diagnostic schemes in the service of particular theoretical orientations, such empirical equanimity has a lot to recommend it. It must be said, however, that as a behavioral scientist, occasional clinician, and psychometrician, I also find their approach to be somewhat bereft. Bereft of what? I don't miss the theoretical rigidity, overstatement, or heaven knows the reductionism of so many diagnostic systems, but I do miss the entities.

Romeijn and van Loo's account of classification does refer to psychiatric categories – depression is their main example – but where do they come from? In fact, the approach they describe appears to forego entities in favor of something more literal. In describing their approach to classification, they say:

> The classification of the individuals must facilitate accurate predictions of, and effective interventions on the phenomena that we care about. Optimizing a psychiatric classification scheme is, at least in part, that kind of exercise: it concerns the selection of criteria for the formation of groups that can serve as reference classes for stable and distinct chance ascriptions to variables of interest, either for the purpose of accurate predictions or for effective intervention. Importantly, this is an empirical issue: we determine the groupings not on the basis of some preconceived notion of natural kind, or on the basis of a preconceived explanatory level, but primarily by the empirical facts of which characteristics facilitate prediction and intervention.

According to this approach, classification problems are actually prediction problems, with clinical course a favored outcome for prediction. One selects a class of patient characteristics as potential predictors, applies a prediction model of greater or lesser granularity, and generates classes of individuals who are relatively homogeneous in terms of the outcome. As a practical matter, this seems unimpeachable, but there is a lot left out that I think would be missed by both clinicians and scientists if this is all there was to it.

The scientific activity that concerns itself with entities is measurement. Measurement entails specification of a domain of individuals (or, more generally, stimuli; they don't have to be people) to be measured, and a domain of characteristics to be applied to them. Romeijn and van Loo's examples skip both of these steps. They propose building models of clinical outcome in depressed patients, but which depressed patients, and how do we know who is "depressed" before we have developed a classification system? If the characteristics to be used as predictors can come from literally anywhere, then some of the most relevant might not be attributes of the individual patient at all (e.g., "lives in a neighborhood without adequate clinical services"). (In their larger body of work they discuss the role of conventions that are typically in place before the measurement process can begin.)

This kind of old school empiricism certainly has its uses, but if it were to be applied literally there would be some consequences that would need to be considered. The first of these is that modeling of this kind does not require classes at all. In the study Romeijn and van Loo describe (van Loo et al., 2014), characteristics of depressed patients were input into statistical models that generated three classes of risk of persistence-severity. But in models of this kind, the classes themselves are incidental, intermediary constructs generated by the prediction model. Ultimately one class of variables, designated as predictors, is input into a statistical system that predicts other variables, designated as outcomes. The classes have no residual meaning outside of their role in the classification scheme. Moreover, given the nature of the results, which is essentially, low-, medium- and high-risk groups, one can wonder why classes *per se* are even necessary. Could continuous models accomplish the same thing?

Another way of putting the same point is to ask whether in a particular domain there is one correct classification system, or several, or even a finite number of them. Romeijn and van Loo refer at times to the "right" categories, input variables, levels of granularity, or statistical models, but won't the optimum categories depend on what it is that is being predicted? Is there reason to think that the categories of depression that optimize prediction of treatment outcome will also be optimal for characterizing

GWAS results? Once again, the alternative to deriving a new classification system for every new prediction problem is to have some degree of realist commitment to entities with enough persistence to have meaning across domains.

Consider a simple example: ski slopes. Ski mountains use a simple ordered categorical system of colors and shapes to inform skiers about the difficulty of the slopes. Where do these categories come from? One presumes that they are generated intuitively, not a strategy to be endorsed for psychiatry, but there are other lessons to be learned. If one were to proceed according to Romeijn and van Loo, one would select an outcome, let's say risk of injury, and a set of potential predictors, like slope, smoothness, narrowness, and grooming. One could then apply statistical models and generate either classes or continuous indicators (this slope rated 7.4 for injury risk). This might work, but thinking it through suggests several important points.

First, the choice of the outcome would be crucial. One would get different results if one predicted average speed, subjective difficulty, or probability of falling, and science will not inform us as to which criterion is "right." Second, the choice of a categorical over a numerical rating system is not a matter of science either; it is a recognition of a cognitive heuristic whereby nervous skiers at the crest of a slope, under severe cognitive load as they attempt to get down, prefer the limited information provided by a crude category to the potentially more precise value of a continuous score. Finally and most important, for all its informality, the actual color-and-shape system that is employed does more than simply generate a numerical prediction of some outcome: it measures a psychological construct that might be called "degree of difficulty." That construct is useful precisely because it has some independence from the local characteristics that were used to generate it. The remainder of this response will suggest that the relationship between raw prediction and psychological measurement is a very old one, with important lessons for modern psychometricians.

A long time ago, the nascent field of clinical psychology was trying to extract itself from the methodological strictures of philosophical operationalism and psychological behaviorism. Neither of these dogmas had much tolerance for entities, especially entities without explicit operational ties to empirical data. Behavioral science still talks casually about "operational definitions," but in those days people meant it. How could one have a science about complex abstractions like depression and anxiety, never mind libido, in a theoretical context that insisted on strict operationalism? It is probably apocryphal, but I have heard it said that it was considered bad form to remark in a faculty meeting that one was "worried" about something. What is the operational definition of a mental construct like worry?

Kenneth MacCorquodale and Paul Meehl (1948) were worried about the theoretical status of Hull's *Principles of Behavior* (1943). It is no longer possible to imagine how important to psychology Hull's work was at the time, with its elaborate equations and postulates describing the course of learning in lower animals and humans. Hull's postulates are mathematical expressions of the relationship between learning parameters like timing of reinforcements on the one hand, and habit strength on the other. They include nothing resembling what we would today recognize as psychological constructs, much less diagnostic entities. They do, however, include intermediary terms that serve to systematize the relationship between prediction parameters and outcomes. So, for example, Hull has an expression for "cumulative reinforcement," written as an exponential function of the total number of reinforcements in the learning history that can then be repeated as a subunit in other expressions.

MacCorquodale and Meehl call this kind of term an "intervening variable." Intervening variables have no meaning other than the operational qualities of the expressions in which they are located. To ask if they are "valid" is simply to ask whether the equation in which they are embedded describes behavior in the way it is intended. In contrast to intervening variables, MacCorquodale and Meehl propose what they call "hypothetical constructs," which are entities that rely on some degree of realist intuition about existence for their meaning. MacCorquodale and Meehl's contribution, which proved to be transformative for clinical psychology, was to show how such entities could be instantiated without resorting to ghost-in-the-machine ephemera.

They say:

> We propose that the term 'hypothetical construct' be used to designate theoretical concepts which do not meet the requirements for intervening variables in the strict sense. That is to say, these constructs involve terms which are not wholly reducible to empirical terms; they refer to processes or entities that are not directly observed (although they need not be in principle unobservable); the mathematical expression of them cannot be formed simply by a suitable grouping of terms in a direct empirical equation; and the truth of the empirical laws involved is a necessary but not a sufficient condition for the truth of these conceptions.

It doesn't seem so today, but hypothetical constructs were a heretical idea at the time. Many of the psychological constructs we discuss nowadays without much thought, like "intelligence," "anxiety," and of course, "depression" are hypothetical constructs in the sense of MacCorquodale and Meehl. Unlike intervening variables, which are willed into existence by the operations that define them, the validity of hypothetical constructs is a legitimate matter for scientific investigation; indeed it is *the* legitimate matter of scientific investigation in post-operationalist psychology. Romeijn and van Loo, in their understandable eagerness to step back from the rigid kinds of realist literalism that too-often afflict thinking about psychiatric categories, have retreated to a theory that seems to posit psychiatric classification as no more than an intervening variable between predictor and outcome, with some black-box machine learning algorithm in the place of Hull's now-forgotten equations.

Romeijn and van Loo, I am certain, would be loath to be characterized as operationalist. They describe their theory of classification as "pragmatic and empiricist." Just as their theory is a-reductionist, it is a-realist. In their empirical practicality, it doesn't matter to Romeijn and van Loo whether the high-, medium- and low-risk groups generated by their algorithm have any meaning outside the context of the particular prediction problem that generated them. But applied strictly, practical empiricism can start to look a lot like operationalism, with hypothetical constructs dismissed as practically unnecessary rather than philosophically out of bounds.

Return to ski slopes for a moment. The reader may not have known where I was headed with the title of this comment, but they knew what the phrase meant, in a sense that would not have been true if the title had been "Middle Risk Group." Two ski slopes labeled double black diamond in very different situations can be effortlessly psychologically equated by a tired skier. One could refer to a philosophy paper as being "double black diamond" to get across the idea that it was difficult and maybe a little risky. A scientist employed by the ski industry could conduct meaningful research into the utility of the slope rating system and its effects on the conduct of skiers. All of this without insisting on the deep existence of slope-categories out there in the real world somewhere. The hypothetical construct of double black diamond, as Meehl would later explain, has construct validity.

Romeijn and van Loo suggest that the greatest benefit of their empiricist model is that it offers a way out of the perpetual concerns about reductionism in category formation, a hope with which I am broadly sympathetic. If all the scientist is doing is selecting among potential predictors of an outcome, they can come from anywhere in the hierarchy of levels, and then be combined Frankenstein-style into multilevel constructs. As

I suggest in my own contribution to this volume, however, that I think there are some good reasons why entities, whether generated by scientists or in lay discourse, are usually intra-level. Humans are not just prediction machines: they are also creators and recognizers of objects. Behavioral science had to find a way out of the rigid constraints of operationalism because forswearing hypothetical constructs worked better as an abstract philosophy of science that it did as a program for actual scientific investigation. Scientists had their worries, and were not willing to give them up in the interest of a strictly operationalist view of what a worry might be. The same, I think, will turn out to be the case for depression. Empirical prediction models can help, but they will not prevent us from perceiving, recognizing and investigating a hypothetical construct called melancholia.

REFERENCES

Hull, CL (1943). *Principles of behaviour* (Vol. 422). New York: Appleton-century-crofts

MacCorquodale K, & Meehl PE (1948) 'On a distinction between hypothetical constructs and intervening variables.' *Psychological Review*, 55(2), 95.

van Loo HM, Cai T, Gruber MJ, Li J, de Jonge P, Petukhova M, Rose S, Sampson NA, Schoevers RA, Wardenaar KJ, Wilcox MA, Al-Hamzawi AO, Andrade LH, Bromet EJ, Bunting B, Fayyad J, Florescu SE, Gureje O, Hu C, Huang Y, Levinson D, Medina-Mora ME, Nakane Y, Posada-Villa J, Scott KM, Xavier M, Zarkov Z, & Kessler RC (2014) 'Major depressive disorder subtypes to predict long-term course.' *Depression and Anxiety*, 31, 765–777.

SECTION 11

31

Introduction

PETER ZACHAR

In his chapter, Ken Schaffner dives into the variety of levels that are invoked in both the traditional fear center model and Joe LeDoux and Danny Pine's (2016) two-system model of fear. In many ways, LeDoux wrote the book on the biology of fear conditioning and for him to claim (with Pine and others) that rodent models can never fully represent the biology of human fear has incredible gravitas.

On the topic of the book, Schaffner points out that there are many different ways something can be a level of analysis, and that psychobiological models always incorporate multiple levels, even though this is not always recognized. For example, consider the fear center model, which is widely considered a reductionist model. Nevertheless, it incorporates multiple levels. There is a threat in the *environment*, which is detected by the *sensory system*, initiating *subcortical activity* in the amygdala, which coordinates a series innate *physiological responses* and fear *behaviors*, and the *experience* of fear.

In the more psychological two-system model, information about the threat is still sent to the amygdala, but there is also a parallel pathway to the cortex. The two-system model adds in a *cognitive circuit* at the cortical level (which involves prefrontal activity and functions such as discrimination, appraisal, language, and so on), and attributes the generation of the *conscious experience of fear* to the higher-level cortical regions. Subcortical activity is responsible for the physiological responses and defensive behaviors only.

As noted, one of the important features of the two-system model for LeDoux and Pine is that the subjective experience of consciousness for human beings is an important part of fear and anxiety disorders, and rodent models cannot account for this feature of the disorders. Schaffner argues that the importance of this innovation cannot be over-emphasized, but it also requires consideration of various theories of consciousness and of self-representations. Schaffner notes that LeDoux has committed to one particular theory of consciousness, a higher-order thought theory (HOT theory). To simplify, according to HOT, a mental state becomes conscious whenever it is represented by another (higher-order) mental state. Pine has not committed to a theory of consciousness, preferring instead to refine the methods than can be used to scientifically study the conscious component of the two-system model.

Schaffner then proceeds to evaluate some leading alternatives to the higher-order thought theory of consciousness with respect to the two-system view in general and to Pine's Chapter 8 more specifically. He does not describe these theories as much as names them and says something about their virtues. One alternative theory holds that consciousness is contingent on the act of attending to something. In contrast to more cognitively advanced HOT theories, this *attention theory* creates a broader notion of consciousness that can be attributed to children, people with developmental disabilities, and some animals. But human adults typically have better, more nuanced appraisals of their emotions than children, so lower-level attentional process cannot tell the whole story. For this, Schaffner prefers what is called a *global neuronal workspace theory* that adds on something like working memory to attention, greatly expanding on the scope of conscious awareness.

Another important feature of the two-system model is that as we develop from infancy to adulthood, our appraisals of our emotions improve because our experiences are understood against a background consisting of a stable concept of the self and coherent self-representations. To address this part of the model, Schaffner first surveys different ways the concept of self has been construed in philosophy and psychology (one approach of which is described in Chapter 17 by Parnas and Zandersen). He then introduces an alternative approach to the self that was developed in the study of personality disorder. Schaffner believes that the two-system model might benefit from thinking about the self as operationalized in the first part of the Alternative *DSM-5* Model for Personality Disorders' Levels of Personality Functioning Scale.

The notion that personality disorder represents a disturbance in the structure of the self was introduced by psychodynamic psychiatrists writing about borderline and narcissistic disorders. These concepts were influential on those members of the Personality and Personality Disorders Work Group who took the lead in developing the first part of the Alternative *DSM-5* Model, which describes disturbances in self and interpersonal functioning (Aaronson, Bender, Skodol, & Gunderson, 2006; Bender & Skodol, 2007; Morey & Bender, 2014). This part of the Alternative *DSM-5* Model fits pretty well with what Pine says in Chapter 8: in development we acquire a more coherent and stable sense of self that allows for accurate self-appraisal. In the Alternative *DSM-5* Model, a more severe personality disorder corresponds to the kinds of disturbances of the self-structure identified with borderline personality disorder: lack of a stable sense of identity, poorly defined boundaries, intense and labile emotions, and so on.

Schaffner briefly mentions the second part of the Alternative *DSM-5* Model, which is a personality trait model based on the factor analytic tradition in psychology. He believes an important virtue of this part of the Alternative *DSM-5* Model is that it can readily incorporate information from behavioral genetics regarding the heritability of traits.

The philosophical core of the chapter is contained in the conclusion where Schaffner looks at the two-system view through the lens of his notion of a temporally extended theory (TET) (Schaffner, 1993). A TET is similar to what Lakatos (1970) called a research program, but it is more diachronic. Rather than hard-core assumptions that cannot be altered, there are high-level central hypotheses which are very general and have varying degrees of centrality. There are also more specific hypotheses that allow for testing of the high-level hypotheses. The lower-level specific hypotheses can (and will) change over time. In Schaffner's view, the role of the cognitive circuit is the most central hypothesis in the two-system view and he makes some suggestions about how this research program may developed in the future as a temporally extended theory.

In his commentary, Bill Bechtel says something more about both levels of analysis and about the self. With respect to levels, he describes how Schaffner's notion of TETs might be coordinated with how the new mechanists in the philosophy of science think about levels. For example, the notion of a central hypotheses seems similar to the notion of a mechanism sketch; both are heuristic guides that are tested by less general models that incorporate more particular details. Bechtel notes that in addition to levels of hypotheses (e.g., general versus intermediate versus detailed) in TETs, the intermediate and detailed levels are also levels of composition.

With respect to the notion of the self, Bechtel is not excited by Schaffner's use of a clinical, psychodynamic model (that does seem to construe the self as a real entity) and offers a more traditionally empiricist alternative where what we call "the self" is typically considered a cluster (or bundle) of various self-representations. The first thing Bechtel does is to unpack something Schaffner only mentioned in his historical survey of self-concepts namely Ulric Neisser's (1988) five kinds of self-knowledge. In Bechtel's view these might be more relevant to the two-system theory because they can be studied experimentally.

Next, Bechtel explores some ideas of the philosopher Wilfred Sellars (1956) regarding the theoretical nature of our self-representations. Contra Gilbert Ryle, Sellars believed that we do have inner episodes to which we have privileged access and in reporting them we are not making category mistakes, but these reports are also dependent on public discourse. Sellars' Myth of Jones describes why it is that a community that has mastered giving descriptions of behavior would come to posit latent mental processes like "thoughts" and "sense impressions." Roughly, they would do so if the "thought theory" or the "sense impression theory" allowed them to attribute intelligence and sensory discrimination to people even when those people are not overtly saying intelligent things or reporting on what they discriminate. What is inner, however, is being modeled on what was previously public. Eventually, the members of this community would learn to use these theoretical posits in their own self-descriptions.

What Sellars is doing here is reconfiguring how philosophers can think about the nature of the gap between the subjective (private) and the intersubjective (public). (Note: If one does not slot Ryle into the behaviorist box – see Zachar, Chapter 23 – Ryle can be seen as engaging in a similar project).

If thoughts and sense impressions have a theoretical aspect, our selves and personalities certainly do as well. Bechtel notes we do not observe a self or even a personality – but we can make inferences to them, and doing so supports our predictive and explanatory goals. With respect to Schaffner's ideas about improving upon the two-system theory, Bechtel notes that "the self" or "the personality" are like general hypotheses in a TET. They can be better understood with a collection of intermediate and more detailed hypotheses of a how person behaves in particular situations.

REFERENCES

Aaronson, C. J., Bender, D. S., Skodol, A. E., & Gunderson, J. G. (2006) 'Comparison of attachment styles in borderline personality disorder and obsessive-compulsive personality disorder.' *Psychiatric Quarterly*, *77*(1), 69–80.

Bender, D. S., & Skodol, A. E. (2007) 'Borderline personality as self-other representational disturbance.' *Journal of Personality Disorders*, *21*(5), 500–517.

Lakatos, I. (1970) 'Falsification and the methodology of scientific research programmes.' In I. Lakatos & A. Musgrave (Eds.), *Criticism and the growth of knowledge* (pp. 91–196). New York: Cambridge University Press.

LeDoux, J. E., & Pine, D. S. (2016) 'Using neuroscience to help understand fear and anxiety: A two-system framework.' *American Journal of Psychiatry, 173*(11), 1083–1093.

Morey, L. C., & Bender, D. S. (2014) 'Articulating a core dimension of personality pathology.' In J. M. Oldham, A. E. Skodol, & D. S. Bender (Eds.), *The American Psychiatric Publishing textbook of personality disorders* (2nd ed., pp. 39–54). Arlington, VA: American Psychiatric Publishing, Inc.

Neisser, U. (1988) 'Five kinds of self-knowledge.' *Philosophical Psychology, 1*(1), 35–59.

Schaffner, K. F. (1993) *Discovery and explanation in biology and medicine*. Chicago: University of Chicago Press.

Sellars, W. (1956) 'Empiricism and the philosophy of mind.' In H. Feigl & M. Scriven (Eds.), *Minnesota studies in the philosophy of science* (Vol. 1, pp. 253–329). Minneapolis: University of Minnesota Press.

32

Approaches to Multilevel Models of Fear: The What, Where, Why, How, and How Much?

KENNETH F. SCHAFFNER

32.1 INTRODUCTION – A PANOPLY OF LEVELS

When we talk of "levels," these can variously be levels of abstraction, analysis, aggregation, behavior, complexity, function, perspective, organization, generality, and processes – including causation and control – as well as description and explanation, and more. Levels can also address the perspectives afforded by different scientific disciplines, such as psychology, genetics, and neurobiology. Thus, the "what" in part briefly addresses this general aspect and provides some preliminary definitions of some of the more salient of these different senses of levels throughout this chapter but especially in the conclusion Section 32.4. The "where" query asks which levels are more prominent, and the "why" gives the reasons. The "how" outlines the methods used for those level(s), and the "how much" the extent to which an investigation has or should be done on that level(s).

Speaking more generally, but also in psychiatry, we are, and should be, concerned with levels that involve *subjective* perceptions and feelings, as well as behaviors. Call that the subjective/behavioral level. In addition, recently, major developments have occurred in the discipline of psychiatric *genetics*, so that level must be added, and also best associated with what might be termed a *neurobiological* level, possibly at the "circuit" level. And we ought not to forget the important role of the *environment*, so add an environmental level to any list of significant perspectives. But this list is only a beginning. . .

I am grateful for many helpful conversations and e-mail comments on the topics in this chapter from Colin Allen, Bill Bechtel, James Bogen, Shaun Gallagher, Joseph LeDoux, Mael Lemoine, Bill Lycan, Bob Krueger, Daniel Pine, and Wayne Wu. Special thanks in addition to Peter Zachar for assistance in editing this MS.

For example, within each of these levels, we could look at more fine-grained analyses; typically these are related by size levels, which also, but not always, track with "levels of organization." And even within the subjective level, we could also fine structure the various aspects of different levels of experience, and include such notions as levels of awareness, personality types, the results of psychological tests and "instruments," and even an analysis of the "self."

That all said, one of my conclusions, albeit yet to be defended after I introduce my main example, is that any analysis of levels will largely *not* be a general one, but rather one tied to specific examples, including specific theories or models, and in this chapter connected with specific psychiatric constructs. I will also argue in the conclusion that an appropriate use of different levels of analysis and organization can be related to the topic of theory or model competition and scientific progress.

32.2 THE LEDOUX AND PINE "TWO-SYSTEM" THEORY OF HUMAN EMOTION, INCLUDING FEAR AND ANXIETY

32.2.1 The "Two System" Model

My main example presented in this chapter is the LeDoux and Pine "two-system" theory or model of human emotion, including fear as well as anxiety (LeDoux & Pine, 2016). (The account is sometimes called a "framework" or "theory" and even a "view", but I will mostly use the term "model.") I selected this two-system model for several reasons. First, it has been developed in considerable detail, some of it with other collaborators, such as Brown and Lau on the theory side and multiple investigators working with Pine on the experimental side. Still, further research on the model, and its competitors, is needed and is currently occurring. Second, the two-system model has a key "consciousness" component along with clinical aspects of consciousness, and thus can serve as a portal to consciousness research that has been so important in recent decades in philosophy of mind. Philosophy, in turn, can utilize this two-system model to further ground its more speculative analyses of consciousness. Third, the two-system model is a significant departure from the received or "traditional" approach to fear and anxiety, and can thus be a source for a discussion of competitive theory analysis and the relation of that type of competition to scientific progress (on this topic, see Schaffner (2020b)).

A diagram or figure is the best way to introduce my main example of the LeDoux and Pine "two-system" theory or model. Figure 32.1, taken

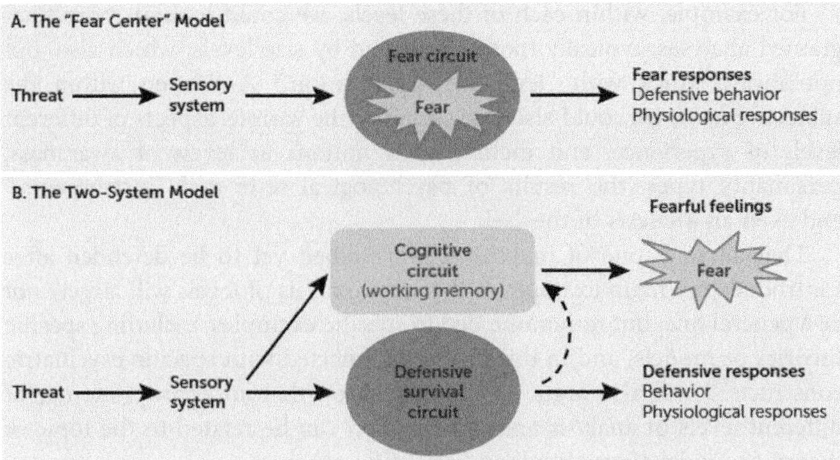

FIGURE 32.1 The traditional fear center model versus the LeDoux and Pine two-system model.

Note: As quoted from LeDoux and Pine (2016, p. 1084): In the traditional "fear center" model, the subjective experience of "fear" in the presence of a threat is innately programmed in subcortical circuits that also control defensive behaviors and physiological responses. The two-system framework views "fear" as a product of cortical circuits that underlie cognitive functions such as working memory; subcortical circuits control defensive behaviors and physiological responses and only indirectly contribute to conscious "fear." The traditional view thus requires different mechanisms of consciousness in the brain for emotional and nonemotional states, whereas in the two-system framework, both emotional and nonemotional states of consciousness are treated as products of the same system. In the two-system framework, what distinguishes an emotional from a nonemotional state of consciousness, and what distinguishes different kinds of emotional states of consciousness, are the input processes by the cortical consciousness networks. Reprinted with permission from the *American Journal of Psychiatry* (Copyright ©2016). American Psychiatric Association. All Rights Reserved

from the article by LeDoux and Pine (2016), then can also be used to identify in a preliminary sense several "levels" of analysis.

The two-system model is an alternative to the current received view of fear emotions. In their article, LeDoux and Pine (2016) picture the two contrasting "models" as in Figure 32.1.

Though at first glance the *traditional or "fear center" model* (shown in A) may appear uni-level, it is vigorously interlevel. It is initiated by "threat" (stage 1) – such as a snake, wasp, avalanche, or virtually anything. This threat then is perceived by an organism's "sensory system" (stage 2) *as a threat* that directly influences a "fear *circuit*" (stage 3), creating in turn a set of *innate* fear *responses* (stage 4). The stage 4 responses are *both* physiological and behavioral. Each of these differing perspectives are "levels" as suggested in the introduction, and each can be further analyzed into both finer-structured levels, as well as exemplified by specific examples from the psychological and psychiatric literature.

In the contrasting two-system model (shown in B), it is critical to note that only at stage 3 does this model becomes more complex, where it is divided into two circuits. In the two-system model, the sensory signal affects a "defensive survival circuit," but it also stimulates a *separate cognitive circuit* involving working memory. Thus, although the traditional fear responses can be the principal consequence of the survival circuit, that survival circuit can also affect the cognitive circuit (dashed line). But it is the *cognitive circuit* that produces *fear* – an extremely important point for LeDoux and Pine. The terms and definitions used to describe the components of the model, including phenomenal experiences, are critical, and LeDoux and Pine state that "fear" is *only* to be *defined* in a *subjective* phenomenological sense. They write:

> Because precise terminology is essential for scientific progress, we propose that the use of mental state terms, like fear and anxiety, be limited to their primary, as opposed to their extended, meanings, that is, to mental states – subjective feelings of fear and anxiety... Confusion also results from interchangeable use of the terms fear and anxiety. To avoid such confusion, we propose using a common distinction consistently – that the mental state term fear be used to describe feelings that occur when the source of harm, the threat, is either immediate or imminent, and anxiety be used to describe feelings that occur when the source of harm is uncertain or is distal in space or time.
>
> (pp. 1083–1084)

32.2.2 The Innate and Traditional Fear Circuit View

The traditional view of fear (and anxiety) causation is based on the central role of the amygdala (and some other brain components) as either a "fear center" or more recently the hub of a fear circuit. This amygdala system is believed to be an *evolutionarily conserved circuit*. The processing is complex, and *interlevel*, or perhaps better *mixed-level*, and also makes a distinction between active or present threats versus threats that are less certain. For LeDoux and Pine, the neurobiological fine-structure of the neural control of reactions and actions elicited by these two types of threats works as follows:

> ...the amygdala is the central hub of circuits that control reactions and actions elicited by an immediately present threat. The lateral amygdala (LA) receives sensory inputs about the threat. Connections from LA to

> the central nucleus of the amygdala (CeA) control reactions, whereas connections from LA to the basal nucleus (BA), and from there to the ventral striatum (nucleus accumbens, NAcc), control the performance of actions, such as escape and avoidance. However when the threat is uncertain, and thus only a possible outcome in the future, connections from the amygdala and hippocampus to the extended amygdala (the bed nucleus of the stria terminalis, BNST) are engaged in the control of reactions, and actions using similar output pathways are used by the amygdala to control responses to present threats."
>
> (2016, p. 1085)

There is an explicit "behaviorist" or *anti-subjectivity* orientation held by at least some of the major proponents of the *traditional circuit.* LeDoux and Pine write concerning this important philosophical and methodological point that:

> For a number of contemporary neuroscientists, emotions are not subjective experiences but central physiological states ("central states" for short) that intervene between trigger stimuli and behavioral and physiological responses . . . [references deleted]. A strong version of the central state view of fear is expressed by Fanselow and colleagues . . . They argue that a goal of science should be to "replace inaccurate subjective explanations . . . with more scientifically grounded explanations." This approach ignores subjective states to avoid the scientific problems that result from attributing subjective experiences to animals. But it does so at the expense of making subjective experience off-limits as a scientific topic in humans.
>
> (p. 1085)

Not only does this behavioralist orientation bracket off human subjective experience, characterizing it essentially as being "non-scientific" and even worse (see Fanselow & Pennington, 2017, 2018; Pine & LeDoux, 2017), but much of this type of traditional research is based on virtually *only* rodent models. This rodent focus also minimalizes the potential role of brains with a more extensive dorsal lateral prefrontal cortex (DLPFC). The more recently evolved DLPFC and its different circuits, such as found in primates and humans, can thus significantly affect an analysis of fear and anxiety.

32.2.3 Some Details of the Two-System Model: The Consciousness Aspect

The two-system model exemplifies a substantive "paradigm shift," if that overused phrase may be permitted, in that it involves extensive appeals to analyses of *phenomenal consciousness*. The radical nature of this modification of the traditional fear circuit model cannot be overemphasized. The *upside* of this paradigm shift is that adding the second system allows a reorientation, not only of the diagnosis of fear-related mental disorders, including panic disorder and generalized anxiety disorder, but it could point the way to better *treatments* both of a pharmacological type and behavioral type (see specific suggestions in LeDoux and Pine (2016)). An inquiry into a fear and anxiety consciousness model may also be a paradigm shift for *analytic philosophy* of consciousness, but it joins a long-standing philosophical phenomenological tradition that has had significant earlier influences in psychosis and schizophrenia studies (Parnas, 2011; Parnas et al., 2005; Zahavi, 2014a, 2018).

The *downside* of this paradigm shift is that appealing to phenomenal consciousness evokes what has been termed "the hard problem," (Chalmers, 1995), and it is only in the last three decades that phenomenal consciousness has begun to be treated as a *scientific* problem. The details of the second system in the two-system model thus may well require deep dives into controversial theories of consciousness, including global workspace, attention theories, and higher-order theories to be discussed below. Each of these consciousness theories contains many non-empirical assumptions, and none has achieved the status of a consensus theory.

In addition, the details of the consciousness theory aspects of the two-system model appeal to circuits that have only been presented in outline form by LeDoux and Brown (2017), which also appeal to yet largely "blackboxed" "cortically based" general networks of cognition (GNC). Though this point is a neurobiologically critical aspect of a yet-to-be developed form of the two-system theory, for reasons of space it cannot be pursued in the extensive detail it deserves in the present chapter.

(Interestingly, Pine views deep dives into theories of consciousness as only the beginning to become relevant for research conducted with patients; theories that LeDoux – and Brown, and Lau – feel are necessary to adequately develop the "two-system" theory. Thus Pine would prefer to concentrate on further development of *better empirical methods* to track the conscious component of the model, especially ones that examine the temporal development of the "self" in children and adolescents – personal communication, May 16, 2018; also see Pine's chapter (Chapter 8) as well as my comments on Pine (Chapter 9) in this volume.)

Not only does the two-system model involve the need to deal with the traditional philosophical "hard problem," a significant elaboration of the two-system theory also involves at least a moderately robust notion of the "self," which is itself a contentious issue. More on this issue later.

LeDoux and Pine introduce their two systems' principal *consciousness* feature noting as follows:

> Significant progress has been made in neuroscience research on the cognitive and neural underpinnings of subjective experiences (references deleted) This work assumes that conscious experience is cognitively derived from nonconscious processes that allow cortical regions to rerepresent [sic] lower-order information, and that this rerepresentation [sic] enables conscious awareness of nonconscious processing about external stimuli.†
>
> (see original article for specific references)

The "references" mentioned here are to a potpourri of recent scientific and philosophical theories of consciousness from Dehaene, through Frith, to Prinz, and others (Dehaene, Charles, King, & Marti, 2014; Frith, Perry, & Lumer, 1999; Prinz, 2012).

LeDoux and Pine add that "...that subjective feelings of fear or anxiety are not products of subcortical circuits underlying defensive responses, but instead depend on the same circuits that underlie any other form of conscious experience – namely, circuits in the so-called higher-order association cortex that are responsible for cognitive processes such as attention and working memory." These typically are the lateral and medial prefrontal cortex and the parietal neocortex, and possibly the insula.

LeDoux and Pine also mention two of the "leading theories" of how these circuits produce conscious experience:

> In global workspace theory, subjective experience emerges through widely distributed reentrant circuitry, with prefrontal areas playing an especially prominent role (refs). In higher-order theory, subjective experience arises from a more delimited circuitry, especially involving a prefrontal hub, which supports thoughts about lower-order information (refs).
>
> (2017, p. 1086)

32.2.4 When You're HOT, You're HOT

In a separate 2017 article on the two-system model, (LeDoux & Brown, 2017), as well as in another article (Brown, Lau, & LeDoux, 2019), these

† The notion of "rerepresentation" here foreshadows the LeDoux (and Brown, and Lau) commitment to a higher-order theory, to be discussed in further detail below.

authors argue strongly for the second approach, a higher-order theory, and more specifically for a higher-order *thought* theory (HOT). This commitment to a HOT account is controversial, and in my view, not necessary for a "two-system" theory, but other investigators in addition to LeDoux and Brown believe HOT is the strongest currently available account of consciousness (Murray, Wise, & Graham, 2017) and (Murray and Wise, personal communication, 2018).

It should be noted, however, that LeDoux and Brown seem somewhat open to alternative theories, as long as they are *some kind* of higher-order account. On this point they write:

> Most cognitive theories call upon similar cognitive processes in accounting for conscious experience, but do so in somewhat different ways. Included are theories that emphasize attention and working memory (references deleted), processing by a global workspace (references deleted), or the interpretation of experience (references deleted). A common thread that runs through various cognitive theories is that processing beyond the sensory cortex is required for conscious experience. In this sense, these other cognitive theories, although not explicitly recognized as HOTs, have a close affinity to the basic premise of HOT...
>
> (2017, p. E2018 – see original article for specific references)

I find this flexibility salutary, since it seems that an alternative theory (or theories) *may* be more acceptable than HOT within which to frame the two-system theory. Perhaps an attention theory, or even a more global workspace theory, might be used as the framework to further explore the implications of the LeDoux and Pine/LeDoux and Brown two-system theory of emotions rather than the more controversial HOT framework. I will pursue this prospect in the next main Section 32.3.1.

32.2.5 A Focus on the "Self"

Perhaps the *most controversial* addition to a HOT theory preferred by LeDoux and Brown involves "Refining the Role of the Self." In the next section, I will also propose my own preferred theory of the self as a complement to the account presented by LeDoux and Brown, and which does not require a HOT account. But the importance of the "self" for LeDoux and Brown should be noted at this point, since they write:

> The modifications of HOT just described allow us to view the phenomenal states we call emotions as HORs [higher order representations].

> Particularly important to our HOT of emotional consciousness (HOTEC) is the notion that *emotions depend on the self. Without the self there is no fear or love or joy.* If some event is not affecting you, then it is not producing an emotion. When your friend or child suffers you feel it because they are part of you. When the suffering of people you don't know affects you emotionally, it is because you empathize with them (put yourself in their place, feel their pain): no you, no emotion. *The self is, as noted above, the glue that ties such multidimensional integrated representations together* (ref). (my italics)
>
> (2017, p. E2021)

The notion of the self in the LeDoux and Brown version of the two-system theory is complex and introduces a quite detailed account of the self involving memories and self-awareness, including what Tulving has termed "autonoetic consciousness" (Tulving, 2005). Self-awareness is viewed as a "uniquely human experience" raising major questions about the use of animal models, and especially rodents.[‡] In terms of functions and circuits, LeDoux and Brown propose that the self involves various cognitive functions (working memory, attention, metacognition, etc.) and neural circuits (especially prefrontal circuits). More generally LeDoux and Brown write:

> When a higher-order state includes information about oneself, it becomes possible for there being something that it is like for "you" to be in that state. This is what we call "self-HOROR," a HOROR [an abbreviation for a higher order representation of a representation] for that includes information about the self. Tulving refers to experiences that include the self as "autonoetic consciousness," and experiences that do not as "noetic consciousness" (refs). The presence of the self in the nonconscious representation allows for an autonoetic conscious (a self-HOROR) state to result from the re-representation.
>
> (p. E2020)

The autobiographical (and thus narrative) dimension of the self is further stressed as follows in which the notion of 'schema' is introduced. Schemas function like personal multidimensional scripts:

> We view the self as a set of autobiographical memories about who you are and what has happened to you in your life, and how you think, act, and feel in particular situations (refs). Such bodies of information are

‡ For brief discussions of the relevance and limits of animal models, see my (Schaffner, 2019, 2020a).

called schema (refs). As part of self-HOROR theory, we thus propose that autobiographical self schema (refs) contribute to conscious states in which the self is involved.

(p. E2020)

32.3 EVALUATION AND ALTERNATIVE FRAMEWORKS FOR THE LEDOUX-PINE AND LEDOUX-BROWN MODELS

In this section of my chapter, I want to explore two possible alternative frameworks within which many of the advances and insights of the LeDoux-Pine and LeDoux-Brown models (hereafter the LeDoux, Pine, and Brown model) might be preserved, but I will only be able to elaborate in detail on one of those frameworks due to space limitations.[§] These two frameworks involve (1) an alternative theory of consciousness or theories to HOT and HOTEC, and (2) a somewhat different, or at least expanded, notion of the "self" as it might be pursued in studies of fear and anxiety. Both of these alternative frameworks tackle enormously broad literatures, and other than in Section 32.3.1 on the "self," I can only offer brief pointers to accounts of consciousness that I plan to pursue elsewhere in more detail (Schaffner, in development).

32.3.1 Alternative Theories of Consciousness to HOT and HOTEC: Attention Theory and Global Neuronal Workspace Theory

32.3.1.1 Attention Theory

The LeDoux, Pine, and Brown model clearly needs *some* theory of consciousness to provide a grounding for its second system of *conscious fear*. It would also seem that the model requires some type of a *second-order theory* as *broadly* defined in the LeDoux and Brown paper, but without the critical defects of HOT theory, but also see Brown et al. (2019) for a defense against some standard critiques of HOT. For a second-order theory, I prefer, as a first step, a type of "attention" theory, which attempts to explain consciousness by appealing to the mental activity or process of "attention." But I would also argue for what we might call a "thin" attention theory, by which I mean an attention theory that does not claim that it explains *all of* consciousness (as does Prinz's well-known theory and

[§] A much longer version of this chapter, including considerably more detail on attention theories and the Dehaene Global Neuronal Workspace theory, is available on request to the author.

perhaps Lycan's newer approach (Prinz, 2012; Saurat and Lycan, 2014)). Such a thin attention theory can be very useful in itself within its bounds and also relates to some empirical work on fear and anxiety by Pine (White et al., 2017) and Pine (Chapter 8), and discussed below. (Philosophers frequently use "thin" in this sense, as opposed to "thick," where a "thick" account means a full, robust, and nearly complete analysis of a concept or subject is available.) But I would additionally want to argue still further that any attention theory, especially this "thin" type, will need to be embedded within *a more general* brain circuit type of theory to permit adequate further neurobiological development. For the latter, I favor the Dehaene, Changeux, and colleagues Global Neuronal Workspace (GNW) theory, about which more is discussed below.

An attention theory in its "thin" version, but also amplified and embedded in an appropriate neuroscientific context such as the GNW, can avoid the many critiques of a HOT account. Jesse Prinz, who as noted favors an attention theory, albeit a strong one, usefully summarizes a long series of objections to both HOT and HOP theories in his 2012 book (pp. 21–29) (see both Prinz, 2002, 2012). Prinz writes:

> The HOT theory has difficulty explaining why consciousness can come in degrees, why it can arise by act of will (we can't choose our beliefs), and why introspecting feels like attention (Lycan, 2004). Another common complaint is that thoughts are more coarse-grained than conscious experiences (Lycan, 2004): the range of things we can consciously discriminate outstrips those we can recognize from one occasion to another (Raffman, 1995). Concepts are generally regarded as endowing us with recognitional abilities (Millikan, 2000; Prinz, 2002), so this suggests that we don't have concepts for the full range of things that we can consciously experience, and hence we can't have thoughts corresponding to every conscious experience.
>
> (2012, p. 24)

In addition, Prinz notes that:

> To have a higher-order thought, we need to deploy mental-state concepts. To think that you are seeing a sunset, you need a concept of seeing. This implies that people who have difficulty with mental-state concepts, such as individuals with autism, should suffer from corresponding deficits in consciousness. There is no evidence for that. People with autism seem to perform normally when it comes to actions that require perceptual consciousness, such as tying shoelaces or spontaneously responding to an object presented before their eyes.
>
> (2012, p. 26)

A "thin" attention theory *can* also be a focus of at least some aspects of the empirical testing of the two-system theory (also see Schaffner, 2019). Here I will only briefly mention several ways that Pine and his colleagues have made use of what is termed both bottom-up as well as top-down forms of attention. More specifically, in Pine's analysis this implicates attention-orienting versus appraisal, where the latter involves an aspect of top-down attention as part of that process; but more on this below.** Readers of the Pine article (Chapter 8) will note that there is significant use of what is termed "attention orienting," which is one component of attention that in connection with danger signals has been well conserved in evolution. In humans, Pine's prototype is its activation upon coming across a dangerous snake during a leisurely forest stroll. Attention orienting can be studied clinically by using the "dot probe task" as discussed in detail in Pine's article. This type of attention can also be affected by a clinical intervention known as Attention Bias Modification Therapy (White et al., 2017).

But humans, and primates at least, also seem to have an additional danger alerting process that involves conscious thought as well as memories, a view motivated by the two-system model. This second process Pine terms "appraisal," and in the framework of the "two-system" model, appraisal will use largely different brain circuits and be addressable by different forms of therapy, including cognitive behavioral therapy (White et al., 2017). Appraisal, however, is not that well understood, especially neurobiologically. It probably involves a form of top-down attention in addition to other related processes, and is the subject of active investigations regarding both clinical and neuroscience research projects. For additional details on this issue see Pine's chapter (Chapter 8) and my commentary (Chapter 9) on Pine's chapter.

** On these two general notions, see Katsuki and Constantinidis (2014) They define them succinctly, writing as follows:

> This process of information selection is referred to as attention. Attention is commonly categorized into two distinct functions: bottom-up (or exogenous) attention, an externally induced process in which information to be processed is selected automatically because of highly noticeable features of stimuli; and top-down (or endogenous) attention, an internally induced process in which information is actively sought out in the environment based on voluntarily chosen factors (refs are in original) (p. 509).

Bottom-up attention is also typically related to the older circuits that signify danger, or possibly related to a novel stimulus.

32.3.1.2 *Global Neuronal Workspace (GNW) Theory*

Higher-order theories and some related brain circuits have been briefly discussed earlier in Section 32.2 in connection with the (LeDoux & Brown, 2017) analysis, but perhaps the two most popular of those general brain circuitry approaches are Tononi's Integrated Information Theory (IIT) (Tononi, Boly, Massimini, & Koch, 2016) and Dehaene's Global Neuronal Workspace (GNW) theories (Dehaene, 2014; Dehaene & Changeux, 2011; Dehaene et al., 2014). Of these two, I find the IIT unpersuasive, in part because it seems to involve a strange form of panpsychism. Dehaene's theory, though somewhat limited in what it can say about *phenomenal consciousness*, seems to be a plausible approach to at least vector in on how consciousness might emerge, and perhaps to offer an alternative framework to the HOT analysis that could provide a stronger and more testable set of experiments than HOT, though the details of that suggestion needs to be pursued elsewhere.

Further, it is worth noting that in a recent article (Dehaene, Lau, & Kouider, 2017), Dehaene and his colleagues usefully distinguish two types of consciousness within the GNW into "Global Availability" abbreviated as C1, and "Self-Monitoring," or C2. They also suggest that C2 is "orthogonal" to C1 but still related to C1. And about C2 they write:

> It (C2) refers to a self-referential relationship in which the cognitive system is able to monitor its own processing and obtain information about itself. ... This sense of consciousness corresponds to what is commonly called introspection, or what psychologists call "meta-cognition" – the ability to conceive and make use of internal representations of one's own knowledge and abilities.
>
> (pp. 486–487)

This proposal is relevant to the alternative to a "self" concept that I develop in the following section.

So here's a proposal emerging from this section (and also drawing on Section 32.3.1): It's beginning to look like the regions, circuits, and information flows may turn out to be a *relatively* common (perhaps partially overlapping) consensus among various theories of consciousness/self-awareness.[††] And perhaps parts of this overlap *constitute* the thus far blackboxed LeDoux, Pine, and Brown's cortically generated networks of cognition (GNC) referred to largely in LeDoux and Brown (2017). Possibly

[††] More detailed arguments for this critical point are available from the author in a considerably longer version of the present chapter.

these other analyses of consciousness can also be drawn on to help open that GNC blackbox and provide more details of the neuroscientific workings of the two-system model. The common overlap would, moreover, seem to be compatible with a thin and psychological attention theory as well as the neuroscientific GNW, but it is highly likely that the implementation in the hardware, or "wetware," is where the "beef" is, and not necessarily in the use of the ill-defined but still heuristic word "attention." Thus in my view, thin attention approaches, but embedded in still further elaborations of the GNW, may be a more fruitful approach for additional development of the two-system approach to fear and anxiety than a HOT theory.

32.3.2 An Expanded Notion of the "Self"

32.3.2.1 Some Historical Background to "Self" Theories

As noted above, the "self" is a central component in the LeDoux and Brown model and also appears in a more implicit form in Dehaene's notion of "self-monitoring" or what he terms C2 consciousness. The range of the literature on the "self" comprises philosophical, psychological, psychiatric, and neuroscientific analyses and it is vast, diverse, and diffuse in all of these four fields. There are broad analyses of the "self," perhaps best typified by William James' definition, who wrote as his preliminary expansive "larger sense" definition:

> *In its widest possible sense*, however, *a man's Self is the sum total of all that he* CAN *call his*, not only his body and his psychic powers, but his clothes and his house, his wife and children, his ancestors and friends, his reputation and works, his lands and horses, and yacht and bank-account. (James, 1890)

Later psychologists were more precise and more focused. For example Neisser (1988) distinguished the self into ecological, interpersonal, extended, private and conceptual aspects of self. (Neisser's analysis has also been elaborated and critiqued recently by Tekin (2016).) Philosophers have also sliced and diced the "self" notion into myriad forms. A 1999 collection by Gallagher and Shear (1999) largely in the philosophical area does provide some useful integration since it is largely directed at a first (target) chapter by Galen Strawson. Still, after reviewing the topics in this 1999 book the editors wrote:

> As Strawson suggests, the many different approaches that can be pursued in addressing the question of the self appear to yield a multitude of

> conceptions of the self: the cognitive self, the conceptual self, the dialogical self, the ecological self, the embodied self, the emergent self, the empirical self, the existential self, the extended self, the fictional self, the interpersonal self, the material self, the narrative self, the physical self, and so on. The more recent psychological literature is also vast, and the neuroscientific literature on the self is growing rapidly.
>
> (p. xviii)

Two fairly broad analyses of the self widely discussed in the "self" literature are the "minimal self" and the "narrative self." Gallagher (2000) defines these as follows:

> Minimal self: Phenomenologically, that is, in terms of how one experiences it, a consciousness of oneself as an immediate subject of experience, unextended in time. The minimal self almost certainly depends on brain processes and an ecologically embedded body, but one does not have to know or be aware of this to have an experience that still counts as a self-experience.
>
> Narrative self: A more or less coherent self (or self-image) that is constituted with a past and a future in the various stories that we and others tell about ourselves.
>
> (2000, p. 15)

Both of these broad approaches have a long history (see William James on the "empirical me," versus other more objective views of the self) and been utilized in psychiatry. Dan Zahavi has argued for the minimal self and the narrative self, but also a social self in a number of books and articles (Zahavi, 2000, 2005, 2014b), as well as worked with psychiatrists such as Parnas on diagnostic and therapeutic aspects of the self. In addition, there are more precise versions of the minimal self developed in several SZ studies by Parnas and the McGorry group, and the narrative self has figured in personality disorder work (see my comments below). Both types will be needed in any account of the LeDoux, Pine, and Brown model, since it comprises both phenomenological consciousness as well as a self model.

In this chapter I can do no more than outline a variation on theories of the self that I think is useful, and also has potential *empirical aspects* within the fields of genetics, psychology, and neuroscience, and that offers a more pragmatic approach to the notion of the self. I also think that the outline I will provide might serve as a framework for further application of the LeDoux, Pine, and Brown model discussed in the previous sections of this article. My approach will utilize the perspective of a self's *personality*, and embed that in a recent still-exploratory model of personality disorders as presented in *DSM-5*.

One aspect of how a person's self might be approached is to consider what is stable over the long term about the person – in a sense what "grounds" that particular person and "what they are like." From a human genetics point of view, in the area of normal individuals, we can obtain a reasonable, initial purchase at such, by examining the nature of the individual's "*personality*." This seems plausible, because, as noted in the Plomin et al.'s canonical text on *Behavioral Genetics*:

> If you were asked what someone is like, you would probably describe various personality traits, especially those depicting extremes of behavior. "Jennifer is full of energy, very sociable, and unflappable." "Steve is conscientious, quiet, but quick tempered." Genetic researchers have been drawn to the study of personality because, within psychology, personality has always been the major domain for studying the normal range of individual differences, with the abnormal range being the provenance of psychopathology.
>
> (Knopik, Neiderhiser, Plomin, & DeFries, 2017, p. 254)

And these authors add: "Personality traits are relatively enduring individual differences in behavior that are stable across time and across situations..." (p. 254)

Further, in terms of a potentially useful genetic component of personality, Knopik et al. also note:

> Genetic research on personality is extensive and is described in several books and dozens of reviews... [and] its basic message is quite simple: Genes make a major contribution to individual differences in personality whereas shared environment does not, especially when assessed by a self-report questionnaire; environmental influence on personality is almost entirely of the nonshared variety (p. 255)

Thus developing an analysis of the "self' by framing that analysis within an account of *personality* offers the promise of providing the resources of psychiatric genetics for a deeper combined genetic and neurobiological approach to the "self."‡‡

‡‡ For more details on various personality theories, see Schaffner (2016, chapter 5). Chapter 8 of this book also contains an outline of a Frankfurt type of model of "free will," and (in principal) a preliminary form of a normative version of a theory of the "self."

32.3.2.2 An "Alternative Approach" to Personality (and Personality Disorders) and the Self

One of the more controversial episodes in the development of the recent *DSM-5* (American Psychiatric Association, 2013) was the proposal of a novel dimensional approach to defining and assessing personality disorders – an approach termed the *Alternative DSM-5 Model of Personality Disorder* (AMPD). Some of the controversy about the AMPD receives a brief mention in my *Behaving* (Schaffner, 2016, p. 147), but a more detailed and recent account can be found in Zachar, Krueger, and Kendler (2016) and an update in Skodol (2018).

The AMPD is introduced using a personality functioning perspective by evaluating two aspects of the self: (1) its integrity and self-direction, and (2) the self's interpersonal relations re: empathy and intimacy. This is developed in the AMPD's Table 1 – in *DSM-5* (American Psychiatric Association, 2013, p. 762), also called Criterion A, to distinguish it from the novel trait analysis developed in the AMPD's Criterion B component. Table 1 follows:

In the *DSM-5* Table 1, the "Self" is characterized by two dimensions:

1. *Identity*: Experience of oneself as unique, with clear boundaries between self and others; stability of self-esteem and accuracy of self-appraisal; capacity for, and ability to regulate, a range of emotional experiences.
2. *Self-direction*: Pursuit of coherent and meaningful short-term and life goals; utilization of constructive and prosocial internal standards of behavior; ability to self-reflect productively.

Further, the "interpersonal" aspect of personality functioning also has two dimensions:

1. *Empathy*: Comprehension and appreciation of others' experiences and motivations; tolerance of differing perspectives; understanding the effects of one's own behavior on others.
2. *Intimacy*: Depth and duration of connection with others; desire and capacity for closeness; mutuality of regard reflected in interpersonal behavior.

Two questions can arise in asking whether an analysis of personality *disorders* is the *right way* to begin to think about the self. But a close analysis of how the AMPD's criterion A is implemented and scored, points to the fact that *normal healthy self-functioning* is the baseline (termed level zero) for an AMPD analysis. The series of topics and questions that flesh out this criterion and provide scoring guidelines uses the *Level of Personality Functioning Scale* (*LPFS*); see Table 2, pp. 775–778 in *DSM-5*). Thus Criterion A constitutes a detailing of features of the self in both healthy (level zero) as well as increasingly compromised and disordered states (levels one through four).

Second, one might ask whether an analysis of self that is relevant to the two-system model should really involve the "interpersonal" aspects of criterion A of the AMPD. But the two-system model's sense of self is quite robust, and includes narratively significant interpersonal aspects of the self. Recall that LeDoux and Brown wrote:

> If some event is not affecting you, then it is not producing an emotion. When your friend or child suffers you feel it because they are part of you. When the suffering of people you don't know affects you emotionally, it is because you empathize with them (put yourself in their place, feel their pain): no you, no emotion.
>
> (2017, p. E2021)

It again needs to be emphasized that this "self–other dimensional perspective" is only the *first* part of the quite complex *Alternative DSM-5 Model of Personality Disorder* (AMPD). In point of fact, in the *DSM-5* Section III pages, the self and interpersonal elements of personality functioning are listed as "Criterion A" (Level of Personality Functioning), and are followed by Criteria B through G for the *more traditional* approach to personality disorders, and by a *different* Criterion B for the *trait-specified* approach. (These additional criteria deal with pathological personality traits, their pervasiveness and stability, and alternative explanations for the observed behaviors.)

Let me elaborate further: A moderate level of impairment in Criterion A is the *sine qua non* for any further diagnosis of a "personality disorder." A complete diagnosis can then be obtained by following *two* divergent diagnostic reasoning pathways. The *first* is the traditional pathway involving a specific personality disorder such as antisocial personality disorder, borderline personality, and avoidant personality disorder. It is also in the analysis of a traditional *avoidant personality disorder* that we can see the role of fear and anxiety. The *second* diagnostic pathway involves a "trait-specified" personality disorder that utilizes five pathological trait domains (further split into twenty-five associated "facets"). The traits (facets) in this pathway are evaluated and scored by the *Personality Inventory for DSM-5 (PID-5) – Adult*.

It is this second trait-specified personality disorder pathway that incorporates traits that are reasonably close analogues of those traits found in the widely accepted Five-Factor Model (FFM) of normal personality, albeit here taken to their pathological extremes of these five dimensional traits.

It should be added, however, that the exact relation of the AMPD's trait structure and the FFM is an active area of discussion, and the trait structure of the AMPD could well further evolve to incorporate traits assessed in other standard instruments of personality assessment. Furthermore, this trait structure can contribute to novel approaches to psychiatric classification, such as in HiTOP. On this latter point see Widiger et al. (2019).

It is quite plausible that the AMPD is a very useful *first and preliminary approximation* to a theoretically rich and clinically applicable account of the self that may be used in connection with the features of behavior developed in this chapter. From a theoretical perspective, and as just noted, the AMPD's second diagnostic pathway intercalates reasonably well with the currently dominant approach to the normal personality Five-Factor Model, described in *Behaving* (Schaffner, 2016, pp. 146–147) and also in the extensive personality literature. Furthermore, because this analysis is also the basis of additional current research into personality disorders, it may well facilitate an account of those aspects of traditional personality disorders that could be addressable by clinical interventions involving talk and even pharmacological therapies to assist with better interventional choices. For one recent analysis of the relation of the AMPD traits to therapeutic interventions, see Bach, Lee, Mortensen, and Simonsen (2016).

On the clinical point, there are also several already mentioned psychological instruments (essentially structured interviews with detailed questions and sample expected responses, along with rating scales) that have been developed in the AMPD and are currently being investigated to delineate specific strengths and weaknesses of the self-concept for any individual's healthy or compromised self. (Sources available here include the PID-5 – on-line at APA_DSM5_The-Personality-Inventory-For-DSM-5-Full-Version-Adult%20(1).pdf – as well as the specific questions used in the LPFS (Bender, Skodol, First, & Oldham, 2018).) These might well be adapted to explore the self-concepts that need to be further developed in the LeDoux, Pine, and Brown model of fear and anxiety. More specifically, Lynam, Loehr, Miller, and Widiger (2012) have developed an instrument, "A five-factor measure of avoidant personality: the FFAvA," that assesses this type of fear-driven personality disorder and that is closely related to the five-factor model of personality, suggesting it could constitute the basis of an instrument to be appropriately tailored to the psychological levels of the LeDoux, Pine, and Brown model.

Insofar as personality *genetics* will continue to be investigated, it will almost certainly take place within the framework of the FFM – see Rosenstrom et al. (2018). Similarly, one might anticipate FFM-related research on the *neurobiology* of personality, though the more traditional *DSM-IV-TR* schema or the similar categorical non-trait-based *DSM-5* Section III approach will also likely continue – see Nostro et al. (2018) – but also Drislane, Brislin, Jones, and Patrick (2018).

Though this AMPD-based model of the self has its strengths in terms of providing a reliable and potentially valid approach to an analysis of the conscious self, it will need to be expanded on psychological and neurobiological fronts to include the *non*conscious aspects of the self, indicated in both the LeDoux, Pine, and Brown models, as well as situated in the context of the "attention" and GNW neurobiological approaches proposed above. In addition, the self has intrinsic *normative aspects*, already represented in Table 1 above covering the "Elements of personality functioning" in the AMPD. Those normative features of the self have been approached in a variety of ways, some of them empirically as in van der Cruijsen, Peters, and Crone (2017) and also in analyses of what is termed the "true self"; see Newman, Bloom, and Knobe (2014); Strohminger, Knobe, and Newman (2017) as well as in Schaffner (2017).

32.4 SUMMARY AND CONCLUSION: ANSWERING THE WHAT, WHERE, ETC. QUESTIONS

The LeDoux, Pine, and Brown model is clearly an *interlevel* or *mixed-level* theory. It mixes environmental (threats) and organismic level (responses) with (blackboxed) sensory response systems as well as some specific circuits. Some of those circuits are believed to be strongly conserved and studiable in animal models, but some are cognitive, perhaps distinctively human, and involve "consciousness." It should be noted, however, that human studies will not be sufficient to uncover the nature of the *circuits* and fine structure of the brain-based processes. For this, relevant animal models will be needed, and there are compelling reasons to believe that this will require primate models, an increasingly ethically and socially controversial area.[§§]

[§§] I discuss some of the arguments for primate research, as well as the social controversy involving such research, in Schaffner (2020a) Also see my Comments on Pine (Chapter 9) in this volume.

Thus the answer to the "*what*" question mentioned in the title of this article is that these are multiple levels that are *intertwined*, often in what might be termed a "zig-zag" fashion as the processes of interest in the model proceeds, moving down or up or sideways in terms of levels of aggregation. Different models will be advanced using different levels characterizing their entities and processes, so *no general checklist* for the levels expected to be found in all models is likely. The "two-system" account also appeals to the type of levels that are found in what I have previously termed "temporally extended theories," (Schaffner, 1993), which leads me to my next general thesis in this section.***

Appealing to what I have termed "temporally extended theories" may well be relevant to the evolving dispute between proponents of the received traditional theory of fear and anxiety and the "two-system" model – see Fanselow and Pennington (2017, 2018); Pine and LeDoux (2017). "Temporally extended theories," or (TETs) (Schaffner, 1993) in addition to containing levels, also have those levels partitioned into *high level* central hypotheses and a *temporal series* characterizing more *specific entities* (possibly cells, circuits, or mechanisms) that instantiate the central hypothesis (details are in Schaffner (1993), pp. 211–215 and 220–231). Thus the structure of TETs involves multilevel and interlevel hypotheses, partly separable but partially intertwined in ways that need to be specifically addressed in terms of specific examples.

In the LeDoux and Pine version of the two-system model, the central high-level hypothesis involves the supplementation of older fear circuits by a consciousness circuit. This high-level hypothesis is also maintained in the LeDoux and Brown variant, but conjoined there with another high-level hypothesis involving an appeal to HOT. In the competing more traditional fear theory, the role of consciousness is downplayed if not denied, as in the Fanselow account. All three of these theories, of which two are variants of the two-system model, appeal to a varying degree to lower-level hypotheses involving more specific entities that instantiate the higher-level hypotheses, such as organs, parts of organs, pathways, circuits, and mechanisms. The *most* specific entities (often but not always *molecular-level* mechanisms), which further specify the central high-level hypothesis and which are eminently empirically testable, can then be subjected to and pass or fail experimental tests of verification.

*** These temporally extended theories are a modification and development of some of Lakatos (1970) See this 1970 chapter for his analyses of scientific progress; for details on this relation of Lakatos and TETs see Schaffner (1993, chapter 5).

If empirical failure happens, then these entities or processes (maybe circuits or mechanisms) usually become patched up and reformulated as alternative mechanisms, and often in ad hoc ways to save the higher-level central hypothesis(es). If this ad hoc strategy occurs, then any *competing* account with a distinctly different central high-level hypothesis can become significantly more attractive, if it has not also failed or had to appeal to an ad hoc strategy. On the other hand, if a TET successfully passes its experimental tests, investigators working with it will try to go on and develop a series of additional rigorous experimental tests that cannot be accounted for by any reasonable and available alternative competing TET with its mechanisms. When that situation (which Lakatos might call a progressive shift) occurs, the TET account suggests that we have attained strong "direct evidence" for the high level central hypothesis (on this notion of "direct evidence" see my (1993), pp. 156ff.). A detailed account of how this testing and falsification process works can be found in my extended example of the clonal selection versus instructive theories of immunology (Schaffner, 1992a, 1992b, 1993). This analysis was also employed when Kendler and I applied this TET approach to the dopamine hypothesis of schizophrenia (Kendler & Schaffner, 2011).

It would seem that this TET framework should presumptively apply to the LeDoux, Pine, and Brown models in its temporally extended competition with the older model alternative defended recently by Fanselow (Fanselow & Pennington, 2017). However, we are not quite there yet, since at present both groups of investigators are continuing additional research under their own two different paradigms, and have not yet fully engaged in an effective sustained debate subsequent to their initial journal exchange in 2017 (Fanselow & Pennington, 2017; Pine & LeDoux, 2017).

My "Where" question in my article's title relates to *which* level of analysis is thought to be fruitful to pursue the research program in which the model of interest is being investigated. This is a historical and pragmatic question, and also involves the "How" question that is dependent on the materials and methods of analysis available at the time. It is likely no *general* set of principles can be articulated to answer at which level in an evolving research program it is best to investigate at that point in time, but detailed *review articles* in the appropriate sub-field provide some answers in specific cases. The same answer, thus, is to be given to the "Why" question asking at which level to proceed. Peer-reviewed results accepted in excellent journals and supplemented by thoughtful editorials can also frequently be a preliminary answer as to "How Much" at any given level can be pursued.

In this conclusion, I should also note that there are many unresolved and difficult issues that I could only briefly address in this article. These include even more details than I could provide of an alternative attention and GNW theory contrasted with the HOT account preferred by LeDoux and Brown. There is also much more to be said about an expanded notion of the "self," as well as arguments that validated primate animal models will be needed to further anything like the "two-system" approach to fear and anxiety. Those developments will need to await two additional in-progress articles of mine and a book project.

That the LeDoux, Pine, and Brown model raises so many fundamental questions in psychology and psychiatry reveals its richness and its promise, both features that will keep philosophers and psychiatrists busy for many future years.

REFERENCES

American Psychiatric Association. (2013) *Diagnostic and statistical manual of mental disorders: DSM-5* (5th ed.). Washington, DC: American Psychiatric Association.

Bach, B., Lee, C., Mortensen, E. L., & Simonsen, E. (2016) 'How do *DSM-5* personality traits align with schema therapy constructs?' *Journal of Personality Disorders, 30*(4), 502–529.

Bender, D. S., Skodol, A. E., First, M. B., & Oldham, J. M. (2018) *Structured clinical interview for the alternative model for personality disorders (SCID-5-AMPD) – Module I – Structured clinical interview for the level of personality functioning scale.* Arlington, VA: American Psychiatric Association Publishing.

Brown, R., Lau, H., & LeDoux, J. E. (2019) 'Understanding the Higher-Order Approach to Consciousness.' *Trends in Cognitive Sciences.* 23(9):754–768. doi: 10.1016/j.tics.2019.06.009

Chalmers, D. J. (1995) 'Facing up to the problem of consciousness.' *Journal of Consciousness Studies*, *2*(3), 200–219.

Dehaene, S. (2014) *Consciousness and the brain: Deciphering how the brain codes our thoughts.* New York: Viking.

Dehaene, S., & Changeux, J. P. (2011) 'Experimental and theoretical approaches to conscious processing.' *Neuron, 70*(2), 200–227.

Dehaene, S., Charles, L., King, J. R., & Marti, S. (2014) 'Toward a computational theory of conscious processing.' *Current Opinion in Neurobiology, 25*, 76–84.

Dehaene, S., Lau, H., & Kouider, S. (2017) 'What is consciousness, and could machines have it?' *Science, 358*(6362), 486–492.

Drislane, L. E., Brislin, S. J., Jones, S., & Patrick, C. J. (2018) 'Interfacing five-factor model and triarchic conceptualizations of psychopathy.' *Psychological Assessment, 30*(6), 834–840.

Fanselow, M. S., & Pennington, Z. T. (2017) 'The danger of LeDoux and Pine's two-system framework for fear.' *American Journal of Psychiatry, 174*(11), 1120–1121.

(2018) 'A return to the psychiatric dark ages with a two-system framework for fear.' *Behaviour Research and Therapy, 100*, 24–29.

Frith, C., Perry, R., & Lumer, E. (1999) 'The neural correlates of conscious experience: An experimental framework.' *Trends in Cognitive Sciences*, 3(3), 105–114.

Gallagher, S. (2000) 'Philosophical conceptions of the self: Implications for cognitive science.' *Trends in Cognitive Sciences, 4*(1), 14–21.

Gallagher, S., & Shear, J. (1999) *Models of the self.* Thorverton, UK: Imprint Academic.

James, W. (1890) *The principles of psychology*. New York: H. Holt and Company.

Katsuki, F., & Constantinidis, C. (2014) 'Bottom-up and top-down attention: Different processes and overlapping neural systems.' *Neuroscientist, 20*(5), 509–521.

Kendler, K. S., & Schaffner, K. F. (2011) 'The dopamine hypothesis of schizophrenia: An historical and philosophical analysis.' *Philosophy, Psychiatry, and Psychology (PPP), 18*(1), 41–63.

Knopik, V. S., Neiderhiser, J. M., Plomin, R., & DeFries, J. C. (2017) *Behavioral genetics* (6th ed.). New York: Worth Publishers.

Lakatos, I. (1970) 'Falsification and the methodology of scientific research programmes.' In I. Lakatos & A. Musgrave (Eds.), *Criticism and the growth of knowledge* (pp. 91–196). Cambridge, England: University Press.

LeDoux, J. E., & Pine, D. S. (2016) 'Using neuroscience to help understand fear and anxiety: A two-system framework.' *American Journal of Psychiatry, 173*(11), 1083–1093.

LeDoux, J. E., & Brown, R. (2017) 'A higher-order theory of emotional consciousness.' *Proceedings of the National Academy of Sciences USA, 114*(10), E2016–E2025.

Lycan, W. (2004). The superiority of HOP to HOT. In R. Gennaro (Ed.), *Higher-order theories of consciousness* (pp. 115–136). Amsterdam: John Benjamins.

Lynam, D. R., Loehr, A., Miller, J. D., & Widiger, T. A. (2012) 'A five-factor measure of avoidant personality: The FFAvA.' *Journal of Personality Assessment, 94*(5), 466–474.

Millikan, R. G. (2000). *On clear and confused ideas : An essay about substance concepts.* Cambridge, England; New York: Cambridge University Press.

Murray, E. A., Wise, S. P., & Graham, K. S. (2017) *The evolution of memory systems: Ancestors, anatomy, and adaptations* (1st ed.). Oxford, UK/New York: Oxford University Press.

Neisser, U. (1988) 'Five kinds of self knowledge.' *Philosophical Psychology, 1*, 35–59.

Newman, G. E., Bloom, P., & Knobe, J. (2014) 'Value judgments and the true self.' *Personality and Social Psychology Bulletin, 40*(2), 203–216.

Nostro, A. D., Muller, V. I., Varikuti, D. P., Plaschke, R. N., Hoffstaedter, F., Langner, R., . . . Eickhoff, S. B. (2018) 'Predicting personality from network-based resting-state functional connectivity.' *Brain Structure and Function, 223*(6), 2699–2719.

Parnas, J. (2011) 'A disappearing heritage: The clinical core of schizophrenia.' *Schizophrenia Bulletin, 37*(6), 1121–1130.

Parnas, J., Moller, P., Kircher, T., Thalbitzer, J., Jansson, L., Handest, P., & Zahavi, D. (2005) 'EASE: Examination of Anomalous Self-Experience.' *Psychopathology, 38*(5), 236–258.

Pine, D. S., & LeDoux, J. E. (2017) 'Elevating the role of subjective experience in the clinic: Response to Fanselow and Pennington.' *American Journal of Psychiatry, 174*(11), 1121–1122.

Prinz, J. J. (2002) *Furnishing the mind: Concepts and their perceptual basis.* Cambridge, MA: MIT Press.

(2012) *The conscious brain: How attention engenders experience.* Oxford/New York: Oxford University Press.

Raffman, D. (1995). 'On the persistence of phenomenology.' In T. Metzinger (Ed.), *Conscious experience.* Paderborn: Schöningh/Imprint Academic

Rosenstrom, T., Gjerde, L. C., Krueger, R. F., Aggen, S. H., Czajkowski, N. O., Gillespie, N. A., . . . Ystrom, E. (2018) 'Joint factorial structure of psychopathology and personality.' *Psychological Medicine,* 1–10.

Saurat, W., & Lycan, W. (2014). Attention and internal monitoring: A farewell to HOP. *Analysis,* 74 (3), 363–370

Schaffner, K. F. (1992a) 'Theory change in immunology. Part I: Extended theories and scientific progress.' *Theoretical Medicine and Bioethics, 13*(2), 175–189.

(1992b) 'Theory change in immunology. Part II: The clonal selection theory.' *Theoretical Medicine and Bioethics, 13*(2), 191–216.

(1993) *Discovery and explanation in biology and medicine.* Chicago: University of Chicago Press.

(2016) *Behaving: What's genetic and what's not, and why should we care.* New York: Oxford University Press.

(2017) 'Neuroethics, free will, self-identity, and neuromodulation.' *Cerebrum.* https://www.dana.org/article/the-first-neuroethics-meeting-then-and-now

(2019) 'Comments on Pine.' In K. S. Kendler, J. Parnas, & P. Zachar (Eds.), *Copenhagen-V.* New York: Cambridge University Press.

(2020a) – Construct Validity in Psychology and Psychiatry (to be submitted; available on request to the author).

(2020b) 'A comparison of two neurobiological models of fear and anxiety: A "construct validity" application?'. *Perspectives on Psychological Science,* under review.

(in development) *Choosing: What Can We Learn about Choice and Flourishing from Behavioral Neurogenetics.*

Skodol, A. E. (2018) 'Can personality disorders be redefined in personality trait terms?' *American Journal of Psychiatry, 175*(7), 590–592.

Strohminger, N., Knobe, J., & Newman, G. (2017) 'The true self: A psychological concept distinct from the self.' *Perspectives on Psychological Science, 12*(4), 551–560.

Tekin, S. (2016). 'The missing self in scientific psychiatry.' *Synthese, 196*(6), 2197–2215.

Tononi, G., Boly, M., Massimini, M., & Koch, C. (2016) 'Integrated information theory: From consciousness to its physical substrate.' *Nature Reviews Neuroscience, 17*(7), 450–461.

Tulving, E. (2005) 'Episodic memory and autonoesis: Uniquely human?' In H. S. Terrace & J. Metcalfe (Eds.), *The missing link in cognition: Origins of self-reflective consciousness* (pp. ix, 364pp., 368 leaves of plates). Oxford; New York: Oxford University Press.

van der Cruijsen, R., Peters, S., & Crone, E. A. (2017) 'Neural correlates of evaluating self and close-other in physical, academic and prosocial domains.' *Brain and Cognition, 118*, 45–53.

White, L. K., Sequeira, S., Britton, J. C., Brotman, M. A., Gold, A. L., Berman, E., . . . Pine, D. S. (2017) 'Complementary features of attention bias modification therapy and cognitive-behavioral therapy in pediatric anxiety disorders.' *American Journal of Psychiatry, 174*(8), 775–784.

Widiger, T. A., Bach, B., Chmielewski, M., Clark, L. A., DeYoung, C., Hopwood, C. J., . . . Thomas, K. M. (2019) 'Criterion A of the AMPD in HiTOP.' *Journal of Personality Assessment, 101*(4), 345–355.

Zachar, P., Krueger, R. F., & Kendler, K. S. (2016) 'Personality disorder in *DSM-5*: An oral history.' *Psychological Medicine, 46*(1), 1–10.

Zahavi, D. (2000) *Exploring the self: Philosophical and psychopathological perspectives on self-experience*. Amsterdam; Philadelphia: J. Benjamins Pub. Co.

(2005) *Subjectivity and selfhood: Investigating the first-person perspective*. Cambridge, MA: MIT Press.

(2014a) *Self and other: Exploring subjectivity, empathy, and shame*. New York: Oxford University Press.

(2014b) *Self and other: Exploring subjectivity, empathy, and shame* (1st ed.). Oxford: Oxford University Press.

(2018) *The Oxford handbook of the history of phenomenology*. New York: Oxford University Press.

33

Schaffner on Levels and Selves

WILLIAM BECHTEL

33.1 INTRODUCTION

Of the very interesting discussions in Schaffner's paper, I will focus on two: that of levels and that of the notion of the self. The discussion of levels bookends the discussion of the self (and of consciousness) as they figure in accounts of fear and anxiety, but Schaffner offers little to connect the two parts. The term *level* is largely absent in the middle sections of the paper,[1] including his discussion of the notion of the self. Accordingly, I take them up independently, but suggest a connection in the conclusion. In Section 2 I focus on Schaffner's *what* question about levels, identifying two conceptions of level that seem to be operative in his analysis. I then turn in Section 3 to the notion of self, arguing that a conception that he largely dismisses in his historical overview is more adequate for filling in theories of fear and anxiety than the one he advances.

33.2 WHAT ARE LEVELS?

A fundamental way humans, including scientists, understand things in the world is in terms of the dimensions of the world we experience – a horizontal plane with things raising or falling vertically from it. These dimensions readily give rise to a distinction between things on a level and things at a higher or lower level. More importantly, metaphors that draw

[1] One context in which they do appear is in explication the traditional *fear center* model. Schaffner treats the stages in processing as levels. It is not clear what sense of level is operative here and what is gained beyond referring to processing stages. Perhaps all Schaffner means is that these processes occur at a particular level of aggregation or perhaps organization as at the end of the paragraph he refers to analyzing these at "finer-structured levels."

upon these dimensions permeate our attempts at understanding, including appeals to levels in science. There is not, however, just one way of extending the two dimensions of our experience onto scientific domains. This is at least part of the explanation for the multitude of conceptions of level with which Schaffner begins this essay: "levels of abstraction, analysis, aggregation, behavior, complexity, function, perspective, organization, generality, and processes – including causation and control – as well as description and explanation."

Ironically, within the large sampling, Schaffner does not include levels of hypotheses, although that seems to be the notion most at work in his discussion of *temporarily extended theories* (TETs) towards the end of his paper. Arguably, though, levels of hypotheses might fall under levels of analysis and the entities discussed in the hypotheses under levels of processes. According to Schaffner, TETs are "partitioned into *high level* central hypotheses and a *temporal series* of more *specific entities* (possibly cells, circuits, or mechanisms) that instantiate the central hypothesis." Schaffner draws upon this framework to explicate LeDoux and Pine's (2016) two-system model of fear and anxiety in which "the central high level hypothesis involves the supplementation of older fear circuits by a consciousness circuit." At an intermediate level Schaffner locates "hypotheses involving more specific entities that instantiate the higher level hypotheses, such as organs, parts of organs, pathways, circuits, and mechanisms." In his discussion Schaffner relates his notion of high-level central hypotheses to Lakatos's (1970) research programs and they also function much like Kuhn's (1970) paradigms. On these accounts, there is a fundamental difference between high- and intermediate-level hypotheses. Those at the intermediate-level are the hypotheses which ordinary scientific inquiry seeks to discover and test. The high-level central hypotheses are not themselves testable, although they might be abandoned if subsequent research fails to produce adequate and confirmed intermediate-level hypotheses. The high-level hypotheses are heuristic guides to the sorts of intermediate-level hypotheses that can fill them in. In this respect, they seem to function much like what Machamer, Darden, and Craver (2000) call *mechanism sketches* – very abstract accounts of mechanisms that, when filled in with specific proposals, result in mechanism schemas.

When one looks within the more specific hypotheses, one finds a different notion of level arising, one involving not hypotheses but entities. Schaffner shifts from talking about specificity of theories to specificity of entities: "*most* specific entities (often but not always *molecular-level* mechanisms) ... further specify the central high level hypothesis..."[2] Although the language of specificity is being used, we seem rather to be talking about composition or aggregation. This is the conception of level that has been foremost in the accounts of the new mechanists (Craver, 2007, chapter 5). Even the simplest examples of mechanistic explanation span compositional levels, including both the mechanism that is responsible for a phenomenon and the components of the mechanism that are appealed to in the explanation. Although this picture is too tidy – in real science researchers take some parts of a system apart, and perhaps even iterate the process several times, while leaving other parts as basic units – the mechanistic notion of level does seem to accommodate what Schaffner says about "where," "how," "why" and "how much." For example, researchers conduct inquiry at a level of aggregation at which the entities seem capable of answering the question about how the phenomenon was generated (this provides the basis for answering the "why" question), but this is often limited by answers to the "how" question by the availability of research tools needed for research to proceed.

Schaffner's account to TETs thus seems to require at least two different conceptions of levels. I turn now to self-concepts before returning to how this fits into these conceptions of levels in the conclusion.

33.3 SELF-CONCEPTS

Schaffner surveys theories of self with an eye to which might satisfy the role self-representations play in LeDoux and Brown's account of fear and anxiety. LeDoux and Brown (2017, p. E2021) assert: "*emotions depend on the self. Without the self there is no fear or love or joy.*" More specifically, LeDoux and Brown incorporate self-representations into their higher-order thought or HOT account of consciousness – part of what the higher-order thought has as its content is a representation of oneself. Before we turn to Schaffner's account, it is worth noting that what is important for LeDoux and Brown is representation of oneself. As with many representations, the representation of oneself may not map onto any one thing in the world. That is, one can represent oneself even if there is no thing that is the self. I will return to this after briefly considering Schaffner's "alternative approach."

[2] Schaffner concludes this sentence with the phrase "and which are eminently empirically testable." Entities, however, are not things we test; rather, we test hypothesis. Perhaps the most charitable interpretation is to assume that when Schaffner is talking about testability, he is talking about hypotheses scientists advance about these entities.

Schaffner's account ties self to personality:

> One aspect of how a person's self might be approached is to consider what is stable over the long term about the person – in a sense what "grounds" that particular person and "what they are like." From a human genetics point of view in the area of normal individuals, we can obtain a reasonable, initial purchase at such, by examining the nature of the individual's "*personality*."

Schaffner's motivation for doing so is not only that personality is considered to be stable, but to have a strong genetic component: "developing an analysis of the 'self' by framing that analysis within an account of *personality* offers the promise of providing the resources of psychiatric genetics for a deeper combined genetic and neurobiological approach to the 'self'."

I find both the claimed stability of personality and the invocations of genetics problematic, especially for the purposes for which LeDoux and Brown invoke the self. Even if we grant that personality is an enduring trait of a person, it is also well known that people can exhibit very different personalities in different environments such as when they interact in different languages. Moreover, appeal to genetics would account for personalities as enduring traits of individuals, not their representation of it. Without denying that personality, however malleable and contextual it turns out to be, is an important component of who a person is, what matters more for the purposes put forward by LeDoux and Pine is how the individual represents herself or himself – the conception of self that is available for use by information processing within the person. A person's representation of their personality may be quite at odds with that which is observed by others in their behavior. Further, as I will suggest below, how people represent their personality can affect their behavior and people can set about trying to change their actions to accord with the representation of the personality they desire to have.

Several of the other concepts of self that Schaffner identifies in his historical review but rejects in favor of appealing to personality will likely be more useful in addressing how individuals represent themselves. In what follows I take up Neisser's (1988) five kinds of self-knowledge, not because his account is exhaustive but because it can point researchers to important aspects of what we know about ourselves that might affect not only our behavior but our emotions. Moreover, these forms of knowledge can be studied experimentally.

A salient feature of Neisser's approach is that he begins with two forms of knowledge that organisms can possess about themselves without possessing what most researchers would consider mental states: knowledge about their relations to their environment, including perspectives on that environment, and their capacities to act on that environment (the ecological self), and their relations to other organisms, including conspecifics and kin (interpersonal self).[3] Bacteria and plants (especially through their root systems) acquire and use such knowledge in directing behavior in their environment, and capacities to acquire such knowledge are found in us and ground our actions. Noting that bacteria and plants can acquire such knowledge indicates, at least to most philosophers and scientists, that representation of such knowledge in the organism need not be conscious, although we can become conscious of, for example, our egocentric perspective on the world and of our relations to other organisms. One of Schaffner's desiderata for a self-concept is that it be extended to include "*non*conscious aspects of the self," and these two types of self-knowledge might be a place to start.

The third and fourth forms of self-knowledge in Neisser's account require greater representational and information processing capacities in the organism. Neisser's temporally extended self involves knowledge of one's own past and possible futures in the form of episodic memories in which one remembers oneself as engaged in the activity. Tulving (1983), who pioneered the study of episodic memory, characterized it as mental time travel and argued that it was a distinctively human capacity. Whether or not non-human organisms have episodic memories, the capacity requires the ability to create and use internal representations of past and future events. Evidence that episodic memories are reconstructed on recall (Schacter, 1996) points even more to the active information processing of representations in recalling the past and envisaging the future (Schacter, Addis, & Buckner, 2007). Likewise, the private self, in which the subject has qualitative experiences which can only be conveyed to others metaphorically, requires complex forms of information processing (and may force a confrontation with the so-called *hard* problem of consciousness).

In many ways, it is Neisser's last form of self-knowledge, which he called the *conceptual self*,[4] that is the most interesting for LeDoux and Brown's purposes. We humans, at least, are able to represent ourselves – attribute characteristics to ourselves and use those representations in part to direct our future behavior. Explaining how organisms can form

[3] Both of these require information processing by the organism, which leads those studying them often to describe them in cognitive terms (Shapiro, 2007; Baluška & Levin, 2016).

[4] What is distinctive of the conceptual self is not the use of concepts, which are required for the third and fourth type of self-knowledge and arguably as well for the first two, but concepts that represent oneself.

representations of themselves presents an interesting challenge. Unlike our ability to represent objects presented to us (consider a child learning words by being presented with various toys or animals), there is no object that constitutes the self that one experiences. The closest object that we do experience is our bodies, and our experiences of our bodies certainly plays a role in how we represent ourselves. But even more than in the case of our knowledge of ourselves as temporally extended and as having private experiences, our conceptual representations of ourselves are constructs, much as our theoretical concepts in science are constructs.

A strategy for thinking about how we construct representations of ourselves that I have found especially valuable is Sellars' *myth of Jones.* Sellars (1956) imagines a mythical past in which people have a rich language for talking about public phenomena but no language for talking about inner experiences. They talk about public actions, including their own, but they do so in behaviorist terms. They have, though, learned to construct theories about phenomena that appeal to hypothetical entities. They have even developed semantic theories in which they can say what their utterances mean and judge their truth and falsity. What, according to Sellars' myth, these people have not done is construct hypotheses about inner mental processes that explain their behavior. Then Jones advances a theory that proposes that covert speech occurs in people's heads. He refers to hypothesized utterances as thoughts and invokes them in his theoretical accounts of people's behavior. These enable more successful predictions that could be made otherwise. Jones employs the same hypotheses to account for his own behavior. He also begins to teach another person, Dick, to give such reports without consulting his overt behavior:

> ... it now turns out – need it have? – that Dick can be trained to give reasonably reliable self-descriptions, using the language of the theory, without having to observe his overt behavior. Jones brings this about, roughly by applauding utterances by Dick of "I am thinking that p" when the behavioral evidence strongly supports the theoretical statement "Dick is thinking that p"; and by frowning on utterances of "I am thinking that p," when the evidence does not support this theoretical statement. Our ancestors begin to speak of the privileged access each of us has to his own thoughts. *What began as a language with a purely theoretical use has gained a reporting role.*

In using language to describe his hypothetical internal states, Dick is picking up on cues, perhaps even ones he has private access to, and this may give him greater abilities to predict his own actions than those around him. He may even come to disagree with their explanations of his behavior. What is important in Sellars' myth is that the language for talking about one's own thoughts is part of a constructed theory, not an observational report. We might ask: of what use is such a theory if it is only a construct? To answer this question, consider the use of scientific theories that are likewise constructs; they are immensely useful not just in predicting events but also designing and building new artifacts. Thoughts can lead to changes in the world. Our hypotheses about ourselves, for example, about our personality traits, can likewise lead to changes in our own behavior. Consider the possibility that you have formed the hypothesis that you are a generous person. It may not be true, but if you are reminded of the hypothesis in a moment when you were about to act non-generously, that may be sufficient to change your action. (I have discussed the Myth of Jones and how thoughts about one's self can regulate ones actions in more detail in Bechtel, 2008, chapter 6.)

33.4 CONCLUSIONS

I have discussed separately Schaffner's treatment of levels and self. In contrast to Schaffner's suggestion that one ground the analysis of self in personality, I have argued that LeDoux and Brown's account of fear and anxiety require focus on how individuals represent themselves. Although all of Neisser's types of self-knowledge may be applicable, his conceptual self is likely to be most relevant. Drawing on Sellars, I have proposed treating a person's self-concept as resulting from hypotheses the person constructs. To tie this to Schaffner's conception of levels, one can consider where such theorizing falls on the hierarchy he offers. I would suggest that it involves both central high-level hypotheses, perhaps high-level representations of one's personality, and more intermediate-level specific information about how one actually behaves in characteristic situations. The latter opens itself up to accounts involving yet more micro-entities and activities. Perhaps if one is highly educated in psychology or neuroscience, one might even incorporate lower-level knowledge about how cognition and neural processes operate into one's self-concept.

REFERENCES

Baluška, F., & Levin, M. (2016) 'On having no head: Cognition throughout biological systems.' *Frontiers in Psychology*, *7*, 902. doi:10.3389/fpsyg.2016.00902

Bechtel, W. (2008) *Mental mechanisms: Philosophical perspectives on cognitive neuroscience*. London: Routledge.

Craver, C. F. (2007) *Explaining the brain: Mechanisms and the mosaic unity of neuroscience*. New York: Oxford University Press.

Kuhn, T. S. (1970) *The structure of scientific revolutions* (2nd ed.). Chicago: University of Chicago Press.

Lakatos, I. (1970) 'Falsification and the methodology of scientific research programmes.' In I. Lakatos & A. Musgrave (Eds.), *Criticism and the growth of knowledge* (pp. 91–196). Cambridge: Cambridge University Press.

LeDoux, J. E., & Brown, R. (2017) 'A higher-order theory of emotional consciousness.' *Proceedings of the National Academy of Sciences, USA, 114*, E2016–E2025.

LeDoux, J. E., & Pine, D. S. (2016) 'Using neuroscience to help understand fear and anxiety: A two-system framework.' *American Journal of Psychiatry, 173*, 1083–1093.

Machamer, P., Darden, L., & Craver, C. F. (2000) 'Thinking about mechanisms.' *Philosophy of Science, 67*, 1–25.

Neisser, U. (1988) 'Five kinds of self-knowledge.' *Philosophical Psychology, 1*, 35–39.

Schacter, D. L. (1996) *Searching for memory: The brain, the mind, and the past*. New York: Basic Books.

Schacter, D. L., Addis, D. R., & Buckner, R. L. (2007) 'Remembering the past to imagine the future: The prospective brain.' *Nature Reviews Neuroscience, 8*, 657–661.

Sellars, W. (1956) 'Empiricism and the philosophy of mind.' In H. Feigl & M. Scriven (Eds.), *Minnesota studies in the philosophy of science. I. The foundations of science and the concepts of psychology and psychoanalysis* (pp. 253–329). Minneapolis: University of Minnesota Press.

Shapiro, J. A. (2007) 'Bacteria are small but not stupid: Cognition, natural genetic engineering and socio-bacteriology.' *Studies in History and Philosophy of Science Part C: Studies in History and Philosophy of Biological and Biomedical Sciences, 38*, 807–819.

Tulving, E. (1983) *Elements of episodic memory*. New York: Oxford University Press.

SECTION 12

34

Introduction

KENNETH S. KENDLER

Woodward, who has for several decades been a leader in the philosophical analysis of causal processes, takes us on a detailed and somewhat demanding tour – a philosophical analysis of "levels talk." While several other essays in this volume explore the implications of multilevel approaches to issues psychiatric, in this essay Woodward leads us into the philosophical/conceptual nitty-gritty of multilevel processes, with a focus on the problem of top-down causation.

But before we get into the details, I need to comment briefly about Woodward's interventionist concept of causation. As he outlines here and in many previous writings,[1] this is a very helpful and levels "friendly" approach to causal inference.[2] Most importantly, it requires the "surgical" manipulation of a variable that impacts on C (aka cause) holding all other relevant covariances stable and then seeing if that change in C produces a change in E or the effect variable. This is a particularly lucid way to form a counterfactual approach to causality and is remarkably flexible. As long as you can meaningfully define C, the approach is agnostic to the level or, indeed, ontological status of C. It could be a social, psychological, neurobiological, or subatomic level variable. As long as manipulating it produces a reliable change in E, it counts as a cause assuming that all the background covariances are stable. This immediately cuts away a range of crusty issues like the mind-body problem. If in psychotherapy, a psychological intervention produces reliable change in brain structure, a biological variable, no metaphysical panic is needed. We can avoid getting ourselves tangled up in the hard problem of how brain could possibly produce mind or mind influence brain, etc.

Now, to this essay which illustrates one primary task of philosophy of science: that is to take a term that scientists frequently use in an explanatory (but sometimes imprecise) fashion and put it under a philosophical microscope to see what is really going on. Many of us working at the philosophy–psychiatry interface bear some guilt in this regard. I recall my enthusiasm when first reading seriously about the idea of explanatory levels. I engaged in many examples of "levels talk." But in the process, my enthusiasm somewhat outran my conceptual precision. I recall using a phrase like this for a rather diverse set of issues: "Oh yes, that's a level's problem."

I want to first focus on Woodward's preliminary section on a simple typology of levels. He outlines three major definitions: compositional, disciplinary, coarse-grained. Composition is the most common-sense idea of levels. The classic expression of this would be statements such as "subatomic particles make up atoms," "cells make up organs," and "people make up societies."

"Disciplinary" is captured by the "wedding cake" model of science that runs something like this: physics, chemistry, biology, psychology, sociology etc. These disciplines can be seen as a hierarchy of lower to higher levels. Of course, this is made more complex by the proliferating number of subdisciplines such as molecular versus systems neuroscience.

Coarse- versus fine-grained is best captured by the example of an experiment that critically depends upon the temperature of a gas. Theoretically, the mean kinetic energy of every single molecule in your gas sample would capture that construct. But in modern terminology that would be "TMI" (i.e., too much information). All you need is the mean temperature. So, by this example, temperature is a higher level than molecular energy of all the molecules. Importantly, for many scientific manipulations, that is all you need.

This issue of coarse- versus fine-grained explanations is an important one for psychiatry because it is on this basis that one can sometimes justify working at higher levels. In the physics example, you could theoretically know what every molecule is doing. But in psychiatry, imagine we are dealing with a variable such as the traumatic unexpected divorce as a predictor of risk for major depression. Underlying this kind of trauma must be all kinds of psychological and neurobiological factors that produce a risk for depression. But in our current state of ignorance, we do not come close to knowing what they were. But equally important, for a lot of what we care about – here, predicting depression – they are no more relevant than the energy of every single molecular in a gas. The event captures the causal power of the subsequent complex mechanism in the same way that temperature captures the molecular activity of a gas. That does not mean that the question of how nasty divorces cause depression is not of interest.

It is, but not knowing that does not invalidate the value of research at that level given our interest in the prediction of major depression.

In thinking about definitions of levels (Woodward outlines only three and there are a lot more), it is important to realize how easy it is to skate from one definition to another. Keeping levels talk focused on one definition is effortful.

Turning finally to Woodward's main topic, he seeks to counter prior theorists who question the plausibility of inter-level and especially top-down causation. I am not going to outline his main lines of argument as they are subtle. But one of them builds out on the "divorce effect on depression" example outlined above. In the end, he advocates strongly for the philosophical coherence and research meaningfulness of such top-down effects. As an empiricist whose day job is working in psychiatric epidemiology and genetics, I would certainly support his conclusion. Our research literature is full of examples of studies that suggest such processes. Loneliness changes gene expression patterns in white blood cells. Being pregnant motivates women to stop using drugs of abuse, thereby overcoming the urgings of their addicted brains. My favorite example comes from the well-demonstrated excess rate of lifetime alcohol abstainers in the children of alcoholics.[3] I have encountered a few such individuals. In one case, as a child, on seeing his drunken alcoholic father beating up his mother, he prayed: "Please, God, never let me turn out like him." He swore then to never drink and kept that pledge till I saw him in his mid-50s. By not drinking, he was effectively nullifying the effect of his high genetic risk for alcohol dependence. As a crass empiricist, one might argue, "If that isn't top-down causation, then what is?"

REFERENCES

1. Woodward J. (2003) *Making Things Happen*. New York: Oxford University Press.
2. Kendler KS, Campbell J. (2009) 'Interventionist causal models in psychiatry: Repositioning the mind–body problem.' *Psychological Medicine*; 39:881–887.
3. Kendler KS. (2012) 'Decision making in the pathway from genes to psychiatric and substance use disorders.' *Molecular Psychiatry*; 18:640–645.

35

Levels: What Are They and What Are They Good For?

JAMES WOODWARD

35.1 INTRODUCTION

As many writers have observed, talk of "levels" (of description, organization, explanation etc.) is common in many areas of science. At the same time, many also complain that such talk is unclear and problematic in many ways. Part of the problem is that researchers operate with many different understandings of levels and how to distinguish them. Often the differences between these various notions are insufficiently appreciated with the consequence that researchers mistakenly attribute features associated with one notion of level to other notions where they do not apply. This may prompt the thought that we would be better off avoiding level talk entirely (so-called levels eliminativism – see Eronen, 2015). I think this conclusion would be a mistake. Despite its multiple meanings (and in some respects, unclarity), level talk does useful work and, as I will illustrate below, there are many important methodological ideas that are naturally expressed in terms of levels.

This chapter begins (Section 2) with a partial typology of some of the different ways in which the notion of level has been understood – these are not wholly independent of each other but they are far from exactly coinciding. Because of this variety, the search for a single general account that captures all legitimate uses of "level" is unlikely to be successful. However, awareness of the important differences among level notions can guard us against various confusions.

A great deal of recent discussion of levels has focused on the implications of this notion (or notions) for causal reasoning. Can there be causal relations between factors at different levels (e.g., can there be "downward causation" from upper to lower levels) or must all causation be intralevel? I explore this issue in Sections 3–5, focusing largely on influential recent discussions by Craver and Bechtel. In contrast to their views, I argue for the intelligibility and importance within science of interlevel causation and in particular downward causation.

Sections 5 and 6 then attempt to put these ideas within a more general framework, linking issues about levels to issues about variable choice. It is a common and I believe entirely correct observation that different systems are best understood at different levels of analysis (or perhaps in terms of some combination of levels) – where this means that the systems are more appropriately analyzed or understood in terms of certain explanatory or causal variables (belonging to different levels) rather than others. I will describe one kind of consideration which has to do with what I call *conditional independence* that bears on this issue and which, I claim, helps to illuminate why "level talk" is often useful.

A general feature of this account is that which level or levels are most appropriate turns out to be an empirical matter, dependent on the details of the behavior of the systems we are trying to understand. Sometimes "lower" or more fine-grained levels of analysis will be most appropriate and sometimes more "upper-level" variables will be most appropriate. In particular, it is a mistake to suppose that we always improve the quality of an explanation or causal analysis by invoking lower-level variables. In addition, as we shall see, the considerations that figure in variable choice will sometimes lead us to accounts which include (in a single model) variables that are at different "levels" on some understandings of that notion – so-called multi-level or mixed-level models. Thus another related theme is the contrast between such multi-level models and theories that appeal to variables that are at least for the most part at a single level.

35.2 SOME DIFFERENT NOTIONS OF "LEVEL"

I begin, then, with a taxonomy of some of the different notions of level that have figured in recent discussion. But before getting started, a brief aside on the language of "upper" and "lower" is in order. Although talk of upper and lower levels can seem very natural, it is, as Denis Noble remarks (2006), puzzling if one tries to take it literally. After all, it is not as though the "lower-level" atoms and molecules that are taken to compose "higher-level" cells are spatially below the latter or that the atoms are part of some edifice in which they function like a basement or ground floor and the cells as the upper stories. Exactly why we find the language of upper and lower in this context so natural is an interesting question; perhaps it is connected to expectations that explanations in terms of lower-level entities will be "deeper" or "more fundamental" than those that appeal to upper-level entities, with "deeper and more fundamental" being associated with what is lower. In any case, I am going to follow others in availing myself of this language, while at the same time, recognizing that it involves a somewhat odd metaphor.

Let me add (as should be obvious) that the list that follows is not meant to be exhaustive. Also the different notions of level that I discuss are not wholly distinct but rather partially overlap and interrelate in various complex ways.

35.2.1 Levels as Compositional

One of the most familiar notions is a compositional or mereological understanding of levels: objects (or entities) at a higher level are "composed of" or "made up of" or "constituted by" objects at lower levels in a way that generates at least a local hierarchy of levels. In a paradigmatic case, the lower-level objects are (or at least are thought of as) spatial parts of higher-level objects: Atoms are composed of protons, neutrons and electrons, molecules are composed of atoms, cells are composed of molecules, organs (like the brain or liver) are made up of different kinds of cells, multicellular organisms are composed of a range of different organs, social groups or societies are composed of organisms and so on. Each item on this list is regarded as at a "higher" level than the items of which it is composed. We find this idea (among others) in Oppenheim and Putnam's classic paper (1958), and it often seems to be the preferred conception of levels both among metaphysically inclined philosophers and among some philosophers of biology, particularly those that stress the role of mechanisms in biological explanation. As noted below, some philosophers extend this compositional notion of level to include items such as processes or "activities" which they take to be related by temporal part/whole or "constitutive" relations, so that, e.g., long-term potentiation is understood as one of the constituents of the formation of memories, with the latter being at a higher level than the former (Craver and Bechtel, 2007).

35.2.2 Levels as Individuated in Terms of Disciplinary Subject Matters

Another common notion links levels to the present organization of disciplines or perhaps to differences among methods or research strategies that are presently characteristic of those disciplines. For example, one might take the "psychological level" to have to do with whatever psychologists study, the "biological level" with whatever biologists study and so on. Or one might take the psychological level to have to do with what can be discovered by research methods that investigate certain aspects of the behavior of whole organisms in contrast to research at the physiological or neurobiological level, which instead involves measurements performed on brains, hormones and so on. Obviously these are not very principled or stable notions of level, but I think they clearly influence how researchers think about levels. One problem with this conception is that changes in research practices or interests (which can occur for any number of different reasons) will, in this conception, change what belongs to a given level; certain molecules will become entities at "the" biological level as biologists begin to study them, the brain will be thought of as at the level of economics to the extent that economists venture into neuro-economics and so on. Moreover, this notion of level is closely tied to how scientific disciplines are individuated in a way that threatens to make it very misleading unless those disciplines are individuated very finely; "biology" may be thought of as a scientific discipline but talk of "the" biological level (or for that matter "the" neurobiological level) is obviously highly problematic. Some would subdivide even subdisciplines – such as the distinction between molecular and systems neuroscience. There is a tendency (see, e.g., Oppenheim and Putnam, 1958) to suppose that levels in this sense (individuated in terms of disciplinary subject matter) will coincide with levels characterized in other ways – e.g., in terms of composition – so that the subject matter of chemistry has to do with "parts" of the objects biologists study but this also is highly problematic.

35.2.3 Levels as Related to Abstractness and Coarse-Graining

A common intuition about levels is that variables that are more fine-grained or specific are at a "lower level" than variables that are related to them by some sort of coarsening operation. "Coarsening" can take many different forms but often the idea is that the lower level more fine-grained variables are related to the more coarse-grained upper-level variables via some many-to-one function – e.g., by averaging.[1] Consider a variable specifying the kinetic energy of each of a number of individual molecules composing a gas. This variable is typically understood to be at a lower level than a variable ascribing an average kinetic energy to the entire collection

[1] Other, more complex forms of coarsening are discussed in Batterman (2019).

of molecules. Similarly, for the relationship between total caloric intake and a more detailed breakdown of the individual foodstuffs making up those calories. As we shall see, coarsening operations of this sort are important in many areas of science – not because coarsening per se is valuable but because it is sometimes associated with other features of good explanations, including what I call conditional independence (Section 6). Coarsening represents one form that "abstraction" can take in science with different degrees of abstraction being associated with different "levels."

35.2.4 Interactionist Conceptions of Level and Conditional Independence

Here, I will focus on one particular kind of case in which considerations having to do with how strength and character of interactions affect assignments of levels. Suppose that some set of variables – *L* – influences some effect *E*, but that we can adequately summarize the impact of the *L* variables on *E* by means of some much smaller number of variables or parameters (or variables with a small number of possible values) *U*, where the *U* variables correspond to a coarsening of the *L* variables. In other words, we find that *conditional* on the values of the *U* variables, further details about the *L* variables don't matter for *E*, so that we can explain *E* just as well (or at least as well) by means of *U*, as we can by appealing to *L*. When this condition holds I will say that the *L* variables are *independent* of *E*, *conditional* on the *U*. (I will make this more precise in Section 6.) When this condition holds, we are likely to think of *U* as at a different (and "higher") level than *L*. I call this conception of level interaction-based because it is based on the idea that the causal impact of the *L* variables on *E* can be fully represented or captured by the impact of the *U* variables on *E* (or at least that this is true to some very high level of approximation). For example, if we are interested in the relation between thermodynamic variables, we don't need a detailed description of the behavior of individual molecules; their aggregate impact as expressed in terms of variables like temperature or volume is all that is needed. Given the values of these thermodynamic variables, further variations in molecular details do not matter to the values of other thermodynamic variables. This is one consideration that leads us to think of the thermodynamic variables as at a different (and higher) level than the variables characterizing the behavior of individual molecules.[2]

[2] In this case, the interactionist and compositional notions of level lead to the same judgments since it is also the case that the gas is composed of molecules, hence that

This interaction-based notion of level is often tied to ideas about the role of considerations having to do with "scales" – spatial, temporal and energetic – in constructing theories and models. Sometimes when nature is kind we have "separation" or near separation of scales, so that what happens at one length or energy scale can be understood largely independently of what happens at other scales, and this in turn leads us to think of interactions at one scale as at a different level than interactions at other scales. Relatedly, in physical contexts, this notion is tied to the idea that "different physics" can be "dominant" at different scales, so that, with respect to many explananda (like rates of flow through a pipe), one can model the behavior of a fluid as though it is continuous, using the Navier-Stokes equations, even though it is made up of discrete molecules, a fact that matters at other scales (Batterman, forthcoming). Here the values of the continuous variables in the Navier-Stokes equations play the role of the *U* variables in the schema above, with variables characterizing the behavior of individual molecules playing the role of the *L* variables.

It is important to understand that "scale" matters in this sort of framework to the extent that it bears on the kinds of interaction that occur; that is, size or the difference between longer and shorter times do not matter in themselves but only because (or to the extent that) they are thought to be related to the strength and nature of causal interactions and to what can be safely ignored (for purposes of understanding such interactions) conditionally on other information. So the idea is *not* that little things cannot interact (or rarely interact) with big things or vice-versa (after all viruses can destroy armies); it is rather that causal interactions often have systematic relations with spatial and temporal relationships, and that this is tied to what sort of causal details can be ignored or summarized by means of other variables.

Put differently, because this conception focuses on causal interactions, it is the character and relata of those interactions that figure in or are relevant to the characterization of levels. Note also that on most accounts of causation, including the interventionist account I will endorse below, *things* (or parts of things) per se don't stand in causal relationships; instead the causal relata are something more like properties or magnitudes or whatever is described by variables. By contrast, paradigmatic cases of compositional relations involve relations among things. This by itself

variables characterizing the gas a whole seem (on a composition-based notion) at a higher level than individual molecules. But as noted below, level assignments based on interactionist and compositional ideas do not always coincide.

marks a fundamental difference between composition-based and interaction-based conceptions of levels.

As another illustration of this interactionist notion of level and its connection to the notion of scale, consider that for the purposes of understanding what is going on within the nucleus and phenomena such as radioactive decay, two of the four fundamental forces – the strong and weak nuclear forces – are crucial. These forces are very strong at very short spatial scales. Gravity, another fundamental force, is effectively irrelevant for most purposes in modeling nuclear behavior. On the other hand, if we are interested in explaining/understanding chemical behavior – how atoms combine and form molecules and compounds – the strong and weak nuclear forces are effectively irrelevant in the sense that detailed features of these forces do not matter as long as they allow for the formation of stable nuclei. Instead, another force, the electromagnetic force, plays a central role in chemical behavior. In many cases, this separation of levels or scales – the fact that nature permits us to construct theories that explain aspects of nuclear behavior that appeal to factors that are different from those that are required to explain chemical behavior, so that we can do nuclear physics without doing chemistry and vice versa – is crucial for successful science. As explained in more detail below, this separation enables us to avoid, at least to some considerable extent, problems of computational and other sorts of intractability that would likely otherwise hamstring scientific understanding. We avoid such problems by neglecting what is going on at other length, time, and energy scales, and we are justified in doing so because what goes on at these other scales either does not matter (much) for the phenomena we are trying to understand or else, to the extent that such goings on do matter, their influence can be summarized in a small number of manageable parameters or variables at the scale at which we are modeling, as in the thermodynamic case.[3]

Both length and temporal scales are also important in biological contexts.[4] Some biological variables may change so slowly with respect to

[3] This general theme of looking for ways of modeling certain features of a system which allow the modeler to avoid having to model other features in any detail is explored in great depth in Wilson (2018).

[4] Alon (2006) provides illustrations of important differences in temporal scale in biological context: inputs change the activities of gene transcription factors on a sub-second scale, in contrast, "binding of the active transcription factor to its DNA site reaches equilibrium in seconds. Transcription and translation of the target gene takes minutes and the accumulation of the protein product can take many minutes to hours" (pp. 10–11).

others and to the explananda of interest that the former can be effectively treated as constants – thus variations in them make effectively no difference for the problem at hand. For example, although large-scale anatomical connections in the brain can change over time, they generally change much more slowly than large-scale "functional" connections and thus the former can be treated as effectively unchanging for purposes of understanding the latter. Other variables may reach an equilibrium so quickly that they can also be treated as non-varying. Again, this can justify ignoring or greatly simplifying interactions involving those variables, as when we summarize the impact of a variable by a single constant.

In my opinion, this interactionist notion is one of the most scientifically interesting and relevant notions of "level" although it can easily mislead us, as discussed below. I emphasize again that this basis for level talk (which interactions are important and which can be ignored) is conceptually distinct from the issues about composition or size that figure in the first notion of level distinguished above. Whether one object X is part of another object Y is obviously a distinct question from whether one can safely ignore features of X in explaining the behavior of Y.[5] Nuclei are "parts" of molecules but, as noted above, nuclear forces can be safely ignored in understanding the chemical behavior of molecules. Electrons are also parts of molecules but aspects of the behavior of electrons that have to do with electromagnetic forces are crucial to understanding chemical behavior. More generally, as noted above, little things can clearly interact with big things and conversely. Things that belong to the same kind or type as things that compose big things can interact with those big things. Proteins in the form of prions can affect brains and people even though proteins are among the constituents of brains and people. Thus strength of interaction considerations and ignorability considerations are only very imperfectly related to size differences or to compositional relationships. Although as noted above, compositional notions of level have been the subject of a lot of recent attention, especially among metaphysicians and philosophers of biology, in my view such notions have less bearing on interaction-based notions of level than many have supposed.

Several other preliminary observations may be helpful at this point. Interactionist conceptions of level are, as I have said, based on the assignment of systems or variables to the same level to the extent that they

[5] Of course, as noted above, sometimes composition-based and interactionist notions of level will coincide or track one another. My point is that this is by no means always the case.

interact strongly with one another and to the extent that various details about what is going on at other levels may be safely ignored or summarized by a much smaller number of variables. In some cases, this rationale for level assignment works smoothly and is very fruitful, as is illustrated by examples discussed above (and below). In these cases, we are able to identify a set of phenomena all of which can be explained in terms of some relatively small set of explanatory factors that interact primarily with one another and this encourages us to think of all these factors as "at the same level." Put differently, in such cases, the phenomena and explanatory factors to which we appeal are relatively self-contained: we don't have to bring in other factors willy-nilly from some arbitrarily long and disparate list to account for what is going on. Thus general considerations based on scale and other factors help to provide principled motivations for restricting the list of possible explanatory factors and regarding them as separable from other explanatory factors. This sort of situation is sometimes described by physicists by means of talk of distinct "regimes" or "protectorates" – the idea being that there is a distinct, separable set of phenomena that can be adequately modeled by some restricted set of variables or explanatory factors. When we are in this sort of situation, level-based considerations can be very heuristically useful in guiding judgments about which causal factors can be safely ignored.[6]

Although it is not uncommon to find explanatory factors and explananda that behave in the way just described – separable regimes and so on – this is by no means always the case. For this to be possible, nature has to cooperate and it does not always do so; an alternative possibility is that the list of possible explanatory factors for some set of explananda may be very open-ended and at different levels (by one or more of the criteria described above) with the kinds of heuristic arguments that in some cases allow us to exclude certain factors unavailable. Arguably, this is the case for

[6] An illustration: My former colleague David Goodstein, a solid-state physicist at Caltech, recounts the reaction of physicists to the claims of the chemists Pons and Fleischmann to have discovered cold fusion. Goodstein observes that one reason why most physicists disbelieved those claims (even in the absence of detailed calculations or failed attempts at replication) was based on a heuristic application of separation of scale/level considerations. The energy supplied in the apparatus these researchers were using was many orders of magnitude too small to produce fusion and the distance relations between atoms that could be achieved by the electrolytic reactions the chemists were employing were many orders of magnitude greater than the distances required to achieve fusion. The processes involved in fusion occur on distance scales and on time scales that are effectively completely separate from anything that might be involved in the kind of experiment the chemists conducted.

many explananda in psychiatry: many different causal factors – social or environmental factors, factors having to do with personality type, as well as genes and brain structure – are relevant to paradigmatic mental illnesses such as depression and we do not have, as we do in the case of the nuclear and electromagnetic forces, strong general arguments that certain factors could not possibly be relevant (or at least any general arguments of this sort are much weaker than they are in the physics case[7]).

This fact can generate lots of misguided expectations and assumptions if we are not careful. As an illustration, consider the causal influence of environmental factors such as stressful life events on gene expression and mental illness. Assuming that such influences are real, what do they imply about levels? Suppose that we adopt a conception of levels according to which factors that interact are automatically at the same level (as one simple version of an interactionist conception might suggest). Then it follows that environmental factors and genes are at the same level. Of course, this is not the way we usually think about environmental events like the death of a parent; intuitively we think of them as at a "higher level" than gene expression. Such intuitive judgments must reflect the influence of other conceptions of level besides the simple interaction-based conception described above: perhaps we are thinking that genes are parts of organisms, that environmental stressors involve whole organisms,[8] hence (via a composition-based notion) that the stressors must be at a "higher level" than genes. Perhaps we are also thinking that environmental stress belongs to the subject matter of the social sciences and psychology and that these disciplines are at a "higher level" than genetics.

Suppose we try to retain the idea that objects and systems at the same level interact preferentially or even exclusively with each other *and* combine this with a notion of level based on something other than interaction (e.g., a size or composition-based notion, as above). Now we have a recipe for confusion: on the one hand, the occurrence of environmental stressors is a higher-level event (based on size and composition considerations) than genes; on the other hand factors at different levels are not supposed to

7 Wimsatt (1994) speculates, plausibly, that what he calls "causal leakage" (that is causal influence across levels and causal explanations employing causes at different levels) becomes more common as one moves to phenomena at "higher levels"; it is more common in, say, psychology than in high-energy physics.

8 Note that an environmental stressor like "death of a parent at an early age" seems to be well-defined and measurable only at the level of whole organisms, rather than at, say, the level of individual genes, even though the environmental event can influence gene expression.

interact (much) with one another, so that it can seem problematic that environmental events can influence genes (so that some special story needs to be told about how to analyze the appearance of such influence – for example, by claiming that what is really doing the influencing is some set of much lower-level events that realize the environmental event). Accordingly, one finds, both in the philosophical literature and elsewhere, a number of arguments to the effect that objects and systems at different levels cannot interact with one another (or that such interaction is problematic and needs to reinterpreted in a way that makes it philosophically respectable, as in the views of Craver and Bechtel, discussed below). My opinion is that such views derive, at least in part, from illegitimately combining expectations that come from an interactionist view of levels with conceptions of level that are based on other sorts of considerations such as part/whole relations. In my view, there is no problem in principle with the notion of interlevel causation, including the notion of downward causation from "upper" to "lower" levels. The temptation to think otherwise results, at least in part, from thinking of levels too exclusively in compositional terms, which helps to makes it seem plausible that downward causation should be modeled in terms of causal relations running from wholes to their parts.

35.3 CAUSATION AND LEVELS

I turn now to some more specific remarks about causal relations between variables at different levels. This requires an account of causation and here I'm going to proceed within the interventionist framework that I have defended elsewhere (Woodward, 2003). According to this framework:

> (**M**) *X* causes *Y* in background conditions B if and only if under some intervention that changes a value of *X* in B, the value of *Y* will change in a regular or stable way. (For our purposes, we can think of "regular" here as meaning either that *Y* takes the same value for the intervention on the value of *X* or that *Y* exhibits the same stable expected value or at least that this is approximately true.)

Here *X* and *Y* are variables which can be either binary (corresponding to the occurrence or non-occurrence of some event) or can take many different values, as with real-valued variables. An intervention on *X* with respect to *Y* can be thought of as an idealized experimental manipulation of *X* which changes *X* in such a way that any change in *Y*, should it occur, occurs only through the manipulation of *X*. Put slightly differently, an intervention on *X* is an unconfounded manipulation of *X*. Interventions can be realized in, for example, randomized experiments among other possibilities.

The idea underlying **M** is that causal relations are relations that are potentially exploitable for purposes of manipulation and control; if *X* causes *Y* then if one wiggles *X* in the right way, *Y* should change. Conversely, if *Y* changes under some intervention on *X* then *X* causes *Y*. This does *not* mean that causal relationships can only be discovered through experimentation or by actually performing interventions – I can certainly learn about causal relationships in non-experimental or "purely observational" contexts by employing various sorts of causal modeling procedures. However, according to (**M**), when I learn about causal relationships in such contexts what I am learning is what the results of a possible experiment involving manipulation of *X* would be, were I to perform the experiment. One consequence of this picture is that the kind of evidence that supports causal conclusions on the basis of non-experimental data should be evidence that would support conclusions about the outcomes of hypothetical experiments. I won't try to defend this idea here but it is becoming increasingly accepted within statistics and econometrics; it underlies the use of instrumental variables and regression discontinuity designs (which involve looking for intervention-like processes in observational data), that are increasingly used in psychiatric epidemiology.

Note that (**M**) by itself imposes no constraints connecting causal claims with the various non-interactionist notions of level. As far as (**M**) is concerned, a variable that is identified as "upper-level" according to some criterion like composition or abstractness – e.g., a variable like environmentally induced stress *S* or famine *F* – can cause a lower-level variable having to do with, e.g., a certain pattern of gene expression *G* as long as it is true that under the right sort of wiggling of *S* or *F*, *G* would change in a regular way. That this is the case might be established either by experimental manipulation of the upper-level variable or from observational studies or a combination of these. For example, experimental manipulation of stressors imposed on laboratory animals can be shown to alter gene expression and observational evidence from a variety of sources (including instrumental variable type reasoning such as observations from the Dutch Hunger Winter) supports the conclusion that famine experienced by mothers can alter gene expression in their offspring. Such procedures can establish that upper-level variables have causal impacts on lower-level variables without having detailed causal information about exactly how the upper-level variables are realized by lower-level variables.[9] Of course, if we say that variables are automatically at the same level as long as they causally interact, we will be led to conclude that *S* and *G* are at the same level but the point is that (**M**) imposes no further level-based constraints on what can cause what. For similar reasons, as far as **M** goes, variables that are "lower level" by some criterion (e.g., variables having to do with gene expression) can causally influence upper-level variables like whole organism psychology or behavior.

In my view, this "level neutrality" is a virtue of (**M**); it allows us to judge that the very common use of theories in the life sciences and the social and behavioral sciences in which there are causal relations holding among variables at different levels is legitimate and unproblematic and it fits naturally with the information on which we often rely to establish such conclusions.[10]

35.4 LEVELS AND DOWNWARD CAUSATION

At this point, non-philosophers may ask, regarding the possibility of causation across levels: Why would anyone suppose otherwise? In fact several different reasons have been advanced (primarily but not exclusively by philosophers) for why causation "across" different levels, and in particular, "downward causation" from an upper to lower levels, is impossible. In this and the following section, I explore and respond to several of these arguments, focusing first on these issues at a general level and then more specifically on an influential recent discussion by Craver and Bechtel (2007).

A common complaint against downward causation is that this involves causation running from a whole to its parts and that this is always incoherent; typically this is claimed to be so because wholes and parts are not "suitably distinct" to stand in causal relationships and/or because whole/part relations are synchronic in a way that causal relationships are not

9 This is not to deny that it is of great interest to discover the mediating variables by which environmental events affect gene expression: they will often do so via the organism's sensory system which will in turn affect neural processing, hormone and neurotransmitter levels and so on. These mediating processes will be "lower-level" but this is compatible with the initial triggering environmental events often being best conceptualized as at a higher level – e.g. as "stress" or perhaps a particular kind of stressor.

10 For a defense of this claim within psychiatric contexts, see Kendler and Campbell (2009).

(because, it is supposed causes must temporally precede their effects).[11] A similar objection would apply to upward causation from parts to wholes. Thus Craver and Bechtel take as an example of a claim of downward causation the claim that "signal transduction" in the visual system causes changes in the "conformation of rhodopsin" and object that, because the latter is a temporal stage in the former, the relation between the two cannot be causal (2007, p. 552). For similar reasons they object to the claim that a mechanism considered as whole (that is, as a collection of parts or constituents standing in ordinary causal relations with each other) can exert downward causation on the parts or constituents of that mechanism. Heil (2017) takes as one of his paradigms of downward causation, the claim that the motion of a whole body of water causes the motion of its component molecules and objects that this involves a whole causing its parts, which is incoherent.

I agree that these (and other similar synchronic whole/part relations) should not be understood as causal relations. However, for the most part, these are *not* the sorts of examples that are described as cases of downward causation in the recent scientific literature. To begin with, as noted above, causal claims in most areas of science (and causal claims as these are understood within the interventionist framework) relate *variables* (or more pedantically what is described by variables) rather than things or thing-like entities such as processes or events. By contrast, whole/part relationships do relate thing-like entities – bodies of water and the molecules that compose such bodies, temporally extended processes and component sub-processes and so on. In my view, the latter are not appropriate candidates for the relata of causal relationships of any kind, whether interlevel or intralevel. In other words, to the extent that whole to part relations relate thing-like entities – and it is unclear what else the relata of such relations might be – this alone is a sufficient reason for disqualifying them as causal.

11 The idea that a causal relationship requires that the relata of that relationship be "distinct" in some appropriate way is a common place of the philosophical literature – see, for example, Lewis (2000). One of his examples is that saying "hello" loudly cannot cause one to say, "hello", because saying "hello" loudly logically entails saying "hello" and this sort of entailment implies that the events in question are not distinct. I agree that causation requires that the causal relata satisfy some appropriate distinctness requirement but, for reasons discussed below, do not think that standard claims of downward causation in the scientific literature violate a reasonable version of such a requirement.

An even more important consideration is that when things stand in whole/part relationships, variables predicated of those wholes and parts need not (and usually do not) stand in whole/part or constitute relations of a sort that are inconsistent with a causal interpretation. As an illustration, consider that in the Hodgkin–Huxley model of the action potential, the potential difference *V* across the cell membrane is treated as a cause of the opening and closing and conductances of the ion channels in the cell membrane and of the various ionic currents through the membrane. The ion channels are literally part of the cell membrane and thus on a compositional conception, one might think of the causal influence of the membrane potential on the ion channels as a matter of upper to lower or downward causation, which indeed is how it is often described (e.g., by Noble, 2006). However, although the ion channels are part of the membrane, it is dubious that it makes sense to describe the strength I_i of the ionic currents as "part" or a "constituent" of the membrane potential *V*. (I will say more about this later.) Moreover, whether or not this "parthood" language is appropriate, it seems clear that *V* and I_i are nonetheless "distinct" in a way that allows them to stand in causal relationships. In fact, the $V \rightarrow I_i$ relation straightforwardly satisfies the interventionist criterion for causation; if one intervenes on the membrane potential the ionic currents will change. Indeed, Hodgkin and Huxley actually did this experiment with the then new device of a voltage clamp which allowed them to impose different potentials across the cell membrane and measure the resulting changes in the ionic currents.

Similarly, even if one thinks that genes are parts of people (or, if this makes sense, "parts" of environmental interactions involving people), and that the former are at a lower level than the latter, according to **M** this is no barrier to the truth of a causal claim according to which some high levels of stress cause changes in gene expression. Again an interventionist framework makes straightforward sense of such downward causal claims – one can, for example, manipulate social stress among laboratory animals and measure corresponding changes in gene expression.

35.5 CRAVER AND BECHTEL ON DOWNWARD CAUSATION AND MUTUAL MANIPULABILITY

So far, I have been objecting to the idea that claims of downward causation are to be understood in terms of part/whole relations (and hence are illegitimate). I want now to flesh out this portion of my discussion by turning to a more detailed look at one of the most developed and influential discussions of "levels" and downward causation in the philosophical literature, which is due to Craver and Bechtel (2007). These authors advance an account of levels according to which a necessary and sufficient condition for components to be at the "same level" is that they all be components or constituents of the same "mechanism." That is, components of the same mechanism and only those components are at the same level. This basically relies on a compositional notion of level but the resulting notion is, as these authors stress, very "local" in the sense that components of different mechanisms will be non-comparable with respect to levels.

Craver and Bechtel advocate the following condition (called **MM** for Mutual Manipulability) for whether something is a component of mechanism or more generally a constituent or part of something.

> (**MM**) X and S are related as part and whole (X is a constituent of S) if and only if *F* is some behavior of X and *J* some behavior of S such that

(i) there is an intervention on X's *F*-ing with respect to S's *J*-ing that changes S's *J*-ing and
(ii) there is an intervention on S's *J*-ing with respect to X's *F*-ing that changes X's *F*-ing (Craver, 2007, p. 153).

In other words, X is a part of S if and only if there is some way of intervening on X to change its behavior that changes S's behavior and some way of intervening to change S's behavior that changes X's behavior. For example, rhodopsin conformation is a constituent of signal transduction because there is a way of intervening on the former that will change the latter and vice-versa. (Here rhodopsin conformation is the behavior corresponding to *F* in the above schema and signal transduction corresponds to *J*. Signal transduction is a behavior of the whole visual system – S in the above schema – and rhodopsin conformation is a behavior of a part X of S.) (**MM**) is satisfied because there is a way of intervening on the extent of rhodopsin confirmation that would alter overall signal transduction and, similarly, appropriate interventions on signal transduction would alter rhodopsin conformation. According to Craver and Bechtel, the presence of this sort of constitutive relationship between X and S precludes that relationship from being causal.

It follows from this picture that there is no such thing as interlevel causation literally speaking; what looks like interlevel causation is really a matter of the operation of intralevel causation and constitution relations, as captured by **MM**. When upper-level *U* appears to cause lower-level *L* what is really going on is that some set of lower-level constituents *C* of *U* (where the *C*s at the same level as *L*) cause whatever happens with respect to *L*. Although in such cases we may observe *L* change after changes in *U*, strictly speaking the real causal action is all at the level of *L* (and *C*); *U* doesn't do any causing. Apparent top-down causation is thus what Craver and Bechtel call a "hybrid" relation, that can be decomposed into a constitution relation between *C* and *U* and a causal relation between *C* and *L*, rather than a causal relation between *U* and *L*. To use another of their examples, the macro-level event *M* of Kane experiencing the loss of a sled leads to various lower-level neural events *N* as traces of a memory of *M* are laid down – an apparent case of downward causation. However, this can be translated into a claim to the effect that *M* itself is constituted by various events *X* at the same level as *N*, which then cause *N*, so that all of the causation involved is intralevel.

My view is that making sense of downward causation (or more generally, interlevel causation) does not require this sort of hybrid picture. Indeed, this picture fails to capture why we often find it so useful to employ interlevel causal claims. I will say more to motivate these claims in Section 6.

Here I want to comment briefly on the **MM** criterion itself. One problem with this criterion is that it does not adequately distinguish part/whole or constitution relations from ordinary causal relations that are cyclic. Causal relations that involve cycles with V_1 causing V_2 which in turn causes V_1 are very common in biological, psychological and social scientific contexts, particularly when there is interlevel causation. This is because, when an upper-level variable causes a lower-level variable, often the lower-level variable will in turn feedback to affect the upper-level variable (or vice-versa). For example, in the HH model, the membrane potential causally affects the channel conductances and the ionic currents and changes in these conductances/currents in turn affect the membrane potential over time – claims that as we have seen have a natural interpretation (and are readily testable) within an interventionist framework. Applying the **MM** criterion to this example, we seem forced to conclude, mistakenly, that the channels/ionic currents are constituents of the membrane potential and thus that these cannot stand in causal relationships. Similarly, as Kendler (2011), among others, notes, not only do environmental events influence gene action which in turn influences psychological states, those psychological states may in turn influence behaviors which help to create (or involve choosing to be in) environments which further influence expression

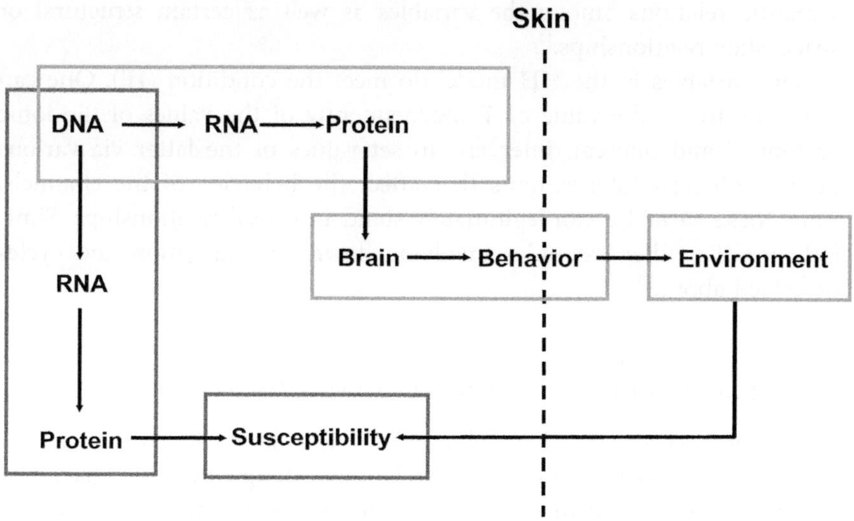

FIGURE 35.1 A combined disease pathway: "Within the Skin" and "Outside the Skin".

of the same genes and so on. For example, environmental stressors may influence the action of genes contributing to depression which may in turn lead to behavior and choices that place the subject in environments which further accentuate gene action associated with depression. This is represented in the above diagram of Kendler's (Figure 35.1) which makes clear the cyclic nature of the process as well as the presence of interlevel causation.

Because causal cycles are so common in the biological and social sciences, it seems to me to be a limitation in **MM** that it appears to classify cases in which cycles are present as cases involving constitution relations which are understood in a way which precludes causation, so that because the ionic channels are constituents of the cell membrane, the membrane potential cannot cause changes in those channels. A better criterion for when variables fail to be distinct in a way that precludes their standing in causal relationships appeals instead to what I have elsewhere called independent fixability (**IF**): variables in set S are distinct in a way that permits their standing in causal relationships if and only if it is "possible" to intervene on each variable independently, holding it fixed at each of its possible values while intervening to hold the other variables to each of their other possible values. Here "possible" includes settings of values of variables that are possible in terms of the assumed, logical, mathematical, or semantic relations among the variables as well as certain structural or space–state relationships.[12]

The variables in the HH model do meet the condition (**IF**). One can intervene to set the value of V independently of the values of the ionic currents I and one can intervene to set values of the latter via various pharmacological interventions that affect the behavior of the channels. Thus these variables can legitimately stand in causal relationships. Similarly for the other examples involving downward causation and cycles described above.[13]

35.6 Levels and Conditional Independence[14]

In my remarks so far, I have objected to views about levels that tie this notion exclusively to compositional relations. Along with this, I have also attempted to respond to objections to the notion of interlevel causation that seem to be motivated by this compositional picture such as interpretations of downward causation according to which it involves a whole acting downwards on its parts. I am very aware, however, that some readers will think that I have failed to get to the heart of the matter. After all, they will say, in the case of, for example, of the HH model, the neuron itself is composed of atoms and molecules which interact locally, mainly through the electromagnetic force. The membrane potential difference, the

[12] For further discussion see Woodward (2015). It is worth explicitly noting the difference between (**IF**) and (**MM**). (**MM**) has to do, roughly, with whether it is true both that Y changes under some intervention on X and that X changes under some intervention on Y (where X and Y correspond to the behaviors F and J in (**MM**). By contrast, **IF** says distinctness fails when it is impossible to intervene to set X and to set Y to some combination of values.

[13] There is a tendency in philosophical discussion to suppose that causal representations with cycles are always illegitimate; indeed another part of Craver and Bechtel's objection to downward causation is that this often involves causal cycles which they take to be objectionable. To the extent that this is a worry, cyclic representations can sometimes be replaced with acyclic representations involving time-indexed variables: X at time t causes Y at time $t + 1$ which causes X at time $t + 2$. Although I lack the space for detailed discussion, I believe, however, that there are legitimate cases involving cycles – e.g., models which describe certain kinds of equilibrium relations – for which this sort of interpretive move is not available. Such models nonetheless can have a straightforward interventionist interpretation.

[14] The ideas in this section regarding conditional independence are in some respects similar to and have been influenced by ideas developed much more formally by Frederick Eberhardt and colleagues in a machine learning context – see, e.g., Chalupka et al. (2017). I am indebted to Eberhardt for helpful discussion.

channel conductances and so on must be the upshot or result of complex patterns of interaction among these atomic and molecular constituents. Thus variables like *V* and *I* do not represent anything "over and above" such constituents and their interactions. Why then do we need to make use of any notion of downward causation from upper-level variables? All that is "really going on" (it will be argued) involves causal interactions among lower-level variables. Talk of downward causation seems (at best) superfluous, if not positively misleading. Similarly for the other examples discussed above.

As I see it, to adequately respond to these worries we need to explain more clearly what legitimate work is done by the notions of downward (and interlevel) causation and by notions of level that are not purely compositional.[15] Here the notion I called conditional independence in Section 2 will play a crucial role.

I begin by filling out a kind idealized or limiting case sketched in Section 2. Suppose *L* is a fine-grained variable (or set of these, although I will ignore this possibility in what follows since it does not really change anything) which is causally relevant to some explanandum *E* characterizing system S (where causal relevance is understood in terms of **M**). Here "fine-grained" means that *L* has many different possible values or states. For example, the values of *L* might represent all of the various possible combinations (all 36×10^{23} of them) of momentum and position of each of the individual molecules making up a mole of gas. Suppose also that there is another variable *U* which also characterizes S, and which corresponds to a "coarsening" of *L*. ("Coarsening" here means that *U* is a function of *L*, in the mathematical sense of "function,"[16] but that *U* has many fewer possible values than *L*, so that the relation between *L* and *U* is that many different values of *L* are mapped into the same value of *U* as when, in the example above, the different possible combinations of momentum and pressure are mapped into a variable like temperature; this is connected to the abstractness notion of level in Section 2.3).[17] Assume that *U* is also causally relevant to the *E* (where again this is understood in terms of **M**) and that, furthermore, *conditional* on the values of *U*, the values of *L* are irrelevant to *E*.

15 I see this as part of a general program of elucidating important notions in science by spelling out what their legitimate function is or what we aim to accomplish in using them.

16 That is, each value of *L* is always mapped into just one value of *U*.

17 In other words, although *F* is a function, it is not 1-1 or injective.

The notion of conditionality here is to be understood in terms of interventionist counterfactuals, rather than conditional probability: if we were to fix the value of *U* via an intervention, further changes in the value of *L* also produced by interventions that are consistent with the value of *U* make no further difference to *E*. For example, given that a gas has pressure $P = p$, then (as a matter of empirical fact) it is true or very nearly true that any variation in the positions and momenta of its component molecules which are consistent with $P = p$ will have no further impact on other thermodynamic variables like the temperature and volume which we take to be our target explananda *E*. In such a case, it is natural to think that all of the causal information about *E* that is in the fine-grained variable *L* is absorbed into the *U* – in this sense *U* "screens off" *L* from *E*. Thus, within an interventionist framework, one can just as well use *U* as *L* in explaining *E*. There is no loss of causal or explanatory information relevant to *E* in using *U* rather than *L* despite the fact *U* is a coarser variable.[18] When, in this sort of case, *U* is taken to be at a different level than *E* (where this judgment may reflect compositional or other sorts of considerations), we may legitimately think of *U* as an interlevel cause of *E*. Thus, on this view of the matter, claims of downward causation (and claims of interlevel causation more generally) can be thought of as claims about the irrelevance of certain kinds of information conditional on other sorts of information – we can legitimately make claims of interlevel causation when such conditional irrelevance relations are present.

Here are some additional illustrations of the basic idea. Returning to the HH model, think of this as embodying the claim that, given the potential *V* across the entire membrane, any further information about how that potential is realized in the electromagnetic forces associated with individual atoms and molecules does not matter for the impact of *V* on the variables measuring the ionic currents and the channel conductances. This does not mean, of course, that such forces do not exist or are not causally operative; rather the point is that they do not *matter* for the behavior of the ionic currents and channel conductances, *given* the value of *V* or at least they do not matter for the overall shape of the action potential. Put differently, this view does not deny that (as claimed in the objection envisioned above) there are causally relevant goings on at the level of individual molecules; rather the claim is that we do not *need* to advert to

18 In other words, although *L* contains more information than *U*, *U* contains all the information that is relevant to *E* in *L*.

such details in explaining certain facts about the channel conductances and ionic currents, given the value of *V*.[19]

Consider another example: some environmental event (famine during pregnancy, death of a parent at an early age) is claimed to causally influence gene expression via some epigenetic process – in a putative case of downward causation. One might imagine an enthusiastic reductionist who resists this claim, insisting instead that what is "really" going on is that there is some molecular-level instantiation of these environmental events with molecular-level interactions involving these molecules being causally responsible via some complicated chain of molecular-level intermediates for the changes in gene expression. According to the reductionist, all of the real causal action occurs at the molecular level. In responding it seems to me that the defender of downward causation should not deny (as some anti-reductionists do) the obvious point that causal (and explanatory) relations are present at the molecular level that influence gene expression. Rather the defender of downward causation should resist the claim that these are the *only* causal relations that are present (as the reductionist's use of "really" seems to insinuate). Downward or interlevel causation will be present in such cases to the extent that is true that the appropriate conditional irrelevance relations hold. Suppose it is true (as it appears to be) that, given that a mother experiences a famine-level reduction in total calories in the first trimester of pregnancy, then, independently of the details of the composition of those calories or their molecular realization, her offspring have changes in gene expression resulting in an increased tendency to obesity later in life. Then reduced caloric intake will be a legitimate downward cause, which indeed is how it is usually described.

The sort of case just described, in which there is complete conditional independence is, as I have said, a limiting case, although I believe that it is not as unusual as some philosophers suppose. One might relax this requirement in various ways: lower-level variable *L* might be conditionally independent of *E*, given *U*, for "almost all" even if not literally all values of *L*. Such conditional independence might hold for those values of *L* that are most likely (as measured in terms of relative frequencies) to occur or at least most likely to occur in environments of interest. Arguably it will be

[19] A number of defenses of upper-level causation (or explanation) in the philosophical literature contend that, when true, the upper-level claims rule out the truth of lower-level causal claims, so that there is "downward exclusion". I reject such views.

legitimate to continue to talk of upper-level causation in such cases, although there will be countervailing considerations.[20]

At this point the readers may wonder whether (and when and why) it is reasonable to expect even approximate conditional independence to hold. The answer to this question is going to depend on empirical facts about the domain under investigation. In physics, for example, there are a number of results that tell us when to expect such independence and even (in some cases) why it occurs. Renormalization group type arguments show why various phenomena having to do with phase transitions are independent of facts about the details of the material composition of the systems undergoing such transitions (Batterman, 2019). Decoupling theorems in high-energy physics show that the correct physics at lower energy scales is effectively (conditionally) independent of the correct physics at higher-energy scales. Turning to macroscopic organisms like ourselves, there are a number of general reasons for expecting that conditional independence relations (or some approximation to them) in which relatively coarse-grained environmental variables screen off more fine-grained variables will sometimes hold. Roughly, this is because it is often the values of such coarse-grained variables rather than variables that make further fine-grained distinctions that are biologically meaningful for us and that we have been shaped, by natural selection and various learning processes, to be sensitive to. For example, it makes biological sense that insofar as the effect of interest is weight gain in adulthood, that this would be sensitive to an upper-level variable like maternal caloric intake rather than tracking further fine-grained variations in how this variable is realized. Of course, with respect to other effects more fine-grained dietary details may matter.[21] Similarly, although different environmental stressors may have different effects on gene expression, it is plausible that these stressors will fall into certain broad groups (e.g., those that involve loss versus threat) having similar effects based on the biological significance of the stressor and the

[20] The countervailing considerations are that as we relax the conditional independent requirement in the ways described, we admit downward causes that have more and more heterogeneous effects. At some point this heterogeneity becomes sufficiently great that we don't have well-defined effects or well-defined responses to interventions on the candidate cause.

[21] Glymour et al. (2011) argue that folate deficiency in the diets of mothers during the Dutch hunger winter is partially responsible for the increased incidence of neural tube defects and schizophrenia in their offspring. If this is correct, then, even conditional on total caloric intake, dietary folate levels are relevant to NTDs so that the downward cause is folate deficiency rather than calorie deficiency.

psychological and neuroendocrine systems it engages. In other words, given that the stressor involves threat, further variation in the details of the stressor may not matter to its genetic effect, in which case the experience of threat is the downward cause. More generally, there are obvious ecological reasons why sensory systems are likely to be sensitive to the values of relatively coarse-grained environmental variables rather than fine-grained realizations of these (the presence of a tiger rather than small variations in the molecular realization of the tiger) and thus that it will be these "upper-level" macroscopic variables that will drive lower-level neural, hormonal and genetic responses. Whenever this is the case, one has a good approximation to conditional independence.[22]

So far my argument has been that causes framed in terms of upper-level variables will sometimes do at least as well, for purposes of causal explanation, as causes framed in terms of lower-level variables – this shows that such claims are not superfluous. There are, moreover, several additional points that help to explain why it is often useful to operate with notions of interlevel causation.

The first is that, in many cases, explanations in terms of lower-level variables are simply not accessible or constructable, both for computational and epistemic reasons. Consider the project of replacing an explanation in terms of an upper-level variable like death of parent with a molecular-level characterization of this cause. Obviously we are in no position to actually exhibit or construct such an explanation – we don't know the molecular details of the realization of the upper-level variable on any particular occasion and even if we did, these details would be different for other episodes of parental death. Furthermore, even if we did have such information, a bottom-up calculation from these details showing how they result in, say, depression, would be (to state the obvious) completely intractable. Similarly for many of the other examples of causal claims involving upper-level variables discussed above. It is thus fortunate indeed that when the appropriate conditional independence relations hold, we don't need to appeal to such lower-level causes. We can establish the truth of upper-level causal claims and that the appropriate conditional independence relations hold by means of the usual methods of experimentation and causal modeling involving such variables without making use of "underlying" lower-level information. We thus have a two-part rationale

22 Put differently, many biological systems operate by neglecting or abstracting away from certain kinds of detail or variation; think of systems that have a binary response to continuous input variables etc.

for appealing to upper-level causes and downward causation: (i) we may lose nothing by doing so in terms of relevant difference-making information and (ii) it may be impossible to actually construct or exhibit explanations in terms of lower-level causes. Note that even if (ii) is regarded as a "merely pragmatic" consideration, (i) is not. Whether conditional independence or something close to it holds depends on what nature is like, not on our calculational and epistemic limitations or other pragmatic considerations. These are among the considerations that show why appeals to upper-level variables as causes (including causes of lower-level variables) is not "superfluous" or a product of some sort of confusion.

Let us now return, in the light of these observations, to Craver and Bechtel's proposal that interlevel causal claims should be understood as hybrid claims that invoke both interlevel constitution relations and intralevel causal relations. As noted above, we often lack information about the compositional and interlevel relations that according to Craver and Bechtel underlie interlevel causal claims. Focusing for the moment on claims of downward causation, we often don't know the necessary details concerning the lower-level constituents of the upper-level causes, or what the laws or causal relations governing the lower-level variables are. Thus their account seems to hide the very reason that we appeal to downward causal claims in the first place: we do so to a substantial extent because we don't have the very information on which their account rests. Put differently, appeals to downward causation are to a considerable extent part of a strategy of avoiding modeling unknown lower details – the very details to which Craver and Bechtel appeal.

Finally, let me return to the question posed in Section 1 (and in the title of this chapter) concerning the function of level talk: what legitimate work does it do? In addition to the role played by compositional considerations, we can think of claims about levels as encoding information about what factors it is permissible to ignore in modeling and causal analysis – either because these factors are unconditionally irrelevant to some effect of interest or (more commonly) because, they are irrelevant, conditional on information represented by other variables.

REFERENCES

Batterman, R. (forthcoming) 'Multiscale Modeling in Inactive and Active Materials.'

(2019) 'Universality and RG Explanations.' *Perspectives on Science* 27(1):26–47.

Chalupka, K. Eberhardt, F., and Perona, P. (2017) 'Causal Feature Learning: An Overview.' *Behaviormetrika* 44:137–164.

Craver, C. (2007) *Explaining the Brain*. Oxford: Oxford University Press.

Craver, C. and Bechtel, W. (2007) 'Top-down Causation without Top-Down Causes.' *Biology and Philosophy* 22:547–563.

Eronen, M. I. (2015) 'Levels of Organization: A Deflationary Account.' *Biology and Philosophy* 30(1):39–58.

Glymour, M., Veling, W., and Susser, E. (2011) 'Integrating Knowledge of Genetic and Environmental Pathways to Complete the Developmental Map.' In Kendler, K., Jaffee, S., and Romer, D. (eds.), *The Dynamic Genome and Mental Health*. New York: Oxford University Press.

Kendler, K. and Campbell, J. (2009) 'Interventionist Causal Models in Psychiatry: Repositioning the Mind–Body Problem.' *Psychological Medicine* 39 (6):881–887.

Kendler, K. (2011) 'A Conceptual Overview of Gene-Environment Interaction and Correlation in a Developmental Context.' In Kendler, K., Jaffee, S., and Romer, D. (eds.), *The Dynamic Genome and Mental Health*. New York: Oxford University Press.

Heil, J. (2017) 'Downward Causation.' In Paoletti, M. and Orilia, F. (eds.), *Philosophical and Scientific Perspectives on Downward Causation*. New York: Routledge, 42–53.

Lewis, D. (2000) 'Causation as Influence.' Reprinted in Collins, J., Hall, N., and Paul, L. (eds.), *Causation and Counterfactuals*. Cambridge, MA: MIT Press.

Noble, D. (2006) *The Music of Life*. Oxford: Oxford University Press.

Oppenheim, P. and Putnam, H. (1958) 'The Unity of Science as a Working Hypothesis.' In Feigl, H., Scriven, M., and Maxwell, G. (eds.), *Concepts, Theories, and the Mind-Body Problem*. Minneapolis: University of Minnesota Press, 3–36.

Wimsatt, W. (1994) 'The Ontology of Complex Systems: Levels of Organization, Perspectives, and Causal Thickets.' In Matthen, M. and Ware, R. (eds.), *Biology and Society: Reflections on Methodology*, Canadian Journal of Philosophy, Supplementary Volume 20. Calgary: The University of Calgary Press, 207–274.

Wilson, M. (2018) *Physics Avoidance: Essays in Conceptual Strategy*. Oxford: Oxford University Press.

Woodward, J. (2003) *Making Things Happen: A Theory of Causal Explanation*. New York: Oxford University Press.

Woodward, J. (2015) 'Interventionism and Causal Exclusion.' *Philosophy and Phenomenological Research* 91:303–347.

(Forthcoming) 'Explanatory Autonomy: The Role of Proportionality, Stability, and Conditional Irrelevance.' *Synthese*.

36

Levels of Analysis in Alzheimer's Disease Research

STEPHAN HECKERS

Scientific explanations use different levels of analysis. Such division of labor allows for a flexible and appropriate reduction of complex phenomena into simpler units. In "Levels: What Are They and What Are They Good for?" James Woodward reviews several meanings of levels, makes the case that levels do good work, and argues that interlevel causation is philosophically defensible.

Here I will use Alzheimer's disease as an example to demonstrate different levels of analysis in the scientific exploration of a psychiatric disorder. I will describe how we have made progress in our understanding of Alzheimer's disease at four different levels of analysis. They evolved over the course of a century, have complemented each other and allowed for an increasingly complex understanding of a progressive neuropsychiatric disorder.

In the introduction to his paper, James Woodward points out that the notion of "upper/lower" as descriptors of increasingly deeper and more fundamental levels of analysis is "a somewhat odd metaphor." It seems to me that this is more straightforward in clinical medicine, including psychiatry. In my view, the ethically appropriate care of an autonomous person defines the highest level of analysis and any sociological, psychological, or biological investigation occurs at a lower level. This is captured well by Sir William Osler: "The good physician treats the disease; the great physician treats the patient who has the disease."

But a scientist studying Alzheimer's disease might turn this hierarchy upside down, putting genes at the top of the hierarchy, with their impact descending down to the level of clinical phenotype. (For a highly instructive example, see Figure 1 in Elahi and Miller 2017.)

36.1 THE STORY OF A PATIENT, A DOCTOR, AND A DISEASE

On November 25, 1901, a 51-year old married woman, Auguste Deter, was admitted to a psychiatric hospital in Frankfurt, Germany, where she was examined by the 36-year-old psychiatrist Alois Alzheimer. Auguste D presented with prominent cognitive deficits and signs of psychosis. Alzheimer continued to follow the case after he left Frankfurt and, when Auguste D died on April 8, 1906, he received her brain and studied it.

Alzheimer presented his findings later that year, on November 4, at the 37th Conference of South-West German Psychiatrists in Tübingen (Alzheimer 1907). He began his presentation with the statement that the clinical features of the case had already been different from known diseases and that the pathological findings then deviated from all previously known disease processes. He described what we now refer to as neurofibrillary tangles and neuritic plaques. (Of note, the brief publication did not include any drawings or microphotographs.) He suggested that he had identified a "peculiar disease process" and concluded, in more general terms, that "histological examination can confirm the distinctiveness of a case." There were about 80 colleagues in attendance. They did not realize the importance of the presentation and proceeded, without any further discussion, to the next presentation.

Alzheimer presented his findings at two levels of analysis: the detailed clinical description of a severe form of dementia and the microscopic study of neuropathological abnormalities (see Figure 36.1). It was not clear to him how they were related. But he conjectured that disease groups can be divided, first neuropathologically and then clinically, into specific diseases.

For the next 70 years, progress in the scientific study of Alzheimer's disease was slow. But there were two major achievements. First, pathologists mapped out degenerative brain changes, especially in the medial temporal lobe, which led to the neuropathological staging of Alzheimer's disease (Braak and Braak 1991). Second, neurochemical investigations revealed a prominent loss of cholinergic neurons in the basal forebrain (nucleus basalis of Meynert), which gave rise to the development of acetylcholinesterase inhibitors as the first FDA-approved treatment for Alzheimer's disease (Vergallo et al. 2018).

In 1984, George Glenner and Caine Wong at the University of California San Diego isolated a novel cerebrovascular amyloid protein from human brains obtained at autopsy (Glenner and Wong 1984). This led to

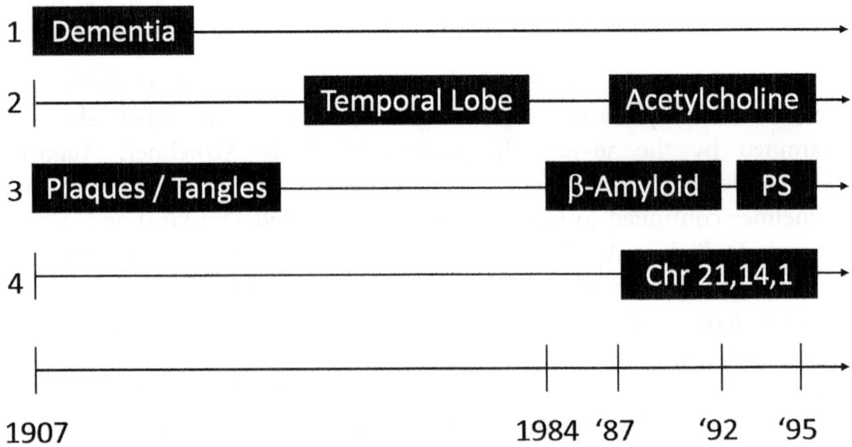

FIGURE 36.1 Levels of AD research.
Note: The scientific study of Alzheimer's disease (AD) research has progressed at several levels of analysis. The initial report juxtaposed the clinical description of dementia (level 1) with the discovery of plaques and tangles (level 3). The pathological and neuroscientific exploration of AD revealed abnormalities of the temporal lobe and the cholinergic system (level 2), leading to a pathological staging system and the development of the first drug treatment. The identification of the beta-amyloid protein (level 3) led to the discovery of disease-causing mutations in chromosome 21 (level 4), which was complemented later by the discovery of additional mutations in chromosomes 14 and 1, coding for the presenilin (PS) proteins.

the identification of the amyloid precursor protein (APP) and the mapping of the APP gene to chromosome 21 (Tanzi 2012). Mutations in the APP gene accounted for the observation that Down syndrome (trisomy 21) patients develop Alzheimer's disease in their 30s and 40s. Linkage studies identified additional genetic loci for Alzheimer's disease on chromosomes 14 and 1 (Bekris et al. 2010).

The biochemical analysis of postmortem tissue and the genetic study of familial Alzheimer disease cases dramatically accelerated the scientific exploration of Alzheimer's disease. It led to the development of transgenic animal models of Alzheimer's disease and to the ambitious project to treat and prevent Alzheimer's disease by halting or preventing the pathological effects of amyloid deposition (Mehta et al. 2017).

Despite these advances at lower levels of analysis, the neuroscientific explanation of dementia has become increasingly complex. There are several dementia syndromes: Alzheimer's disease, vascular dementia, frontotemporal dementia and related syndromes, Lewy body dementias, and prion diseases, creating a "tangled web of neurodegenerative disease" (Elahi and Miller 2017). While the underlying pathology is often used to classify the dementias, mapping the anatomical location of the pathology across the cortical mantle is crucial for proper subtyping of patients.

36.2 Composition, Subject Matter, and Abstractness of Alzheimer's Disease Research

The scientific exploration of plaques and tangles is a good example of higher and lower levels of analysis. Alzheimer used a light microscope to discover neuritic plaques and neurofibrillary tangles. This level was sufficient to develop a neuropathological staging of Alzheimer's disease. But it was the isolation and biochemical characterization of amyloid plaques, including the discovery that the misfolded proteins are toxic to the brain, that accelerated the scientific exploration of Alzheimer's disease.

Furthermore, the identification of proteins allowed for the identification of disease-causing mutations and the characterization of familial (Mendelian) forms of Alzheimer disease.

Closely related to the compositional nature is the subject matter. The scientific discovery of the dementias has been pursued by different professional groups, including psychiatrists, neuropsychologists, neuroscientists, neuropathologists, biochemists, and geneticists. Each of them studied Alzheimer's disease at the level of analysis that suits their training.

However, alignment of subject expertise was necessary. For example, scientists who want to develop animal models of dementia by creating toxic levels of a misfolded protein need to appreciate the cognitive deficits seen in Alzheimer's disease in order to study the behavioral consequences of their intervention. Similarly, clinical trialists who want to show that blocking the deposition of a misfolded protein prevents or ameliorates dementia need to define a cognitive function in Alzheimer's disease patients as their primary clinical outcome (Mehta et al. 2017).

Related to subject matter and professional expertise is the degree of abstractness at each level. For example, the clinical syndrome of dementia and the cognitive neuroscience of memory are complex. In fact, there is no comprehensive systems neuroscience framework that can explain all of the facets of Alzheimer's disease. In contrast, the impact of mutations in the amyloid precursor protein (APP) and the subsequent generation of abnormal protein fragments is considerably more accessible, allowing for targeted manipulation in animal models.

36.3 WHAT DO LEVELS OF ANALYSIS DO FOR ALZHEIMER'S DISEASE RESEARCH?

Some of the biological factors identified in Alzheimer's disease have proven to be invariant, i.e., they are stable and robust. The most compelling example is familial Alzheimer disease, which can be linked to specific mutations which cause misfolded proteins. In contrast, the effect of allelic variation (e.g., the APOE-e4 allele, the strongest risk gene for Alzheimer's disease) is less invariant in the sporadic cases of Alzheimer's disease.

It is important to note that the deposition of amyloid plaques is not an invariant feature of Alzheimer's disease. In fact, some patients with prominent amyloid plaques do not show the clinical picture of Alzheimer's disease (De Jager et al. 2018). The role of neurotransmitters in Alzheimer's disease is even less invariant, limiting the effects of treatment with acetylcholinesterase inhibitors (Vergallo et al. 2018).

Related to the invariant nature of levels of analysis is their specificity. Here again, the genetic findings in familial Alzheimer's disease are rather specific, i.e., mutations in APP and presenilins are associated with Alzheimer's disease but no other brain disorders. In contrast, the allelic variation in the ApoE gene is less specific: there are several brain and non-neural phenotypes associated with the various ApoE alleles.

36.4 CONDITIONAL INDEPENDENCE OF LEVELS IN ALZHEIMER'S DISEASE RESEARCH

The scientific study of human neurodegeneration is an excellent example of the power and limits of scientific reductionism, at both higher and lower levels of analysis. We have come a long way from the single case of Auguste D, reported in 1907, to the population-level exploration of genetic and environmental risk factors of neurodegenerative brain disorders (De Jager et al. 2018). But we are still far away from a personalized medicine of dementia, which proposes to identify all risk factors and accurately predicts disease trajectory, morbidity and mortality in each person (Hampel et al. 2017).

The misfolding of proteins is at the core of many dementias, but it does not provide a simple template for the nosology of dementias. It is even more difficult to imagine how the current levels of analysis can provide sufficient information for a complete model of cognition in the healthy brain and, as a consequence of pathology, in Alzheimer's disease patients.

In fact, further progress at the level of genes and proteins might lead to a scenario where we can prevent and treat Alzheimer's disease, without ever having reached a sufficiently detailed analysis of the cognitive deficits seen in Alzheimer's disease patients. Would this not be a great example of the conditional independence of levels of analysis?

For now, scientists studying Alzheimer's disease are emboldened by the new knowledge gained at the lower levels of analysis. At the same time, clinicians are humbled by the inability to explain the cognitive and behavioral changes in Alzheimer's disease patients and the disappointments in developing effective drugs treatments.

Practitioners and scientists alike are well served to employ multi-level or mixed-level models of analysis. Such levels of analysis allow for the appropriate blending of approaches and provide hope that we can discover the causes of psychiatric illness, necessary for intervention, and ultimately, prevention of mental illness.

REFERENCES

Alzheimer, A. (1907) 'Über eine eigenartige Erkrankung der Hirnrinde', *Allgemeine Zeitschrift für Psychiatrie*, 64, 146–48.

Bekris, L. M., et al. (2010) 'Genetics of Alzheimer disease', *Journal of Geriatric Psychiatry and Neurology*, 23 (4), 213–27.

Braak, H. and Braak, E. (1991) 'Neuropathological stageing of Alzheimer-related changes', *Acta Neuropathologica*, 82 (4), 239–59.

De Jager, P. L., Yang, H. S., and Bennett, D. A. (2018) 'Deconstructing and targeting the genomic architecture of human neurodegeneration', *Nature Neuroscience*, 21 (10), 1310–17.

Elahi, F. M. and Miller, B. L. (2017) 'A clinicopathological approach to the diagnosis of dementia', *Nature Reviews Neurology*, 13 (8), 457–76.

Glenner, G. G. and Wong, C. W. (1984) 'Alzheimer's disease: Initial report of the purification and characterization of a novel cerebrovascular amyloid protein', *Biochemical and Biophysical Research Communications*, 120 (3), 885–90.

Hampel, H., et al. (2017) 'A Precision Medicine Initiative for Alzheimer's disease: The road ahead to biomarker-guided integrative disease modeling', *Climacteric*, 20 (2), 107–18.

Mehta, D., et al. (2017) 'Why do trials for Alzheimer's disease drugs keep failing? A discontinued drug perspective for 2010–2015', *Expert Opinion on Investigative Drugs*, 26 (6), 735–39.

Tanzi, R. E. (2012) 'The genetics of Alzheimer disease', *Cold Spring Harbor Perspectives in Medicine*, 2 (10), a006296. doi: 10.1101/cshperspect.a006296

Vergallo, A., et al. (2018) 'The cholinergic system in the pathophysiology and treatment of Alzheimer's disease', *Brain*, 141 (7), 1917–33.

SECTION 13

37

Introduction

PETER ZACHAR

One of the defining claims of so-called post-positivist approaches to the philosophy of science is that observation is theory-laden (Hanson, 1958; Kuhn, 1962). According to the strongest versions of this claim, theories do not just influence what we attend to, they actually influence what we observe – and people with different theoretical frameworks can look at the same stimuli, but observe different things. If correct, this undermines the notion that there is something called raw observation.

Against this backdrop, Ken Kendler examines the view that nineteenth-century alienists, with the advantage of asylums that presented them with many clinical cases that could be observed for prolonged periods, were able to carefully describe symptoms in a way that previous generations could not. Based upon this raw clinical data, they then inductively grouped them into kinds, culminating in diagnostic systems like those of Kraepelin.

Kendler rejects this simple inductivist story. If so, how then should we understand the development of psychiatric nosology in the nineteenth century? By studying the historical development of diagnostic categories such as paranoia in Kraepelin's textbooks, Kendler (2018, 2019) has discovered that patterns that seem obvious to us now slowly coalesced for Kraepelin through an iterative reshuffling of symptom clusters guided by evolving conceptual considerations. This process was much more conceptually elaborate than observing symptoms and inductively generating diagnostic categories.

He suggests that folk psychology played a role the development of psychiatric nosology, but not exactly the folk psychology of the person-in-the-street. In his view, two different elaborations of folk psychology were important. The first was the faculty psychology of the academic philosophers such as Christian von Wolff and Immanuel Kant. In the first part of the chapter, Kendler provides examples of clinicians writing about the derangement of particular mental faculties, which were considered innate structures of the mind rather than something acquired in development. Their idea was that that the most advanced theories about the nature of mind should inform how medical doctors understand what they would have called insanity.

It should be noted that faculty psychology also had a contender for dominance, namely the associationism of the empiricists (Berrios, 1996). In terms of the contrast, faculty psychology would put more emphasis on innateness, biological reductionism, canalization, modularity, and internalism, whereas associationism would put more emphasis on development, causal pluralism, plasticity, domain generality, and relationalism.

The second elaboration of folk psychology was a consequence of the first. If the mind was composed of distinct faculties, it was important to have some grasp of how disturbances in more than one faculty complicated things, or how disturbances in one faculty would influence the other faculties. Kendler illustrates these elaborations using early theories of paranoid delusions and mania. Paranoid delusions were thought to result from the disturbance of a cognitive faculty, and the altered cognitive appraisals would "cause" dysfunctional emotional reactions. Mania was a disturbance of an emotional faculty, which would in turn influence the patient to make distorted appraisals. Kendler notes that this notion of primary disturbance and secondary symptoms does not differ much from how disorders are currently conceptualized. This way of looking at faculties came into clearer view once Kraepelin started emphasizing the importance of clinical course (i.e., how symptoms develop over time).

Kendler also suggests, somewhat provocatively, that the nineteenth-century notion of innate psychological faculties that are likely localized in the brain might be considered the historical forebears of the RDoC initiative's emphasis on psychological processes implemented in neural circuits. However, says Kendler, in the faculty psychology model, the relationship between faculties were governed by the relationship between mental contents. (See Campbell Chapter 14 for a further exploration.) And as Borsboom, Cramer, and Kalis (2018) have argued, disorders whose descriptions depend on transitions between mental contents are not really brain disorders.

In response, Greg Miller agrees that faculty psychology played an important role in the history of nosology, but rather than tracing a line from the innate, localized, and modular status of the faculties to the basic psychological processes and neural circuits of RDoC, he calls attention to the categorical nature of the faculties. Rather than focusing on the primarily categorical systems of the *DSM* and *ICD*, however, he stays on Kendler's topic and examines the categorical and dimensional distinctions both between cognition and emotion, and within the domain of emotion itself. One of his main points is that, for both psychiatric classification and the classification of emotion, these categorical structures can be readily and usefully mapped in multidimensional spaces.

The interesting backstory to this exchange is that Miller takes Kendler's history and turns it into an indictment of categorical diagnoses, knowing that Kendler managed one of the primary roadblocks to the inclusion of dimensions in the *DSM-5* (Kendler, 2013). It is fascinating to follow how diverse background assumptions and commitments lead to such different interpretations.

Miller also articulates how faculty psychology and RDoC differ. One important difference is that the faculties were assumed to be localized in the brain, whereas in RDoC, constructs are only admitted to the matrix if there is already evidence that they are implemented in the brain. In addition, the faculties at best were analogous to general domains whereas RDoC constructs are more fine-grained.

REFERENCES

Berrios, G. E. (1996) *The history of mental symptoms*. Cambridge, UK: Cambridge University Press.

Borsboom, D., Cramer, A., & Kalis, A. (2018) 'Brain disorders? Not really... Why network structures block reductionism in psychopathology research.' *Behavioral and Brain Sciences*, 42, 1–54.

Hanson, N. R. (1958) *Patterns of discovery*. Cambridge, UK: Cambridge University Press.

Kendler, K. S. (2013) 'A history of the *DSM-5* scientific review committee.' *Psychological Medicine*, 43, 1793–1800.

(2018) 'The development of Kraepelin's mature diagnostic concepts of paranoia (Die Verrücktheit) and paranoid dementia praecox (Dementia Paranoides): A close reading of his textbooks from 1887 to 1899.' *JAMA Psychiatry*, 75(12), 1280–1288.

(2019) 'The genealogy of dementia praecox I: Signs and symptoms of delusional psychoses from 1880 to 1900.' *Schizophrenia Bulletin*, 45, 296–304.

Kuhn, T. S. (1962). *The structure of scientific revolutions*. Chicago, IL: University of Chicago Press.

38

The Impact of Faculty Psychology and Theories of Psychological Causation on the Origins of Modern Psychiatric Nosology

KENNETH S. KENDLER

38.1 INTRODUCTION

In this essay, I will first marshal historical evidence for two theses. The first is as follows:

> During the formation of psychiatric nosology during the 19th century, faculty psychology typologies played a strong role in the conceptualization of psychiatric diagnostic categories. These typologies were often derived from the work of philosophers.

For a definition of faculty psychology, let me turn to the "Oxford Companion to the Mind" (and see Hilgard, 1980; Albrecht, 1970; Brooks, 1976; Müller-Freienfels, 1935 for other useful discussions):

> The theory, in vogue, particularly during the second half of the eighteenth and first half of the nineteenth centuries, that the mind is divided up into separate inherent powers of "faculties" such as memory, learning, intelligence, perception, and will. The faculties might be contrasted with those other powers which the individual could acquire through use, exercise, or study, and which were generally known as "habits".
> (Gregory, 1987, p. 253)

I am not the first to posit a close relationship between faculty psychology and psychiatric nosology (e.g., Radden, 1996). The second thesis follows from the first:

> In clarifying how possible disorders in different faculties might interrelate, 19th century psychiatric nosologists made frequent references to

Drs. Peter Zachar and Gregory A. Miller provided helpful comments on earlier versions of this chapter.

causal influences of one faculty on another using the implicit folk criteria of understandability.

By "understandability" I mean the intuitive sense that individuals possess about their own mental functioning and those of their relatives and friends. Specifically, here, this means that when observing a patient with a disorder of mental functions A and B, the alienist can draw on his or her prior experience to judge the plausibility of a dysfunction in faculty A causing a dysfunction in faculty B or vice-versa.

I then argue that these approaches were sensible and predictable as experienced clinicians tried to "reverse engineer," using the folk psychological categories with which they were familiar, the nature of the disorders they were seeing in their asylum patients. The idea that psychiatric nosologists would work in a "purely" inductive manner without prior conceptions of the key mental functions that might be disturbed is implausible. I conclude with some thoughts about the philosophical implications of these findings for a "levels-based" view of psychiatric science, including RDoC, and the significance of this story for our current efforts to use our diagnostic categories in etiologic research.

38.2 PART 1: FACULTY PSYCHOLOGY AND PSYCHOPATHOLOGY

To vastly oversimplify a complex history, the first time in Western civilization that trained physicians had the opportunity to see, on a daily basis, hundreds of insane individuals, was in the large asylums that were established in the late eighteenth and early nineteenth centuries in Western Europe. As detailed in several reviews (Kendler, 2016b, 2016c, 2017a, 2017b), by 1900, largely under the influence of Emil Kraepelin, our major psychiatric diagnostic categories – particularly mania, depression (or melancholia), dementia praecox (or schizophrenia) and paranoia – were formed. Indeed from 1900 up until 1980 and the publication of *DSM-III* (American Psychiatric Association, 1980), there has been a considerable, albeit incomplete, consensus on the key symptoms and signs for these syndromes. How did this happen? What conceptual framework did these early alienists adopt in trying to understand the nature of the disorders they were confronting in their asylum work?

We begin with William Cullen (1710–1790), a Scottish physician who counted David Hume among his patients. Cullen proposed, over several editions from 1769 to 1785, an early and highly influential general medical nosologic system. He defined the major order of "Vesanie" (which included a number of "mental" disorders such as amentia, melancholia and mania) as "A disorder of the functions of the judging faculty of the mind, without fever or sleepiness" (Cullen, 1808). He mentioned other faculties in his disease description including will, memory, imagination and perception (Eigen, 2016, p. 61). So, from the early days in the development of modern Western medicine, future psychiatric disorders were described as disorders of particular mental faculties.

Moving half a century forward in time and across the Atlantic in space, let us consider some remarks made by Rufus Wyman, M.D. to the Massachusetts Medical Society on June 2, 1830 in a talk entitled "A Discourse on Mental Philosophy as Connected with Mental Disease (Wyman, 1830)." He said

> Writers on mental philosophy arrange the mental operations or states under two heads, one of which regards our knowledge, the other our feelings. The former includes the functions of intellect, or the intellectual powers or states. The latter includes the affections, emotions or passions, or the pathetical powers or states... This division of the mental states or functions has suggested a corresponding division of mental diseases – diseases of the intellect and diseases of the passions... As there is disease of intellect, without disease of the passions, so there may be disease of the passions, without apparent disease of intellect... To exhibit clear and exact views of an insane mind, it seemed necessary to consider separately diseases of the intellect, and diseases of the passions.
>
> (Wyman, 1830, pp. 12–13 and 19)

Three points are of interest. First, Wyman starts by a reference to the philosophical literature. Wyman understands that the first task of the physician is "to learn of chemistry and natural philosophy the laws of inanimate matter – to toil, at the risk of life, in learning the structure of the body, and the functions of its organs (Wyman, 1830, p. 21)." But in addition, for those physicians who seek to study insanity, it is just as vital to turn to a different field – that of "mental philosophy" about which he writes "Nowhere does it cast a clearer or a stronger light, than it throws upon the darkness of a disordered mind (Wyman, 1830, p. 22)." So as general medicine turns to the physiologist and anatomist to understand the basis of classical medical disorders, so alienism (aka psychiatry) needs to turn to the mental philosopher to learn the basis for their diseases. Second, Wyman assumes, analogous to distinct physiological systems (e.g., cardiac, respiratory, skeletal, etc.) that can individually cause distinct diseases, the faculties of the mind can be independently disordered. There can be "a disease of intellect, without diseases of the passions." Third, the findings of mental philosophy – in this case the two key faculties of the mind, intellect and emotions – have a clear and immediate impact on nosology. As a typical physician might want to separate disorders of the kidney from those of the liver, so would an alienist, Wyman argues, want to divide disorders of the intellect from disorders of passion.

Let's now turn to lecture IV on "Varieties of Insanity," in an 1853 textbook written by Daniel Noble, a lecturer on psychological medicine at the Chatham-Street School of Medicine in Manchester England (Noble, 1853). In his treatment, he proposes anatomical bases for the faculties:

> I have said that the peripheral grey matter of the cerebral hemispheres forms, in the highest degree of probability, the organic structure wherewith the inherent conscious principle exercises itself with ideas and intellectual processes generally; and that certain ganglionic masses nearer the base – most likely the corpora striata and the so-called optic thalami – are concerned in the production of emotional sensibility.
>
> (Noble, 1853, p. 125)

He then goes on to propose his diagnostic framework based on these faculties:

> I propose, then, in the further discussion of the symptoms of mental disease, to recognize three divisions. In the first place, I shall group together those cases in which some false or perverted idea so rivets itself in the mind as to constitute an illusion which gives rise to confusion between the products of imagination and positive realities, . . . such a state of things, for my present purpose, may be called notional insanity, involving some derangement of the hemispherical ganglia. Next, I shall speak of instances in which, from some weakening or depravation of intellectual energy, there is a primary perversion of the intelligence . . . and this mental condition we may designate intelligential insanity. Lastly, I shall treat of that larger class which comprises the great majority of cases, where the prominent derangement is obviously in the emotive sense and correlated ganglia, and which may be said to constitute emotional insanity.
>
> (Noble, 1853, pp. 126–127)

He proposed an anatomical basis for psychological faculties: "notional" or as one might now say cognitive, "intelligential" which probably represents what one would now call intellectual disability, and "emotive." He postulates that these three faculties underlie key diagnostic groups.

One important advantage that faculty psychology provided to these early alienists is a "place to locate their pathology." The rise of the clinical-pathological model in medicine in the first half of the nineteenth century was a frustrating experience for these alienists. With the possible exception of the early observations of general paresis of the insane, efforts to obtain a clear 1:1 relationship between psychiatric symptoms or syndromes and brain pathology were met with frustration. Faculty psychology provided a "next best" alternative. They could argue that a particular patient was suffering from a "destruction of the faculty of thought." While not as good as an anatomic location, it was better than nothing.

Let us, on this brief tour, now jump 30 years ahead to one of the most prominent American neuropsychiatrists of late nineteenth century, William Hammond. In his widely read "Treatise on Insanity" (Hammond, 1883), Hammond presents a typology of psychiatric nosologies, reviewing six in total. He describes number 4 as follows:

> The Psychological. – A classification from a psychological stand-point is one in which the pathology of the mind is arranged in accordance with the several categories of mental faculties. Hence, there is a perceptional, an intellectual, an emotional, and a volitional insanity, corresponding to the four divisions of the mind.
>
> (Hammond, 1883, p. 286)

In this textbook, he adopts this system with slight modifications. Here are his definitions:

> Perceptional Insanities – Insanities in which there are derangements of one or more of the perceptions... II. Intellectual Insanities – Forms in which the chief manifestations of mental disorder relate to the intellect, being of the nature of false conceptions (delusions), or clearly abnormal conceptions... III. Emotional Insanities – Forms in which the mental derangement is chiefly exhibited with regard to the emotions.... IV. Volitional Insanities – Forms characterized by derangement of the will, either by its abnormal predominance or inertia.
>
> (Hammond, 1883, pp. 292–293)

While I provide here four Anglophonic sources on the role of faculty psychology in framing nineteenth-century psychiatric nosology, let me give two quotes from secondary sources which place these trends in a broader historical context. In reviewing developments in early to mid-twentieth century psychiatric nosology, Radden traces key categories back to Continental philosophical traditions:

> The distinction between affective and more cognitive disorders mirrors one of the entrenched – we would now say "modernist" – philosophical classifications which dominated seventeenth-, eighteenth- and nineteenth-century thought in the West, in particular, the contrast between Passion or Emotion, and Reason or Cognition. In Kantian theory and subsequent "Kantianism," this duality is associated with – and often reified through – a pervasive faculty psychology. The distinct categories of affect and cognition were understood to reflect distinct, independent functions. Increasingly these came to be regarded as distinct parts of the human mind, and later, to be identified with distinct areas of the brain.
>
> (Radden, 1996, p. 3)

In discussing the origins of the diagnostic categories of psychosis, Berrios writes

> The rebirth of faculty psychology during the early part of the 19th century was to offer for the first time a new possibility of classification. Insanities could be classed as intellectual, emotional or volitional (moral), according to what faculty was assumed to be involved.
>
> (Berrios, 1987, p. 491)

From this historical sketch, I conclude, with some confidence, that faculty psychology played a significant and likely quite central role in the efforts by alienists/psychiatrists working in the eighteenth, nineteenth and early twentieth centuries to develop scientifically useful and clinically meaningful diagnostic categories of the insane patients they were seeing (Grob, 2011; Scull, 2005; Engstrom, 2003; Goldstein, 1987).

38.2.1 Causal Relationships between Disordered Faculties

Let me now turn to my second point, i.e., that psychiatric nosologists had to figure out a way to deal with causal influences of one disordered faculty on another. Today, many of the severely psychiatric ill patients present with abnormalities both in the reasoning (i.e., they describe delusional beliefs) and in mood or emotions (i.e., prominent depressive or manic symptoms and signs). Such cases are also frequently described in textbooks of psychiatry from the nineteenth century. So, our alienist precursors would often have confronted patients with abnormalities in several faculties (especially cognition and mood). In figuring out a nosology to describe them, they had to develop a way to understand how these faculty disturbances causally interrelated to each other.

To illustrate this story, let me first turn to the major German mid-nineteenth century figure of Wilhelm Griesinger, the first university professor of "psychiatry" in Europe. In his section on Elementary Disorders in Mental Disease from his textbook (2nd edition, translation published 1867) he writes, describing delusional ideas as commonly having two possible emotional themes "...joyous, sublime, brilliant ideas ... [or] somber, sad, and painful" (Griesinger, 1867, p. 71). How then do delusions emerge from these primary mood states? He writes

> The false ideas and conclusions, which are attempts at explanation and vindications of the actual disposition [mood]... are spontaneously developed in the diseased mind according to the law of causality ... At first the delirious [delusional] conceptions are fleeting; the I perceives them, it may be terrified by them, acknowledge their absurdity, and yet feel quite unable to rid itself of them, and struggles with them; gradually, by continued repetition, they gain more body and form, repel opposing ideas and form connections with similar masses of perceptions of the I; then they become constituent parts of it, and the patient cannot divest himself of them...
>
> (Griesinger, 1867,p. 71)

In a psychologically sophisticated manner, Griesinger describes a process whereby persistent severe depressed or euphoric mood could produce first transient cognitive distortions (that is "false ideas") that develop under continued "affective pressure" to become delusions (that is "constituent parts" of their mental functioning). So, Griesinger is, I suggest, proposing a mood → cognition cross-faculty causal pathway in this passage.

To review a quite different formulation, we turn to the writings of Friedrich Scholz in his 1892 textbook (translated from the German by Astrid Klee and KSK) (Scholz, 1892). In his chapter on paranoia (German – Verrücktheit – which at this time referred to a broad class of nonaffective delusional psychoses), he begins, in accord with decades of earlier writers, by dividing up the cases into primary and secondary paranoia. Secondary paranoia is, he notes, always "an outcome stage for the unhealed affective insanity (Affekt-Irresein)." That is, like Griesinger, he hypotheses a mood → cognition cross-faculty causal pathway for secondary paranoia.

In describing primary paranoia, he writes

> Paranoia is distinct from melancholia and mania mainly in its lack of affect. This, of course, does not mean that there is no change in mood at all. Instead, all perceptions as a whole and the vehemence with which they impose themselves onto consciousness are always determined by

> the contents of the delusions (Wahnvorstellungen). The paranoid patient may also be sad, cheerful or angry, like a healthy person who reacts naturally to perceptions, irrespective of whether they are objectively true or erroneous. However, pathological affects with inhibition or acceleration of psychological activity do not occur. Due to the lack of affective foundation, paranoid delusions (Wahnideen) are distinct from melancholic and manic delusions.

In our framework, Scholz is postulating a cognition → mood cross-faculty causal pathway for primary paranoia. In this syndrome, mood disturbances arise from the delusional content. If an affected individual has grandiose delusions, perceives everyone bowing to him in the streets and worshiping him, it is understandable, he claims, that he might develop a euphoric mood. On the other hand, if he has persecutory delusions, and most people he meets in public are derisive, critical and threatening, it is understandable that he may become irritable, aggressive and possibly depressed. But, he claims, such moods do not indicate a primary "pathological affect." So, in his final sentence, he makes the clear distinction between paranoid delusions which are primarily a result of disturbances in the cognitive facilities and melancholic or manic delusions, which arise via a mood → cognition pathway from primary affective disturbances.

We now turn to the pre-eminent nosologist Emil Kraepelin in the opening paragraph of his chapter on Paranoia (Verrücktheit) from his famous 6th edition (Kraepelin, 1899, 1990). It was in this edition that he provided, for the first time, his mature vision of both dementia praecox and manic-depressive insanity. Echoing themes from Scholz, we quote him in full here:

> A great number of German psychiatrists group all those functional mental diseases where the disorder chiefly or exclusively concerns the fields of mental activity ["cognition"] under the name of paranoia. Therefore, the occurrence of delusions and hallucinations is considered the essential characteristic of this disease. The true cause of this vague definition is to be found in the history of its origin. According to Griesinger's older theory, paranoia was always the outcome of a preceding affective mental disorder. Only the investigations of Snell, Westphal and Sander resulted in the general recognition "primary" form of paranoia. Under the influence of this undeniable progress, the new form of disease as a primary illness of the mind was opposed to mania and melancholia where the decisive disorders were considered to be in the field of emotional life. The emotional variations occasionally observed in the first form were supposed to be exclusively brought about "secondarily"

> through the intervention of delusions or hallucinations, just as the occurrence of the disorders of reason in affective diseases were believed to be derived as mere consequences from the primary cheerful or sad changes in mood. This is why it was of major importance for the prognosis to know in the individual case whether disorders in affect or in reason had formed the starting point of the pathological symptoms.

Kraepelin is clear in his exposition about the diagnostic importance of causal relations between disorders of the faculty of cognition and mood. He distinguished delusional cases where the illness began with a disorder "in affect" as Griesinger had first suggested from those which began with a disorder "in reason" as Scholz postulates.

Lest we think that the issues I raise here are merely dusty irrelevances of nineteenth-century alienism, I have two final points to make in this section, one small and one large. For the small one, I quote from the *DSM-5*, published in 2013 (American Psychiatric Association, 2013, p. 186). One of the multiple specifiers listed for the diagnosis of depressive disorders (and mania which we don't here examine) is "with psychotic features." Two types are listed which are defined as follows:

> **With mood-congruent psychotic features:** the content of all the delusions and hallucinations is consistent with the typical depressive themes of personal inadequacy, guilt, disease, death, nihilism or deserved punishment.
>
> **With mood-incongruent psychotic features:** the content of all the delusions and hallucinations is consistent does not involve typical depressive themes of personal inadequacy, guilt, disease, death, nihilism or deserved punishment...

Mood-congruent psychotic features are directly analogous to what Kraepelin saw as a result of "disorders ... considered to be in the field of emotional life," that is by a mood → cognition pathway. By contrast, mood-incongruent features cannot be understood in that causal framework, with the implications that they reflect, at least partially, a primary disorder of cognition.

Now to the large point. Our sketchy story suggests that the leading faculties that European alienists were concerned with through most of the nineteenth century were cognition and emotion. (Volition was also an important faculty but plays a minor role in this sketch). In 1899, Kraepelin's 6th edition divided the hitherto rather disorganized nosology of major psychiatric disorders into two broad categories: dementia praecox and manic-depressive illness. Might there be a relationship between these two observations? Berrios and Radden both think so. In at least two of his essays (Berrios, 1987; Berrios & Hauser, 1988), Berrios makes this point explicit – that Kraepelin's nosology – dividing the broad array of psychotic disorders into one form that emphasizes problems of thinking and perceiving (dementia praecox) and another on disorders of mood (manic-depressive illness) was not an accident but a direct result of the increasing influence of faculty psychology in psychiatric thinking. Berrios specifically traces this back to Kant and his contributions to faculty psychology (Berrios & Hauser, 1988). So, assuming these scholars are broadly correct, faculty psychology was not only important at the fringes of psychiatric nosology (e.g., defining possible subtypes of paranoia), but rather was central to what is widely considered the most prominent hallmark of modern psychiatric nosology – the distinction between dementia praecox and manic-depressive insanity.

38.3 PART 2: A SCHEMA FOR THE DEVELOPMENT OF PSYCHIATRIC NOSOLOGY

The naïve Whigish view of the history of psychiatric nosology is that our diagnostic concepts arose from a raw inductive process practiced by the great clinicians of the nineteenth century culminating in Kraepelin. They carefully examined and followed over years large numbers of hospitalized patients with severe illness. From these observations, they developed, by an intuitive sorting system from raw clinical data, our diagnoses. One explicit example of this is Kraepelin taking hundreds of his "index cards" to his holiday home in the Alps as he worked on new editions of his textbook. This is how he describes this process:

> I went through all the available index cards relating to the different pathological forms I had to refer to. The index cards contained in a very condensed resume of all essential information on each case. . .. The most similar cares were collected into larger or smaller groups and the clinical characteristics of these subtype were defined more precisely.
>
> (Kraepelin, 1987, p. 156)

He then described looking at the tentative groupings as a function of heredity, external causes, age, sex, course and outcome. By examining these external variables, "I gained criteria to judge whether the trial group arrangement was justified or should be altered" (Kraepelin, 1987, p. 156).

I have outlined elsewhere, from a study of many psychiatric textbooks from 1900 to 1960, that there is a robust connection between the categories of dementia praecox/schizophrenia, mania and depression as articulated by Kraepelin in his 1899 6th edition and the relevant *DSM* categories (Kendler, 2016a, 2016b, 2017a). So, a possible history of psychiatric nosology path would look something like

Symptoms, signs, course of illness → Clinical syndromes → *DSM* categories

This framework, which can be characterized as a raw inductivist account, is overly simplistic. Human behavior, whether healthy or disturbed, is far too complex for simple induction to possibly work. I am, of course, here simply restating a popular view in the philosophy of science about the "theory-laden" nature of observations – that they are always impacted upon by the theoretical presuppositions of the investigator – here our nineteenth-century alienist.

But we have an interesting wrinkle here regarding the theory-laden nature of observations. Typically, this point is made about observations in the physical world as in astronomy or biology. But here, the object of observations is "us" – that is other humans. The everyday person does not likely have strongly held specific theories about star formation, electron clouds or the evolution of species of *Drosophila melanogaster*. But as humans, we all develop, from a very early age, theories about how other humans "work." Such theories are critical to our survival, our ability to mate, make friends, get along with our chairperson and obtain tenure. Often such theories are referred to as "folk psychology."

So, I suggest that our great nineteenth-century alienist clinicians could not approach their task of developing a nosology for their patients without some theory to organize their observations. I have produced evidence that a good number of them relied on what we might see as a common-sense elaboration of folk psychology into the concept of mental faculties or what we could call "faculty psychology." This means that we need to modify our diagram as follows:

Symptoms, signs, course → Faculty Psychology → Clinical syndromes → *DSM* categories

But our readings suggest tentatively a further modification. There is good evidence that many alienists wanted to base their faculty theories not on generic folk wisdom, but rather the writings of philosophers who had posed specific faculty psychology theories. As one example, I quote a passage from Wyman whom we met above:

> Mental philosophy, then, is an indispensable study of an accomplished physician. Such are the mutual dependencies and influences of the mental and organic functions, that diseases of either cannot be well treated without a knowledge of both. But I would not go back to the vagaries of the ancient metaphysicians. It is sufficient to begin with Locke, and proceed with Brown, Stewart, and Reid.
>
> (Wyman, 1830, pp. 8–9)

We can call this roughly a "Philosophic Theory" by which I mean a developed theory about how best to understand what the mind does. So, our picture would now look like this:

Philosophic Theories

↓

Symptoms, signs, course → Faculty Psychology → Clinical syndromes → *DSM* categories

But, as I suggest above, we are not quite finished. The model needs to be more complex because our alienist forbearers frequently saw patients who demonstrated dysfunction in several faculties. To build a nosology, they had to develop a way to nosologically assign such patients. They did that largely by proposing tentative causal interrelationships between the faculties. Assume we have mental faculties A and B, the disturbances of which produced psychiatric disorders a and b. If we see a patient with disturbances of both A and B, the argument is that if we can show that the causal link went A → B, then the patient should be assigned a diagnosis of a. However, if the causal link went B → A, then the correct diagnosis was b.

While I do not have space here to adequately defend my position, I want to suggest that they used two major methods: the folk psychological reasoning outlined above (e.g., when I am sad my view of the world gets distorted negatively and if the mood change is severe and persistent, that can develop into delusions) and something not previously introduced in this discussion: longitudinal observation. These were rare in writers before the late nineteenth century but became particularly prominent in the work of Kraepelin. He was the master of the longitudinal study and used this data in forming his nosology (Kendler, 2018). I suggest, but cannot prove, that the folk psychological reasoning used by the alienist can be best explained by an extrapolation to psychiatric ill individuals of our everyday observations of ourselves, our loved ones, and our friends and colleagues. Think of all the common attributions we make about the behavior of the humans around us in a week. We often assume changes in "reasoning" on the basis of "mood" (my wife is being especially critical of my being home late because she is irritable from her hip hurting all day) and changes in "mood" on the basis of cognitive content (my assistant is especially happy in our meeting today because he is expecting a positive evaluation.) This is the stuff of our lived human lives. It is hard for me to imagine that our alienist ancestors would *not* use these kinds of approaches in understanding the behaviors of their insane patients?

So, the final sketch of this historical story looks as follows:

Philosophy of Mind ↓ Temporal Observation and Folk Psychological Attribution ↓

Symptoms, signs, course → Faculty Psychology → Causal Attribution → Clinical syndromes → *DSM* categories.

38.4 PART 3: IMPLICATIONS FOR OUR THEORY OF THE LEVELS OF PSYCHIATRIC INQUIRY

So, what then do we learn from this sketch of a story about the role of levels in the history of nosology? A levels analysis of the naïve story, especially as told by "hard-nosed" biological psychiatrists, would look something like this

Raw clinical observations → *DSM* syndromes → Biological research to understand brain etiologies.

Note that this is a "mindless" story. The biological psychiatric paradigm can be understood as getting "straight to the biology" of psychiatric illness.

But the story I have told looks quite different. Instead of biological psychiatrists getting "straight to the biology" of the syndromes defined from raw clinical facts, the syndromes they are researching reflect clinical observations *translated through* mentalistic constructs of how philosophers divided up the major functions of the human mind into faculties and the folk psychology of causal attribution in human behaviors.

The naïve story assumes a simplistic inductivist approach as if our alienist forebears could observe and classify their patients from raw clinical observations without any theory of mental functioning to guide and organize their perceptions. This is implausible and not supported by the texts we have reviewed.

I suggest that the naïve story of the origin of our nosology is false. What then are the implications of this on the reductionist agenda of the "hard" biological psychiatrists? Does it undermine their goal of keeping psychiatry on a neurobiological level, free of the "softness" and uncertainties of the mental world?

What we can be reasonably confident of is that the pathway to biological discoveries about the etiology of our *DSM* categories have "passed through" a mentalist level that was required to define these disorders. I cannot help but be amused at thinking about how such a hard-nosed neurobiologist psychiatric researcher – who would react with scorn about suggestions that philosophy had anything to teach psychiatry – would respond to the revelation that the creation of the categories which she is investigating were substantially influenced by the writing on mental functioning by philosophers!

The hard reductionists may wish to eschew psychological or sociological levels of inquiry about psychiatric disorders, arguing that they are at the "wrong level" to provide useful etiologic insights. But the force of that argument is somewhat undermined by the argument I have made here that the origin of these categories is inextricably linked with the mental world.

At the other extreme, the mentalistic origin of our diagnostic categories should provide at least some solace to those whose scientific work focused on the role of psychological processes in the etiology and treatment of these disorders.

There are two elephants in the room that we need to acknowledge before concluding. The first is "Where do we situate RDoC – examined in several other chapters in this volume – in this story?" RDoC postulates five domains: (i) Negative Valence Systems, (ii) Positive Valence Systems, (iii) Cognitive Systems, (iv) Systems for Social Processes and (v) Arousal/Regulatory Systems. Do these domains seem eerily reminiscent of earlier faculty psychological systems? The domains – rows in the RDoC matrix – are defined by Insel et al. as representing "various constructs grouped hierarchically into broad domains of function (e.g., negative emotionality, cognition)." (Insel et al., 2010) (Is it accidental that he refers here to the two faculties that dominated psychiatric nosology in the late nineteenth century?) Our faculties are defined as "separate inherent powers" of the mind. While not a perfect match surely, these definitions seem somewhat related, although I cannot claim any deep knowledge about the degree of historical connection between the two.

What are the implications of this potential homology for our story? Can we suggest (as food for thought rather than as any definitive claim) an historical drama of psychiatric nosology in three acts? These would be: (i) eighteenth and early nineteenth-century philosophers proposed a faculty psychology which articulated specific mental functions, (ii) these functions served as the basis for the major psychiatric nosologic systems of the late nineteenth century and (iii) the categories created by these systems were seen as too heterogeneous to support research progress and so the NIMH proposed to switch the research focus to an early twenty-first century version of a neuropsychology and systems neuroscience-informed faculty psychology.

The second elephant in the room is "How well do the faculty psychological and causal mentalistic theories utilized in the creation of psychiatric diagnoses actually capture, in a meaningful fashion, underlying neurobiological processes?" Insel claims that his RDoC domains – which have some likely parallels with our faculties are created in part because of their relationship with known underlying neurobiological and genetic mechanisms. Certainly, systems neuroscience has been able to trace specific pathways in rodents, primates and sometimes humans that underlie various emotions such as anxiety and disgust. Progress on a more abstract "faculty" will likely be harder but progress is being made. I suspect that the understanding of pathways underlying higher cognitive concepts like "belief" are in a much earlier stage so success is harder to judge. As an informed non-expert, I would suggest some likely parallels between our faculty psychological functions and the underlying neurobiology of the human mind/brain system.

But what about the hypothesized mental causation from emotion to cognition or cognition to emotion? Could these be easy or even possible to understand neurobiologically? This, of course, puts us in the middle of the mind-body problem and the casual relationships over time between mental and brain states, a nearly perpetual conundrum. I regard this issue as largely terra incognita to this day.

In conclusion, this project needs further work and a deeper rooting in a wider array of historical texts and a deeper reading in the literature on faculty psychology. My hope is that, nonetheless, this essay has shed some useful light on our current debates about which levels are optimally appropriate for the understanding of psychiatric illness. This discussion has largely been rooted in the long-running debate about the applicability of current research approaches from molecular neuroscience through epidemiology. I argue here that we seem to have forgotten, in our "presentist" focus, that part of this discussion should also consider the "levels" involved in the conceptual birth of our diagnostic categories. I hope this essay has contributed to a strengthening of this historical voice. Knowing where we have been is nearly always helpful in understanding where we are.

REFERENCES

Albrecht, F. M. (1970) 'A reappraisal of faculty psychology.' *Journal of the History of the Behavioral Sciences, 6*, 36–40.

American Psychiatric Association. (1980) *Diagnostic and Statistical Manual of Mental Disorders* (3rd ed.). Washington, DC: American Psychiatric Association.

(2013) *Diagnostic and Statistical Manual of Mental Disorders: DSM-5* (5th ed.). Washington, DC: American Psychiatric Association.

Berrios, G. E. (1987) 'Historical aspects of psychoses: 19th century issues.' *British Medical Bulletin, 43*, 484–498.

Berrios, G. E. & Hauser, R. (1988) 'The early development of Kraepelin's ideas on classification: A conceptual history.' *Psychological Medicine, 18*, 813–821.

Brooks, G. P. (1976) 'The faculty psychology of Thomas Reid.' *Journal of the History of the Behavioral Sciences, 12*, 65–77.

Cullen, W. (1808) *A Methodical System of Nosology*. Translated from Latin by Dr. Eldad Lewis. Stockbridge, MA: Cornelius Sturtevant.

Eigen, J. P. (2016) *Mad-Doctors in the Dock: Defending the Diagnosis, 1760–1913* (1st ed.). Baltimore, MD: Johns Hopkins University Press.

Engstrom, E. J. (2003) *Clinical Psychiatry in Imperial Germany: A History of Psychiatric Practice*. Ithaca, NY: Cornell University Press.

Goldstein, J. (1987) *Console and Classify: The French Psychiatric Profession in the Nineteenth Century*. New York: Cambridge University Press.

Gregory, R. L. (1987) *The Oxford Companion to the Mind*. Oxford and New York: Oxford University Press.

Griesinger, W. (1867) *Mental Pathology and Therapeutics*. London: The New Sydenham Society.

Grob, G. N. (2011) *The Mad among Us: A History of the Care of America's Mentally Ill* (1st ed.). New York: The Free Press.

Hammond, W. A. (1883) *A Treatise on Insanity in Its Medical Relations*. New York: D. Appleton and Company.

Hilgard, E. R. (1980) 'The trilogy of mind: Cognition, affection, and conation.' *Journal of the History of the Behavioral Sciences, 16*, 107–117.

Insel, T., Cuthbert, B., Garvey, M., Heinssen, R., Pine, D. S., Quinn, K. et al. (2010) 'Research domain criteria (RDoC): Toward a new classification framework for research on mental disorders.' *American Journal of Psychiatry, 167*, 748–751.

Kendler, K. S. (2016a) 'Phenomenology of schizophrenia and the representativeness of modern diagnostic criteria.' *JAMA Psychiatry, 73*, 1082–1092.

(2016b) 'The phenomenology of major depression and the representativeness and nature of DSM criteria.' *American Journal of Psychiatry, 173*, 771–780.

(2016c) 'The phenomenology of schizophrenia and the representativeness of modern diagnostic criteria.' *JAMA Psychiatry, 73*(10), 1082.

(2017a) 'The clinical features of mania and their representation in modern diagnostic criteria.' *Psychological Medicine, 47*, 1013–1029.

(2017b) 'The clinical features of paranoia in the 20th century and their representation in diagnostic criteria from DSM-III through DSM-5.' *Schizophrenia Bulletin, 43*, 332–343.

(2018) 'The development of Kraepelin's mature diagnostic concepts of paranoia (Die Verrücktheit) and paranoid dementia Praecox (Dementia Paranoides): A close reading of his textbooks from 1887 to 1899.' *JAMA Psychiatry*, *75*(12), 1280–1288.

Kraepelin, E. (1899) *Psychiatrie: Ein Lehrbuch fur Studirende und Aerzte* (6th ed., 2 vols.). Leipzig: Barth.

(1987) *Memoirs*. Berlin: Springer-Verlag.

(1990) *Psychiatry: A Textbook for Students and Physicians* (Volume 2: Clinical Psychiatry), J. Quen (ed.) (Translation of the 6th Edition of Psychiatrie, Translator Volume 2 – Sabine Ayed). Canton, MA: Science History Publications.

Müller-Freienfels, R. (1935) *The Evolution of Modern Psychology* (1st ed.). New Haven: Yale University Press.

Noble, D. (1853) *Elements of Psychological Medicine: An Introduction to the Practical Study of Insanity, Adapted for Students and Junior Practitioners*. London: John Churchill.

Radden, J. (1996) 'Lumps and bumps: Kantian faculty psychology, phrenology, and twentieth-century psychiatric classification.' *Philosophy, Psychiatry and Psychology*, 3, 1–14.

Scholz, F. (1892) *Lehrbuch der Irrenheilkunde: Für Aerzte und Studirende*. Leipzig: Eduard Heinrich Mayer (Einhorn & Jäger).

Scull, A. (2005) *Most Solitary of Afflictions: Madness and Society in Britain, 1700–1900*. New Haven, CT: Yale University Press.

Wyman, R. (1830) *A Discourse on Mental Philosophy as Connected with Mental Disease: Delivered Before the Massachusetts Medical Society, June 2, 1830*. Boston, MA: Daily Advertiser.

39

Commentary on "The Impact of Faculty Psychology and Theories of Psychological Causation on the Origins of Modern Psychiatric Nosology"

GREGORY A. MILLER

Kendler's essay (Chapter 38), on which I have been asked to comment, prepares us for the radical case that his essay goes on to make about the continuity of important themes across the history of modern psychiatric nosology. Respecting centuries-old terminology, he discusses psychological "faculties" – a set of theoretically or at least traditionally differentiated categories of mental operations that constitute "faculty psychology." His analysis shows that the major outlines of modern psychiatric nosology became mainstream in the nineteenth century and, remarkably, have changed little since then. His analysis focuses on the *DSM* tradition, but he also raises questions about the much more recent Research Domain Criteria (RDoC) initiative of the U.S. National Institute of Mental Health, which I will address.

Scholars of faculty psychology, with more or less interest in psychopathology as conceived and perceived in their time, differed somewhat in

Based on an invited lecture presented at the "Philosophical Issues in Psychiatry V: The Problems of Multiple Levels, Explanatory Pluralism, Reduction and Emergence" conference, Copenhagen, May 29, 2018. This chapter benefited from the formal lectures and oral commentaries as well as the informal discussions at the conference and from comments by Morgan E. Bartholomew, Bruce N. Cuthbert, Paul B. Sharp, and Peter Zachar on an earlier draft of this written commentary. This chapter is dedicated to Michael J. Kozak, recently deceased, who contributed broadly and deeply to many scholars' conceptualizations of psychopathology, including the psychology/biology controversies engaged here, and who contributed substantially to early stages of the RDoC initiative. The author acknowledges current support from grant R01 MH110544S1 from the U.S. National Institute of Mental Health to Gregory A. Miller, Keith H. Nuechterlein, and Cindy M. Yee-Bradbury. The author is a member of the U.S. National Institute of Health (NIH) National Advisory Mental Health Council (NAMHC) and is one of two co-chairs of its Workgroup for Revisions to the RDoC Matrix. The views expressed herein are those of the author and do not necessarily reflect the official policy or position of NIH or its NAMHC.

the map of faculties offered to characterize mental function and dysfunction. Kendler (Chapter 38) shows that the differences were small, with scholars commonly relying on two, sometimes three, broad faculties that in modern terminology we would call cognition and emotion. A premise of that early scholarship was that cognition and emotion are distinct domains of mental function – a categorical framing. Furthermore, for the major scholars Kendler discusses, mental disorder was not just a matter of degrees of dysfunction in the two domains. A given type of dysfunction was frequently assigned exclusively to one domain. Accordingly, the map of disorder was organized categorically. Those scholar clinicians could have conceived of such a map dimensionally – identifying multiple dimensions (conceptually distinct axes, not necessarily orthogonal, but in the same space) and placing a given normal or clinical phenomenon (a symptom, a syndrome, an entire disorder) somewhere in that multidimensional space. But the dominant practice was to assign a given phenomenon and its causal domain to either cognition or emotion (e.g., the occasional term "affective psychosis").

The simplicity of such a cognition/emotion dichotomy in psychopathology has considerable appeal. Even within frameworks focused on emotion, scholars have proposed several ways of parsing emotional phenomena using distinct categories or dimensions that can and usually do co-occur. Large portions of modern scholarship on emotion similarly assume one of two (sometimes overtly competing) models. In one view, there is a small set of distinct core emotion categories (joy, fear, etc.), with arguments about whether there are six (Ekman) or nine (Izard) or some other number of categories. In the other view, there is a small set of core dimensions that describe the space in which diverse emotional phenomena occur, with arguments about the labels but rarely about the number of dimensions, often labeled valence, arousal, and dominance (Osgood, Suci, & Tannenbaum, 1957, with successors in this tradition often emphasizing the former two such as Heller, 1993; Lang, Bradley, & Cuthbert, 1990; Russell, 1980, 2003). Zachar (2006; Zachar & Ellis, 2012) provided systematic discussions of categorical vs. dimensional approaches to emotion.

The categorical view of emotions allows that "blends" (co-occurrences) of distinct emotions occur, but the premise remains that the fundamental emotions themselves are distinct. Not being on dimensions, they cannot be summarized via a Euclidean distance score, positioning a given experience or syndrome at a particular distance from some default emotional status or from some other emotion blend. But dimensionally inclined scholars have no problem plotting such blends of categorically conceived emotions in multidimensional space. Authors using a dimensional view of emotion sometimes rotate the valence and arousal axes, yielding a dimension of positive affect and a dimension of negative affect (e.g., Watson & Tellegen, 1985), but the two sets of axes are readily intertranslatable. Authors sometimes declare one or the other set of axes pair superior, either more parsimonious or at least a better fit to some scope of data, but in fact there are so many data in support of each axis pair that pursuit of such a dispute in order to declare a victor is unproductive (Miller et al., 2013). Let the rotations continue.

Both in common/folk psychology and in the academy, the language of both ways of parsing emotional phenomena is widespread. But emotion remains almost always distinct from cognition, although the need for such segregation has been questioned (Miller, 1996, 2010). Modern psychiatric nosology almost always assumes a categorical model, and Kendler demonstrates in his review of a variety of nineteenth-century and earlier psychiatric scholars that cognition and emotion are the dominant categories that structured their thinking. To his examples, we can add Hume (1738): "We speak not strictly and philosophically when we talk of the combat of passion and of reason. Reason is, and ought only to be the slave of the passions, and can never pretend to any other office than to serve and obey them."

The long-running dispute between categorical and dimensional models of emotion strongly parallels the dispute between categorical and dimensional models of psychopathology. The fact that most instances of emotion can readily be placed in both the categorical model or the dimensional model has, oddly, not led to the victory of one model or a merger of the two. Similarly, the *DSM* and ICD diagnostic frameworks are thoroughly categorical, yet researchers commonly supplement them with dimensional rating instruments – now ironically more often touted *because of* their transcategorical value – and recent biological research on psychopathology almost uniformly employs dimensional dependent variables. The latter discrepancy sets up a fundamental problem. The faith that biological reductionism in psychopathology research will lead us to the right categorical structure, widespread across the Decades of the Brain (Miller, 2010) with echoes in a longer and broader history in science (e.g., Keating & Cambrosio, 2004), stumbles when categorical diagnoses are studied with dimensional measures (biological or psychological). Unless the histograms of data provide clear cutpoints, continuous distributions of dependent variables raise doubts about stark categorical distinctions in our independent variables – our diagnostic concepts.

As *DSM-5* (American Psychiatric Association, 2013) was taking shape, a number of clinical scientists tried valiantly to bridge this divide, especially in the domain of personality disorders, but this effort was ultimately rejected by the American Psychiatric Association leadership. Zachar, Krueger, and Kendler (2016, p. 1) set the stage for the fascinating and somewhat tragic story they reported:

> At the beginning of the *DSM-5* revision process, it was widely expected that the personality disorders would have a dimensional component. In the closing weeks of the revision process those with final authority decided that the categorical personality disorder model contained in *DSM-IV* would be reprinted in *DSM-5* – with essentially no changes to the criteria. A hybrid model containing dimensions and categories that was intended to be the new *DSM-5* model is printed in a section on 'Emerging Measures and Models'.

Zachar, Regier, and Kendler (2019) document the enthusiasm for bringing dimensions to other portions of *DSM-5* early in its development, though those efforts were later abandoned.

Just two weeks before the American Psychiatric Association debuted *DSM-5*, the Director of the National Institute of Mental Health, psychiatrist Thomas Insel, blogged that, essentially, the *DSM* series was of little value and that "Patients with mental disorders deserve better" than *DSM-5* (www.nimh.nih.gov/about/director/2013/transforming-diagnosis.shtml). This attack prompted a furious response and eventually a superficial peace, but it pushed further apart adherents to the categorical tradition embodied in the *DSMs* and advocates of dimensional representations of psychopathology. In particular, it turned some traditional opinion leaders in academic psychiatry against NIMH's RDoC initiative (Cuthbert & Insel, 2010, 2013; Cuthbert & Kozak, 2013; Insel et al., 2010; Kozak & Cuthbert, 2016; Sanislow et al., 2010) and its emphasis on dimensional constructs and measures, even though, as noted above, dimensional constructs and measures were by then widespread in psychiatric research, if not practice.

This dispute is critical background for the thoughtful questions Kendler (Chapter 38) asks about RDoC. A fair appraisal of RDoC requires putting aside what had become a political turf dispute (would the American Psychiatric Association or the National Institute of Mental Health determine what is worthy in psychopathology research and practice?). Frances (2014, p. 48), the leader of the *DSM-IV* development effort, noted about NIMH Director Insel's post shortly before the release of *DSM-V* in 2013: "Although the RDoC strategy is sound and necessary, the way it was recently announced to the public was badly muddled – misleading, poorly timed, and damaging to the credibility of both NIMH and the practice of clinical psychiatry." The ensuing firestorm fostered diverse misrepresentations of RDoC (for discussions of such distortions of RDoC see Lake, Yee, & Miller, 2017; Miller, Rockstroh, Hamilton, & Yee, 2016; Miller & Yee, 2015; Yee, Javitt, & Miller, 2015).

RDoC is a fresh bootstrapping using the nineteenth-century faculty psychology that (as Kendler, Chapter 38, shows) underlies the *DSMs* to provide an initial set of driving psychological constructs. Thus, RDoC's Cognitive Systems, Positive Valence Systems, and Negative Valence Systems domains trace directly to the cognition and emotion dichotomy of nineteenth-century faculty psychology, with the valence dimension foregrounded to begin to subdivide emotion. In each domain, RDoC elaborates a broad super-construct (such as cognition) into more specific constructs (such as perception, language, declarative memory, working memory, cognitive control) and in some cases subconstructs, using modern psychological and biological science, especially evidence of neural circuits, as criteria to determine which psychological constructs have sufficient research support for generative inclusion in the RDoC matrix.

Crucial to understanding the relationship between *DSM* and RDoC approaches is that RDoC is not conceived as a nosological system, attempting to characterize psychopathology. It is an experimental framework attempting to identify phenomena that contribute to psychopathology and to foster that identification process. The matrix that the RDoC initiative produced and continues to refine is not a map of psychopathology. One should not ask of it, as some have, "where does a diagnosis of X fit?" Furthermore, one cannot fault it simply for not offering much about a given traditionally defined disorder. What goes in the RDoC matrix reflects consensus judgments that the research literature has produced a meaningful confluence of (1) psychological construct(s) and (2) biological and psychological data.

The RDoC matrix does not (yet) attempt to be comprehensive. Important clinical phenomena for which clear psychological constructs and adequate understanding of supporting circuits are lacking are intentionally left out until the science advances to clarify and substantiate relevant psychological and biological mechanisms. In contrast, *DSM-III*, *DSM-IV*, and *DSM-5* were not driven by twentieth-century (let alone twenty-first-century) neuroscience. They were developed in hopes that a reliable and eventually valid descriptive map of clinical phenomena (almost entirely psychological) would lead to a valid biological map, one so sound and tractable that many believed that the field could do without psychological constructs. However, with Kendler showing that the *DSM* map is based heavily on nineteenth-century folk psychology instead (see also Lang, 1984), it is not surprising that the *DSMs'* biological yield has been so paltry (Frances, 2013, 2014; Hyman, 2010; Lilienfeld & Treadway, 2016; Yee et al., 2015; many others).

RDoC's eventual yield may or may not be better. Its fresh start, however, harvests decades of psychological and biological research filtered through the stark criterion of confinement to psychological constructs for which there is a good story about the implementing neural circuitry. Cuthbert (2014, p. 28) wrote that the RDoC initiative seeks "fundamental circuit-based behavioral dimensions. . .useful for eventual clinical work." By design, RDoC sacrificed initial comprehensiveness (and thus adequate utility for clinical practice) in order to deploy a richer psychological construct map with strong biological support.

In contrast, the *DSM* series has not merely been unsuccessful in fostering science that vastly improves clinical practice; Kendler's (Chapter 38) analysis of the historical roots of the *DSM* tradition in faculty psychology reveals a major factor that has undermined the *DSMs*' ability to reach its biological aspirations. Rather than basing *DSM* categories or symptoms substantially on the best available psychological and biological science, *DSM* has remained thoroughly grounded in earlier clinical traditions and has also been limited by the understandable practical need to try to cover the full terrain that practicing clinicians deal with. Lacking compelling (validating) biological findings, many proponents of the *DSM* tradition have declared its connection to biology by fiat, such as by announcing that psychopathology is a brain disease (see Miller, 2010, for examples). At present, there are no compelling empirical grounds for this claim, against which there are significant logical barriers. Ironically, the most successful enterprises mapping biological implementations of psychological disorders require psychological/algorithmic accounts (Sharp & Eldar, 2019). Reliance on *DSM* categories has understandably been unsuccessful in fostering research connections between clinical phenomena characterized in (old-fashioned folk) psychological terms and modern biological findings. Again, RDoC starts where research has already connected psychological and biological constructs and phenomena. It thus has an almost unfair head start in fostering discovery of biological maps in psychopathology, in that what goes into the RDoC matrix is held to a standard of biological support to which entries in the *DSM*s are not held.

In preparation for responding further to Kendler's (Chapter 38) questions about RDoC, it can be noted that RDoC has what may seem to be surprising roots in the troubled efforts that produced *DSM-5*. Zachar et al. (2019) document that at the outset *DSM-5* leadership advocated a paradigm shift, argued that "*DSM-IV* constructs misrepresent psychopathology by defining disorders as pure categorical types," and convened a 1999 conference "at which participants were encouraged to think beyond the *DSM-IV* framework, especially with respect to data emerging from genetics and neuroscience. . ." Such an effort to ground a map of psychopathology in the best available biology – without necessarily hoping to reduce psychopathology (which is inherently psychological) to biology – presages a central tenet of the RDoC initiative. Zachar et al. describe what unfolded in the development of *DSM-5* when that goal was lost, leading them to conclude that significant advancement of the *DSM* series awaits "substantial scientific breakthroughs in biomarker availability," which is part of what RDoC is built to foster.

Crucial to the nature of RDoC is its avoidance of the hyperbiological reductionism often associated with modern *DSMs'* brand. (*DSM-III* and *DSM-IV* leadership arguably was not particularly committed to such reductionism, but many picked up the banner, e.g., Andreasen, 1984, and by the declaration of the Decade of the Brain in 1990, it was a widely held premise.) NIMH leadership has been problematically inconsistent in its messaging about such reductionism, such as suggesting that more "micro" explanations in neuroscience are superior to more "macro" explanations in psychology (Insel, 2014; see Sharp & Miller, 2019, for an explanation of why that claim is untenable; see Miller and Bartholomew, Chapter 20, for an analysis of the inconsistency in messaging more generally). But the best articulations of the RDoC approach (e.g., Kozak & Cuthbert, 2016) have been explicit that the RDoC initiative neither assumes nor intends such reductionism, assumes no primacy between psychology and biology, does not cast biology as "underlying" psychology, and strives for hybrid constructs without the traditional psychology/biology opposition (see Miller et al., 2016) grounded in both the best psychological science and the best biological science.

RDoC's explicit agnosticism about psychology/biology relationships suits well the new NIMH Director, Joshua Gordon, foregrounding so-called computational psychiatry (which could be more precisely characterized as that portion of computational psychobiology or computational cognitive neuroscience [with "cognitive" understood very broadly] that has aspirations of application to the phenomena of psychopathology, thus computational psychopathology). Computational psychiatry involves a growing variety of methods for modeling and predicting psychological and biological data often based on large psychological and/or biological data sets subjected to formal statistical modeling. Such formal modeling fosters quantitative tests of theory rather than simply determining whether one can reject the null hypothesis that two samples are from the same population (Meehl, 1978; Miller, 2004; Miller & Yee, 2015). This emphasis conforms superbly to RDoC efforts to drive clinical science forward from locations where the available data signal is relatively strong. In fact, those in pursuit of computational psychiatry will need to address questions of normality and abnormality. Does one's algorithm development start with *DSM* categories (and clinician diagnoses of cases) as a gold standard? That would be a very twentieth-century strategy – or in light of Kendler's (Chapter 38) analysis a very nineteenth-century strategy. RDoC or something very much like it will be needed to provide bootstrap criteria for computational psychiatry.

The RDoC path is nevertheless quite challenging. The current RDoC matrix (www.nimh.nih.gov/research/research-funded-by-nimh/rdoc/constructs/rdoc-matrix.shtml) is under active development, at a pace quite different from that of the *DSM*s. In 2018 the Positive Valence Systems domain was substantially revised, in early 2019 a Sensorimotor Systems domain was added, and as of late 2019 the Negative Valence Systems domain is under review and revision. The latter effort is especially challenging, in part because of the broad range and high prominence of negative emotional phenomena in psychopathology. Those factors make it difficult to distill a vast literature into a set of psychological constructs and subconstructs that are representative, adequately distinct, yet well grounded in knowledge about neural circuits and other biological data. How far, at each iteration of the RDoC matrix, to extend the psychological constructs into areas where the biological literature is thin or in contention? The literature does not yet support comprehensive coverage of negative emotion. Overreach in revising the Negative Valence Systems domain would violate the principle that RDoC constructs be well supported in terms of what is known about implementing (not underlying!) circuitry. Yet excessive caution risks limiting research that can push the edges forward. A balance must be found that is optimally generative of high-impact clinical research.

Kendler (Chapter 38) asks "Where do we situate RDoC?" and correctly notes that its "domains seem eerily reminiscent of earlier faculty psychological systems." In remarks above I have argued that RDoC, like the *DSM*s, indeed has roots in nineteenth-century faculty psychology but that

RDoC is built on differentiated constructs developed by modern psychological science judged to be well supported by the implementing biology, such as brain structures and mechanisms in what has come to be called the "reward system." Both of those features distinguish it fundamentally from *DSM* categories and symptom criteria. "Cognition" and "emotion" and their progeny in the *DSMs* are much too coarse as guidance to find the important implementing (not underlying!) biology in psychopathology. Fortunately, over a century of psychological science (including a very rich and diverse psychophysiology literature) is available to guide design and revision of the rows of the RDoC matrix.

Kendler (Chapter 38) also asks how to understand causation between cognition and emotion and whether such causal relationships could "be easy or even possible to understand neurobiologically?" The latter brings us to the tougher question of how to understand causation between psychology and biology more generally. I have argued that, at best, we do not have a clue of how psychology/biology causation works in any comprehensive sense and perhaps that, as commonly conceived, no such causal relationship is possible (I have hastened to explain that the latter does not entail dualism; Miller, 1996, 2010; Miller & Keller, 2000). Miller and Bartholomew (Chapter 20), Sharp and Miller (2019), and Thomas and Sharp (2019) borrow heavily from a movement in recent philosophy of science called the "new mechanists" to suggest more viable (and nonreductionistic) ways to conceive psychology/biology causation. Borsboom, Cramer, and Kalis (2019) and Schwartz, Lilienfeld, Meca, and Sauvigné (2016) provide additional nonreductionist alternatives for conceiving the roles of psychological and biological phenomena, on an equal footing, in psychopathology. For now, I share the humility of Kendler's (Chapter 38) judgment that relevant versions of the mind-body causation problem are "largely terra incognita to this day."

Kendler's essay (Chapter 38) shows convincingly that intellectual history may not merely repeat itself, nor does it simply constrain the present: it sometimes does not evolve at all. He makes clear that some of the concepts and premises dominating modern psychiatric nosology that are firmly rooted in the seventeenth century have not budged much at all from the nineteenth century. One hopes for better at some point in the twenty-first century. To answer succinctly his question of how RDoC fits into this long vector, its strategy is to work from neuroscience and other biological data without seeking reduction to it of the phenomena of psychopathology, which remain conceived in largely psychological terms.

REFERENCES

American Psychiatric Association (2013) *Diagnostic and statistical manual of mental disorders (DSM-5)*. Washington, DC: American Psychiatric Publishing.

Andreasen, N.C. (1984) *The broken brain: The biological revolution in psychiatry*. New York: Harper & Row.

Borsboom, D., Cramer, A.O.J., & Kalis, A. (2019) 'Brain disorders? Not really: Why network structures block reductionism in psychopathology research.' *Behavioral and Brain Sciences, 42*, e2: 1–63.

Cuthbert, B.N. (2014) 'The RDoC framework: Facilitating transition from ICD/ DSM to dimensional approaches that integrate neuroscience and psychopathology.' *World Psychiatry, 13*, 28–35.

Cuthbert, B.N., & Insel, T R. (2010) 'Toward new approaches to psychotic disorders: The NIMH Research Domain Criteria project.' *Schizophrenia Bulletin, 36*, 1061–1062.

Cuthbert, B.N., & Insel, T.R. (2013) 'Toward the future of psychiatric diagnosis: The seven pillars of RDoC.' *BMC Medicine, 11*, 126.

Cuthbert, B.N., & Kozak, M.J. (2013) 'Constructing constructs for psychopathology: The NIMH research domain criteria.' *Journal of Abnormal Psychology, 122*, 928–937.

Frances, A. (2013) *Saving normal: An insider's revolt against out-of-control psychiatric diagnosis, DSM-5, Big Pharma, and the medicalization of ordinary life*. New York: William Morrow.

(2014) 'RDoC is necessary, but very oversold.' *World Psychiatry, 13*, 47–49.

Heller, W. (1993) 'Neuropsychological mechanisms of individual differences in emotion, personality, and arousal.' *Neuropsychology, 7*, 476–489.

Hume, D. (1738) *Treatise of human nature. Book 2. Of passions. Part 3. Section 3*. https://en.wikisource.org/wiki/Treatise_of_Human_Nature/Book_2:_Of_the_passions/Part_3/Section_3, accessed 06/29/19.

Hyman, S.E. (2010) 'The diagnosis of mental disorders: The problem of reification.' *Annual Review of Clinical Psychology, 6*, 155–179.

Insel, T. R. (2014) 'The NIMH research domain criteria (RDoC) project: Precision medicine for psychiatry.' *American Journal of Psychiatry, 171*, 395–397.

Insel, T.R., Cuthbert, B.N., Garvey, M.A., Heinssen, R.K., Pine, D.S., Quinn, K.J., . . . Wang, P.S. (2010) 'Research domain criteria: Toward a new classification framework for research on mental disorders.' *American Journal of Psychiatry, 167*, 748–751.

Keating, P., & Cambrosio, A. (2004) 'Does biomedicine entail the successful reduction of pathology to biology?' *Perspectives in Biology and Medicine, 47*, 357–371.

Kozak, M.J., & Cuthbert, B.N. (2016) 'The NIMH research domain criteria initiative: Background, issues, and pragmatics.' *Psychophysiology, 53*, 286–297.

Lake, J.I., Yee, C.M., & Miller, G.A. (2017) 'Misunderstanding RDoC.' Mechanisms of mental disorders special issue. *Zeitschrift für Psychologie, 225*, 170–174.

Lang, P.J. (1984) 'Dead souls: Or why the neurobehavioral science of emotion should pay attention to cognitive science.' In T. Elbert, B. Rockstroh,

W. Lutzenberger, & N. Birbaumer (Eds.), *Self-regulation of the brain and behavior* (pp. 255–272). New York: Springer-Verlag.

Lang, P.J., Bradley, M.M., & Cuthbert, B.N. (1990) 'Emotion, attention, and the startle reflex.' *Psychological Review, 97*, 377–395.

Lilienfeld, S.O., & Treadway, M.T. (2016) 'Clashing diagnostic approaches: DSM-ICD versus RDoC.' *Annual Review of Clinical Psychology, 12*, 435–463.

Meehl, P.E. (1978) 'Theoretical risks and tabular asterisks: Sir Karl, Sir Ronald and the slow progress of soft psychology.' *Journal of Consulting and Clinical Psychology, 46*, 806–834.

Miller, G.A. (1996) 'How we think about cognition, emotion, and biology in psychopathology.' *Psychophysiology, 33*, 615–628.

(2004) 'Another quasi-thirty years of slow progress.' *Applied and Preventive Psychology: Current Scientific Perspectives, 11*, 61–64.

(2010) 'Mistreating psychology in the decades of the brain.' *Perspectives on Psychological Science, 5*, 716–743.

Miller, G.A., Crocker, L.D., Spielberg, J.M., Infantolino, Z.P, & Heller, W. (2013) 'Issues in localization of brain function: The case of lateralized frontal cortex in cognition, emotion, and psychopathology.' *Frontiers in Integrative Neuroscience, 7*, 2.

Miller, G.A., & Keller, J. (2000) 'Psychology and neuroscience: Making peace.' *Current Directions in Psychological Science, 9*, 212–215.

Miller, G.A., Rockstroh, B.S., Hamilton, H.K., & Yee, C.M. (2016) 'Psychophysiology as a core strategy in RDoC.' *Psychophysiology, 53*, 410–414.

Miller, G.A., & Yee, C.M. (2015) 'Moving psychopathology forward.' *Psychological Inquiry, 26*, 263–267.

Osgood, C., Suci, G., & Tannenbaum, P. (1957) *The measurement of meaning.* Urbana: University of Illinois.

Russell, J. A. (1980) 'A circumplex model of affect.' *Journal of Personality and Social Psychology, 39*, 1161–1178.

(2003) 'Core affect and the psychological construction of emotion.' *Psychological Review, 110*, 145–172.

Sanislow, C.A., Pine, D.S., Quinn, K.J., Kozak, M.J., Garvey, M.A., Heinssen, R.K., . . . Cuthbert, B.N. (2010) 'Developing constructs for psychopathology research: Research domain criteria.' *Journal of Abnormal Psychology, 119*, 631–639.

Schwartz, S.J., Lilienfeld, S.O., Meca, A., & Sauvigné, K.C. (2016) 'The role of neuroscience within psychology: A call for inclusiveness over exclusiveness.' *American Psychologist, 71*, 52–70.

Sharp, P.B., & Eldar, E. (2019) 'Computational models of anxiety: Nascent efforts and future directions.' *Current Directions in Psychological Science, 28*, 170–176.

Sharp, P.B., & Miller, G.A. (2019) 'Reduction and autonomy in psychology and neuroscience: A call for pragmatism.' *Journal of Theoretical and Philosophical Psychology, 39*, 18–31.

Thomas, J.G., & Sharp, P.B. (2019) 'Mechanistic science: A new approach to comprehensive psychopathology research that relates psychological and biological phenomena.' *Clinical Psychological Science, 7*, 196–215.

Watson, D., & Tellegen, A. (1985) 'Toward a consensual structure of mood.' *Psychological Bulletin, 98*, 219–235.

Yee, C.M., Javitt, D.C., & Miller, G.A. (2015) 'Replacing DSM categorical analyses with dimensional analyses in psychiatry research: The research domain criteria initiative.' *JAMA Psychiatry*, *72*, 1159–1160.

Zachar, P. (2006) 'The classification of emotion and scientific realism.' *Journal of Theoretical and Philosophical Psychology*, *26*, 120–138.

Zachar, P., & Ellis, R. D. (Eds.). (2012) *Categorical versus dimensional models of affect: A seminar of the theories of Panksepp and Russell.* Amsterdam: John Benjamins.

Zachar, P., Krueger, R. F., & Kendler, K. S. (2016) 'Personality disorder in *DSM-5*: An oral history.' *Psychological Medicine*, *46*, 1–10.

Zachar, P., Regier, D.A., & Kendler, K. (2019) 'The aspirations for a paradigm shift in DSM-5: An oral history.' *Journal of Nervous and Mental Disease*, *207*(9), 778–784.

SECTION 14

40

Introduction

KENNETH S. KENDLER

Stephen Heckers, a psychiatrist and neuroscientist, who began pursuing a philosophy degree before changing his mind and attending medical school, provides a succinct and multifaceted introduction to the problem of *levels* and the attractions and problems of *reduction* in psychiatric research and practice. On first reading, this essay is deceptively simple. It repays a second visit.

He frames this paper around a typology of the kinds of reductions that happen in psychiatry: (i) from first person personal experiences by patients to third person accounts by clinicians, (ii) from third person accounts of signs and symptoms to decisions about the presence of mental illness and the assignment of a specific diagnosis, (iii) from the mental disorder to biological (usually brain) correlates and maybe even disease mechanisms, and (iv) the use of diverse individuals as research subjects in clinical and research trials.

Heckers begins with the first-person experiences of the patient and then describes what he calls the "psychiatric situation" – the face-to-face interview between the psychiatric clinician and the patient. It is here that the reductive process begins as the clinician must abstract from the many complexities of this interaction to obtain key signs, symptoms and historical information. The personal richness is lost but the data reduction is needed for both clinical care and research. In the next step, the richness is reduced yet further as we go from the historical information and symptoms and signs to a psychiatric diagnosis. This in turn forms a zero or one in a data column or an ICD code in an electronic medical record.

Then Heckers switches to review a different kind of reduction: the attempt to map the mind to the brain. As he notes, this has been tried in many different ways during the history of psychiatry. To ground us in this discourse, he briefly cites the neurological and clinical approaches of

Wernicke and Kraepelin, respectively. This has been an extraordinarily challenging problem, subject to repeated over-promising in our history, and the actual progress has been very slow. To see a "best case scenario," he summarizes the status of our understanding of auditory verbal hallucinations – a classical psychiatric symptom of first importance where we have had real substantive progress in linking this to neurologic processes using both functional (fMRI) and anatomic approaches.

He then raises the hard problem of the reduction and explanation of the mental, quickly reviewing classical approaches of Jaspers, Engel and, more recently, McHugh and Slavney. We share this hard problem with the metaphysics community and it is unlikely to see resolution any time soon.

Finally, he raises the problem of causal inference, treating people – with all their complexity – as subjects, numbers in data files as we might do for a large cohort or double-blind study. He relates this to the question of the personal agency of our patients. How does that figure in our approaches? How do we treat patients who do not buy into their patient status? At the same time, as we want to reduce our patients' problems to genetic and/or neuroscientific malfunctions, they also demonstrate agency, have wants and often express specific preferences for treatment or non-treatment.

In summary, Heckers in this essay takes us on a wide tour of the psychiatric landscape – from clinical interviewing to basic neuroscience – pointing out philosophical "hot-spots" especially with respect to the broad focus of this book, the problem of levels in psychiatric discourse.

41

Psychiatric Discourse: Scientific Reductionism for the Autonomous Person

STEPHAN HECKERS

41.1 REDUCTIONISM IN PSYCHIATRY

Psychiatric problems are complex. The problems are mental states and human behaviors, defined as abnormal and in need of treatment. Psychiatry, a branch of medicine, has embraced scientific reductionism to simplify these problems. Here I propose that psychiatrists engage in several forms of scientific reductionism in order to manage clinical problems. I will then advance the idea that, even with the greatest possible success of reducing the complexity of psychiatric problems, the autonomy of a person limits the power of scientific reductionism in psychiatry.

Medicine has made remarkable progress by applying scientific reductionism to solve complex clinical challenges. It was therefore reasonable, in the middle of the nineteenth century, to propose that psychiatry should pursue a path similar to the rest of medicine (Engstrom, 2004; Schmitt, 1983). Neurology and neurosurgery embraced the clinico-pathological correlation as gold standard for reducing clinical problems to abnormalities in the brain. This well-established method has given rise to translational medicine: the ability to move from bed to bench and back again, from laboratory data to clinical populations (Solomon, 2015).

Initially, clinicians described neurological cases and validated their diagnoses with studies of brain tissue. More recently, neuroimaging, biomarker and genetic studies have provided additional evidence. Increasing knowledge of brain anatomy and physiology has guided remarkable progress in early detection, effective treatment and even prevention of neurological disorders caused by infections, tumors and strokes (Helmers, Phillips, & Esper, 2010). The growing knowledge of brain circuitry is now also paving the way for an increasingly reductionist approach to complex behavioral syndromes such as the dementias (Honig, 2012).

TABLE 41.1 *Scientific reductionism in psychiatry*

	Object of study	Scientific disciplines
Situation	(Ab)normal mental states and behaviors	Phenomenology, psychopathology
Diagnosis	Diagnosis	Nosology
Mapping	Brain mechanism	Neurobiology
Testing	Causality	Genetics, randomized clinical trial

Some psychiatrists have argued that they should join the neurologists and neurosurgeons and become clinical neuroscientists (T. R. Insel & Quirion, 2005). This would change the education of psychiatrists considerably and distinguish their scope of practice more clearly from other mental health care providers (e.g., psychologists and psychiatric nurse practitioners) (Chung & Insel, 2014). But the impact of neuroscience discoveries on the practice of psychiatry has been limited (Heckers, 2017). Many attribute the slow progress in psychiatry to the difficulty of mapping mental phenomena to the brain, i.e., the mind–brain problem. Consequently, there has been a long tradition in psychiatry to refute the definition of psychiatry as clinical neuroscience (Schneider, 1919).

In the first part of this chapter, I argue that scientific reductionism in psychiatry does not begin with and is not limited to the mind–brain problem. Several other reductionist simplifications are needed for the practice of psychiatry. Here I will outline four forms of scientific reductionism in psychiatry (see Table 41.1).

Initially, the first-person experience of mental phenomena is translated into a third-person account during the psychiatric situation. As a next step, the psychiatric diagnosis separates normal from abnormal mental states/behavior. Then it is either the psychopathological construct or the diagnosis (not the complex first-person experience) that is correlated with the person's body (mainly brain, but also endocrine/humoral and genetic features). Finally, human subject experiments and randomized clinical trials make considerable simplifications for the sake of causal inference testing in psychiatry.

41.2 THE PSYCHIATRIC SITUATION

Psychiatry begins with the encounter of two persons. They are often referred to as the patient/client/consumer/service user (person 1) and the clinician (person 2). Person 1 is being evaluated for the lived experience of abnormal mental states and behaviors. Person 2 has two tasks. First, assess person 1. Second, decide whether person 1 experiences mental states and demonstrates behavior that can be considered outside of the normal range. (There might be more than two persons involved, e.g., when a couple or a family are evaluated.)

To distinguish it from a simple conversation between two persons, I refer to this encounter as the *psychiatric situation*. The psychiatric situation is the origin of all clinical descriptions, diagnostic formulations and therapeutic interventions in psychiatry.

Person 2 is not just an observer and person 1 is not simply the object of clinical observation. This psychiatric situation is dyadic and interactional. Person 1 is expected to engage with person 2 to allow for the exploration of temperament and personality, sensory experiences, moods, beliefs and behaviors. Ideally, person 1 articulates live goals, reports about spiritual/religious practices and shares deeply personal preferences.

The interactions during the psychiatric situation are crucial for the diagnostic assessment. Person 2 interprets the interactional styles, cognitive and emotional capabilities, and volitional acts displayed by person 1 during the psychiatric situation. It is this interpretation of lived experience that is the first step in the scientific reductionism of psychiatric problems. The three other reductionist approaches in psychiatry that I review below are all built on data gathered during the psychiatric situation.

There are different settings for the psychiatric situation. The most conducive for a dyadic and interactional encounter is the voluntary office visit. Nowadays, this often occurs in a mental health clinic, a less personal setting than the private office. Psychiatric crises may lead to encounters in emergency rooms and inpatient units, many of them locked and associated with forced treatment. Finally, the forensic setting introduces an additional layer of social and legal considerations into the psychiatric situation. The setting shapes the psychiatric situation and leads to remarkably different approaches. In fact, most practitioners of psychiatry favor one setting, seek specialized training for it and then limit their practice to this setting.

It is helpful to compare person 1 in the psychiatric situation with the typical patient who receives medical attention. Parsons identified four aspects of the *sick role* for the person in a clinical situation: the person is (1) exempted from normal responsibilities, (2) not held responsible and not expected to recover by an act of will, (3) obliged to get well and (4) cooperating with a competent treater (Parsons, 1951). This description of the sick role holds true for most medical settings, including the person who seeks psychiatric help in a voluntary setting. However, the person in forced treatment settings usually rejects roles 3 and 4. As a result, details of the person's mental state are often inferred by observation (e.g., facial expression and body posture might indicate that the person is depressed) or by comparison to an established norm (e.g., delayed responses and furtive glances might indicate that the person is responding to internal stimuli).

Each of the various settings in which the psychiatric situation may occur has developed a local culture of diagnostic biases and heuristics. At the most basic level, the reimbursement for clinical services requires a standard set of clinical data and a diagnostic code. The standard set, known as the "mental status exam," is a less than perfect summary of the clinical encounter, often ignoring crucial clinical information. In educational settings, the trainee is expected to formulate the case using a shared theoretical framework. Finally, since most psychiatric treatments are managed by the person who completed the psychiatric assessment, the psychiatric situation is usually framed by the therapeutic milieu (e.g., therapy versus medication, voluntary versus involuntary). The cultural biases among practitioners in psychiatry are not trivial. In fact, they can lead to academic and entrepreneurial competitions and might result in sectarian isolation (Havens, 2005; Makari, 2008).

Only after mental states and behaviors have been observed or inferred during the psychiatric situation can they be reduced further. Phenomenological psychiatrists have long been concerned about a simplification of the epistemological and ethical problems that arise from the psychiatric situation (Jaspers, 1913). Some have chosen to direct all of their analytical focus on the first-person account, often seeking guidance from philosophy, especially phenomenology (Binswanger, 1957; Broome, Harland, Owen, & Stringaris, 2013). Some have argued that psychiatry should limit itself to the scientific exploration of the psychiatric situation, as a pure form of psychiatry (Schneider, 1919, 1959). More recently, this has been complemented with research projects that aim to better understand the lived experience of persons with mental illness (Zolnierek, 2011).

Even with considerable disagreements about psychiatry as a pure discipline or a form of clinical neuroscience, there is agreement among psychiatrists that the lived experience of person 1 needs to be translated during the psychiatric situation. This translation of a first-person into a third-person account is a necessary form of reductionism. In contrast to the biological reductionism of relating mental to brain states, the reductionism of the psychiatric situation is subtler. Here are two examples from the rich psychopathology literature: mood/affect and reality testing.

The exploration of mood begins with a verbatim report of person 1. Person 2 is simply asking "How do you feel?" and records the response of person 1 in quotation marks. Mood is then contrasted/compared with the affect of person 1, which includes features such as lability/stability, range and appropriateness to the situation.

For the assessment of reality testing, person 2 interprets the utterances and behaviors of person 1 within a culturally appropriate concept of reality. This is a crucial step in assessing distortions of reality such as delusions and hallucinations.

There is growing awareness that the complex first-person experience has to be reduced in a scientific way, not just as an exercise guided by diagnostic coding rules (Andreasen, 2007).

41.3 THE PSYCHIATRIC DIAGNOSIS

The psychiatric diagnosis goes beyond the reductionism of the psychiatric situation in two ways. First, the diagnosis serves as a summary statement of all the observations and interactions during the psychiatric situation. The experiences of Person 1 are transformed into standardized ratings and criteria-based categorization. Second, the psychiatric diagnosis is categorical with respect to normality. In the transition from psychopathology to nosology, the person disappears. For example, "the person with schizophrenia" becomes "the schizophrenic" (Sass, 2007).

The differential diagnosis among several psychiatric labels can be categorical or dimensional, but the demarcation of psychiatric illness from normality is categorical. In his dissection of psychiatric power, Michel Foucault reduces psychiatric nosology to a simple dichotomy:

> Psychiatric diagnosis does not involve a differential diagnosis but, if you like, a decision, or an absolute diagnosis. . . . the real question posed in every diagnosis of madness (. . .) is not whether it is this or that form of madness, but whether it is or is not madness.
>
> (Foucault, 2006, 266)

The categorical separation of abnormal from normal mental states/behavior by a diagnosis is relevant for several clinical and forensic settings. For example, some diagnoses justify the forced application of psychiatric treatment (e.g., medication or electroconvulsive treatment), while other diagnoses do not. Similarly, some psychiatric diagnoses have an impact on sentencing in court proceedings (e.g., the diagnosis of schizophrenia excludes the death penalty in some states of the United States, but not others).

Psychiatric diagnoses serve as gatekeeper for access to and reimbursement for health care services, eligibility for social services (e.g., housing) and application for disability benefits. The emerging sociology of diagnosis (Jutel, 2009) is especially relevant for psychiatry:

> Medicine in general and psychiatry in particular remain boundary managers: border police examining and certifying transit documents in an unceasing battle over depression and anxiety, sexuality and addiction. Psychiatry remains the peculiar legatee of such problems, an obligate participant in every generation's particular cultural negotiations – a kind of canary at the pitface of cultural strife.
>
> (Rosenberg, 2006)

The sociological and legal dimensions of psychiatric diagnosis make psychiatric problems a topic of intense debate in the general public. The stigmatization of mental illness is, to a large part, linked to the impact a psychiatric diagnosis has for the role of a person in society.

In addition, psychiatrists are also acutely aware of the limited validity of psychiatric diagnoses (Kraemer, 2013). There are several validators for a psychiatric diagnosis: some are antecedent (e.g., familial pattern), some are concurrent (e.g., biological test) and some are predictive (e.g., response to treatment) (Kendler, 1990). The strength of the validators varies within and between diagnoses. The validator arguably of greatest value for the person who is given a psychiatric diagnosis is overall functioning over time (Fusar-Poli, Hijazi, Stahl, & Steyerberg, 2018). For example, the majority of patients diagnosed with mild cognitive impairment will progress to dementia, but less than 30% of persons at clinical high risk for psychosis progress to a psychotic disorder (Fusar-Poli, 2015).

Szasz has argued that the limited validity of psychiatric diagnoses makes them ineligible for their current use in society (Szasz, 1961). His strong antipathy against psychiatric diagnoses is the result of disillusionment about limited validity and a rigid libertarian philosophy.

While the current diagnostic systems in psychiatry, the ICD-10 (World Health Organization, 1992)and *DSM-5* (American Psychiatric Association, 2013), do not endorse a hierarchy of validators, most users of psychiatric diagnoses do. On the one hand, patients want a psychiatric diagnosis to capture their experience, guide selection of treatment, predict course and, if possible, prevent onset or remission. On the other hand, clinicians are primarily interested in predicting treatment response (both therapeutic and adverse) and projecting disease course and outcome. Finally, researchers expect that psychiatric diagnoses guide their study of disease mechanism, e.g., when selecting cohorts for studies of genetic risk factors or neural correlates.

These diverging viewpoints regarding the value of psychiatric diagnoses have led to the proposal to replace the current diagnostic system with a more valid one (T. Insel et al., 2010). Academic psychiatry, in particular, has embraced the proposal that psychiatry should become clinical neuroscience (Reynolds, Lewis, Detre, Schatzberg, & Kupfer, 2009).

41.4 MAPPING THE MIND TO THE BRAIN

The gold standard in clinical medicine is the clinico-pathological correlation: the clinical diagnosis is validated by pathological examination of the body. The exam may occur post-mortem or, during the lifetime, with the help of tissue biopsy, clinical laboratory test of body fluid or radiological examination. Such a biomarker can be used for the prospective assessment of risk and the staging of disease progression and treatment response. More recently, the assessment of allelic variation and epigenetic modulation of the human genome has been added.

There is a long-standing debate about the merits of scientific reductionism in psychiatry. Carl Wernicke proposed an approach that was informed by his success of explaining the aphasias with a neural circuitry model: a complete map of human brain function will reveal the mechanism of psychiatric signs and symptoms (Wernicke, 1880, 2000). In contrast, Emil Kraepelin proposed that psychiatrists can find mechanisms for clinically defined syndromes, even those with considerable clinical heterogeneity, as long as disease progression and outcome are different (Kraepelin, 1913).

Whether neuroscience or clinical psychiatry should take the lead for scientific reductionism in psychiatry is unclear, since mental phenomena and behaviors may be reduced in more than one way. It is not necessary to map out the *complete* pathway of *all* experiences of a person. Some reductionist models focus on a single psychopathological sign or symptom, others aim to explain a highly heterogeneous syndrome. Some models aim to reduce signs, symptoms or syndrome to a brain region, others to a gene. There is no a priori defined causal pathway for a lived experience.

The reduction of mental states and behaviors to the person's body is shaped by what the psychiatric situation has provided. For example, reducing depression to a neurochemical abnormality in the brain begins with the first-person account of mood and the description of affective states (e.g., labile, irritable, constricted). The reduction from the higher mental to the lower neural level can occur in several ways, ranging from statistical association (weak hypothesis testing) to randomized clinical trials (strong hypothesis testing).

Here I briefly review the neuroscientific exploration of auditory verbal hallucinations (AVH) as an example for the challenge in reducing clinical features in psychiatry to abnormalities in the brain. More than 5% of the general population endorse the experience of AVH at some point in their life (Linscott & van Os, 2013). If the experience interferes with social function at home or at work, the person is likely to seek help from a clinician.

Functional neuroimaging studies have contributed to mapping AVH to structural and functional variants of the human brain (Jardri, Pouchet, Pins, & Thomas, 2011). Just like behavioral neurologists, psychiatrists have benefited from the mapping of auditory perception in the primary auditory cortex (A1, located on the dorsal surface of the superior temporal cortex) and its unimodal and multimodal representations in adjacent association areas (Brewer & Barton, 2016). Functional neuroimaging studies have identified increased brain activity during the experience of AVH in A1 of the left hemisphere (Dierks et al., 1999). In addition, persons who have a history of AVH show smaller left superior temporal cortex volumes (Allen et al., 2012). Together, the symptom-capture studies of AVH and the association of AVH with volume changes in the brain region primarily coding for auditory information provide compelling evidence for their involvement in the experience of AVH.

Despite this compelling evidence of a clinico-pathological correlation, there are many questions. First, does the activation of A1 drive the experience of AVH or is it a secondary recruitment of the primary sensory cortex by the multimodal association cortex? Second, does the volume difference indicate an abnormality at the cellular level? Third, how can the individual features of the AVH experience (i.e., loudness and vividness) be mapped to brain activation pattern? Most importantly, how can the content of the AVH and the limbic valence of such experience be explained by structural and functional variants of the human brain?

The mapping of AVH to the brain is one of the most promising examples in contemporary psychiatric neuroscience (Waters et al., 2012). The study of beliefs, language and motor behavior to explain delusions, disorganization of thought and abnormal psychomotor behavior are more complex challenges (Strik & Dierks, 2011). We can safely conclude that the translation of psychopathology into neuropathology will be slow. But psychiatric research can pursue another goal, even without a complete mapping of the mind to the brain: the search for the causes of abnormal mental states and behavior.

41.5 CAUSAL INFERENCE TESTING

The testing of causal relationships is a prominent goal of scientific reductionism. Medical research has successfully employed experiments (in humans and animals) and randomized clinical trials to test causal relationships.

Experiments have also played an important role in psychiatric research. An excellent example is studying the effect of illicit and therapeutic drugs on cognition, affect and motor behavior in humans and animals. But there are several significant constraints for the experimental exploration of psychopathology. First, many psychiatric symptoms and signs are difficult (or simply impossible) to replicate in animal models. Second, many features of psychiatric diagnoses are stressful or induce suffering, preventing their exploration in humans. Third, even the study of psychiatric signs that are ideal for an experimental exploration, e.g., cognitive deficits, depend on engagement and motivation by the person experiencing psychiatric symptoms, which can make it difficult to disambiguate the effect of illness (e.g., psychomotor slowing) from the experimental manipulation of the variable under study (e.g., speed of processing).

Randomized clinical trials have been considered the gold standard for causal inference testing in clinical populations. When combined with neuroscientific studies, the intervention can reveal crucial mechanisms of disease. For example, the L-dopa therapy provided crucial evidence that a hypo-dopaminergic state causes the hypertonic–hypokinetic motor syndrome in Parkinson's disease patients (Obeso et al., 2017). Similarly, the administration of GABA-agonists to treat ictal events provided compelling evidence for an excitation–inhibition imbalance in seizure patients (Jones-Davis & Macdonald, 2003).

There are also compelling examples of causal inference testing in psychiatric disorders, but the impact on the development of new treatments has been less impressive. For example, both cognitive-behavioral therapy and pharmacological treatment reduce the symptoms of obsessive-compulsive disorder by normalizing striatal activity (Baxter et al., 1987), but this finding has not lead to the development of new treatments.

41.6 THE HARD PROBLEM

The scientific reduction of abnormal mental states and behaviors is a hard problem. Psychiatry runs the risk of making matters too simple: when the clinician limits the psychiatric evaluation to just one hour, when the teacher employs a single theoretical framework for every case, or when the researcher looks only at data ascertained with a readily available method. There is also a risk to make matters too complex: when psychopathology becomes so esoteric that clinicians do not understand it or when a nosology becomes so complex that it is no longer clinically feasible.

There is a multitude of explanatory models in psychiatry and it is not clear how they can be integrated (Luhrmann, 2001). Some have proposed that levels of explanation in psychiatry should be kept separate, as complementary approaches to the psychiatric situation.

Jaspers identified two distinct goals for psychiatry: understanding the person (*Verstehen*) and explaining the mental disease (*Erklären*). Ignoring such distinct domains of knowledge leads to mythology (Fuchs, 2014).

Engel developed the biopsychosocial model primarily for the proper recognition and management of psychiatric problems in medically ill patients (Engel, 1980). Similarly, the *Perspectives of psychiatry* teaches the psychiatrist to understand what the patient "has" (disease), "is" (dimension), "does" (behavior) and "encounters" (life story) (McHugh & Slavney, 1998).

These heuristics are embraced in the education of psychiatrists because this avoids a premature reduction of psychiatric problems. Some have argued for a pluralistic view (Ghaemi, 2003), but do the different reductionist approaches in psychiatry all have the same explanatory power?

Even with the greatest success of scientific reductionism in psychiatry, there will be one hard constraint: the agency of person 1. While the psychiatric situation results in an objectivation of person 1, it does not negate the autonomy of person 1. Every person, including one who experiences abnormal mental states and demonstrates abnormal behavior, has agency and the ability for self-efficacy.

41.7 AGENCY IN PSYCHIATRY

Agency is the capacity of the person to act independently and to make free choices. Self-efficacy is the person's belief in the innate ability to achieve goals. Both concepts emanate from the enlightened view that a person can think independently and rationally (Foucault, 1984; Kant, 1784). How is this relevant for scientific reductionism in psychiatry?

Many persons given and subsequently treated for a psychiatric diagnosis agree with the assessment and treatment plan derived from the psychiatric situation. But not all do. Consider the question: Does person 1 seek a diagnosis and require treatment? There are four possible scenarios (see Figure 41.1).

		Person 1	
		YES	NO
Person 2	YES	YES/YES	NO/YES
	NO	YES/NO	NO/NO

FIGURE 41.1 Psychiatric matrix.

Here I will not review the agreements (YES/YES and NO/NO). I will also not review the scenarios where the self-assessment of a problem by person 1 is not validated by person 2 (e.g., somatoform disorders, factitious disorder, malingering). I will focus on scenarios in which person 1 rejects a psychiatric diagnosis and does not endorse a need for treatment.

A person might reject a psychiatric diagnosis when the normal/abnormal boundary is not clear. Similarly, a person might refuse a recommended treatment, especially if it is associated with more than minimal risk of adverse reactions. Here I will briefly review three psychiatric disorders that have seen recent moves with the psychiatric matrix toward disagreement (i.e., person 1 does not seek a diagnosis or disagrees with the assessment of person 2): personality, neurodevelopmental and psychotic disorders.

Personality disorders are defined as an abnormal pattern of inner experience and behaviors that lead to distress and impairment in functioning. When stress becomes distress (i.e., when a personal style becomes maladaptive) is open to debate and the definition of impaired function depends on the social/legal context. This has led some clinicians and researchers to reject the categorical definition of personality disorders in favor of a dimensional approach (Trull & Durrett, 2005). Persons with personality disorders might avoid diagnostic assessments and, when seeking treatment, disengage easily.

Neurodevelopmental disorders have been reinterpreted as neurodiversity: brain structure and function outside a previously defined "normal range" are now interpreted within a more comprehensive, evolutionary view of brain development. Persons might be wired differently, with no simple boundary between normal and abnormal. This shifts the focus away from disorder (requiring treatment) to differences and disability (deserving adjustment by society) (Baron-Cohen, 2017).

Psychotic disorders often include reality distortion. Mean lifetime prevalence of psychotic experiences in the general population is above 5%, with hallucinations being more common than delusions (McGrath et al., 2015). But many of these experiences are transient and do not become plans for action. The transition from normal reality testing to reality distortion is not permanent and individuals can make sense of even marked distortions.

What is the common feature in these three scenarios of disagreements between the two persons in the psychiatric situation? Most importantly, there is a significant move away from a disease/deficit model of mental illness to a recovery model (Slade et al., 2014). Related to this, the paternalistic attitude of medicine is giving way to a shared decision-making model (Slade, 2017).

There is growing realization that agency is a constraint for scientific reductionism in psychiatry (Bracken et al., 2012). This is in stark contrast to the traditional model of medicine, which explained signs and symptoms of disease by physical changes in the body. Psychiatric patients see themselves increasingly as service users who can push the boundaries of normalcy and negotiate the need for treatment.

But discontent with the current paradigms in psychiatry arises not only when the search for clinico-pathological correlation and the testing for causal inference is rejected by person 1. It is present already during the initial step of scientific reductionism, the psychiatric situation (Parnas, Sass, & Zahavi, 2013). Only a person with agency can engage in a dyadic/interactional encounter with another person in such a way that observations and inferences can lead to a psychiatric diagnosis. A paternalistic attitude might lead a "clinician" to diagnose a "patient" and establish a need for treatment. But it does not remove the agency of person 1.

41.8 PROGRESS IN PSYCHIATRY

Scientific reductionism has great potential for psychiatry, but it may fail at various stages. Here I have outlined at least four forms of scientific reductionism in psychiatry that have been embraced, to varying degrees, with the goal to make progress in psychiatry as a medical specialty. But each of these four steps is fraught with errors. We need to proceed carefully and successfully from the psychiatric situation to a mechanistic explanation of disease. Only a respectful and ethical acceptance of human agency will allow scientific reductionism to be successful in psychiatry.

REFERENCES

Allen, P., Modinos, G., Hubl, D., Shields, G., Cachia, A., Jardri, R., . . . Hoffman, R. (2012) 'Neuroimaging auditory hallucinations in schizophrenia: From neuroanatomy to neurochemistry and beyond.' *Schizophrenia Bulletin*, *38*(4), 695–703.

American Psychiatric Association. (2013) *Diagnostic and statistical manual of mental disorders*. Arlington, VA: American Psychiatric Publishing.

Andreasen, N. C. (2007) '*DSM* and the death of phenomenology in America: An example of unintended consequences.' *Schizophrenia Bulletin*, *33*(1), 108–112.

Baron-Cohen, S. (2017) 'Editorial perspective: Neurodiversity – A revolutionary concept for autism and psychiatry.' *Journal of Child Psychology and Psychiatry*, *58*(6), 744–747.

Baxter, L. R., Jr., Phelps, M. E., Mazziotta, J. C., Guze, B. H., Schwartz, J. M., & Selin, C. E. (1987) 'Local cerebral glucose metabolic rates in obsessive-compulsive disorder. A comparison with rates in unipolar depression and in normal controls [published erratum appears in *Arch Gen Psychiatry* 1987 Sep;44(9):800] [see comments].' *Archives of General Psychiatry*, *44*(3), 211–218.

Binswanger, L. (1957) *Der Mensch in der Psychiatrie*. Pfullingen: Neske.

Bracken, P., Thomas, P., Timimi, S., Asen, E., Behr, G., Beuster, C., . . . Yeomans, D. (2012) 'Psychiatry beyond the current paradigm.' *British Journal of Psychiatry*, *201*(6), 430–434.

Brewer, A. A., & Barton, B. (2016) 'Maps of the auditory cortex.' *Annual Review of Neuroscience*, *39*, 385–407.

Broome, M. R., Harland, R., Owen, G. S., & Stringaris, A. (Eds.). (2013) *The Maudsley reader in phenomenological psychiatry*. Cambridge, UK: Cambridge University Press.

Chung, J. Y., & Insel, T. R. (2014) 'Mind the gap: Neuroscience literacy and the next generation of psychiatrists.' *Academic Psychiatry*, *38*(2), 121–123.

Dierks, T., Linden, D. E., Jandl, M., Formisano, E., Goebel, R., Lanfermann, H., & Singer, W. (1999) 'Activation of Heschl's gyrus during auditory hallucinations.' *Neuron*, *22*(3), 615–621.

Engel, G. L. (1980) 'The clinical application of the biopsychosocial model.' *American Journal of Psychiatry*, *137*(5), 535–544.

Engstrom, E. J. (2004) *Clinical psychiatry in imperial Germany: A history of psychiatric practice*. Ithaca, NY: Cornell University Press.

Foucault, M. (1984) 'What is enlightenment?' In P. Rabinow (Ed.), *The Foucault reader* (pp. 32–50). New York: Pantheon Books.

(2006) *Psychiatric power. Lectures at the College de France, 1973–1974*. New York City: Picador.

Fuchs, T. (2014) 'Brain mythologies. Jasper's critique of reductionism from a current perspective.' In T. Fuchs (Ed.), *Karl Jasper's philosophy and psychopathology* (pp. 75–84). New York: Springer.

Fusar-Poli, P. (2015) 'The enduring search for the Koplik spots of psychosis.' *JAMA Psychiatry*, *72*(9), 863–864.

Fusar-Poli, P., Hijazi, Z., Stahl, D., & Steyerberg, E. W. (2018) 'The science of prognosis in psychiatry: A review.' *JAMA Psychiatry*, *75*(12), 1280–1288.

Ghaemi, S. N. (2003) *The concepts of psychiatry: A pluralistic approach to the mind and mental illness*. Baltimore, MD: Johns Hopkins University Press.

Havens, L. (2005) *Psychiatric movements. From sects to science*. New Brunswick: Transaction Publishers.

Heckers, S. (2017) 'Project for a scientific psychiatry: Neuroscience literacy.' *JAMA Psychiatry*, *74*(4), 315.

Helmers, S. L., Phillips, V. L., & Esper, G. J. (2010) 'Translational medicine in neurology: The time is right.' *Archives of Neurology, 67*(10), 1263–1266.

Honig, L. S. (2012) 'Translational research in neurology: Dementia.' *Archives of Neurology, 69*(8), 969–977.

Insel, T., Cuthbert, B., Garvey, M., Heinssen, R., Pine, D. S., Quinn, K., . . . Wang, P. (2010) 'Research domain criteria (RDoC): Toward a new classification framework for research on mental disorders.' *The American Journal of Psychiatry, 167*(7), 748–751.

Insel, T. R., & Quirion, R. (2005) 'Psychiatry as a clinical neuroscience discipline.' *JAMA, 294*(17), 2221–2224.

Jardri, R., Pouchet, A., Pins, D., & Thomas, P. (2011) 'Cortical activations during auditory verbal hallucinations in schizophrenia: A coordinate-based meta-analysis.' *The American Journal of Psychiatry, 168*(1), 73–81.

Jaspers, K. (1913) *Allgemeine Psychopathologie* (9th ed., 1973). Berlin: Springer-Verlag.

Jones-Davis, D. M., & Macdonald, R. L. (2003) 'GABA(A) receptor function and pharmacology in epilepsy and status epilepticus.' *Current Opinion in Pharmacology, 3*(1), 12–18.

Jutel, A. (2009) 'Sociology of diagnosis: A preliminary review.' *Sociology of Health and Illness, 31*(2), 278–299.

Kant, I. (1784) 'Beantwortung der Frage: Was ist Aufklärung?' *Berlinische Monatsschrift, 12*, 481–494.

Kendler, K. S. (1990) 'Toward a scientific psychiatric nosology. Strengths and limitations.' *Archives of General Psychiatry, 47*(10), 969–973.

Kraemer, H. C. (2013) 'Validity and psychiatric diagnoses.' *JAMA Psychiatry, 70*(2), 138–139.

Kraepelin, E. (1913) *Psychiatrie. Ein Lehrbuch für Studierende und Ärzte. Achte, vollständig umgearbeitete Auflage. 3. Band. Klinische Psychiatrie. 2. Teil.* Leipzig: Verlag von Johann Ambrosius Barth.

Linscott, R. J., & van Os, J. (2013) 'An updated and conservative systematic review and meta-analysis of epidemiological evidence on psychotic experiences in children and adults: On the pathway from proneness to persistence to dimensional expression across mental disorders.' *Psychological Medicine, 43*(6), 1133–1149.

Luhrmann, T. M. (2001) *Of two minds: The growing disorder in American psychiatry*. New York: Knopf.

Makari, G. J. (2008) *Revolution in mind: The creation of psychoanalysis*. New York: Harper Collins.

McGrath, J. J., Saha, S., Al-Hamzawi, A., Alonso, J., Bromet, E. J., Bruffaerts, R., . . . Kessler, R. C. (2015) 'Psychotic experiences in the general population: A cross-national analysis based on 31,261 respondents from 18 countries.' *JAMA Psychiatry, 72*(7), 697–705.

McHugh, P. R., & Slavney, P. R. (1998) *The perspectives of psychiatry*. Baltimore, MD: Johns Hopkins University Press.

Obeso, J. A., Stamelou, M., Goetz, C. G., Poewe, W., Lang, A. E., Weintraub, D., . . . Stoessl, A. J. (2017) 'Past, present, and future of Parkinson's disease: A special essay on the 200th anniversary of the shaking palsy.' *Movement Disorders, 32*(9), 1264–1310.

Parnas, J., Sass, L. A., & Zahavi, D. (2013) 'Rediscovering psychopathology: The epistemology and phenomenology of the psychiatric object.' *Schizophrenia Bulletin*, *39*(2), 270–277.

Parsons, T. (1951) *The social system*. New York: Free Press.

Reynolds, C. F., 3rd, Lewis, D. A., Detre, T., Schatzberg, A. F., & Kupfer, D. J. (2009) 'The future of psychiatry as clinical neuroscience.' *Academic Medicine*, *84*(4), 446–450.

Rosenberg, C. E. (2006) 'Contested boundaries: Psychiatry, disease, and diagnosis.' *Perspectives in Biology and Medicine*, *49*(3), 407–424.

Sass, L. A. (2007) "Schizophrenic person' or 'person with schizophrenia'?' *Theory & Psychology*, *17*(3), 395–420.

Schmitt, W. (1983) 'Das Modell der Naturwissenschaft in der Psychiatrie im Übergang vom 19. zum 20. Jahrhundert.' *Berichte der Wissenschaftsgeschichte*, *8*, 89–101.

Schneider, K. (1919) 'Reine Psychiatrie, symptomatische Psychiatrie und Neurologie.' *Zeitschrift für die gesamte Neurologie und Psychiatrie*, *49*, 159–166.

(1959) *Clinical psychopathology*. New York: Grune & Stratton.

Slade, M. (2017) 'Implementing shared decision making in routine mental health care.' *World Psychiatry*, *16*(2), 146–153.

Slade, M., Amering, M., Farkas, M., Hamilton, B., O'Hagan, M., Panther, G., . . . Whitley, R. (2014) 'Uses and abuses of recovery: Implementing recovery-oriented practices in mental health systems.' *World Psychiatry*, *13*(1), 12–20.

Solomon, M. (2015) *Making medical knowledge*. Oxford: Oxford University Press.

Strik, W., & Dierks, T. (2011) *Biologische Psychopathologie*. Stuttgart: Verlag W. Kohlhammer.

Szasz, T. S. (1961) *The myth of mental illness: Foundations of a theory of personal conduct*. New York: Dell.

Trull, T. J., & Durrett, C. A. (2005) 'Categorical and dimensional models of personality disorder.' *Annual Review of Clinical Psychology*, *1*, 355–380.

Waters, F., Allen, P., Aleman, A., Fernyhough, C., Woodward, T. S., Badcock, J. C., . . . Laroi, F. (2012) 'Auditory hallucinations in schizophrenia and nonschizophrenia populations: A review and integrated model of cognitive mechanisms.' *Schizophrenia Bulletin*, *38*(4), 683–692.

Wernicke, C. (1880) *Über den wissenschaftlichen Standpunkt in der Psychiatrie*. Kassel: Fischer.

(2000) *Grundriss der Psychiatrie*. Nijmegen: Arts & Boeve Verlag.

World Health Organization. (1992) *ICD-10 classifications of mental and behavioural disorders*. Geneva: World Health Organization.

Zolnierek, C. D. (2011) 'Exploring lived experiences of persons with severe mental illness: A review of the literature.' *Issues in Mental Health Nursing*, *32*(1), 46–72.

42

Commentary on Stephan Heckers, 'Psychiatric Discourse: Scientific Reductionism for the Autonomous Person'

JOHN CAMPBELL

I very much admire Stephan Heckers' way of framing what he calls 'four forms of scientific reductionism in psychiatry', and the issue of their relation to the autonomy of the patient. Although Stephan says that '[p]sychiatry . . . has embraced scientific reductionism" (p. 3), he thinks that there is some important relation between reductionism and patient autonomy that has to be respected for reductionism to be successful. I think it is immediately persuasive that there is an interesting relation between reductionism and patient autonomy, and I applaud Stephan for raising the question, I think it is quite difficult to explain what the relation is. On Stephan's way of explaining the relation between 'forms of reductionism' and the autonomy, the issue arises in the context of the psychiatric interview, where, he says, 'Only a person with agency can engage in a dyadic/interactional encounter with another person in such a way that observations and inference can lead to a psychiatric diagnosis' (p. 19). However, at first glance it is not quite obvious that this identifies a distinctive role for patient autonomy in psychiatry specifically. Any doctor, even one engaged only in physical medicine, typically relies on an initial discussion in which the patient is expected to be voluntarily forthcoming with information, although there are of course exceptions in both the physical and the psychiatric cases. After all, any medical professional should acknowledge patient autonomy. Stephan stresses the point at which patient and clinician might disagree over whether a particular diagnosis applies, and whether the patient is in need of treatment (p. 17ff.), and says that 'there is a significant move away from a disease/deficit model of mental illness to a recovery model (Slade et al., 2014). Related to this, the paternalistic attitude of medicine is giving way to a shared decision-making model' (Slade, 2017, p. 17). However, as I understand him, Stephan's position is not that the clinician should yield authority over diagnosis or possibilities of treatment to the patient, who after all may not have a great deal of insight into their own condition. Rather, just as a doctor treating a patient with a cancer diagnosis might collaborate with the patient in choosing one among various possibilities of treatment, the psychiatrist should collaborate with the patient in 'shared decision-making' as to how to proceed with treatment, respecting patient autonomy.

I think that there is a way of explaining the relation between 'reductionism' and patient autonomy that is special to psychiatry, but that takes some explaining; in particular, we need to know a bit more about what is meant by 'reductionism', and what is meant by 'autonomy'. I think Stephan is using 'reductionism' in a somewhat non-standard way, so let's begin with that. Typically, if one says that 'A can be reduced to B', what one means is something like 'A is nothing over and above B'. This can be reported in one of two ways. One might say, 'A's exist all right, it turns out that they are nothing but B's'; 'mental states exist, but they are nothing but neural states'. Or one might say, 'it turns out there are no A's, there are nothing but B's'; 'it turns out that mental states don't exist, there are only neural states'. Arguments over which of these responses is correct can of course occupy a great deal of time in one domain or another. I think that Stephan is not using 'reductionism' in this sense. What he means by 'reduction' has to do rather, on the face of it, with (as he says) 'simplification' (p. 5–6), or perhaps a bit more generally, 'loss of information'. Of course, a classical reduction, if one says, for example, 'heat is motion of molecules', or 'the valence of an element is the maximum number of hydrogen atoms that can combine with an atom of the element', this is not intended as a *simplification,* the idea is that the definition captures all, or at any rate, all that was important, about the phenomenon being reduced. But let's look a bit at Stephan's 'four forms' of reductionism, to get a bit more of a sense of the kind of simplification that he is talking about.

Stephan's picture, I think, is that we begin with the 'first-person experience of mental phenomena' (p. 5), the 'complex first-person experience' (p. 5; cf. p. 10) of the patient. There are then four reductive steps:

(1) There is the 'psychiatric situation' which is the clinical encounter between therapist and patient. Here the patient's experience is 'translated into a third-person account' (p. 5). Stephan notes that the 'translation' here should not be understood as a mechanical exercise in applying coding rules (p. 9). Stephan notes that many theorists, such as phenomenological psychiatrists, are concerned about the loss of information, or simplification, one finds at this

stage. But, he says, this kind of 'reduction' of the patient's lived experience into a third-person report, is 'a necessary form of reductionism' (p. 9). The other types of reductionism he identifies all depend on this one (p. 7).

(2) There is the classification of the patient as having some particular disorder. This depends, of course, on the choice of a particular set of diagnostic classifications, presumably with some kind of validation behind them. But again, information will be lost here.

(3) There is the finding of biological, presumably in particular neurobiological, correlates of the diagnostic classification. Stephan gives the example of auditory verbal hallucinations, and their correlates in the primary auditory cortex (p. 13). Stephan notes how far we are from explaining the psychological characteristics of such hallucinations in terms of the behavior of the auditory cortex, but remarks that nonetheless the finding of such a biological marker of auditory-verbal hallucinations is of value (p. 14). So he is not thinking of this as what would usually be called a 'reduction' of the psychological phenomenon, as when someone says, 'auditory-verbal hallucinations are nothing but disordered firings in the auditory cortex'; the point is rather the loss of information involved in moving to the biological level.

(4) The final type of 'reduction' Stephan considers is causal inference testing, when one uses laboratory experiments or randomized controlled trials to find the causal relationships implicated in disorders (p. 15). Stephan mentions testing of the impact of drug use on cognition, or the observations of the upshot of L-dopa therapy for Parkinson's patients (p. 15). Here again there is an element of 'simplification': there may be no attempt in such an experiment to deal comprehensively with all aspects of the disorder, but progress can be made by selecting one aspect of it for further study.

I think it's helpful to have these four types of exercise separated so cleanly. Still, before considering the relation of patient autonomy to these four forms of 'reduction', it seems worth making a bit more explicit just what is going on. Why should we bother engaging in this kind of 'simplification'?

Stephan does not explicitly consider this question. Let us look at a kind of answer that I do not think he would endorse, the answer of a biological essentialist about psychiatric disorders. In this approach, the four steps above are not properly described as 'simplifications'. Rather, from the first moments of the 'psychiatric situation', the clinician is asking whether there is a biological disorder, and if so, what it is. So the task of the clinician here is to separate out what, in the dialogue with the patient, is relevant to the specification of an underlying biological condition. The diagnostic steps – applying a classification and the finding of the underlying biological marker of the condition – are on this approach steps at which we get more and more traction on what that biological condition is, in the case of this patient. This is not really a 'simplification' of the patient's condition, it is, rather, finding more and more information about the biological condition that has to be treated. Similarly, a doctor of physical medicine, confronting a patient with a broken leg, may have to listen to a great deal of circumstantial information as to how the patient came by this condition and how they feel about it, filter out most of this information as irrelevant, and use the diagnostic classifications they have, and their knowledge of the underlying bone biology, to home in specifically on the problem to be addressed. Stephan's fourth step, the finding of causal relationships, is on this reading simply discovering more about the causes and consequences of the underlying biological condition.

Now Stephan does not explicitly reject this biological essentialism about disorders, but the paper seems written to accommodate, at any rate, a quite different picture. In this picture, the condition that has to be treated is the 'lived first-person experience' of the patient, in all its richness and idiosyncrasy. Questions about the underlying biology are merely instruments to, eventually, enable us to address the first-person experience of the patient. So the four 'reductions' that Stephan identifies are to be assessed as ways of doing that, and there is a concern running through all his remarks that these 'simplifications' may be missing out crucial aspects of the phenomenon to be addressed. In this picture, there is really no strong analogy with what is going on in physical medicine; the type of disorder being treated is identified in a quite different way, in terms of the 'lived experience of the patient', and everything else is merely a way of getting to that.

Still, however we think of it, it is puzzling how the 'autonomy' of the patient is supposed to fit in. Of course, in a clinical interview, one hopes that the patient will autonomously volunteer information, just as the patient with a broken leg ought to autonomously volunteer information, and hopefully collaborate with the therapist on a course of treatment. But even if we think that what constitutes the disorder as such is the 'lived experience of the patient', it is hard to see where there is a role distinctive to psychiatry of the autonomy of the patient. A patient who reports a life filled with melancholy and suicidal ideation has no more authority over their own diagnosis or treatment than does a patient reporting an inability to use their left leg to walk on. Of course, in both cases, the patients should be taken on board to discuss what courses of treatment would work best for them, be most practical and so on. But there is here nothing distinctive about psychiatry.

I want to suggest another way of thinking of Stephan's four types of reduction and their relation to patient autonomy. It seems to me that each of Stephan's four types of reduction can be viewed as an attempt to find generalizations under which the patient falls. In the 'psychiatric situation', such as a clinical interview, the therapist is looking for 'relevant' information, this being facts about the patient that can fit with already known generalizations (generalizations established quite independently of anything to do with this patient) to yield helpful conclusions about prognosis or treatment. The first way in which these generalizations can be helpful is in providing a diagnostic classification; there may be further generalizations to be had about the likely underlying biology of the patient, as the example of auditory-visual hallucinations and the auditory cortex suggests. And causal generalizations, derived from laboratory experiments or randomized controlled trials, may be of value in predicting the course of the disorder and helpful possible treatments.

The role of generalization here misses out what Jaspers took to be core of the clinical situation and the exercise of imaginative understanding in the interaction with the patient: the following of idiosyncratic, one-off causal connections in the mental life of the patient. This is not a matter of generalizations at all. In fact, as Jaspers pointed out, following the one-off causal connections in a patient's mental life may lead one to run counter to established generalizations. As he said, one can follow the train of thought and feeling of someone who, oppressed by the dark and cold of a northern winter, turns to suicidal ideation and suicide, even though the generalizations suggest that suicide typically happens in the spring. Similarly, consider the elaboration of complex secondary delusions. The therapist interacting with a patient might follow the thought of the patient perfectly well here ('so you found that the cameras were always being installed in your house in the evenings rather than the mornings?'), even though there are no relevant generalizations to be found behind the patient's thoughts here.

It seems to me that though it would take too long to try to establish the point here, a lot of what we typically mean by human 'autonomy' or 'freedom' has to do with our capacity to engage in idiosyncratic, one-off causal trains of thought and feeling. What distinguishes us from an animal like a dog that does not have autonomy is that the animal, in so far as it has a psychology, has a psychology that is entirely governed by causal generalizations, and that does not engage in one-off causation.

I am sketching this view very briefly, but if it is correct, is brings out one key way in which the autonomy of a human patient is in tension with the four reductions that Stephan describes. Those are all attempts, I have suggested, to exhibit the generalizations under which the patient falls. But the idiosyncrasy of human motivation, thought and feeling is a threat to any such attempt. At its most extreme, the threat would be decisive: there would be no significant generalizations to be had about human psychology, only accidents, hard to replicate, in which there happened to be a number of incidents which all fell under a single general type, but without there being any explanatory force to the generalization. But even if the point is not pressed so hard, and we acknowledge that there may nonetheless be some explanatory psychological generalizations governing people's mental lives, the capacity for one-off mental causation in the autonomous human will still be a pervasive problem for the attempt to find significant generalizations governing people's psychology, whether they are patients or not.

REFERENCES

Slade, M. (2017) 'Implementing shared decision making in routine mental health care.' *World Psychiatry*, *16*, 146–153.

Slade, M., Amering, M., Farkas, M., Hamilton, B., O'Hagan, M., Panther, G. et al. (2014) 'Uses and abuses of recovery: Implementing recovery-oriented practices in mental health systems.' *World Psychiatry*, *13*, 12–20.

SECTION 15

43

Introduction

JOSEF PARNAS

Imagine a society, which strongly disapproves of divorce. It is not illegal, but it is considered as a very bad, transgressive and immoral thing. Due to the activist pressure from certain well-organized groups, a National Psychiatric Association introduces to its diagnostic manual of mental disorders a new category Divorce Tendency Disorder (DTD). You suffer from the DTD if you have divorced more than once. DTD is further divided into subtypes: (1) divorce on your own initiative, (2) divorce on your spouse's initiative, (3) mixed type and (4) not otherwise specified. The creation of this diagnostic category stimulates a lot of scientific research. National Institute of Health and Prevention invests large sums of money into epidemiological and biological research. It turns out that DTD may be comorbid with a Personality Disorder, a Suicidal Behavior Disorder or Drug and Alcohol Dependence. Genetic-epidemiological studies show that DTD runs in families and twin data indicate genetic and earlyenvironmental effect. A genetic consortium using large sample studies shows that DTD is massively polygenic.

This fictional story, inspired by Turkheimer (2015, 2017) and far removed from reality, shows a possible way of addressing the issue of divorce. Another possible research pathway to the problem of divorce would be to study social, economic and cultural issues involved in this problem. If we considered divorce as a harmful phenomenon for the couple involved, their children and the society at large, perhaps wide-ranging social and economic reforms would be more suitable for preventing divorce than investing in molecular genetic research.

In this chapter, Eric Turkheimer, using a metaphor of the lens, is advocating for studying psychopathological disorders at a level where they are most sharply in focus. In other words, notwithstanding the likelihood of biological correlates to divorce, a molecular genetic approach to this issue would not be appropriate. Something entirely different would be the case in dealing with Huntington's chorea, which is a heritable, monogenic, dominant brain disease. Turkheimer's chapter touches upon the fundamental issue concerning the object of psychiatry, its classification and scientific and therapeutic implications. His present contribution can be considered as a follow-up on his previous thoughtful discussions of our common metaphysical assumptions involved in biological and statistical approaches in psychiatry.

REFERENCES

Turkheimer, E. (2015) 'The nature of nature.' In K. S. Kendler & J. Parnas (Eds.), *Philosophical Issues in Psychiatry III: The Nature and Sources of Historical Change* (pp. 227–244). Oxford: Oxford University Press.

(2017) 'The hard question in psychiatric nosology.' In K. S. Kendler & J. Parnas (Eds.), *Philosophical Issues in Psychiatry IV: Classification of Psychiatric Illness* (pp. 27–44). Oxford: Oxford University Press.

44

Entity Focus: Applied Genetic Science at Different Levels

ERIC TURKHEIMER

Twenty years ago, I wrote a paper entitled "Heritability and Biological Explanation" (Turkheimer, 1998) that examined the then nascent trend for theories of psychopathology to head ever further down in Comte's hierarchy of the sciences. My ultimate concern in that paper was with quantitative genetics: this was the heyday of twin studies, and as one disorder after another, and ultimately one behavior after another, was found to be substantially heritable, it seemed to many psychopathologists that the path ahead was going to lead first to quantitative and finally to medical genetics. It wasn't only genetics, of course: the turn of the last century was also a time of great excitement in brain imaging, where for the first time scientists could visualize the anatomical and then physiological processes that accompanied disordered or normal cognition. A new generation of psychiatric medications had produced a tidal wave of research into the role of neurotransmitters in psychopathology; the dopamine hypothesis of schizophrenia was in full flower. The selective serotonin reuptake inhibitor (SSRI) Prozac was then introduced in 1987, part of a new, more effective generation of psychiatric medications, the first ever to have been informed by brain science.

It was a heady time for biological psychiatry. Nancy Andreason's *The Broken Brain* was published in 1987, announcing a hegemony of brain-based theories of psychology that continues to the present day. Completion of the Human Genome Project was around the corner. Brain imaging technology proceeded from CT to MRI to PET to fMRI. New SSRIs appeared every month. Nevertheless, beneath all the excitement lay an unexamined theoretical problem. All of the great biological methodologies of the day – the quantitative genetics, the brain imaging, the pills – didn't only apply to the *DSM*-enshrined, uncontroversially pathological syndromes for which they were originally intended. Schizophrenia is heritable, but so are marital status and its pathological form, divorce (Jocklin, McGue, & Lykken, 1996). One can identify characteristic neurological activity in the brains of schizophrenics, but once again the same is true for any behavioral activity that can be reliably defined, for example, holding hands with a loved one (Coan, Schaeffer, & Davidson, 2006). Psychiatric drugs help the mentally ill, but psychiatric drugs have effects on everyone, often with side effects that patients do not want or recreational effects that patients want too much. The benzodiazepines and narcotics that offered help to so many genuinely suffering patients became drugs of abuse in the general population (Fraser, 1998).

A similar theoretical problem extended in the opposite direction. As the bioscientific tools of the time turned out not to apply specifically to their intended targets – all behavior is heritable, everyone processes dopamine, no one is immune to valium – it was also the case that none of the biological modalities had a crisply curative or explanatory relation to their intended objects. The onset of the Human Genome era was a disappointment. As was already becoming obvious in 1998, there are no "genes for" schizophrenia or depression, only genes that are (minutely) correlated with them, and conversely there *are* genes associated with marital status. Contemporary genome-wide association studies (GWAS) or functional magnetic resonance imaging (fMRI) have only made the situation more obvious: although they have produced vast networks of variously useful and interesting science, the mysteries of major psychopathology have not, despite repeated promises, been unlocked (Visscher, Wray, Zhang, Sklar, McCarthy, Brown, & Yang, 2017). Dopaminergic genes do not have a prominent place in recent GWAS of schizophrenia (Edwards, Bacanu, Bigdeli, Moscati, & Kendler, 2016). SSRIs and benzodiazepines have helped millions of people, but, likewise, hardly solved the problems of anxiety and depression. One can sum up the successes and failures of biological and genetic psychiatry this way: they are unfocused. They explained some limited aspects of their intended targets, but the explanations pertained to other targets as well, many of them having nothing to do with psychopathology. In any case, the explanations that were offered were always incomplete theoretically and clinically. One cannot point to a single psychiatric syndrome that has been decisively solved or cured.

This essay will suggest that the accomplishments, shortcomings, and disappointments of biological psychiatry can be understood in terms of a misunderstanding – or more acutely, an avoidance – of a theoretical question about when and how biological explanations and interventions do and don't apply to behavioral syndromes. Table 44.1 describes a

TABLE 44.1 *A proposed hierarchy of complexity for human problems, psychiatric disorders and brain diseases*

- Problems in living
  - Marital status, bankruptcy
- Complex psychiatric
  - Neurosis, dysphoria
- Clinical complex
  - Depression, GAD
- Low-level behavioral
  - OCD, panic
- Major psychiatric
  - Schizophrenia, BPD
- Neuropsychiatric
  - Tourette's, autism
- Complex neurological
  - Dementia, Parkinson's
- Major genetic disorders
  - Huntington's, Down's
- Frank brain disease
  - Stroke, tumors

hierarchy of human behavioral disorders; anyone could construct one much like it. At the top of the hierarchy are complex human activities that have often been characterized as "problems in living" or those that Freud described as *lieben und arbeiten*. Humans strive to get along with their families and acquaintances, and to perform happily and productively at work. Failures in these domains are the business of certain kinds of psychiatry and clinical psychology, but also the domain of counselors and clergy. At the bottom of the hierarchy are problems not pertaining to complex human lives but instead to physical bodies. Human brains suffer injury and illness just like any other body part. Those kinds of problems sometimes fall within the purview of psychiatrists and clinical psychologists, but they also receive attention from neurologists and neuroscientists.

Our intuitions about hierarchies of this kind are more complex than they may at first appear, leading eventually to a dilemma. On the one hand, it seems natural that different kinds of scientific understanding, and by extension, different kinds of treatment regimens, are appropriate for constructs at the top and bottom of the hierarchy. It would be perverse to expect insight-oriented psychotherapy to remediate the language problems of brain-injured patients, or to perform brain surgery on people struggling with their marriage, not that such things have never been tried.

Nevertheless, in the modern era, it is universally accepted that humans are integrated physical organisms from genes and neurons to emotions, intentions, and marriages. The days are long gone when human exceptionalism was animated by some variety of extra-materialist psychology, let alone a soul. Humans are evolved physical organisms, as subject to chemistry as any other object and as subject to biology as any other species; the neologistic hegemony of the *biopsychosocial model* is unquestioned.

The entire discussion of biological levels in psychopathology is made intractable by the absence of a coherent applied analysis of what if anything is at stake in the hierarchy. Questions of where particular conditions should be located in the hierarchy are fiercely debated (Leshner, 1997; Satel & Lilienfeld, 2014), yet when the question is addressed on a theoretical level, it is usually dismissed as falsely dualist (Greenberg & Bailey, 1994; Lipowski, 1989). The general problem of levels of analysis in science has been widely and deeply explored in philosophy (Wimsatt, 2007), and although much of that work is of course relevant to the psychopathology problem, my concerns here are more local and practical. The declarations that "X is a brain disease" that have become so commonplace usually proceed in the complete absence of analysis of what it means for something to be a brain disease, or not to be a brain disease, or even what the alternative to being a brain disease might be. One can infer some of the issues that are thought to be important from the evidence, such as it is, that is routinely brought forward. Most of this evidence, I will contend, is not decisive or even relevant.

After reviewing several of the brain disease papers as a way of gaining access to extant theories of the hierarchy of psychopathology, I will propose a novel way of thinking about levels in psychopathology: psychiatric levels are about entities and their boundaries. Even though it is obviously true that people in bad marriages have brains and use them to conduct their marriages, and that people with brain injuries have good or bad marriages which they experience psychologically; even though our genes are related to everything we are, simple and complex; even though drugs have effects, good or ill, on the human condition, whether or not the condition in question is enshrined in the *DSM*; even though all these things are true, none of them provides a method for thinking about where a condition should be located in the hierarchy.

44.1 THE PHYSICS OF CARPETS

When I first wrote about the problem of levels of analysis in Turkheimer (1998), I borrowed, almost in passing, an example from the Harré, Clarke, and DeCarlo (1975): the physics of carpets. My account of the example, in its entirety, was as follows: "Although carpets may have characteristic physical components, what makes something a carpet is its relationship, at a much higher level of analysis, with the world of human beings. No amount of physics would ever lead to an explanation of why some objects are carpets" (Turkheimer, 1998, p. 784). I assumed naively that the question of whether there existed a physics of carpets was a self-evident "No," and that the negative response had important implications for, say, a neuroscience of marriage. In the years that followed, I have often returned to this example as an argument against the blind reduction of complex behavioral syndromes to biological or genetic terms; so often, in fact, that the phrase, "physics of carpets" became almost an argument in itself, or a code for one, rather like the old story about the lifers in prison who retell their stale jokes in the lunchroom by shouting out numbers.[1]

My penchant for repetition notwithstanding, it is safe to say that the physics–of-carpets argument has not won the day in contemporary psychopathology, as evidenced by the ongoing enthusiasm for "brain disorder" models of all manner of human behavioral suffering. The reason is informative: there *is* a physics of carpets. An unironic paper titled precisely, "The Physics of Carpets," (Carnaby & Wood, 1989), in its technical sophistication, utter lack of interest in theoretical questions about what exactly a carpet is, and its optimism about new technologies to come, sounds exactly like a contemporary paean to the neurogenetics of depression or addiction. It concludes:

> This review paper has highlighted some of the fascinating and urgent topics in the physics of carpets. As understanding of the scientific principles that govern the mechanics and optics of the pile material unfolds, it is to be hoped that it will be possible to design carpets that perform better and to design better tests that will quantify these gains. Because carpets represent a large budget item in any refurnishing programme, it is important to the industry and the consumers that products on the market will give long-term satisfaction. Future improvements in understanding of the physics seem imminent. Comfort testing of carpets seems likely to be available soon. Improved construction-based formulae that incorporate fibre mechanical behaviour (e.g., fibre-fatigue properties) also seem possible. The rapid progress in the measurement of carpet appearance should enhance the

1 A newcomer decides to give it a try, and yells out, "Twenty-three!" only to be met with unamused silence. "It was the way you told it," an old-timer assures him.

> control of carpet texture in manufacture and the retention of the carpet's new look longer during use. The old problem of carpet shading is beginning to yield to the new techniques of analysis, although no panacea is yet evident. A reliable, accurate, and precise abrasion test, capable of predicting the performance across the full range of fibres and carpet styles, remains a challenge in carpet-testing.
>
> (p. 89)

What could be going on here? How is it that an intuition which on its surface seems so natural – that the study of carpets is a matter not for physicists but for anthropologists, decorators, or other human-level professionals – is so easily undermined by the unironic, practical, and technically sound efforts of a couple of engineers from the Wool Research Institute of New Zealand?

No one, of course, has ever disputed that carpets were physical objects, subject to the same physical laws as everything else. Indeed that is the point of the carpet example: to insist that even indisputably physical things like carpets are better studied with the tools of social science than they are with nuclear physics. Once Carnaby and Wood point it out, it becomes perfectly natural that physics informs issues like color saturation and fiber strength that are crucial to the manufacture, care, and improvement of carpets. The biologically oriented psychopathologist is entitled to a feeling of vindication at this point. Of course biology (although, tellingly, not physics) is relevant to the understanding of psychopathology. Just as the physics of color saturation, applied to the manufacture of dyes, is relevant to creating carpets, the brain circuits involved in negative emotions, the genes involved in their construction, and their potential for modification with drugs is relevant to our understanding of depression. For that matter, it is no different for marital status: there are widely studied genetic variants, discovered in voles but homologous in humans, that are related to hormonal pathways involved in mating and fidelity (Walum et al., 2008). Are such genes the explanation of why some people get divorced? Obviously not (exactly why not to be discussed below), but just as obviously they are relevant to it.

44.2 THE EVIDENTIARY BASIS FOR BRAIN DISEASES

One might be tempted to leave the issue there. The intuition that complex human behaviors are somehow immune to biological analysis was just wrong, a vestige of dualist or even vitalist philosophy, or a holdover from psychoanalysis. The problem is not so easily dismissed, however. The tension between an intuitively leveled, but ultimately unanalyzed, view of human function and dysfunction on the one hand, and a unified biopsychosocial science on the other, is manifest in many of the unsolved theoretical problems and recalcitrant empirical disappointments in modern psychopathology. The most obvious of these involves the status of the middle of the hierarchy, where in fact the most interesting problems – schizophrenia, depression, addiction – are to be found. Is addiction a problem in living or a brain disease? Apparently it is a little of both, but how are such questions to be specified and adjudicated? Moreover, although there may have once been a time when it was commonplace to overshoot the hierarchy on the high end, submitting the delusions of schizophrenic patients to Jungian analysis or something of the sort, nowadays the methodological trend is relentlessly downward. Addiction, as a matter of fact, is commonly declared to be a brain disease (Leshner, 1997), as is schizophrenia (van Haren, Cahn, Pol & Kahn, 2008), and as we will see below, pretty much the entire range of *DSM*-validated psychopathology. The difficulties of such persistent downward pressure on the psychopathological sciences are explored at several places in this volume.

In my 1998 paper on this topic, I analyzed a paper by Samuel Guze (1989), then President of the American Psychiatric Association and a pioneer of biological psychiatry. The paper was titled, "Biological psychiatry: Is there any other kind?" His answer, predictably, was no. He reached his conclusion on the grounds I have outlined here: problems are biological if they involve brains, and all human problems involve brains: "If it could be asserted that few if any of the states or conditions that constitute the focus of psychiatry are the result of differences in the development or physiology of the brain, biology would seem to be of only marginal interest (p. 316)." He concluded, "Psychopathology thus involves, biology." Obvious as this conclusion may seem I demurred, on physics-of-carpets grounds: "Had Guze titled his article, 'Why Psychiatrists Should Know Something about Neuroscience,' [Contemporary note: Why carpet designers should know something about color physics] there would be no basis for argument. It is nevertheless necessary to insist that it is entirely possible for psychiatry to be too biological. What would you say to a programmer, assigned to correct a factor analysis program that was misestimating the communalities of the observed variables, who started out with a pile of chips and a soldering iron?"

I rehash this old argument to make the point that nothing has changed. In 2013, Thomas Insel, then the director of the National Institute of Mental

Health, and Story Landis, the Director of the National Institute of Neurological Disorders and Stroke, published a paper in *Neuron*, titled, "Twenty-Five Years of Progress: The View from NIMH and NINDS." Noting the recent "explosive growth" of knowledge in molecular neurobiology, they set their task as follows: "Our charge is to relate these changes to the state of brain disorders in 2013, identifying the best bridges for translational research. We conclude that progress on brain disorders will require a significantly deeper understanding of fundamental neurobiology." This seems reasonable enough, but what exactly is to be counted as a brain disorder? As is typical for articles of this type, they don't say, but we can infer what they have in mind by listing the conditions they refer to as brain disorders in the course of the article. In order of first appearance, they are Parkinson's disease, autism, epilepsy, schizophrenia, intellectual disability, stroke, ALS, Huntington's disease, bipolar disorder, suicide, Alzheimer's disease, multiple sclerosis, depression, obsessive-compulsive disorder, posttraumatic stress disorder, migraine, essential tremor, and dystonia. So, it seems safe to say, everything. Nothing is excluded as *not* a brain disorder, and from their brief discussion of psychotherapy one can infer that the domain of brain disorders includes indeed all activities for which people might use their brains:

> In 1988, treatments in psychiatry were largely divided between psychotherapy and pharmacotherapy. While it would be naive to suggest that this division no longer exists, cognitive neuroscience in the past decade has begun to put psychotherapy into the context of neural plasticity, with studies of how the brain changes during psychotherapy and the development of cognitive therapies based specifically on feedback from fMRI signals.

In the same spirit as the Guze piece, the Insel and Landis article illustrates the most common outcome of incompletely analyzed ideas about the hierarchy of levels, which is that it can quickly lead to the conclusions that (a) in a materialist biopsychosocial universe the hierarchy doesn't really exist and (b) one might as well start at the bottom, where the scientific ground seems the most solid. If brain disorder is the class of disorders involving activities that people conduct with their brains, then it includes depression and anxiety (and, one presumes, bad marriages and poor budget management) just as much as ALS and stroke. Of course, NIH institute directors are not generally in the business of defining domains that do not come under their domain, so it is to some extent natural that they would be so inclusive. Nevertheless, there is a price to be paid for a theory-free acceptance of the idea that everything is a brain disorder.

44.3 COMPOSITION AND CLASSIFICATION

We are seeking a theory that allows us to maintain our sense that high-level human constructs and the problems of living associated with them are different than brain and other physical disorders, while also maintaining our commitment to the psychophysical integration of human beings and the universality of the scientific method. We want carpets to be carpets, things that people use to cover floors, while freely admitting the knowledge about carpets that can be generated by the physical sciences. The answer is to be found in the original source: Harré, Clarke, and DeCarlo (1975). Here is the full context of Harré, Clarke, and DeCarlo's invocation of the physics of carpets:

> First, familiar categories of phenomena do not always correspond one-to-one with sensible divisions of the under-lying process. In other words, although every product is produced by a process, the same kind of product is produced sometimes by one kind of process, sometimes by another. This is why there is no 'physics of carpets'. Of course, every feature of every particular carpet is produced by some particular physical and chemical processes, which could serve as an explanation for colour (why this carpet is just this colour), but there are all sorts of ways of making carpets of a given colour and texture. Furthermore, carpets are human artefacts, and what makes something a carpet is a human convention. So no coherent branch of physics could, in its own right, represent the study of carpets and all the processes that go to make them what they are, taken as a set. To put it another way, carpets are not a natural kind. For the same reasons, the psychological explanation for social explananda may not form a coherent and profitable topic for a branch of scientific psychology. The same social behaviour may be the product of diverse psychological and social processes; and what is to count as the same type of social behaviour (say, mourning) may be collected up into a category by a human social convention, which differs from one society to another.

We see immediately that the reason Harré, Clarke, and DeCarlo (1975) deny the possibility of a physics of carpets doesn't involve the relation between individual carpets and the laws of physics. Their book, which is titled *Motives and Mechanisms*, is an attempt to establish a scientific method suitable for the study of interpersonal interaction. That method focuses on what they call "processes," rule-governed sequences that lead to the outcomes of interest, which for them are varieties of social behavior. Those explanatory sequences are themselves social behaviors, or the cognitive processes that underlie them; they reject the possibility of finding explanations of social behavior in the physical sciences or biology, or for that matter within individual humans at all.

Harré, Clarke, and DeCarlo (1975) would have no reason to object to or be surprised by the actual physics of carpets as laid out by the wool engineers. Their concern would be with the question: What are the processes by which some objects become carpets? For that question, issues of color optics or fiber durability would have very little relevance. In the same way, one presumes, the wool engineers would be nonplussed by a question like, "What is it about the physical and chemical properties of an object that makes it be a carpet?" The physical characteristics that describe the composition of objects is one thing, and the social (if such they are) processes that lead to the designation of objects as being a certain kind of thing in a decorating scheme are another. Harré, Clarke, and DeCarlo (1975) see the problem as a straightforward instance of token identity: "Even though the approach of this book is materialist in general, the fact of token identity means that there must always be a place for an autonomous psychological account of human action and thought." So carpets have physical properties, which are crucial to the manufacture, understanding, performance, and improvement of carpets. On the other hand, the physical properties cannot explain the boundaries of the category, "carpet." That is reserved for the human processes that define carpetdom.

So there are two kinds of questions that can be asked about a class of complex objects like carpets. First, one can ask inter-level questions about composition. Such questions could be atomic or subatomic or chemical; in the case of organisms they might also be genetic or neurological. Individual objects, persons or carpets, are necessarily inter-level: it's just the way an integrated universe works. Individual carpets are, in principle, made of something. Conversely, a big pile of molecules is a thing, an object, however humans choose to classify it; a bunch of protoplasm is an organism. You can't have a carpet-sized object that isn't made of molecules or a human being who doesn't have genes or neurons. One can ask scientific questions about the small things large objects are composed of, or about the characteristics of objects made out of particular elements, but such questions are not essential: wool engineers don't have any reason to care where the boundaries of the class of carpets are to be found, or why they are located there.

Alternatively, one can ask questions about the nature of classes of individual objects. Because classes are created by humans who live at a particular level and think in terms of levels, classes are usually intra-level. Carpets are objects that are used by humans in a certain way. The *DSM* criteria for depression comprise behavioral and phenomenal characteristics. Once again, although individual people being diagnosed are necessarily integrated across levels from atom to gene to neuron to feeling to culture, as a matter of official policy, the criteria that admit them to the class "depressed" are the behavioral criteria listed in the *DSM*, and those criteria, at least for the time being, are at the level of human cognition, affect, and action.

What, then, are the scientific activities associated with the understanding of classes? On the one hand, there are the literal classificatory sciences, forms of cladistics like cluster analysis. As I discussed in the previous volume of this series (Turkheimer, 2017), however, such methods have not proved particularly interesting or decisive, at least in psychopathology. The problem is that classification and clustering are two different things because classes don't necessarily imply clustering, i.e., regions of multivariate density surrounded by relatively empty space. Carpets are undoubtedly a class, but there is no reason to think they are a cluster: the border with other kinds of things like tapestries or drop cloths is, one expects, smooth and continuous, like the border between depression and anxiety.

Another kind of question about classes, this one inter-level and much more interesting but also much more problematic, is the source of the perpetual confusion about the hierarchy of psychopathological categories with which this essay began. Although as I have noted, classes are usually defined within a level, they are detectable across them, albeit in a somewhat degraded form. Analysis of a large number of objects, some carpets and some not, would certainly identify chemical (or atomic or subatomic) regularities among the things we call carpets: they would be more likely to be made of wool than of fiberglass, for example. Conversely, looking upward instead of down, a class defined at the level of chemistry – wool objects or fiberglass objects – might have some very rough correspondence to carpets as people define them, but the correspondence would not and could not replace the human-defined class of carpet. If a flat object is spun out of steel wool and put on the floor under an armchair it is a carpet, chemistry be damned. This was Harré, Clarke, and DeCarlo's point: "familiar categories of phenomena do not always correspond one to one with the underlying process." Classes that are defined at one level of analysis are detectable but fuzzy at another. I will say that a class is *focused* at the level of analysis at which it is defined, and *blurry* elsewhere.

All of this becomes more difficult and more interesting as one proceeds from carpets to the characteristics, components and classes of human beings. The carpet problem is a useful example because it is easy: we know at the outset that carpets are a human creation, and that as a consequence carpets can't be defined by their chemical composition. When we encounter an entity in the actual conduct of science, however, we are faced with a problem: perhaps this is a focused entity at the level at which we have encountered it, but then again maybe it isn't. Even at their best, psychological constructs are prone to be blurry, so maybe what we are encountering is actually a blurred version of a class that is in focus at a different – in practice usually lower – level of analysis. This is the hypothesis that biological psychiatry can never seem to abandon. Depression *seems* like a human-level thing when encountered casually, and it is certainly enshrined as such in the *DSM*, but like most behavioral constructs it can also be frustratingly blurry. Maybe in reality *DSM* depression, or something related to depression, is actually a blurry version of a focused category unobserved at a lower level of analysis, a pattern of genes or a dysfunctional neural circuit.

Our intuitions about the level-focus of classes are the real basis of the hierarchy of psychopathology. There are two reasons why those intuitions are so difficult to turn into empirical science. The first is that focus questions are persistently confused with compositional questions, usually in the interest of moving something down in the hierarchy. *Of course* carpets are more likely to be made out of some materials than others; *of course* depressed people are more likely to have certain alleles than others. In a universe integrated from small to large, it can't be otherwise. Humans at their most complex and abstract are nevertheless instantiated in biology, so biological differences are inevitable even across the most complex and abstract of human classes. There is nothing wrong with science directed at observations like these if it is recognized for what it is, and like carpet physics such science might be very useful, but it doesn't – can't, isn't designed to – lead to decisive understanding about the level at which psychopathological categories are focused.

The second reason questions about level-focus are hard to turn into science is that the scientific methods that *are* suited to the purpose are diverse, difficult, and ill-defined. In the previous volume of this series (Turkheimer, 2017), I examined how Paul Meehl dedicated the last half of his career to developing a statistical method for detecting unobserved focused classes at lower levels of analysis, a method he called taxometrics (Meehl, 1995). The method was ingenious, sophisticated, and briefly popular, but it never caught on and has now been largely abandoned. As I discussed in that previous chapter, there were two reasons for this outcome: probably no one other than Meehl fully understood the method, and more importantly because it turned out there aren't many undiscovered taxa down there. If compositional hypotheses about are too easy to confirm, indeed almost tautological, the problem with low-level focus hypotheses is that they are almost never true; no wonder the scientific establishment is usually content with composition.

44.4 INTER-LEVEL CAUSATION: MOTIVES AND MECHANISMS REVISITED

Parts and wholes are obviously related, sometimes in ways that seem uncontroversially causal. Carl Craver and William Bechtel (2007) have developed a sophisticated account of part–whole relations that makes it clear when cause, or something very much like it, can be attributed to them. Their model encompasses both "top-down" and "bottom-up" causes; given our interest in biology and behavior we will be primarily concerned with the latter. The key to Craver and Bechtel's account is the notion of a mechanism. Mechanisms are "organized collections of entities and activities" that link (usually symmetrically) larger parts of a hierarchy to smaller ones. If you open a wind-up clock and twiddle a certain tiny gear inside it, the hands of the clock go around as if they were telling time. If you move the hands of the clock, the gear turns. Craver and Bechtel explain that one would not want to say that the moving gear causes the hands to turn or vice-versa; they happen simultaneously, two parts of a single mechanism observed at two different levels. One could speak of an exogenous cause of the gear turning, like a person's decision to twiddle it, which would then, via the mechanism, produce simultaneous motion in the clock hands. In this way, Craver and Bechtel avoid the many problems of inter-level causation that have been discussed by philosophers: causes are exogenous, temporally sequential, and intra-level, and mechanisms are endogenous, simultaneous, and inter-level.

Most important for current purposes, the existence of a mechanism is a *hypothesis* about hierarchical organization. Not all part–whole relations are mechanisms, in fact it seems safe to say that few of them are. Routine part–whole relations are, in Craver and Bechtel's terms, constitutive, simply the observation that large objects on one level are made up of certain kinds of small objects on another. Smashed clocks might have gears inside them, but they don't contain mechanisms. Carpets may be often made of wool, but wool is not part of a mechanism that turns things into carpets. A scientist encountering a clock for the first time would have to *discover* the mechanism linking the gears and the hands. The frequent occurrence of gears inside clocks might be an interesting clue, but it wouldn't be definitive.

A more conceptual and less mechanical way of saying this is that mechanisms are a means of expressing identities between entities at different levels of analysis. Mechanical clocks telling time are the same thing as objects with gears that behave in a certain way. Carefully specified interactions among gears don't cause clocks to tell time, they *are* clocks telling time. So for a psychopathologist interested in the relation between genes (a part) and depression (a whole), there are two possibilities. Clearly the constitutive relation holds: depressed people are more likely to contain certain kinds of genes than others. The mechanistic hypothesis, however, is much more difficult to establish. Maybe depression is the high-level manifestation of a mechanism in which a gene is a tiny gear, but maybe not, and probably not. Trying to establish bio-behavioral mechanisms of that kind is a worthy enterprise for a scientific psychopathologist, but it has not been a particularly successful one to date.

44.5 THE VIEW FROM GENETICS: HUNTINGTON'S DISEASE

In 1872, when George Huntington published his discoveries about what would soon become known as Huntington's disease (HD), genetics was unknown, but chorea itself was already a well-established neurological phenotype. The paper, titled, "On Chorea," was not primarily concerned with what we now call Huntington's chorea: it was about chorea generally. Huntington spent the majority of the famous paper detailing chorea's diverse potential causes of which the Huntington's gene is only one of many:

> The causes predisposing to chorea are various: Improper and indigestible articles of diet, confinement in illy ventilated apartments, with want of proper exercise; disordered digestion, etc. While the exciting causes are irritation from dentition, irritation in the stomach and alimentary canal; by worms, retained faeces, etc., anger, fright, rheumatism and injuries to the head. It is, also, singular as it appears, sometimes the result of mitation.

Those diverse causes were associated with an equally diverse set of treatments:

> The treatment of chorea now most generally adopted is by purgatives, tonics, counter-irritants, and anti-spasmodics. The first indication is, if possible, to remove the exciting cause and it will probably be different in

> each individual case. Bleeding used to be employed, and it is said with good results, but it is rarely used at present, except in cases when there is much pain in the head, or along the spine, when it may be taken moderately by cups or leeches.

It is only in the very last section of the paper that Huntington arrives at his eponymous discovery:

> The hereditary chorea, as I shall call it, is confined to certain and fortunately a few families, and has been transmitted to them, an heirloom from generations away back in the dim past. It is spoken of by those in whose veins the seeds of the disease are known to exist, with a kind of horror, and not at all alluded to except through dire necessity, when it is mentioned as "that disorder." It is attended generally by all the symptoms of common chorea, only in an aggravated degree, hardly ever manifesting itself until adult or middle life, and then coming on gradually but surely, increasing by degrees, and often occupying years in its development, until the hapless sufferer is but a quivering wreck of his former self.

Huntington's anticipation of the pattern of transmission of an autosomal dominant gene is truly remarkable, but not the main point here, where we are more concerned with the structure of the discovery itself. Huntington did not discover the cause of chorea in general, and in fact there is no cause of chorea in general. Notwithstanding Huntington's extraordinary perspicacity, he had no knowledge of genetics, and no insight into the neurological mechanisms underlying hereditary chorea. What he did perceive is that amidst the multivariate domain of chorea symptoms caused by all sorts of things and taking all kinds of forms, there was one subdomain that was a slightly out-of-focus image of a hereditary syndrome with crisp edges at an unobserved lower level of analysis. Huntington's discovery was about classification, not causation or genetics or biology.

Once Huntington had established that this form of chorea was an unfocused reflection of something better understood in (necessarily primitive) hereditary terms, it was no longer necessary or desirable to discuss *this kind* of chorea as a matter of hysterical contagion in schools, as he did elsewhere in the manuscript. The association he observed between motoric chorea and "insanity" in the hereditary form were now presumed to be mutually determined by the heredity, rather than being mutually causal on the phenotypic level. (The conditional covariance between two "indicators" of hereditary chorea would have been a perfect target for Meehlian taxometrics.) Huntington couldn't quite know it, but he had turned one form of chorea into a genetic disease of the brain. Today there is no controversy about the proper level of analysis for HD: an article with a title like, "Huntington's Is a Brain Disease, And It Matters" would be pointless.

It is also important to notice that the discovery of hereditary chorea did not replace the older, more general category of chorea, which was and remains defined behaviorally. Chorea is a focused class of motor behavior. Only one part of behavioral chorea is a blurry representation of Huntington's chorea. Other aspects of chorea are an unfocused image of classes focused at a neuropsychological level. Chorea of this kind, although almost certainly heritable in a statistical sense (more on this below) is not crisply associated with any particular genetic variant.

The hysterical form of contagious chorea that Huntington cites is particularly interesting because it is a class of chorea that is not focused at either the genetic or neurological levels, and is probably an instance of a behavioral class that turns out to be focused at a higher level than the behavioral level at which it is observed. Why are there occasional breakouts of hysterical motor disturbances, for example in schools (Goldstein & Hall, 2015)? It isn't easy to say, but it is certain that it is not the result of a segregating gene or a focused neurological pathway. Hysterical conversion was the origin of Freud's psychoanalytic hypotheses about complex human behavior, and whatever one now makes of Freudianism in general, hysteria remains the most plausible place to apply it. Hysterical conversion, mysterious and unfocused when observed behaviorally, is a blurry image of a focused class of motivations and desires at a higher (unconscious) level of analysis. At the very least, it must be admitted that no genetic, neurological, or rationally cognitive accounts can provide a focused account of hysterical contagion.

44.6 POLYGENICITY, THE FOURTH LAW, AND OMNIGENICS, AND GENERALIST GENES

Modern complex genetics has imported terminology from older, classical genetics in ways that are superficially sensible but prone to breaking down as the distance between genotype and complex phenotype becomes ever greater. The most obvious of these is "polygenic." The original notion of polygenicity involved countable sets of variants with biologically traceable causal relations with structured phenotypes in model organisms, for example, involving patterns of veins in *Drosophila* wings. From a modern-day perspective, it is hard to believe that not so long ago, many genetic theories of behavioral phenotypes included genes of large effect (e.g., Weiss, 1992). Such theories were slowly abandoned in favor of briefly popular "oligogenic" theories involving genes of relatively large effect against a polygenic background, but with a few rare exceptions the genes with the relatively larger effects were never found. The field then retreated further to the notion of quantitative trait loci (QTL), polygenes of small but statistically quantifiable and biologically traceable biological effects. These, too, have proven easier to theorize about than they are to actually find.

Finally, Chabris et al. (2015) made it official, adding to the previously enumerated three laws of behavior genetics a fourth: "A typical human behavioral trait is associated with very many genetic variants, each of which accounts for a very small percentage of the behavioral variability." Note that the word "cause" does not appear in this formulation; neither does the proposed law offer any expectation that the number of variants is quantifiable, even in principle. It is just very many variants accounting for variance. The process of generalizing the genetics of complex phenotypes did not stop here. Several years later, Boyle, Li, and Pritchard (2017) introduced the concept of "omnigenics," breaking down the notion of even a very complex causal chain between genetic variation and complex (and not all that complex; Pritchard et al. are biologists, and mostly talking about diabetes and height) phenotypes.

There is much to be said about this exponentiating polygenic complexity, but for present purposes, the point is that we are witnessing the slow motion collision of human genetics with the physics of carpets. By now, I hope that this assertion has a more specific meaning than it did at the outset. Complex (omni) genetics is no longer a search for causal pathways between genetic variants and behavioral outcomes, it has become a means of observing the blurry correspondence between entities defined at behavioral and genetic levels. That correspondence, it should be noted, is neither arbitrary nor spurious. Variants associated with behavioral phenotypes are "enriched" for expression in the brain, for example. It is not impossible that some psychological equivalent of color saturation or fiber durability will eventually be discovered, and if that happens, the discovery may be relevant to behaviorally defined entities.

44.7 PLEIOTROPY AND GENERALIST GENES

The degeneration of polygenicity has been widely noted (if not often appreciated for its importance), but the situation regarding polygenicity's inverse, pleiotropy, is more acute but so far under the radar. Polygenicity refers to phenotypic entities that are related to multiple genetic variants;

pleiotropy refers to variants that are related to multiple phenotypic entities. As the causal basis for thinking about relations between genetic and phenotypic levels has slowly been replaced with a definitional one about level relations between entities, pleiotropy has become so obviously pervasive, and the possibility of variants with specific causal effects on complex phenotypes so implausible, that the very notion no longer applies to the complex world of behavioral entities. Once again: pleiotropy made sense when biologists were tracing upward the causal effects of individual variants, but once the enterprise turned into describing the blurry correspondence between genetic entities and behavioral ones, pleiotropy was both inevitable and uninteresting. Color saturation applies to curtains just as much as carpets.

Robert Plomin has conducted an extended effort to rescue the genetic concept of pleiotropy from the causal irrelevance imposed by the extreme complexity of inter-level analyses, in the form of the concept of "generalist genes" (Plomin & Kovas, 2005). Plomin, along with a variety of junior investigators, was working on educational psychology and learning disabilities at the time, and most of the examples are from that domain:

> This [quantitative genetic] research suggests that most genes associated with common learning disabilities – language impairment, reading disability, and mathematics disability – are generalists in 3 ways. First, genes that affect common learning disabilities are largely the same genes responsible for normal variation in learning abilities. Second, genes that affect any aspect of a learning disability affect other aspects of the disability. Third, genes that affect one learning disability are also likely to affect other learning disabilities.
>
> (Plomin & Kovas, 592)

Note, first of all, that in 2005 causal notions of relations between polygenes and phenotypes had not yet been abandoned in favor of fully acknowledged variance partitioning. Although the studies to which Plomin and Kovas refer are twin studies that don't and can't specify causal pathways at the level of DNA, they nevertheless refer to "genes" that "affect" phenotypic outcomes.

A more appropriately non-causal account of the relation between genetic and phenotypic variance is the concept of genetic correlation, as Plomin and Kovas also explore. Genetic correlation is simply the observation that genetic variance associated with one entity is also associated with another. For all the reasons cited above, genetic correlations are universal in complex genetics, but they don't actually inform us about the causal effects of individual genes; they just describe the overlap between the blurry genetic images of behavioral phenotypes. But Plomin and Kovas impose a causal interpretation on the relation:

> One of the genetic causes of correlation is that the same genes influence both traits, an effect called *pleiotropy*. The key concept in the present context is the genetic correlation, which indicates the extent to which genetic effects on trait *X* correlate with genetic effects on trait *Y* regardless of the heritabilities of *X* and *Y*. The genetic correlation, which is described in greater detail below, can be considered as the probability that a gene found to be associated with *X* will also be associated with *Y*.

The "genes" (I will remove the scare quotes in the next paragraph) associated with learning phenotypes don't "affect" learning; there is no known mechanism linking any actual gene with learning; what Plomin and Kovas call genes are blurry genetic images of behaviorally focused entities. Various learning disability entities, of course, are not independent of each other at the behavioral level either, and genetic correlations, generalist genes if you will, are simply a reflection of that overlap, amplified by the blurriness that results from looking at the entities at the wrong level of analysis. Most of the time, the pattern of overlap, the structure of the matrix of genetic correlations, cannot be distinguished from the pattern at the phenotypic level, a phenomenon called the phenotypic null hypothesis (Turkheimer, Pettersson & Horn, 2014). Failure to reject the phenotypic null hypothesis is an indication that genetic variance is nothing more than a blurry image of the phenotype.

The reader may protest at this point that my contention that genetic effects are merely correlational variance components, without concrete biological meaning, has been supplanted by modern developments in DNA-based genomics. Nowadays genome-wide association studies (GWAS) can identify individual units of DNA (single-nucleotide polymorphisms, or SNPs) that are (statistically) significantly correlated with phenotypes, and SNPs can sometimes be associated in turn with whole genes and biological pathways associated with them. I note, however, that associations between phenotypes and small components of phenotypes are inevitable under a physics-of-carpets model, as I made clear in Turkheimer (1998) before GWAS was imagined.

> ...modern molecular genetics has made it possible to detect small covariations between alleles and behavior that span the complexity of the causal network... Such associations are real and potentially interesting, but they remain correlations – and small ones – not evidence of

substantial causal pathways between individual alleles and complex behavior.

(p. 789)

Although there is no doubt that GWAS would identify a Huntington-like major allele that explains some portion of a complex behavioral phenotype of chorea, and some non-behavioral examples where it has done so, it is hard to point to a behavioral example where this has happened in a decisive way. The current trend in GWAS is very much away from identification and interpretation of individual variants, moving instead in the direction of summation of variants into atheoretical sums called polygenic scores (PGS). And PGS are generalists! A PGS originally estimated with respect to a particular phenotype is often correlated almost as highly with other phenotypes as it is with the original target. Indeed, computation of genetic correlations has become one of the main activities of contemporary GWAS.

44.8 CONCLUSION: TOP-DOWN, BOTTOM-UP, AND RDOC

Do schizophrenia, depression, or addiction qualify as brain or genetic disorders? No, they don't, and I am tempted to say of course they don't. Behavioral syndromes that are brain disorders are entities observed in behavior that are linked via Craver and Bechtel mechanisms to genetic or neurological entities at a lower level of analysis. Huntington's chorea is a genetic disorder of the brain. The reason is not that a gene makes it more likely that one will acquire HD, or that choreaform motor function and dementia are things that happen in brains. Thinking like that only serves to turn all human problems into brain disorders. The Huntington gene is linked via a mechanism to brain disorders that are linked via a mechanism to dementia and chorea. One might say, with Craver and Bechtel (who don't address behavioral syndromes of this kind) that the Huntington gene doesn't cause Huntington's disease; it *is* Huntington disease, a part of the integrated mechanism that is Huntington disease in hierarchically organized whole organisms.

Could it be that some subset of behaviorally focused mental illness is a brain disorder, in the same sense that Huntington's disease, a subset of chorea, is a genetic disorder? Yes, of course, and indeed there are many obvious examples. Drugs can cause psychosis, and strokes can cause depression. Instances of this kind of mechanistic identity between psychiatric symptoms with known neurologic or metabolic causes are interesting and uncontroversial when they occur, but they cannot be counted on to provide a comprehensive account of psychiatric syndromes generally, any more than HD provides a comprehensive account of chorea. Biologically oriented psychopathologists who wish to pursue such hypotheses must start with the recognition that hypotheses are indeed what they are, or we will wind up back on the same slippery slope downward, toward explaining essentially everything in terms of essentially nothing, as Wimsatt (2007) famously remarked.

Meaningful research strategies for testing hypotheses about biology and behavior can be either top-down or bottom-up. The top-down strategy is the Meehlian taxometric approach or some variant of it, in which covariances among indicators of entities are examined for evidence of lower-level focused taxa. These approaches are ingenious and appealing, but as I have already mentioned they have not been very successful.

The alternative, bottom-up approach has a name: it is RDoC, and thinking about RDoC in terms of focused and blurry categories provides a helpful way to evaluate its value and its limitations. RDoC was formulated by Thomas Insel (Insel et al., 2010; for the sake of simplicity I will credit the concept to Insel alone), the same Director of NIMH who implicitly endorsed a model in which all forms of human behavioral suffering could be characterized as "brain disorders." RDoC was originally justified and formulated in terms of entities, in particular by the neuroscientist's frustration with "clinical" entities that seemed to map so poorly onto more biological constructs:

> Diagnostic categories based on clinical consensus fail to align with findings emerging from clinical neuroscience and genetics. The boundaries of these categories have not been predictive of treatment response. And, perhaps most important, these categories, based upon presenting signs and symptoms, may not capture fundamental underlying mechanisms of dysfunction. One consequence has been to slow the development of new treatments targeted to underlying pathophysiological mechanisms.

Insel is correct that clinical categories fail to align with neuroscientific ones, but characteristically he sees the alignment problem only from the point of view of a neuroscientist. So-called clinical categories are not infallible, but they exist for a reason: psychiatric problems are encountered on a human level of analysis and, as a consequence, that is where they are focused. Neuroscience that is badly aligned with clinical categories is not necessarily an indictment of the categories, and in fact it is often a sign that one has identified a domain in which neuroscience may not be especially useful.

If RDoC had been implemented in a more generous spirit, encouraging biological scientists to investigate the blurry behavioral images of focused genetic or neurological processes, it could have been to psychopathology what the New Zealand Wool Institute is to carpet design, producing results like fiber chemistry in the carpet mill to elucidate the basic processes that inform (but can't replace) meaningful large-scale human constructs. It might even have discovered some portions of behavioral entities that turn out, like Huntington's chorea, to be unfocused images of focused low-level processes. It might have finally shown the way out of psychiatry's mindless-brainless dilemma. But in the absence of a meaningful theory of entities and levels, RDoC has been used as an instrument for replacing clinical categories with neuroscientific ones (and clinical grants with neuroscientific ones), leading inexorably to broad dissatisfaction among investigators on the more psychological side of the ledger (Parnas, 2014).

Recently, in an interview, Insel (2017) uttered a remarkable *mea culpa*: "I spent 13 years at NIMH really pushing on the neuroscience and genetics of mental disorders, and when I look back on that I realize that while I think I succeeded at getting lots of really cool papers published by cool scientists at fairly large costs – I think $20 billion – I don't think we moved the needle in reducing suicide, reducing hospitalizations, improving recovery for the tens of millions of people who have mental illness. I hold myself accountable for that." (Rogers, 2017). Insel's failure was not essentially empirical. Behavioral science is hard, and scientific breakthroughs of any kind are rare. The real problem was theoretical: if we don't understand the hierarchical relationships between neuroscience and genetics on the one hand to mental disorders on the other, we will be stuck in the endless rhetorical mind–brain tautology that has persisted from at least Guze to the present time. Scientists who do not study theory are bound to repeat it.

REFERENCES

Boyle, E. A., Li, Y. I., & Pritchard, J. K. (2017) 'An expanded view of complex traits: From polygenic to omnigenic.' *Cell, 169*(7), 1177–1186.

Carnaby, G. A., & Wood, E. J. (1989) 'The physics of carpets.' *Journal of the Textile Institute, 80*(1), 71–90.

Chabris, C. F., Lee, J. J., Cesarini, D., Benjamin, D. J., & Laibson, D. I. (2015) 'The fourth law of behavior genetics.' *Current Directions in Psychological Science, 24*(4), 304–312.

Coan, J. A., Schaefer, H. S., & Davidson, R. J. (2006) 'Lending a hand: Social regulation of the neural response to threat.' *Psychological Science, 17*(12), 1032–1039.

Craver, C. F., & Bechtel, W. (2007) 'Top-down causation without top-down causes.' *Biology & Philosophy*, *22*(4), 547–563.

Edwards, A. C., Bacanu, S. A., Bigdeli, T. B., Moscati, A., & Kendler, K. S. (2016) 'Evaluating the dopamine hypothesis of schizophrenia in a large-scale genome-wide association study.' *Schizophrenia Research*, 176(2–3), 136–140.

Fraser, A. D. (1998). Use and abuse of the benzodiazepines. *Therapeutic Drug Monitoring*, 20(5), 481–489.

Goldstein, D. M., & Hall, K. (2015) 'Mass hysteria in Le Roy, New York: How brain experts materialized truth and outscienced environmental inquiry.' *American Ethnologist*, *42*(4), 640–657.

Greenberg, A. S., & Bailey, J. M. (1994) 'The irrelevance of the medical model of mental illness to law and ethics.' *International Journal of Law and Psychiatry*, 17, 153–173.

Guze, S. B. (1989). Biological psychiatry: is there any other kind? *Psychological medicine*, 19(2), 315-323

Harré, R., Clarke, D., & De Carlo, N. (1975) *Motives and mechanisms: An introduction to the psychology of action*. New York: Routledge.

Huntington, G. (1872) 'On chorea.' *The Medical and Surgical Reporter*, *26*(15), 317–321.

Insel, T., Cuthbert, B., Garvey, M., Heinssen, R., Pine, D. S., Quinn, K., . . . Wang, P. (2010) 'Research domain criteria (RDoC): Toward a new classification framework for research on mental disorders.' *The American Journal of Psychiatry*, *167*(7), 748–751.

Insel, T. R., & Landis, S. C. (2013) 'Twenty-five years of progress: The view from NIMH and NINDS.' *Neuron*, *80*(3), 561–567.

Insel, T. R. (2017) Star Neuroscientist Tom Insel Leaves the Google-Spawned Verily for . . . a Startup? Retrieved from https://goo.gl/JX2Qyf, March 28, 2019.

Jocklin, V., McGue, M., & Lykken, D. T. (1996) 'Personality and divorce: A genetic analysis.' *Journal of Personality and Social Psychology*, *71*(2), 288.

Meehl, P. E. (1995) 'Bootstraps taxometrics: Solving the classification problem in psychopathology.' *American Psychologist*, *50*(4), 266.

Leshner, A. I. (1997) 'Addiction is a brain disease, and it matters.' *Science*, *278*(5335), 45–47.

Lipowski, Z. J. (1989) 'Psychiatry: Mindless or brainless, both or neither?' *The Canadian Journal of Psychiatry*, *34*(3), 249–254.

Parnas, J. (2014) 'The RDoC program: Psychiatry without psyche?' *World Psychiatry*, *13*(1), 46–47.

Plomin, R., & Kovas, Y. (2005) 'Generalist genes and learning disabilities.' *Psychological Bulletin*, *131*(4), 592–617.

Rogers, A. (2017) 'Star Neuroscientist Tom Insel Leaves the Google-Spawned Verily for . . . a Startup?.' *Wired*. Retrieved from https://goo.gl/JX2Qyf, March 28, 2019.

Satel, S., & Lilienfeld, S. O. (2014) 'Addiction and the brain-disease fallacy.' *Frontiers in Psychiatry*, *4*, 141.

Turkheimer, E. (1998) 'Heritability and biological explanation.' *Psychological Review*, *105*(4), 782.

(2017) 'The hard question in psychiatric nosology.' In K. S. Kendler and J. Parnas (Eds.), *Philosophical issues in psychiatry IV: Classification of psychiatric illness* (pp. 27–44). Oxford: Oxford University Press.

Turkheimer, E., Pettersson, E., & Horn, E. E. (2014) 'A phenotypic null hypothesis for the genetics of personality.' *Annual Review of Psychology*, *65*, 515–540.

van Haren, N. E. M., Cahn, W., Pol, H. H., & Kahn, R. S. (2008) 'Schizophrenia as a progressive brain disease.' *European Psychiatry*, *23*(4), 245–254.

Visscher, P. M., Wray, N. R., Zhang, Q., Sklar, P., McCarthy, M. I., Brown, M. A., & Yang, J. (2017) '10 years of GWAS discovery: Biology, function, and translation.' *The American Journal of Human Genetics*, *101*(1), 5–22.

Walum, H., Westberg, L., Henningsson, S., Neiderhiser, J. M., Reiss, D., Igl, W., . . . Lichtenstein, P. (2008) 'Genetic variation in the vasopressin receptor 1a gene (AVPR1A) associates with pair-bonding behavior in humans.' *Proceedings of the National Academy of Sciences*, *105*(37), 14153–14156.

Weiss, V. (1992) 'Major genes of general intelligence.' *Personality and Individual Differences*, *13*(10), 1115–1134.

Wimsatt, W. C. (2007) *Re-engineering philosophy for limited beings: Piecewise approximations to reality*. Cambridge, MA: Harvard University Press.

45

Commentary on "Entity Focus: Applied Genetic Science at Different Levels" by Eric Turkheimer

KATHRYN TABB

I go to buy a carpet, and brush up against a world of technicalities. Theories have been generated, falsified, improved upon – about the best and cheapest way to manufacture a carpet, about consumer preferences, about safety. Some of the terms which facilitate these efforts will make their way to me, words like "pile," "millennial pink," and "flammability," but most won't. I was unproblematically unreflective about "fiber fatigue properties," for example, before Eric's intervention. My ignorance is facilitated by the fact that the properties I care about in a carpet are, as philosophers of science would put it, *multiply realized* by their underlying causes. These multiple realizations are "screened off" from the final product, insofar as their details are irrelevant to its ultimate function. There are many combinations of dyes and processes that can turn a material millennial pink, for example, and there are many chemical compositions that are both flame-retardant and softer than flooring. I ignore these possibilities when selecting my trendy, safe, comfortable carpet. On the other hand, for materials engineers working to create a durable yarn, whether the material they produce contributes to items sold in the carpet section or the bathmat section is beside the point. For them, while some of the realizations of carpet properties are of central interest, there is no meaningful question about the causal pathways to "being a carpet." Due to this division of labor, no one has in their heads a "physics of carpets."

Arguments from multiple realizability have been wielded with great effect in the philosophy of mind to reject the claim of mind-brain identity, that is, the view that every mental phenomenon corresponds to a physical phenomenon, such that one might abandon all talk of the mental (e.g. psychological theory) in favor of talk of the physical (e.g. neuroscientific theory) (see Bickle 2019 for an overview). But Harré et al. (2015) are using multiple realizability to make a different point in their example that Eric relies on, and therefore need a further premise. A comprehensive physics of carpets would require an enormously unwieldy disjunction of possible realizations of carpet properties, too diverse to bring to heel under a set of natural laws. If one tried, one would end up with something that looked much like the physics of anything else. This is a different story from, e.g., samples of slate, which tend to share the same set of properties and have been produced by the same set of processes, which might be enumerated. But this in-practice awkwardness only becomes an in-principle impossibility with an additional component: "carpets are human artefacts, and what makes something a carpet is a human invention" (57). The reason there can't be a physics of carpets is not only because one might not be willing to call the theoretical scrape pile of all the disjunctive processes that go into carpet-making a science. One couldn't even assemble such a set because what is considered a carpet is ambiguous, subject to social convention and fashion; in philosophy-speak, "carpet" is not a *natural kind*, meaning, crudely, that it does not feature in the laws of any science (which is not to say one can't make generalizations about carpets).

This latter step of Harré et al.'s argument is importantly distinct from the former one; multiple realizability and artificial kindhood need not go together. In his chapter, Eric writes, "The carpet problem is a useful example because it is easy: we know at the outset that carpets are a human creation, and that as a consequence carpets can't be defined by their chemical composition" (p. 531–532). But Play-Doh is a human creation, and its chemical composition is surely a known formula. On the other hand, pain, a natural phenomenon, is a favorite case of multiple realizability for philosophers. Harré et al. are offering conditions for assessing the viability of reductive projects. The problem with carpets is that they are *both* defined by convention *and* multiply realized. For Eric's analogy to go through, his analog for carpets would also need to be a constructed kind displaying multiple realizability – like the social behaviors that are the actual subject of Harré et al.'s discussion.

In Eric's original employment of the physics of carpets analogy, the analog was behavior, writ large. In the current discussion, he is interested in the potential reducibility of "behavioral syndromes," or types of psychopathology – "schizophrenia, depression, addiction" (p. 527) – to genes or neural circuits. The question of whether or not most diagnostic kinds are, in any significant sense, natural has been the subject of extensive debate among philosophers of psychiatry, with the consensus being that despite the robustness of some symptom clusters gathered together by the *DSM*'s diagnoses, its categories don't correspond with precision to discrete divisions in the real world (see Kincaid and Sullivan 2014 for discussion). On the other hand, there is widespread consensus that, natural or no, they are multiply realized with respect to lower physiological levels – genes implicated in a specific mental disorder, for example, are not necessary, and certainly not sufficient, to cause all cases of disorders of that type.

Categories of mental disorder may, therefore, be analogous in the appropriate sense to carpets. Assuming with Eric that they are, it nonetheless seems to be begging a substantial question – a question that has generated a huge amount of scientific and philosophical debate – to assume that *all* of psychiatry's explananda are socially constructed and multiply realized. Elsewhere Eric claims that "Classes that are defined at one level of analysis are detectable but fuzzy at another. I will say that a class is *focused* at the level of analysis at which it is defined, and *blurry* elsewhere" (p. #). But not all natural phenomena defy reduction; some we can focus on at diverse levels. Unless one believes that science never successfully reduces a phenomenon to its underlying mechanisms, one must acknowledge that some blurriness is rectifiable. Goldfinches are blurrier at the atomic level than samples of gold these days, but it wasn't always so. And elsewhere, Eric grants that it makes fine sense to search out physical causes for traditional carpet properties. It is worth asking what the analog for this scientifically coherent project might be in psychiatry, in order to consider whether there may be an alternative to "the slow-motion collision of human genetics with the physics of carpets" (p. 537).

A consensus has formed that the answer doesn't lie with diagnostic kinds. The case has been made stridently by psychiatrists at the reins of the NIMH, most explicitly perhaps by its past director Steven Hyman, who wrote an influential paper in 2010 identifying the reification of diagnostic categories – that is, the treating of them as real entities, or natural kinds – as the major barrier to psychiatric progress. The Research Domain Criteria (RDoC) project grew out of this sort of worry. Its aim was to liberate researchers approaching the NIMH for funding from the need to frame their research in terms of the traditional targets of psychopathology (Tabb 2015). In the terms of the current discussion, we might see RDoC as intending to redirect psychiatric researchers toward, in Harré et al.'s language, "products" for which there is reason to assume "processes" can be discovered, in part because, taken together as a class, they form a manageable number of possible realizations of a single kind of thing.

"So-called clinical categories are not infallible," Eric argues, "but they exist for a reason: psychiatric problems are encountered on a human level of analysis and, as a consequence, that is where they are focused." That's right, an apologist for RDoC might respond, but syndromes and the distress they cause are not the only psychiatric objects we can investigate; where psychiatry is reconceived as "a clinical neuroscience discipline" (Insel and Quirion 2005), or where optimism reigns that genetic correlations will resolve into causal pathways, finding the mechanisms is only a matter of narrowing in on an appropriate target. If neuroscience is "badly aligned with clinical categories," as Eric says, it should move on from them to a domain where it holds more promise. But this need not mean leaving psychiatry, insofar as mechanistic discoveries at the level of the neural circuit might have substantial translational value for medicine. What might this look like? – that is, what could it mean for psychiatry to study entities that aren't the *DSM* categories, but are instead appropriate targets for reduction by sciences like neuroscience and genetics?

Some philosophers have suggested that multiple realization is a pseudo-problem, arising from an allegiance to folk categories rather than scientific ones. Shapiro has argued that judgments about whether different tokens are taken to be realizers of the same type are often made on the basis of shared function, rather than an identity relation among causally significant properties. But functional kinds whose members share few causal properties, while potentially legitimate cases of multiple realizability, are mostly useless for the doing of science; it is only once such kinds are disaggregated and their members rearranged into causally relevant categories that explanation and prediction become possible (Shapiro 2000). This is when causal mechanisms, in the sense Eric discusses, come into view. In some cases, such rearrangement won't be possible; there are no mechanistically significant groupings to be found, and each member will require its own "science." In psychiatry, this would mean that each patient would be in a class by him- or herself; this, quixotically, is the seductive promise of precision medicine (Tabb, Chapter 26). But maybe psychiatry's objects can be fruitfully disaggregated into new kinds – at the level of a specific endophenotype, neural network, genetic profile, or symptom cluster – such that mechanisms might be discovered. This proposal may seem similar to Eric's plea that we bring entities into focus at the "right" level, but it differs importantly. It suggests that psychiatry's way forward is not looking at the same entities – that is, the traditional diagnostic categories – at different levels of focus, but rather looking at different entities altogether.

Turkheimer has the expertise in behavioral genetics to assess this sunny sort of stance and find it Pollyannaish. The challenge of finding gene variants that have clinical relevance is too great, in his view; in particular, the search for genetic causes of *any* psychopathological behavior – *DSM* syndrome or otherwise – is doomed. Why? Drawing on the account of mechanistically mediated effects introduced by Craver and Bechtel (2007), Eric argues it is because the relationships between genes and behaviors are for the most part constitutive, not causal. Within this mechanistic framework, efforts to attribute behaviors to genetic causes are *all*, technically, doomed from the start – talk of *any* genes "causing" behavior misunderstands the constitutive relationship between the genetic level and the doings of the human organism. The case of Huntington's chorea shows that, nonetheless, intralevel causation on the level at which genes operate mechanistically can mediate effects that are hugely significant at the level of the organism. While not, properly speaking, "causes," some genes are, in Craver and Bechtel's language, "enlisted" in the activities of higher-level mechanisms, while others are simply along for the ride, like hotdogs pushed about in a hotdog cart. So Eric's point is perhaps best put this way: research confirming that certain gene variants are constitutive of systems displaying certain behaviors does *not* amount to a discovery of an interesting causal mechanism at the genetic level, and most certainly does *not* amount to a discovery of bottom-up causation from the genetic level to the behavioral, the former for in-practice reasons, the latter for in-principle ones.

Furthermore, on the basis of a pessimistic meta-induction from history, Eric expects that the vast majority of research on psychiatric genetics will not generate novel mechanistic discoveries. (See Stegenga 2018 for a more sweeping example of this kind of medical nihilism.) And as Thomas Insel himself acknowledges in the quote Eric provides, there are grounds for an analogous case about psychiatric neuroscience: while scientists are getting better and better at discovering brain abnormalities that correlate with pathological behaviors, these have not resulted in the discovery of causal mechanisms at the level of the neural circuit on which psychiatrists and other clinicians might intervene. But will the future resemble the past?

Going back to our imagined RDoC apologist, he might respond to all this by noting that while the aspirational rhetoric has maybe gotten overblown, the past failure of the basic sciences to inform psychiatry is no reason for a global pessimism like Eric's. He might respond that science often requires a dogged persistence on the part of would-be reductionists; disappointments often pile up, as Kuhn noted, along the path to a paradigm shift. On these grounds, he might argue that the way to settle whether there are useful intralevel causes to be discovered is to try and see. Whether basic sciences like neuroscience and genetics will rewardingly contribute to psychiatry in the future is an empirical question, one that is too important to beg. Precisely what is at issue is whether the person-level entity can be fruitfully explanatorily reduced to underlying causes at one or the other biological level; while we can't just assume that psychiatric phenomena are like carpets, we also can't assume that they aren't. What is necessary is an investigation of whether, in the language of Harré et al., psychiatry has products for which new source processes can be effectively proposed, investigated, and ultimately translated into clinically fruitful knowledge. After all, as Shapiro puts it, "[i]t is quite possible that some special sciences are more susceptible to reduction than others, depending on how the world turns out to be" (2000, 641).

I agree with Eric's characterization of the theoretical fallacies that have led scientists like Insel to treat discoveries of inter-level correlations as proof that impressive intralevel mechanistic discoveries have been made, or are just around the corner. But I don't think that this line of criticism is enough to convince our apologist that RDoC should be given up, if he is really an optimist, and believes in the ultimate forward march of science toward the truth. He will simply insist that social constructions need to be forsaken for natural kinds, and that multiple realizability needs to be tamed through a regrouping of the phenomena, and that all this will take more hard work. However, a stronger case can be made, an ethical one, in line with Eric's musing that RDoC would have been less problematic had it been "implemented in a more generous spirit" (p. 542).

Very briefly, the ethical argument could go something like this (I motivate it further in the conclusion of Chapter 26). As Eric shows, when we say mental illnesses are brain diseases, we are acting as though the work of discovering psychiatric mechanisms is complete, or at least manageable. As Insel admits, this optimism has not been rewarded over the years since RDoC kicked off. On the following page is a graphic representation (Figure 45.1) of Insel's own errors in calculation on this front, taken from a paper he wrote in 2005 with Remi Quirion.

Anyone following the state of the art in psychiatry will know we are already over a decade behind here; since Insel wrote, there has been little progress toward a biodiagnostic revolution. Personalized or "precision" medicine has had some successes in oncology and immunology, but not psychiatry. One can't be sure, of course, that the discovery of core pathological features of psychopathology won't be forthcoming – and if they come, they may indeed be transformative. The ethical question is whether betting on this kind of future success is worth the present costs. During Insel's time as director of the NIMH, according to his own estimates, spending on epidemiology and clinical care was reduced in order to

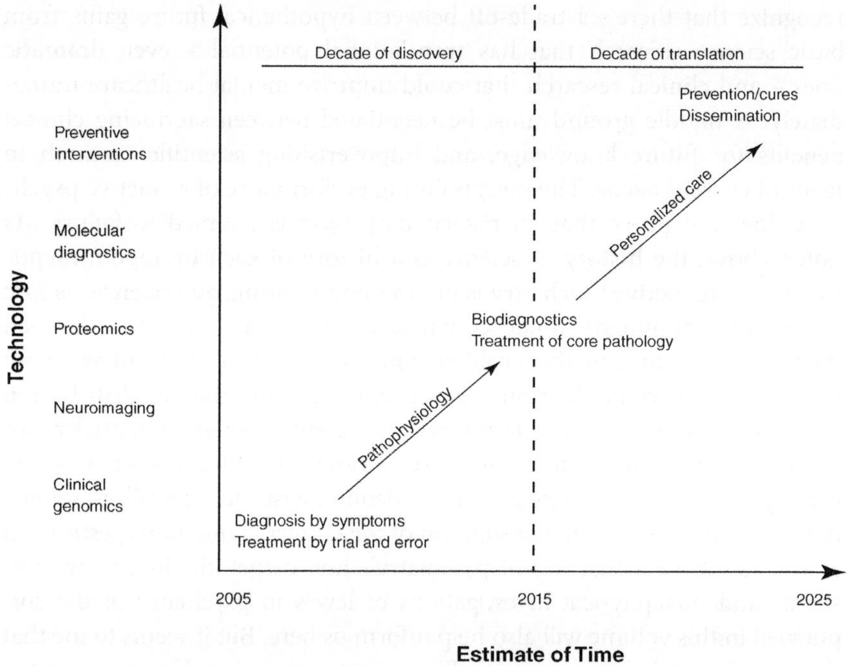

FIGURE 45.1 A vision for mental health research.
Note: Pathophysiologic descriptions of mental disorders will permit diagnoses validated by biological measures and treatments aimed at core pathology. Care will become personalized via an understanding of individual risk, allowing for strategic approaches to prevention and treatment. These ambitious goals require application of genomics and proteomics to mental disorders. Reprinted from Insel TR, Quirion R. "Psychiatry as a clinical neuroscience discipline." JAMA. 2005;294(17):2221–2224

increase basic science (neuroscientific and behavioral) funding by a fourth. (See my chapter, this volume, for more discussion, and Teachman et al. (2019) for more quantitative analysis.) The prioritizing of basic science over translational and clinical research has been a growing source of alarm among psychologists and others who depend on the NIMH for funding (Lewis-Fernendez et al. 2016, Schwartz et al. 2016, Teachman et al. 2019). Globally, NIMH funding supports about 9% of all published work in psychiatry (Pollitt et al. 2016), so its priorities have world-wide ramifications.

While a dose of stubborn optimism about the wandering upward arc of scientific inquiry might be enough to offset Eric's gloomy theoretical prognostications, it can't dispel the worry that *any* delay in reductive psychiatry's payouts is an ethically loaded act. Even our apologist should recognize that there's a trade-off between hypothetical future gains from basic science research that has translational potential – even dramatic ones – and clinical research that could improve mental healthcare immediately. A middle ground must be negotiated between sacrificing clinical benefits for future knowledge, and impoverishing scientific research in favor of current needs. The disappointing performance of reductive psychiatry does not prove that, *in theory*, its project is doomed to failure. As noted above, the history of science is a history of such disappointments. But even if reductive psychiatry is not as disappointing, *qua* science, as Eric suggests, his argument should convince us that it can be, *in practice*, bad medicine. We can put the problem more formally in terms of what we might call diachronic distributive justice, concerning the fair distribution of health resources across temporally different (though potentially not distinct) populations. One could take a variety of ethical approaches to solving this problem – consequentialist, deontologist, etc. Regardless, solving it well will also depend on a resolution of the empirical questions gestured at above, about the actual size of psychiatry's non-carpet-like inventory. Epistemic and metaphysical investigations of levels in psychiatry of the sort pursued in this volume will also help inform us here. But it seems to me that the most worrying impact of calling mental disorders "brain diseases," calling psychiatry "clinical neuroscience," and talking about gene variants as "causing" psychopathology is ethical, not metaphysical.

REFERENCES

Bickle, J. (2019) 'Multiple realizability.' *The Stanford encyclopedia of philosophy* (Spring 2019 Edition), Edward N. Zalta (ed.), https://plato.stanford.edu/archives/spr2019/entries/multiple-realizability/.

Craver, CF and Bechtel, W. (2007) 'Top-down causation without top-down causes.' *Biology & Philosophy* 22(4): 547–63.

Harré, R, Clarke, D, and De Carlo, N. (2015) *Motives and mechanisms: An introduction to the psychology of action*. Routledge.

Hyman, S. (2010) 'The diagnosis of mental disorders: The problem of reification.' *Annual Review of Clinical Psychology* 6: 155–79.

Insel, TR and Quirion R. (2005) 'Psychiatry as a clinical neuroscience discipline.' *JAMA* 294(17): 2221–24.

Kincaid, H and Sullivan, JA, eds. (2014) *Classifying psychopathology*. Cambridge, MA: MIT Press.

Lewis-Fernendez, R, Rotheram-Borus, MJ, Betts, VT, Greenman, L, Essock, SM, Escobar, JI, Barch, D et al. (2016) 'Rethinking funding priorities in mental health research.' *The British Journal of Psychiatry* 208(6): 507–9.

Pollitt, A, Cochrane, G, Kirtley, A, Krapels, J, Larivière, V, Lichten, CA, Parks, S, and Wooding, S. (2016) 'Project ecosystem: Mapping the global mental health research funding system.' Santa Monica, CA: RAND Corporation. www.rand.org/pubs/research_reports/RR1271.html.

Schwartz, SJ, Lilienfeld, SO, Meca, A, and Sauvigné, KC. (2016) 'The role of neuroscience within psychology: A call for inclusiveness over exclusiveness.' *The American Psychologist* 71(1): 52–70.

Shapiro, L. (2000) 'Multiple realizations.' *Journal of Philosophy* 97: 635–54.

Stegenga, J. (2018) *Medical nihilism*. Oxford: Oxford University Press.

Tabb, K. (2015) 'Psychiatric progress and the assumption of diagnostic discrimination.' *Philosophy of Science* 82(5): 1047–58.

Teachman, BA, McKay, D, Barch, DM, Prinstein, MJ, Hollon, SD, and Chambless, DL. (2019) 'How psychosocial research can help the National Institute of Mental Health achieve its grand challenge to reduce the burden of mental illnesses and psychological disorders.' *The American Psychologist* 74(4): 415–31.

Index